Oracle Press™

Oracle9*i* Mobile

Alan Yeung
Philip Stephenson
Nicholas Pang

McGraw-Hill/Osborne

New York Chicago San Francisco
Lisbon London Madrid Mexico City
Milan New Delhi San Juan
Seoul Singapore Sydney Toronto

McGraw-Hill/Osborne
2600 Tenth Street
Berkeley, California 94710
U.S.A.

To arrange bulk purchase discounts for sales promotions, premiums, or fund-raisers, please contact **McGraw-Hill/Osborne** at the above address. For information on translations or book distributors outside the U.S.A., please see the International Contact Information page immediately following the index of this book.

Oracle9*i* Mobile

1234567890 FGR FGR 0198765432

ISBN 0-07-222455-X

Publisher
Brandon A. Nordin

Vice President & Associate Publisher
Scott Rogers

Acquisitions Editor
Jeremy Judson

Project Editor
Elizabeth Seymour

Acquisitions Coordinator
Athena Honore

Technical Editors
Martin Graf, Jean Sini

Copy Editor
Bart Reed

Proofreader
Cheryl Abel

Indexer
Jerilyn Sproston

Computer Designers
Tabitha M. Cagan, Michelle Galicia

Illustrator
Michael Mueller, Lyssa Wald

Cover Series Design
Damore Johann Design, Inc.

This book was composed with Corel VENTURA™ Publisher.

This book is dedicated to our families, especially our wives, Stella, Lisa, and Sophie, whose patience, support, and understanding made this possible.

About the Authors

Alan Yeung is Co-Founder, President and CEO of Where2Net, a software provider of multichannel development tools and web applications. Before establishing Where2Net, Dr. Yeung held executive and technical positions at PointCast, a pioneering push technology company, and at Raychem Corporation. A frequent speaker on the subject of technology, Dr. Yeung has taught wireless and engineering courses at San Jose State University, Stanford University and University of Wisconsin-Madison. Dr. Yeung received an MBA from University of California at Berkeley, a PhD from Stanford, and a BSChE degree from University of Wisconsin.

Philip Stephenson is Director of Mobile Architects at Oracle Corporation's Mobile Products and Services Division. At Oracle, Mr. Stephenson has concentrated on mobile and embedded products, including Oracle Lite database, Web-to-Go disconnected environment, Oracle9*i* Application Server Wireless Edition, Oracle Mobile Online Services, and Mobile Studio. Currently, Mr. Stephenson leads a team of mobile architects in providing consultative technical solutions to Oracle customers, using Oracle's wireless, voice, and synchronized mobile technologies. Before coming to Oracle, Mr. Stephenson worked at IBM, Amdahl, Ernst & Young, EMC, and Sequent Computer Systems. Mr. Stephenson holds a B.S. degree in Business Administration and an M.S. degree in Computer Science with an emphasis on distributed computing. He is a member of the adjunct faculty of Webster University's Graduate School of Computer Science.

Nicholas Pang is Co-Founder and Chief Knowledge Officer (CKO) at Where2Net. As CKO, Mr. Pang has been instrumental in building Where2Net's tools and applications, creating its intellectual property suite, and driving service development around Oracle technologies. Before founding Where2Net, Mr. Pang held management, consulting, and systems engineering positions at PointCast, Cadence Design Systems, Redwood Design Automation, and Amdahl Corporation. A mobile expert with in-depth experience in client and server side programming, Mr. Pang holds an M.S. degree in Electrical Engineering from the University of Wisconsin-Madison, where he single-handedly built a cycle-accurate Cray 1 Supercomputer simulator. He also holds a B.S. degree in Electrical Engineering from Arizona State University.

Contents

PART II
Oracle9*i* Application Server Wireless

PART III

Developing and Deploying Dynamic Applications

Foreword

As people have become more productive using Internet technology at their desks, these same benefits can be extended to those away from their desks—using mobile technology. Oracle believes the most cost-effective and productive mobile architecture supports a single model that can provide access to information in a variety of ways, matching roles and requirements to the application.

Integrated at the application server level, the mobile features of Oracle9*i* Application Server let you develop, deploy, and manage applications that can be accessed from any mobile device through any communication mode: voice or text. It is a powerful platform with facilities for offline, messaging, mobile office, voice and location-based services, and a wide range of device support. Oracle9*i* Application Server offers a complete platform for building multichannel, multi-modal mobile applications.

The authors provide a great service to the development community by clearly explaining and demonstrating the unique mobile features and benefits of Oracle9*i* Application Server. With sample code and extensive examples, developers and service designers can quickly exploit the mobile features of Oracle9*i* Application Server to build and deploy applications and enhance their mobile development environment.

I highly recommend this book for those looking to mobile technology as a way to streamline processes, drive revenue, and increase efficiencies. I especially recommend it to those considering using the mobile features and services of Oracle9*i* Application Server.

Denise Lahey, Senior Vice President,
Oracle Mobile Products and Services Division

Acknowledgments

A book on new technologies like this is never easy to write without the help of many people.

Our thanks go to Martin Graf and Jean Sini, who provided us with lots of insight into Oracle9*i*AS Wireless while serving as our technical editors. We want to thank Denise Lahey for penning the foreword; Jacob Christfort for his comments and ideas; and John Dolan for his insights into Oracle's mobile strategy. We also want to thank Zhou Ye and Xiaolin Zang for helping out on Push/SMS; Rushan Jiang on Location-Based Services; Johnny Wong on Mobile Commerce; Sam Rehman for his help with Oracle9*i* Lite APIs and development environments; Jonathan Hauland for providing detailed information on replication and synchronization; Harald Collet for sharing with us his thoughts on business impacts of technologies; PV Subramanvian Peruvenda for helping us with Oracle9*i*AS Wireless; Norman Adams on Oracle Lite ADOCE; Lisa Alms for branding and positioning; and Kirk Gustafson for his views on the religious impacts of technology.

We'd like to thank our editorial team, including Jeremy Judson, Acquisitions Editor, for his inspiration and confidence in us; Athena Honore, Acquisitions Coordinator, for keeping us from going astray; Elizabeth Seymour, Project Editor, for making the editorial process as easy as possible; Bart Reed, Copy Editor, for making our book better than it would have been without his comments. Jeremy, Athena, Elizabeth, Bart, and other members of the McGraw-Hill/ Osborne production and editorial teams have been a real pleasure to work with.

Alan Yeung
Phil Stephenson
Nicholas Pang

I would like to thank my wife, Stella, for putting up with my days at work, and my nights and weekends at writing a book that, I believe, needs to be written. Her support and care energize my writing, and the muse never left me.

Watching my son, Austin, who started from learning how to walk, to being able to climb all over my chair in the study, to finally being able to pound on the keyboard and click on my mouse at barely 18 months of age—are special things I will always remember. May this book mark the beginning of many wonderful things that come in life, courtesy of new and exciting technologies—which Austin obviously has a love for.

I would also like to thank Jean-Claude Michaca, Oracle EMEA, for introducing me to the world of Oracle9*i*AS Wireless; and Todd Berkowitz, Oracle Marketing, for helping me navigate through it. Both have made an impact on how we embrace this leading-edge product platform.

Finally, my thanks to my parents for their support, and to my parents-in-law, whose accommodation kept my writing on track even when I was traveling.

Alan Yeung
San Francisco, California
June 2002

I'd like to thank my understanding wife Lisa, daughter Caitlin, and brother Mike for all their support. Special thanks to my colleagues in Server Technologies at Oracle who contributed materials or support for this text: Martin Graf, Jean Sini, Denise Lahey, Gaurav Juchhal, Alyson Fryhoff, John Dolan, Sam Rehman, Jonathan Hauland, Atilla Bodis, Harald Collet, PV Subramanvian Peruvenda, Kirk Gustafson, and Norman Adams.

Phil Stephenson
Saint Louis, Missouri
June 2002

First and foremost, I want to thank my wife, Sophie, who quietly put up with all my late nights and early mornings, day in and day out, while I was writing this book and dealing with the frustrations that came with using beta software. Most importantly, she brought me down to earth by having me spend time with our three kids, Nathan, Jeremy, and Claire, through taking them to Aikido, swimming, and piano lessons. I truly thank her for making me *not* miss nine months of our dear kids' lives.

Amidst all the chaos three energetic kids create in our house, I especially remember my four-year-old daughter stopping everyone by saying, "Read me a book!" She knows the best way to a calm house is by sitting down and reading a storybook.

Finally, I want to thank my parents, Tet Tshung and Nyuk Kong, for their encouragement and support. I would not be where I am today without them.

Nicholas Pang
San Francisco, California
June 2002

Introduction

The idea of writing this book came to us one afternoon when we were discussing building mobile applications. We marveled about the lack of reference materials and books that would go beyond WAP and single channel wireless publishing. Jeremy Judson of McGraw-Hill/ Osborne encouraged us to share what we know best: how to build mobile applications with the Oracle platform. Thus, the concept of this book was born.

About This Book

In this book, we strive to provide an overview of Oracle9*i*AS Wireless Release 2, including its core technologies, mobile studio, and linked services. We focus on exposing the key features and core differentiators of Oracle9*i*AS Wireless, and reviewing its architecture. Our goal is to help others understand mobile development and successfully build and manage their own applications and services.

Throughout this book, we discuss the concepts and terminology for building mobile solutions that are server platform agnostic, and provide references and examples to help you understand multichannel XML applications. By sharing with you the code snippets, and covering the design rules for building scalable solutions, we hope you will have the requisite information to architect, develop, and deploy your own mobile services.

Who Should Read This Book

Our targeted audiences are developers who want to use Oracle9*i*AS Wireless to build mobile applications and services, and system administrators who need to manage mobile users, devices, platforms, and applications. Service designers will find it useful in understanding and exploiting features in Oracle9*i*AS Wireless. Oracle DBAs who want to mobile enable data and content will benefit from this book as well. Finally, program managers, content providers, wireless project leaders, and IT managers will find the information helpful for their roles and can gain insights from the knowledge imparted in this book.

How to Use This Book

This book can be used as both a reference and a developer's guide. To follow its examples and run the code, you may want to install Oracle9*i*AS Wireless Release 2.

There are three parts in this book. **Part I** provides the background and an introduction to mobile technologies in general, and the Oracle Mobile environment in particular. It helps you understand the Oracle strategy as well as the underlying technology and XML application model. **Part II** illustrates the servers, facilities, integration components, and various Wireless Services of Oracle9*i*AS Wireless. In **Part III**, we pull together the basic concepts of mobile application design and development, and examine cases of building applications with Oracle9*i*AS Wireless. We also look at successful applications that can be built with Oracle9*i*AS Wireless, and emphasize their business and technology needs, as well as key benefits. We conclude by looking at what products and technologies may lie ahead, and discuss what Oracle may offer and support in the future.

Part I: The Mobile Environment

Chapter 1: The Mobile Economy—Chapter 1 discusses the whys and wherefores of mobile communication, and explores its market drivers and benefits. It outlines the features and functions of mobile services and applications, and examines what makes mobile services unique in terms of opportunities and challenges.

Chapter 2: Introducing Oracle9*i*AS Wireless—Chapter 2 examines the background of the mobile technology stack of Oracle Corporation and takes a glimpse at its strategy. It introduces the Oracle9*i*AS Wireless framework and its components. It examines the so-called "Oracle9*i*AS Wireless accelerators" that help speed up service development, and highlights what differentiates Oracle's product offerings from other mobile platforms.

Part II: Oracle9*i* Application Server Wireless

Chapter 3: Oracle9*i*AS Wireless Architecture—Chapter 3 reviews the overall architecture of Oracle9*i*AS Wireless in terms of its core and services. It goes into details on the Wireless Core, including the functionality and needs for network and device adaptation, and the Oracle9*i*AS XML application model. It reviews adapters, transformers, and tools for administering wireless object components, users, applications, and devices.

Chapter 4: Servers and Integration—Chapter 4 focuses on the integration of Oracle9*i*AS Wireless with other components of Oracle9*i* Application Server, such as Single Sign-On (SSO), Oracle Internet Directory (OID) and WebCache. It covers session management and device detection, as well as the underlying servers within Oracle9*i*AS Wireless. It also goes through an example on how to design a multichannel XML application using the Service Designer and publish this service via the Content Manager.

Chapter 5: Advanced Customization—Chapter 5 introduces the customization framework that offers advanced personalization features, such as presets, and covers the web-based graphic interface to centrally manage users, groups, profiles, and devices. It also covers the alert engine that drives the event- and time-based alert services that Oracle9*i*AS Wireless supports.

Chapter 6: Push and SMS—Chapter 6 explains the unique capabilities of the push modality, and illustrates the Oracle9*i*AS Wireless Messaging architecture. It covers the Push and PushLite Java APIs, Push drivers, and the Push WSDL Web service. It also includes an example application that uses a Push WSDL (SOAP) API to deliver an SMS message to a mobile phone.

Chapter 7: Transcoding—Chapter 7 discusses the web content adaptation and WML translation capabilities of Oracle9*i*AS Wireless Transcoding Service. It explains the benefits and limitations of transcoding, and introduces the Web Integration Developer as an environment to create and test Web Integration services written in Web Interface Definition Language (WIDL). This chapter provides an example JSP application that generates XML and uses the Web Integration Bean to execute a FedEx WIDL service.

Chapter 8: Offline Management: Develop and Deploy Mobile Applications—Chapter 8 introduces the Offline Management Service of Oracle9*i*AS Wireless —Oracle9*i* Lite— and reviews the lifecycle of creating, testing, and deploying an offline application. It explains the Oracle9*i* Lite architecture and reviews its components, especially the Mobile Development Kit and Mobile Server. It reviews the three application models—native, Java and Web —and illustrates how to use the Packaging Wizard and mSQL utility, and how to manage replication and snapshots. It also includes detailed explanations on how you can build a native Windows application using Visual Basic for Oracle9*i* Lite.

Chapter 9: Offline Management: Advanced Features—Chapter 9 continues to discuss the advanced features of Oracle9*i* Lite. It illustrates how to build a Windows CE application using ActiveX Data Objects and Embedded Visual Tools. It introduces the Oracle9*i* Lite synchronization and replication architecture, and explains its capabilities including the Mobile Generator and Processor (MGP). This chapter also reviews the support of Oracle9*i* Lite for branch offices, as well as its support for internationalization and different chipsets in mobile devices. It also discusses issues related to performance tuning and scalability.

Chapter 10: Location-Based Services—Chapter 10 reviews the Location-Based Service (LBS) capabilities of Oracle9*i*AS Wireless and highlights its core features including Location Picker, Driving Directions, Business Directory, and Mapping. Included is an LBS application to find a local restaurant, obtain its operating hours, retrieve driving directions, and get a map of the surrounding area.

Chapter 11: Mobile PIM and E-Mail—Chapter 11 explains how you can build messaging and communication services through the Personal Information Management (PIM) and E-Mail services of Oracle9*i*AS Wireless. It depicts how corporate e-mail, directory, address book, calendaring, and instant messaging applications are integrated with other Oracle components like LDAP and Oracle iFS. It introduces the Jabber Instant Messaging server as well as the SMS and Fax modules.

Chapter 12: Mobile Commerce—Chapter 12 introduces the Oracle9*i*AS Wireless Mobile Commerce architecture. It explains how profiles are stored securely, and illustrates how to integrate m-commerce services with third party applications via a Mobile Wallet server. It introduces the Form Filler module to fill out forms for shopping carts and the Translator module to transcode existing WML commerce applications into XML. The example application shows how you can use the Mobile Wallet to enable a "single-tap" checkout from a shopping cart.

Chapter 13: Mobile Studio—Chapter 13 introduces the Mobile Studio, a web-based development environment that is shipped with Oracle9*i*AS Wireless. Along with a set of mobile modules, the Mobile Studio enables you to quickly prototype and test applications in a live environment within your firewall in an intranet environment. In an extranet setting, an instance of Mobile Studio can be launched as a public developer portal and be accessible by any developer from the Internet.

Part III: Developing and Deploying Dynamic Applications

Chapter 14: Application Design and Development—Chapter 14 provides a development methodology for designing and developing mobile applications. It discusses architecture design and use case development, and goes into some depth on choosing between wireless and offline applications, and between single-channel and multichannel.

Chapter 15: Case Studies—Chapter 15 reviews three cases where Oracle9*i*AS Wireless is implemented: Field Data Acquisition, Mobile Enabling Dynamic Content, and Sales Force Automation. These cases provide you with insights into the *what* and *why* aspects of the application design. It walks through the complete lifecycle of building wireless and offline applications with Oracle9*i*AS Wireless, with emphasis on choices and decisions made in service development.

Chapter 16: Mobile Applications: A Survey—Chapter 16 provides an overview of mobile enterprise information services and reviews successful applications like Field Force Automation, Field Service Automation, etc. and how you can leverage Oracle9*i*AS Wireless to build and deploy many of these vertical and horizontal mobile applications.

Chapter 17: Looking Ahead—Chapter 17 provides a glimpse at what devices, technologies, and networks may prove significant and relevant to Oracle mobile developers. Topics reviewed include J2ME, XHTML, MMS, and VoiceXML.

Part IV: Appendixes

Appendix A: Glossary—Appendix A consists of terms and definitions used throughout this book.

Appendix B: Oracle9*i*AS Multichannel XML—Appendix B contains a complete listing of XML tags of Oracle9*i*AS Wireless Release 2.

Additional information about this book is available from the Oracle Press website at http://www.osborne.com/oracle. You may download the latest Oracle9*i*AS Wireless software at http://otn.oracle.com.

PART I

The Mobile Environment

CHAPTER 1

The Mobile Economy

any of you have heard about the great promises of mobile communications and computing: the freedom of receiving information anytime, communicating with friends and colleagues anywhere, and getting work done and receiving alerts through any devices. Maybe a personal interest prompted you to pick up this book. Perhaps your needs are business oriented: You must wirelessly enable your corporate intranet or mobilize a business intelligence module. Whatever the case may be, you are intrigued by the potential of mobile communications. In this chapter, we discuss the whys and wherefores of mobile communications (sometimes referred to as just *mobile*). We explore its market drivers and benefits. We look at what makes mobile unique in terms of opportunities and challenges. Here are the topics we cover in this chapter:

- Is Mobile Really Different from Wired Communications?
- Mobile vs. Wireless: Basic Concepts
- Key Challenges
- Ideal Experience and Key Points
- New Developments

Is Mobile Really Different from Wired Communications?

The answer to this question is, yes! To explain why, a reference to Oracle is appropriate: A senior executive at Oracle's Mobile Products and Services Division likened the use of personal computers (PCs) and mobile devices to watching a film in a theater and a program on television. Although both media display moving pictures, theaters and TVs are fundamentally different channels and devices. We venture to take this argument further. PCs and mobile devices differ not only because of their form factor but also in their usage and application. You wouldn't put a 25-meter wide screen in your living room to watch the world premiere of *Star Wars III,* but you would watch a special TV program on a 31-inch television screen.

The same is true for extending web browser or PC-based applications to mobile devices. You can't expect to fit a web page designed for an 800x600-pixel monitor screen into that of a wireless phone. Televisions bring entertainment and information to your living room. Likewise, mobile devices bring communication and resources to your pocket. You get 24-hour news coverage from CNN on your television in the living room—not in the theater. You get personal alerts and location-based services with the wireless phone in the palm of your hand—not on your desktop PC.

From Client/Server to Mobile Internet

In some ways, the route to "going mobile" parallels how mass media has changed from radio and broadcast TV, to cable television and 24-hour coverage of news and sporting events. Similarly, the emergence of computer software as an automation tool has brought tremendous productivity gains and revenue growth to many businesses, starting with client/server computing. With this growth has come a new discipline called *business process reengineering*, which changes the way people use computers in much the same manner radio and television changed the way people receive news. The advent of the Internet and web-based computing has made the delivery of these solutions widespread and economic, much like price declines for TV sets and cable TV subscriptions. Now, with the new devices, you can access a vast amount of information and online services, so you can afford to be mobile, keeping in touch with the resources and support you need. Let's examine the market drivers and why we would want to build mobile solutions.

Market Drivers

You are probably familiar with client/server and Internet computing. For most enterprises, the evolution of this relationship has taken place over the past 10 to 15 years. Let us review the key drivers that underpin the changes in the information technology marketplace:

- **Business Process Reengineering** Computer software has brought tremendous productivity to business enterprises and our daily lives through automation and process reengineering. With software, you no longer have to rely solely on "paper-based" processes to key in data, retrieve results, and perform analyses. When companies moved from paper-based systems to mainframe or client/server computing, the changes involved more than technology. They involved a mindset change as well. Many business processes were reviewed, challenged and re-architected to streamline operations and reduce costs. Instead of being paper-based and centralized, business processes became more and more paperless and distributed, leveraging the availability of client/server computing. However, these client/server-based systems lacked scalability, efficiency, and cost effectiveness. The next stage in the evolution led companies to transfer business functions to the Internet, away from proprietary networks, platforms, and hardware systems.
- **Direct Access to Information** With the Internet, and the evolution of personal computers and web browsers, companies can enable ordinary workers to directly access information and benefit from technology, instead of limiting the resources and capabilities to specially trained workers using

proprietary terminals. With the multi-tier Internet architecture, access to these systems and resources become more cost effective. The introduction of web browsers makes it easy for everyone, especially non-computer people, to "use" the Internet and all web-based resources. For instance, employees can access and manage their retirement and pension benefits accounts. Banking customers can review and manage their bank accounts. Businesses can trade and transact deals with each other electronically. With the Internet, the delivery of these software applications, along with e-mail and personal information management (PIM), has revolutionized the way people communicate and work.

- **People Are Mobile** Once you step out of your office or away from your PC, you are no longer connected. All the resources—the richness of the Internet and corporate resources—are taken away from you. Working at your desk, you are "plugged in" to the organization's resources. On the road or away from your PC, you have to rely on others—those who have access to the network through their PCs. Sales personnel may have to rely on an inside sales rep to look up account information, confirm appointments, or retrieve prices and documents. Using the same resources on the road can be difficult due to a number of issues including network availability, compatibility, and security. Nevertheless, mobile workers and business managers alike want the ability to access enterprise data and applications wherever and whenever they are, to help them do their job.

While mobile applications bring benefits to road warriors and others, we shouldn't look at mobile devices as simply an extension of the desktop. The size of the mobile device, its input mechanisms, and the types of tasks people want to complete all require companies to develop a well-thought-out strategy for going mobile. Wireless technology can bestow a number of benefits, as detailed in the next section.

Benefits

In general, you gain the most when paper-based tasks are moved to the web-based, paperless office because it increases the availability of business information from a few users to many. Mobile expands upon this concept by making an enterprise's information available beyond the connected desktop. Information now becomes available to many, anywhere, anytime, thus resulting in greater productivity and efficiency. We discuss some of the benefits here:

- **Enhance Productivity** The biggest driver for mobile devices is to allow web-based applications and person-to-person communication to become pervasive. You don't have to be in front of the desktop to be productive.

You become more successful when you are in front of the customer—but with the same or even more enhanced resources to tap into using mobile devices, thus making you more productive!

- **Improve Business Processes** With mobile devices, you can take out the intermediate steps or interactions with people that are not needed but are there because you are on the go or because a desktop computer is not at hand. Data entry and acquisition—in terms of timeliness and accuracy—are prime examples.
- **Drive Revenue Growth** Allowing your customers to look up product catalogs and inventory availability, providing a new means to serve or entertain, and enabling anywhere, anytime communication are just a few examples of how you and your enterprise can grow your business and increase sales.
- **Reduce Cost** An obvious result of mobile computing is its ability to bring cost savings to enterprises by reducing the latency and manual steps involved. It also lowers the cost of communication; perhaps the most obvious is long-distance or toll calls. Witness how Europeans and Asians are using Short Messaging Service (SMS) to communicate. It's efficient, easy, and inexpensive. It doesn't replace face-to-face meetings or personal phone calls, but it sure complements them.

Unique Features

From the user's perspective, a number of features make mobile usage advantageous:

- **Presence** With mobile devices, the services you need are always there. Because these services are always present (the so-called "always on" or "always available" services), you don't have to wait for a long bootup like the PC. And you can come to rely on them and use them often.
- **Location** You can be wherever you want because you can carry these mobile devices with you. With location-based technologies, you expect these services to know where you are and provide you with the information relevant to your location needs.
- **Personalized** Unlike desktop computers, your mobile devices comprise a unique, personal lifestyle extension. Your phone company or wireless provider knows your preferences. You or your service provider, through usage patterns, can proactively personalize your user interface, services, and information needs.

- **Automated** You may want to access web-based content from multiple devices, ranging from a desktop PC to a handheld PDA, smart phone, or regular voice-based phone. You will need ways to handle and synchronize the multitude of e-mail messages, phone numbers, and web addresses for you and your enterprise. Mobile services can simplify your life by offering transparent access to your data and content while being agnostic to device types.

Mobile vs. Wireless: Basic Concepts

Many use the terms *mobile* and *wireless* interchangeably. Oracle Corporation defines *mobile* as the combination of wireless, offline, push and voice. Wireless represents the mobile online services that are always-on and rendered in a synchronous fashion, with state and session control. Wireless online services include information portals offered by operators or business intelligence portals provisioned by enterprises.

Offline applications, sometimes referred to as disconnected applications, are asynchronous in nature. Typical examples are PDA applications that allow users to capture data or retrieve information in a disconnected mode, then later on uplink or "sync" up with a database server when wired or wireless connection is achieved.

Push services generally refer to applications that send information, alerts and actionable messages to users, based on pre-defined criteria or events. And voice applications cover a broad range of speech-oriented services including automatic speech recognition (ASR), text-to-speech (TTS) translation and other telephony capabilities.

Now that we have outlined the definition of *mobile*, let us examine the key concepts of mobile computing and communications.

Mobility and Bandwidth

You can look at mobile computing from local and wide area perspectives, as shown in Figure 1-1. You can consider accessing the web through an IEEE 802.11b local area network as untethering your dial-up desktop computer and giving it a turbo charger. At the same time, the network infrastructure for wide area access is evolving from second generation (2G) networks, such as Global Systems for Mobile Communication (GSM), to Global Packet Radio System (GPRS), the so-called 2.5G network, and Universal Mobile Telecommunication Systems (UMTS), a third generation (3G) network. In all cases, bandwidth is greatly improved and access is "always on"! It is an important milestone for the mobile industry to finally be able to make mobile data services affordable for practically everyone. It can be likened to the delivery of TV programming via cable and satellite.

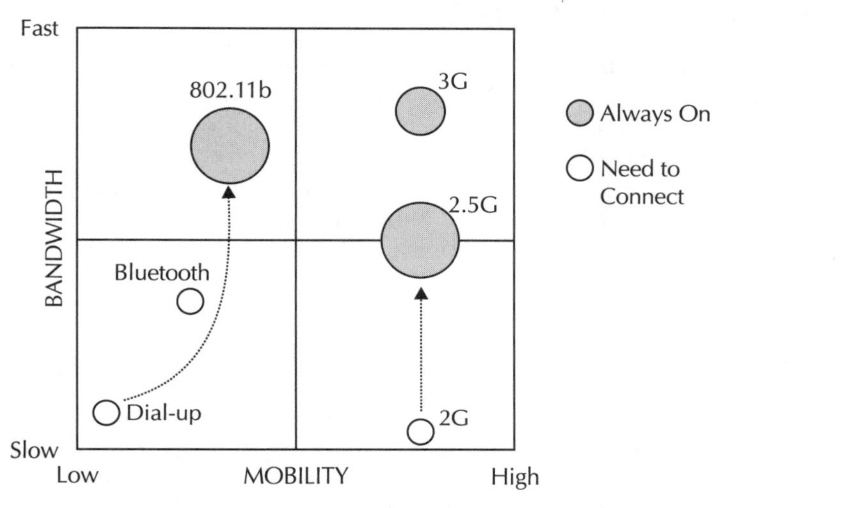

FIGURE 1-1. *Bandwidth improvement*

Data, Content, and Applications

Mobile devices allow you to access data, content, and applications anytime, anywhere. Data can be retrieved, acquired, and synchronized. Content may reside in an intranet, the Internet, or an extranet, or it may be aggregated as a wireless portal. Applications might be assessable via a single channel, or you can tap into the applications via multiple channels. Together, mobile data, content, and applications can uniquely bring value to you and your workgroup. Here are some examples:

- **Data** When data is coupled with automation, you can eliminate paper and manual data reentry. With its ease of use, you can eliminate latency issues and avoid propagation of errors.
- **Content** You can pull information from wireless portals. Intranet services can push alerts to you based on time or value events.
- **Applications** Horizontal applications such as Customer Relationship Management (CRM), Enterprise Resource Planning (ERP), workgroup collaboration, and e-mail communication can be leveraged with mobile access. Vertical applications, such as law-enforcement command and communication, can be enhanced with mobile devices.

Online and Offline

For both 802.11b and wireless Internet access, you may come across situations where you don't have network access or coverage. Most wireless operators provide services that are meant to be always on or online. For other applications, such as warehousing or package delivery, you may want to enter data or review downloaded information in a disconnected mode, to reduce connection charges, for instance. In other words, you want to have an "offline" management capability that can provide persistent access on the client device and can synchronize with the server when the network is available.

Right Time, Place, and Information

Wireless communication means providing the user with the right information at the right time and at the right place. For developers, this is an opportunity and a challenge. The growing needs to manage personal information and access business resources with mobile devices present an opportunity. The constraints in network bandwidth and availability, as well as device user interface and capability, represent a set of unique challenges.

Alerts, Messaging, and E-Mail

As with desktop computing, you can receive alerts, send messages, and read e-mail with your mobile devices. However, unlike the traditional PC approach, your device is personal and mobile—and you can expect the push technology to play a major role. Also, messaging, especially instant messaging, short messaging, and mobile e-mail, will become more compelling to mobile communications.

Key Challenges

Mobile computing and communications cut across and draw upon many disciplines and requirements: network infrastructure, hardware devices, and application software development. It is no wonder that confusion is rampant and that quite a number of wireless projects never reach their intended goals and wind up as catastrophic flops. To avoid these pitfalls, let's take a look at a key question: What issues arise when designing mobile applications to leverage the pervasive wireless technology?

In general, you can summarize these issues under cost and complexity. When you look at the myriad of infrastructure issues, hardware, and software involved, as shown in Figure 1-2, it's not surprising that high cost and complexity result.

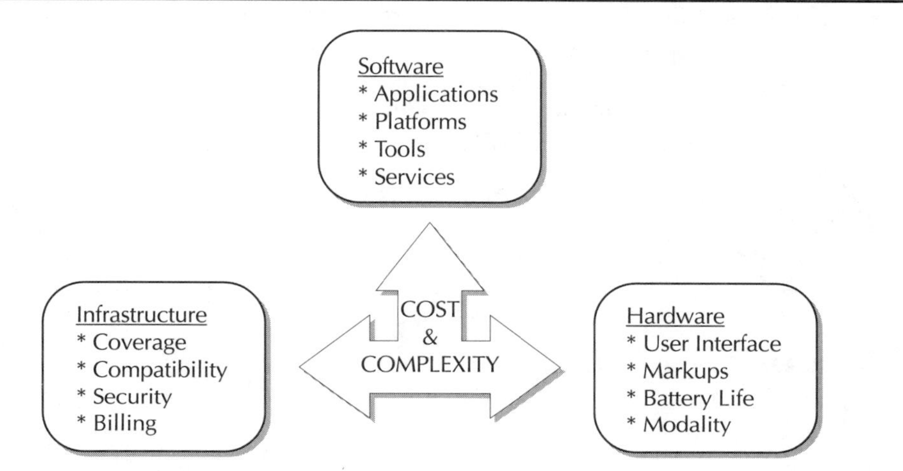

FIGURE 1-2. *Cost and complexity*

Devices

In recent years, many kinds of device technologies have emerged: web-enabled PCs, personal digital assistants (PDAs), Wireless Application Protocol (WAP) phones, and pagers—and the number is growing. These devices support different protocols, have different capabilities, and use different browsers. Starting with web browsers on desktop and laptop PCs, multi-channel applications are now being made available through an increasing array of devices, including touch-screen terminals, voice-only telephones, PDAs, Java devices, pagers, smart phones, and interactive TVs. Key development issues include:

- **User Interface** Providing customized and rich applications for all device types is challenging. Information-access terminals have continued to proliferate and take new shapes. Therefore, you have a rapidly rising number of devices and a challenging design and development environment.
- **Markup Language and Protocol** Many devices are designed to work with different markup languages and protocols—for example, WAP, cHTML, HDML, GSM, TDMA, CDMA, AMPS, CDPD, just to name a few. Therefore, understanding what they are and how to support them are major issues.

- **Battery Life** A key factor for designing mobile services for handheld devices is battery consumption. The heavy use of some device functions and inefficient applications requiring multiple packets can drain battery life quickly. As a developer, you have the responsibility to factor this into your application development work.
- **Modality** Different devices support multiple kinds of modalities, each behaving differently. For example, with text-to-speech and speech recognition technologies, voice applications accessed through any telephone will open up new ways to communicate, but they also present a new set of challenges.

Network Infrastructure

A typical network infrastructure for mobile computing may comprise different network domains, including wide area networks (WANs), local area networks (LANs), the Internet and various intranets. Although all these domains may eventually meld into a single IP network, individual networks, with their intrinsic characteristics that differ from each other, can add cost and complexity to mobile computing. Even within a single IP network, a number of design and deployment issues exist:

- **Coverage** Wireless coverage is still evolving, and mobile users must be able to count on always being connected to their network when applications are designed as "always on." Users can work in out-of-coverage areas if there are offline management modules and features. Users expect instant and constant access to their online services, whereas mobile networks are still working on delivery of always-on packet services. Congestion and uneven coverage within radio networks will remain an issue for a while. Constant outages present challenges for an application developer to account for data protocol implementations.
- **Compatibility** Securing the best-quality internetworks is imperative to achieving seamless end-to-end services. Because the wireless world is evolving so rapidly, no global standards exist for mobile phones. If you are based in Europe and have a GSM phone, and you take it to the U.S., you'll find your phone won't be compatible with many U.S. networks. The "i-mode", a highly successful wireless data service offered by NTT DoCoMo, may be popular in Japan, but it will take some time before it is offered widely elsewhere around the world.
- **Security** How secure is transmitted information? Can the information be tapped or intercepted? Can someone impersonate a different user? It's one thing to receive alerts on stock prices, but it's another thing to retrieve

your sales and expenses reports on your division, or conduct banking transactions with your mobile devices. Will your applications compromise the secure systems of the entire enterprise?

- **Bandwidth and Transmission Cost** Unlike broadband Internet access, wireless content will still have bandwidth limitations in the near term. It is unclear whether flat rates will apply to wireless Internet access. Therefore, by minimizing the packet requirements of your applications, you not only make them easier to use but less costly to run.
- **Billing and System Management** With a variety of network infrastructures and transmission and integration points, tracking usage and managing systems, applications, and users can be challenging. It's not enough to have excellent applications if there are no means to support system management and provide resource accounting and billing.

Software

Compounding developers' task to build mobile applications is a marketplace that includes hundreds of software vendors and wireless application service providers. Let us look at the key issues that developers need to address:

- **Applications** When you understand the current state of mobile services and delivery, you soon realize that the biggest barrier to mobile deployment is a lack of good apps. That doesn't mean there are no good mobile applications. It means most applications built to date are not specifically written to be mobile. The mobile user experience is incredibly important, and it is different from that on your PC. Wireless is about process transforming, and it engenders a completely different venue from desktop. You need to keep this in mind when you build your apps. Many enterprise information services can be delivered to sales, services, support, marketing, and distribution in a mobile context. The important consideration is what subset of this content is appropriate in a mobile context and what value it brings to a mobile user. Each of these issues has specific characteristics that need to be factored into the design of a mobile application, and the characteristics can vary widely.
- **Platforms** Most software platforms for wireless computing stem from a niche or monolithic approach in solving specific business problems. A comprehensive, integrated approach is needed to ensure availability, scalability, and performance. For example, how will the platform and applications respond to hundreds of concurrent users? Can you connect your wireless portal with your enterprise portal? How can you integrate your wireless applications with legacy systems?

- **Tools** Mobile application development is a new field. Many tools that developers use are not designed or meant for this purpose. Developers want flexibility, power, and ease of use. Designers, line-of-business managers, and software developers are only starting to work together. How do they collaborate and what tools are available for development as well as content and system management?
- **Services** Mobile applications mean personal and location services, which in turn mean leveraging third-party content and resources intelligently. How can you, as a developer, build a useful application quickly by accessing online road reports with delivery scheduling of the "goods and services?" How can you easily build SMS or instant-messaging applications without writing code from scratch?

Ideal Experience and Key Points

The same mindset change is required to fully realize the opportunities that mobile devices provide. Let's look at what will be ideal and key points to address for a user, a developer, and a system administrator for wireless applications.

User

People want to interact much differently with mobile devices than they do with PCs. They do want to access some of the same applications they do on the Web, such as e-mail, expense reports, address books, and calendars, but they have no desire to write lengthy documents. Other pieces of information, such as driving directions, real-time traffic, and alerts about critical pieces of data are far more important on a mobile device than on a PC. More importantly, people use mobile devices when they are not at their home or office, and, as a result, their locations are not fixed. So to provide your audience (whether they're employees, customers, or partners) with mobile applications with the greatest utility, you need to understand where they are, where they've been, and where they are going. Incorporating location-based services with your mobile applications can help you complete these requirements.

Developer

A mobile application normally flows from one mobile page to another, where each page typically corresponds to a screen displayed on a mobile device. When designing wireless applications, ask yourself a few questions:

- **Direct** What is the goal of this interaction? What is the easiest way for the user to complete this task?

- **Interruption** The network goes down. The user gets sidetracked. Can the application handle an interruption and resume interaction later?
- **Duration** Battery life is limited. Voice-activated applications demand short and clear interactions. How long does it take for users to accomplish their goals?
- **Intuitive Usage** Most users don't have time or the patience to learn to use new devices, let alone new applications. How easy is it for them to use your application? Are the user interface features familiar or strange to them?

System Administrator

Much like building and implementing a corporate website or an enterprise application, the real challenge for a system administrator is management and maintenance after the designers and developers are done with their assignments. What infrastructure and support are available? Are there facilities that can help the system administrator manage devices, users, roles, services, and applications? Ideally, these challenges will not be met by using a great many point servers and solutions. An integrated approach, preferably web-based, would be ideal.

New Developments

Notwithstanding the challenges we described earlier, mobile developers are now witnessing new and exciting developments that address the key issues. New gateways and new networks have been built and are in place. New devices, with vastly improved form factors and user interfaces, are now available and affordable. Mobile strategies are being addressed and application needs clearly identified. Finally, comprehensive, robust software platforms and toolkits are made available. Let us take a look at some of these new developments.

Improved Gateways and Networks

Wireless LAN standard 802.11b looks poised for growth as it continues to gain traction in the market. The biggest boon came when cafes began wiring stores with 802.11b technology so that customers can access the Internet with their PDAs and laptops.

802.11b offers at least as much capacity as 3G, at a limited mobility. One key advantage of the technology is that 802.11b cards are powerful, enabling wireless connectivity from relatively long distances. Its real potential is in the workplace and in the home—turning factories, hospitals, warehouses, and stores into 802.11b-based local area networks (LANs). Users can access the Internet at 11 Mbps—much faster than DSL or cable modems.

The GPRS and 3G networks are now being put in place across Europe and Asia, and the rollout of CDMA2000 (the U.S. version of 3G) is proceeding rapidly. GPRS is replacing the slow and unreliable 2G networks, and can be installed as an overlay over GSM networks. Installation and deployment will cost less, and the cost savings are passed along to users. In addition, the "always-on" feature of GPRS eliminates the 30–45 second wait time that has hindered wireless data services for current GSM or CDMA networks.

On local area networks, IEEE 802.11 (a, b, and g) are emerging as the standard bearers for enterprise back-end operations, fulfilling the promise of increasing productivity and reducing costs through data access for any site location. These developments lower the cost of ownership for mobile application implementation.

New Devices

One of the reasons for excitement about mobile applications is the fact that devices capable of running the technology properly are coming onto the market. Products that support the next generations of WAP, SMS, instant messaging, and offline applications include the Nokia Communicator and Samsung's integrated color Palm Powered Phone. The latter is one of the first devices to truly combine the features of a mobile phone with a PDA. Mobile e-mail access is gaining popularity as BlackBerry handheld devices become more popular. Also, Java phones are showing up everywhere after proving their value in Japan.

Emerging Standards

There is no doubt that standards reduce the overall cost of computing and allow for better returns on investments. The trend away from proprietary systems toward standards has been gathering steam with Java/J2EE, Extensible Markup Language (XML), Web Services, J2EE Connector Architecture (JCA), SyncML and Simple Object Access Protocol (SOAP), to name a few. Recently, a handful of providers and vendors have agreed to support Liberty Alliance, the mobile identity initiative, and Open Mobile Architecture, the mobile extension of Java 2 standard.

The IT industry's commitment to the Open Mobile Architecture initiative marks the beginning of the next phase of mobile services, by incorporating a mobile extension for Java 2 Platform, Enterprise Edition (J2EE) based application servers. These companies intend to focus on creating interoperable server solutions for service providers, corporations, and mobile operators. Joint specifications are being developed in compliance with the guidelines provided by the relevant industry standardization bodies.

This effort will lead to the development of uniform mobile application programming interfaces (APIs), providing developers with optimal tools for incorporating mobility into their applications, thus fueling worldwide growth of mobile services and third-party software innovation.

New products and solutions will be based on Open Mobile Architecture enablers, such as Java- and 3GPP-compliant technologies, such as WAP2.0/XHTML, Multimedia Messaging Service (MMS), and SyncML. Joint specifications will result in the creation of mobile services using J2EE application servers. Leading the charge is Oracle, whose mantra is to combat the complexity of dealing multiple point solutions, devices, protocols and networks.

The emergence of markup languages such as VoiceXML and XHTML will finally allow service providers and technology vendors to focus on their core competencies, instead of expending efforts to create competing standards and protocols. Mobile applications built by different service providers will interoperate with each other. Services built with current technologies will work with future platforms. As a result, the cost of building and managing mobile enterprise solutions is reduced. A good example can be found in the widely acceptable IEEE 802.11b standard, on which many offline applications are based and interoperability is assured.

Software Platform and Tools

Software platforms, along with new applications and greater choices of tools and kits, are making the lives of mobile developers easy—easy not because building mobile applications will be a cinch but rather because developers will be offered more resources and so-called *accelerators* to rapidly build mobile solutions. For example, Oracle has one of the most complete platforms to build your solutions on. You can utilize the open standards approach in XML, J2EE, and SQL, yet leverage the unique and value-creating characteristics of Oracle9*i* Application Server (Oracle9*i*AS). Because all Oracle's e-business applications will run on Oracle9*i*AS, you can take advantage of the well-defined integration points and interface specifications that Oracle publishes, if you ever need to modify or enhance these applications.

Summary

Mobile applications will become available at lower prices and become accessible to an increasingly wider audience. Wireless is about setting people free to interact with each other and with systems wherever they are and whenever they like. It's also about simplicity and a new way of thinking about software. It's about turning the next-generation devices into simple things that perform meaningful tasks for people. This has always been the vision at Oracle. In this book, we will show you how to design and develop mobile applications on the Oracle platform by leveraging its tools, accelerators, and modules to accomplish this goal.

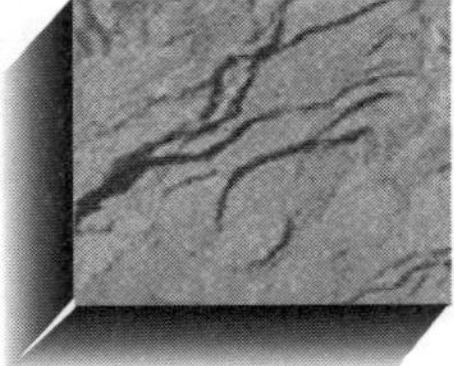

CHAPTER 2

Introducing Oracle9*i*AS Wireless

racle has been involved in mobile computing since the mid-1990s. To understand how the pieces fall into place, we'll look at the background of the mobile technology stack of Oracle Corporation and take a glimpse at its strategy. We'll also review various components within the mobile architecture and highlight what makes Oracle's product offerings different from others. In this chapter we will discuss the following topics:

- 9*i*AS Wireless
- Oracle Mobile Strategy
- Oracle Mobile and Wireless Architecture
- Oracle Differentiators

Oracle9*i*AS Wireless

Since 1999, Oracle9*i* Application Server Wireless (Oracle9*i*AS Wireless), the mobile technology stack from Oracle Corporation, has been enabling the development of open, standards-based applications that can be deployed once and are instantly accessible from any device. To drive growth and technology adoption, Oracle created a Products and Services Division, dubbed Oracle Mobile, to offer a complete mobile solution. A complete solution means the entire platform supports anytime, anywhere, computer-hiding the complexity related to network infrastructure, devices, protocols, markup languages, and software platforms. This solution is meant to help developers, enterprises and wireless carriers build mobile applications easily and deploy them in-house or with a hosting partner.

Project Panama

Oracle9*i*AS Wireless is a story of meeting customer needs. Started in 1997 as a joint project between Oracle and Telia AB in Sweden, this wireless application server undertaking was known as *Project Panama* because the server linked two oceans of opportunities: wireline content and wireless access. The product was subsequently named Portal-To-Go (PTG) and later integrated with the Oracle9*i* Application Server product and renamed Oracle9*i*AS Wireless. As a result, you will see names and references within the URLs and code to *panama* and *ptg*. Because Oracle9*i*AS Wireless owes its heritage to wireless portals, the platform is carrier grade and scalability proven. This also means usability has been at the top of Oracle's design considerations.

Oracle9*i* Lite

In reality, enterprises have adopted wireless for quite a while, particularly for remote communications with field engineers and vehicles using properietary analog systems, and for warehouse and inventory management, and car rental returns/check-ins using wireless LAN (WLAN). Even with WLAN, wireless coverage is not ensured at all times in all areas. Enterprises have learned that they need a solution that can run in an offline mode with PDAs and laptops. Oracle's answer to the challenge is Oracle9*i* Lite, a proven platform consisting of a mobile server on the server side and a lightweight relational database management system (RDBMS) on the "smart" client side. Now branded Oracle9iAS Wireless Offline Managment, Oracle9*i* Lite originated from Omniscience Object Technology with strong Oracle input. Subsequently, Oracle has done a complete revamp and built a very robust product. It supports wireless and wireline synchronization as well as deployment and application management, and it provides persistent data access on the client device if and when there is no wireless coverage.

Oracle Mobile Online

As the market tends toward delivering software as services, Oracle offers an online service, called Oracle Mobile Online, that includes wireless application hosting and an online developer studio. The delivery of Oracle software and intellectual property as an online service enables better support, management, and delivery of applications. As a Wireless Application Service Provider (WASP), Oracle Mobile Online provides hosting service with easy access to modules and resources. You can get your mobile applications up and running quickly, without investment in wireless network and server infrastructure. As a hosted development environment, Oracle Mobile Online offers a Mobile Studio (developer portal) that allows you to build, test, and deploy your applications.

Oracle Mobile Strategy

Three essential elements constitute Oracle's mobile strategy (see Figure 2-1):

- **Oracle9*i*AS Wireless** The thrust of Oracle's entrée into mobile computing is its mobile and wireless platform, Oracle9*i*AS Wireless, which includes the wireless application server that runs in a Java 2 Platform, Enterprise Edition (J2EE) container, an offline management service known as Oracle9*i* Lite, a mobile studio that enables online application development within an intranet or an extranet, along with a plethora of mobile services, modules, and tools.
- **Online Services** To provide testing and deployment alternatives to building infrastructure in-house, Oracle offers its online services in Oracle Mobile Online for application hosting and an online studio for developers, currently hosted on the Oracle Technology Network (OTN).

- **E-Business Suite** Who knows better how to mobile enable an Oracle e-business application than Oracle itself? The entire Oracle11*i* E-Business Suite will have mobile modules that are built on the Oracle9*i*AS platform.

Underpinning all these are Oracle's consulting efforts—which at the time of this writing are dubbed *mSpeed Consulting*. If you don't have sufficient resources or prefer to leverage Oracle's mobile experts, they are your hired guns in mobile!

Write Once, Publish Everywhere

The Oracle Mobile Application Framework makes it easy to develop mobile applications by providing a development model that clearly separates the different tiers of your application (presentation, logic, and data) and allows for parallel development of each tier. The Oracle9*i*AS Wireless Core is the framework that gives application developers independence from the underlying networks, protocols, devices, gateways, and other wireless complexities. The Oracle9*i*AS Wireless Core normalizes the wireless complexities to primarily one protocol, HTTP, for synchronized applications (SMTP/SMS for asynchronized applications), and one language, XML, thus enabling applications to be accessed by any device, including voice phone, while exploiting different device features. All this can be accomplished by writing each application only once.

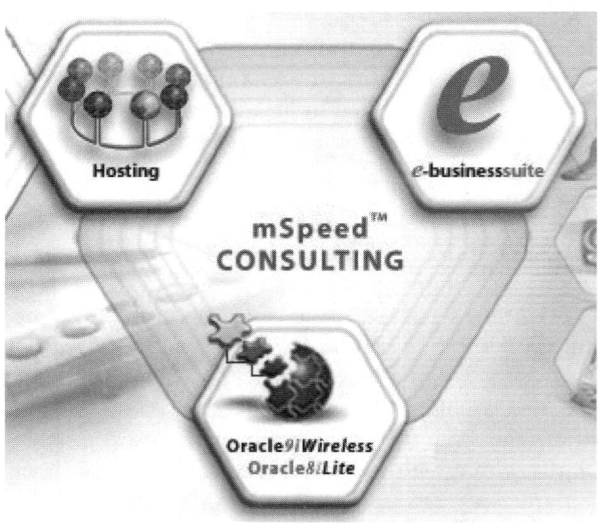

FIGURE 2-1. *The triad of Oracle Mobile Strategy*

Integration with 9*i* Application Server

Oracle9*i*AS Wireless consists of components that are deployed as Oracle9*i*AS Containers for Java (OC4J) applications and standalone Java applications. The OC4J applications include the following:

- **Wireless Web Server** Handles requests from mobile devices via HTTP.
- **Async Servers** Handles requests from mobile devices via non-HTTP (for example, e-mail and SMS).
- **Module Servers** Provides built-in services that can speed up application development, such as PIM and m-wallet. Services and modules are used interchangeably in this context. For their differences, refer to Appendix A.
- **Push Server** Supports push messages to any devices with any protocol.

The standalone Java applications within Oracle9*i*AS Wireless include the following:

- **Data Feeder** Fetches data from providers through any protocol.
- **Alert Engine** Handles alert services through subscriptions.
- **Messaging Server** Delivers messages to any device in any protocol.
- **Performance Logger** Writes usage logging data asynchronously to the database for performance monitoring.

Mobile E-Business Suite

In response to market demand, Oracle has mobilized its E-business Suite 11*i*, which is a tightly integrated collection of individual modules across functional areas, such as customer relationship management (CRM), human resources, supply-chain planning, logistics, and financials. The initial focus for mobile development has been on applications in which customer demand is greatest, including CRM and enterprise resource planning (ERP), and could be easily used with the current generation of mobile devices and networks.

Hosted, In-house, or Hybrid

Offering hosting services represents a strategic transformation of Oracle from an offline vendor of enterprise business software to a complete provider of online and offline enterprise-class business services through the Internet. Oracle Mobile Online gives you much faster time to market with a solution, because you immediately get your application connected to live devices and other network services. This way, you don't have to worry about infrastructure issues involving the network and gateway, as well as managing the production process for wireless provisioning.

For instance, a company that is not an expert in wireless may want to have Oracle host its mobile applications, whereas some other high-tech companies may want to manage their own platforms and host their own mobile services. Oracle9*i*AS Wireless offers complete flexibility in how you want to deploy your infrastructure. It is possible to take a hybrid approach: use the Oracle Mobile platform for hosting mobile E-business Suite applications and run your custom mobile solutions in-house.

XML, J2EE, and SOAP

Oracle has a long history of provisioning carrier and enterprise customers with open-standards support for the development and deployment of Internet applications. Based on open J2EE, OC4J, and XML standards, Oracle9*i*AS Wireless is no exception. Intended for easy integration with existing and future technologies, you can create interoperable server solutions for service providers, corporations, and mobile operators.

To render an application to any device, you just need to create any application that outputs XML and point the Oracle9*i*AS Wireless Core to the application with a URL. The Oracle9*i*AS Wireless Core will automatically alleviate the complexities associated with wireless technologies. On J2EE, Oracle9*i*AS Wireless is a J2EE-compliant option and component of its application server, Oracle9*i*AS. To leverage web services, you can quickly add services via Simple Access Object Protocol (SOAP), Universal Description, Discovery, and Integration (UDDI), and Web Services Description Language (WSDL) because Oracle9*i*AS Wireless is integrated with other components within Oracle9*i*AS, including Web Services.

Oracle Mobile and Wireless Architecture

Oracle recognizes that creating applications for the mobile context poses unique challenges. By adopting a proven methodology and leveraging the unique capabilities of Oracle9*i*AS Wireless, you can reduce development and deployment costs. In this section, we'll review a typical mobile and wireless architecture that is based on Oracle technologies (see Figure 2-2).

Devices, Markups, and Protocols

The goal of Oracle9*i*AS Wireless is to support any device with any markup language and protocol. To accomplish that, Oracle9*i*AS Wireless handles the style sheets that present content in WML, cHTML, tinyHTML, and VoiceXML to be served into such devices as WAP phones, PDAs, and voice phones.

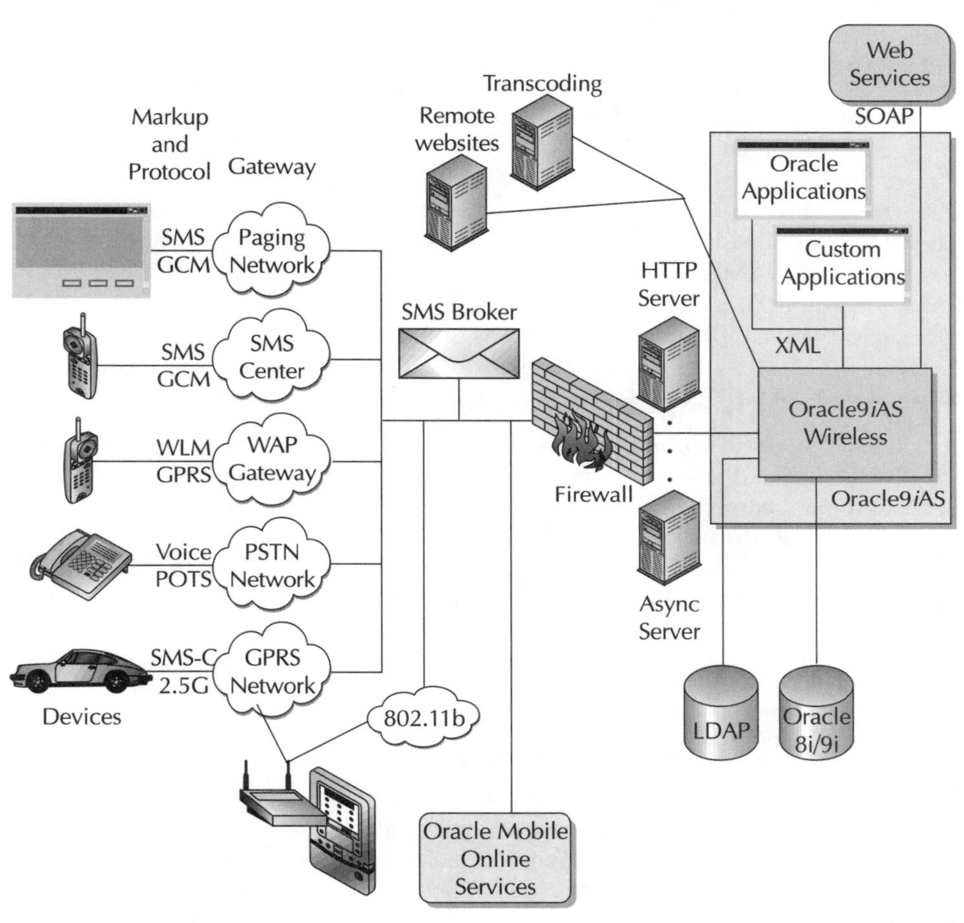

FIGURE 2-2. *Oracle wireless and mobile architecture*

Networks

To succeed in providing a "write once, publish everywhere" platform, you need to shield developers from the complexity of supporting various networks and infrastructure. As depicted in Figure 2-2, you may come across a range of networks such as pager, SMS, voice, and WAP, and these networks may add an SMS broker to boot. Devices may access a GPRS network at a point but sync up with an 802.11b wireless LAN at another. Oracle9*i*AS Wireless provides services to easily call upon these networks with mobile services, modules, and Java classes.

Online Services

Because Oracle offers a hosting service, you can link your applications to the hosting site via Oracle Mobile Online Services and have your application live quickly. Oracle Mobile Online is indifferent to the mechanism used to generate the presentation logic of your mobile application. You can build your applications in CGI, PHP, JavaServer Pages, ColdFusion, and Active Server Pages and deploy them in your own server environment. You can also leverage your investment in code and programmer skills. For Oracle Mobile Online to work, you just need to ensure your application will return content in XML. For in-house applications, you have the added benefit that you can code against lower-level APIs and customize your applications deeper using XML. It also gives you a bit more control in terms of deployment.

Framework Architecture

In Chapter 3, we will cover the Oracle9*i*AS Wireless Core and services in more detail. You can leverage Oracle9*i*AS Wireless to aggregate content through transcoding services, or you can provision location-based services (LBS) using Web services from an LBS provider. Armed with HTTP and async servers, the Oracle9*i*AS Wireless framework allows you to support Oracle applications as well as your own. These applications could be on the sell side (for example, managing sales leads), on the buy side (for example, monitoring inventory), or on the inside (for example, receiving workflow notifications).

Oracle Differentiators

Enterprises face a number of challenges when it comes to building and deploying mobile applications for their employees, customers, and partners. The eternal questions IT managers and developers face also apply here: Are packaged applications available? Can we customize? Should we use an existing platform or build our own?

Let's look at the key factors in evaluating and choosing wireless platforms. In some cases, some key characteristics of Oracle9*i*AS Wireless are included—and you can decide whether it is worth writing about (we thought so) and worth building applications on (we hope you think so).

Platform

The answer to the eternal "make or buy" question almost always revolves around another question: Do you want to become a mobile expert, or would you be content with becoming the beneficiary of someone's hard work and focus on your business objectives instead? We believe, unless you are a wireless carrier, you probably want to concentrate on your core competency and let infrastructure vendors such as Oracle tackle the development and support of such systems.

Having said that, even wireless carriers, such as Telia, Sprint, Verizon, AT&T Wireless, and Telefonica Moviles (just to name a few), leverage some aspects of Oracle9*i*AS Wireless.

Another question to ask is, is the wireless platform written in a proprietary language? As a developer, you know that learning a proprietary language will slow you down—and it is not even clear the skills will help you down the road. The system you select should not put you in the situation where you have to completely rebuild your middleware layer due to system complexity and/or cost. You're better off with a middleware developed in a standard language, such as Java. This way, you have a standards-based solution, and your platform will be compatible with other enterprise systems.

Core and Services

If you decide you want to buy, and your choices are standards based, you of course need to choose a platform from a vendor who will stand behind it. Someone once said that when you choose a platform, you are choosing a long-term partner. Let's look at Oracle again in this context.

Oracle9*i*AS Wireless simplifies development and deployment by providing the ability to deliver any content to any device, with any protocol, and across any wireless network with the Oracle9*i*AS Wireless Core. Oracle9*i*AS Wireless includes a set of wireless services, such as PIM (and e-mail), push, and location-based services, that enhance the capabilities of your application and leverage its traits. It uses open standards, such as XML, OC4J, and J2EE, which allow for the delivery of a high-performance and scalable mobile infrastructure. What's more, you can add or write your services on top of the platform.

Integration

How does the middleware integrate with other products? A middleware product that supports XML would be ideal, given that integration methods based on XML tags are in common use today. If there is no XML support, check to see what other connectors exist and what products the middleware can integrate with.

In choosing integrated applications and solutions, you want to minimize the need for complicated and costly systems integration. Imagine having to hire hundreds of consultants to connect CRM to ERP across multiple platforms, including desktops and mobile devices. Additionally, choosing a mobile middleware solution that is designed to work seamlessly with a particular application package means that applications go to market quicker, and the end solution is a seamless one.

With Oracle's integration points and interface specifications, you can easily integrate and enhance e-business offerings.

Scalability

Any application initiative must be scalable to change with the growing needs of a business, especially in its support of users and new technology. When choosing a platform, you must consider application growth and the platform's ability to increase capacity to meet future demands. The platform you choose must be scalable enough to accommodate support for new devices by building on open standards. This will help ensure that your mobile initiatives are built to last.

Security

How secure is the middleware product itself and how secure is its delivery to the mobile device? The product you choose should support some type of security—either data encryption or user validation at the beginning of each session.

When you build solutions for delivering mobile Internet content and applications to wireless users, you want an end-to-end security model designed to meet the security needs of diverse applications, including banking, e-commerce, self-service, and CRM.

Oracle9*i*AS Wireless utilizes data-encryption technologies such as Wireless Transport Layer Security (WTLS), Secure Sockets Layer (SSL), virtual private networks (VPNs) and Public Key Infrastructure (PKI) to deliver solid end-to-end security across the Internet and the wireless network to include PDAs, RIM devices, voice, and WAP phones.

Oracle9*i*AS Wireless has a number of ways to assure you that your data remains secure; however, the wireless gateway (WAP, Palm.Net, and so on) operated by the carrier or service provider is outside of the Oracle9*i*AS Wireless server's control. The wireless gateway and the Oracle9iAS Wireless server are both security trust points.

During the encryption/decryption phase, the data at the Application layer is in the "clear", i.e., unencrypted and exposed, in the wireless gateway server's memory for a short time interval. This is being addressed by Openwave in WAP 1.2 and in the interim by Secure Enterprise Proxy, which is supposedly addressing this concern in WAP 1.1. To prevent any possible leakage of "clear" data, the carrier is responsible for setting up its gateways so that they never store decrypted content on secondary media. The carrier also uses a single decryption/re-encryption optimized process that clears the gateway's server internal memory as soon as re-encryption is done, and the carrier ensures that the server is physically secure so that only authorized personnel have access to it.

Oracle also provides third-party security partners access to published APIs, allowing them to architect and provide external security solutions. These solutions include encrypted tunneling, as well as other VPN and PKI solutions, and support encryption at the Application layer in the server and client device, thus eliminating any possibility for "clear" data at the Application layer.

Fault Tolerance

What is the level of fault tolerance? You should remember that for these complex distributed systems, the level of fault tolerance is very important, because the cost of redelivering may be expensive. This is true not only for the entity maintaining the system but also for wireless users in the form of access time, because they have to reload lost screens and data.

Adaptability

Last but not least, you must assess the adaptability and extensibility of the mobile middleware. That is, what's its ability to either modify or extend the existing available APIs to additional or future enterprise systems? What adapters and transformers are available? Do you want to write adapters if it will take you weeks and cause you lots of headaches? The latest middleware systems allow you to support storing complete documents in XML form (or in your application's form) directly in the specific binary data type. This decreases the time needed to incorporate a relational structure into your systems. You can parse the data out to various displays using Extensible Stylesheet Language Transformation (XSLT) and caching the data in objects for faster display.

Summary

Hopefully, we have set the stage for you to explore Oracle9*i*AS Wireless. If you are new to Oracle or to its wireless stack, hopefully we have convinced you to look further— because Oracle9*i*AS Wireless is comprehensive, easy to learn, and simple to use. Integrated with other Oracle infrastructure (Oracle9*i*AS and Oracle8*i*/Oracle9*i* Database) and Oracle11*i* E-Business Suite applications, Oracle9*i*AS Wireless is extensible for advanced development and customization as well.

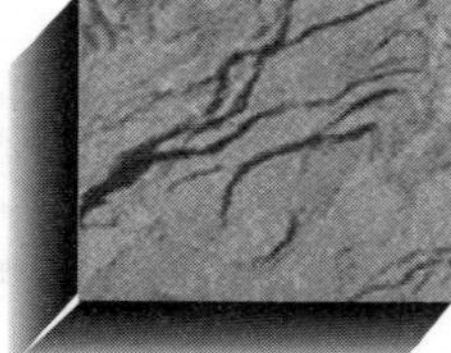

PART II

Oracle9*i* Application Server Wireless

CHAPTER 3

Oracle9*i*AS Wireless Architecture

This chapter introduces the Oracle9*i*AS Wireless architecture—in terms of its core and services as well as the tools you can use. We will dig into the Wireless Core, with emphasis on adapters and transformers, Oracle9*i*AS multichannel XML, devices, and networks. This chapter also provides a brief introduction to each of the eight major services and the web-based wireless tools. We will progress to advanced features, such as integration with other Oracle technologies, in Chapter 4. Chapters 5 through 13 will cover each of the eight Wireless services in detail. For now, here are the topics we will discuss:

- Overview
- Oracle9*i*AS Wireless Core
- Oracle9*i*AS Wireless Services
- Oracle9*i*AS Wireless Tools and Roles

Overview

As shown in the illustration, Oracle9*i*AS Wireless is a component of the Oracle9*i* Application Server (Oracle9*i*AS). It consists of the Wireless Core and a set of Wireless Services, including E-Mail and PIM, Push, Location-Based Services, and Mobile Commerce, which run "out of the box" or can be extended with custom capabilities. These services, when used with the Oracle9*i*AS Wireless tools and Mobile Studio, help developers simplify the task of wirelessly enabling their applications and also free developers from the burden of tackling the complexity of the underlying wireless infrastructure.

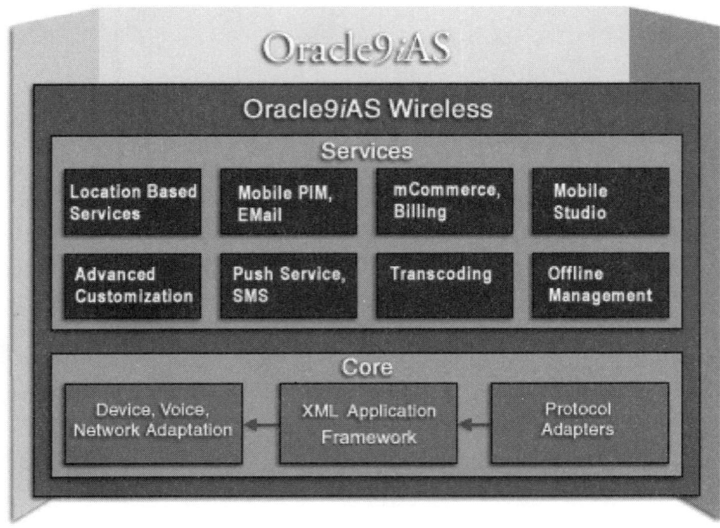

Wireless Core

The Oracle9*i*AS Wireless Core is the framework that enables the "write once, publish everywhere" capabilities for any device, protocol, gateway, or network. Oracle strives to normalize the wireless complexity to essentially one protocol, HTTP/HTTPS, and one meta-language, Oracle9*i*AS multichannel XML. A developer simply creates an application that outputs XML and points Oracle9*i*AS Wireless to the application with a URL.

NOTE
The meta-language Oracle9iAS multichannel XML is evolving and you will see Oracle's documents refer to it as Mobile XML, Wireless XML, iASW XML, and 9iAS XML. They are all the same meta-language.

In accessing an application, the device makes a request to the HTTP listener, which relays the request to the Wireless Core. Within the Wireless Core, the XML Application framework authenticates the user, determines the browser type from the request header, identifies the services associated with the authenticated user, and makes a fetch of the content from the data source or the application layer. The protocol adapters provide facilities to fetch the XML content. Through the use of device-specific transformers using XSL style sheets, the XML representation is converted into a markup language that is compliant with the protocol for the network and specific to a particular device. The Device and Network Adaptation framework, better known as *transformers*, helps deliver the content back to the HTTP web server (or any other server, such as the Async Server) and eventually back to the requesting mobile device.

Wireless Services

Oracle9*i*AS Wireless ships with a set of prebuilt services, or *business components*, that can accelerate application development. You no longer need to write commonly used code and popular services. Oracle has done this for you. These services include Location-Based Services, Mobile PIM and E-Mail, mCommerce and Billing, Push and SMS, Transcoding, and Offline Management. These components can be easily integrated with existing applications. Additionally, the Mobile Studio service is added in Release 2 to allow developers to test and deploy wireless applications in an environment that requires a minimal learning curve. Voice-based services have been added recently and, most likely, they will be formally included as one of the Wireless Services in a future release.

Wireless Tools

Associated with the Wireless Core and Services is a complete set of web-based tools to help you build, deploy, and manage wireless and mobile applications.

The Service Designer is used by developers to create and manage applications; the Content Manager is used to manage the end users; the User Manager is used to control user and group access; and the System Manager monitors and administers the servers. Separately, the Customization Portal is used to administer and customize the end user's profiles.

Oracle9*i*AS Wireless Core

The Oracle9*i*AS Wireless Core is the component that manages the Oracle9*i* Wireless repository and service requests. It is built on top of proven Oracle technologies, including OC4J Container, Distributed Configuration Management (DCM), Enterprise Management Daemon (EMD), XML, Oracle Internet Directory (OID), Single Sign-On (SSO) Server, Oracle Process Management and Notification (OPMN), WebCache, and Oracle9*i* (see the illustration).

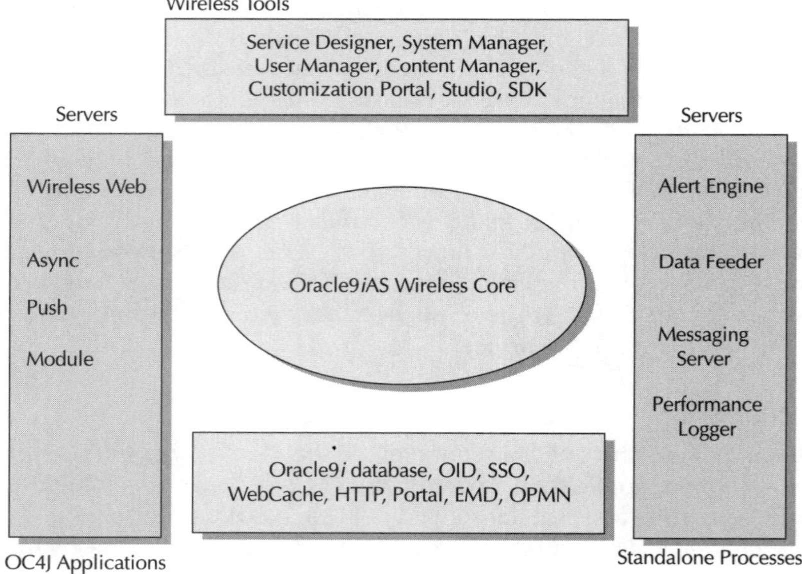

The Oracle9*i*AS Wireless Core integrates with various servers, including the following:

- **Wireless Web Server** Services wireless requests through the HTTP protocol
- **Async Server** Services wireless requests through non-HTTP protocols such as Short Messaging Service (SMS) and e-mail
- **Push Server** Provides push capability to push a message to any device through any protocol

- **Module Server** Provides built-in modules such as Personal Information Management (PIM), Mobile E-Mail, mCommerce, and so on
- **Alert Engine** Provides alert services to subscribers
- **Data Feeder** Provides content-fetching capability from content providers in any protocol and in any format. The fetched content can be used as a data source for the alert engine or mobile applications.
- **Messaging Server** Provides message delivery in any protocol
- **Performance Logger** Writes usage logs from Wireless Web Server, Async Server, Messaging Server, Alert Engine, and Data Feeder to the database for performance monitoring and business intelligence analysis

We'll now take a more in-depth look at each of the components that make up the Oracle9*i*AS Wireless Core.

Protocol Adapters

As mentioned earlier, the Oracle9*i*AS Wireless architecture is designed to adapt content from websites, Internet applications, databases, and other data sources to an Oracle9*i*AS multichannel XML representation. The design goal is to allow for the abstraction of any content from any source and to be content agnostic. Protocol adapters fetch application XML content, and Oracle9*i*AS Wireless provides a number of protocol adapters, including the two primary ones: HTTP and OC4J. Included previously, but de-emphasized in Release 2, are adapters for Web Integration and SQL. You can also create your own custom adapters in Java and use them to integrate any application. The newly created adapter can be a self-contained application, or it can invoke external applications.

You can see the list of available adapters in the Service Designer's Adapters panel, shown here.

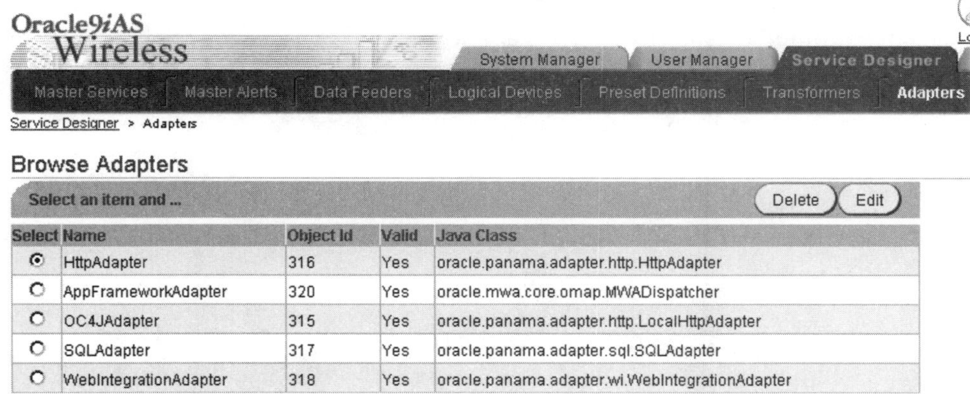

Select	Name	Object Id	Valid	Java Class
⦿	HttpAdapter	316	Yes	oracle.panama.adapter.http.HttpAdapter
○	AppFrameworkAdapter	320	Yes	oracle.mwa.core.omap.MWADispatcher
○	OC4JAdapter	315	Yes	oracle.panama.adapter.http.LocalHttpAdapter
○	SQLAdapter	317	Yes	oracle.panama.adapter.sql.SQLAdapter
○	WebIntegrationAdapter	318	Yes	oracle.panama.adapter.wi.WebIntegrationAdapter

Descriptions of the various protocol adapters shipped with Release 2 of Oracle9*i*AS Wireless are provided in the following subsections.

HTTP Adapter

This primary adapter is used to mobile enable any URL, thus acting as a wireless proxy. It supports the HTTP and HTTPS protocols, session cookies, absolute and relative URLs, GET and POST methods, and HTTP proxy servers.

Using the HTTP adapter is the *preferred* way for building an Oracle9*i*AS multichannel XML-aware application. The application can be built using any web programming language, such as JavaServer Pages (JSP), Active Server Pages (ASP), Perl, or ColdFusion markup language, among others, and can be hosted on any web server. As an example, the Oracle customer relationship management (CRM) applications use the HTTP adapter to enable wireless e-business transactions.

OC4J Adapter

Known as the *Java servlet adapter* in Release 1.0, the OC4J (J2EE) adapter fetches content from Java servlet/JSP-based applications running within the same J2EE container as Oracle9*i*AS Wireless. Therefore, it is used internally and primarily to fetch XML by invoking JSP pages in the same Java Virtual Machine (JVM).

SQL Adapter

SQL adapter is for enabling database queries and PL/SQL. Databases that have a JDBC driver are supported. Therefore, SQL adapter enables developers to create services based on SQL statements and stored procedures. It's a particularly useful content adapter for the expert Oracle DBAs.

Web Integration Adapter

The Web Integration adapter is used to retrieve and adapt existing HTML web applications. This adapter works with Web Interface Definition Language (WIDL) files to map existing HTML content into Oracle9*i*AS multichannel XML. See Chapter 7 for full details on using this adapter.

To address scalability issues, Oracle9*i*AS Wireless loads a specific adapter only once, even if a number of service requests have invoked it. By pooling access to various services, Oracle9*i*AS Wireless provides a scalable, secure way to handle multiple incoming requests and instances.

Oracle9*i*AS Wireless XML Application Model

Prior to Oracle9*i*AS Wireless, most developers built separate markup pages to support different devices. For example, if the goal was to support web browsers, WAP phones and PocketPCs, separate versions of the same page in HTML, WML and cHTML, respectively, had to be created. And you had to do that for the entire application. As devices and markups began to multiply, or the need to support different channels changes, developers had to make changes on the code. Hence, a more scalable way was needed to generate content and support devices.

Oracle's solution is to focus on the middle tier and separate the presentation layer from the application logic. Normally, your application may retrieve data from one or more back-end sources, and present the result in HTML to the web browser. In the case of Oracle9*i*AS Wireless, your application outputs the result in an Oracle9*i*AS multichannel XML document. Using XSLT style sheets, Oracle9*i*AS Wireless transforms the XML document into the markup language format appropriate for the specific device (see the illustration).

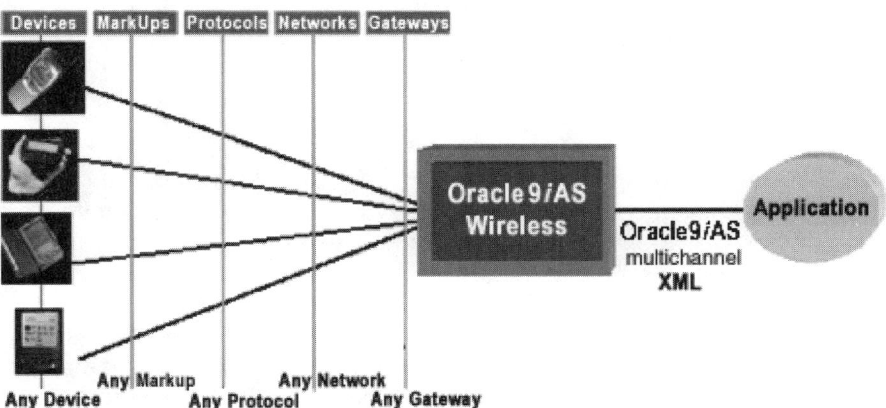

This way, your code is insulated from any changes that may take place at the presentation side. You can add support for new devices (and markup languages) when they come along. Focusing on the business logic and creating only multichannel XML outputs shield developers from the complexity and headaches of creating and maintaining numerous style sheets for the growing list of new mobile devices coming into the market. Therefore, you are "future proof" with Oracle9*i*AS Wireless, and you can protect your investment by allowing developers to build once and deploy across all devices—truly device-agnostic development!

Typically, the Oracle9*i*AS Wireless Core handles all incoming service requests by identifying and authenticating a user. It manages the interaction between data sources and content adapters, dynamically loads various service classes as needed, and schedules and manages their execution. It also manages user sessions and ensures all processing is load balanced. Finally, it invokes the appropriate device/network transformer to serve up the appropriate content in XML or another markup language to the appropriate modal(s).

As a result, each application created in the Oracle9*i*AS XML application model will be automatically "multichannel" and can be accessed wirelessly through Push, Offline, and Voice services. This is the way Oracle achieves "Write once, publish everywhere" for any device, any markup, any protocol, any network, or any gateway.

The complete list of Oracle9*i*AS multichannel XML tags can be found in Appendix B and also online at http://otn.oracle.com, the Oracle Technology Network (OTN). The Document Type Definition (DTD) file can be found locally in the $ORACLEiASW_INSTALL/wireless/DTD folder. As of this writing, the DTD file is SimpleResult_1_1_0.dtd.

Network and Device Adaptation

Device and network adaptation is nothing more than using the appropriate device transformer to convert content from Oracle9*i*AS multichannel XML into the target format. The user agent in the HTTP Request header is used to help determine the browser, device type, and which transformer to use. The user agent identifies the browser client to a server, and the server can then decipher the client and act accordingly. With Oracle9*i*AS Wireless, the default implementation is to take advantage of the "user agent string to logical device" mappings. These mappings, stored in the logical device model object, are used to identify the logical device from the request. You can edit user agent strings with the Service Designer Logical Devices panel.

A logical device is an object that describes either a physical device, such as a Motorola mobile phone, or an abstract device, such as an e-mail server. A default device transformer exists for each logical device. Oracle9*i*AS Wireless transformers are Java programs or XSLT style sheets that convert a document into either the target format or another Oracle9*i*AS Wireless format by mapping to a device-specific XSL style sheet.

Oracle9*i*AS Wireless supports both the prebuilt (default) transformers and custom transformers. You can see the list of the prebuilt transformers in the Service Designer's Transformers panel, shown here.

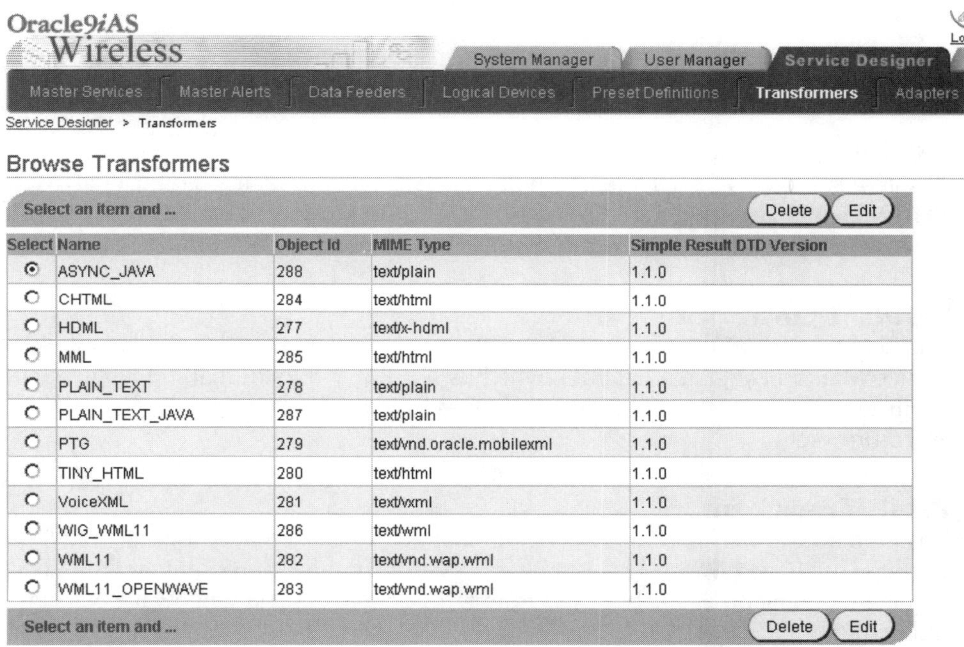

Select	Name	Object Id	MIME Type	Simple Result DTD Version
◉	ASYNC_JAVA	288	text/plain	1.1.0
○	CHTML	284	text/html	1.1.0
○	HDML	277	text/x-hdml	1.1.0
○	MML	285	text/html	1.1.0
○	PLAIN_TEXT	278	text/plain	1.1.0
○	PLAIN_TEXT_JAVA	287	text/plain	1.1.0
○	PTG	279	text/vnd.oracle.mobilexml	1.1.0
○	TINY_HTML	280	text/html	1.1.0
○	VoiceXML	281	text/vxml	1.1.0
○	WIG_WML11	286	text/wml	1.1.0
○	WML11	282	text/vnd.wap.wml	1.1.0
○	WML11_OPENWAVE	283	text/vnd.wap.wml	1.1.0

Oracle9*i*AS Wireless publishes device-transformation rule files so that anyone can create support for any type of device and markup language. Initially, the Oracle9*i*AS Wireless Repository includes transformers for several target formats, such as cHTML, HDML, HTML, VoiceXML, and WML. By modifying the transformers provided with Oracle9*i*AS Wireless or by creating new ones, you can target new device platforms and optimize content presentation for specific devices. Transformers not only map source tags to target format tags, they can manipulate content, including rearranging, filtering, and adding text (such as boilerplate text). This enables you to present content in the format, as well as the form factor, that is best suited for the target device. When you create a transformer, you map the elements in the source content to the result format.

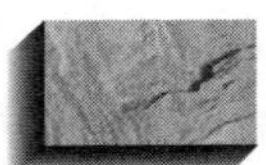

NOTE
Oracle9iAS Wireless requires you to associate a transformer to each logical device.

The following subsections provide brief descriptions of some of the popular prebuilt device transformers that come with Oracle9*i*AS Wireless Release 2.

cHTML Transformer

This item transforms the Oracle9*i*AS multichannel XML format into compact HTML (cHTML), a markup language used by NTT DoCoMo browsers running on the i-mode network in Japan, as well as the microbrowsers in Microsoft PocketPCs.

HDML Transformer

This item transforms the Oracle9*i*AS multichannel XML format into the Handheld Device Markup Language (HDML), which is still the dominant markup language in North America on older mobile WAP phones running the Openwave version 3.*x* micro-browser.

WML Transformer

This item transforms an Oracle9*i*AS multichannel XML document into the Wireless Markup Language (WML). This is the world's most popular and dominant markup language running on micro-browsers from Ericsson, Nokia, and Openwave (version 4 and higher).

Tiny HTML Transformer

This item transforms Oracle9*i*AS multichannel XML into a subset of the HyperText Markup Language (HTML). Used by the latest web-enabled smart phones with built-in Palm OS or personal digital assistants (PDAs) based on the Palm OS or Microsoft Pocket PC OS.

VoiceXML Transformer

This item transforms the Oracle9*i*AS multichannel XML format into VoiceXML. It's used by most voice gateways currently in production.

Custom Transformer

You can implement Oracle9*i*AS Wireless transformers as either Java transformers or XSLT style sheets. XSLT style sheets are XML documents that specify the processing rules for other XML documents. The XSLT processor included with the Oracle XML processor conforms to the final W3C XSLT specification (Working Draft of August 13, 1999). Refer to the W3C document for details on writing XSLT style sheets. Java transformers are beyond the scope of this book—refer to the Oracle javadoc files for the available methods of the RtTransformer interface.

Extensible HyperText Markup Language (XHTML)

XHTML is a family of current and future document types and modules that reproduce, subset, and extend HTML 4 in order to support a wide range of new devices and applications by defining modules and specifying a mechanism for combining these modules. XHTML Basic (W3C), XHTML Mobile (Openwave), or flavors of these will be supported in future micro-browsers—Openwave's Universal Browser (version 5.1) supports both WML and XHTML.

Oracle will most likely provide tools to convert Oracle9*i*AS multichannel XML to XHTML or build and include XHTML in a subset of Oracle9*i*AS multichannel XML in the near future when more modules are available that can support both voice and presentation markup in mobile devices.

Oracle9*i*AS Wireless Services

Eight Wireless Services are shipped with Release 2 of Oracle9*i*AS Wireless. This section touches on each of them briefly. However, they are also covered in more detail in subsequent chapters.

Customization and Alerts

The Oracle9*i*AS Wireless Customization framework offers large-scale personalization options, including presets. Presets can store the user preference settings, personal information, and frequently used input parameters on the server side so that applications can use them to generate personalized responses. End users can customize their presets from any PC or mobile device.

The Oracle9*i*AS Wireless Alert Engine provides an extensible and scalable solution to developing mobile alert services. Alerts generate delivery events from a content source based on an event/value or time condition. The notification of alerts is through the Push, E-Mail, SMS, Instant Messaging (IM), or Voice service. A data feed engine within Oracle9*i*AS Wireless provides inputs for alerts or applications. The engine accepts data through HTTP, local files, FTP, SQL, and so on—and in many different formats (delimited, HTML, or XML).

For full details on this Advanced Customization Service, refer to Chapter 5.

Push and SMS

The Oracle9*i*AS Wireless Push service provides a highly scalable mechanism for delivering messages to all mobile devices. These messages are delivered to the mobile devices in a protocol that is native to each device—for example, via SMS to a mobile phone or via an audio message to a regular phone. Additionally, this service is implemented as a Web service (WSDL) and uses SOAP over HTTP. This enables applications to invoke the Push service from anywhere on the Internet, using any programming model.

For full details on this Push and SMS Service, refer to Chapter 6.

Transcoding

The Oracle9*i*AS Wireless Transcoding Service dynamically translates web content and applications into XML and optimizes these applications for delivery to mobile devices, such as mobile phones, PDAs, and voice devices. This service also has a WML translator that allows for the interpretation of content authored in WML and translates the content for access from all web-enabled devices.

For full details on this Transcoding Service, refer to Chapter 7.

Offline Management

The Oracle9*i*AS Wireless Offline Management Service offers users the ability to use applications without any network access, in a so-called *offline* or *disconnected environment*. When the Internet connection is available again, the device user can synchronize to update the server with any new information. Oracle9*i* Lite's Synchronization Server forms the basis of Offline Management and provides this capability. Oracle9*i* Lite's Synchronization Server, used in conjunction with the Oracle9*i* Lite small-footprint database on the client device, complements the wireless (or online) push and voice capabilities of Oracle9*i*AS Wireless. Offline Management provides the necessary framework needed to provide persistent storage and synchronization to client applications that run on all of today's popular mobile platforms, including Palm OS, Symbian EPOC, Microsoft Windows CE, and Microsoft Windows 95/98/NT/2000.

For full details on this Offline Managment Service, refer to Chapters 8 and 9.

Location-Based Service

The Oracle9*i*AS Wireless Location-Based Service enables access to maps, driving directions, traffic reports, nearby businesses and services, and so on. The user's location can be easily passed to any application with XML. Users can view and edit their privacy settings to enable or disable the positioning operation themselves. Users can also authorize one or more people to obtain their positioning information within certain time frames.

For full details on this Location-Based Service, refer to Chapter 10.

Mobile PIM and E-Mail

The Oracle9*i*AS Wireless Mobile Personal Information Management (PIM) services allow customers to integrate corporate e-mail, directory, address book, calendar, and instant messaging applications into their mobile enterprise portals. The services are built as modules that can be called either directly by mobile users or by other applications.

The Oracle9*i*AS Wireless Mobile E-Mail services provide access from any mobile devices to any IMAP4 or POP3 server. These services support popular mail servers such as Microsoft Exchange and Lotus Domino.

For full details on the Mobile PIM and E-Mail Service, refer to Chapter 11.

mCommerce and Billing

The Oracle9*i*AS Wireless mCommerce and Billing Service enables easy input and secure storage of user information, such as credit cards, bank accounts, and billing/shipping addresses, while allowing authorized applications to receive this information at any time from any device.

For full details on this service, refer to Chapter 12.

Mobile Studio

The Oracle9*i*AS Wireless Mobile Studio is a web-based development environment for quickly building, testing, and deploying wireless applications. This bundled developer studio allows mobile designers and developers to reap the benefits of an easy-to-use studio in an internal corporate setting. Enterprises can set up and run the Mobile Studio within their firewalls to allow collaboration without exposing their applications to the external world.

For full details on this service, refer to Chapter 13.

Oracle9*i*AS Wireless Tools and Roles

Oracle9*i*AS Wireless provides a set of web-based tools to help you create, manage, and deliver mobile services. Oracle9*i*AS Wireless Release 2 provides the following tools:

- Service Designer
- System Manager

- User Manager
- Content Manager
- Customization Portal

Note that these tools are role specific, meaning that users can only access tools associated with their given roles as assigned by the User Administrator. We'll discuss each of these tools in depth, but first let's look at the definitions of all the different wireless roles relative to Oracle9*i*AS Wireless.

Wireless Roles and Users

Depending on what role has been assigned by the User Administrator, the user has access limited to the relevant tools. For example, a user assigned to the Content Management role can only access the Content Manager tool, and a user assigned the Content Developer role can only access the Service Designer. Application developers would most likely not use any of these tools. Instead, they will be using Mobile Studio and the Wireless SDK. The Wireless SDK is a lightweight development version of Oracle9*i*AS Wireless and provides an environment for application developers to test and simulate multichannel XML applications, XSLT style sheet transformers, and new device descriptions.

Here's a basic guide to the role of each Oracle9*i*AS Wireless user and the tools available to them:

- **Administrator** A super user who can access all the web-based wireless tools
- **System** Manages the wireless system using the System Manager tool
- **HelpDesk** Manages user profiles, services, groups, and access privileges using the User Manager tool
- **Designer** Manages the master services, alerts, and deployment using the Content Manager tool
- **Organizer** Manages master services, alerts, adapters, transformers, data feeders, presets, and so on using the Service Designer tool

NOTE
End users, or consumers, only have access to the Customization Portal to customize their services from a desktop PC or mobile device.

We'll now move on to the web-based wireless tools available in Oracle9*i*AS Wireless Release 2.

Service Designer

The Service Designer tool, shown in the illustration, is used to create and manage Oracle9*i*AS Wireless users, groups, adapters, transformers, and services in the repository.

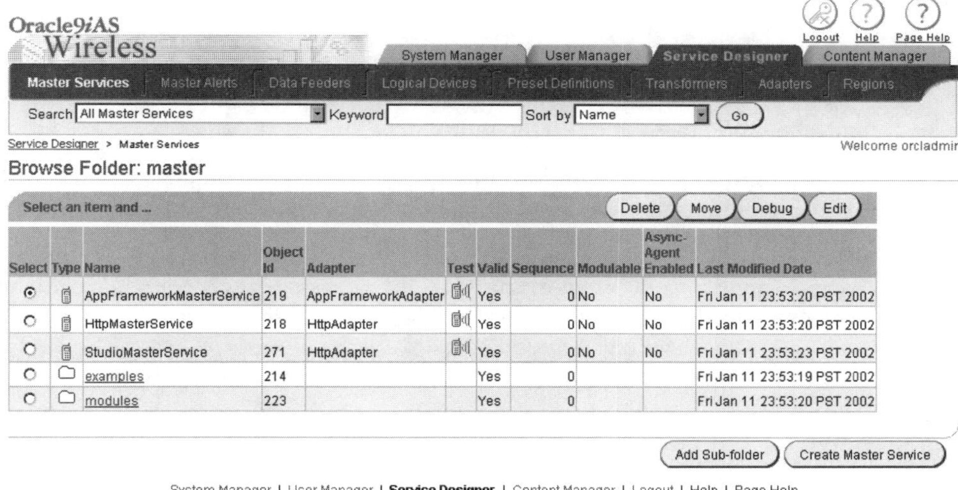

Specifically, the tool allows you to create the following:

- **Master Services** The actual implementations of services. You specify the adapter used for a service and any service-specific parameters. By mapping an adapter to device transformers, master services link mobile content sources to delivery platforms. Each master service is based on one adapter; a master service creates its own instance of the adapter it uses. Therefore, several services can use the same type of adapter, and each can pass its own service-specific argument values.
- **Async Agent Services** Services whose devices only support two-way messaging or e-mail. You can provide users access to web content by using

listeners to intercept messages and routing them to the correct service or application and then sending the requested information back to the users.

- **Master Alerts** A notification service delivered to users based on the trigger condition and a specific data feeder they set when subscribing to an alert service.
- **Data Feeder** A repository object that retrieves content from both internal and external content sources and then converts that content into a standard XML format for publishing to alert engines.
- **Logical Devices** Repository objects that represent either physical devices, such as a Sony Ericsson mobile phone, or abstract devices, such as an e-mail server. Logical devices represent the interface between transformers and the target devices or applications.
- **Preset Definitions** Definitions that allow users to personalize services with their own input parameters for an application. Presets are presented to the users by the service for selection in order to execute the application.
- **Transformers** Java programs or XSLT style sheets that convert a document into either the target format or another XML format. The transformer associated with a logical device is that device's default transformer. Although several devices can use a single default transformer, a custom transformer can be associated with only one master service and one device. This is because a custom transformer optimizes the presentation of that service to a particular device, and it can only be used for that device.
- **Adapters** Java applications that retrieve data from an external source and render it in Oracle9*i*AS multichannel XML. When invoked by a master service, an adapter returns an XML object that contains the service content. This XML object is processed by the Oracle9*i*AS Wireless Core and then delivered to the user's device in response to the user's service request.
- **Regions** Used to assign a location to a service, making the service location based (unique to a specified area).

System Manager

The System Manager, shown in the illustration, provides configuration-management and performance-monitoring capabilities for various wireless servers.

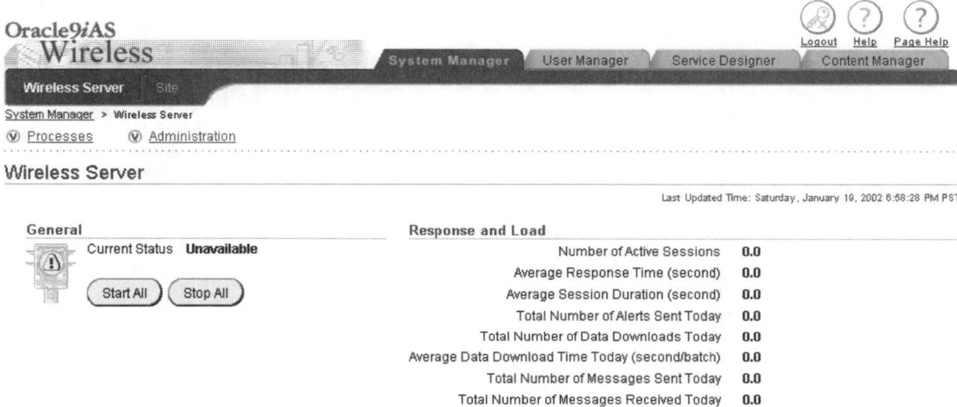

Specifically, this tool allows you to manage the following views:

- **Wireless Server** Allows you to monitor and manage system performance for each server-level process and to start and stop the server processes, both as a group and individually.
- **Site** Provides an overall look at all processes and their respective machines and enables you to create a common configuration for these machines.

User Manager

The User Manager tool, shown in the illustration, enables you to perform help desk functions such as creating and modifying users and groups and assigning services to users and groups.

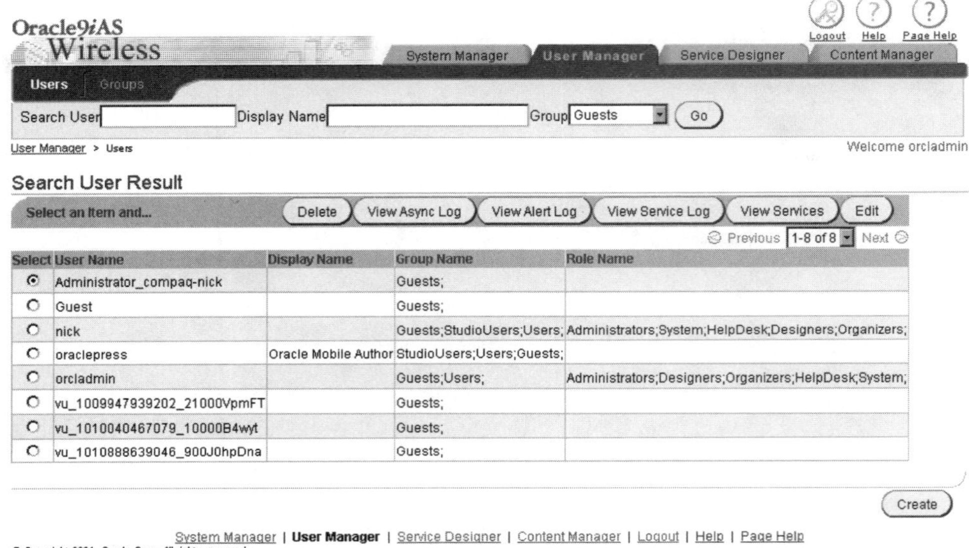

Specifically, this tool allows you to manage the following:

- **Users** You can create and modify users as well as assign services to users.
- **Groups** You can create and modify groups as well as assign services to groups.

Content Manager

The Content Manager tool, shown in the illustration, enables you to create services and alerts based on the master services and master alerts created by content developers. This tool enables you to assign services, alerts, and topics to each user group. Using the Content Manager tool, you can organize the wireless portal in a business context appropriate to a user group.

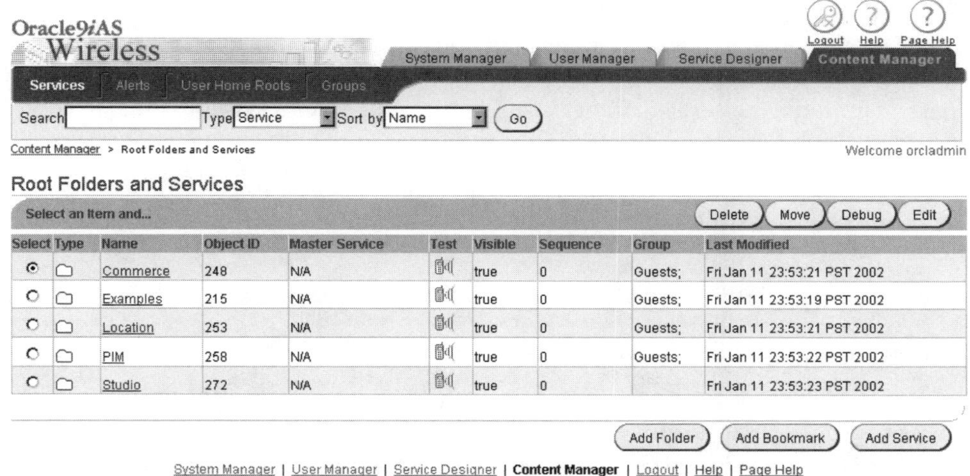

Specifically, this tool allows you to manage the following:

- **Folders** You can organize objects such as services and bookmarks. When you assign a folder to a user group, you make its subfolders, services, and bookmarks accessible to users.
- **Services** You can inherit a master service or a "module-able" master service, thus enabling you to distribute service access to multiple users or groups. You can also "specialize" master services by setting default parameter values that override values initially set for the master service in the Service Designer.
- **Modules** Reusable services that can be invoked as normal services or by another service to return a result to that service.
- **Bookmarks** Bookmarks give the user quick access to an external resource. The bookmark appears as a menu selection in the device portal. The format of the target content must be supported by the user's device.

■ **Alerts** An alert inherits a master alert created from the Service Designer. You can organize alerts by topics or containers that group alerts.

Customization Portal

The Customization Portal tool, shown in the illustration, enables users to personalize their device portals from a desktop computer or mobile device. By providing default pages for modifying service, folder, user, group, and other repository objects, the Customization Portal tool also enables users to set frequently entered parameters, such as e-mail addresses, passwords, and PINs.

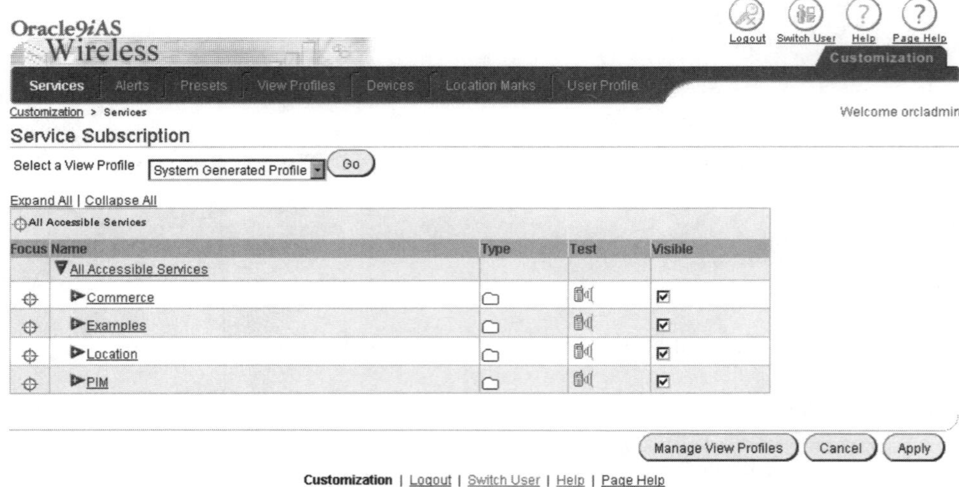

Specifically, this tool allows you to manage the following:

■ **Services** You can create a quick link to a service or edit, create, or delete the service through the Service Subscription screens.

■ **Alerts** You can edit the properties of a selected alert, such as enabling an alert or setting the frequency of an alert.

■ **Presets** You can add, delete, or edit preset values (the user-defined inputs for a service).

■ **View Profiles** You can create different views of the service trees that are suited to the display capabilities of a device or to a connection profile.

■ **Devices** You can add or disable alerts sent to wireless devices.

- **Location Marks** You can create, delete, edit, or change the default status of a location mark. A location mark is spatial information—a name of a location that is meaningful to you.
- **User Profile** You can set up or edit basic user information.

Because the form factor of mobile devices limits the entry and display of spatial information such as street addresses and location coordinates, having the Customization Portal and being able to set up user profiles in advance using a desktop PC or small form factor device truly makes Oracle9*i*AS Wireless–hosted services usable without having to enter those lengthy alphanumeric strings.

Summary

You have been introduced to the Oracle9*i*AS Wireless Core and its associated services. You have also seen the available wireless tools shipped with Release 2 of Oracle9*i*AS Wireless. In a nutshell, the Wireless Core is the basis for administering all the wireless object components, including users, wireless applications, and devices—all of which are stored in a database repository using Oracle's database server. This infrastructure was designed to be a highly scalable and high-performance server that supports tens of thousands of users. The Wireless Services represent prebuilt components and resources that can accelerate your development work, without you having to write code for basic building blocks. Proceed to Chapter 4 and learn more about the underlying servers of Oracle9*i*AS Wireless and how they integrate with other Oracle technologies.

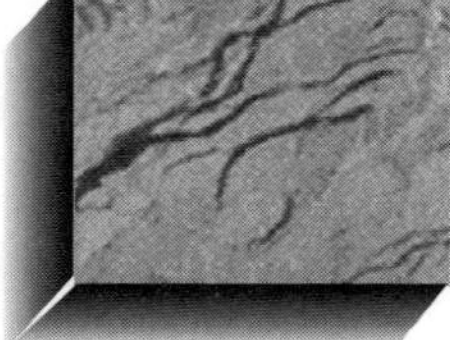

CHAPTER 4

Servers and Integration

Now that you have some familiarity with the basic principles and technologies of Oracle9*i*AS Wireless, we'll continue to look at the Oracle9*i*AS Wireless Core, focusing on its integration with other components of Oracle9*i* Application Server and the underlying servers that drive the functionality of Oracle9*i*AS Wireless. Specifically, we focus on the following topics:

- Integration with Oracle9*i*AS
- HTTP, Async, and Other Servers
- Creating Mobile Applications

Before going into depth with the Oracle9*i*AS Wireless servers, we will discuss how Oracle implements Single Sign-On (SSO), directory, cache, session management, and device detection. We then follow with an overview of the various settings and default configurations for Oracle9*i*AS Wireless servers. With the basics under your belt, you will be equipped to build your first Oracle9*i*AS Wireless application. We will go through a complete example and show you how to create a mobile application on Oracle9*i*AS Wireless using the tools and technologies you have learned about thus far.

Integration with Oracle9*i*AS

As discussed in Chapter 3, Oracle9*i*AS Wireless is a component of Oracle9*i* Application Server (Oracle9*i*AS). As an integral part of Oracle9*i*AS, the wireless platform integrates seamlessly with other Oracle9*i*AS components, including WebCache, Oracle HTTP Server, Single Sign-On (SSO), Oracle Internet Directory (OID), Enterprise Manager (EM), and Oracle9*i*AS Portal. This section describes Oracle9*i*AS Wireless integration with SSO, OID, and WebCache.

Single Sign-On (SSO)

Oracle9*i*AS Single Sign-On (SSO) addresses the problem of "too many passwords" and multiple sign-ons for different applications supported within an enterprise. Not only do multiple sign-ons create inconvenience for the users, they present administrative and security issues to the enterprise. Oracle9*i*AS SSO resolves this problem by providing centralized administration of user name and password combinations for all users in an enterprise. It provides a framework for secure, one-time "signing-on" to any web-based applications from any client device through standard protocols. SSO prompts users for a user name and password when they access the system for the first time in a given time period and then verifies the password submitted by the user. The SSO framework authenticates users and passes their identities securely to partner applications. In the context of SSO, partner applications are defined as those applications that have been designed or modified to delegate user authentication to the SSO framework and accept the user identities presented to them. As a result, all web-based Oracle9*i*AS Wireless applications running behind Oracle HTTP Server are treated as a single partner application by SSO.

Users authenticate only once and can access any SSO partner applications. Because partner applications take advantage of the SSO authentication services, they no longer need to implement their own authentication modules. User administration is greatly simplified because there is no need to manage passwords. Deploying an application as a partner application can reduce both development time and ongoing administrative expenses. This SSO framework is especially compelling for mobile applications where user key-ins must be minimized and personalized.

Another advantage of SSO is its ability to provide centralized management and provisioning of user information in a directory so that administrators can easily create and manage user accounts. Centralizing the authentication process also makes it possible to support additional authentication mechanisms in a localized manner. For example, you can implement an LDAP-based authentication, such as Oracle Internet Directory (OID), and the change would be localized to the SSO server. Oracle9*i*AS SSO also supports Public Key Infrastructure (PKI) client authentication, thus enabling secure identification management to a wide range of applications.

User authentication in Oracle9*i*AS Wireless can be summarized in the following steps:

1. The user sends a login request or accesses a private service.
2. Oracle9*i*AS Wireless sends the login request (with no user credentials) to the SSO server.
3. The SSO server checks for an SSO cookie. If one is present, the SSO server identifies the user from the encrypted cookie and sends the SSO Redirect form (advancing to step 7). This happens if the user is already authenticated by an external partner application. If the SSO cookie is not present, the SSO server sends the Oracle9*i*AS multichannel XML Login form to the Oracle9*i*AS Wireless server.
4. Oracle9*i*AS Wireless transforms the XML Login form to the appropriate device markup and sends the login page to the device browser.
5. The user enters a user name and a password and submits the Login form.
6. Oracle9*i*AS Wireless forwards the login request (this time with the user credentials) to the SSO server.
7. The SSO server authenticates the user. If the authentication is successful, the SSO server sends the SSO Redirect form. If the authentication is

unsuccessful, the SSO server sends the Oracle9*i*AS multichannel XML Login Form to the Oracle9*i*AS Wireless server (go back to step 3).

8. The Oracle9*i*AS Wireless server sends the home page of the user (or the private service result) to the device browser.
9. The user is now authenticated and can access any SSO-enabled application without further authentication.

Oracle Internet Directory

Oracle Internet Directory (OID) is the single repository for storing all user-related information. Oracle regards OID as a critical component of the Oracle9*i*AS management and security infrastructure. OID makes the task of managing users, groups, configurations, and other user information easier. Tightly integrated with the Oracle9*i* database, OID ensures that user accounts and groups are managed centrally via the LDAP version 3 standard with high availability, scalability and security. Through LDAP, OID offers both access and update capabilities and can be managed and queried securely via an access controller. With Oracle9*i*AS Release 2, user accounts can be created centrally in OID and shared across all components in Oracle9*i*AS. When users log in, they are authenticated once by SSO against their OID credentials and can thus access multiple applications seamlessly. The user information is synchronized between Oracle9*i*AS Wireless and OID.

WebCache

Web caching is critical for implementing scalable mobile applications because it provides efficiency and can save bandwidth. This is especially significant for enterprises and carriers alike in supporting a growing user base and transaction volume. To boost performance, availability, and scalability, Oracle9*i*AS Wireless is integrated with Oracle9*i*AS WebCache, which have several significant features. First, Oracle9*i*AS WebCache significantly improves performance and scalability of web applications by caching *both* static and dynamic content. Oracle9*i*AS WebCache operates as a caching reverse-proxy server that is situated in front of the Oracle HTTP server. It improves performance by storing frequently accessed pages in memory, thus eliminating the need to repeatedly process requests for these pages from the web server, the applications, or the Oracle database.

In addition, Oracle9*i*AS WebCache provides administrative tools to create custom rules for validation and the refreshing of cached content. To reduce overhead, you can leverage the intelligent cache miss routing and failover support of Oracle9*i*AS WebCache.

It is noteworthy that WebCache is not deployed in the traditional sense of web caching in the framework of Oracle9*i*AS Wireless. WebCache is usually deployed in front of web servers serving HTML content and interacting with HTML clients and the web server to cache dynamic content. However, with Oracle9*i*AS Wireless, the wireless runtime determines what content needs to be inserted into WebCache and when to expire content in the cache. WebCache, in this case, acts as a device-adaptation cache rather than as a reverse-proxy cache. By caching the markup content with WebCache, you improve performance and scalability by reducing device-adaptation costs, and more significantly, adapter-invocation costs.

You achieve savings in device-adaptation costs because content is now shared across users, and sessions are essentially transformed only once (per logical device) from their Oracle9*i*AS multichannel XML format. Moreover, because you don't need to generate the content every time through an adapter, you drastically lower the total adapter-invocation cost, especially for applications or websites with a large subset of cacheable pages.

Caching Dynamic Content

To cache dynamic content, it is necessary to enable the WebCache. Follow these steps to enable this feature:

1. From the System Manager, click the Site tab. Under the Administration section, in the Configuration subsection, click the WebCache Configuration link.
2. To enable WebCache, check the Enable WebCache check box (see Figure 4-1).

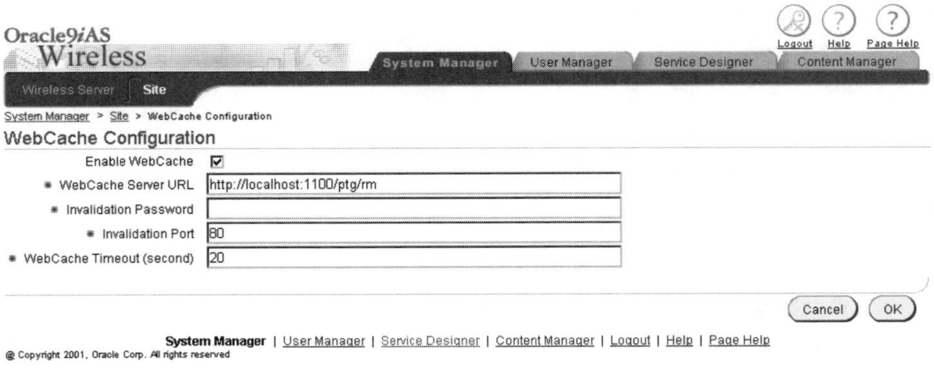

FIGURE 4-1. *WebCache configuration*

3. Next, enter the complete URL that corresponds to the WebCache installation. Be sure to include the port number at which WebCache listens (the default port is 1100) and the servlet path to the wireless runtime (the default is /ptg/rm).
4. Supply an invalidation password (the default is Administrator). This should be the same as the WebCache invalidation password that is set from the WebCache administration console of Oracle9*i*AS.
5. Provide an invalidation port (the default is 4001). This should be the same as the invalidation port specified from the WebCache administration console of Oracle9*i*AS.
6. Enter a timeout value for requests made to WebCache (the default is 20 seconds). Ensure that this is at least 5 seconds less than the request timeout value from the WebCache administration console of Oracle9*i*AS.
7. Click OK after the changes have been made.

Cache Enabling a Service

In order to use the cache, you need to enable a particular service to be cacheable. Two areas need further configuration:

- In step 2 of the Master Service Creation Wizard, check the Cacheable check box. See the section titled "Creating the Master Service with the Service Designer" for more details.
- By checking this box, the Invalidation Frequency section appears. Specify the frequency at which pages must be removed from the cache (see Figure 4-2).

Invalidating Cache Content

Once your service content is cached, it is necessary to perform invalidation of the cache contents at appropriate intervals. Invalidation of wireless content residing in WebCache can be either policy-based or asynchronous, as described in the following list:

- **Policy-Based Invalidation** You can invalidate a cache automatically based on predefined policies. For example, you can invalidate and refresh content in the cache based on the Invalidation Frequency setting described earlier. When a page is inserted into the cache, the invalidation frequency of the service defines how long the page should live in the cache.
- **Asynchronous Invalidation** It may be necessary to invalidate a cache explicitly. It is possible to invalidate and refresh content in the cache

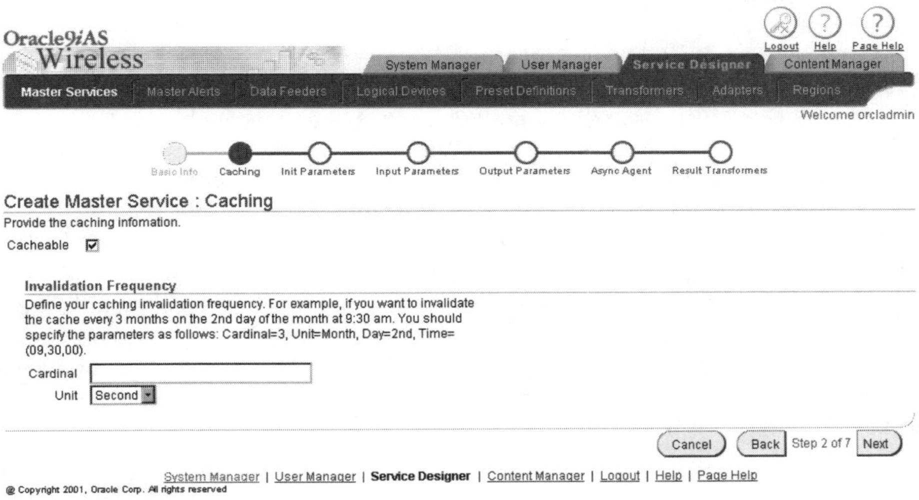

FIGURE 4-2. *Create Master Service: caching*

based on a master service or a device. Follow these steps to refresh a service or device:

1. From System Manager, click the Site tab. Under the Administration section, in the Configuration subsection, click either the Refresh WebCache | Master Service or Refresh WebCache | Device link.
2. To invalidate all pages belonging to a master service, click Refresh WebCache | Master Service, select a master service by clicking a radio button corresponding to the master service, and click Refresh.
3. To invalidate all pages with a given device markup, click Refresh WebCache | Device, select a device by clicking a radio button corresponding to the device, and click Refresh.

Session Management and Device Detection

As discussed in Chapter 1, session management for mobile devices is a unique challenge because not all client devices support cookies. Robust application development and implementation must therefore presume no cookie is supported. To complicate matters, your applications need to be able to initiate, manage, and terminate user sessions in a sporadically connected wireless network.

Session Management

Let's look at how Oracle9*i*AS Wireless handles session management. Upon receiving requests from a user, Oracle9*i*AS Wireless creates a session for the user. Unlike in HTTP, where session information is kept by the cookie (through an IE or Netscape browser), all session states are kept in the backend, either through the WAP gateway or the wireless server itself. If the device or the gateway does not support cookies, the OC4J servlet container can use a mechanism called *URL rewriting,* which basically appends the session ID to the end of the URL using a GET or POST parameter.

When a user session is initiated, the server creates and assigns a session identifier to the instance. Because no cookie is available, the session ID is "coded" on the page sent by the server to the browser. Any subsequent requests will include the session ID to allow the server to recover the session information. It should be noted that the session ID can be rather long and could exceed the 128-character limitations of many WAP devices for URL strings. To resolve that, you may have to change and limit the length of the session ID.

NOTE
Because the Oracle9iAS Wireless runtime also tracks the session, it is possible to have more than one runtime session bound to a single servlet session.

Device Detection

Device detection is handled by the Oracle9*i*AS Wireless Core. We will review the basics and briefly mention one way to customize its capabilities. In general, you can determine the device type by checking which MIME type of documents the browser explicitly accepts. This is easily done by looking up the special HTTP request header with the name Accept. Another method is to check for the identity of the device browser, which is used by the Oracle9*i*AS Wireless Core to transform Oracle9*i*AS multichannel XML to the appropriate device markup page.

The device detection can be customized by implementing a hook class. The default implementation is in the **oracle.panama.rt.hook.DeviceIdentificationPolicy** class. The interface class is **oracle.panama.rt.hook.DeviceIdentificationHook**. It uses the user agent string–to–logical device mappings that are stored in the LogicalDevice Model object. Writing a custom device-detection interface hook is beyond the scope of this book. Therefore, refer to the Oracle9*i*AS Wireless document for more information.

Servers

Behind the scenes of Oracle9*i*AS Wireless are many servers deployed as either OC4J applications or standalone Java applications. We will touch on each of them briefly in this section and go into some details on how to manage them using the System Manager web tool.

Servers Deployed as OC4J Applications

The OC4J applications within Oracle9*i*AS Wireless include the Wireless Web Server, Async Server, Push Server, and the various Module Servers. Although these servers are deployed as OC4J applications, only the Wireless Web Server and Async Server are configured to be auto-started. The Push Server and Module Server are started upon the first received request. Deployed as a single-process group, these OC4J applications can also be started or stopped as a group. Let's review these servers in more details:

- **Wireless Web Server** This server handles wireless requests through the HTTP protocol. The devices that make these requests include WAP phones with WAP gateways, fixed voice lines with VoiceXML gateways, and others. If the response for the request from the particular requesting device is cached by WebCache, the response is returned immediately. If the request is to access a private service, the Wireless Web Server redirects the request to the SSO server (see the earlier section on SSO to see how this is handled). After user authentication, the mobile application processes the request and returns the Oracle9*i*AS multichannel XML to the Wireless Web Server. The Wireless Web Server adapts the received content to the network and device markup and returns it to the requesting device. The mobile content is visible on the requesting mobile device in its most native format.
- **Async Server** This server handles wireless requests through non-HTTP protocols such as e-mail and Short Messaging Service (SMS). The response is returned immediately. An execution flow similar to that of the Wireless Web Server occurs when private service is accessed. The Async Server adapts and returns the mobile content in its native format.
- **Push Server** This server provides the capability to push a message to any device through any protocol. Any message can be pushed out as an e-mail, SMS message, voice mail, or fax, or it can be pushed to the Oracle Mobile message gateway.
- **Module Server** This server provides the built-in mobile applications in the areas of personal information management (PIM), mobile commerce, and location-based services.

Servers Deployed as Standalone Java Applications

The standalone Java applications include the Alert Engine, Data Feeder, Messaging Server, and Performance Logger. These applications can be started, stopped, and configured through the System Manager. The default installation only enables the Performance Logger, so the performance of various wireless servers on this machine can be monitored through the System Manager. Other processes should only be started manually if their respective functionality is desired. Let's look at these Java applications more closely:

- **Alert Engine** This application provides alert services to subscribers. An alert service generates alert message delivery events from a content source based on certain conditions, such as a value-based predicate—for example, sending an auction bid alert to a user when the bid price has reached a predefined value. A condition can also be a time-based predicate with or without a value-based predicate. For example, a user can request the Dow Jones or S&P market index every day at 8 A.M. PST, if the index has reached a predefined value. The delivery mechanism of the alert message is through the Oracle9*i*AS Wireless message gateway, which allows notification to be sent through push, e-mail, SMS messages, instant messaging, or voice. The end user creates alert subscriptions using either the Oracle9*i*AS Wireless Content Manager or the Oracle9*i*AS Wireless alert subscription APIs.
- **Data Feeder** This application enables you to fetch content from content providers through any protocol in any format. The fetched content can be used as a data source for the alert engine or any mobile application. The Data Feeder runs periodically, independently of service invocations. The feed framework is designed to download content for an Oracle9*i*AS Wireless process. The downloaded content can be used for asynchronous alerts as well as cached data for synchronous services.
- **Messaging Server** This application handles sending and receiving messages to and from devices as well as all message routing functions. The Messaging Server can asynchronously query the delivery status of a message or choose to be notified upon delivery. More on this in Chapter 6 in our discussion of push services.
- **Performance Logger** This application writes usage logging data of the Wireless Web Server, Async Server, Messaging Server, Alert Engine, and Data Feeder asynchronously to the database for performance-monitoring purposes. Furthermore, the information stored in the performance logger database tables can be utilized for business-intelligence analysis.

Creating Mobile Applications

We will now go through the complete design of a multichannel mobile application using the Service Designer and then use the Content Designer to publish this service.

We will first mobile enable some static JSP code to display information about an employee in Oracle9*i*AS multichannel XML. Once that is working, we can modify the code to dynamically use the Oracle database to generate the same XML page. Specifically, here are the steps to follow in the design of a wireless service using the Oracle9*i*AS Wireless web tools:

1. Create the JSP code for static content in Oracle9*i*AS multichannel XML.
2. Create an HTTP Adapter master service using the Service Designer web tool.
3. Create a new user group and new user account using the User Manager.
4. Publish the service using the Content Manager web tool.
5. Create the service folder, configure the parameters, and assign them to the user group.
6. Test the newly created service on mobile devices.
7. Modify the static JSP code to use an Oracle database for dynamic content in XML.
8. Test the modified service on mobile devices.

Creating the JSP Application

Using your favorite editor, create the following JSP application, named *static.jsp*:

```
<?xml version="1.0" encoding="UTF-8" standalone="yes" ?>
<%@ page contentType="text/vnd.oracle.mobilexml; charset=UTF-8"
session="false" language="java" import="java.util.*, java.text.*,
java.net.*, java.sql.*" %>
<SimpleResult>
   <SimpleContainer>
      <SimpleText>
         <SimpleTextItem halign="left" mode="nowrap">
         <SimpleStrong>EMPLOYEE INFO:</SimpleStrong>
         </SimpleTextItem><SimpleBreak />
         <SimpleTextItem halign="left" mode="nowrap">SMITH
         </SimpleTextItem><SimpleBreak />
         <SimpleTextItem halign="left" mode="nowrap">7369
         </SimpleTextItem><SimpleBreak />
         <SimpleTextItem halign="left" mode="nowrap">CLERK
         </SimpleTextItem><SimpleBreak />
         <SimpleTextItem halign="left" mode="nowrap">800
         </SimpleTextItem><SimpleBreak />
         <SimpleTextItem halign="left" mode="nowrap">20
         </SimpleTextItem><SimpleBreak />
```

```
        <SimpleTextItem halign="left" mode="nowrap">12/17/1980
        </SimpleTextItem>
      </SimpleText>
    </SimpleContainer>
</SimpleResult>
```

After you create the *static.jsp* file, place it in a folder under your web server. Under a running web servlet container file, do the following with the static.jsp file:

1. Create a subfolder called "book" under $ORACLE9iASW_INSTALL\wireless\j2ee\applications\examples\examples-web.
2. Copy static.jsp to the book folder.

NOTE
The static.jsp file must be accessed from a web browser. For example, the book folder is created under an OC4J application, called examples, that runs at localhost port 9000. In a browser, you access static.jsp by entering the URL http://localhost:9000/examples/book/static.jsp.

Creating the Master Service with the Service Designer

We will now step through the details of creating an HTTP Adapter master service and its attribute settings. Here are the steps to follow:

1. Log into the Wireless web tool. From the Wireless web tool, select the Service Designer tab. The Browse Folder screen of the Service Designer appears.
2. Folders are used to organize your master services. To create a folder, click Add Subfolder. The Create Folder screen appears. Complete the Create Folder screen by entering **TestBookApp** in the Folder Name field. This is a required field. Select Valid so that the Content Manager can publish this folder to user groups. Click Create. The folder TestBookApp now appears in the Browse Folder screen (see Figure 4-3).
3. Next, add a master service to the TestBookApp folder. To create a master service, click TestBookApp and then click Create Master Service. The Master Service Creation Wizard appears, displaying the Basic Info screen (the first screen of the master service creation sequence). Fill in only the

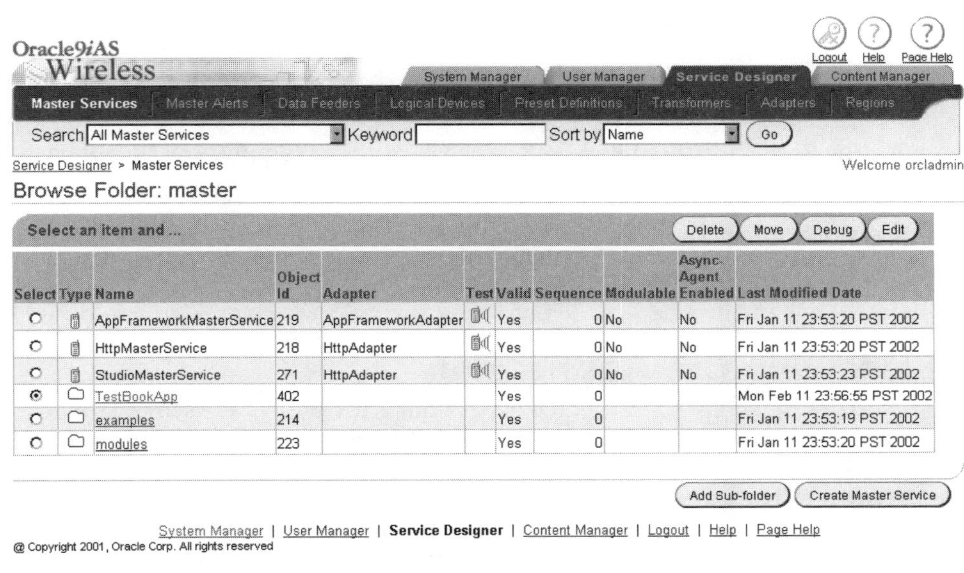

FIGURE 4-3. *TestBookApp folder in Service Designer*

required fields for this example. Enter **EmployeeInfo** in the Name field, select HTTP Adapter from the drop-down list of adapters, and then select the Valid check box so that we can publish this master service to user groups using the Content Manager later on. Click Next.

4. The Caching screen appears. Select the Cacheable check box if you would like to cache the master service with the WebCache server. Leave the check box clear if you do not want to cache this master service. If you want to cache the master service, set the frequency of the invalidation. For this example, we will not use the cache, so click Next.

5. The Init Parameters screen appears. The HttpAdapterInvokeListener field is optional and for detailed debugging only. For this example, we will leave it clear. Click Next.

6. The Input Parameters screen appears. For this example, enter http://localhost:9000/examples/book/static.jsp in the URL field, set the REPLACE_URL field to False, and leave the INPUT_ENCODING field clear.

If you specify an encoding, it's used between the Wireless server and the static.jsp application. Click Next.

7. The Async Agent screen appears. Do *not* select the Async-Enabled check box. Click Next.
8. The Result Transformer screen appears. For this example, you do not have to specify a result transformer.
9. To complete the master service, click Finish. The master service, EmployeeInfo, appears in the Browse Folder screen under TestBookApp (see Figure 4-4).

Previewing the Application

From the Browse Folder screen, you can do a quick preview of the sample service you just created by clicking the phone icon under the Test column. The Oracle9*i*AS Wireless PDA Simulator will appear (see Figure 4-5).

To view the generated XML, click the Debug button on the same Browse Folder screen. In the Debug screen, choose View Wireless XML Result. Click Set Parameters and then click Run Service. The PDA Simulator appears, displaying the result, which is generated by static.jsp. The Service Result section of the screen

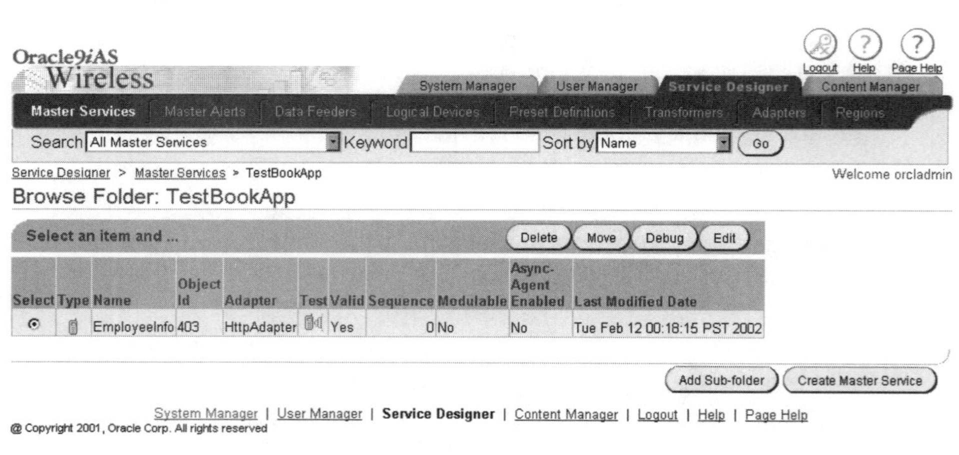

FIGURE 4-4. *EmployeeInfo Master Service*

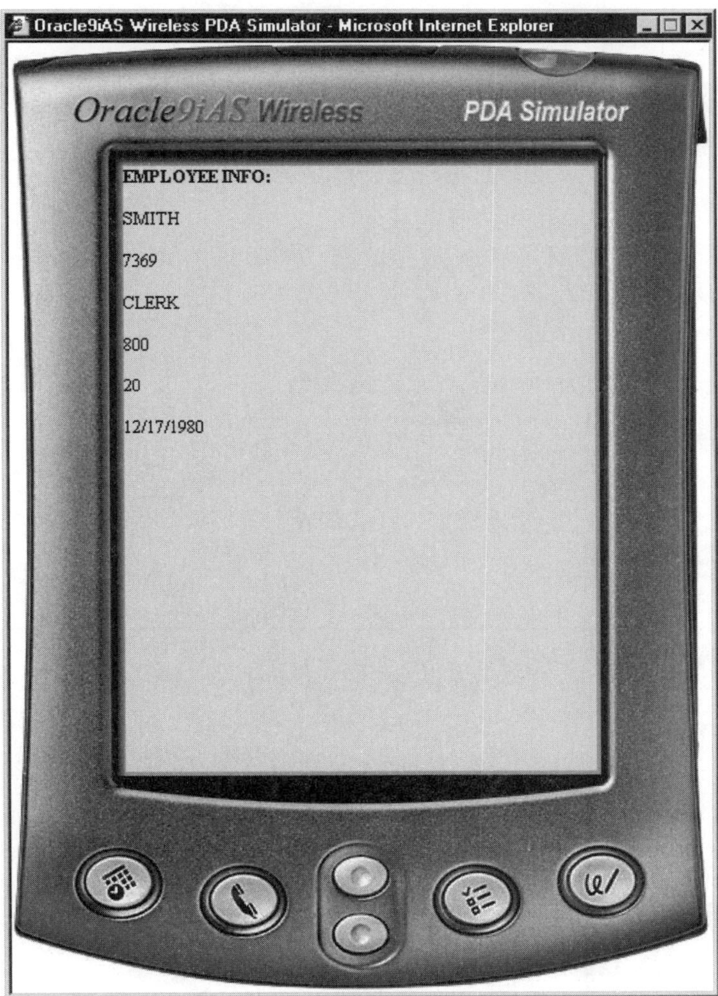

FIGURE 4-5. *Oracle9iAS Wireless PDA Simulator*

displays the intermediate result in Wireless XML, enabling you to see whether this is the result you want to generate (see Figure 4-6).

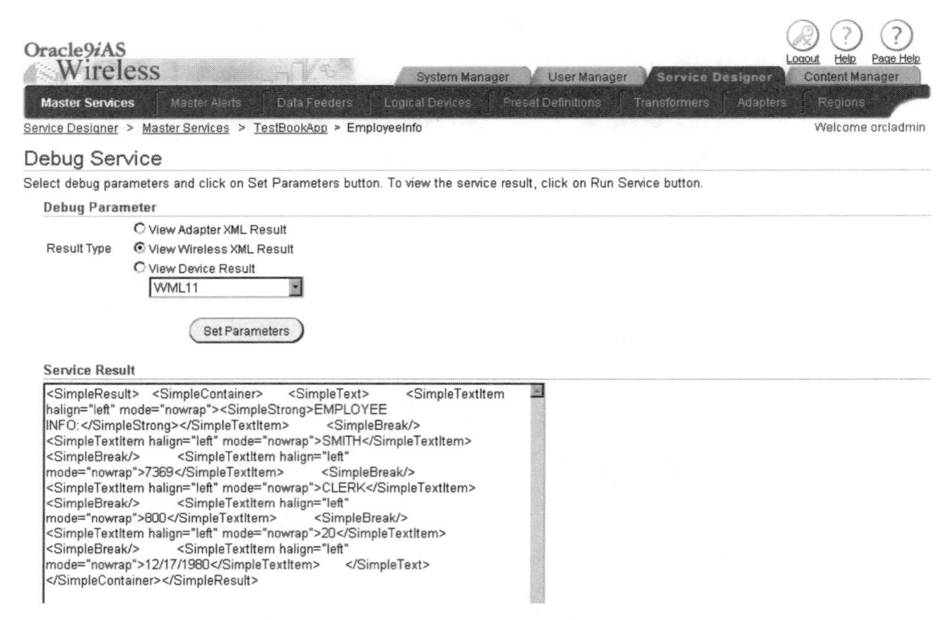

FIGURE 4-6. *Viewing the Wireless XML result*

If you want to see a device result other than Wireless XML for EmployeeInfo, select View Device Result in the Debug Parameter section and from the drop-down list select a device result type, such as SMS or VoiceXML. Click Set Parameters and then click Run Service. The Service Result section will now display the device result.

Creating the User Group and User with the User Manager

Before we can use the Content Manager to publish the folder and the service to the user group, TestGroup, we must first use the User Manager to create this group. We will now step through the details of creating the user group and the user:

1. Log into the Wireless web tool. From the Wireless web tool, select the User Manager tab and then click the Groups tab. The Groups screen of the User Manager appears, showing the current user groups.

2. Click the Create New Group button and enter **TestGroup** in the Group Name field. Click Create. TestGroup now appears in the Group Name section.

3. We will now create a user for TestGroup. Click the Users tab. The User screen appears, displaying the current users. Click Create. The Create a New User screen appears. Complete the Basic Information section for the new user. Fill in only the mandatory fields for this example, such as User Name and Password (use "testuser" for both). For the User Preference section, leave everything with its default setting. For the Group and Role section, select (using the right-arrow button) TestGroup from the Group list. Do not assign any roles. Click Finish.

4. The User screen reappears, displaying testuser.

Publishing a Service Using the Content Manager

We now publish a master service to a user group by creating a service. A *service* is based on a master service and inherits its values. Services enable you to specialize a master service by modifying its values. We will now step through the details of publishing the service:

1. Log into the Wireless web tool. From the Wireless web tool, select the Content Manager tab. The Root Folders and Services screen appears.

2. Click the Add Folder button. The General page of the New Folder screen appears. Fill in only the mandatory fields for this example. Enter **TestService** in the Folder Name field and select System from the Renderer Type drop-down list. The System option sorts folders by sequence number, then by name. Click Continue.

3. The Rendering screen appears. From the drop-down list, select Name Ascend. Click Finish.

4. The Root Folders and Services screen reappears, displaying TestService. Click TestService. The Service Browse screen for TestService appears. Because TestService is new, the Browse Service screen for TestService displays no services. Add a new service to it now by clicking Add Service.

5. The General screen of the Service Creation Wizard appears. Enter **EmployeeInfoService** in the Service Name field and leave everything in its default state. Click Next.

6. The Master Service screen appears. Drill down to the TestBookApp folder. Select EmployeeInfo using its corresponding radio button. Click Next.
7. The Input Parameters screen appears. The Input Parameters screen displays the input parameters you set for EmployeeInfo using the Service Designer. You do not have to change the input parameters. Click Next.
8. The Async Services screen appears. The Async Services screen enables you to set the parameters for an async service. Because the master service, EmployeeInfo, is not async-enabled, you do not have to enter any values in this screen. Click Submit to complete the EmployeeInfo service.
9. We will now assign the EmployeeInfo service to the user group TestGroup, which you created with the User Manager. Click the Groups tab. The Groups List screen appears. Use the radio box to select TestGroup. Click Assign Services. The Service Content screen for TestGroup appears. This screen includes two tables: a table of the services accessible to TestGroup and the Available Services table, which lists services that currently exist in the repository. Using the Select check box, select TestService from the Available Services table. Click Add to Group. The TestService folder now appears in the available services for TestGroup. Click Finish.

Testing the Published Service

Let's test what we have created thus far for the sample static.jsp multichannel application. Running the EmployeeInfo service from Wireless Web Server enables you to see the device-level view of the service. Here are the steps to follow:

1. Starting with a web browser, enter the URL of your Wireless Web Server (for example, http://localhost:9000/ptg/rm).
2. To access the Login page, click the key icon. In the Login page, enter **testuser** as your user name and password. Your home page appears, displaying the default settings. Click the TestService folder. The EmployeeInfo service appears. Click the EmployeeInfo service.
3. You have now invoked the HTML version of the EmployeeInfo service. Let's repeat steps 1 and 2 using a mobile device browser such as the Openwave WAP 4.*x* browser. The content is now rendered as shown in Figure 4-7.
4. Taking it one step further, let's repeat steps 1 and 2 using the MS PocketPC mobile browser. The content is now rendered as shown in Figure 4-8.

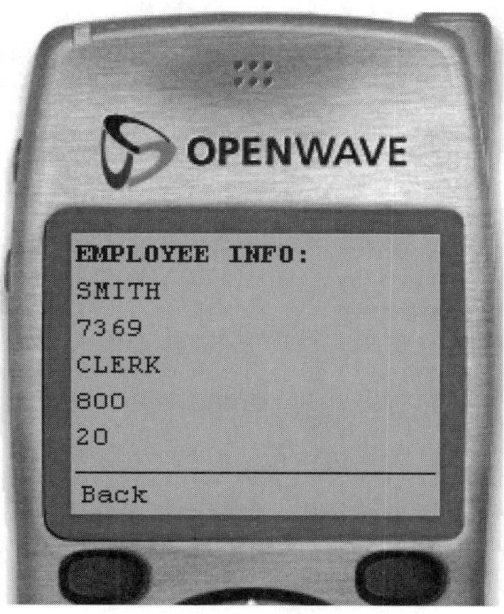

FIGURE 4-7. *EmployeeInfo service in WML device format*

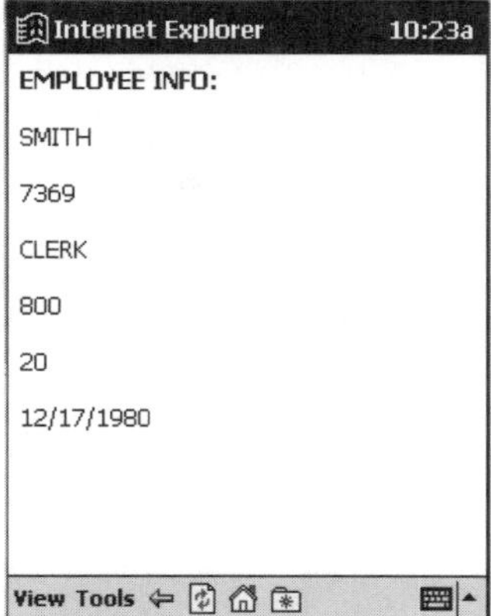

FIGURE 4-8. *EmployeeInfo service in compact-HTML device format*

Creating a Dynamic JSP Application

Our initial JSP application was created using static content for the employee information. Let's make a simple change to the code and name the file dynamic.jsp and then store it in the same web folder as static.jsp (see the "Creating the JSP Application" section earlier). This application will query an Oracle database and grab the content dynamically. The code follows:

```
<?xml version="1.0" encoding="UTF-8" standalone="yes" ?>
<%@ page contentType="text/vnd.oracle.mobilexml; charset=UTF-8"
   session="false" language="java"
   import="java.util.*, java.text.*, java.net.*, java.sql.*" %>
<%
   String URL_id = request.getParameter("id");
   if (URL_id == null) {
      URL_id = "7369";
   }
%>
<%!
public String getQueryString( String queryString )
{
   if ( queryString == null )
      return "";
   return queryString;
}
%>
<%
   Class.forName("oracle.jdbc.driver.OracleDriver");
   String url_qryOracle = "jdbc:oracle:thin:@localhost:1521:oracle";
   String query_qryOracle = "SELECT * FROM EMP WHERE EMPNO = "
      + URL_id + "";
   Connection conn_qryOracle = DriverManager.getConnection
     (url_qryOracle, "scott", "tiger");
   Statement stmt_qryOracle = conn_qryOracle.createStatement(
      ResultSet.TYPE_SCROLL_SENSITIVE, ResultSet.CONCUR_READ_ONLY);
   ResultSet rset_qryOracle =
stmt_qryOracle.executeQuery(query_qryOracle);
%>
<SimpleResult>
   <SimpleContainer>
   <SimpleText>
      <SimpleTextItem halign="left" mode="nowrap">
      <SimpleStrong>EMPLOYEE INFO:</SimpleStrong>
      </SimpleTextItem><SimpleBreak />
<%
```

```
   rset_qryOracle.absolute(1);
   int CurrRow = rset_qryOracle.getRow();
%>
      <SimpleTextItem halign="left" mode="nowrap">
      <%=getQueryString( rset_qryOracle.getString("ENAME") )%>
      </SimpleTextItem><SimpleBreak />
      <SimpleTextItem halign="left" mode="nowrap">
      <%=getQueryString( rset_qryOracle.getString("EMPNO") )%>
      </SimpleTextItem><SimpleBreak />
      <SimpleTextItem halign="left" mode="nowrap">
      <%=getQueryString( rset_qryOracle.getString("JOB") )%>
      </SimpleTextItem><SimpleBreak />
      <SimpleTextItem halign="left" mode="nowrap">
      <%=getQueryString( rset_qryOracle.getString("SAL") )%>
      </SimpleTextItem><SimpleBreak />
      <SimpleTextItem halign="left" mode="nowrap">
      <%=getQueryString( rset_qryOracle.getString("DEPTNO") )%>
      </SimpleTextItem><SimpleBreak />
      <SimpleTextItem halign="left" mode="nowrap">
      <%=getQueryString( rset_qryOracle.getString("HIREDATE") )%>
      </SimpleTextItem><SimpleBreak />
      <SimpleTextItem halign="center" mode="nowrap">
      *** oracle dynamic results ***</SimpleTextItem>
      </SimpleText>
   </SimpleContainer>
</SimpleResult>
```

We are using the sample employee database that comes configured for the Oracle8 or Oracle9 database.

Running the Final Test

To run the modified JSP application, simply replace the static.jsp URL with the dynamic.jsp URL within the Service Designer. Here are the steps to follow:

1. Select the Service Designer tab. The Browse Folder screen appears. Click TestBookApp folder. Check the radio button for EmployeeInfo and then click Edit.

2. The Basic Info screen appears. On the left side of this screen, click the Input Parameters link. The Input Parameters screen appears. Edit the URL to use dynamic.jsp instead of static.jsp and save your changes by clicking Apply. You are now set to test the new application.

3. With the MS PocketPC mobile browser, enter the URL of your Wireless Web Server (for example, http://localhost:9000/ptg/rm).

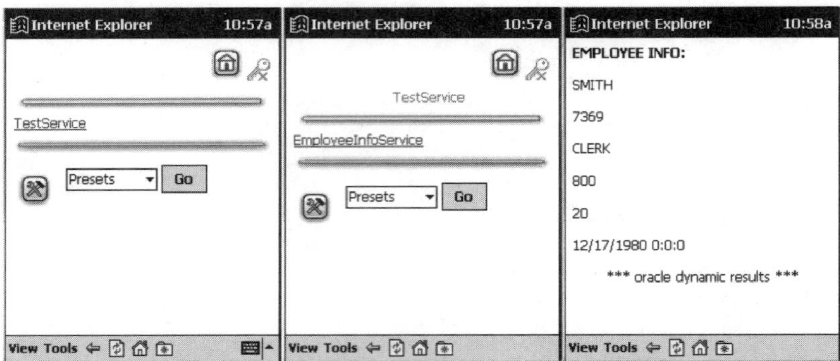

FIGURE 4-9. *Dynamic EmployeeInfo service in compact-HTML device format*

4. To access the Login page, click the key icon. In the Login page, enter **testuser** as your user name and password. Your home page appears, displaying the default settings. Click the TestService folder. The EmployeeInfo service appears. Click the EmployeeInfo service.
5. You have just invoked your dynamic EmployeeInfo service using the PocketPC browser! The content is now rendered as shown in Figure 4-9.

Summary

By now, after going through Chapters 2 through 4, you should be able to build applications in XML and Java/JSP using the tools provided with Oracle9*i*AS Wireless Release 2. Your one-page static (or dynamic) application is now a multichannel application because it can be accessible via a web browser, an Openwave 4.*x* WAP browser, and an MS PocketPC mobile browser, along with other browsers supported. This chapter is meant to illustrate the use of the web tools and the steps it takes to create an Oracle9*i*AS multichannel XML application. For the sake of simplicity, we have neglected to address any design issues. Chapters 14 through 16 focus on multichannel design methodology, and all related design issues will be addressed there.

CHAPTER 5

Advanced Customization

his chapter describes the Advanced Customization Service of Oracle9*i*AS Wireless. Although Chapters 5 through 13 are not meant to be read sequentially, the Advanced Customization features are essential for developers to build services and applications that are seamless and easy to use and navigate. For system administrators, Advanced Customization offers a web-based graphical interface to centrally manage users, groups, profiles, and devices. For users, this service allows self-directed customization that can be particularly useful for a wireless portal or content service provider. Here, we define *customization* as the process by which the system adapts to the needs and preferences of its users, and vice versa. The user-centric customization features give users control over how they adapt the system to their needs and preferences. Specifically, we'll discuss the following topics:

- Customization: What and Why?
- Customization Portal
- Presets
- User, Profile, Device, and Service Management
- Alerts
- Data Feeders

Customization: What and Why?

Customization is needed to make applications manageable by understanding end users' needs based on their roles and preferences—for example, it is beneficial to present information in many different and diverse ways to suppliers, consumers, and your own employees. Ultimately, you want to know enough about a customer's preferences and needs to intelligently suggest new services that they can use on return visits or new usages of your service. The result is to turn a series of single transactions into a series of interactions that leads to an enduring, mutually profitable relationship.

NOTE
Advanced Customization is not to be confused with Oracle9iAS Personalization, which is an option of Oracle9iAS. Oracle9iAS Personalization provides real-time personalization for e-business sales channels, such as web stores, application hosting environments, and call centers. Oracle9iAS Personalization provides an integrated real-time recommendation engine. Oracle9iAS Personalization uses data-mining technology to sift through the mountains of e-business data generated from customers' clicks, transactions, demographics, and ratings information gathered from web sites.

Release 2 of Oracle9*i*AS Wireless has added presets, flexible data-feed capabilities, and multiple profiles in the Advanced Customization Service. User management is based on OID/LDAP and has support for Single Sign-On (SSO). In addition, a scalable new alert engine is available with condition and time alerts that can be pushed to any device.

Mass Customization

The system can also introduce mass-customization techniques that apply automatic user profiling, sometimes by associating a user with a like-minded group of users, to predict the user's needs and preferences, and adapt the system accordingly. This facilitates a role-based association of like-minded users to applicable information domains.

NOTE
The usage history of the users can be found in the PTG_SERVICE_LOG and PTG_SESSION_LOG tables in the Oracle9iAS Wireless repository (Oracle database). The log tables contain records with information of the service ID, service name, user ID, timestamp, and many related values.

Customization Portal

Oracle9*i*AS Wireless includes a default Customization Portal developed in JavaServer Pages (JSP). It allows end users to customize folders, services, bookmarks, alerts, location marks, and profiles via PC browsers. You can reuse these JSP files to rebrand the Customization Portal. You can also develop your own Customization Portals or integrate the customization tools to your existing portals.

The Oracle9*i*AS Wireless Customization Portal is both a framework for the customization interface and a sample implementation of that framework. The framework consists of JSP files, JavaBean modules, JavaScript, images, XSL stylesheets, and HTML files. Another element of the framework is the logical sequence in which the elements execute. You can rebrand the Customization Portal based on the existing framework or restructure the framework itself by altering the logic in the JSP files and JavaBeans.

The device-based Customization Portal targets the customers who want to customize their mobile services directly from mobile devices such as mobile phones and PDAs. The device Customization Portal presents these services in edit mode and also includes the user's preferences settings, landmark creation, and alert creation in the menu list. Because of the limited size of the display screen and the restricted input methods, the user interface and user interaction will be simplified to fit in those device form factors.

The Customization Portal API enables you to create your own JavaServer Pages. The classes are categorized by specific function. Combining these functions is one method of creating your own JSP framework, which provides a self-branded Customization Portal. For detailed information regarding the Customization Portal API, see the Oracle9*i* Application Server Wireless Javadoc.

Accessing the Customization Portal from a PC Browser

The web-based Customization Portal for desktop PCs can be accessed as follows:

1. Point your browser to the following URL:

   ```
   http://hostname:9000/customization/Login.jsp
   ```

2. Supply your administrator or user ID and password to log in. After you successfully log in, the Customization Portal defaults to the Services tab (see Figure 5-1). The Services tab displays the Service Subscription screen, which enables you to select a service and perform such functions as editing a service and creating a quicklink, bookmark, or folder.

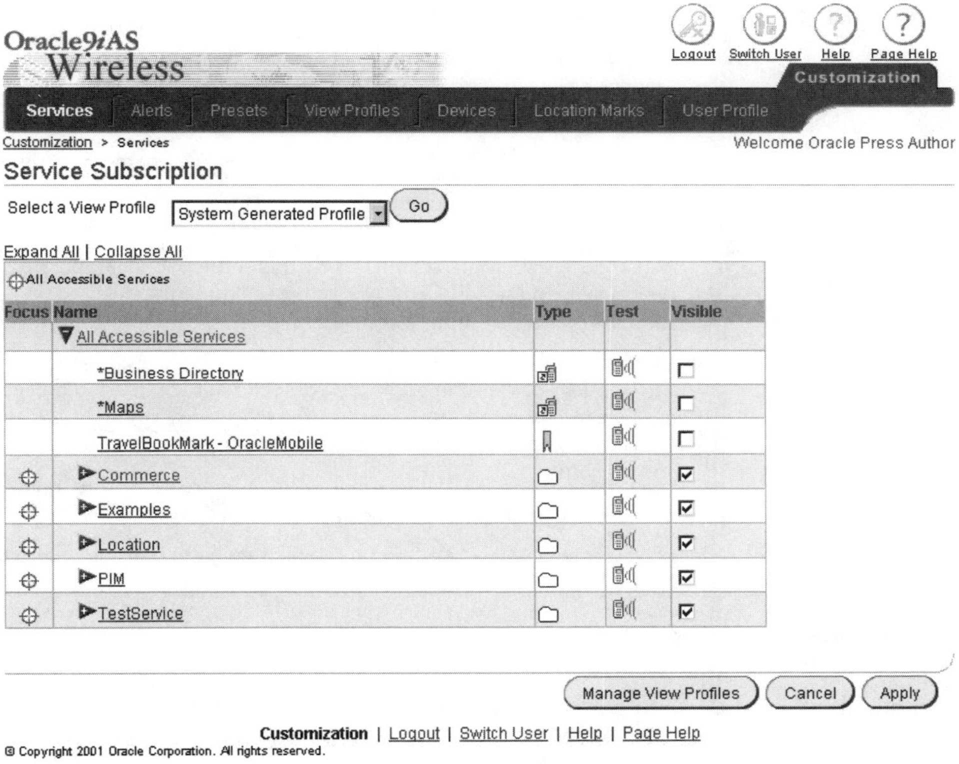

FIGURE 5-1. *Customization Portal services*

A brief description of each of the tabs is provided in Table 5-1.

We will visit the Alerts, Presets, View Profiles, and Location Marks features of the Customization Portal in subsequent sections of this chapter.

Accessing the Customization Portal from Mobile Devices

Accessing the Customization Portal from a mobile device is slightly different than from a desktop PC. Additionally, the features available are slightly different. The device-based Customization Portal provides a subset of the current browser-based

Tab Name	Description
Services	Displays the Service Subscription screen. You can create a quicklink of a service as well as edit, create, or delete an object.
Alerts	Displays the Alerts screen. You can edit the properties of a selected alert, such as enabling an alert and setting its frequency.
Presets	The current preset definitions available to the user group. Users can add, delete, or edit preset values (the user-defined inputs for a service).
View Profiles	Displays the View Profile screen. Using this screen, you can create different views of the service trees that are suited to the display capabilities of a device or to a connection profile.
Devices	Displays the Wireless Device screen. You can add or disable alerts sent to wireless devices. In addition, you can validate that the device is set up correctly, send test pages, set the WAP provisioning profile, and set the maximum number of alerts sent per day.
Location Marks	Displays the LocationMark List screen. You can create, delete, edit, or change the default status of a location mark on this page.
User Profile	Displays a screen where users set up or edit their basic user information.

TABLE 5-1. *Customization Portal Tabs*

functionality that you use to perform such user administration functions as creating quicklinks, presets, alerts, and devices. The device-based Customization Portal for mobile devices can be accessed as follows:

1. Point your mobile browser to the following URL:

   ```
   http://hostname:9000/ptg/rm
   ```

   Notice that this is the wireless web server!

2. Supply your administrator or user ID and password to log in. After you successfully log in, the standard wireless services menu will be displayed on your home page (see Figures 5-2 and 5-3). Your home page, which bears your user name or display name, displays a set of default services and folders. From your home page, you can customize your services.

A brief description of the functionalities available to the user is provided in Table 5-2.

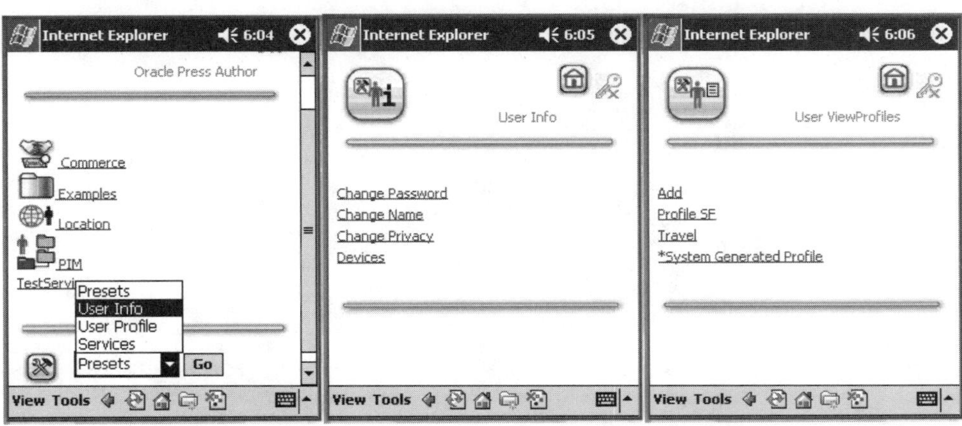

FIGURE 5-2. *Device-based Customization Portal home page on a PocketPC*

FIGURE 5-3. *Device-based Customization Portal home page on a WAP phone*

Functionality	Description
User Info	This option enables you to change your user information and add or delete devices.
Presets	The current preset categories available to the user group. Users can add, delete, or edit preset values (the user-defined inputs for a service).
User Profile	With this option, you can create different views of folders and services for different purposes or scenarios. You can also switch between profiles.
Services	This option enables you to create, edit, reorder, or delete folders, bookmarks, and quicklinks.

TABLE 5-2. *Device-Based Customization Portal Functionality*

Configuring the Customization Portal

A newly created user has an empty home folder bearing the user's name. All new users are assigned to the default group, Users, and have end-user privileges. Using the Customization Portal, users can customize their services through such functions as creating quicklinks, creating folders, and organizing services. In addition, users can schedule the delivery of alerts as well as create or edit wireless devices. We will cover the management of these functions next.

Offline Customization

We have covered online wireless customization thus far. Offline applications can be customized both from the end user's prospective (Mobile Workspace) and from the administrator's prospective (Mobile Server). Refer to Chapters 8 and 9 for details.

Presets

One of the key Advanced Customization facilities in Oracle9*i*AS Wireless is presets. Presets are used for the storage of users' personal information, preference settings, and frequently used input parameters on the server side so that the services can use them to generate the personalized responses. Presets are persistent objects in the Oracle9*i*AS Wireless repository that can be used to extend repository schemas, especially to incorporate new persistent attributes for the User objects in the repository.

Presets enable users to customize services by defining their *own* input parameters for an application or service. When a user requests a service, an adapter loads the user-defined parameters, or *presets*. The executed application then uses the presets as the input parameters. Although the preset definitions are available to the user group, the presets themselves belong to the user and cannot be seen by other users.

Service developers have the control to manage the types of presets available to particular users and groups and the input values used. Developers create preset categories for managing the presets that are available to end users. Each preset category consists of a preset category name (for example, AddressForm) and any number of preset attributes. This will give end users the ability to create presets called Home, Work, and so on, and each will have their own values for the preset attributes (Street, City, and so on).

Individual end users can also customize some of the capabilities of the user agent. The user agent types and the logical device models in the repository describe the capabilities of the devices. The presets for user agent profiles can be used to let the end users customize the capabilities of the user agent—for example, to enable or disable sound, select background color, select quality of service, and disable images to minimize packet transmissions, even though the device supports images.

The user agent profiles also control the format of the content, but more general user preference profiles can affect the selection of the services and response of the services. The user preference profiles for sports, entertainment, technology, privacy requirements, and so on can be used by the services to filter the contents. The presets architecture enables the development of adaptive web services based on emerging Composite Capability/Preference Profile (CC/PP), User Agent profile (WAP UAProf), and Platform for Privacy Preferences (P3P) standards.

Oracle9*i*AS Wireless gives you the option to save the input values that a user has entered as a preset value for future invocations. Furthermore, Oracle9*i*AS Wireless provides options to enter a symbolic name to represent a preset group. These symbolic names allow easy selection if there is more than one group of preset values.

Managing Presets

You can check out some of the preset definitions on the web-based Wireless server under the Service Designer tab by selecting Preset Definitions (see Figure 5-4).

Note that presets are made available to end users as part of the bundled services, such as Location-Based Services, Mobile PIM, and Mobile E-mail.

The users can manage their presets from either a PC or a mobile device. The Presets screen, invoked by selecting the Presets tab on the Advanced Customization Portal with a PC browser or by tapping the Presets link from the user's home page on a mobile device (see Figures 5-5 and 5-6), enables the user to create, edit, and delete preset values.

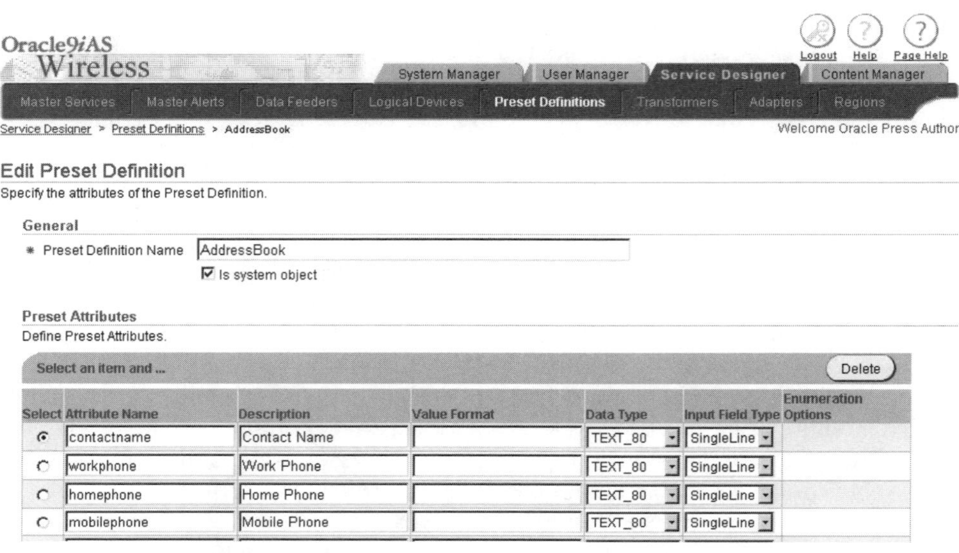

FIGURE 5-4. *Preset definitions for AddressBook*

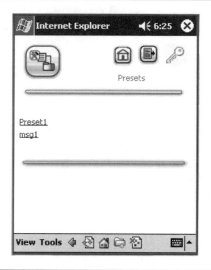

FIGURE 5-5. *Presets on a PC browser*

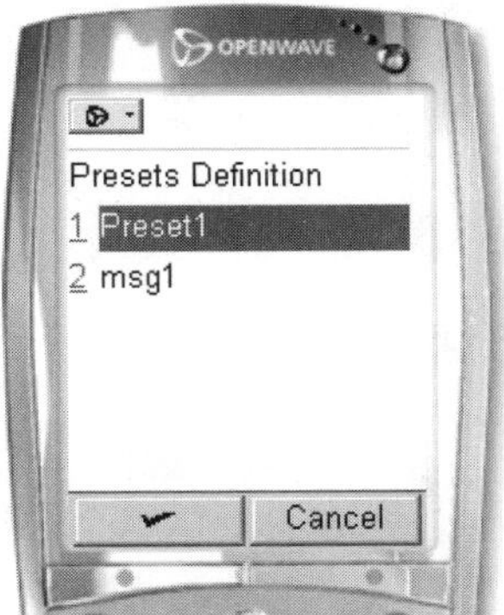

FIGURE 5-6. *Presets on a mobile device*

User, Profile, Device and Service Management

Oracle9*i*AS Wireless enables the development of user-centric web services that adapt the contents not only to the device and network capabilities but also to the end user's references. The device portals typically provide a menu of services that may be organized under several folders and subfolders. Menu-driven device portals are designed to optimize the interactive efficiency of wireless devices. Service menus are usually static, but the portal may intelligently suggest new services to the user as it learns more about the user's needs and preferences.

The Oracle9*i*AS Wireless server lets end users personalize the portal by controlling the arrangement of the services in the menus. The portal can suggest new services to the users, but the users still control when to include or exclude each service in their personalized portal. System administrators can explicitly prevent the end users from rearranging or removing certain services, such as promotions, preferred partners, emergency services, and so on, from their personalized portals. The system administrators may also apply the location-based filtering of the services in the location-enabled folders. This filtering function offers additional dynamism to the views that vary with the users' mobile position.

Managing Users

Oracle9*i*AS Wireless has advanced group and user management. Any user who is granted User Manager capabilities is able to create, delete, and modify groups and users through any device or PC. Note that such a user is created using the User Manager of the web-based Wireless WebTool. Any group or user can be restricted or granted access to any folder or service. The advanced Access Control List (ACL) used with the user and group management allows for fine-grained access control that takes advantage of the flexible user or group policies that may be applied to services or folders.

Managing Services and Folders

Oracle9*i*AS Wireless offers complete control to the developer for managing what end users can do in terms of folder management. Developers can offer groups or users complete flexibility with their service management or restricted use of service management. Services and folders may be organized in the following ways:

- User-specified sequence numbers (ascending or descending)
- Creation date (ascending or descending)
- Frequency of access (ascending or descending)
- Dynamic ordering based on frequency of access or last access (ascending or descending)

By default, Oracle9*i*AS Wireless has the following user groups: Administrator, Guest, and Users. A new user is automatically assigned to the Users group and has default privileges to all the services that the Content Manager has assigned to the Users group. The Service Subscription page does not reveal group membership to users, nor does it display other users belonging to the user's group. Whereas an administrator can alter any service in the Advanced Customization Portal, non-administrator-level users, such as end users, can only alter the services they own. Users own services belonging to the user groups to which they have membership (via the Content Manager of the web-based Wireless WebTool). End users can create, edit, and delete subfolders. Unless users have the administrator role, they can only edit or delete the folders that they have created.

End users also have the ability to customize their mobile experience with bookmarks (links to a URL) and quicklinks (aliases to services). This gives users the ability to link frequently accessed services to the home deck or any other desired folder. Users can create, edit, and delete quicklinks and bookmarks.

Managing Devices

Oracle9*i*AS Wireless gives users with multiple devices the ability to easily manage and optimize their mobile experience for each device. The users can manage their devices from either a PC or a mobile device. The Devices screen, invoked by selecting the Devices tab on the Advanced Customization Portal with a PC browser (see

Figure 5-7) or by tapping the Devices link from the User Info menu (see Figure 5-8), enables you to create, edit, and delete a device.

NOTE
You must have at least one of the devices registered with the Advanced Customization Portal for alert subscriptions in order to deliver content appropriate to the display capacities of the device.

Multiple Profiles

The Advanced Customization Portal enables you to create a personalized view of folders, quicklinks, and bookmarks. The User's View Profile screen (or User Profile on mobile devices) enables you to create different view profiles, such as separate views for home and office use. These views hold the selected settings, including the visibility status and ordering of folders. You can also create views for different devices, depending on their display capabilities. This makes the mobile experience much more efficient.

Oracle9*i*AS Wireless

Logout Switch User Help Page Help

Customization

Services | Alerts | Presets | View Profiles | **Devices** | Location Marks | User Profile

Customization > Devices

Welcome Oracle Press Author

Device

Device List

For Selected Device — WAP Provisioning | Disable All Alerts | Delete | Set Default | Apply | Validate

Select	Device Name	Alerts/Day	Address	Data Delivery Type	Carrier	Model	Validated	Default	Has Alert Dependency
◉	SMS	0	6505551212	SMS			false	false	false
○	iaswe	0	iaswe@where2net.cc	Email			false	false	false

Create Device

* Device Name
* Address
Data Delivery Type: Email
Carrier
Model
Maximum Alerts to Send per Day
Default

TIP After creating this Device, a validation number is sent to you.
TIP Click the Validate button and type in the validation number to validate your Device.

Create

FIGURE 5-7. *Device management on a PC browser*

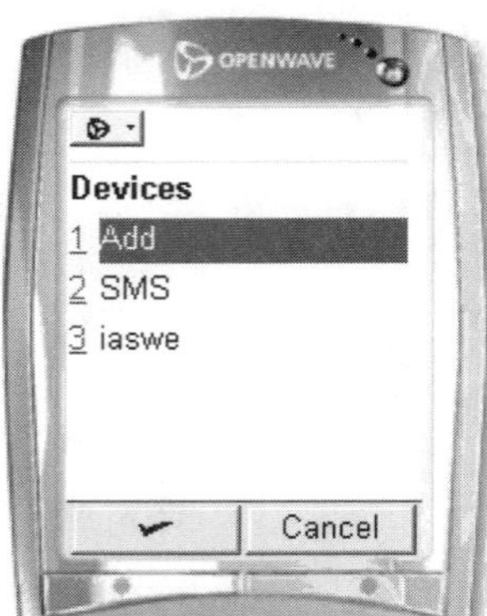

FIGURE 5-8. *Device management on mobile devices*

Multiple profiles can be created for different roles, locations or contexts, device and network characteristics, or any other taxonomy. For a telecommuter who frequents multiple metropolitan cities, the profiles may be created for each location (see Figure 5-9). For example, a user's customization profile for Travel may include services for theaters, sporting events, maps, directions, and train schedules.

Location Marks

Location awareness is a key feature of Oracle9*i*AS Wireless. A user's location can be obtained from E911 or GPS units or *location marks,* which are user-defined locations. For example, end users may enter into their location-aware applications addresses for their home, work, and headquarters office. Then, a movie theater lookup application, for example, can use the current location to provide driving directions. To ensure security and privacy, users can control which applications can access their locations.

Due to the limitations of certain mobile devices, such as telephones, it is difficult to input or display lengthy alphanumeric strings. A location mark stores a piece of spatial information identified by a concise, easy-to-understand name. For example, My Home might be the name of a location mark, but the underlying spatial information might be "12345 Main Street, My City, CA, 94402, Lon = -122.42, Lat = 37.58". Users can select, create, delete and modify location marks with any

FIGURE 5-9. *Multiple profiles*

mobile device or PC browser. Using location marks, you do not have to enter lengthy alphanumeric strings on your mobile devices. Instead, you enter and manage the underlying spatial information (see Figure 5-10). For example, to generate a map for a certain address on a mobile device, you select a predefined location mark instead of tediously typing in the full address (see Figure 5-11).

Alert Engine

The Oracle9*i*AS Wireless Alert System provides extensible and scalable solutions to develop mobile alert services. An alert service can generate alert message delivery events from a content source based on certain conditions. Such a condition can be a value-based predicate (for example, a stock price reaches a predefined value). The delivery mechanism of the alert message is through the Oracle9*i*AS Wireless Messaging System, which allows notifications to be sent via WAP push, fax, e-mail, SMS, two-way pager, one-way pager, or voice.

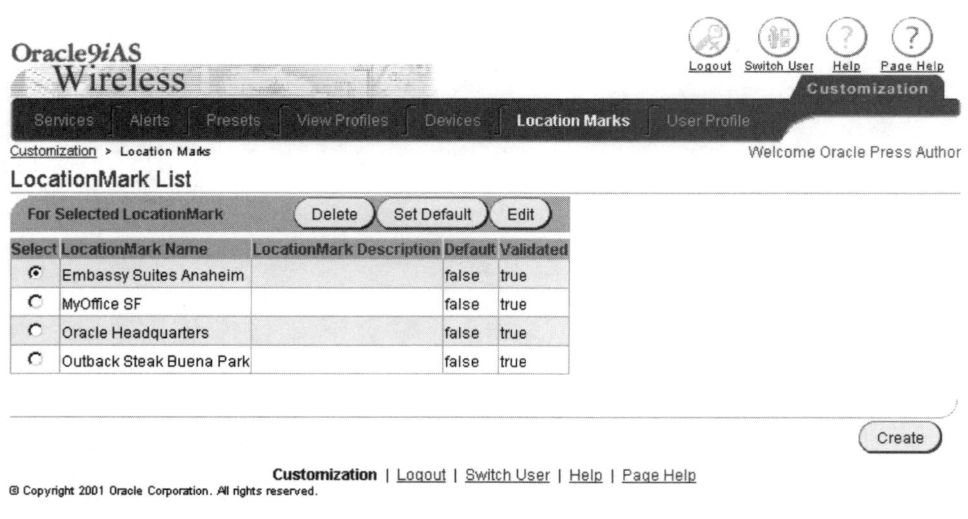

FIGURE 5-10. *Location marks management*

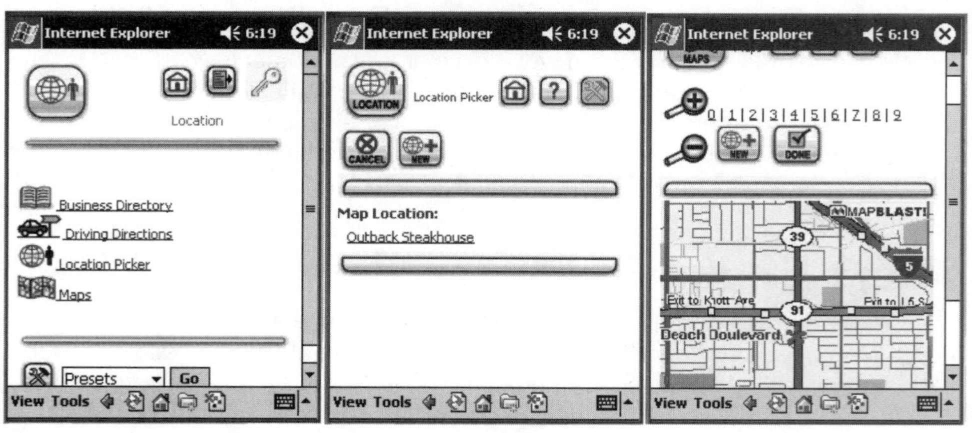

FIGURE 5-11. *Using location marks in maps*

Alert Architecture

At design time, each master alert service selects a content descriptor, known as a *data feeder*, as its content source and becomes a subscriber to a content-arrival event from that content source. Upon a content-arrival event, which is generated by either data feeders or custom applications, the alert engine will notify all the content event handlers whose associated master alert services have subscribed to that content-arrival event. Once the list of alert subscribers has been determined, the message formatter generates the outgoing alert message by either applying the message-formatting template to the content or invoking the message-formatter hook (Java) with the content and alert subscriber information. Finally, the alert message dispatcher communicates with the Oracle9*i*AS Wireless Messaging System to deliver the message to the alert subscriber's device address.

End users can create their alert subscriptions using either the Oracle9*i*AS Advanced Customization Portal or Oracle9*i*AS Wireless alert subscription APIs. If a master alert service is set to be time-based enabled, the user will also be able to specify the time and the frequency for evaluating their alert subscriptions. The time event handler will request the content from the data feeder based on the user's time-based setting and generate the content-arrival event for the content event handler.

Data Feeder and Alert Service Design Process

Here are the steps you would go through to develop a turnkey system, from the data feeder to an alert service for end users (subscribers) using Oracle9*i*AS Wireless:

1. *Create a data feeder.* This could be sourced from various protocols, including the local file system, FTP, HTTP, SQL, or a custom program. Use the Service Designer Data Feeder Wizard (web-based Wireless WebTool) to create and specify the source and update the policy, input parameters, and output parameters. See the "Data Feeder" section later in this chapter for additional details.
2. *Create a master alert.* The Service Designer Master Alert Wizard requires you to define the data feeder source, the trigger conditions, and the notification message XML template.
3. *Publish the master alert as an alert.* Use the Content Manager Alerts Wizard to add a subtopic for the alert folder and add the newly created alert service to the folder. Specify the input parameters and trigger conditions that you want your end users or subscribers to be able to customize. Remember to use the Content Manager Groups Wizard to grant access (assign an alert) to that alert service for the users.
4. *Start the Messaging Server.* Make sure the Messaging Server is started, if it is not already. Refer to the Oracle9*i*AS Wireless System Administration documents on configuring the Messaging Server.

5. *Configure and start the data feeder process.* Use the System Manager Wireless Server Wizard to select the Data Feeder Server, add the data feeder process created in step 1, and explicitly start that process.

6. *Configure and start the alert engine process.* Use the System Manager Wireless Server Wizard to select the Alert Engine Server, add the alert service process created in step 3, and explicitly start that process.

7. *Register a device and subscribe to the alert.* This is the most crucial part of the process. From the Advanced Customization Portal, select the Devices tab. Create your new device (use any name) using one of the many delivery types (WAP push, fax, e-mail, SMS, two-way pager, one-way pager, or voice) and enter the relevant configuration information for that specific device. After you click Create, you will be notified with a validation number. Click the Validate button for this device and supply the validation number (click Validate again in that new dialog).

8. You are done and ready to subscribe to alerts!

NOTE
Without a validated device, you will not be able to receive alerts. A device must be validated using the validation number sent to you when you finished creating the new device.

Managing Alerts

Users can manage their alerts from a PC browser through the Advanced Customization Portal. The Alert Subscription screen, invoked by selecting the Alerts tab on the Advanced Customization Portal, lists the alerts available to your user group. In order to create an alert subscription, you must have at least one validated device. If you do not have a validated device, the Devices screen will be displayed instead.

Data Feeder

A data feeder is an agent that downloads content and runs periodically, independently of service invocations. The feed framework is designed to download content for an Oracle9*i*AS Wireless process. The downloaded content can be used both for asynchronous alerts and for cached data for synchronous services.

The download schedule for the data feeder is maintained in the update policy for that data feeder. The update policy determines the update interval (how often the data feeder runs). The update policy can be the time of day as well as which days of the week to run the data feeder.

Each data feeder has a content provider, which is the source of the content. The content provider maintains information about the URL of the content, the protocol to use for downloading the content, and the format of the data to be downloaded. For example, when data is downloaded from a content provider using HTTP, the input parameters will be used either to construct a GET URL or as POST parameters in the HTTP request.

Building a Data Feed

You can create a data feed using the Service Designer Data Feeder Wizard or programmatically using a Java/JSP program. Follow these steps to create a data feed using the Service Designer Data Feeder Wizard:

1. *Create a named data feeder.* All data feeders must have a name (these names may be modified later).
2. *Set the content provider parameters.* Set the protocol and format for the content provider.
3. *Create input parameters.* A data feeder must have at least one input parameter. For each input parameter you specify, you must give an internal name and data type. Parameters may have options that depend on the chosen format. If the format chosen is delimited text, you have the option of specifying the column number in which the input parameter appears. This is useful if the input parameter is also included in the output from the content provider. The index for the columns starts at 1, as SQL. If 0 is specified, the input parameter is assumed to not be in the output.
4. *Create output parameters.* A data feeder must have at least one output parameter. The output parameter can be customized in the same manner as an input parameter.

Yahoo! Stock Quotes Data Feed Example

Let's now go through a complete example of how to create a data feeder process using delayed stock quotes feed from Yahoo!. This feed is being used only for the purpose of this example. You can create a similar feed using your own content source.

NOTE
For all intent and purposes, the delayed quotes feed from Yahoo! is provided for informational purposes only and is not intended for trading purposes or redistribution.

The Yahoo! Finance website allows any user to freely download a series of stock quotes in a comma-separated CSV format. For example, the URL

```
http://finance.yahoo.com/d/quotes.csv?s=ADBE+BEAS+MACR+OPWV+ORCL+QQQ+
   SEBL+WEBM+YHOO&f=sl1d1t1c1ohgv&e=.csv
```

will download the following *dynamic* CSV content:

```
""ADBE"",37.64,""4/9/2002"",""4:00pm"",-1.22,39.05,39.79,37.63,3094800
""BEAS"",11.88,""4/9/2002"",""4:00pm"",-0.64,12.61,12.92,11.80,9468600
""MACR"",18.10,""4/9/2002"",""3:59pm"",-0.74,18.63,18.75,17.70,770600
""OPWV"",5.39,""4/9/2002"",""4:00pm"",-0.27,5.71,5.76,5.33,1855400
""ORCL"",11.98,""4/9/2002"",""4:00pm"",-0.36,12.33,12.38,11.83,36219100
""QQQ"",33.59,""4/9/2002"",""4:15pm"",-1.21,34.78,34.98,33.498,80941904
""SEBL"",27.56,""4/9/2002"",""4:00pm"",-1.33,29.40,29.64,27.36,15131100
""WEBM"",17.51,""4/9/2002"",""4:00pm"",+0.51,17.41,18.64,17.26,2327400
""YHOO"",18.46,""4/9/2002"",""4:00pm"",-0.38,18.95,19.15,18.39,10826200
```

You can interpret the quote format as follows:

```
Ticker, Closing Price, Trade Date, Trade Time, Change, Open, High,
   Low, Volume
```

Let's get started creating data feed. Here are the steps to follow:

1. *Create a named data feeder.* Let's call our data feed **YahooQuotes** and update it throughout weekdays from 6:30 A.M. PST to 1:30 P.M. PST as illustrated here.

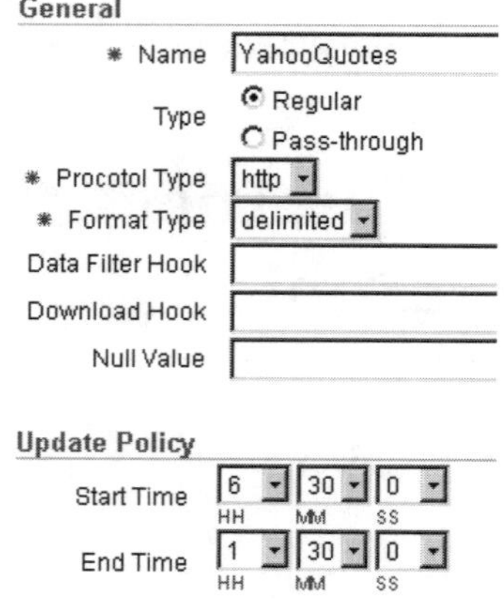

2. *Set the content provider parameters.* Enter the URL to the Yahoo! quotes feed using the HTTP protocol with a GET method. Use "," (the comma character) as the separator as illustrated here.

Init paramters for the protocol type you have selected

* HTTP URI	http://finance.yahoo.com/d/quotes.csv?s=ADBE+BEAS+MACR+OF
Username	
Password	
HTTP Method	(•) GET ( ) POST

Init parameters for the format type you have selected

Delimiter	,

3. *Create input parameters.* Enter **symbol** for the input parameter, **TEXT_80** for the data type, **1** for the column number, and **ticker** for the caption as illustrated. Leave everything else blank.

Input Parameters

Select an item and ...

Select	Internal Name	Data Type	External Name	Return Content Column Number	Caption
(•)	symbol	TEXT_80		1	ticker

Add Another Row

4. *Create output parameters.* Enter a row for each of the quote feed content columns that you're interested in using for your alerts, such as price, change, volume, and so on. Enter **Number** for the data type and specify the appropriate column number for each variable as illustrated here.

Output Parameters

Select an item and ...

Select	Internal Name	Data Type	Return Content Column Number	Caption
(•)	price	NUMBER	2	Price
( )	change	NUMBER	5	Change
( )	volume	NUMBER	9	Volume

Add Another Row

5. *Finish the wizard.* Click the Finish button. You now have a data feeder created as illustrated here.

Browse Data Feeders

Select an item and ...

Select	Name	Object Id	Procotol Type	Format Type	Data Filter Hook
( )	StockDF	569	file	delimited	none
(•)	YahooQuotes	584	http	delimited	

6. *Activate the data feeder.* In order to activate this data feed, you have to configure it and start the process. Using the System Manager Wireless Server panel, select Data Feeder from the process table. In the Process Name field, enter **YahooQuotesDF**. Click Add. YahooQuotesDF appears in the process table as illustrated here.

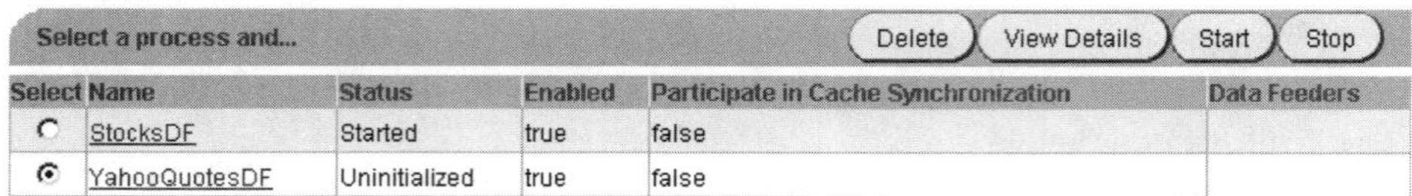

Data Feeder Processes
On this page, you can click on the process name link to configure and view details of the process. You can also start, stop or delete one process, or create a new process.
Select a process and...
Delete
View Details
Start
Stop
Select
Name
Status
Enabled
Participate in Cache Synchronization
Data Feeders
StocksDF
Started
true
false
YahooQuotesDF
Uninitialized
true
false

Click YahooQuotesDF. The overview screen for YahooQuotesDF appears. From the Data Feeder Name drop-down list, select YahooQuotes. Click Add. YahooQuotes appears in the data feeders table. In the General section, click the Start button as illustrated.

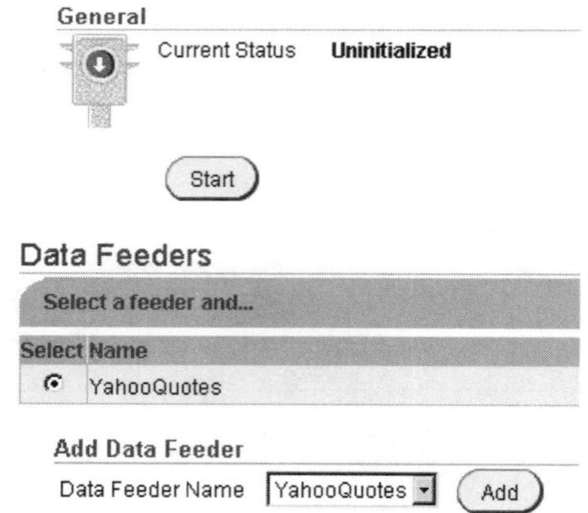

7. *The data feeder begins running.* You now have a live data feeder process running on Oracle9*i*AS Wireless Server!

Yahoo! Stock Quotes Alert Example

Let's now cover how to design an alert service that utilizes the YahooQuotes data feeder from the previous section. We will go through these four steps in detail:

1. Creating a master alert
2. Publishing the master alert as an alert service
3. Configuring and starting an alert engine process
4. Registering a device and subscribing to the alert service

Creating a Master Alert

To create a master alert, follow these steps:

1. *Create the master alert.* Log into the Wireless WebTool and select the Service Designer Master Alerts tab. To create a new master alert, click the Create Master Alert button. You will be presented with the Basic Info screen of the Master Alert Creation Wizard.
2. *Enter the basic information.* Enter **YahooQuotesMA** in the Name field, **Yahoo Quotes Alert** in the Description field, and then check the Time-Based Enabled box. From the Data Feeder drop-down list, select YahooQuotes as shown in the illustration. Click the Next button to advance to the next screen.

Create Master Alert : Basic Info

Provide the basic infomation.

* Name: YahooQuotesMA

Description: Yahoo Quotes Alert

* Data Feeder: YahooQuotes

Subscriber Filtering Hook:

[x] Time-Base Enabled

3. *Set the trigger conditions.* Let's add a few trigger conditions now. Click the Add Another Row button and enter **MaxPrice**, select Price, and then select

Greater Than for the Condition Name, Trigger Parameter, and Condition Type fields, respectively. Repeat this action for another row with MinPrice, Price, and Less Than for the Condition Name, Trigger Parameter, and Condition Type fields, respectively. Finally, repeat this action for another row with Change, Change, Greater Than Absolute Value for the Condition Name, Trigger Parameter, and Condition Type fields, respectively as shown in the illustration. Click the Next button to advance to the next screen.

Create Master Alert : Trigger Conditions

Define trigger conditions.

Select an item and ...

Select	Condition Name	Trigger Parameter	Condition Type	Default Value
◉	MaxPrice	price	Greater Than	
○	MinPrice	price	Less Than	
○	Change	change	Greater Than Absolute Value	

Add Another Row

4. *Create the message template.* Select XML Template, as shown in the illustration below, and enter the following template for formatting the alert message that is sent to the end user:

```
<SimpleText>
Stock Alert for &symbol;
Price: &price;
Change: &change;
Volume: &volume;
</SimpleText>
```

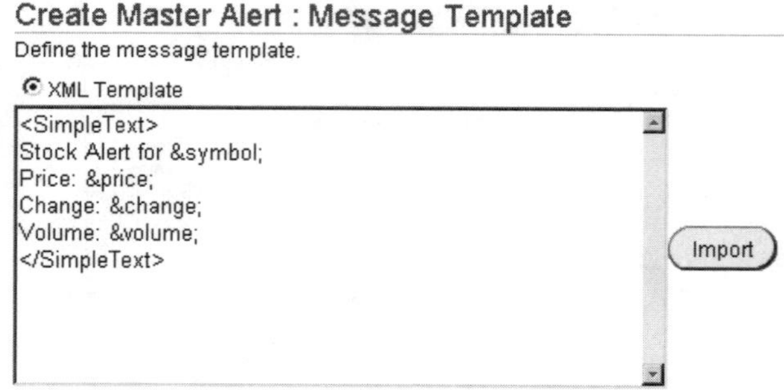
Create Master Alert : Message Template
Define the message template.
XML Template
<SimpleText>
Stock Alert for &symbol;
Price: &price;
Change: &change;
Volume: &volume;
</SimpleText>
Import

5. *Finish the wizard.* Click the Finish button. The screen now shows all the master alerts available in the wireless server as shown in the illustration.

Browse Master Alerts

Select an item and ... (Delete) (Edit)

Select	Name	Object Id	Data Feeder	Time-Base Enabled
○	StockMA	572	StockDF	Yes
◉	YahooQuotesMA	600	YahooQuotes	Yes

Publishing the Master Alert as an Alert Service

Next, we will use the Content Manager to publish the master alert YahooQuotesMA as an alert service to certain user groups. Follow these steps:

1. *Create the alert.* Log into the Wireless WebTool and select the Content Manager Alerts tab. Click the Add SubTopic button and enter **StockQuotes** for the topic name. Click Finish. Now click the StockQuotes folder (subtopic) and then click the Add Alert button to start the Alert Creation Wizard.
2. *Enter the general information.* Enter **YahooAlert** in the Alert Name field and **Yahoo Stock Alert** in the Description field. Click Next.
3. *Select a master alert.* Using the radio button, select YahooQuotesMA and click Next.
4. *Set the input parameter(s).* Only one input parameter, Symbol, is defined by the data feeder. Set this input parameter by entering **StockTicker** in the Caption field as illustrated. Click Next.

New Alert

Name	Caption	DataType	Value
symbol	StockTicker	TEXT_80	

Set the trigger conditions. Enter the following for the Caption fields of Change, MaxPrice, and MinPrice, respectively: **Change**, **MaxPrice**, and **MinPrice** as illustrated here.

New Alert

Name	Caption	TriggerParameter	ConditionType	Value
Change	Change	change	Greater Than Absolute Value	
MaxPrice	MaxPrice	price	Greater Than	
MinPrice	MinPrice	price	Less Than	

Click *Submit* to finish the wizard. You should see the newly created alert for the StockQuotes subtopic as seen in the illustration.

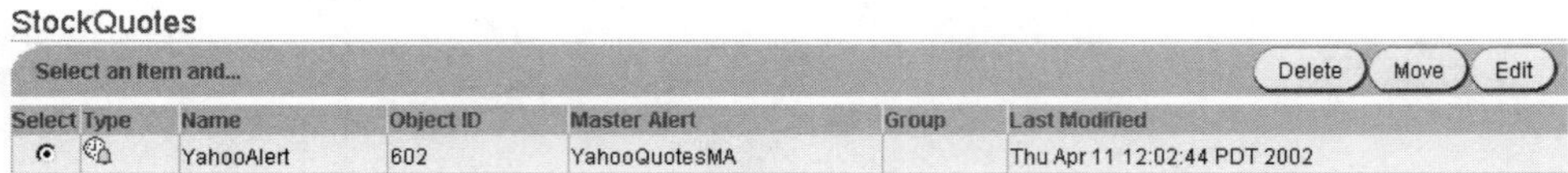

5. *Publish the alert to a user group.* Finally, we will publish YahooAlert to a user group. Click the Groups tab and select the TestGroup radio button, as shown in the illustration, or any other group you want to test with.

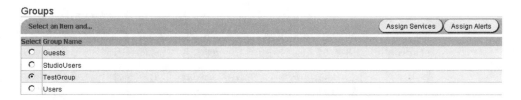

Click the Assign Alerts button next. The alert content of TestGroup appears. The top table lists the topics and alerts that TestGroup can currently access, whereas the bottom table lists all the existing alerts and topics in the repository. Select StockQuotes using the check box in the Select column of the bottom table (as shown in the illustration).

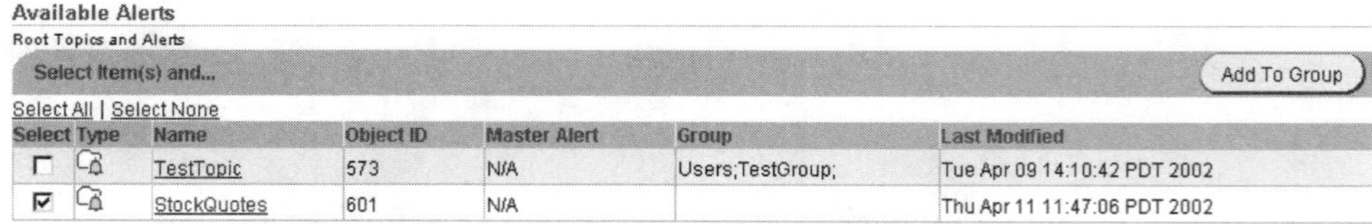

Available Alerts
Root Topics and Alerts
Select Item(s) and...
Add To Group
Select All | Select None
Select Type Name Object ID Master Alert Group Last Modified
TestTopic 573 N/A Users;TestGroup; Tue Apr 09 14:10:42 PDT 2002
StockQuotes 601 N/A Thu Apr 11 11:47:06 PDT 2002

Click the Add to Group button. StockQuotes now appears in the top table because TestGroup can now access it (as illustrated). Click the Finish button.

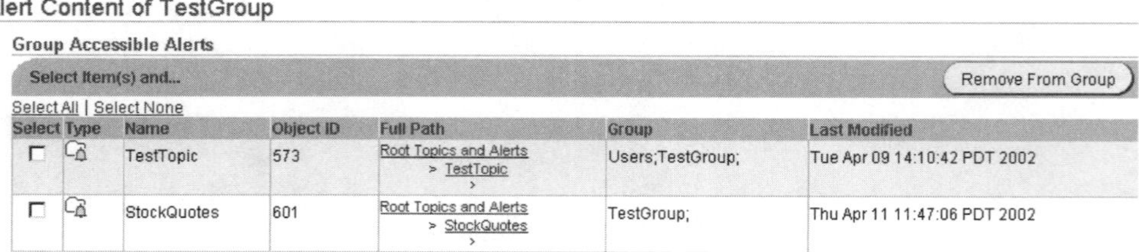

Alert Content of TestGroup
Group Accessible Alerts
Select Item(s) and...
Remove From Group
Select All | Select None
Select Type Name Object ID Full Path Group Last Modified
TestTopic 573 Root Topics and Alerts > TestTopic > Users;TestGroup; Tue Apr 09 14:10:42 PDT 2002
StockQuotes 601 Root Topics and Alerts > StockQuotes > TestGroup; Thu Apr 11 11:47:06 PDT 2002

Configuring and Starting an Alert Engine Process

We will now use the System Manager Wireless Server Wizard to select the Alert Engine Server and add the alert service and explicitly start that process. Here's how:

1. Log into the Wireless WebTool and select the System Manager Wireless Server tab. From the process table, click the Alert Engine hyperlink. The Alert Engine processes screen appears.
2. Enter **YahooAlertEngine** in the Process Name field and click the Add button (see Figure 5-12). YahooAlertEngine now appears in the alert processes table (see Figure 5-13).
3. Click YahooAlertEngine. The overview page for YahooAlertEngine appears. From the Master Alert Name drop-down menu, select YahooQuotesMA (see Figure 5-14). Click Add. YahooQuotesMA now appears in the alert engine table.
4. In the General section, click Start. The YahooAlertEngine process is now running on Oracle9*i*AS Wireless Server!

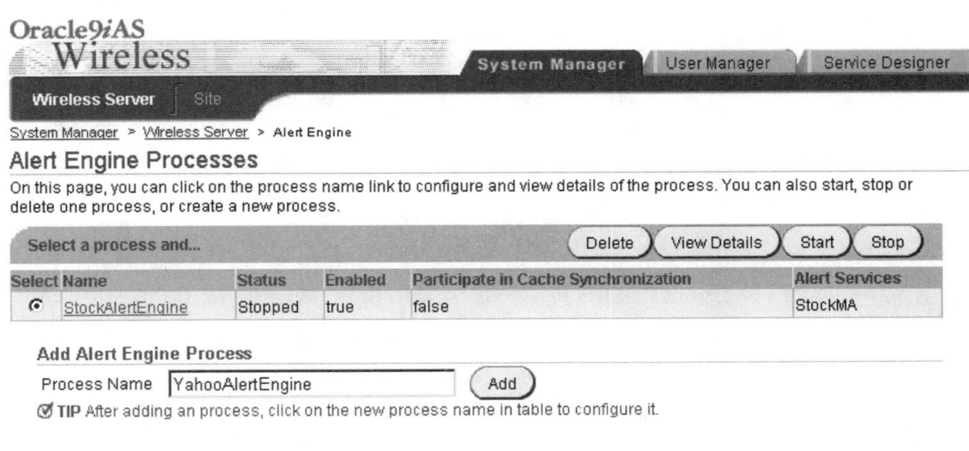

FIGURE 5-12. *Adding YahooAlertEngine to the alert engine*

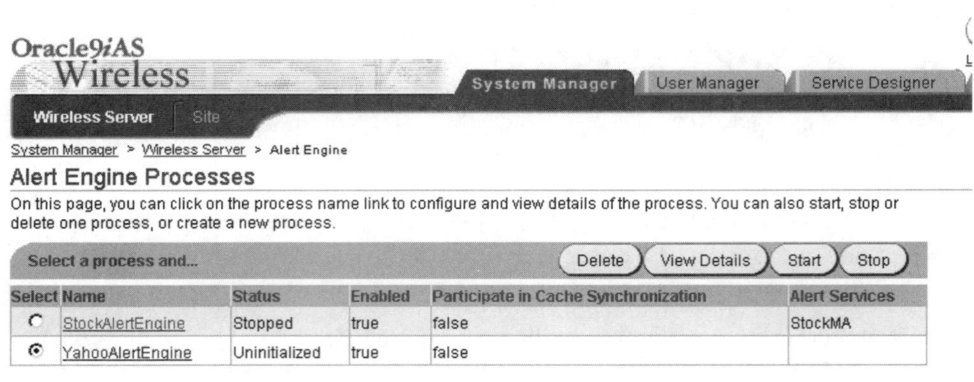

FIGURE 5-13. *Listing of alert engine processes*

Registering a Device and Subscribing to YahooAlert

Let's finish up our example by registering one of our mobile devices and subscribe to receive a YahooQuote alert. Here's how:

1. Log into the Advanced Customization Portal using your PC browser and select the Devices tab. Let's create a new device by entering **MyVoice**, **16505551212**, **Voice**, **Cingular**, **Nokia3390**, and **10** into the Device Name, Address, Data Delivery Type (pull-down), Carrier, Model, and Maximum Alerts to Send per Day fields, respectively (see Figure 5-15). Also check the Default box to make this the default device. Click the Create button. You will be sent a validation number using the data delivery type you've selected to use. In this example, you will get a voice phone call that states the following:

   "This message is from Oracle9*i*AS Wireless Customization. The number to validate your device of my voice is one one three three three four seven eight four nine."

NOTE
If you enter 0 (zero) or leave blank the Maximum Alerts to Send per Day field, you will not *receive any alerts.*

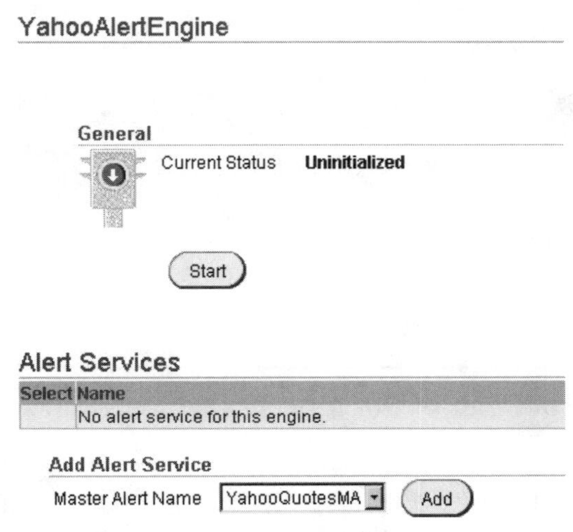

FIGURE 5-14. *Adding the YahooQuoteMA master alert*

2. Validate the MyVoice device by clicking the Validate button and entering the validation number from the previous step (see Figure 5-16). Once this device is validated, you are ready to subscribe to alerts.

Create Device

* Device Name	MyVoice
* Address	16505551212
Data Delivery Type	Voice
Carrier	Cingular
Model	Nokia3390
Maximum Alerts to Send per Day	10
Default	☑

TIP After creating this Device, a validation number is sent to you.
TIP Click the Validate button and type in the validation number to validate your Device.

FIGURE 5-15. *Creating a new MyVoice device*

FIGURE 5-16. *Validating the MyVoice device*

3. Subscribe to the YahooAlert alert service by clicking the Alerts tab. You will be shown a list of all your alert subscriptions. Under the Name column for StockQuotes, you should see YahooAlert listed (an alert type bell image is associated with it). Configure your triggers by clicking the YahooAlert link. The Alert Subscription appears. Create a new subscription by entering **MySubscription**, **ORCL**, **1**, **15**, **10**, **07/04/2002**, **Weekday**, **6**, and **35** into the Alert Subscription Name, StockTicker, Change, MaxPrice, MinPrice, Expiration Date, Frequency, Hour, and Minutes fields, respectively. You'll get alerts starting at 6:35 A.M. PST (or whatever your time zone setting is). Click Create.

You're done! With the data feeder and alert processes for YahooQuotes running, you will be alerted with a voice message to your telephone (mobile or landline) whenever any of your trigger conditions are met!

Summary

Advanced Customization in Oracle9*i*AS Wireless has made it easy for developers to build services and applications that are seamless and easy to use and navigate. The Customization Portal allows end users to customize their folders, services, bookmarks, alerts, location marks, and profiles using PC browsers. The device-based Customization Portal allows end users to customize their mobile services directly from mobile devices such as cell phones and PDAs. In this chapter, you have learned how easy it is to build data feeders using the Service Designer Data Feeder Wizard as well as how to use the Service Designer Master Alert and Content Manager Alerts Wizards to create and publish alert services to your end users or subscribers.

CHAPTER 6

Push and SMS

racle9*i*AS Wireless Push and SMS (Short Message Service) offer a versatile, yet simple set of services for building powerful application design and implementation. They provide a highly scalable and flexible mechanism to "push" text and multipart messages to all mobile devices and PCs. They support cross-platform and cross-operator delivery of messages to devices in protocols native to the mobile devices—for example, sending SMS to a mobile phone, or an audio message to a regular phone, or a facsimile to a fax machine. In this chapter, we review what makes Oracle9*i*AS Wireless Push and SMS services so useful for users, easy to build for developers, and easy to manage for administrators. We will cover the following:

- Push: A Unique Modality
- Oracle9*i*AS Wireless Messaging Architecture
- Push Drivers
- Building Push Applications

Push: A Unique Modality

Push has been around for quite some time. Perhaps many of you recall PointCast, Inc., and other push pioneers from the late nineties. What makes push, especially SMS, so unique is its simplicity. It is simple for users to use, for developers to develop, and potentially, for administrators to administer. And that is also why Push and SMS services have been so successful. Users can access them from their GSM phones and send messages by tapping in a text message and tapping a button. Using a web-based tool, a user can easily set up an alert via SMS. By creating a service that sends out short messages, based on certain event- or time-based predicates, a developer can build very powerful push applications to serve millions of subscribers. By implementing a scalable, flexible, and extensible system, administrators can manage a push platform, not just for SMS, but also for such other modalities as voice, fax and e-mail. And let's not forget—the cost of sending SMS messages is minimal, and that makes the service very economical (and profitable).

SMS: Background and Success

SMS derives from the Digital Wireless Interface standard of GSM, which has become exceedingly popular first in Europe and then Asia. It has gained popularity in North America recently. Short messages in text form of up to 160 characters can be sent in large volume. Because the service is text based, you can expect SMS receipt service and delivery almost instantly. You can save SMS messages, like e-mail, and send a message and expect it to be delivered quickly or queued easily. The appeal of SMS goes beyond person-to-person; for example, with state and session control, SMS is becoming a transaction enabler.

The Technology Need

While SMS may be simple to use and develop for, you must address a number of technical challenges in order to successfully implement Push and SMS services, including the lack of mobile devices that support SMS (PDAs don't necessarily support it) and the need to support different phones, protocols, and message types. Not all phones, especially in U.S., can "do SMS," let alone EMS (Enhanced Messaging Service). Also, for the service to be useful, you may opt for a cell-broadcast mode, which essentially sends the message to any SMS phone within a cell. Future message formats must be supported, such as EMS, which provides for animated pictures, rich text, and polyphonic ringtones, as well as MMS (Multimedia Messaging Service).

In terms of implementation and deployment, the key issue is scalability. Any SMS services may easily involve tens of thousands, and even millions, of messages per month with peak use. To make things complex, devices are not universal.

Also, different SMS modes are implemented at different operators. Hence, any Push and SMS services need to account for cross-operator capabilities. SMS may not roam between coverage areas or interoperate between phone users from different wireless operators. Besides protocols and gateways, you need capabilities for tracking and billing—especially for determining how you bill senders and receivers. In terms of pricing and billing of services, either on a per-message fee/flat rate or a sender pay–versus–receiver pay plan, the ability to track and bill becomes critical for wireless operators to consider for implementation. It is therefore not a luxury, but a prerequisite for any SMS service.

Oracle9*i*AS Wireless Features

The Push and SMS services built into Oracle9*i*AS Wireless enable you, as a service developer, to easily and quickly build stand-alone push applications, or to incorporate push and other services, such as alerts, into your wireless solution. Let's examine several key features of Oracle9*i*AS Wireless Push and SMS:

- **Scalability** Push services in Oracle9*i*AS Wireless can handle large volumes of messages to many devices. Scalability is achieved by dispatching messages to the appropriate transport/protocol driver implementation. The driver interface delivers the message to the device in the native device protocol. It can support multiple drivers in a single instance. Also, the drivers are very fast, and they can be easily administered for load balancing.

- **Extensibility** Push services are based on an extensible architecture and design that can be extended to support a variety of devices and push protocols. Oracle9*i*AS Wireless Push services are based on transport APIs that are independent of the network protocols required to communicate with mobile devices. Push Simple Object Access Protocol (Push SOAP) messages are handled by a messaging subsystem that supports a driver-based architecture. Drivers can be plugged into the transport system rather easily, extending network protocol support to the base product. Also, if users and service developers would like to link SMS with voice alerts, Oracle9*i*AS Wireless has them built in and easily implemented.
- **Flexibility** Flexibility is critical, especially for wireless operators. Once the services are implemented and people are used to the services, operators will have to revisit performance levels to adjust services to meet rapidly changing demand. Oracle9*i*AS Wireless offers Java, Java API, and SOAP as three transport options. You can write Java code to access the push services and build receive-send applications. The Java Push APIs provide two simple ways to deliver push services. Finally, the SOAP service allows push applications to be written in any programming language as long as the applications can invoke remote SOAP object methods over the HTTP protocol. This enables applications to be hosted anywhere on the Internet.
- **Ease of Use** Oracle9*i*AS Wireless offers a web-based environment for users to customize presets (see Chapter 5) and sign up for alerts. It is easy for users to set up and use. And it is also easy for administrators to manage and install. For service developers, its use of SOAP/HTTP as the transport layer, and the availability of Push and PushLite for building Java/JSP push applications, makes it easy to build services.

Oracle9*i*AS Wireless Messaging Architecture

Take a look at the Oracle9*i*AS Wireless Messaging system architecture, as shown in Figure 6-1. The Messaging system handles all messaging runtimes, including message routing functions, load balancing, and fault tolerance, and it supports a highly scalable subsystem including a Transport API and a Driver API. These APIs allow developers to customize various functions of the transport system. The Messaging system supports multiple drivers for different wireless protocols and also allows multiple drivers that support a given network protocol.

Transport APIs are independent of the underlying network protocols (implemented by the drivers) required to communicate with mobile devices. Drivers implement device-specific and wireless communication-specific messaging stacks. To deliver

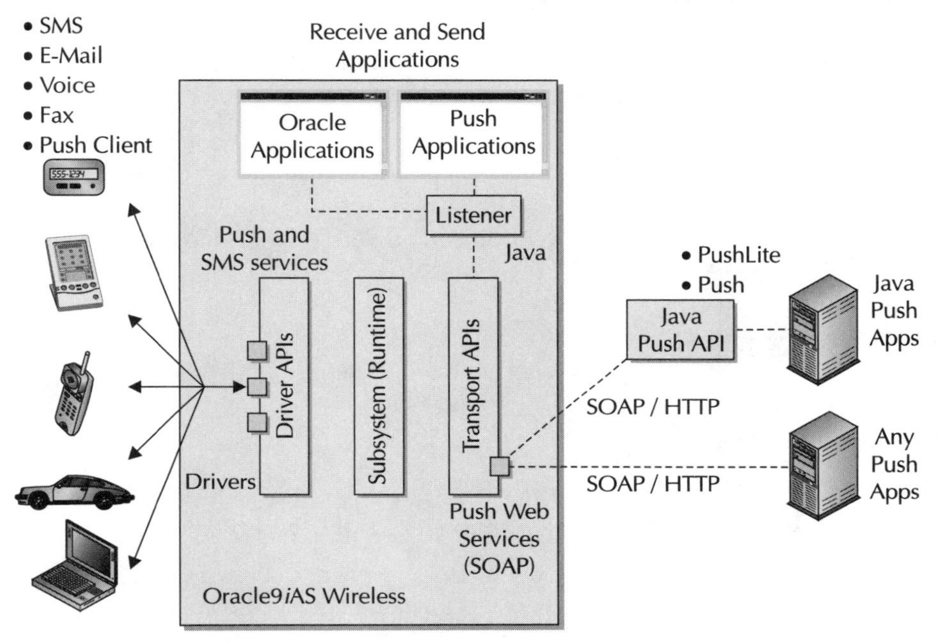

FIGURE 6-1. *Oracle9iAS Wireless Messaging system architecture*

messages, the Messaging system uses the appropriate driver to deliver messages to the device.

The Driver API provides an extensible interface for network- and protocol-specific drivers to be plugged into the Messaging system. A driver implementation wraps required network protocol routines and must implement the interface defined by the Messaging system. For example, an e-mail driver can implement an IMAP/SMTP interface or use a MAPI interface.

Push Java API

Oracle9*i*AS Wireless supports a simple Push API, in Java, that abstracts any protocol-specific (SOAP) implementation from the application Java code. This is the preferred API for application developers who need a clear and simple interface to deliver messages. The Java Push API uses SOAP over HTTP to communicate to the Oracle9*i*AS Wireless server instance. If you run your application and the Java Push API within the Oracle9*i*AS Wireless server JVM, the Java Push API will not use SOAP to communicate. Instead, it will use interprocess communication to handle message delivery.

The Oracle9*i*AS Wireless Java Push API supports two different push clients:

- **PushLite** A lightweight messaging client that can only send out text messages or query delivery status.
- **Push** An advanced client that sends out messages of any MIME (Multipurpose Internet Mail Extensions) type and queries delivery status.

We offer examples of using the PushLite and Push Java APIs in the "Building Push Applications" section, later in this chapter.

PushLite Java API

This is a lightweight push messaging client, which sends out messages and obtains query status of delivery to recipients. Transparent to the developer, two push servers are implemented:

- **Public Push Gateway Server** This server provides messaging services to network users. The communication protocol between a Push client and the Push gateway is via SOAP.
- **Private Local Installed Server** A Push client calls the Push server class through Java method calls directly without using SOAP or Remote Procedure Call (RPC)—no SOAP gateway is needed.

The APIs are identical for both implementations. The Push client must provide the gateway URL, username, and password for the SOAP Push gateway; none is required for the local Push server.

The PushLite Java API has the following features:

- Text messaging only; no binary data is allowed.
- All e-mail recipients are sent in "To:" mode; "Cc:" and "Bcc:" are not supported.
- Multipart messages are not supported.

The available methods are shown here:

```
PushLite Java API

Classname:
oracle.panama.messaging.push.PushLite

Available Methods:
```

```
getStatus(java.lang.String messageID)
   Get current status of the single message ID
getStatus(java.lang.String[] messageID)
   Get current status of a set of message IDs
getSupportedTransports()
   Get the names of available transports from the Messaging Server
getVersion()
   Get the version of the Push API
send(java.lang.String[] senders, java.lang.String[] recipients,
      java.lang.String message)
   Sends out a text message
send(java.lang.String[] senders, java.lang.String[] replyTOs,
      java.lang.String[] recipients, java.lang.String[] associatedKeys,
      java.lang.String subject, java.lang.String message,
      java.lang.String encoding)
   Sends out a message
setProxy(java.lang.String host, int port)
   Proxy setting for push clients behind firewalls
```

The parameters for the methods are described in Table 6-1.

A detailed description of the Java PushLite API interfaces can be found in the Oracle9*i*AS Wireless Push Javadoc (*oracle.panama.messaging.push*).

The available transport methods (defined in *oracle.panama.messaging .common.TransportType*) are as follows:

```
EMAIL - static.java.lang.String
FAX - static.java.lang.String
ONE_WAY_PAGER - static.java.lang.String
SMS - static.java.lang.String
TWO_WAY_PAGER - static.java.lang.String
VOICE - static.java.lang.String
WAP_PUSH - static.java.lang.String
```

In general, there are two different ways to use this Java API. The first and more simple way sends out a text message with a default encoding of "text/plain" and no subject, reply-to, content type encoding, or key parameters. For example, the first *send()* method is used as shown in this listing:

```
String wo[] = null;
try
{
   wo = pushLite.send(senders, recipients, messageString);
}
```

The second way sends out a message and allows the developer to set the subject, reply-to, content type encoding, and key parameters. Use the overloaded

Name	Description	Field
senders	An array of senders' addresses. It has a transport type and an address, separated by colons (:). Only one sender is allowed per transport type. The latest sender of the same transport type will override earlier senders of the same transport type in the array.	Required
recipients	An array of recipients' addresses (e-mail address or phone number). The format is: [transport]:[recipient address1],[recipient address2],… where the comma (,) separates the addresses in the list.	Required
replyTOs	An array of reply-to addresses (e-mail addresses or phone numbers). Only one *reply to* is allowed per transport type. The latest *reply to* of the same transport type will override an earlier *reply to* of the same transport type in the array.	Optional
associatedKeys	An array of text strings used by client applications to do message tracking. Only one key is allowed per recipient, and each key can be up to 64 bytes in length. The order of the keys is the same as the order of the recipients.	Optional
subject	Subject of the message	Optional
message	Body of the message	Required
encoding	MIME type with optional charset encoding of the message	Required
messageID	Message ID of the messages sent as returned by the messaging server after it accepts the request. One message ID is assigned for each instance of the recipient's address.	Required
host	Host name of proxy server	Required
port	Port number of proxy server	Required

TABLE 6-1. *PushLite Methods Parameters*

send() method to accomplish this. For example, the overloaded method is used as shown in this listing:

```
String wo[] = null;
try
{
   wo = pushLite.send(senders, null, recipients, associatedKeys,
        subject, messageString, "text/html; charset=us-ascii");
}
```

Push Java API

The Push Java API is a superset of the PushLite Java API and is an advanced client that sends out messages of any MIME type and queries to obtain the status of delivery to recipients. The available methods are shown here:

```
Push Java API

Classname:
oracle.panama.messaging.push.Push

Available Methods:

   getStatus(WorkOrder workOrder)
      Get current status of a work order
   getStatus(WorkOrder []workOrders)
      Get current status of a set of work orders
   getSupportedTransports()
      Get the names of available transports from the Messaging Server
   getVersion()
      Get the version of the Push API
   removeStatusListener()
      Unregister the status listener if any is registered
   send(Packet pkt)
      Sends out a message
   setProxy(java.lang.String host, int port)
      Proxy setting for push clients behind firewalls
   setStatusListener(StatusListener listener)
      Set the status listener of this Push
```

The parameters for the methods are described in Table 6-2.

A detailed description of the Java Push API interfaces can be found in the Oracle9*i*AS Wireless Push Javadoc (*oracle.panama.messaging.push*).

Push Web Service (SOAP)

The Oracle9*i*AS Wireless Push service is deployed as a Web service using SOAP with HTTP as the transport layer. WSDL (Web Services Definition Language) is a standard

Name	Description	Field
pkt	The message packet to be delivered	Required
listener	The status listener	Required
workOrder	A work order. Each work order has one address and the message ID of that address. One work order is returned for each instance of the recipient's address.	Required
host	Host name of proxy server	Required
port	Port number of proxy server	Required

TABLE 6-2. *Parameters of Push Methods*

XML interface that defines a Web service application. With a valid WSDL, developers can build applications in any programming language, such as Java and Visual Basic, that will communicate over the Internet using the Oracle9*i*AS Wireless Messaging interface. Developers can use any WSDL toolkit to quickly implement push applications and send messages to mobile devices using any Oracle9*i*AS Wireless instance on the Internet. Your application logic is developed using your favorite tools and programming languages, e.g., Java/J2EE, C/C++, or Visual Basic and ASP.

With Release 2 of Oracle9*i*AS Wireless, a stand-alone package to facilitate development using the Push server is included in a file named *push_client.zip* located at:

```
$IASW_INSTALL\iaswv20\wireless\push
```

The WSDL file is provided in the *wsdl* subdirectory.

Transport API

The Transport API is a set of client-side messaging APIs used for both sending and receiving messages, including message routing and status tracking. The Transport API provides Push applications with the abstraction required from the wireless protocols and allows the Push application to be device and network agnostic. The Transport API also allows applications to track message status and change message routing with the available drivers, even at runtime.

NOTE
Like the Async Server and Alert Engine, the Transport API application must be running on the same Java VM as the Oracle9iAS Wireless instance in order to use the Transport API. The Push API, however, does not have this requirement.

To receive messages, the Push application must register listening endpoints and a message callback listener to the transport system. An endpoint essentially is in the form of an address such as a phone number. It identifies to the transport system how a message should be dispatched. When a message is received for a targeted address, it is dispatched to the listener associated with an endpoint with a matching address. When a message delivery request is submitted, the transport system performs analysis of the recipients and routes the message to the appropriate protocol drivers for delivery.

A single message can be delivered to multiple recipients of different communication protocols. Before routing messages to drivers, the transport must analyze and group recipients by their delivery categories. To send the messages, the transport system has to find the best driver (message routing) in terms of conditions such as delivery category (e.g., SMS, e-mail), protocol (SMPP, UCP), or carrier (e.g., SprintPCS, Cingular).

Driver API

As mentioned earlier, the Driver API provides an extensible interface for network- and protocol-specific drivers to be plugged into the Messaging system. The Driver API provides the necessary decoupling to achieve the required abstraction. A driver implementation wraps the required network protocol routines and must implement the interface defined by the Messaging system. We will describe the prebuilt drivers that are shipped with Oracle9*i*AS Wireless Release 2 in the next section.

Push Drivers

Oracle9*i*AS Wireless Push drivers are *plug-able,* meaning these drivers are plug-in components to Oracle9*i*AS Wireless that extend protocol-specific support of the system. These drivers are responsible for making your applications device-specific or communication protocol–agnostic. The Oracle9*i*AS Wireless Release 2 Server ships with prebuilt drivers that support communication protocols such as SMS (SMPP and UCP), voice, e-mail and fax.

Usually, each driver identifies the type of protocol it handles such as e-mail or fax, but a single driver can handle more than one protocol. Use the Oracle9*i*AS Wireless Webtool to configure the protocol a driver handles, the implementation class, and the various parameters. To access the configuration screen, follow these steps:

1. Log into the Wireless Webtool and select the System Manager Site tab. Select the Messaging Server link to the Site Processes screen, followed by the Messaging Server Drivers link at the bottom of that screen (see Figure 6-2).

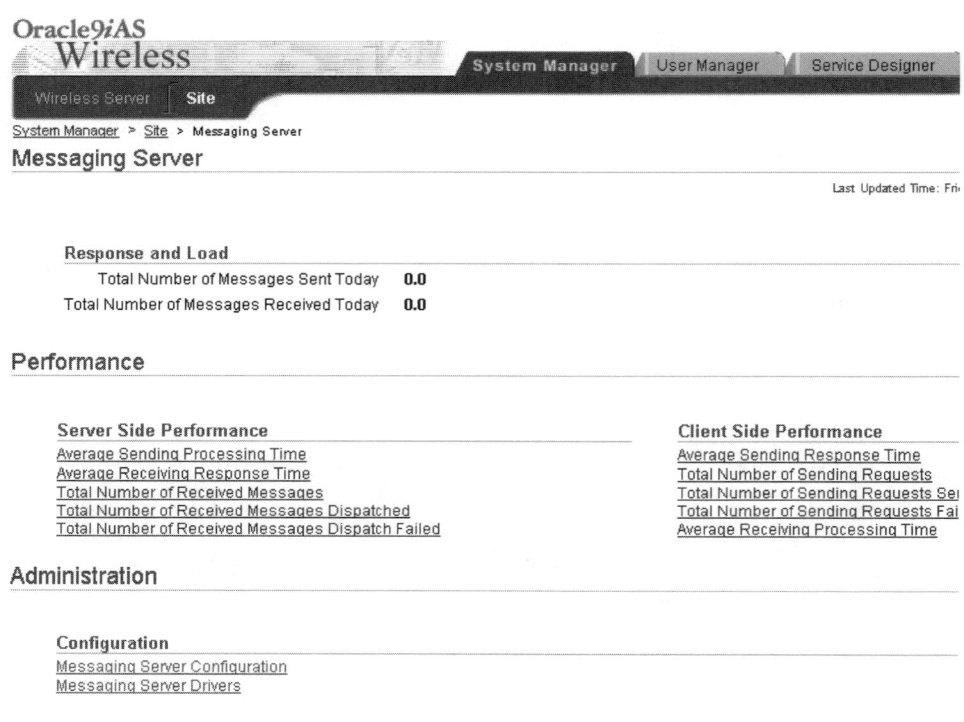

FIGURE 6-2. *Messaging server*

2. From the Messaging Server Drivers screen (see Figure 6-3), you can add, edit, or delete a driver. Drivers are site-level properties in the Oracle9*i*AS Wireless installation. The individual driver configuration page (see Figure 6-4) allows you to provide details of a driver name, the implementation class, and other driver-specific properties (see Figure 6-5 for Push driver).

The drivers are configured as a site-level property for an Oracle9*i*AS Wireless installation and can be registered with one or more messaging servers. Such a configuration allows administrators to load-balance and manage hardware resources according to the usage of individual drivers. Once a driver is made available on the site level, instances of the driver can be created and associated with individual messaging servers. You can have multiple instances of a driver running on different messaging servers, and these different instances can have

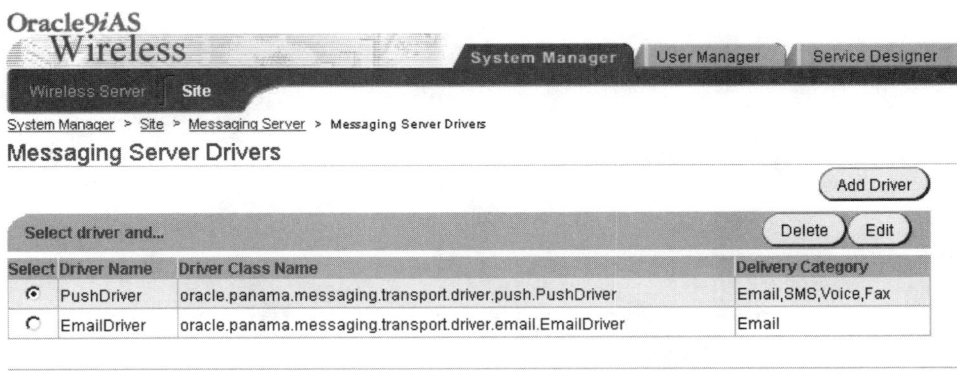

FIGURE 6-3. *Messaging server drivers*

Oracle9iAS
Wireless
System Manager
User Manager
Wireless Server
Site
System Manager > Site > Messaging Server > Messaging Server Drivers > PushDriver
PushDriver: Properties
* Driver Name PushDriver
* Delivery Category Wap Push
SMS
Voice
Email
Fax
Two Way Pager
One way Pager
Protocols *
Protocol list, separated by ','
Carriers
Carrier list, separated by ','
Speed Level 3
Cost Level 1
Capability SEND
Number of Message Queues 1

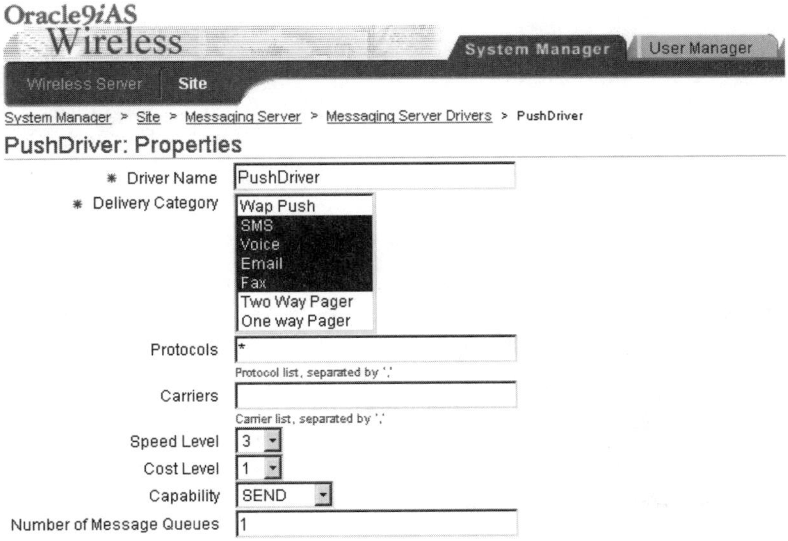

FIGURE 6-4. *Driver configuration*

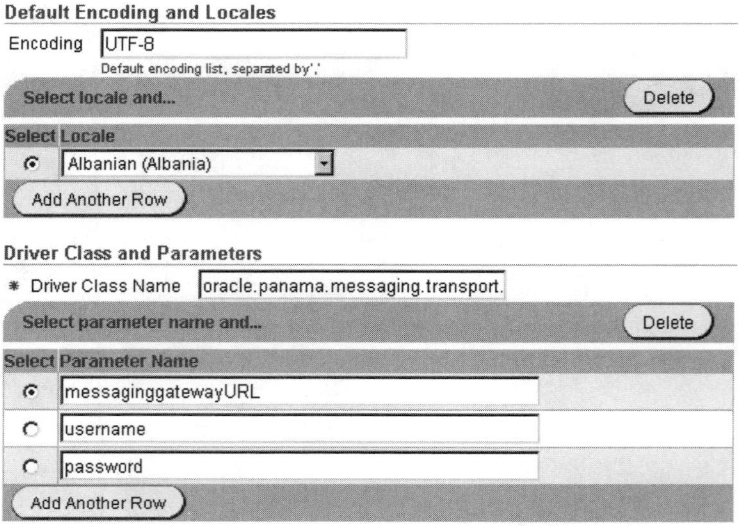

Default Encoding and Locales
Encoding UTF-8
Default encoding list, separated by','
Select locale and... Delete
Select Locale
Albanian (Albania)
Add Another Row
Driver Class and Parameters
* Driver Class Name oracle.panama.messaging.transport.
Select parameter name and... Delete
Select Parameter Name
messaginggatewayURL
username
password
Add Another Row

FIGURE 6-5. *Push Driver additional parameters*

distinct driver parameter settings. For example, you could have one e-mail driver and create instances of the driver that point to different SMTP servers. The same is true for other protocols, such as multiple instances of the SMPP driver with different values for the various "telcos" to which your server connects.

PushClient

This driver uses a hosted push service, by default the service hosted by Oracle Corporation. This driver essentially acts like a push client to an Oracle9*i*AS Wireless server hosted on the Internet; it can be configured to point to any service that supports the Oracle9*i*AS Wireless Push Web Service (e.g., your own instance running locally). The PushClient driver uses the SOAP protocol over HTTP. This service, hosted by Oracle, does not require an account for access. If you have not signed up, you can use "" (empty or blank) as both *username* and *password.* The URL for the Oracle-hosted push server is:

```
http://messenger.oracle.com/push/webservices
```

You can also try your own messaging server if you have started it:

```
http://localhost:9000/push/webservices
```

The following are specifics for this driver:

```
Driver Name:
   PushClient - send only, all content types supported

Class Name:
   oracle.panama.messaging.transport.driver.push.PushDriver

Configuration Parameters:
   messaginggatewayURL - URL to the hosted push web service
                        (required)
   username - Name to use to authenticate against the Push Service
   password - Password to use to authenticate against the Push
              Service
```

E-Mail

The e-mail driver supports sending and receiving messages: SMTP for delivering messages, and either IMAP4 or POP3 for receiving messages. The following are specifics for this driver:

```
Driver Name:
   Email - send and receive

Class Name:
   oracle.panama.messaging.transport.driver.email.EmailDriver

Configuration Parameters:
   server.incoming.protocol - the receiving protocol (IMAP | POP3)
   server.incoming.host - host name of the incoming mail server
   server.incoming.usernames - list of mail account user names
   server.incoming.passwords - list of corresponding passwords
   server.incoming.emails - list of corresponding email addresses
   server.incoming.receivefolder - name of folder (default to INBOX)
   server.incoming.checkmailfreq - frequency to retrieve messages
   server.incoming.autodelete - indicates if the driver should mark
        the messages "deleted" after they have been processed
        (true | false)
   server.incoming.deletefreq - frequency to remove the deleted
        messages
   server.outgoing.host - name of the SMTP server
   default.outgoing.from.address - default from address
```

NOTE

*Only **server.outgoing.host** must be configured if the driver is going to be sending e-mail only.*

SMS-UCP

SMS-UCP (SMS-Universal Communication Protocol) is one of the most popular GSM SMS protocols. Oracle9*i*AS Wireless Release 2 ships with a prebuilt implementation of the UCP driver. This driver is capable of both sending and receiving messages. The following are specifics for this driver:

```
Driver Name:
   UCP - send and receive, content types of RING_TONE, GRAPHICS,
         WAP_SETTINGS, and URL supported

Class Name:
   oracle.panama.messaging.transport.driver.sms.UCPDriver

Configuration Parameters:
   sms.account.id - account id for SMS service center (SMSSC)
                    (required)
   sms.account.password - password assigned by the operator
   sms.ucptype - command to use in sending a message (01 | 51)
   sms.server.host - SMSSC server for TCP/IP connection
   sms.server.port - SMSSC server port
   sms.receiver.listener.port - used by the SMSSC to initialize
                    the TCP/IP connection
   sms.server.url - URL of SMSSC for sending messages using HTTP
   sms.message.maxchunks - maximum chunks for any single message
                    (default is -1 or no limit)
   sms.message.chunksize - maximum size for each chunk in byte
                    (default is 150)
```

NOTE
If you have a direct TCP connection to the SMSSC, ***sms.server.url*** *is not used. If your connection to an SMSSC is HTTP-based,* ***sms.server.host*** *and* ***sms.server.port*** *are not used.*

SMPP

The Oracle9*i*AS Wireless Server Release 2 product ships with a prebuilt SMPP (Short Message Peer to Peer) driver. SMPP is one of the most popular GSM SMS protocols. The SMPP driver is capable of both sending and receiving. The driver opens a TCP connection to the SMSSC as a transceiver; hence, only one connection (initiated by the driver) is needed for all communication between the driver and the SMSSC. The following are specifics for this driver:

```
Driver Name:
   SMPP - send and receive, content type of URL supported
```

```
Class Name:
   oracle.panama.messaging.transport.driver.sms.SMPPDriver

Configuration Parameters:
   sms.account.id - account id for SMS service center (SMSSC)
                   (required)
   sms.smpp.system.id - SMPP system id
   sms.smpp.system.type - SMPP system type
   sms.smpp.system.password - SMPP system password
   sms.server.host - SMSSC server for TCP/IP connection
   sms.server.port - SMSSC server port
   sms.message.maxchunks - maximum chunks for any single message
                   (default is -1 or no limit)
   sms.message.chunksize - maximum size for each chunk in byte
                   (default is 150)
```

This driver can handle only content type of URL.

Fax

Oracle9*i*AS Wireless supports fax messages and the RightFax fax protocol (by Captaris). The Fax driver depends on the RightFax software package and the availability of a RightFax Fax server to deliver fax messages. The following are specifics for this driver:

```
Driver Name:
   Fax - send only, all content types supported
       - MIME type specifically supported are:
         text/xml
         application/msword
         application/msexcel
         application/msppt
         application/postscript
         application/octet-stream

Class Name:
   oracle.panama.messaging.transport.driver.fax.RightFAXDriver

Configuration Parameters:
   server.URL - URL to the RightFax server
            (required)
   server.account - Account name to the RightFax server
            (required)
   default.sender.name - cover sheet
   default.sender.corporation - cover sheet
   default.sender.fax - cover sheet
```

```
default.sender.phone - cover sheet
default.sender.address - cover sheet
default.sender.notes - cover sheet
```

Voice

The voice driver supports the outbound calling functionality of the VoiceGenie VoiceXML gateway. You can set up the server to place a voice message based on time- or event-based predicates. Although the driver can send messages only, it should be configured to have both sending and receiving capabilities for the driver to work. The following are specifics for this driver:

```
Driver Name:
   Voice - send only, content types supported are:
           MOBILE_XML_URL
           MOBILE_XML_URL_REMOTE
           MOBILE_XML
           URL

Class Name:
   oracle.panama.messaging.transport.driver.voice.VoiceGenieDriver

Configuration Parameters:
   voicegenie.outbound.servlet.uri - URL for the VoiceGenie
                Outbound Call Servlet (required)
   voicegenie.outbound.servlet.username - username for VoiceGenie
   voicegenie.outbound.servlet.password - password for VoiceGenie
   voicegenie.outbound.servlet.dnis - phone number to be set as
                the caller
   voicegenie.urlservice.path - servicepath to the pre-built
                VoiceGenie service (default is "VoiceGenieURLService")
               (required)
   voicegenie.driver.receive.host - IP host for the HTTP adapter to
               receive Oracle9iAS multi-channel XML format
   voicegenie.driver.receive.port - IP port for the HTTP adapter to
               receive Oracle9iAS multi-channel XML format
```

Custom Driver

You can, of course, build your own custom drivers. Drivers can be plugged into the transport system, thereby extending network protocol support to the base product. A driver is expected to be a very thin layer and to handle only the protocol-specific details. It should not deal with load balancing or scalability issues, as the transport system will handle them. The driver can be capable of sending only, or receiving only, or both. Please refer to your Oracle9*i*AS Wireless documentation for details on implementing a custom Java driver.

Building Push Applications

Oracle9*i*AS Wireless can support push content of different MIME types such as Microsoft Word documents or ringtones. A message can consist of text only or can be a complex multipart message. Oracle9*i*AS Wireless identifies the message types from the MIME, and hence delivering document such as Microsoft Word or Adobe PDF is possible if the target device supports the message MIME type.

We will now go through three sample push applications using the Oracle9*i*AS Wireless Push APIs provided in Release 2: PushLite Java API, Push Java API, and Push WSDL API (web service). For a detailed description of the Java Push API interfaces, refer to the Oracle9*i*AS Wireless Push Javadoc (*oracle.panama.messaging.push*).

NOTE
Oracle9iAS Wireless Release 2 ships with a fully functional sample application, Short Messaging, that illustrates how to send messages using the messaging APIs over voice, fax, SMS, and e-mail.

PushLite Java API Example

Here is a simple and straightforward example showing how to use the PushLite Java API to send an SMS text message to two mobile phones and an e-mail message to two recipients:

```
import java.io.*;
import java.util.*;
import java.net.*;
import oracle.panama.messaging.common.*;
import oracle.panama.messaging.push.*;
public class PushSMSToMessenger {
   public static void main(String args[]) {
      System.out.println("Hello Mobile Push");
      try
      {
         PushLite pl = new PushLite("http://messenger.oracle.com/
            push/webservices","","");
         String senders[] = {"VOICE:1-650-5551212"};
         String recipients[] = {"EMAIL:info@acme.com",
            "EMAIL:sales@acme.com","SMS:1-415-5551212,1-650-1234567"};
         String messageID[] = null;
         messageID = pl.send(senders, recipients,
            "::Hello Mobile Push >> PushLite To Messenger!");
         if (messageID != null)
```

```
            for (int i=0; i < messageID.length; i++)
               System.out.println(messageID[i]);
         else
            System.out.println("messageID is null");
      }
      catch(Exception e)
      {
         System.out.println("*** PushException *** ");
         e.printStackTrace();
      }
   }
}
```

The code is pretty self-explanatory. Two items bear emphasizing. First, we're using the Oracle-hosted Push Messaging Server with a null ("") username and password as shown in this code listing:

```
PushLite pl = new PushLite("http://messenger.oracle.com/
   push/webservices","","");
```

The Oracle-hosted Push server does not require an account for access. You can use a null for both username and password. Second, we're sending messages to multiple recipients (four, in our simple example) with a single *send()* call:

```
String recipients[] = {"EMAIL:info@acme.com", "EMAIL:sales@acme.com",
   "SMS:1-415-5551212,1-650-1234567"};
```

Notice the different format and delimiters for the input parameters *senders* and *recipients,* as described in the earlier section "PushLite Java API."

Push Java API Example

In this example, we will be using the Push Java API to send ringtones to mobile phones:

```
import java.io.*;
import java.util.*;
import java.net.*;
import oracle.panama.messaging.common.*;
import oracle.panama.messaging.push.*;

public class PushRingTonesToMessenger {
   public static void main(String args[]) {
      System.out.println("RingTones Push");

      // Ringtone recipients
```

```
    AddressData rtRecipients[] = new AddressData[2];
    rtRecipients[0] = new PhoneAddressData("1-650-5551212");
    rtRecipients[1] = new PhoneAddressData("1-415-5551212");

    // Packet object
    Packet pkt = new Packet();

    AddressData rtSender = new PhoneAddressData("1-650-1234567");
    pkt.setFrom(TransportType.SMS,rtSender);
    pkt.addRecipients(TransportType.SMS,rtRecipients);
    Message msg = new Message();

    // Ringtone message
    msg.setContentType(RingTone.MIME);
    msg.setSubject("Your Ring tones!");
    RingTone ringtone = new RingTone();
    ringtone.setRingToneEncoding(RingTone.RINGTONE_ENC_OTA_ASCII);
    ringtone.setPhoneModel("Nokia 3360");
    ringtone.setRingTone(
       "024A3A51D195CDD008001B20550590610560558550548540820849900 0");
    msg.setContent(ringtone);
    pkt.setMessage(msg);
    String gatewayURL =
"http://messenger.oracle.com/push/webservices";

    // create a push client instance
    Push push = null;
    try
    {
       push = new Push(gatewayURL,"","");
    }
    catch(PushException e)
    {
       System.out.println("*** PushException: Push Gateway ***");
       e.printStackTrace();
    }
    WorkOrder wo[] = null;
    try
    {
       // send message packet to the oracle push server
       wo = push.send(pkt);
    }
    catch(Exception e)
    {
       System.out.println("*** PushException: Send Push ***");
       e.printStackTrace();
    }
    if(wo != null)
```

```
        {
           for(int i=0;i < wo.length;i++)
              System.out.println(wo[i]);

           // get sending statuses
           Status status[] = null;
           try
           {
              status = push.getStatus(wo);
           }
           catch(PushException e)
           {
              System.out.println("*** PushException: GetStatus ***");
              e.printStackTrace();
           }
           if(status != null)
           {
              for(int i=0;i < status.length;i++)
                 System.out.println(status[i]);
           }
        }
}
```

Again, the code is pretty much self-explanatory. A few items here may require some comments and background information. First, we build our message packet using this code:

```
Packet pkt = new Packet();
```

A *packet* represents a generic message. It has a *subject* and one *body* or a set of message bodies (multipart). It also has one sender for every transport method and a set of recipients. Next, we set the sender address for the specified transport and add recipients to the packet using this code:

```
pkt.setFrom(TransportType.SMS,rtSender);
pkt.addRecipients(TransportType.SMS,rtRecipients);
```

We next build our message packet using:

```
Message msg = new Message();
```

and set its content type for a ringtone and message subject using:

```
msg.setContentType(RingTone.MIME);
msg.setSubject("Your Ring tones!");
```

We next build our ringtone message using:

```
RingTone ringtone = new RingTone();
ringtone.setRingToneEncoding(RingTone.RINGTONE_ENC_OTA_ASCII);
ringtone.setPhoneModel("Nokia 3360");
ringtone.setRingTone(
   "024A3A51D195CDD008001B20550590610560558550548540820849900 0");
```

by creating the ringtone object, setting its encoding, setting the phone model, and then loading the content.

A little background on ringtones is needed. *Over-The-Air,* or OTA, is an advanced feature of SMS technology that means you can install ringtones on your phone from anywhere in the world. RTTTL, or *Ringing Tones Text Transfer Language,* is a special format for coding the notes of a ringtone. RTTTL is currently recognized only by Nokia phones but is also the most common ringtone format seen on the Internet. With those two definitions (OTA and RTTTL) set, we now go into the ringtone object. The ringtone object supports these encoding types:

- RingTone.RINGTONE_ENC_OTA_ASCII
- RingTone.RINGTONE_ENC_RTTL

In our example, we use the *RINGTONE_ENC_OTA_ASCII* encoding type, which is just a hex dump of the ringtone message. Refer to the *Nokia Smart Messaging Specification* for details. We could have also used the *RINGTONE_ENC_RTTL* encoding, which is a little more common. For example, the following is a sample Flintstones ringtone in the RTTTL format:

```
Flintstone:d=4,o=5,b=200:g#,c#,8p,c#6,8a#,g#,c#,8p,
g#,8f#,8f,8f,8f#,8g#,c#,d#,2f,2p,g#,c#,8p,c#6,8a#,g
#,c#,8p,g#,8f#,8f,8f,8f#,8g#,c#,d#,2c#
```

This RTTTL format consists of three parts, which are separated by colons (:). Spaces within the RTTTL string are ignored:

```
Song Name : Defaults : Note Sequences

Song Name - may consist up to 15 letters, digits, and spaces
          - anything longer is truncated

Defaults - default values for in the form "x=y" and separated by commas
         - duration (d), note scale (o), beats per minute (b), style (s),
           and repeat count (l)
```

```
     - default is d=4, o=6, b=63, s=n, l=0
```

Note Sequences - the actual melody where notes are separated by commas

Finally, back to our example, we set the message body of the packet and push the packet and its content (ringtones) to the mobile phone:

```
pkt.setMessage(msg);
```

Detailed descriptions of the Java Push API interfaces can be found in the Oracle9*i*AS Wireless Push Javadoc (*oracle.panama.messaging.push*).

Push WSDL API Example

Our final example uses the non-Java Push WSDL (SOAP) API to push an SMS message to a mobile phone. This is the same SOAP API used by the Push Java API (which acts as a wrapper around the SOAP API) when the Push client is used with a public Push server. Based on the WSDL file, *PushLite.wsdl,* shipped within the *push_client.zip* archive located at

```
$9iASW_INSTALL\wireless\push
```

We will make a SOAP Request to the Oracle-hosted Push server with the following:

```
<?xml version="1.0"?>
<SOAP-ENV:Envelope
   xmlns:SOAP-ENV="http://schemas.xmlsoap.org/soap/envelope/"
   xmlns:xsi="http://www.w3.org/1999/XMLSchema-instance"
   xmlns:xsd="http://www.w3.org/1999/XMLSchema">
   <SOAP-ENV:Body>
      <ns1:sendTextMsg xmlns:ns1="urn:OracleMobile-PushServer"
         SOAP-ENV:encodingStyle="http://schemas.xmlsoap.org/soap/
         encoding/">
         <senders xsi:type="xsd:string[]">
            SMS:1-650-5551212
         </senders>
         <recipients xsi:type="xsd:string[]">
            SMS:1-415-5551212
         </recipients>
         <messageBody xsi:type="xsd:string">
            SMS Push from SOAP API
         </messageBody>
```

```
      </ns1:sendTextMsg>
   </SOAP-ENV:Body>
</SOAP-ENV:Envelope>
```

This SOAP Request is a valid XML fragment. A few items to note here:

- The SOAP envelope attributes are standard for any SOAP request.
- The namespace used, *ns1,* is the one defined in the *PushLite.wsdl* file,

```
<operation name="sendText">
   <soap:operation soapAction="http://PushServer.com/sendText"/>
      <input>
         <soap:body use="encoded"
         encodingStyle="http://schemas.xmlsoap.org/soap/encoding/"
         namespace="urn:OracleMobile-PushServer"/>
      </input>
      <output>
         <soap:body use="encoded"
         encodingStyle="http://schemas.xmlsoap.org/soap/encoding/"
         namespace="urn:OracleMobile-PushServer"/>
      </output>
</operation>
```

The input parameters are the same as those used in the Java Push API as defined in the *PushLite.wsdl* file:

```
<message name="sendTextMsgInput">
   <part name="username" type="xsd:string"/>
   <part name="password" type="xsd:string"/>
   <part name="senders" type="xsd:string[]"/>
   <part name="recipients" type="xsd:string[]"/>
   <part name="messageBody" type="xsd:string"/>
</message>
...
<message name="sendTextMsgOutput">
   <part name="output" type="xsd:string[]"/>
</message>
...
<operation name="sendText">
   <input message="tns:sendTextInput"/>
   <output message="tns:sendTextOutput"/>
</operation>
```

On a successful request, the mobile phone should receive the SMS message and the Push application will receive a SOAP Response (XML fragment) back that will contain the variable *output* and the status of the request.

Summary

We have just shown you how to build push services using Oracle9*i*AS Wireless. You are well on your way to sending SMS to mobile phones, audio messages to regular phones, or faxes to fax machines. Oracle9*i*AS Wireless has provided a messaging system that handles all messaging runtimes, including message routing functions, load balancing, and fault tolerance, and that supports a highly scalable subsystem including Transport API and Driver API. With the Push Java APIs, you can quickly develop powerful push applications. Or if you are using a non-Java development environment, Oracle has provided a Push WSDL Web service that is freely available for developing push applications.

CHAPTER 7

Transcoding

During the early days of wireless development, a typical project might involve mobilizing an existing website or web application written in HTML. The approach invariably involved explicit coding of markup languages that were device or gateway specific, e.g., WML. This way, the HTML content would be served to PCs, and WML content would be served to WAP phones. This was understandable as developers wanted to leverage their investment in HTML, exploit existing digital content, as well as shorten development cycle time. As wireless development techniques matured, this strategy has since changed to include techniques for XML/XSLT transformations so that their efforts could be more universal and device indifferent. Nonetheless, this means some legacy wireless applications remaining to date may be device dependent.

Oracle offers a transcoding service within Oracle9*i*AS Wireless for easily adapting, translating, and repurposing these older applications. In essence, Oracle9*i*AS Wireless Transcoding Service dynamically translates elements of web content and applications into XML and allows for rapid migration of legacy applications. This way, Oracle9*i*AS Wireless Core can optimize their delivery to mobile devices, such as wireless phones, PDAs, and pagers. Although this transcoding technique is not intended for first-time or primary development, it does help preserve an enterprise's investment in legacy wireless applications.

The Oracle9*i*AS Wireless Transcoding Service supports web content adaptation and WML translation. Through the Web Interface Definition Language (WIDL), you can adapt web content and build transcoding services that are published to the Web Integration Server. Similarly, the WML Translator is a module service that repurposes WML content and applications into Oracle9*i*AS multichannel XML dynamically. In this chapter, we focus on Web Integration and how we can create Web Integration services that can be invoked by using the Web Integration Adapter or Oracle9*i*AS Wireless Web Integration Beans. Specifically, we discuss the following topics:

- Transcoding: Benefits and Limitations
- How Does Oracle9*i*AS Wireless Transcoding Service Work?
- Building and Deploying Transcoding Services
- Invoking WIDL Services with Mobile Applications
- Transcoding WML Sites

Transcoding: Benefits and Limitations

Transcoding, otherwise known as *web scraping*, has been used by early adopters of wireless development to quickly build sites and applications. To date, this approach is still popular in select cases. Most common is the adaptation of certain elements of an HTML site into WML and/or other markup language(s).

The following list provides some of the key benefits of transcoding:

- **Fast** Remote content from existing websites can be adapted and parsed into other markup formats with little development time.
- **Easy** The Web Integration Developer environment is relatively straightforward to learn and intuitive to use.
- **Aggregate** Third-party Internet content can be extracted and aggregated according to your desired specifications.

The limitations of transcoding include:

- **Not Standards Based** WIDL is a proprietary standard. SOAP is becoming the open standard of choice.
- **Easily Breakable** Any changes in the source tags will cause the parsing rules to fail.
- **Not Efficient** Every line of code from all the sources that make up the final page will have to be parsed in order to extract any elements. This results in increased processor utilization from the additional effort required to break down existing components and reassemble the exposed content in a form that will allow subsequent reformatting for multidevice delivery. System management also has inefficiencies because existing logic may need to be refined in its HTML format to ensure a better rendering for small form-factor devices.

Early on, transcoded applications were built to the WML specification, and content was extracted and delivered to WAP devices only. As more devices (such as PocketPC and Palm handhelds) and markup languages (such as cHTML, VoiceXML, and XHTML) gain popularity, this approach becomes less scalable because developers have to support multiple devices and protocols. A clean separation of presentation and application logic, via XML, allows Oracle to make transcoding more scalable. Even then, the only things Oracle uses (and recommends) transcoding for are prototyping and extremely fast-to-market implementation. What's more, this technique is mostly used for data feeding, not application logic.

How Does the Oracle9*i*AS Wireless Transcoding Service Work?

The Oracle9*i*AS Wireless Transcoding Service owes its origin to WIDL, pioneered by webMethods (Oracle's strategic partner). webMethods' technology was licensed and incorporated in Oracle9*i*AS Wireless's Integration Developer and Server to provide developers a framework for extracting HTML and XML documents, along with JDBC-compatible relational databases. Written in WIDL, a transcoding service is a powerful tool for quickly extracting information from an assortment of web and legacy documents. In this section, we look at the Web Integration architecture and the steps for creating and deploying these services.

Architecture and Information Flow

To illustrate the function of the Oracle9*i*AS Wireless Web Integration framework, we'll look at the information flow of a typical request from a mobile device to a mobile application and how the transcoding service can be called out:

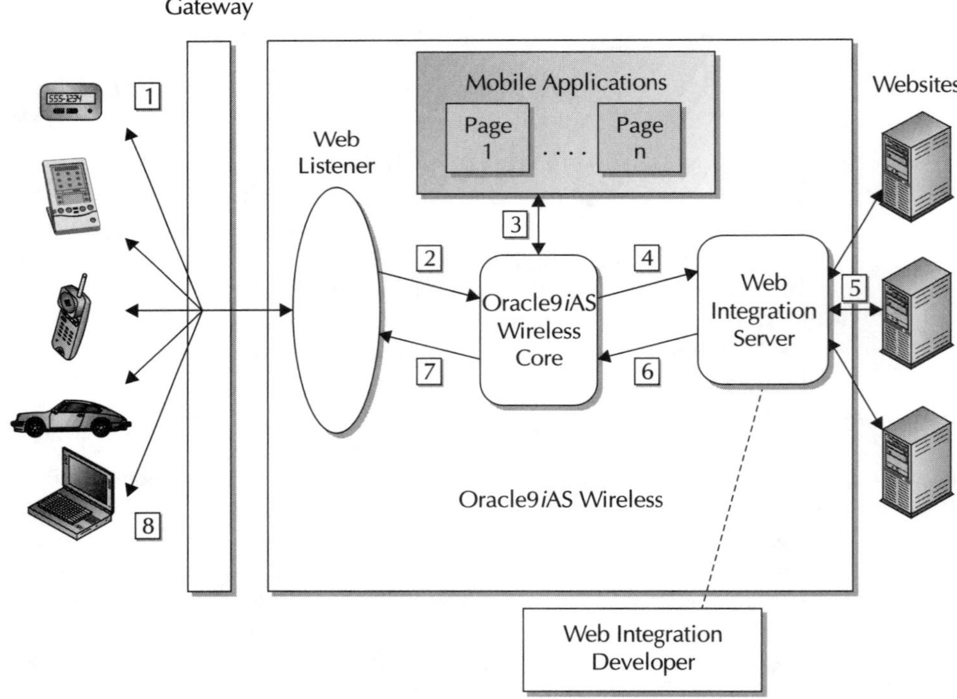

1. A mobile device makes a client request to the web server (listener) via a wireless gateway.
2. The web listener relays the request to the Core of Oracle9*i*AS Wireless.
3. The Wireless Core authenticates a user for a defined transcoding service and invokes the Web Integration Adapter. As defined by the URL of the page requested, the content is adapted from the HTML website or application.

4. The Web Integration Adapter makes a call to the Web Integration Server for service.
5. The Web Integration Server invokes the WIDL service.
6. Through the chain of service calls to one or more sources, the Web Integration Server dynamically extracts the content and sends the output, binding back to the Web Integration Adapter.
7. The Wireless Core makes the final transformation, assembles the markup page, and returns it to the web server.
8. The web server delivers the markup page to the client device via the wireless gateway.

NOTE
In lieu of the Web Integration Adapter, you can achieve the same result with Web Integration Beans. We will cover Web Integration Beans when we create a JSP application and invoke a WIDL service.

Web Integration Developer

Before you can access any transcoding services, you need to generate the Web Interface Definition Language (WIDL) files and publish them to the Web Integration Server. The process is quite simple. Oracle provides the Web Integration Developer as a development environment to create and test Web Integration services written in WIDL. Within the Web Integration Developer, you can retrieve a Web page from the Internet, parse it, and add it to the Document Browser. Then, you can selectively decide what components to extract and return them to the applications that invoked the Web Integration services.

Release 2 of Oracle9*i*AS Wireless is bundled with webMethods' Integration Server release 2.5.1 and Developer release 2.5.1.

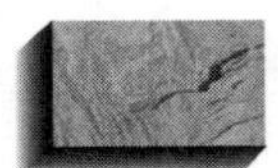

TIP
You can chain multiple WIDL services together to extract information from multiple documents and from multiple sources to create your final document.

WIDL

WIDL is the language you use to write services for extracting information from HTML or XML documents. It's a metadata language that defines interfaces to web-based data and services. WIDL enables automatic and structured web access by compatible applications without requiring complex programming. A WIDL file associates input and output parameters with the source content you want to make available in an Oracle9*i*AS Wireless service.

Now let's look at a generic WIDL file. A WIDL file contains the following basic elements:

- **Header Info** Specifies the name of the service and the bindings it uses as well as identifies the URL of the web document from which it extracts information. We will look at a sample WIDL file (shown later on in Figure 7-8) that extracts information from the document produced by the URL http://www.fedex.com/us/tracking.
- **Input Binding** Defines the input requirements of the service. It also associates those inputs with the input requirements of the web document (usually a CGI application that accepts input in the form of *name=value* pairs). In the example that follows, the input binding defines a single input, tracknumbers, that provides the value for the variable named "tracknumbers" in the web document.
- **Output Binding** Defines the desired outputs. The service produces and associates each output variable with a specific object—a specific piece of information within an element of the web document.

Web Integration Server

For a WIDL file to "become" a service, you need to publish it to the Web Integration Server. The Web Integration Server automates the exchange of data between applications, Internet sites, and legacy data sources. You can use the Web Integration Server to host a set of *services*, such as PlaceOrder and TrackShipment, that applications can use to exchange data and information sources via the web.

Requests to the Web Integration Server can originate from any of the following types of clients:

- An application that incorporates the Web Integration thin client. This might be an Excel spreadsheet, a C++ program, a Java applet, or a Java/JSP application.
- Any application capable of generating XML.
- A web browser.

Building and Deploying Transcoding Services

Building a WIDL service requires some planning. You must determine what elements you want to extract from the web page, and you must decide on the inputs and outputs. If multiple sources or multiple pages are involved, you can chain the WIDL services together.

In this section, we will build a starter application and deploy it to the Web Integration Server. Once it is published, we can either create a master service using the Web Integration Adapter or take advantage of the Oracle9*i*AS Wireless Web Integration Beans that can be invoked within JSP applications.

First, let's use the Web Integration Developer to build our WIDL service for tracking an express package shipped via FedEx.

Choosing Components to Adapt

In this example, we want to build a package-tracking application that takes a Federal Express tracking number as an input. By invoking the WIDL service through a URL, our mobile application extracts the result from the FedEx website and returns information about the status of the package being tracked.

Two web pages are of interest. First, we need a web page to enter our tracking number. Second, we need to extract specific information from the results generated by that request. Starting from the request page URL (http://www.fedex.com/us/tracking, in our example), we can build our input and output bindings with Web Integration Developer.

Again, the purpose of an input binding is to define the input variables that the client passes to the WIDL service and associate those inputs with the variables that are passed as *name=value* pairs to the web application. In this case, it is the tracking number, as shown in Figure 7-1. Notice that we can selectively choose and delete the bindings and variables as required for our application.

Figure 7-2 shows complex HTML tables in the "results" web page from which we are extracting information. Using the Web Integration Developer, however, we can easily identify the desired content and choose only the elements we want for our final page.

Building the WIDL File

Let's walk through the steps required to create the input and output bindings for our example:

1. Start the Web Integration Developer if it is not already running.
2. Select Open URL from the File menu. Type in **http://www.fedex.com/us/tracking** for the URL and click OK. The web page is requested and parsed by the Developer tool and input bindings are automatically created for the user to choose from in the Document Browser (left window pane).
3. Select the ThirdForm node in the Document Browser. We need to generate the service from the form node because it defines the input variables the web application requires. Notice the Name and associated Value.

Track Shipments

Enter any combination of up to **25 FedEx Express** and/or **FedEx Ground** tracking numbers:
(one per line)

Track It

FIGURE 7-1. *Tracking number submission form*

Track Shipments

Detailed Results

Quick Help

Tracking Number	830971089382
Reference Number	
Ship Date	11/29/2001
Delivered To	Guard/Security sta
Delivery Location	VOORBURG ZH2274RJ NL
Delivery Date/Time	12/03/2001 14:37
Signed For By	S.SOBNATH
Service Type	Priority Letter

Tracking Options

- Obtain a Signature Proof of Delivery
- Email these tracking results to one or more recipients
- Track More Shipments

Scan Activity	Date/Time	Comments
Delivered RIDDERKERK NL	12/03/2001 14:37	
On FedEx vehicle for delivery RIDDERKERK NL	12/03/2001 09:01	
Arrived at FedEx Destination Location RIDDERKERK NL	12/03/2001 08:01	
Package status RIDDERKERK NL	12/03/2001 08:00	Release by customs
Package status RIDDERKERK NL	12/03/2001 07:59	Package available for clearance
Arrived at Sort Facility PARIS FR	11/30/2001 20:34	
Left FedEx Sort Facility INDIANAPOLIS IN	11/30/2001 04:47	
Left FedEx Sort Facility INDIANAPOLIS IN	11/30/2001 03:29	
Package status UNION CITY CA	11/29/2001 21:18	In transit
Picked up by FedEx UNION CITY CA	11/29/2001 15:32	

FIGURE 7-2. *Results web page for extraction*

We will use them "as is." Also, a WIDL input variable is generated for each form input and given the same names as in the form.

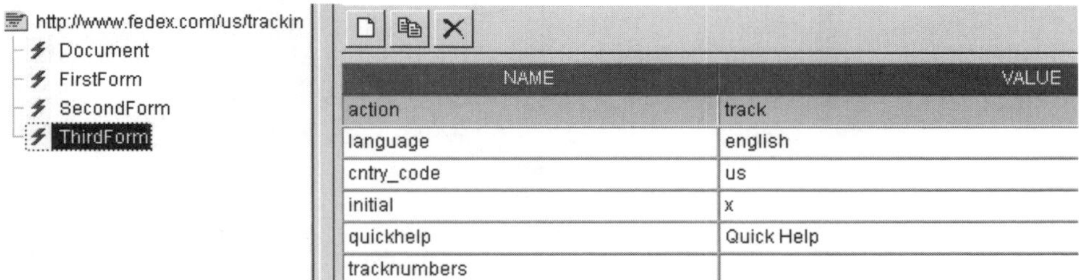

4. Select the WIDL command from the Generate menu and complete the Create New Service dialogs. For the Interface field, type in **FederalExpress**, and for the Service field, type **TrackingPackage**. This generates the initial WIDL code for the service we are creating.

5. Once the initial WIDL is created, the subsequent dialog will ask for a tracking number to try to test out the newly created service. Enter a tracking number, such as 830971089382, and click Submit.

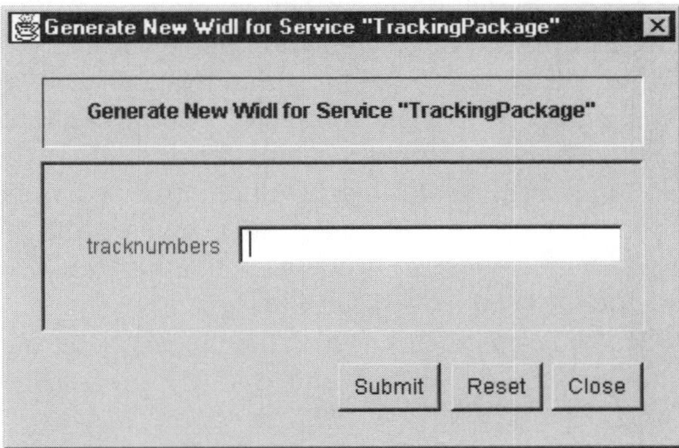

6. You now see the interface FederalExpress, with the service TrackingPackage, and the input as Output Bindings in the Document Browser. Click TrackingPackageOutput under Bindings. The right pane will show the fully parsed results document variables from which we will extract the relevant information. Scroll down the variable list to table14, which contains the information we want. This may be different for you as the Federal Express website is constantly being updated. Notice that the variable has a type of "Table of Strings."

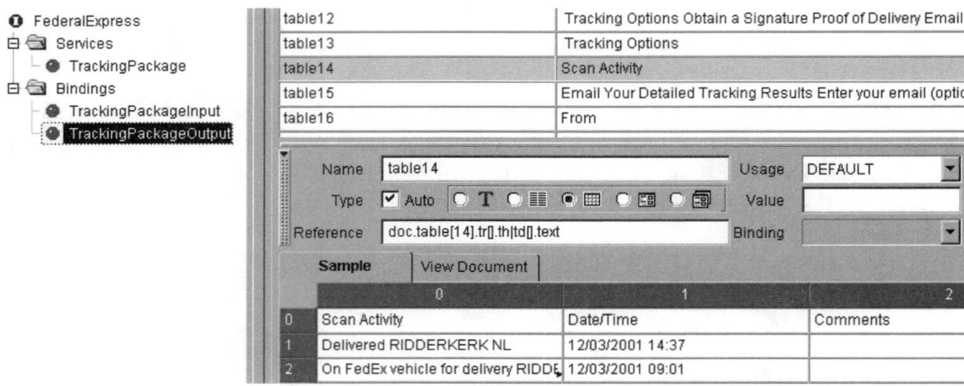

7. Now that we have identified the variable (table14) in which we are interested in the output variable list, we can optionally delete the rest from the list. Save the WIDL file generated as **FederalExpress** (the .widl extension is automatically added).

We have now created our basic WIDL code, and we can view it within the Web Integration Developer by using the View menu and selecting WIDL (see Figure 7-3).

Congratulations! You have just created your first WIDL file. You can add many other features to make this service more user friendly, such as a failure condition to handle cases when the Federal Express web server is unavailable or defining how much time to allow for the remote server before timing out. You could also make the output variable, such as table14, an array of records for further processing with advanced output templates, you could chain two services together so that one invokes the other when it finishes. To find out more about these advanced features, refer to the Oracle documentation.

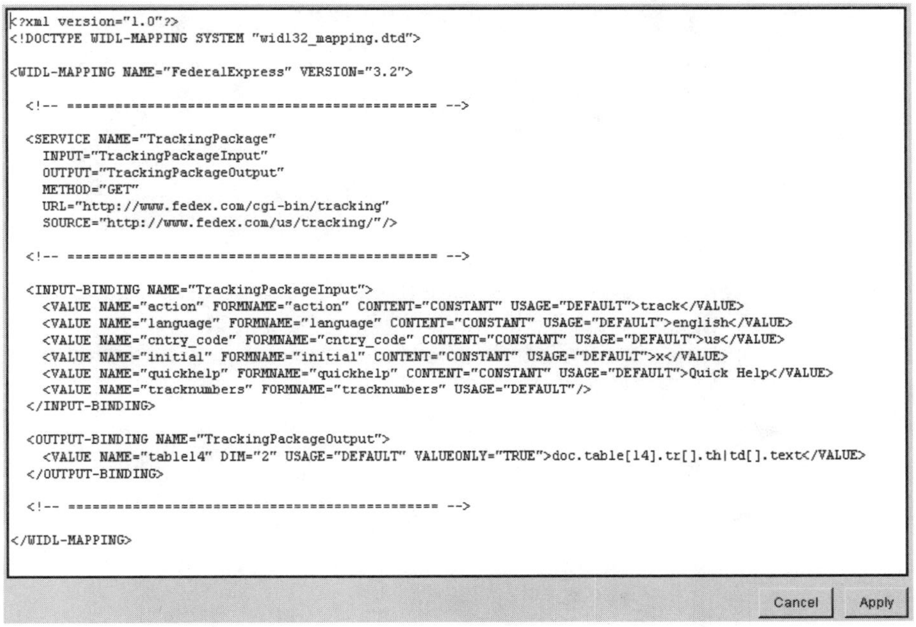

```
<?xml version="1.0"?>
<!DOCTYPE WIDL-MAPPING SYSTEM "widl32_mapping.dtd">

<WIDL-MAPPING NAME="FederalExpress" VERSION="3.2">

  <!-- ============================================ -->

  <SERVICE NAME="TrackingPackage"
    INPUT="TrackingPackageInput"
    OUTPUT="TrackingPackageOutput"
    METHOD="GET"
    URL="http://www.fedex.com/cgi-bin/tracking"
    SOURCE="http://www.fedex.com/us/tracking/"/>

  <!-- ============================================ -->

  <INPUT-BINDING NAME="TrackingPackageInput">
    <VALUE NAME="action" FORMNAME="action" CONTENT="CONSTANT" USAGE="DEFAULT">track</VALUE>
    <VALUE NAME="language" FORMNAME="language" CONTENT="CONSTANT" USAGE="DEFAULT">english</VALUE>
    <VALUE NAME="cntry_code" FORMNAME="cntry_code" CONTENT="CONSTANT" USAGE="DEFAULT">us</VALUE>
    <VALUE NAME="initial" FORMNAME="initial" CONTENT="CONSTANT" USAGE="DEFAULT">x</VALUE>
    <VALUE NAME="quickhelp" FORMNAME="quickhelp" CONTENT="CONSTANT" USAGE="DEFAULT">Quick Help</VALUE>
    <VALUE NAME="tracknumbers" FORMNAME="tracknumbers" USAGE="DEFAULT"/>
  </INPUT-BINDING>

  <OUTPUT-BINDING NAME="TrackingPackageOutput">
    <VALUE NAME="table14" DIM="2" USAGE="DEFAULT" VALUEONLY="TRUE">doc.table[14].tr[].th|td[].text</VALUE>
  </OUTPUT-BINDING>

  <!-- ============================================ -->

</WIDL-MAPPING>
```

Cancel Apply

FIGURE 7-3. *WIDL code*

Creating an Output Template

To complete our example, we will create an output template that presents our extracted content in XML. Here are the steps to follow:

1. Log into the Web Integration Server using your web browser. For this example, the URL is http://localhost:5555/invoke/wm.server.admin/adminPage.
2. Select Services and then the FederalExpress interface. Then drill down to the TrackingPackage service name.

Statistics
Settings

Packages
Services
Specifications
Database

Users
Groups
ACLs

Service Information		
Service Name	FederalExpress:TrackingPackage	
Package	Default	Caching
Type	MAPPING	Cache Expiration
Extended Type	widl	Prefetch
Stateless	○ Yes ⊙ No	Prefetch Activat
Access Control		
ACL Group	<Default>	Binding Name
		Output Template
		Template Type

3. Click the Edit Template button and type in the Oracle9*i*AS multichannel XML code of your choice. Note that because the output variable table14 is a table of strings, we are using the loop construct to cycle through the table.

Edit Template (FederalExpress_TrackingPackage.html)

```
<SimpleResult>
   <SimpleContainer>
      <SimpleText>%loop table14%
      <SimpleTextItem>%value%<SimpleTextItem>
      %endloop%</SimpleText>
   </SimpleContainer>
</SimpleResult>
```

This pretty much wraps it up. You can test your output template by pointing your browser to the WIDL service: http://localhost:5555/invoke/FederalExpress/TrackingPackage/tracknumbers=830971089382

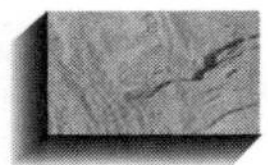

NOTE

The Interface and Service names are both case sensitive.

You could perform a View Source from your browser to see the XML code based on your output template. A sample code listing follows:

```
<SimpleResult>
   <SimpleContainer>
   <SimpleText>
      <SimpleTextItem>Scan Activity</SimpleTextItem>
      <SimpleTextItem>Delivered RIDDERKERK NL</SimpleTextItem>
      <SimpleTextItem>
         On FedEx vehicle for delivery RIDDERKERK NL
      </SimpleTextItem>
      <SimpleTextItem>
```

```
         Arrived at FedEx Destination Location RIDDERKERK NL
      </SimpleTextItem>
      <SimpleTextItem>Package status RIDDERKERK NL</SimpleTextItem>
      <SimpleTextItem>Package status RIDDERKERK NL</SimpleTextItem>
      <SimpleTextItem>Arrived at Sort Facility PARIS FR</SimpleTextItem>
      <SimpleTextItem>
         Left FedEx Sort Facility INDIANAPOLIS IN
      </SimpleTextItem>
      <SimpleTextItem>
         Left FedEx Sort Facility INDIANAPOLIS IN
      </SimpleTextItem>
      <SimpleTextItem>Package status UNION CITY CA</SimpleTextItem>
      <SimpleTextItem>Picked up by FedEx UNION CITY CA</SimpleTextItem>
   </SimpleText>
   </SimpleContainer>
</SimpleResult>
```

Now, let's publish it to the Web Integration Server.

Publishing the Interface

Publishing a WIDL interface makes the WIDL file accessible as a transcoding service, after which you can invoke it with the Service Designer or via a JSP application that runs on a Java/J2EE server. You must have Administrator authority on the Web Integration Server to perform this publishing procedure.

NOTE
The Administrator (note the capital A*) user ID has a default password of "manage" (without the quotes).*

When you publish an interface, you are submitting the service interface to the Web Integration Server, along with other transcoding services already published. Follow these steps to publish our WIDL file (FederalExpress) to the Web Integration Server:

1. Select FederalExpress in the Document Browser pane.
2. From the File menu, select Publishing | Publish Interface.
3. In the Specify Server field in the Publish Interface dialog, type the name of the Web Integration Server to which you want to publish this interface. Specify the server name using the format *ServerName:Port.* By default, the Web Integration Server runs on port 5555.

4. The Web Integration Server uses packages to organize services. You can click Update Packages to view a list of packages on the specified server and then add the service to a specific package. In this case, however, you can add the FederalExpress service to the Default package. Click OK.

5. If the User Name and Password dialog appears, enter a user name and password for the selected server. This user must have Administrator privileges. Click OK. You should get a dialog indicating that the FederalExpress interface is published to localhost:5555 if the Web Integration Server is running at localhost on port 5555.

The Web Integration Developer then copies the interface to the selected package on the Web Integration Server. It should notify you that the interface has been successfully published.

NOTE
If you create a service with the same name as an existing service on the Web Integration Server, the existing service is overwritten.

Invoking WIDL Service with Mobile Applications

Now that your WIDL service has been published and made accessible as part of the master services in the Wireless repository, you can create a JSP application to invoke it. Oracle provides two different ways to invoke these WIDL services. You should use the Web Integration Adapter only when you have basic tags in the outputs. With the Web Integration Adapter, you don't have to write a single line of code. For complex output results, you will need to turn to Web Integration Beans by writing a JSP application. This is also the Oracle-recommended way of implementing transcoding.

Web Integration Adapter

The Web Integration Adapter retrieves and adapts web content by mapping source content to Oracle9*i*AS multichannel XML. Typically, the source format for the Web Integration Adapter is HTML, but you can also use the adapter to retrieve content in other formats, such as WML and XML.

We will not cover the creation of a master service using the Web Integration Adapter in detail in this section. It is a simple process that's identical to the creation of other master services using the Oracle9*i*AS Wireless WebTool, which we covered in

Chapter 4. Just ensure that you have made the following associations before you build the service:

- Create a new master service with the Web Integration Adapter.
- Specify the Web Integration Server (for example, localhost:5555), the interface (FederalExpress, in this example), and the location of WIDL file.
- Choose RawResult for the output type if you have an output template created for XML. If not, choose Oracle9*i*AS multichannel (or *i*ASW XML).
- Make the service available to a group of your choice.

Now that you have created the service, you can test it by pointing your browser to http://localhost:9000/ptg/rm or wherever your wireless application portal is located. Navigate to and test the FederalExpress link with a tracking number. If successful, you will see detailed information returned by the service for the package you are tracking.

Web Integration Beans

Web Integration Beans are new to Oracle9*i*AS Wireless Release 2. Their main functions are to connect the Wireless Core with the Web Integration Server (via the HTTP adapter) and execute the WIDL service. For our example, you can create a JSP application that generates Oracle9*i*AS multichannel XML and uses the Web Integration Bean to execute the FederalExpress WIDL service. This JSP application will be deployed as an HTTP application and rendered to the mobile device.

Here's a snippet of code for the FederalExpress example (note that the JSP application expects a request parameter named tracknumbers—a separate page with a form input can be created to accept the tracking number input):

```
<?xml version="1.0" encoding="UTF-8" standalone="yes" ?>
<!DOCTYPE SimpleResult PUBLIC "-//ORACLE//DTD SimpleResult 1.1//EN"
"http://xmlns.oracle.com/ias/dtds/SimpleResult_1_1_0.dtd">
<%@ page language="java" session="false%>
<%@ page import='java.util.*' %>
<%@ page import='oracle.panama.tools.webbean.*' %>
<%
//Set the Input
   HashMap inputs = new HashMap();
   inputs.put("tracknumbers", tracknumbers);
//Define the Service and ServiceContext
//Set the Service
   WebBeanContextDelegator context = null;
   context = new WebBeanContextDelegator();
   context.setService("FederalExpress");
```

```
   context.setSubService("TrackingPackage");
//Connect to the Server and Invoke the Service
   WebBeanDelegator webBean = null;
   webBean = new WebBeanDelegator();
   HashMap outputs = webBean.invokeWebService(context,inputs);
   String Results = (String)outputs.get ("table14");
%>
<SimpleResult>
   <SimpleContainer>
   <SimpleText>
      <SimpleTextItem>Package Tracking Info:</SimpleTextItem>
      <SimpleBreak></SimpleBreak>
      <%=Results%>
      </SimpleTextItem></SimpleTextItem>
   </SimpleText>
   </SimpleContainer>
</SimpleResult>
```

Deploy this JSP on your J2EE application server and access it using various mobile devices to see the results rendered in these different devices.

Transcoding WML Sites

Oracle provides the Wireless Markup Language (WML) Translator in anticipation of the need for a migration and conversion mechanism for applications written in WML. Using the WML Translator, you can protect your investment in WML applications and extend their use to any device supported by Oracle9*i*AS Wireless.

First, the WML Translator enables legacy WML applications to be transcoded into Oracle9*i*AS multichannel XML format. Second, it translates the same XML into any one of the appropriate device-specific markup languages supported by Oracle9*i*AS Wireless. This makes the WML content available to all wireless web-enabled devices.

The WML Translator is deployed as an Oracle9*i*AS Wireless Module service (refer to modules in Chapter 12), with its module URL being omp://oracle/services/commerce/translator. As such, it is a regular service that may be exposed in a service tree without requiring invocation from a separate application.

To use the WML Translator, applications may invoke the translator module, with the URL to the WML server passed in as a parameter. The default parameter name is XLTORSITE.

For example, to invoke the WML Translator service on behalf of a WML application server named myWMLserver.com, you can use the following URL in your Oracle9*i*AS multichannel XML:

omp://oracle/services/commerce/translator?XLTORSITE=http://myWMLserver.com

Summary

Transcoding, despite its limitations, has its place as a way to quickly mobilize web content, especially for data feeds. Oracle9*i*AS Wireless provides a rapid development service for building applications and leveraging public or third-party web documents. By binding these content and application feeds to your own mobile applications, you can generate interesting intranet, Internet, or extranet applications for employees, suppliers, or trading partners.

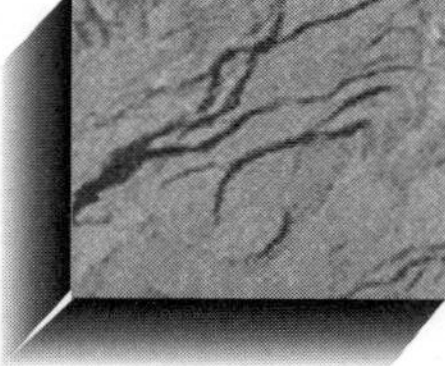

CHAPTER 8

Offline Management: Develop and Deploy Mobile Applications

ost business applications have only been accessible from network-tethered PCs in offices. A majority of the mobile employees are, however, members of the field and sales forces and are away from business information and operations. Recently, business enterprises have recognized the need to rapidly deploy applications to mobile employees who are untethered from the corporate network.

A new generation of lightweight and powerful mobile devices with wireless data connections (Internet HTTP, 802.11b, Bluetooth, and so on) promises to extend the reach of enterprise applications. Leading business enterprises worldwide are now offering their employees anytime, anywhere access to business data, information, and applications.

To meet such challenges, Oracle's mobile strategy includes an offline management solution in Oracle9*i*AS Wireless, also commonly known as Oracle9*i* Lite. It delivers mobile applications that are occasionally connected or seldom connected using wired or wireless networks. These applications can be centrally managed, distributed, and executed for both thick and thin network users alike. Oracle9*i* Lite provides infrastructure and application services that enable the delivery of secure and personalized applications using a broad range of mobile devices. Web-based applications can run in offline or online mode without any change, and from the user's perspective, they behave the same and present a consistent interface regardless of the connection status.

This chapter introduces the Oracle9*i*AS Wireless–Offline Management Service and reviews the lifecycle of creating, testing, and deploying an offline application. Chapter 9 further examines the development and management aspects of offline mobile applications. We will look into issues related to application and user management as well as dive into the replication and synchronization aspects of Oracle9*i* Lite. For now, let's discuss the following topics:

- Challenges of Building Offline Applications
- Oracle Lite Platform
- Mobile Development Kit
- Mobile Server
- Creating a Development Environment
- Building a Native Application

Challenges of Building Offline Applications

IT managers face a number of issues in considering deployment of offline mobile applications. Key challenges include the high cost of building and maintaining a multitude of mobile applications specific to each device, the network overhead associated with multiuser synchronization, and systems integration difficulties across access points. Another major concern that's often mentioned is the need to future-proof any investment in infrastructure, especially with regard to new corporate requirements, technologies, and applications. Here are some key questions to answer when considering any offline application platform:

- How easy is it for developers to build and deploy applications onto various devices?
- How can IT managers ensure the offline applications built will be portable across tomorrow's platforms?
- How can administrators effectively support multiple users accessing offline and online applications that have been provisioned to thousands of devices?
- How easy is it to synchronize and replicate data across hundreds of users at once?
- How can administrators ensure data integrity, scalability, and security across the entire information system while provisioning and supporting these applications?
- How do developers, administrators, and IT managers deal with the cost and complexity associated with offline application development and management?

Let's examine the features and architecture of Oracle9*i*AS Wireless–Offline Management and look at how Oracle answers some of these challenges.

Oracle Lite Platform

Oracle9*i* Lite is an integrated framework that simplifies the development, management, and deployment of offline mobile applications on all of today's popular mobile platforms, including Palm OS, Symbian EPOC, Microsoft Windows

CE/PocketPC (2.x, 3.0 and 2002), and Microsoft Windows 95/98/NT/2000. By using Oracle9*i* Lite, enterprises can enable their mobile workers to access data and applications where they are needed most—in the field and close to the customers—by storing and making available these resources inside their laptop PCs, PDAs, smart phones and handheld computers.

Mobile offline applications are rather different from wireless applications. Consider the following: Whereas wireless applications run with thin clients and are browser based, mobile offline applications are typically self-contained and network independent. A great deal of wireless applications are traditionally targeted toward mobile phones. On the other hand, offline applications are more geared toward thick or smart clients, such as laptop PCs, smart phones and PDAs. Also, wireless applications depend on WML, VoiceXML, and other markup; offline applications owe their heritage to data synchronization and replication. Knowing these differences, let's briefly look at a typical use case of offline mobile applications.

Typically, Oracle9*i* Lite enables enterprises to extend mobile applications to occasionally connected users who are armed with laptop PCs, PDAs, and the like. Application developers may choose from a variety of application models using many different tools. This is possible because the Mobile Server accommodates all applications, regardless of their implementation, by providing packaging, provisioning, deployment, data synchronization, and management, thus presenting a seamless single-system appearance for all applications.

Features

Out of the box, Oracle9*i*AS Wireless supports the building, packaging, provisioning, deployment, and management of offline applications. The main features of the Offline Management Service include the following:

- **Integrated Support** By integrating the application server, a relational database, a local persistent data store, and a local web server, along with replication/synchronization technologies, Oracle9*i* Lite makes it easy to develop offline applications. By incorporating Oracle9*i* Lite into Oracle9*i*AS Wireless, Oracle has made it possible for mobile application developers to build seamless applications that feature both online and offline access.
- **Integrated Set of Technologies** Oracle9*i* Lite provides an integrated set of technologies that offers an infrastructure for developing, deploying, and managing offline mobile applications and extending the enterprise applications to all of today's popular mobile platforms, including Palm OS, Symbian EPOC, Microsoft Windows CE, and Microsoft Windows 95/98/NT/2000.
- **Mobile Server** Oracle9*i* Lite Mobile Server is an offline mobile application server that runs on Oracle9*i*AS Wireless. This allows administrators to centrally

provision, deploy, manage, and synchronize offline mobile applications to a wide range of devices. Using Mobile Server's centralized application deployment, IT departments are freed from the worry about how to roll out new or updated mobile applications to thousands of mobile devices.

- **Asynchronous Data Synchronization** Mobile Server offers robust, highly scalable, bidirectional, asynchronous data synchronization between the Oracle9*i* database and thousands of mobile devices over any wired or wireless network. This enables mobile users to have access to the latest enterprise data and applications at all times.
- **Centralized Management and Provisioning** Oracle9*i* Lite also offers centralized provisioning and management of mobile applications, allowing IT departments to control access to mobile applications from anywhere using the powerful web interface.
- **Mobile Development Kit** The Mobile Development Kit is a set of tools, APIs, and sample code that accelerates the development of mobile applications that access the Oracle9*i* Lite database on mobile devices. The Mobile Development Kit offers a fast and convenient way to develop and package enterprise-class offline, mobile applications for Palm Computing Platform, Microsoft Windows CE, Symbian EPOC, and Windows 95/98/NT/2000.
- **Web-to-Go** This unique feature of Oracle9*i* Lite enables browser-based applications to seamlessly shift between online and offline mode. Web-to-Go lets enterprises invest in one unique browser-based application that services online and offline mobile users alike.

Benefits

Some of the main benefits of Oracle9*i*AS Wireless–Offline Management Service include the following:

- **Reduced Complexity** Oracle's goal is to simplify the development, provisioning, and management of offline applications by hiding and offloading the complexity into the middleware infrastructure. Although the complexity, in terms of replication schema, synchronization latency, and application schema entities, may not be reduced, developers and administrators no longer have to deal with these issues, because data synchronization and software distribution can be handled in a transparent fashion. For example, Oracle9*i* Lite automatically sets up and maintains all necessary software on the client machine. Essentially, application management has been moved to the server, thus eliminating client maintenance and centralizing system management.

- **Lower Total Cost of Ownership** A key objective of implementing Oracle9*i* Lite is to reduce the cost of building and maintaining offline mobile applications. Also, Oracle9*i* Lite allows developers to lower the network overhead stemming from data synchronization, and it greatly reduces the time and expenses related to systems integration and application and user management.
- **Integrated Features** The integrated features found in Oracle9*i* Lite allow developers to focus on development of business logic and solutions rather than building one of a kind infrastuctures.
- **Future-Proof Technology** Oracle9*i* Lite uses industry-standard Internet technologies, including HTML and Java, and offers the choice and flexibility of building native, Java, and web applications that suit different enterprise needs. This offline development platform is indeed future-proof, even with new technologies, such as J2ME, and new requirements, such as always being available.

Architecture

This section introduces the "deployment" architecture of Oracle9*i*AS Wireless–Offline Management Service and examines the key components of this Internet client/server architecture (see Figure 8-1):

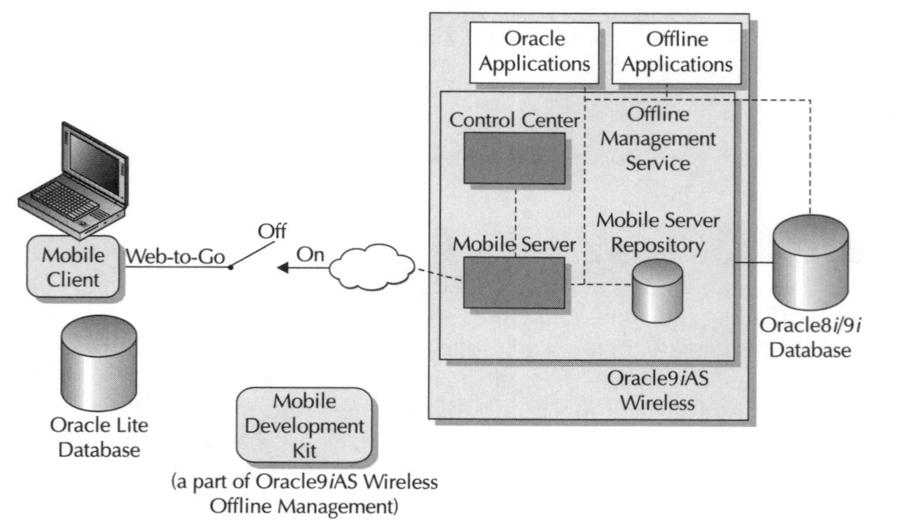

FIGURE 8-1. *Oracle9*i *Lite architecture*

- **Mobile Client** The Mobile Client software can be downloaded into a mobile device during the installation and provisioning of offline applications. For Oracle9*i* Lite, the Mobile Client includes Oracle Lite Database, a device-specific runtime environment, and the client for specific platforms, including Win32, WinCE, Palm/OS and Symbian's EPOC.
- **Oracle Lite Database** A small relational database (or "persistent store") that resides in the mobile device. It is a small-footprint object-relational database designed to be used with small form-factor devices, for single users, in situations where resources are limited. The database also has one of the lightest memory footprints of all mobile databases on the market—50KB to 1MB, depending on the platform. Oracle Lite is not a small or shrunken version of Oracle9*i* Database Enterprise Edition. However, Oracle Lite Database is capable of running in a standalone mode, acting as a persistent data store for small devices or embedded in OEM situations. It is most often configured to connect to a back-end Oracle database for synchronization and replication in push, pull, or push/pull mode. As a local data store, it offers complete transactional support, data-integrity constraints, support of native JDBC and ODBC on all mobile platforms, and the ability to construct queries on the fly.
- **Client Version of Mobile Server** A lightweight, embedded web server that allows browser-based applications (Web-to-Go) to shift between online and offline mode seamlessly. Web-to-Go Server does not exist anymore. It has been morphed into what is known as Mobile Server.
- **Mobile Server** Mobile Server is a multithreaded module extension that is part of Oracle9*i* Application Server; it is used to accomplish data replication between Oracle Lite Database and a back-end Oracle database. Oracle9*i* Lite Mobile Server also provides a comprehensive set of facilities to centrally deploy, manage, and synchronize offline applications and users.
- **Mobile Server Repository** All offline mobile applications are published to the Mobile Server Repository for deployment. Native, Java, Web-to-Go, and Branch Office applications can be centrally managed. Currently, a major integration effort is underway to unify Oracle9*i* Lite and Oracle9*i*AS Wireless to consolidate repositories, among other things. At the present time, the application database and the Mobile Server Repository must exist in the same database instance.
- **Applications** Applications, regardless of their implementation, are packaged and published to the Mobile Server. Once they're published, the Mobile Server allows the applications' characteristics and user affinities to be managed and controlled.

- **Oracle9*i* Database** The Oracle database server must be Oracle8*i* Release 8.1.6/7 or later. It runs the Mobile Server Repository and supports the applications. As mentioned, the Oracle database and Mobile Server Repository should be in the same database instance.
- **Mobile Development Kit** This software development kit provides the facilities, tools, APIs, and sample code to develop mission-critical mobile, disconnected applications. The Mobile Development Kit also offers the Packaging Wizard, which easily packages all mobile application components (executables, DLLs, images, and so on) into a unique self-executable file and deploys them to mobile devices.

We will now take a detailed look at the Mobile Development Kit and Mobile Server, as a prelude to walking through the lifecycle of developing, deploying, testing, and publishing an offline mobile application with Oracle9*i* Lite.

Mobile Development Kit

The Mobile Development Kit provides the facilities, tools, APIs, and sample code to develop field-worthy, production-quality, disconnected mobile applications. Developers can choose from among these different application models:

- **Native Applications** Native applications use ODBC to access Oracle Lite Database on a mobile device. C++, Visual Basic for Windows CE (ADOCE), and MetroWerks CodeWarrior are typically used to build native, device-specific applications. A native application developed in C++ might be recompiled and run on multiple devices without recoding.
- **Java** Java offline applications invoke JDBC functions to access Oracle Lite Database on a mobile device. The user interface might be built via AWT or SWING classes. Java provides reusability and cross-platform capability, thus making it the programming language of choice for developing applications to run on multiple devices.
- **Web** Using J2EE Java servlets/JSP, existing browser-based applications can be run in a disconnected mode without modifying the code base. This unique feature makes it very easy to extend web applications to mobile, disconnected devices.

Native Applications

Native applications are executed via the native operating system of the mobile device. Native applications are developed using C, C++, Visual C++, Visual Basic,

Microsoft's Embedded Visual Tools, ActiveX Data Objects (ADO), MetroWerks CodeWarrior, or AppForge. An application must be compiled against a mobile device's operating system—for example, Windows CE or Palm Computing Platform.

Developers may choose from among several development environments for native Win32 applications. These include C and C++ from GNU, MetroWerks CodeWarrior, and Microsoft's Visual Basic and Microsoft Foundation Classes (MFC).

As shown in the illustration, Oracle Lite provides different interfaces for developing relational database applications.

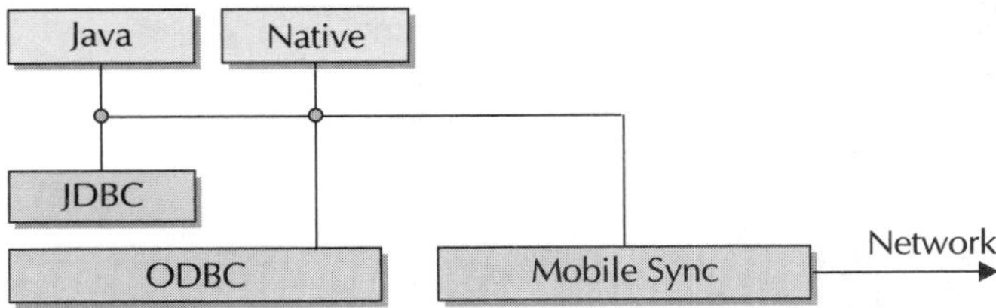

- **JDBC** The Java Database Connectivity (JDBC) interface specifies a set of Java classes that provide an ODBC-like interface to SQL databases for Java applications. Oracle Lite supports JDBC through an Oracle Lite type-2 JDBC driver that interprets the JDBC calls and passes them to an Oracle Lite database.
- **ODBC** Microsoft's Open Database Connectivity (ODBC) interface is a procedural, call-level interface for accessing SQL databases, and it's supported by most database vendors and OEM vendors. ODBC specifies a set of functions that allows applications to connect to databases so they can prepare and execute SQL statements and retrieve query results. Oracle9*i* Lite supports Level 3–compliant ODBC 2.0 and the ODBC 3.5 drivers through Oracle9*i* Lite ODBC drivers that interpret ODBC calls, passing them to Oracle Lite.

Choosing a development environment is ultimately a personal choice and is fairly subjective. However, if you are not already committed to a development platform, you may want to decide which broad category your application falls into—prototype, production, or heavy UI/CPU—and consider the rules of thumb shown in Figure 8-2.

Java Applications

Java applications use a fast, ultra-thin, native JDBC driver to access the Oracle9*i* Lite database on mobile devices. The database, for the Win32 platform, also supports Java stored procedures and triggers, thus simplifying application programming and

Win32 Native Application Development Rules of Thumb

PROTOTYPE APPLICATIONS	**USE:** EVT Visual Basic + Oracle Lite + rSync for COM**
	• You are writing a prototype or quick demo that uses few forms • You want to build an application in the quickest timeframe • Your application does not involve complex database operations
FULL PRODUCTION APPLICATIONS	**USE:** EVT MFC + Oracle Lite ODBC + mSync COM
	• Your application needs to be professional looking • Your application needs a very good user interface and is relatively large • Your development staff has lots of good MFC programmers available
HEAVY UI and **CPU APPLICATIONS**	**USE:** EVT MFC or Win32API + Oracle Lite OKAPI + mSync COM
	• Your application is very UI and CPU intensive and requires optimal response time • You have lots of excellent engineering resources to spend

FIGURE 8-2. *Native applications' rules of thumb*

improving data integrity. Using AWT or SWING Java classes, you can rapidly build the user interface for your offline applications.

A Java/JDBC application must be compiled for a particular mobile device's JVM environment that is different across the various client devices. It may be possible to create one Java source code and run it on different devices.

Oracle9*i* Lite supports two Java Virtual Machines, as shown in Table 8-1.

When developing Java programs, you may follow these steps:

1. Check the environment. Verify that olite40.jar is in your CLASSPATH. The CLASSPATH environment should have been modified to include olite40.jar during Oracle Lite installation. If it was not, add olite40.jar. Make sure your machine environment has a JDK.

Java Virtual Machine	Supported Chipsets
Insignia's Jeode	ARM
Sun	SH3

TABLE 8-1. *Supported JVMs*

2. Load the JDBC driver into your application. Your application must first load the Oracle9*i* Lite JDBC driver. Here's an example of how to do this:

```
Class.forName("oracle.lite.poljdbc.POLJDBCDriver");
```

3. Connect to an Oracle Lite database. There are two ways to do this. If your database is on the same machine as the JDBC application, connect to the database using the native driver connection URL syntax. A connect string for the native driver takes the following form:

```
Jdbc:polite[:userid/password]:dsn
```

   If your database is on a server and you are connecting from a client computer, use the Type2 driver connection URL syntax:

```
Jdbc:polite[:userid/password]@[hostname]:[port]:dsn
```

   Both drivers are components of olite40.jar.

Web Applications

The Web application development model of Oracle9*i* Lite enables developers to run existing web applications using the J2EE Java servlets/JSP in a disconnected mode without modifying the code base. This makes it very easy to extend web applications to mobile, disconnected devices.

Browser-based web applications can be run in either online or offline mode, and they can shift seamlessly between modes (see the illustration). As discussed later, the Mobile Client for Web-to-Go lets enterprises invest in one unique browser-based application that services online and offline mode mobile users alike.

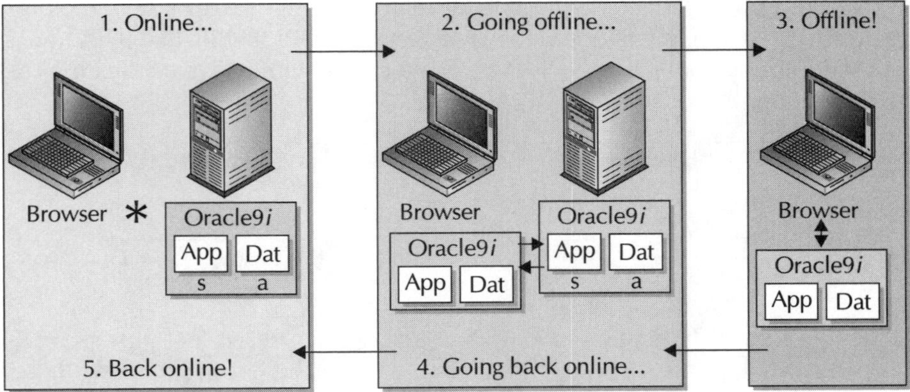

The web application development environment provides a high-level Java API that offers easy-to-use functionality to developers of mobile applications. By using this API, developers no longer need to write code for such functions as replication of database tables, online and offline database connections, security, directory locations, and deployment of applications to client devices. It also allows developers to create and debug web applications that contain Java applets, Java servlets, and JavaServer Pages (JSP).

The web application model comprises three major features:

- **Single Application Program Interface** To shield developers from system complexity, Oracle provides an application program interface (API) on top of Java to abstract issues related to replication and multiple databases and directories. You only have to deal with one high-level API and don't need to deal with runtime, deployment, security, and other issues.
- **Distribution or Deployment Transparency** Because the application code is now decoupled from the distribution model, you do not have to make adjustments in the code every time the offline application is deployed onto a different platform.
- **Write Code Once** Each mobile application will behave the same regardless of deployment mode—with no changes in code. Multiuser client/server and single-user/embedded mode will run the same way and seamlessly for the mobile user. No longer will you need to write and maintain multiple source codes for a particular distribution model.

As mentioned earlier, Web-to-Go is a development option for Web applications and is part of Mobile Server. Web-to-Go is currently available on laptops running Windows 95/98/NT/2000. The Mobile Development Kit enables you to rapidly create Web-to-Go applications via Java servlets and JSPs that invoke JDBC, as opposed to using application APIs, which is the case with native applications (see the illustration).

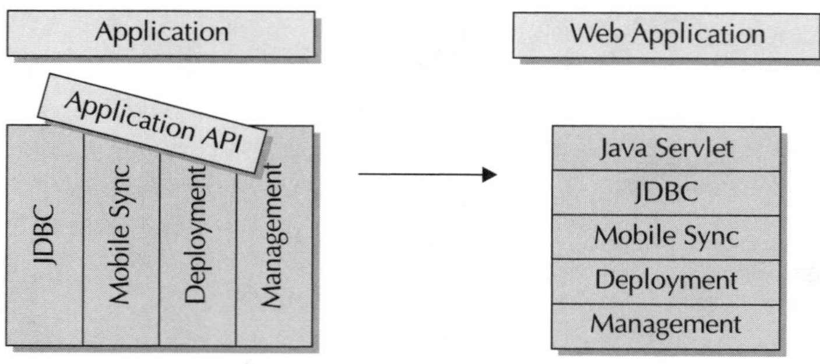

Lifecycle of Developing and Deploying Web Applications

We will now go over the steps involved in building an offline web application and review some of the key aspects related to the Mobile Client, including important features of the persistent store, Oracle Lite Database, as well as the nuances of the offline and online mode.

The following is the lifecycle of the development and deployment of an offline/online web application:

1. Create the database objects of your application in Oracle9*i* Lite before publishing to the Mobile Server.
2. Write, compile, test, and debug your JSP/Java web application code.
3. Package the web application into a .jar file using the Packaging Wizard (see the next section for details) in development mode. In development mode, panels used exclusively for deployment are disabled.
4. Publish the .jar file into the Mobile Server Repository.
5. Create users and user profiles using the Mobile Server Control Center.
6. Set up the application properties.
7. Set up Mobile Client for Web-to-Go. Client-side components are installed on the mobile device.
8. Run the web application in both online and offline mode by pointing to the application's URL.
9. Modify the application as needed and repeat the development loop.

Database Components

Three types of database components are supported: tables, snapshots, and sequences. These components must be registered using the Packaging Wizard. This enables Web-to-Go to create the necessary offline support for the components on the local client. Web-to-Go creates this support the first time a client is in offline mode. In addition, Web-to-Go executes custom Data Definition Language (DDL) statements, thus enabling the creation of database objects such as views and indexes.

Tables

The Mobile Client for Web-to-Go creates offline support for tables. On the client side, a snapshot is created for each database table. These snapshots refresh the data each time the client synchronizes with the server. Web-to-Go propagates the data changes automatically.

Sequences

Sequences allow you to generate unique identifiers. You can use sequences to generate unique primary key values when inserting new records in a database table to ensure unique inserts. This is very important when multiple clients in disconnected mode insert new rows into tables. Replication uses the primary key values to identify records. Duplication of primary keys causes replication conflicts, which must be manually resolved by the administrator. Because avoiding these conflicts is important, Web-to-Go provides a mechanism to ensure that sequence values generated in disconnected mode are unique (valid). To this end, Web-to-Go assigns each disconnected client a unique window of sequence values for each sequence.

DDLs

In addition to replication support for tables and sequences, Web-to-Go executes custom DDL statements on clients. You can use DDLs to create any database object, such as a view or an index. DDLs are part of Web-to-Go applications and are defined using the Packaging Wizard. Web-to-Go executes DDLs only once on each client when the client synchronizes the first time.

Mobile Client for Web-To-Go

Mobile Client must be installed on a separate machine from the Mobile Server for testing on a Windows platform such as your desktop PC or laptop. After installing Mobile Client on the mobile device or your test desktop/laptop environment, an embedded web server (Mobile Client Web Server), a local database, and a local repository are now resident on the device.

Offline Mode

Every HTTP request is directed to the local embedded web server, regardless of whether the client is running online or offline. Once the user logs into the system by providing a user name and password, the user is presented with a mobile workspace, dynamically generated by the local server, showing each application that the user has Execute privileges for. The user just has to click the application icon to launch it. Offline is the default mode.

To work in offline mode, the user clicks the Go Offline button. The mobile platform will look into the repository and retrieve the entire application and replicate it down to the client. Every URL is no longer redirected to the online server but rather executed locally. The embedded web server will access the local repository and local database. All transactions are stored in the local queue. Everything that happens is autonomous from the network, thus allowing the same application to be executed both on the server and client sides.

Online Mode

To work in the online mode, the user clicks the Go Online button. This triggers a refresh process. The queue transactions in the local database are first uploaded and applied to the server database. A new image of the consolidated database gets replicated down to the client. The embedded web server recognizes that it is in the online mode and redirects every URL to the online server.

Mobile Server

This middle-tier infrastructure server acts like a gateway between the mobile devices (such as PDAs, cellular phones, automotive computers, as well as traditional laptops) and the e-business application services accessed by the client devices (see the illustration).

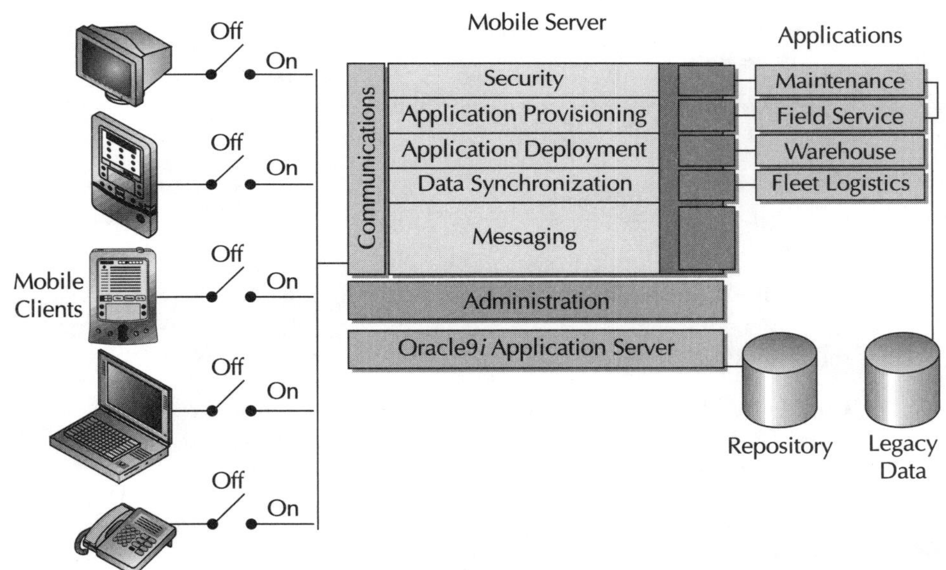

Mobile Server provides the necessary functions required to support mobile devices. The following major functional areas are provided:

- **Data Synchronization** Enables mobile devices to operate applications "offline" and synchronize offline activities with an Oracle database server when connectivity is reestablished.
- **Application Distribution** Synchronization of corporate data requires that related applications be deployed on the mobile device. This service enables

the IT department to centrally control and manage secure application and file distribution.

- **Software Distribution** Provides the capability to manage and distribute runtime libraries or Mobile Client bundles. Over 30 preconfigured bundles are ready with each installation of Mobile Server.
- **Application Provisioning** Enables administrators to centrally register and provision mobile, offline applications.
- **Mobile Persistency** A small relational database resides on the mobile device. Oracle Lite Database is a lightweight, Java-enabled database designed for laptops, handheld computers, PDAs, and smart phones.
- **User Management/Security** Provides user- and device-authentication capabilities, which enable a single, device-independent user logon and pass-through of authentication information to any directory server, such as Oracle Internet Directory or LDAP.
- **Client Authentication/Encryption** Mobile Server and Mobile Client are designed to enable comprehensive end-to-end security.
- **System Management** Provides a comprehensive set of management services, including server status, activity log, remote site inspection, and remote job control.
- **Reliability and Scalability** Mobile Server provides highly scalable caching functions. In addition, Mobile Server load-balances HTTP requests across multiple Mobile Servers for better scalability and performance.
- **Connectivity** Provides security-rich wired and wireless connectivity, such as HTTP, HTTPS, Hotsync, and IP-based wireless transports, including CDPD and 802.11b.

Development and Packaging

By using the Mobile Development Kit, you can implement the business logic of an offline application. After that, you must package the offline application before it can be uploaded into the Mobile Server Repository.

Recall that an offline application is a collection of executables, database information, and other resources that can be bundled into a self-contained archive file. As a result, each of these archive files includes application resources as well as an application deployment descriptor. The deployment descriptor conveys the elements and configuration information of an application between developers and administrators.

Packaging Wizard

A Java application called Packaging Wizard is part of the Mobile Development Kit. Application developers use the wizard to perform the following tasks:

- Create a new Mobile Server application for the Win32, Windows CE, Palm, or EPOC platform
- Edit an existing Mobile Server application

When you create a new Mobile Server application, you define its components and publish them to the Mobile Server Repository. In some cases, you may want to edit the definition of an existing Mobile Server application's components. For example, if you develop a new version of your application, you can use the Packaging Wizard to update your application definition. The Packaging Wizard also enables you to package application components in a .jar file.

Each supported mobile device platform has its own native Packaging Wizard, but they all go through the same logical steps to create, edit, or open a packaged application.

Creating a New Packaged Application

As a developer, you will go through the following sequence to create a packaged application:

1. Start the Packaging Wizard.
2. Choose "Create a New Application."
3. Choose the client platforms your application will be packaged for.
4. Name the Mobile Server application and its associated packing properties, such as the local directory where the files are located, the application CLASSPATH, a description, the server virtual path, connectivity information, and so on.
5. Enter information about the database on the Mobile Server.
6. If you are performing replication, you will need to create a snapshot. Snapshots are copies of application data that Web-to-Go captures in real time from the Oracle database and downloads to the client before it goes offline. A snapshot can be a copy of an entire database table or a subset of rows from the table. The first time a user goes into offline mode, Mobile Server automatically creates the snapshots on the client machine. Each

subsequent time a user goes online or offline, Mobile Server either refreshes the snapshots with the most recent data or re-creates them, depending on the complexity of the snapshots. A snapshot must be unique across all applications, and they can be defined for each client platform.

7. You are now ready to create all the files and publish the application. The Packaging Wizard will create an XML file with detailed application information. The Packaging Wizard retains the XML file and provides you with the option of publishing it to the Mobile Server. You can only publish the XML file to the Mobile Server when the server is running.
8. You have the option to also publish your application components to a .jar file or generate SQL scripts for database objects. (The default output from the Packaging Wizard is a .jar file.)
9. Once your files are created and packaged with publishing privileges, you can publish your application to a specific Mobile Server by specifying a URL, user name, password, and repository directory (more details are available in the next section).
10. Your mobile application now resides on the Mobile Server and is available to be provisioned and deployed to all or a select group of users.

Application Management

Each application must be uploaded and registered with the Mobile Server. This task, also called *publishing*, reads the information provided by the deployment descriptor. An application will be created, and affiliated information for this application will be stored in the repository.

An administrator uses the Mobile Server Control Center to manage applications, users, sites, and other resources. Mobile Server provides a central place to provision offline applications while abstracting implementation details from the administrator. Application management includes defining application properties, such as the application name, the repository directory, the application database name, and more. Users and user groups must be created because Mobile Server enforces authentication and authorization. An Access Control List (ACL) is required to give users access privileges to offline applications. Site management allows for the inspection of remote sites (also called *snapshot sites*) to get useful configuration and client setup information.

The Mobile Server Control Center is a graphical web-based application used by the administrator. A shell utility allows the administrator to inspect and navigate through the repository in case application resources must be inspected or even altered directly within the repository.

Managing Access Control Lists

Access Control Lists enable administrators to grant access to applications for individual users or user groups. Administrators can determine which users and groups have access to an application's executable files and data. The ACL of an application also enables administrators to determine the type of access users and user groups have to an application.

A developer can create roles in the application's code. This is an attribute of the user and of the application. A role is a privilege level that is specified within the application. The Packaging Wizard is used to define these application roles.

Managing Replication and Snapshots

Mobile Server enables Mobile Clients to download a local copy of the application data before going offline. Local copies of the data are called *snapshots,* because the information is captured at a point in time. A snapshot can be a copy of an entire database table or a subset of rows from a table. When a user synchronizes the Mobile Client, the snapshots are automatically created.

For example, after installing Mobile Client for Web-to-Go, when a user logs into the Mobile Client for the first time, Web-to-Go automatically creates snapshots on the client machine. Each subsequent time the user synchronizes, Web-to-Go either refreshes the snapshots with the most recent data or re-creates them, depending on the complexity of the snapshots.

A snapshot is a full set or a subset of rows of a table or a view of a point in time. Executing a SQL query against the base table creates the snapshot. Snapshots are either read-only or updateable, and they vary in complexity.

Tracking Client Sites

A client is a physical machine, such as a laptop or PC, that can be used by one or more users. On the Mobile Client for Web-to-Go, each user has a directory. This directory contains a database file for each of the applications that the user has access to. This directory is called a *site*. A Mobile Client for Web-to-Go can contain multiple sites, but only one site per user. Users can have multiple sites on different clients.

User Management

Mobile Server users are managed in two ways: via the web-based Mobile Server Control Center and via a mobile management scripting language for Mobile Server. The Control Center provides an excellent interface for the following user and group tasks:

- Listing users and groups
- Creating users

- Modifying or dropping users
- Creating user groups
- Modifying or dropping user groups

Administrators will find that the web-based Control Center is useful for these administrative tasks on an ongoing or ad-hoc basis for maintaining a running system.

The Mobile Server scripting language provides a scripting technique useful for the initial creation of large numbers of users and applications. Scripts can be used to create, modify, and delete users, groups, access privileges, registry entries, and snapshot variables. Administrators use scripting to perform batch processing of the administrative tasks performed most often.

Administrators write scripts for the Mobile Server in an INI text file and then use the WSH shell utility to run the INI script. For example, you can use the following scripting syntax to create users and groups:

```
Creating a User:
The syntax for creating a user is as follows:
[USER]
NAME=<User's Name>
PASSWORD=<User's Password>
ENCRYPTED=<True or False; True if the password is encrypted, False if not>
FULLNAME=<User's Full Name>
PRIVILEGE=<User's privilege level as P, C,S, or null>
There are four options for setting the value of PRIVILEGE.
These options are:
P – for publishing an application
C – for connecting to Web-to-Go
S – for administering Web-to-Go
NULL – for no privileges

Creating a Group:
This entry creates a new group (if this group does not already exist)
and adds the listed users to this group. If you use this entry and
specify the name of a group that exists, all the users in the existing
group will be removed and the users who are listed will be added to
this group. If you want to add users to an existing group you have to
use
[ADDUSERTOGROUP].
The syntax for a creating a group is as follows:
[GROUP]
NAME=<Group Name>
USER=<User's name you want to add to this group>

Adding a User to a Group:
This entry creates a new group (if this group does not already exist)
```

```
and adds the listed users to this group. You can also use this entry
to add users to an existing group.
[ADDUSERTOGROUP]
NAME=<Group Name>
USER=<User's name you want to add to this group>

Removing a User from a Group:
This removes the listed users from the group which you specify.
[REMOVEUSERFROMGROUP]
NAME=<Group Name>
USER=<User's name you want to remove from this group>

Creating Access Privileges:
This creates a new ACL (if this ACL does not already exist).
After creating this ACL, all the existing users will be removed
and all the listed users will be added to this ACL. If you want
to add users to the existing ACL, you have to use
[GRANTACCESS].
The syntax for creating access privileges for users and/or groups
is as follows:
[ACL]
APPLICATION=<Name of the application you want to create ACL for>
ROLE=<Role of the user; set the value as DEFAULT ROLE or ADMINISTRATIVE ROLE>
USER=<User's name>
ACCESS=<Set access status as ENABLED>
ROLE=<Role of the user>
USER=<User's name>
ACCESS=<Set access status as ENABLED>
ROLE=<Role of the group>
GROUP=<Groups's name>
ACCESS=<Set access status as ENABLED>

Granting Access:
This entry creates a new ACL (if this ACL does not already
exist) and adds the listed users to this ACL.
[GRANTACCESS]
APPLICATION=<Name of the application you want to add ACL for>
ROLE=<Role of the user>
USER=<User's name>
ACCESS=<Access Status ENABLED/DISABLED>
ROLE=<Role of the group>
GROUP=<Groups's name>

Revoking Access:
This entry removes the listed users from the specified ACL.
[REVOKEACCESS]
APPLICATION=<Name of the application you want to revoke ACL for>
ROLE=<Role of the user>
USER=<User's name>
ACCESS=<Access Status>
ROLE=<Role of the group>
```

```
GROUP=<Groups's name>

Creating Registries:
The syntax for creating registries is as follows:
[REGISTRY]
APPLICATION=<Name of the application>
NAME=<Registry Variable Name>
VALUE=<Value for this variable>

Creating Snapshot Variables:
The syntax for creating snapshot variables is as follows:
[SNAPSHOTVAR]
NAME=<Name of the publication item>
PLATFORM=<Platform for which this publication item is>
VIRTUALPATH=<Virtual path of the application this publication
item belongs to>
USER=<Name of the user who subscribes to this application>
VAR=<Name of the Data Subsetting parameter, value of this parameter>
USER=<Name of the user who subscribes to this application>
VAR=<Name of the Data Subsetting parameter, value of this parameter>
GROUP=<Name of the group which subscribes to this application>
VAR=<Name of the Data Subsetting parameter, value of this parameter>

Deleting a User:
The syntax for deleting a user is as follows:
[DROPUSER]
NAME=<User's Name>

Deleting a Group:
The syntax for deleting a group is as follows:
[DROPGROUP]
NAME=<Group's Name>

Deleting Access Privileges:
The syntax for deleting access privileges for users and/or groups
is as follows:
[DROPACL]
APPLICATION=<Name of the application you want to delete ACL for>
ROLE=<Role of the user; set the value as DEFAULT ROLE or ADMINISTRATIVE ROLE>
USER=<User's name>
ACCESS=<Set access status as DISABLED>
ROLE=<Role of the group; set the value as DEFAULT ROLE or ADMINISTRATIVE ROLE>
GROUP=<Groups's name>
ACCESS=<Set access status as DISABLED>

Deleting a Registry:
The syntax for deleting a registry is as follows:
[DROPREGISTRY]
APPLICATION=<Name of the application>
NAME=<Registry Variable Name>
VALUE=<Value for this variable>
```

```
Deleting Snapshot Variables:
The syntax for deleting snapshot variables is as follows:
[DROPSNAPSHOTVAR]
NAME=<Name of the publication item>
PLATFORM=<Platform for which this publication item is>
VIRTUALPATH=<Virtual path of the application this publication item
belongs to>
USER=<Name of the user who subscribes to this application>
VAR=<Name of the Data Subsetting parameter, value of this parameter>
USER=<Name of the user who subscribes to this application>
VAR=<Name of the Data Subsetting parameter, value of this parameter>
GROUP=<Name of the group which subscribes to this application>
VAR=<Name of the Data Subsetting parameter, value of this parameter>
```

To run a script INI file using the shell utility WSH, use the following command:

```
WSH -c <filename.ini> mobileadmin/manager@webtogo.world
```

NOTE
*In this command, -c tells **WSH** to use the Connect privilege with the positional parameter, administrator ID and password,* (mobileadmin/manager *in the example) followed by the "@" sign and then the Web-to-Go TNS connect string* (webtogo.world *in our example).*

Deployment

Deployment is the physical distribution of runtime libraries, application resources, and data. Runtime libraries embrace the entire Mobile Client stack, including Oracle Lite Database, the ODBC driver, JRE, and the synchronization client. Setting up a Mobile Client is a two-step approach:

1. Mobile Server comes with a set of prepackaged client bundles called Mobile Client, which is managed and provisioned by the Mobile Server. A Mobile Client is a self-contained executable that can be downloaded over HTTP and executed on the mobile device. The Mobile Server, by default, displays all available Mobile Clients, listed by client platform, such as Windows CE, Windows 32, Palm Computing Platform, EPOC, and Web.

2. After completion of the initial setup, the user is able to execute a synchronization process, which distributes application resources and affiliated data to the mobile device. A mobile database is automatically created by the synchronization client called Mobile Sync.

The administrator can customize Mobile Client bundles.

Creating an Environment for Oracle Lite Development

Oracle Lite developers set up a development environment that allows programmers to create native, Java, or web-based applications. This environment requires that developers install the Oracle Lite MDK on their development machines. The MDK installs an Oracle SQL/Net client, the Application Packaging Wizard, administrative tools, and sample code for each platform. The MDK supports Windows, Palm Computing, EPOC, and different flavors of Windows CE, such as Pocket PC, and HPC-Pro on different chipsets, including StrongARM, MIPS, SH3, SH4 and Intel.

The user's development environment should also include a test or development instance of the Mobile Server. It is important to note that installation of the Mobile Server requires access to an Oracle8*i* or Oracle9*i* database instance. This access is necessary because the Mobile Server installation will build a schema for the Mobile Server Repository, including tables that define meta data about applications and users, as shown here:

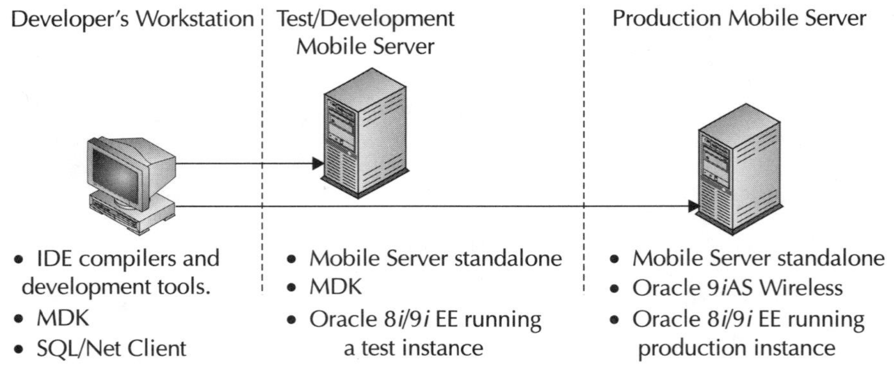

Design methodology can be summarized in the following steps:

1. The developer builds and tests the application code on their individual workstations until the code is ready to test.
2. The developer uses the Packaging Wizard to package and publish the application to the test/development Mobile Server.
3. After complete testing in the development environment, the developer may publish the completed application to the production instance of the Mobile Server.

Building a Native Windows Application Using Visual Basic

The example we'll discuss in this section comes from the Mobile Development Kit and can be found in the Visual Basic code examples. If you have installed the Oracle 9*i* Lite MDK, you can find the source for this example in the following folder:

```
D:\your_Oracle_home_directory\Mobile\Sdk\Examples\VB\UPDATE.frm
```

This application was written using Microsoft's Visual Basic 6.0. This example uses the POLITE.odb starter database included in the MDK, and you will find this starter database in the following folder:

```
D:\ your_Oracle_home_directory\Mobile\Sdk\OLDB40\polite.odb
```

This Visual Basic Update application example provides the basic business logic you will need to add, delete, update, and browse the rows in a simple table called EMP, found in the POLITE.odb sample database. This provides you with a pattern to create just about any type of Field Force application.

In this example, you will see the steps needed to package the application to the Mobile Server as well as the steps necessary to deploy this application to a client device and test the application.

Introduction to the Mobile SQL Utility

It might be useful at this point to introduce the Mobile SQL utility. Mobile SQL, or *mSQL,* is a utility application that provides a command-line interface for users, very much like Oracle's SQL*Plus utility. It allows you to execute SQL statements against the local Oracle Lite database. mSQL allows you to access functionality provided by ODBC or JDBC, and a version of mSQL is available for each operating system supported. The mSQL utility is started from a command window with the following command:

```
msql userid/password@driver:DSN:DBname or msql system/x@odbc:polite:polite
```

Here, *userid* is the name of the database user, *password* is the password for that user (if the Oracle Lite database was created by replication, then the actual mobile user password is used). Be sure to specify a connect string that includes either a JDBC or ODBC driver, the DSN, and database name.

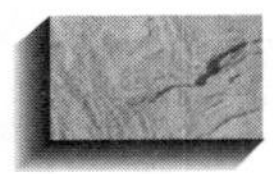

NOTE
There is no password for the user system, *but you must use an alpha character, such as x.*

Once you are in a session with the mSQL utility, you will find a couple SQL commands useful. The command **SELECT * from CAT;** will return a result set that shows the database objects found in this database; this includes all tables, views, indexes, and stored procedures (see Figure 8-3). Another useful command is DESCRIBE, which lists the characteristics of the database objects and describes them. In this example, we ask DESCRIBE to describe the characteristics of the EMP table, and you can see the column names and a description of the data types as well as whether or not they can be null. (DESCRIBE is only available on the WIN 32 platform.) Once you have listed and described the table the application is using, it might be useful to see how the rows are populated and what records exist in the table. The SQL command **SELECT * from EMP;** will display the contents of all rows in the table named EMP (see Figure 8-4).

The mSQL utility will accept SQL commands, and it is possible to create tables, delete them, and define table relationships. Developers can populate tables they

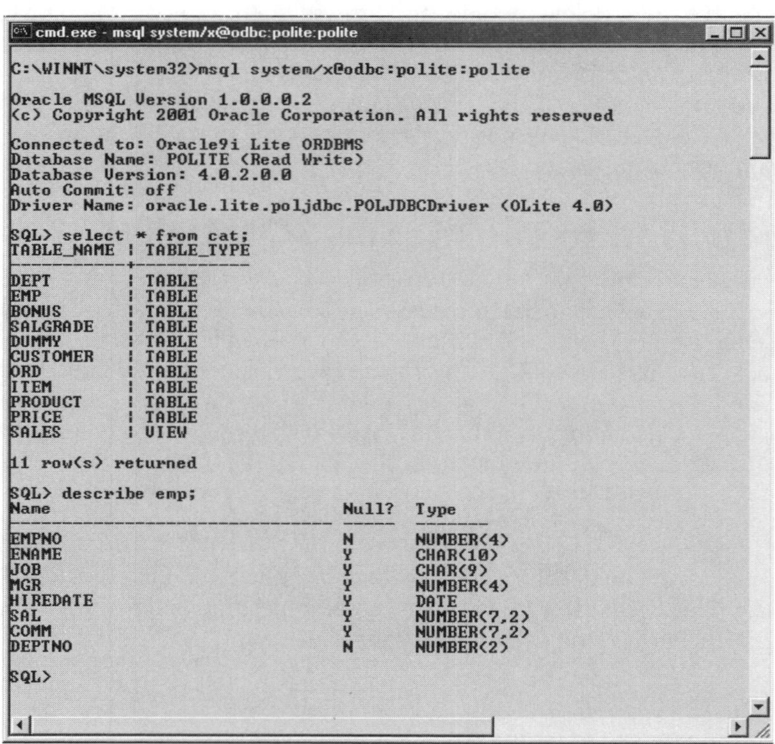

FIGURE 8-3. *Sample commands using mSQ*

```
cmd.exe - msql system/x@odbc:polite:polite

SQL> quit
Disconnected from POLITE

C:\WINNT\system32>msql system/x@odbc:polite:polite

Oracle MSQL Version 1.0.0.0.2
(c) Copyright 2001 Oracle Corporation. All rights reserved

Connected to: Oracle9i Lite ORDBMS
Database Name: POLITE (Read Write)
Database Version: 4.0.2.0.0
Auto Commit: off
Driver Name: oracle.lite.poljdbc.POLJDBCDriver (OLite 4.0)

SQL> select * from emp;
EMPNO | ENAME  | JOB       | MGR  | HIREDATE                   | SAL     | COMM    | DEPTNO
------+--------+-----------+------+----------------------------+---------+---------+-------
7839  | KING   | PRESIDENT |      | 1981-11-17 00:00:00.000000 | 5000.00 |         | 10
7698  | BLAKE  | MANAGER   | 7839 | 1981-05-01 00:00:00.000000 | 2850.00 |         | 30
7782  | CLARK  | MANAGER   | 7839 | 1981-06-09 00:00:00.000000 | 2450.00 |         | 10
7566  | JONES  | MANAGER   | 7839 | 1981-04-02 00:00:00.000000 | 2975.00 |         | 20
7654  | MARTIN | SALESMAN  | 7698 | 1981-09-28 00:00:00.000000 | 1250.00 | 1400.00 | 30
7499  | ALLEN  | SALESMAN  | 7698 | 1981-02-20 00:00:00.000000 | 1600.00 | 300.00  | 30
7844  | TURNER | SALESMAN  | 7698 | 1981-09-08 00:00:00.000000 | 1500.00 | .00     | 30
7900  | JAMES  | CLERK     | 7698 | 1981-12-03 00:00:00.000000 | 950.00  |         | 30
7521  | WARD   | SALESMAN  | 7698 | 1981-02-22 00:00:00.000000 | 1250.00 | 500.00  | 30
7902  | FORD   | ANALYST   | 7566 | 1981-12-03 00:00:00.000000 | 3000.00 |         | 20
7369  | SMITH  | CLERK     | 7902 | 1980-12-17 00:00:00.000000 | 800.00  |         | 20
7788  | SCOTT  | ANALYST   | 7566 | 1982-12-09 00:00:00.000000 | 3000.00 |         | 20
7876  | ADAMS  | CLERK     | 7788 | 1983-01-12 00:00:00.000000 | 1100.00 |         | 20
7934  | MILLER | CLERK     | 7782 | 1982-01-23 00:00:00.000000 | 1300.00 |         | 10

14 row(s) returned

SQL> _
```

FIGURE 8-4. *Results of the SQL command SELECT * from EMP;*

have created with rows by using the correct SQL statements. The mSQL utility provides an interface to all database objects and can be considered the "Swiss Army knife" database utility for developers.

NOTE
*The SQL statements are documented in the Oracle9*i *Lite SQL Reference, part number A95915-01.*

Application Logic

The application is written in Visual Basic, and when it runs on your Windows machine, it will provide a user interface, as shown in Figure 8-5. As you browse or page through the individual records, you can see that they are the same rows listed when you selected all rows from the table with the mSQL utility. If you run the application forms and you modify the table data, the changes will be reflected and can be observed using mSQL utility. This is a good way to confirm table modifications that your application makes while you are testing.

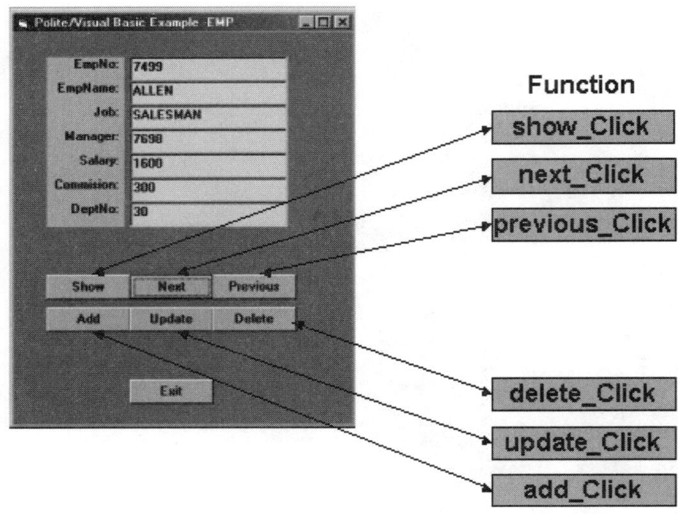

FIGURE 8-5. *User interface for the Visual Basic application*

Each one of the buttons displayed on the Visual Basic form has code that invokes a call to the Oracle Lite database. There are subroutines that show data from the table (show_Click) and provide navigation from the previous to next row in the table (next_Click and previous_Click). There's also a subroutine to delete a row of data (delete_Click), a subroutine to update or modify a row within a table (update_Click), and a subroutine to add a new row to the table (add_Click).

The Visual Basic source code for these subroutines follows:

```
Private Sub show_Click()
    Dim Conn As String
    Dim thissql As String
    MousePointer = 11
    If Not DBOpen Then
        Conn = "ODBC;UID=SYSTEM;PWD=aa;DSN=POLITE;database=POLITE"
        Set Db = OpenDatabase("", True, False, Conn)
        'first open database
        DBOpen = True
    Else
        DynaInfo.Close
    End If
    thissql = "select empno,ename,job,mgr,sal,comm,deptno from EMP
```

```
    order by empno"
Set DynaInfo = Db.CreateDynaset(thissql)
    TotalRec = GetNumbRecsSnap(DynaInfo)
    CurRec = 1
    DoRefresh
    MousePointer = 0
End Sub
Private Sub Next_Click()
    MousePointer = 11
    If TotalRec > 0 Then
       If CurRec < TotalRec Then
            DynaInfo.MoveNext
            CurRec = CurRec + 1
       Else
            DynaInfo.MoveFirst
            CurRec = 1
       End If
    DoRefresh
    Else
        MsgBox "First do a Show please!"
    End If
    MousePointer = 0
End Sub
Private Sub Previous_Click()
     MousePointer = 11
     If TotalRec > 0 Then
        If CurRec > 1 Then
            DynaInfo.MovePrevious
            CurRec = CurRec - 1
        Else
            DynaInfo.MoveLast
            CurRec = TotalRec
        End If
    DoRefresh
    Else
        MsgBox "First do a Show please!"
    End If
    MousePointer = 0
End Sub
Private Sub Add_Click()
    Dim thissql As String
    Dim rows As Integer
    Dim Conn As String
    If Not DBOpen Then
        MsgBox "First do a Show to open the Database please"
        Exit Sub
    End If
    MousePointer = 11
```

```
    For i = 0 To 6
        If Text1(i).Text = "" Then
            Text1(i).Text = "NULL"
        End If
    Next I
   On Error Resume Next
    thissql = "insert into EMP(EMPNO,ENAME,JOB,MGR,SAL,COMM,DEPTNO)
       values ("
    thissql = thissql & Int(Text1(0)) & " , '" & Text1(1) & "' , '"
       & Text1(2) & "' , " & Text1(3) & " , " & Text1(4) & "," & Text1(5)
       & " , " & Text1(6) & ")"
    rows = Db.ExecuteSQL(thissql)
    Db.ExecuteSQL ("COMMIT")
DynaInfo.Close
    thissql = "select empno,ename,job,mgr,sal,comm,deptno from EMP order
       by empno"
    Set DynaInfo = Db.CreateDynaset(thissql)
    TotalRec = GetNumbRecsSnap(DynaInfo)
    If TotalRec > 0 Then
        CurRec = 1
        While DynaInfo(0) < Text1(0).Text
                DynaInfo.MoveNext
                CurRec = CurRec + 1
        Wend
    DoRefresh
    End If
    MousePointer = 0
Exit Sub
```
Private Sub update_Click()
```
    Dim thissql As String
    Dim rows As Integer
    Dim i As Integer
    If TotalRec < 1 Then
        MsgBox "Please do a Show first!"
        Exit Sub
    End If
    MousePointer = 11
    For i = 0 To 6
        If Text1(i).Text = "" Then
            Text1(i).Text = "NULL"
        End If
    Next I
    On Error Resume Next
    thissql = "update EMP set EMPNO="
    thissql = thissql & Text1(0) & ", ENAME='" & Text1(1) & "' ,JOB='"
       & Text1(2) & "',MGR=" & Text1(3) & ",SAL=" & Text1(4) & ",COMM="
       & Text1(5) & ",DEPTNO=" & Text1(6)
    thissql = thissql & " where EMPNO = " & TEMPNO
```

```
    rows = Db.ExecuteSQL(thissql)
    Db.ExecuteSQL ("COMMIT")
    DynaInfo.Close
    thissql = "select empno,ename,job,mgr,sal,comm,deptno from EMP order
       by empno"
    Set DynaInfo = Db.CreateDynaset(thissql)
    TotalRec = GetNumbRecsSnap(DynaInfo)
    If TotalRec > 0 Then
        CurRec = 1
        While DynaInfo(0) < Text1(0).Text
                DynaInfo.MoveNext
                CurRec = CurRec + 1
        Wend
    DoRefresh
    End If
    MousePointer = 0
Exit Sub
Private Sub Delete_Click()
    Dim thissql As String
    Dim rows As Integer
    If TotalRec < 1 Then
        MsgBox "Please do a Show first!"
        Exit Sub
    End If
    MousePointer = 11
    thissql = "delete from emp where empno = " & TEMPNO
    On Error Resume Next
        Row = Db.ExecuteSQL(thissql)
    Db.ExecuteSQL ("COMMIT")
    DynaInfo.Close
    thissql = "select empno,ename,job,mgr,sal,comm,deptno from EMP
       order by empno"
    Set DynaInfo = Db.CreateDynaset(thissql)
    TotalRec = GetNumbRecsSnap(DynaInfo)
    If TotalRec > 0 Then
        If CurRec <= TotalRec And CurRec > 1 Then
            For i = 1 To CurRec - 1
                DynaInfo.MoveNext
            Next I
        Else
            DynaInfo.MoveFirst
            CurRec = 1
        End If
        DoRefresh
    End If
    MousePointer = 0
End Sub
```

Client-Initiated Synchronization

Synchronization in Oracle9*i* is initiated by the client. One of two methods can be used to initiate client synchronization: The mSync client can be used on the client device, as shown earlier, or the synchronization can be initiated programmatically in Visual Basic by using the mSync COM API.

The mSync COM API allows the calling application to start synchronization and establish various settings. The COM API performs the following basic functions:

- Allows the caller to program to start synchronization
- Allows the caller to trap progress information of the sync process
- Allows the caller to access the user profile saved on the client
- Allows the caller to set table-level sync options (Selective Sync)
- Allows the caller to close the transport

The mSync COM API has a self-registering DLL, MSync_DLL, and will install in the D:*your_oracle_home*\mobile\sdk\mSync\COM directory. Once it is installed, you'll find two classes: the ISync class, which is the main interface for the mSyncZCOM API and allows the user to instantiate a synchronization process, and the ISyncOption class.

Interface ISync (MSync.Sync) This is the main interface for the mSync COM API. It allows the user to instantiate the synchronization process. Here's a description of its public method:

Name	Description
HRESULT doSync()	Starts the synchronization process and blocks until the sync process is completed

The following code (in VB) demonstrates how to start a sync session using the default settings:

```
Dim sync As MSync.sync
 Set sync = CreateObject("MSync.Sync")
sync.DoSync
```

Note that if you do not provide a SyncOption, one will be loaded with the last saved information to perform the sync.

Interface ISyncOption (mSync.SyncOption) The SyncOption class is used to define the parameters for the sync process. It can be constructed manually, or it can save or load data from the user profile. Here are its public methods:

Name	**Description**
void load()	Loads the profile for last synced user
void save()	Saves the settings to the user profile

Here are its public properties:

Name	**Description**
username	The name of the user
password	The user's password
transportType	The type of transport to use; only "HTTP" is supported for now
transportParam	The parameters for the transport

The following VB code demonstrates how to start a sync session using the default settings:

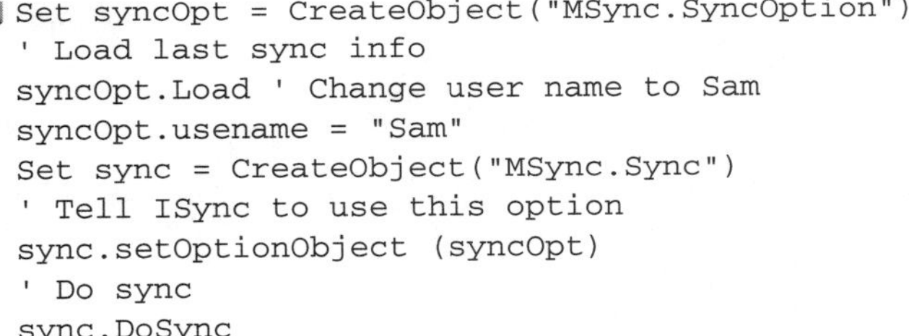

```
Set syncOpt = CreateObject("MSync.SyncOption")
' Load last sync info
syncOpt.Load ' Change user name to Sam
syncOpt.usename = "Sam"
Set sync = CreateObject("MSync.Sync")
' Tell ISync to use this option
sync.setOptionObject (syncOpt)
' Do sync
sync.DoSync
```

The Connection Points Container and ISyncProgressListener ISync implements a connection point container to allow callers to track progress information on the synchronization process. The caller needs to implement ISyncProgressListener to capture the call progress to get updates from the ISync interface.

The ISyncProgressListener has the following abstract method:

Name	**Description**
HRESULT progress([in] int progressType, int param1, int param2);	Called by the engine when new progress information is available. Here, progressType will be set to one of the progress type constants defined next. Current is the current count completed, and Total is the maximum. When Current equals Total, the stage is complete. The unit for Total and Current differs, depending on the progress type.

Here's a list of the constants:

Name	Description
PT_INIT	Progress type. States that the sync engine is in the initializing stage. The Current and Total counts are both set to 0.
PT_PREPARE_SEND	Progress type. States that the sync engine is preparing local data to be sent to the server. This includes getting locally modified data. For streaming implementations, this will be much shorter.
PT_SEND	Progress type. States that the sync engine is sending the data to the network. The Total count denotes the number of bytes to be sent, and Current is the currently sent byte count.
PT_RECV	Progress type. States that the engine is receiving data from the server. The Total count denotes the number of bytes to be received, and Current is the currently received byte count.
PT_PROCESS_RECV	Progress type. States that the engine is applying the newly received data from the server to the local data stores.
PT_COMPLETE	Progress type. States that the engine has completed the sync process.

The following sample code demonstrates how to trap the events in VB:

```
' Define the ISync object with events
Dim WithEvents sync As MSync.sync
' Create the callback.
' The name of the call back is the name of the ISync object (not the class),
' and underscore
' and then the function name - progress
Private Sub sync_progress(ByVal progressType As Long, ByVal param1 As Long,
   ByVal param2 As Long)
    Desc = ""
    ' Decipher the progressType
    Select Case progressType
    Case PT_SEND
      Desc = "Sending data..."
    Case PT_RECV
      Desc = "Receiving..."
    End Select
End Sub
```

Packaging Your Application with the Packaging Wizard

At the point in development when you are convinced that your application is compiled, tested, and running correctly, you are ready to use the Packaging Wizard to create and publish your new application. The Packaging Wizard is a utility found in the MDK that allows you to perform the following tasks:

- Create a new Mobile Server application
- Edit an existing Mobile Server application
- Publish an application to the Mobile Server Repository

When you create a new mobile application with the Packaging Wizard, it will define the application's components and files. A secondary use for the Packaging Wizard is to create SQL scripts that can be run to create base tables on the Oracle9*i* back-end database.

The following steps are needed to define applications to the Packaging Wizard:

1. Select a platform.
2. Name the new application.
3. List the application files.
4. Enter database information.
5. Define snapshots for replication.
6. Publish the application.

Starting the Packaging Wizard

To begin using the Packaging Wizard, you must first start it. To start the Packaging Wizard, you will need a command window. In the command window, from the command line, enter the following:

```
wtgpack
```

This will launch the Packaging Wizard, and you will see the initial Welcome panel (see Figure 8-6). The Welcome panel enables users to create, delete, edit, or open a packaged application.

The Packaging Wizard maintains an XML file that contains meta data about published applications, and it is found in the following folder:

```
D:\your_Oracle_home\wtgsdk\bin\wtgapp.xml
```

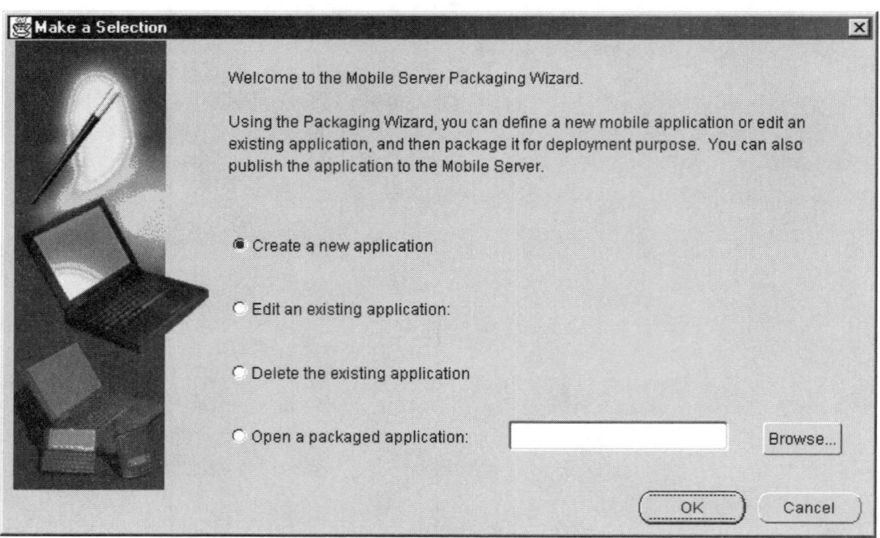

FIGURE 8-6. *The Packaging Wizard's Welcome panel*

You should not modify this file, but you may find it useful to browse when determining problems with publications. In addition to creating this meta data file, the Packaging Wizard will create table entries in the schema owned by the user mobileadmin, which is created when Mobile Server is installed. This schema has a variety of tables that contain information about users, applications, snapshots, and all the elements that make up the Mobile Server environment. All the application setup just described will happen on the developer's behalf when you publish using the Packaging Wizard. It is not important that you know exactly how it all works, but you should know that the publishing process sets up lots of information about the application in several places.

From the initial Welcome panel, developers are able to create their new applications. If you had previously defined applications, this is the place where they may be edited or deleted, or packaged applications can be opened. It's important to point out that if an application has been published to the Mobile Repository, it will also be necessary to remove the application using the Mobile Server Control Center (we will visit the Control Center later in this chapter). Also, if you choose to open a packaged application, this option enables you to select an application that has been packaged as a Java archive or .jar file. You can enter the name of the packaged .jar file in the adjacent field or use the Browse button to search for the application you wish to edit.

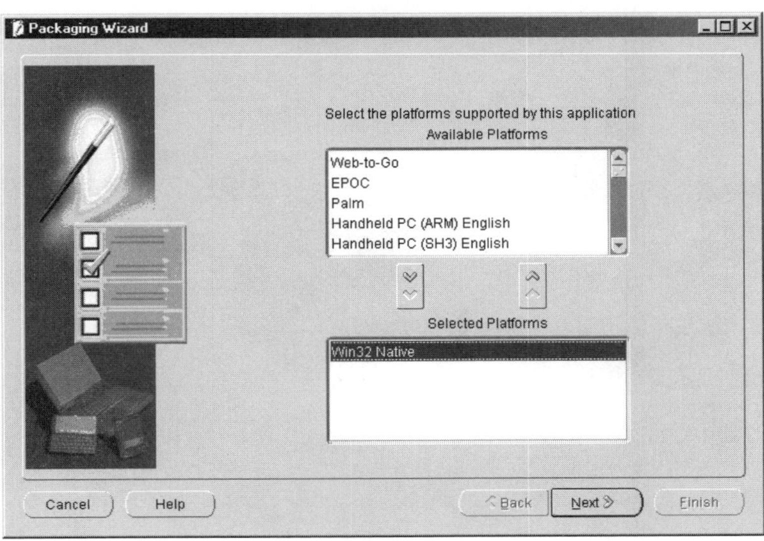

FIGURE 8-7. *Selecting the application platform*

Selecting a Platform

Once you click the OK button on the Welcome panel, you will see a screen that allows you to select the platform type (see Figure 8-7). This platform type refers to the target client operating system environment or Java. You must select at least one platform, but you can select several if your application runs on more than one platform. Highlight the platform of your choice from the list of available platforms and use the down-arrow button to move it to the list of selected platforms.

For the sample Visual Basic application, we'll select Win32Native as the application platform. After selecting the platform, it's time to name the new application.

Naming the Application

Use the Application panel to name the Mobile Server application and specify where you want to store your application on the Mobile Server (see Figure 8-8). This panel includes the following fields:

- **Application Name** The display name of the application when you log into Mobile Server.
- **Virtual Path** Provides the application with a unique identity. This is a path that is mapped from the root directory of the Mobile Server Repository to

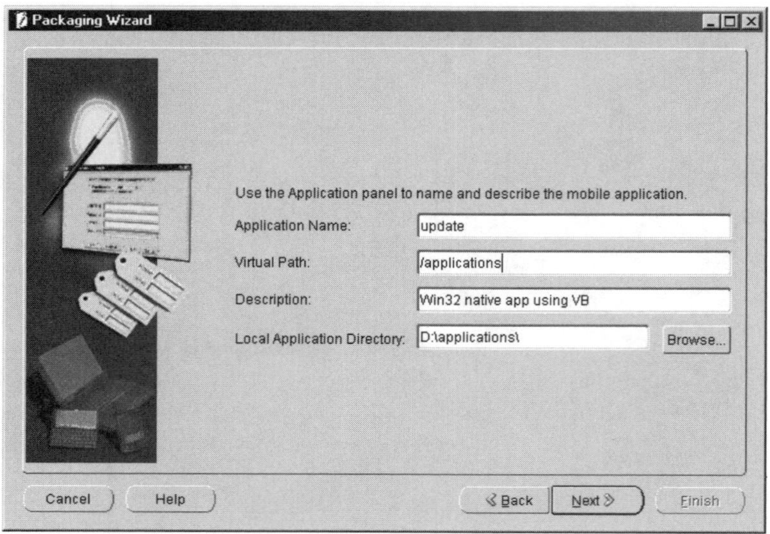

FIGURE 8-8. *Naming the application with the Application panel*

the location of the application itself. The virtual path eliminates the need to refer to the application's entire directory structure.

- **Description** A brief description of the Windows application.
- **Local Application Directory** The directory on the local machine that contains all the components for this application. You can type this location or select it by clicking the Browse button.

The local application directory is required. If the application contains Win32, Palm, EPOC, or Windows CE files, place the files in the following subdirectories of the local application directory (see the illustration):

- Create a subdirectory for Win32 applications named "win32."
- Create a subdirectory for Windows CE applications named "wince."
- Create a subdirectory for Palm applications named "palm."
- Create a subdirectory for EPOC applications named "epoc."

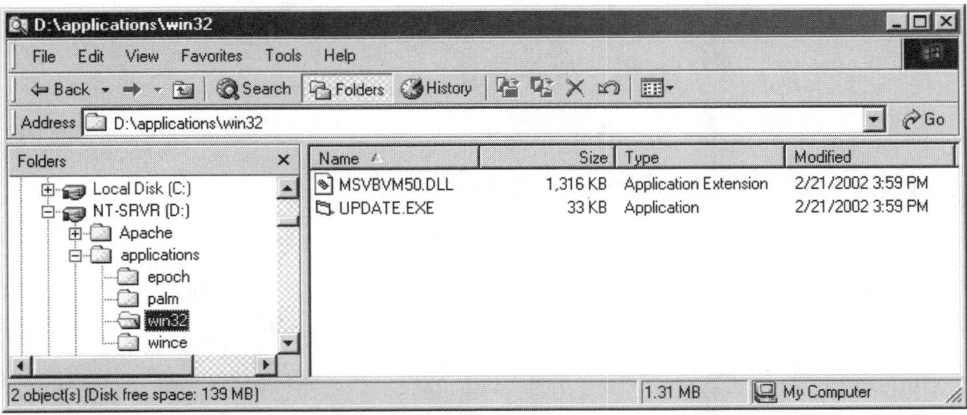

Mobile Server allows multiple versions of the same application to be published and managed in the Mobile Server Repository. You can have multiple implementations of the same application, and each of them can access the same application database tables in the Oracle database server. This means you could publish a C or C++ application for both Win32 and Compaq iPAQ. If your application is able to use the same or similar source code, you will still need to recompile the files for each different target platform, creating separate executables for Win32 and iPAQ. You will not be able to correctly publish your application unless application files are stored in a dedicated subdirectory with these distinct names. The local application directory is the directory on the Windows development system where the different application versions are stored; this can be of your own naming convention as long as the subdirectory structure just described is correctly created (refer to the preceding illustration). The Packaging Wizard recursively reads the application files under this arbitrary application (root) directory.

A local application directory called "Applications" stores the different application versions:

```
C:\Applications
```

The executable files for Win32 must be stored under the \win32 subdirectory:

```
C:\Applications\win32
```

The executable files for iPAQ must be stored under the \wince\Pocket_PC\us\arm subdirectory:

```
C:\Applications\wince\Pocket_PC\us\arm
```

If you place files in the root application subdirectory and don't specify a directory for a particular platform, the Packaging Wizard will assume they are to be used for Web-to-Go applications. No specific directory is needed for Web-to-Go files; they may reside at the root level in the local application directory.

Listing Applications Files

Use the Files panel to list your application files and to specify where they are located on the local machine. The Packaging Wizard analyzes the contents of the local application directory and displays each file's local path.

The File Name entry describes the absolute path of each Mobile Server application file—in this example, MSVBVM50.DLL and UPDATE.EXE. Each entry in the list includes the complete path of the individual file or directory (see Figure 8-9).

You have a couple of ways to sort files. Files may be sorted by extension, in which case files will be displayed alphabetically by extension. Files may also be sorted by directory, which displays the applications files alphabetically by directory. The applications files will be stored in the Mobile Server Repository in a BLOB

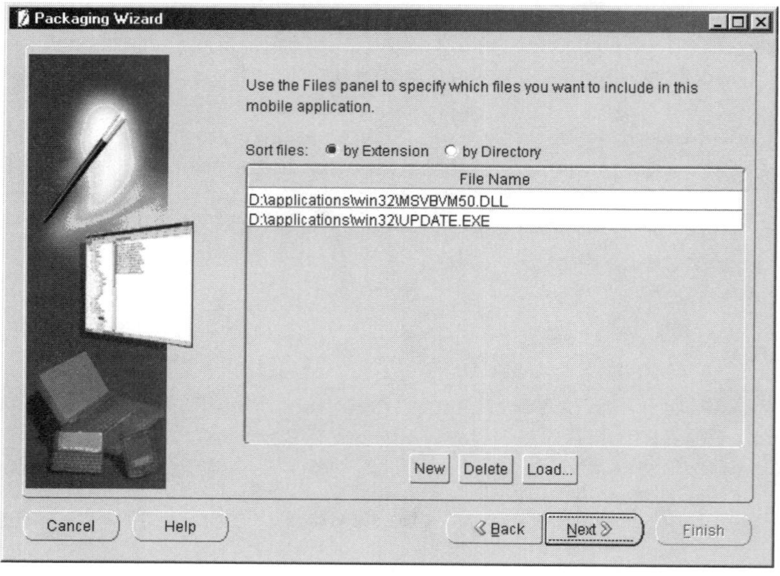

FIGURE 8-9. *Listing application files*

(Binary Large Object) data type. This BLOB is actually the home of an embedded files system—one that very much resembles Oracle9*i* server's *i*FS (Internet File System). The virtual directory name creates a subdirectory off the default (root) file system in the repository, and a subdirectory structure resembling the local application directory will be built in the repository.

After you publish your application, you may want to examine the directory structure built for your application in the repository. The Mobile Server shell utility WSH allows you to examine directories and objects in the file system contained in the BLOB data type.

You invoke the WSH utility from a command-line prompt using the following command (see the following illustration):

```
wsh -O mobileserver_ID/mobileserver_password@webtogo_connect_string
```

or

```
wsh -O mobileadmin/mobileadmin@webtogo.world
```

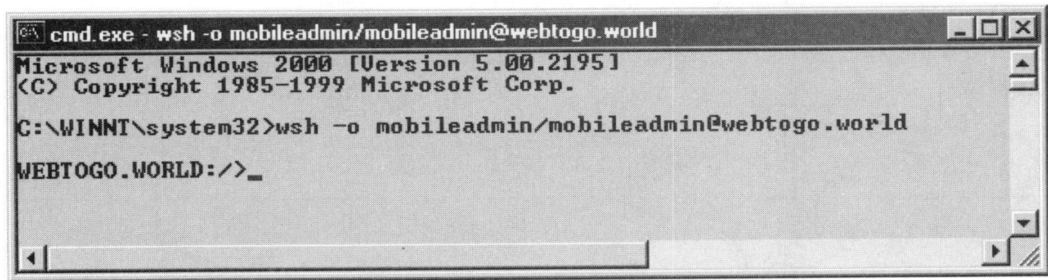

A successful invocation will result in a command-line prompt indicating that you can enter any of the commands listed in Table 8-2. Two options are available when you invoke WSH. The first option, -o, is used to examine the Oracle database repository. Here's an example:

```
wsh -o mobileadmin/mobileadmin@webtogo.world
```

The other option, -l, is used to examine Oracle Lite databases. Here's an example:

```
wsh -l system/x@odbc:polite:polite
```

Several "Unix-like" commands are available once you invoke the WSH utility. These are listed in Table 8-2.

Command	Description
cp	Copies one or more files to another location.
edit	Launches Notepad for editing a file.
del	Deletes one or more files.
rm	Deletes one or more files.
cd	Displays the name of or changes the current directory.
md	Creates a directory.
rd	Removes (deletes) a directory. Use the option -s to remove a directory and all its files/subdirectories.
type	Displays the contents of a text file or files.
exit	Quits the command shell.
quit	Quits the command shell.
help	Provides help information for shell commands.
sync	Synchronizes the file system with the database.

TABLE 8-2. *WSH Commands*

Entering Database Information

You'll use the Database panel, shown in Figure 8-10, to define how the application will interact with the Oracle server and client databases. Two parameters must be specified:

- **Server-Side Database Username** Specifies the name of the server-based user who owns the schema that contains the table you are replicating to.

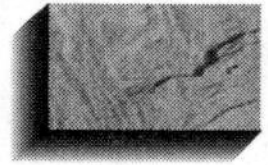

NOTE
The server-side database user must be defined in the same Oracle instance used by the Mobile Server.

- **Client-Side Database** Specifies the name of the database to be defined on the client. This is an arbitrary name, and it will also be part of a concatenated DSN created to define the database and its location on the client.

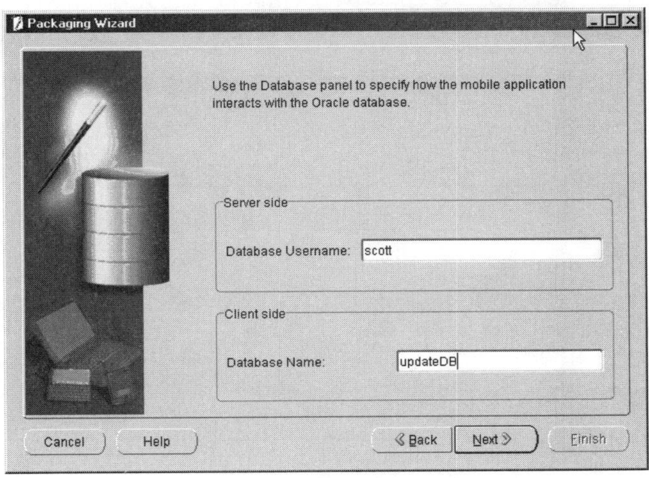

FIGURE 8-10. *Database panel*

Defining Snapshots for Replication

The Snapshots panel allows your mobile application to define database tables and lets you specify the relationship between the tables on the server and the tables replicated to the client (see the illustration). This panel allows you to create simple snapshots for individual tables, but when you are required to create snapshot publications for more complex schema, such as views and updateable views, you will find it necessary to use the Java API. We will also discuss the use of the Java API for more complex snapshot publications. The Snapshots panel gives you an opportunity to define the platform in use, and it's possible to define multiple platforms or all platforms that replication will be set up for.

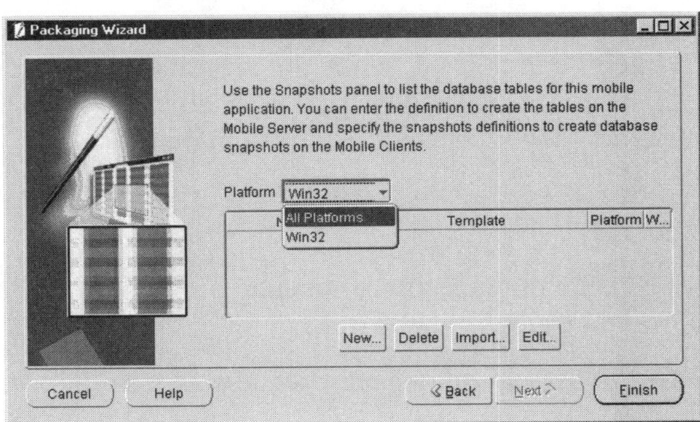

Once you have selected the appropriate platform(s), it is simple to set up a new snapshot by selecting the New button. You'll receive the New Snapshots panel.

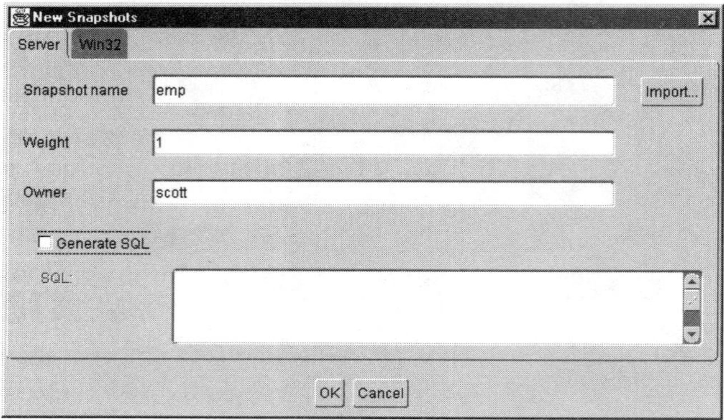

The definition of snapshots requires the specification of the following parameters:

- **Snapshot Name** Must be the name of the database server table that the snapshot definition is based on.

NOTE
The Snapshot name is not the Oracle Lite table name.

- **Generate SQL** If the table you want to take a snapshot of does not exist on the Mobile Server, you may select this option. The Packaging Wizard will collect information that is output to a SQL script that creates a database table on the database server associated with Mobile Server. However, if the table exists on the database server, you should leave clear this check box.
- **Weight** Table weight is used to resolve conflicts when synchronizing. This field allows you to set the weight for this table. Table weight is an integer property that helps describe the association between publications and publication items. Mobile Server uses table weight to determine in which order to apply client operations to master tables:
    1. Client INSERT operations are executed first, from lowest to highest table weight order.
    2. Client DELETE operations are executed next, from highest to lowest table weight order.
    3. Client UPDATE operations are executed last, from lowest to highest table weight order.

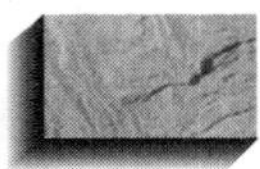

NOTE
You must specify an integer value for Weight even if you only have a single snapshot.

- **SQL** Displays the "create table" SQL statement that defines the named table. You can modify this statement. This SQL statement will be included in the SQL script created if the "Generate SQL" box is checked.

Once you have completed the options under the Server tab, select the Win32 tab, and you will be presented with the options listed here (see the illustration).

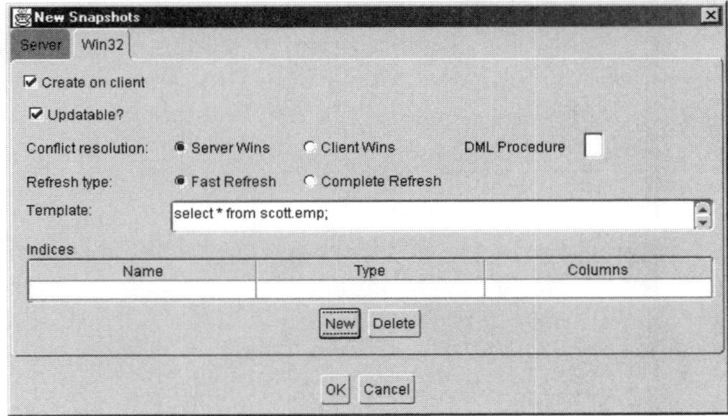

- **Create on Client** This check box allows you to perform the following actions:
  - Create an updateable snapshot. (An updateable snapshot implies bidirectional replication.)
  - Create a snapshot template. You can instantiate variables for different users of this template using the Mobile Server Control Center (you'll find a description on the next page).
- **Updateable** This check box defines the snapshot to be created as updateable.
- **Conflict Resolution** This option defines whether the server or the client wins all conflicts, and you may specify a DML procedure for custom conflict detection and resolution. Note that the default setting is "Server Wins." Conflict resolution is necessary when a conflict error is detected. These errors include nullity violations or foreign key constraint violations. The Mobile Server does not automatically resolve replication errors. When an error is detected, the Mobile Server rolls back the transactions in error and moves the transaction operations to the Mobile Server error queue. At

this point, you can change these transaction operations and reexecute them or purge them from the error queue. Mobile Server replication conflict occurs when any of the following situations occur:

- Client and the server update the same row
- Client and server create rows with the same primary key values
- Client deletes the same row that the server updates

- **Fast Refresh** Default. Only modified data is transferred.
- **Complete Refresh** All data is refreshed.
- **Template** Displays the snapshot template for the named table. You can create a snapshot template with your own DML statement, usually in the form of a SQL SELECT statement. It is also possible to instantiate variables for different users of this template using the Mobile Server Control Center; this is a technique used to partition data based on a variable substituted in the WHERE predicate of the SELECT statement. A snapshot template is a SQL statement used to create a snapshot. The SQL statement contains substitutable variables. After the template is published to the Mobile Server, you can specify substitutions for these variables in the Mobile Server Control Panel.
- **DML Procedure** After you have created a publication item, you can use Java to build a customized PL/SQL procedure, which is stored in the Mobile Server Repository to be called in place of all DML operations for a publication item. There can be only one mobile DML procedure for each publication item. The procedure should be created with the following structure:

```
AnySchema.AnyPackage.AnyName(DML in CHAR(1), COL1 in TYPE, COL2 in
   TYPE, COLn..,PK1 in TYPE, PK2 in TYPE, PKn..)
```

In this syntax, **DML** is the DML operation for each row. Values can be "D" for DELETE, "I" for INSERT, or "U" for UPDATE. Next, **COL1 ... COLn** is a list of columns defined in the publication item. The column names must be specified in the same order in which they appear in the publication item query. If the publication item was created with **"SELECT * FROM example"**, the column order must be the same as in the table "example." Finally, **PK1 ... PKn** is a list of primary key columns. The column names must be specified in the same order as in the base or parent table.

For example, suppose you want to have a DML procedure for the publication item "example"," which is defined by the following query:

```
select A,B,C from publication_item_example_table
```

Assuming "A" is the primary key column for "example", your DML procedure would have the following signature:

```
any_schema.any_package.any_name(DML in CHAR(1), A in TYPE, B in TYPE
   C inTYPE,A_OLD in TYPE)
```

During runtime, this procedure will be called with "I", "U", or "D" as the DML type. For INSERT and DELETE operations, A_OLD will be null. In the case of updates, it will be set to the primary key of the row that is being updated. Once the PL/SQL procedure is defined, it can be attached to the publication item through the following API call:

```
Consolidator.AddMobileDmlProcedure("PUB_example","example",
   "any_schema.any_package.any_name")
```

Here, "example" is the publication item name, and "PUB_example" is the publication name.

The following piece of PL/SQL code defines an actual DML procedure for a publication item in one of the sample publications. The query was defined as

```
SELECT * FROM ord_master
```

where ord_master has a single-column primary key on "ID" (see the illustration).

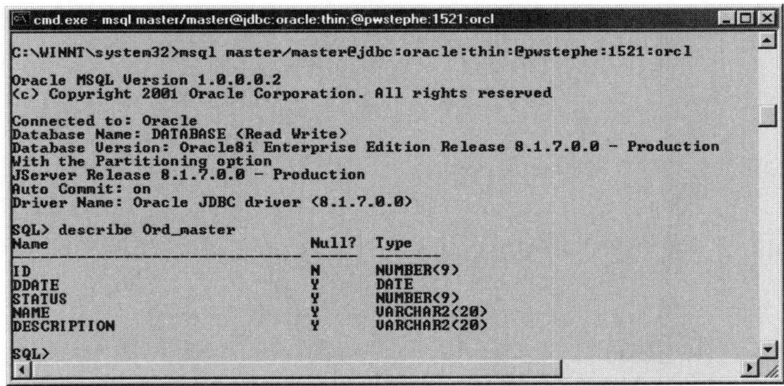


```
CREATE OR REPLACE PACKAGE "SAMPLE11"."ORD_UPDATE_PKG" AS
procedure UPDATE_ORD_MASTER(DML CHAR,ID NUMBER,DDATE DATE,STATUS
NUMBER,NAME VARCHAR2,DESCRIPTION VARCHAR2, ID_OLD NUMBER);
END ORD_UPDATE_PKG;
/
CREATE OR REPLACE PACKAGE BODY "SAMPLE11"."ORD_UPDATE_PKG" as
procedure UPDATE_ORD_MASTER(DML CHAR,ID NUMBER,DDATE DATE,STATUS
NUMBER,NAME VARCHAR2,DESCRIPTION VARCHAR2, ID_OLD NUMBER) is
Begin
   if DML = 'U' then
      execute immediate 'update ord_master set id = :id,
         ddate = :ddate,
      status = :status, name = :name, description = '||''''||'from
```

```
      ord_update_pkg'||''''||' where id = :id_old'
      using id,ddate,status,name,id_old;
   end if;
   if DML = 'I' then
   begin
      execute immediate 'insert into ord_master values(:id, :ddate,
         :status, :name, '||''''||'from ord_update_pkg'||''''||')'
      using id,ddate,status,name;
      exception
      when others then
      null;
   end;
   end if;
   if DML = 'D' then
      execute immediate 'delete from ord_master where id = :id'
      using id;
   end if;
   end UPDATE_ORD_MASTER;
end ORD_UPDATE_PKG;
/
```

Completing the Application

At this point, you have correctly completed all the Packaging Wizard panels, and the final remaining panel, Application Definition Completed, appears with the following options:

- Create Files
- Publish the Current Application
- Restart Wizard

As mentioned previously, an application file is created as meta data in XML, and this definition will be saved if you select the Create Files option. In addition to this application file, you may elect to package the files into a Java archive (JAR) file. Once the application has been packaged, the Packaging Wizard creates a .jar file. Anyone with administrator privileges on the Mobile Server instance can publish to the Mobile Server Repository using the Control Center.

The Create Files option allows you to package your application components in a .jar file. To do this, click Create Files and then click "Package Applications in a JAR File". You are prompted to specify the location for the .jar file. You will also have the option to generate the SQL to build tables if you select the Generate SQL Scripts for Database Objects option.

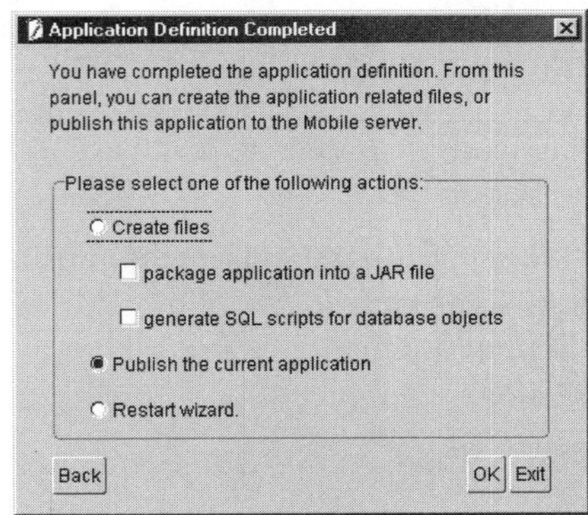

FIGURE 8-11. *Completing the application definition*

If you are ready to publish your application, you simply select the Publish the Current Application option (see Figure 8-11), and your application will be published to the Mobile Server Repository and schema.

The Publish Application panel option enables you to publish the application that you built and defined in the Packaging Wizard. To publish, click the Publish the Current Application option and then click "OK". The Publish Application window will appear, as shown here, offering the following list of options.

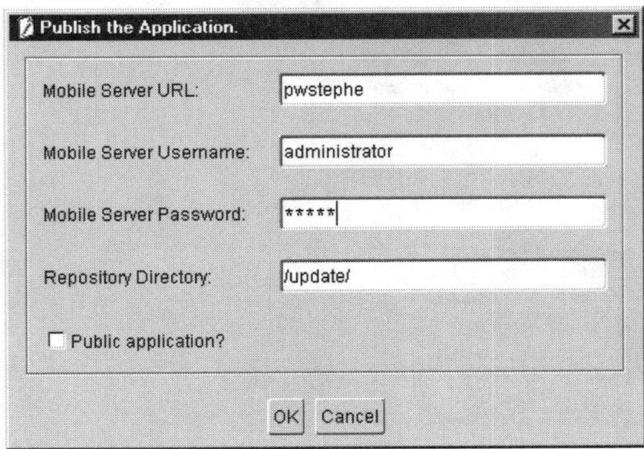

- **Mobile Server URL** Specify the local hostname of the Mobile Server and the port number.

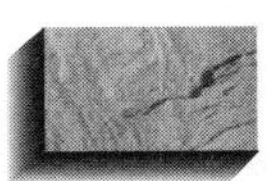

NOTE
Port 80 is the default port number.

- **Mobile Server Username** This is the name of a Mobile Server user who has admin or publish privileges. (The Administrator account is available by default; its password is manager.)
- **Mobile Server Password** Supply the password for the Mobile Server user repository.
- **Repository Directory** Specify the destination directory of the Mobile Server Repository. The Packaging Wizard publishes your application files to this directory in the Mobile Server Repository directory structure on the local application directory.
- **Public Application?** To allow all users access to this application, select the Public Application? check box. This application will be published as a public application. (This option should only be selected if every user needs the application.)

After clicking the OK button, you will receive indication that the Packaging Wizard is registering your application on the Mobile Server. When the registration is complete, you will receive a message that your application has been successfully published (see Figure 8-12). You are now ready to test the application.

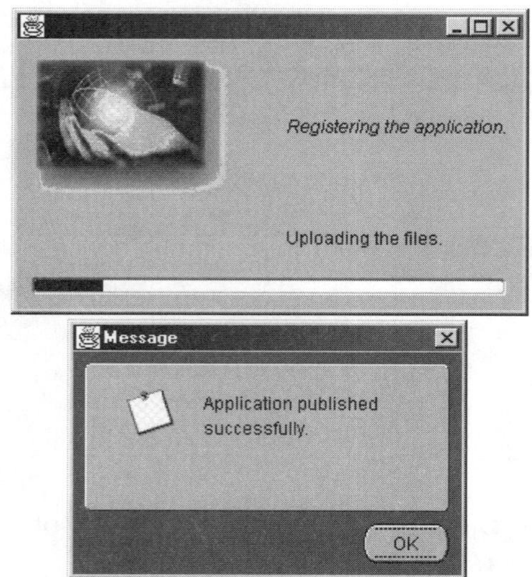

FIGURE 8-12. *Publishing and registering your application*

Invoking the Mobile Server to Test Applications

You are now ready to test the application, so it will be necessary to launch Mobile Server to perform some administrative tasks.

The configuration of the Mobile Server for development and testing is different from the final production configuration. The configuration described here uses a test version of the Mobile Server without the Oracle9*i*AS configured in the form of the webtogo.exe program. Invoking Mobile Server in the form of webtogo.exe provides a listener and sufficient application server support for testing with one or several users. It also provides a diagnostics option and logging so that developers can diagnose problems with applications. When you invoke webtogo.exe, it assumes you have a connection to the Oracle instance where you installed the Mobile Server Repository. We want to perform the following tasks:

- Invoke the Mobile Server
- Log onto the Control Center and check the application definition
- Define a test user
- Associate the test user with the application
- Install the Oracle Lite software environment on the target client device by using setup.exe from the Mobile Server for the appropriate platform
- Run Mobile Sync in the form of mSync.exe on the client device and authenticate as the test user as well as provision the client with the native application and database. (If your target device is the Palm/OS, use mSync.prc.)

Developers will find it useful to use the MDK web server by invoking the webtogo.exe version of Mobile Server and always start it in debug mode, as shown here.

cmd.exe - webtogo.exe -d0
Microsoft Windows 2000 [Version 5.00.2195]
(C) Copyright 1985-1999 Microsoft Corp.
C:\WINNT\system32>webtogo.exe -d0
log0: Mount point WEBTOGO.WORLD oracle.lite.web.ifs.OBFS@750159
log0: pwstephe.us.oracle.com 80

If the invocation is successful, the webtogo.exe version of Mobile Server will indicate that there is a mount point for webtogo.world, the TNSname connect string, and that the listener is listening on the hostname and domain name at port 80. This is a clear indication that the Mobile Server is up and running and waiting for requests. You will not be able to bring the Mobile Server up if there are problems with your Oracle instance, especially the Oracle instance's SQL/Net listener. You should ensure that no other services are currently using port 80, because if port 80 is in use, the Mobile Server will not start. Frequently on NT systems, a copy of Microsoft's IIS is running on port 80. If this is an issue, you should resolve the port conflict.

While the Mobile Server is up and running, log into the Mobile Server as the user Administrator (password admin), as shown in Figure 8-13. The next panel you see will allow you to launch the Mobile Server Control Center, shown in Figure 8-14. Once in the control center you will see the Control Center panel, Figure 8-15, that has an upper frame (the function tabs), a left frame (search

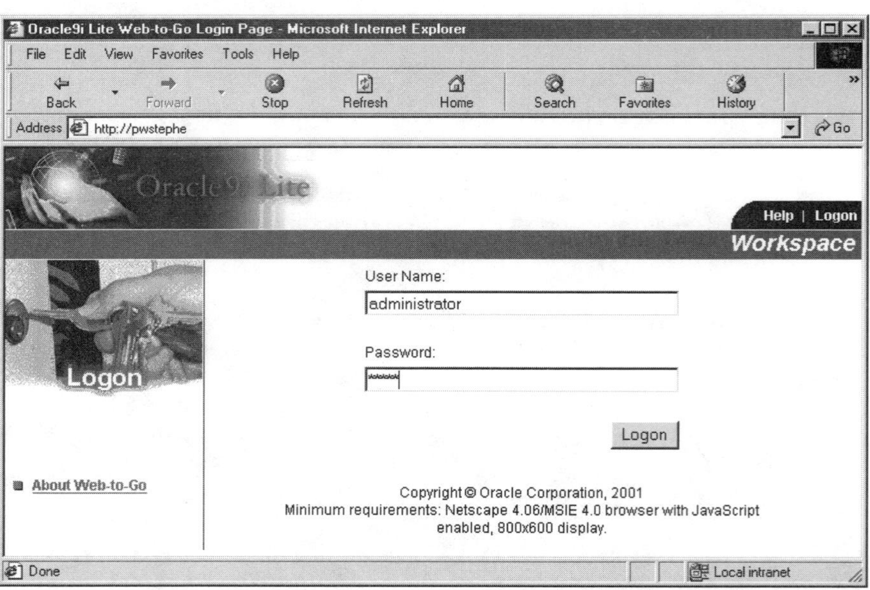

FIGURE 8-13. *Logging into the Mobile Server as Administrator*

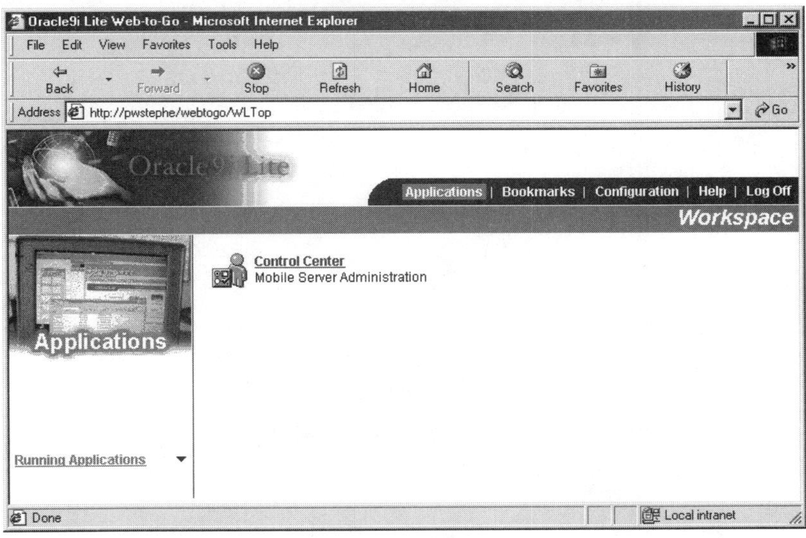

FIGURE 8-14. *Launching the Mobile Server Control Center*

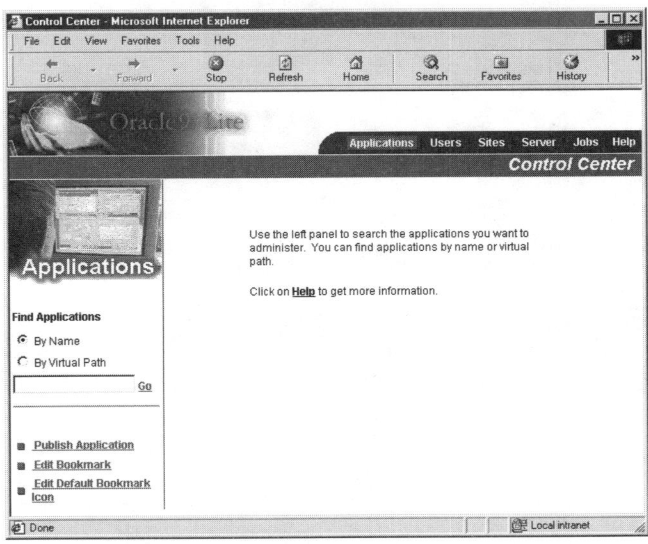

FIGURE 8-15. *Control Center display*

options), and a right frame (administration tasks). The upper frame contains the following function tabs:

- Applications
- Users
- Sites
- Server
- Jobs

Before you can test the newly published application, you must create a Mobile Server user and give that user access to the application. Let's create a new user with the Control Center.

From the Control Center display, select the Users tab at the top of the display. Once you are in the Users panel, select the option on the left side of the panel to create a new user. From this panel, you will be asked to supply a full username for identification as well as a Mobile Server login user name and password. You must also define a privilege for the user (usually Connect for most users). Refer to Figure 8-16.

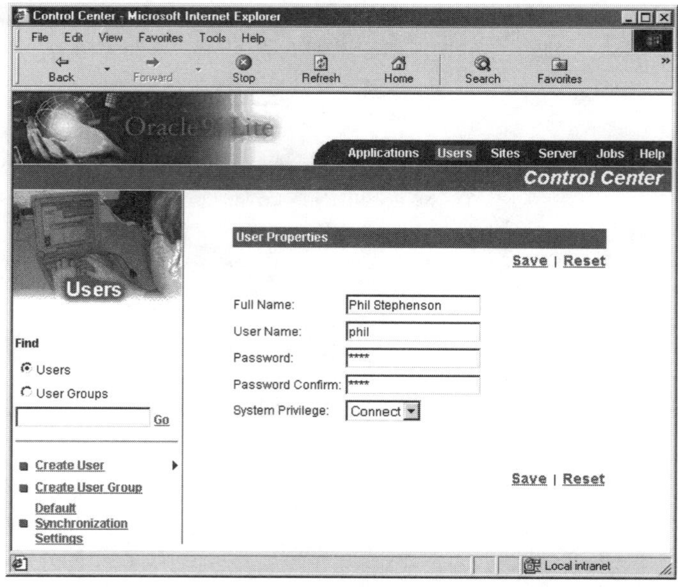

FIGURE 8-16. *Creating a new user using the Control Center*

You may choose from the following options for the privilege:

- **Connect** Enables users to connect to Web-to-Go
- **Admin** Enables users to modify Web-to-Go resources
- **Publish** Enables users to publish applications
- **None** Prevents users from having privileges

After you complete the forms on the User panel, make sure you click Save. When the new user is saved to the Mobile Server Repository, you will receive a confirmation window. You can also display users from the User panel by clicking Go in the left side of the panel. This way, you can see your newly created user (see Figure 8-17).

Now that you have a user defined, you need to associate this new user with an application. Once again from the Control Center, choose the Applications tab at the top to display information about applications. While you are here, you can validate that the application was published (see Figure 8-18).

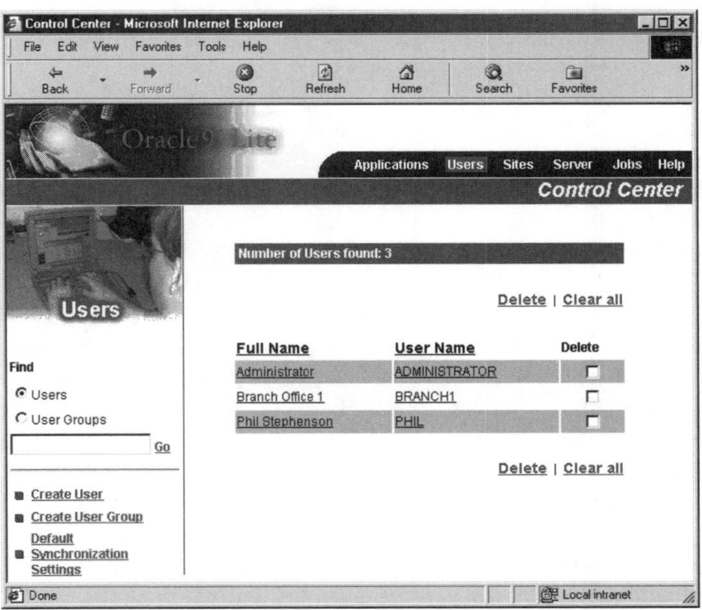

FIGURE 8-17. *Newly created user*

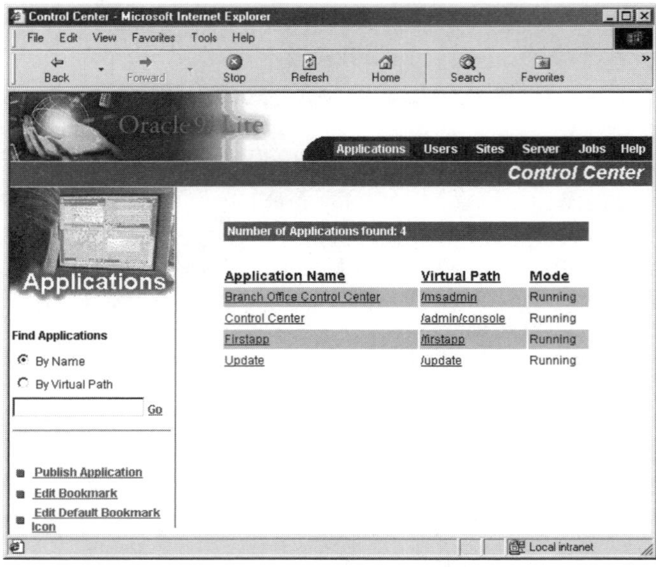

FIGURE 8-18. *Published applications*

To assign users to an application, as shown in Figure 8-19, select the check box underneath the label Access? and click Save. After the save operation is complete, you will be notified, and the user will have access to the application. When a user has access to an application, that user will be eligible to have the application deployed to their client device. Deployment causes the Mobile Server to download the applications the user has access to, builds the necessary DSNs, creates the Oracle Lite client database and the runtime environment, and on the second synchronization replicates the user's data changes made locally to the Oracle8*i* or Oracle9*i* data server. Data changes made to the data in the Oracle8*i* or Oracle9*i* data server are applied to the data in the Oracle Lite database on the Mobile Client. In addition, any application changes are downloaded to the Mobile Client on subsequent syncs.

It is now time to test the deployed application on the client device, but first you must set up the client's mobile device. Because you have deployed a Win32 native application, it is assumed you'll be using a Windows OS. You can set up this device by launching a browser such as Netscape or MS Internet Explorer and specifying a URL in the form http://*your_hostname*/setup. You will be presented with a choice of platform setups to choose from (see Figure 8-20).

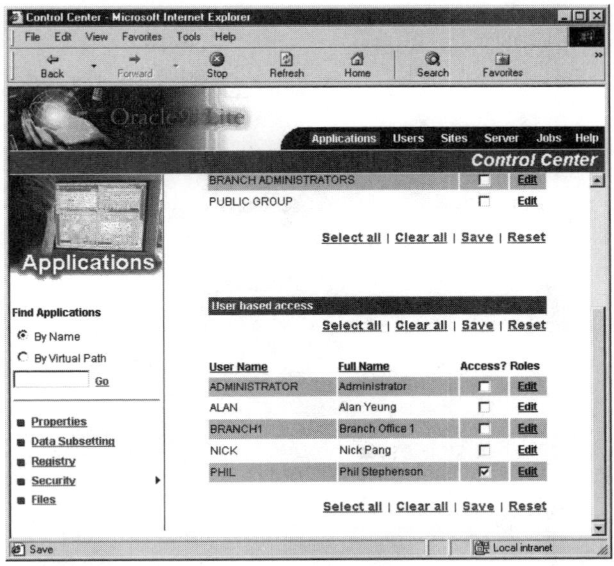

FIGURE 8-19. *Assigning users to an application*

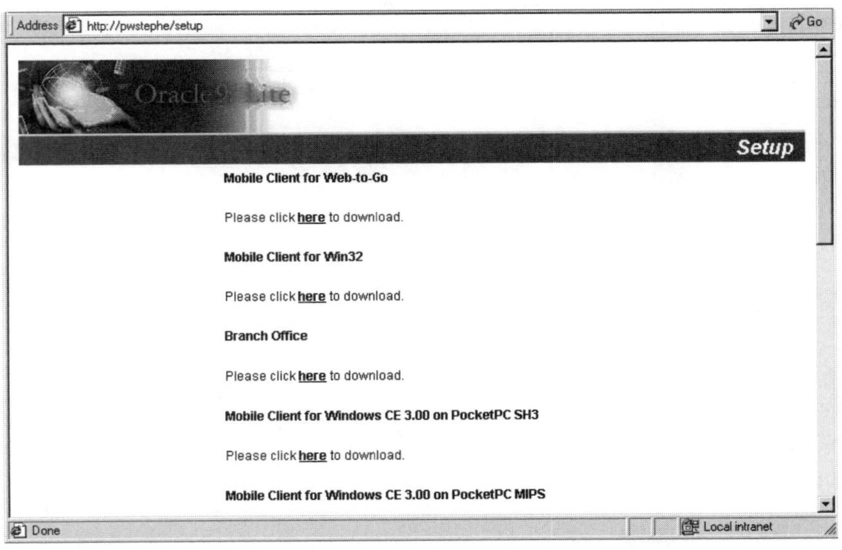

FIGURE 8-20. *Launch pad for Mobile Client*

For this Windows client, select Mobile Client for Win32. When you select this option, you will be presented with a download dialog that requires you to specify the location of a directory to download a self-extracting setup.exe file that builds the environment for the client device. You will be asked to supply a directory for the environment, as shown here.

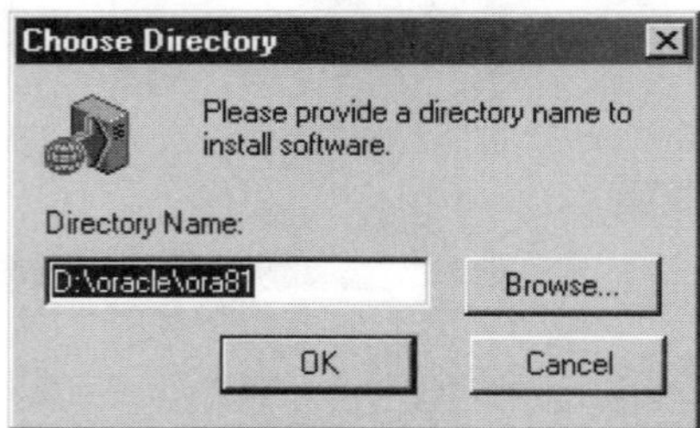

If a conflict on port 80 is detected, you will asked to select a unique port, as shown here.

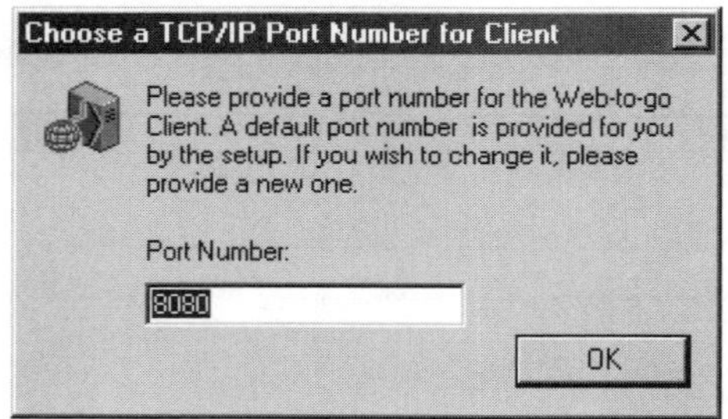

Once the environment has been built, you will have all the client software necessary to connect to the Mobile Server and communicate. The setup builds a local PATH

```
D:\olite_client\Mobile\bin\;%path%
```

and a CLASSPATH

```
D:\olite_client\Mobile\bin\olite40.JAR;%classpath%
```

in your local user environment.

Before you can synchronize data between the Mobile Server and Mobile Client for Windows, you must configure a TCP/IP network connection. The Mobile Client downloads and formats data from the Mobile Server. Use a command window to start the mobile application using the following format for the command (see the following illustration):

```
Oracle_Home\Mobile\SDK\Bin\msync.exe
```

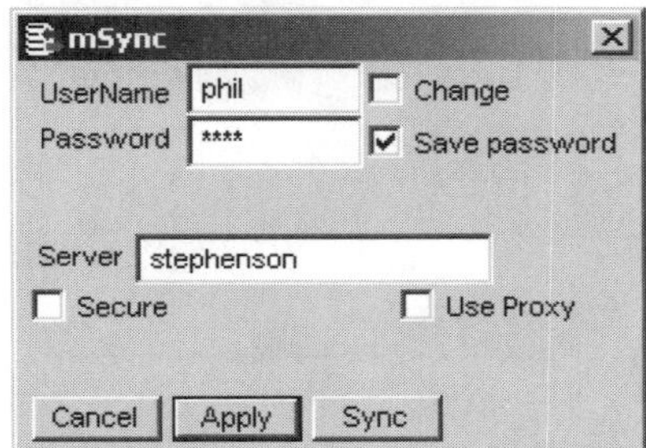

You must specify the following parameters in the mSync client to perform synchronization from the Mobile Client:

- **UserName** Mobile Client user name. (This field is not case sensitive.)
- **Password** Mobile Client password. (This field is case sensitive.)
- **Change** Leave this box clear.
- **Save Password** Select this check box to save the password.
- **The Mobile Server IP address** http://<your_mobile server>
- **Use Proxy** Select if appropriate.

This will allow you to perform the first synchronization with the Mobile Server. Click the SYNC button to start the first sync. During the sync, you will see progress bars that indicate the progress of your synchronization followed by an indication that your synchronization was successful. (See the illustration on the next page). You should also examine the directory structure of the Oracle Lite environment. You should see the files associated with the application in the following directory:

```
Oracle_Home/Mobile/oldb40/your_client_username
```

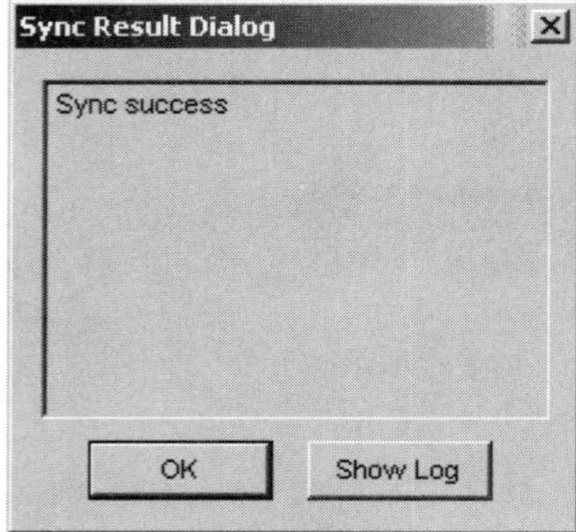

The application has now been provisioned to the client device, and the user may use the application and replicate to the Mobile Server.

Summary

Oracle9*i* Lite provides infrastructure and application services that enable the delivery of secure and personalized applications using a broad range of mobile devices. In this chapter, we have examined the features and architecture of Oracle9*i* Lite and have gone through a complete lifecycle of creating, testing, and deploying an offline application. We also looked at the use of the Mobile Server Control Center and how you can run mSync for synchronization.

CHAPTER 9

Offline Management—Advanced Features

In this chapter, we continue to discuss some of the features of Oracle9*i*AS Wireless—Offline Management, or Oracle9*i* Lite. In particular, you'll learn how to build a Windows CE mobile application to access employee information, focusing on the use of ActiveX Data Objects (ADO) with Oracle9*i* Lite and its support for internationalization and different chipsets. We'll explore issues related to performance tuning and scalability, and discuss the synchronization and replication technology in details. Finally, we'll look at the design issues in building distributed applications and take a close-up look at an Oracle9*i* Lite feature called Branch Office. In a nutshell, we cover the following topics:

- Building a Native CE Application with Visual Basic and EVT
- Server Configuration for Performance and Scalability
- Synchronization and Replication Architecture
- Distributed Design Considerations
- Branch Office

Building a Native CE Application with Visual Basic and EVT

It seems that interest in the PocketPC platform really took off when Compaq introduced the iPAQ model PocketPC. This device has generous display real estate, plenty of memory, and a powerful processor—all in an attractive package. Enterprise application developers have given the nod to the PocketPC platform for applications ranging from field force automation to service and maintenance. Microsoft's PocketPC 3.0 operating system is also known as PocketPC 2000, PocketPC 2002, and the HandheldPC Pro.

The Oracle9*i* development environment for CE supports C/C++, Java, and Visual Basic with Microsoft's Embedded Visual Tools 3.0 (EVT 3.0). To recap, you can choose the development model in accordance with your choice of application development tools:

- **ADOCE** Used with Visual Basic (VB) applications. Active Data Objects for Windows CE (ADOCE) supports a relatively simple development environment, but the performance is not optimal when compared with C/C++ and Microsoft Foundation Classes (MFC).
- **JDBC** Used for Java applications and offers portability for applications.
- **ODBC** ODBC and MFC provide good performance and are used to create applications that use dynamic SQL.

In this example, we'll use Visual Basic and MS EVT 3.0 with Oracle's ActiveX Database Objects for CE (ADOCE). ADOCE is an object-oriented programming interface that enables Visual Basic applications to access an Oracle Lite database. The ADOCE API is based on the COM interface and provides functions to access the underlying database engine. ADOCE is designed to run in the Windows CE environment, and it contains a subset of the full ActiveX Data Objects.

Visual Basic developers can develop applications using the same Microsoft ActiveX Data Objects for Windows CE against Oracle9*i* Lite databases. To support the ADOCE, the Oracle9*i* Lite database implements a module that provides the same interface as Microsoft, and Oracle's ADOCE follows the specification for Microsoft Windows CE ADO v2.0 SDK, which is based on the desktop version of ActiveX Data Objects 1.0 (there are some differences).

Oracle's ADOCE can be accessed using almost any programming language, but Oracle9*i* Lite's implementation is tailored for the Visual Basic EVT environment. Oracle's ADOCE interface exists on top of the Oracle9*i* Lite ODBC interface and provides a COM interface to application programs.

ADOCE control has three objects: ActiveConnection, Recordset, and Field. In this example, we use CreateObject to create an ActiveConnection object and activate a connection based on the DSN entry contained in ODBC.txt. We also use the Polite.odb database table EMP and a complete set of VB subroutines. The following code example is similar to the previous VB for Windows sample application given in Chapter 8:

```
'------------------------------------------------------------
' Module1
'
Option Explicit
'Declare conn as connection variable
Public conn
'Declare currentEmp as currently selected Employee ID
Public currentEmp As Integer
'Declare Recordset variable
Public RS
'------------------------------------------------------------
'
'Main Form
'
Option Explicit
'i Variable used as counter to clear the grid control
Dim i As Integer
'intI variable used as counter to loop through the Recordset
Dim intI As Integer
'Create an Oracle Lite ADOCE Active Connection
Set conn = CreateObject("oladoce.ActiveConnection")
'Connect to the Oracle Lite Database
conn.Connect ("empodb")
'Create the Recordset
Set RS = CreateObject("oladoce.Recordset")
```

```
Private Sub cmdDisplayData_Click()
Set conn = CreateObject("oladoce.ActiveConnection")
Set RS = CreateObject("oladoce.Recordset")
conn.Connect ("empodb")
'Clear the Grid
For i = 1 To GridCtrl1.Rows
    GridCtrl1.RemoveItem 0
Next
'Get all the rows from the emp table
'Active connection, Cursortype=1(Keyset Cursor),Locktype=3(RWED)
RS.Open "select emp.* from emp", "", 1, 3
'Display the Column Headers in the first row
'vbTab separates entries into next column
GridCtrl1.AddItem "EmpNo" & vbTab & _
                    "EName" & vbTab & _
                    "Job" & vbTab & _
                    "Mgr" & vbTab & _
                    "HireDate" & vbTab & _
                    "Sal" & vbTab & _
                    "Comm" & vbTab & _
                    "DeptNo"

' Loop through Recordset to populate Grid
    For intI = 0 To RS.recordcount - 1
        GridCtrl1.AddItem RS.Fields("EMPNO").Value & vbTab & _
                         RS.Fields("ENAME").Value & vbTab & _
                         RS.Fields("JOB").Value & vbTab & _
                         RS.Fields("MGR").Value & vbTab & _
                         RS.Fields("HIREDATE").Value & vbTab & _
                         RS.Fields("SAL").Value & vbTab & _
                         RS.Fields("COMM").Value & vbTab & _
                         RS.Fields("DEPTNO").Value
        RS.MoveNext
    Next intI
'Close the Recordset
'RS.Close
'Set RS = Nothing
End Sub
Private Sub cmdHideData_Click()
'Clear the Grid
For i = 1 To GridCtrl1.Rows
    GridCtrl1.RemoveItem 0
Next
End Sub
Private Sub Form_OKClick()
'On closing the Form - Close the Recordset and disconnect from the database
    RS.Close
    Set RS = Nothing
    conn.disconnect
    Set conn = Nothing
    App.End
End Sub
Private Sub GridCtrl1_Click()
```

```
'Select the current Employee ID in the Grid, except for the Header row.
If GridCtrl1.RowSel > 0 Then
    currentEmp = GridCtrl1.TextMatrix(GridCtrl1.RowSel, 0)
    Detail.Show
End If
End Sub
'-------------------------------------------------------------------------------
'
'Detail Form
'
Option Explicit
'The Cancel button will set the currentEmp to 0 and Display the Form Main
Private Sub cmdCancel_Click()
currentEmp = 0
Main.Show
End Sub
'Subrouting to run when the Detail Form is activated.
Private Sub Form_Activate()
'Dim intI
'Create connection
Set conn = CreateObject("oladoce.ActiveConnection")
'Create the Recordset
Set RS = CreateObject("oladoce.Recordset")
'Connect to the empodb Oracle Lite Database
conn.Connect ("empodb")
'Open the Recordset and execute SQL to find the selected Employee Number
RS.Open "SELECT * FROM EMP WHERE EMPNO = " & currentEmp, "", 1, 3
'Display the Edit Fields with the select Employee
    EmpNoText = RS.Fields("EMPNO").Value
    ENameText = RS.Fields("ENAME").Value
    EmpJobText = RS.Fields("JOB").Value
    EmpMgrText = RS.Fields("MGR").Value
    EmpHDateText = RS.Fields("HIREDATE").Value
    EmpSalaryText = RS.Fields("SAL").Value
    EmpCommText = RS.Fields("COMM").Value
    EmpDeptText = RS.Fields("DEPTNO").Value
End Sub
'Save the Current record with any modifications that have been made.
'Populate the db fields values with the contents of the Forms edit fields.
Private Sub cmdSave_Click()
    RS.Fields("EMPNO").Value = EmpNoText.Text
    RS.Fields("ENAME").Value = ENameText.Text
    RS.Fields("JOB").Value = EmpJobText.Text
    RS.Fields("MGR").Value = EmpMgrText.Text
    RS.Fields("HIREDATE").Value = EmpHDateText.Text
    RS.Fields("SAL").Value = EmpSalaryText.Text
    RS.Fields("COMM").Value = EmpCommText.Text
    RS.Fields("DEPTNO").Value = EmpDeptText.Text
    'Update and commit the record in the db
    RS.Update
    MsgBox "Record has been saved", vbOKOnly, "Record Updated"
    'Close the Recordset
```

```
    RS.Close
    'Display the Form Main
    Main.Show
End Sub
```

Compile the Visual Basic code and use Microsoft's ActiveSync utility to install the program on your PocketPC machine. You will be able to launch the application and navigate the rows in the EMP table as well as add, delete, and modify the table data (see Figures 9-1 and 9-2). You can modify this code to add your own unique user interface and business logic to create just about any forms-based application for field force needs.

Once you're convinced the program is running correctly, you will want to package your CE application using the Packaging Wizard and follow the same steps listed previously in Chapter 8. It is important to place your compiled files in a very specific directory structure, mentioned previously. For CE applications, files are distributed in the Mobile Development Kit based on the structure

```
<AppRoot>/wince/<Form Factor>/<Language>/<Chipset>
```

where:

- <Form Factor> is "PocketPC" or "HPCPro".
- <Language> is one of the supported languages shown in Table 9-1.
- <Chipset> is one of the supported chipset types shown in Table 9-2.

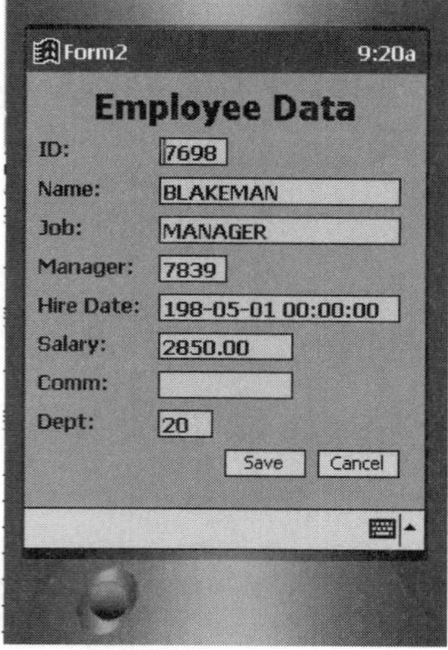

FIGURE 9-1. *Navigating the rows and records in the EMP table*

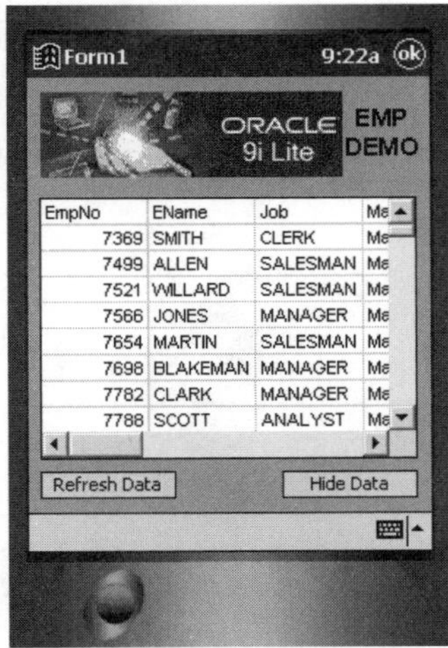

FIGURE 9-2. *Displaying a single record or row for modification*

If, for example, you create an application for the PocketPC in U.S. English for a device using a StrongArm processor chip, such as iPAQ, you might create a directory structure such as the following:

```
D:\applications\wince\Pocket_PC\us\arm
```

Locale	Abbreviation
U.S. English	us
Japanese	ja
Chinese	cn
Korean	ko
Taiwanese	tw

TABLE 9-1. *Supported Languages*

Chipsets	PocketPC	HPC Pro	Subdirectory Descriptor
SH3	Yes	Yes	sh3
SH4	No	Yes	sh4
MIPS	Yes	Yes	mips
ARM	Yes	Yes	arm
X86	No	No	x86

TABLE 9-2. *Supported Chipsets*

Server Configuration for Performance and Scalability

Mobile Server performance and scalability are determined by two major factors:

- The maximum number of concurrent users synchronizing together at one time
- The maximum amount of data that is being synchronized and flowing through at a time

In theory, the maximum number of concurrent users and data is unlimited, but the practical reality is how long the sync process takes, given a maximum number of concurrent users and the amount of data they synchronize. The number of concurrent users is always less than the total number of defined users. If you have 1,000 defined users spread geographically over at least four time zones, then the number of peak concurrent users may range from 25 to 40 percent of total defined users, which would mean 250–400 concurrent users. It is also important to design applications so that the synchronization payloads are minimal. It is possible to arrange for partitioning communities of users and mandating a synchronization window based on time or date or some other arbitrary method to keep the number of concurrent users to a minimum.

Sizing Considerations

Because the preceding parameters are wildly varied among applications, the synchronization payload can be a few records or several hundreds of megabytes in database size. The payload usually is between 5 and 50kB, and the number of tables can range from 10 to 200. As with any performance and capacity issue, you must size the server configuration in a way that utilization stays below 70 percent; otherwise, response time will rise at an increasing rate until the time to sync is extremely long and unacceptable. The implications for resource, processor, memory, disk storage, and bandwidth all affect both the middle tier (Mobile Server) and the back-end database. Because the Mobile Server is using Java to exploit multiple threads, it makes good use of the multiprocessing features of operating systems and SMP machine architectures.

It is advisable that you configure your server with plenty of processor memory for connection pools and spawned threads. You should ensure there is sufficient bandwidth between the Mobile Server and the back-end Oracle instance. It is very important to configure the back-end Oracle instance correctly for optimal performance. This is probably best left to your Oracle database administrator, who will understand how to configure the instance so that there are no system resource constraints.

For typical applications and configurations, Table 9-3 can be used as a rule of thumb for sizing based on the number of concurrent users. This is only a rough estimate, and extreme care should be taken when using this information for sizing, because the behavior of your applications will be unique. It would be best to use this table as a starting point and benchmark your application to measure utilization metrics before determining an ultimate production configuration.

Concurrent Users (Not Defined Users)	Processors for the Mobile Server	Processors for the 9*i* Database
50	2	1
100	2	2
200	2	4
400	2 × 2*	4
800	3 × 2**	6
1600	4 × 3***	8+

* 2 × 2 indicates two separate instances of the Mobile Server on two separate NT dual CPU servers.

** 3 × 2 indicates 3 separate instances of the Mobile Server on three separate NT dual CPU servers.

*** 4 × 3 indicates 4 separate instances of the Mobile Server on four separate NT 3-way CPU servers.

TABLE 9-3. *Rule-of-Thumb Guide for Sizing*

Load Balancing

The best configuration for scalability can be accomplished by using multiple Mobile Servers and adjusting the number of MGP threads to match the load generated by the Mobile Server. Oracle9*i* Lite Mobile Server must use Oracle9*i* Application Server as its front end and listener; as such, Oracle9*i*AS provides load balancing at HTTP Server (Apache) or OC4J levels. Oracle9*i* Application Server also provides additional features, including the following:

- Integration with third-party load-balancing products
- Automatic connection rerouting
- Automatic death detection and restart
- Transparent application failover
- HTTP clustering
- Session state replication and failover
- Static IP-based multicast
- No single point of failure

The Mobile Server environment benefits from these features, and many of them will enhance performance and scalability.

Synchronization and Replication Architecture (MGP and Async Queue)

Because Oracle9*i* Lite was designed to support a large number of concurrent users connected to the Mobile Server infrastructure, replicating data all at once, performance has always been the paramount design parameter. The goal is to allow a large number of simultaneously connected users to replicate data changes to an Oracle8*i*/9*i* database server and complete their transactions in a matter of minutes rather than hours. Scalability and reliability are the most critical requirements for large enterprises that have thousands of mobile workers.

Oracle9*i* Lite uses an asynchronous replication model to enhance performance and scalability (see the illustration). The underlying principle behind asynchronous replication is to divide the entire replication process into two loosely coupled transactions that operate independently of each other. This ensures load balancing, because a heavy load in one process will not impact the performance of the second transaction, and vice versa. Oracle's asynchronous model uses a store-and-forward architecture in which the information payload is temporarily stored in a queue before the data gets applied to the database server. This queue is persistent, which ensures that data is not lost during a server failure. Persistent queues can be inspected at any time, and useful monitoring information about the system status can be easily obtained using the standard SQL programming language.

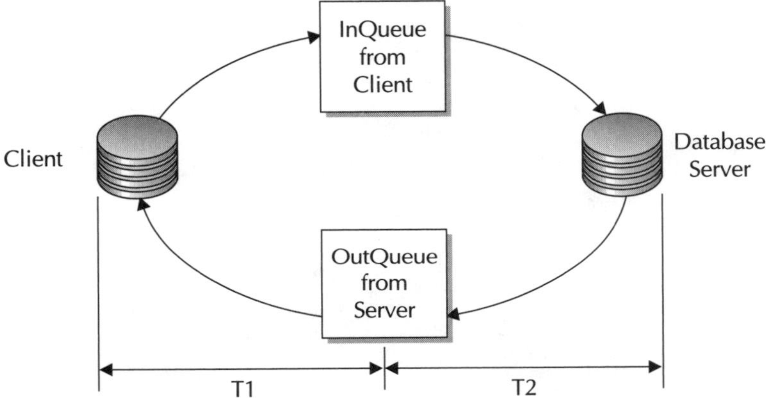

Fundamentally, the replication process consists of two distributed transactions:

- **T1** Transaction 1—Mobile Client, Mobile Server
- **T2** Transaction 2—Mobile Server, database server

T1 executes several subtasks that handle the communication and information exchange between the Mobile Client and the Mobile Server. Remember, the Mobile Server is a highly specialized mid-tier module extension to Oracle9*i* Application Server, which accepts incoming transactions from the client and sends outgoing transactions to the client. In this scheme, the Mobile Server uses INQUEUES to store data from the Mobile Client and OUTQUEUES to store data from the database server.

T2 manages the communication and data-exchange process between the Mobile Server (IN/OUTQUEUE) and the Oracle database server. In addition, several subtasks are performed during T2 (these are described later).

T1 also manages communication between the Mobile Client and the Mobile Server, which typically uses the HTTP transport. More important than the network transport are the characteristics of the network that greatly affect the overall end-to-end response time experienced by users. These characteristics include the following:

- Narrow bandwidth
- High latency
- Network reliability

These factors determine how much data can be pushed through the network and how many retry attempts are necessary before data can be exchanged successfully. Each T1 and T2 transaction embraces a number of subprocesses, as depicted in here.

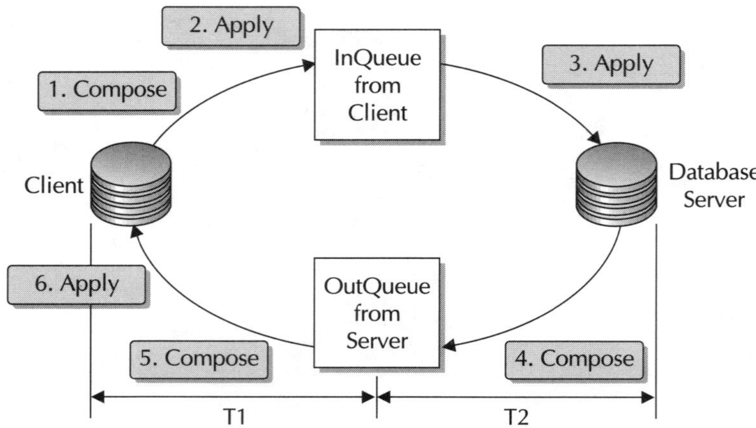

Phase A

Phase A involves queuing transactions from the Mobile Client to the INQUEUE object. In essence, Phase A includes the following subprocesses:

- Client compose
- Apply to Mobile Server
- Compose from Mobile Server
- Apply to Oracle Lite database

Let's dissect these subprocesses and review the underlying tasks here.

Client Compose

The Client Compose subprocess establishes a secure connection between the Mobile Client and the Mobile Server. The Mobile Server then allocates a JDBC connection from the JDBC connection pool that connects the Mobile Server and the Oracle database server. The user credentials (user name/password) are authenticated using the Mobile Server user profile information in the Mobile Server Repository.

The second task reads the changed records from the Oracle Lite database and creates a "virtual change file." The file is virtual because it uses an in-memory data structure rather than a physical file to store the changed data records. An internal communication protocol (OPCODE) is added to the records; it specifies the operation to be performed, such as [I]nsert, [U]pdate, [D]elete, or [R]eturn. This data is automatically encrypted and compressed for maximum security and efficiency.

Apply to Mobile Server

The changed data records arrive at the Mobile Server using an HTTP post method. This server decompresses and decrypts the data and then parses the OPCODE and applies (or populates) the data to the INQUEUE.

You have already been introduced to the Mobile Server replication API that is used to create replication objects, such as Publication, Publication Item, Subscriptions, and supporting objects such as the INQUEUE and map tables. These objects are created prior to the synchronization process, and we'll assume they are defined properly.

On the first sync, the map tables (one map table per replicated base table) are filled with the data from the server in the fashion ClientID, RowIDServer, and Primary Key. RowIDClient is empty because the client has not yet sent any data.

On the second sync, the map tables are updated with the RowIDClient, which provides a way to tell the replication system what records have been populated on the client. The map tables contain information about the server data and the client data. Remember, Oracle uses an asynchronous replication system, and the second sync is the first opportunity for the client to inform the server about its replicated payload. Updating the map tables consumes a lot of CPU and I/O capacity, especially when there are thousands of users and large amounts of client data. Table 9-4 depicts the situation after the first sync.

Table 9-5 depicts the situation after the second sync.

Compose from Mobile Server

The Compose process prepares the data set for each user, placing it into the OUTQUEUE. Interestingly, the OUTQUEUE is not a table at all but just a term

ClientID	RowIDClient	RowIDServer	Primary Key
John	–	1	67
John	–	2	89
John	–	3	56

TABLE 9-4. *Map Table After the First Sync*

ClientID	RowIDClient	RowIDServer	Primary Key
John	1′	1	67
John	2′	2	89
John	3′	3	56

TABLE 9-5. *Map Table After the Second Sync*

used to describe the functionality of an OUTQUEUE. The OUTQUEUE differs from the INQUEUE because it does not contain the actual payload but only the reference to the server base tables. Checking OUTQUEUES uses processing resources because the client data is dynamically collected from the base tables using SQL JOIN operations.

During the first sync, the DDL for the client database is created, based on the information in the Mobile Server Repository, and then the client data is collected. The map tables are populated with data from the server, as described earlier. Finally, the data is encrypted, compressed, and added to HTTP response object.

The second sync operation is slightly different from the first sync because there is no need to create the Oracle Lite database DDL anymore. The second sync merely checks the OUTQUEUE for client-specific data.

Apply to Oracle Lite Database

In the final step in Phase A, the data is sent to the client and then changes are applied to the Oracle Lite database. Databases are created automatically using the DDL information provided by the previous process. If indexes were defined, they are built on a predefined set of columns after the data has been applied to the client database.

Phase B

Phase B involves queuing transactions to the OUTQUEUE from the back-end Oracle instance and includes the following subprocesses:

- Apply to Oracle database
- Compose from Oracle database.

Apply to Oracle8*i*/9*i* Database

The Apply process reads the INQUEUE and applies the records to the Oracle database server using a JDBC connection. During this application, Apply detects conflicts and attempts to resolve them based on the information found in the replication catalog in the Mobile Server Repository.

Compose from Oracle8*i*/9*i* Database

Composing data from the Oracle8*i*/9*i* database server can take just a few seconds or up to several hours, depending on the volume of changed data from the server. The Compose task is primarily responsible for populating the OUTQUEUE. The OUTQUEUE does not carry the data payload itself. Instead, it uses the primary key as a pointer to the base table. The OUTQUEUE basically has two primary keys—one for the ClientID and one for the data record. If your application updates 1,000 records on the server base tables, affecting 1000 users, it would create one million records in the OUTQUEUE (a thousand records for a thousand users is 1,000 X 1,000 = 1,000,000 records total).

Replication Software Architecture

Each of these three replication software components implements the two main subprocesses Apply and Compose, as depicted in here.

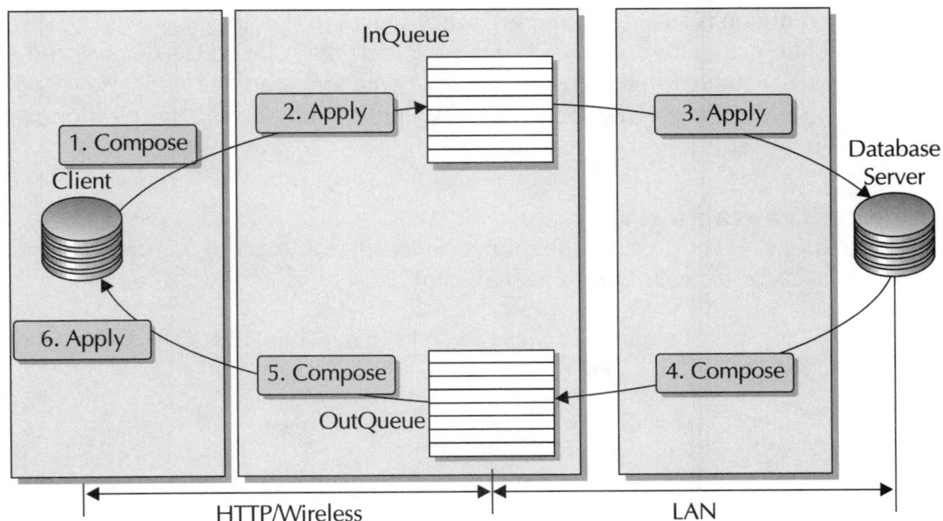

The Mobile Server is the middle tier between the mobile devices and the back-end Oracle database system. The Mobile Server applies the client records to the INQUEUE and composes the client data from the server database. Multiple Mobile Servers can be installed to improve scalability. Oracle9*i* Lite 5.0.1 contains a new software load-balancing feature that allows for the dynamic load-balancing of HTTP replication requests based on a least-used algorithm. Mobile Server will run on Microsoft NT 4.0, Windows 2000, or Sun Solaris.

Message Generator and Processor (MGP) is a multithreaded background process that is configurable. MGP periodically wakes up and starts processing records in the INQUEUE. The majority of the replication logic (conflict detection and resolution, call-outs, error reporting, and so on) is implemented by the MGP process, which runs either on the middle tier or directly on the database server. There can only be one MGP per replication system.

Mobile Sync is a small-footprint client for communications that runs on the client device. It is written in C++ for maximum performance. The client application invokes the Mobile Sync API that initiates the replication session as well as data upload and download. Mobile Sync also applies the data from the Mobile Server to the local Oracle Lite database.

Resolve Conflicts Using the Error Queue

For each publication item created, a separate and corresponding error queue is created. This queue is used to store transactions that fail due to unresolved conflicts. Your application can attempt to resolve the conflicts by using a DML Java-stored procedure, either by modifying the error queue data and then attempting to reapply the transaction via the Execute Transaction API call, or by purging the error queues using the Purge Transaction API call.

Execute Transaction API

You may use the ExecuteTransaction function to reexecute a transaction in the Mobile Server's error queue. Here's an example:

```
public static void ExecuteTransaction(String clientid, long tid)
   throws Throwable

Parameter Description:
  clientid - The Mobile Sync Client name
   tid - The Transaction ID. These are generated strings which appear
         in the error queue


Java Methods Example:

Consolidator.ExecuteTransaction("DAVIDL", 100002);
```

Purge Transaction

The PurgeTransaction function purges a transaction from the Mobile Server's error queue. Adding a DML procedure overrides the selection in the Conflict Resolution option.

Create a New Snapshot Using the Import Option

The preferred method for creating a snapshot uses the Import option. Because the tables you are using in your snapshots most often exist on your Oracle database server, it is very simple to import these table definitions to build the client snapshot. From the Snapshot panel, select the IMPORT button, and you will be asked to connect to the Oracle database instance where your table exists. This will launch a dialog that requests you to enter the name of the database or schema owner (in this example, "scott" with the password "tiger," as in Figure 9-3). You will also be required to specify a connect string in the following form:

```
Driver:Driver_source:driver_type:@your_mobileserver_name:
   your_port:your_Oracle_SID
```

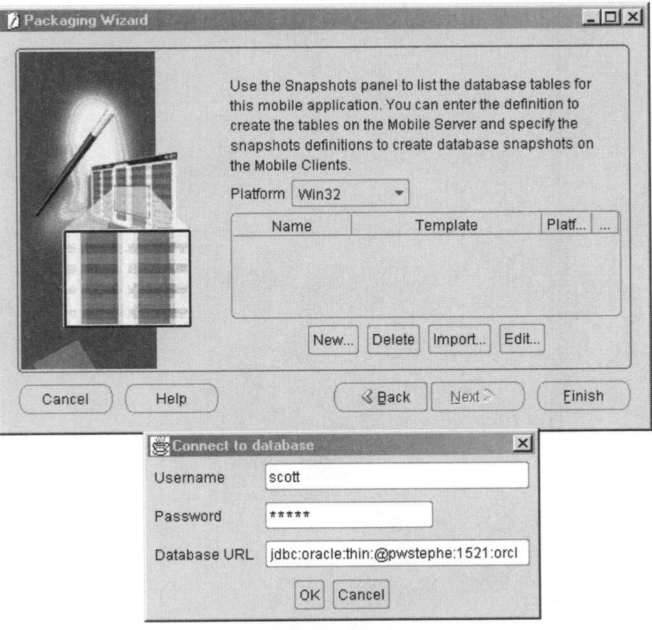

FIGURE 9-3. *An example of the Import snapshot*

Here's an example:

```
JDBC:Oracle:driver_type:@pwstephe:1521:orcl
```

NOTE
The colon after driver_type and before the @ sign is not a mistake.

When the connection is made, you will see a dialog that allows you to specify the table you wish to take a snapshot of (see Figure 9-4). In this dialog, only tables are visible. Views and other database objects are not visible or eligible for snapshots using the Packaging Wizard. If you need to create a snapshot for a view, you'll need to use the Consolidator API Java interface.

Consolidator API for Java

The Consolidator API Java interface exposes another way to programmatically create databases, populate tables, define users, create publications, change passwords, drop users, define publication items, and, as mentioned previously, define conflict detection and resolution. This is a complement to the Packaging Wizard, and in some cases you must use the Consolidator API. In future releases, much of the method functionality found in the API will be built into the Packaging Wizard.

NOTE
*The complete documentation for the Consolidator API can be found in HTML form in the Oracle9*i *Lite 5.0.1 documentation set.*

Tables
Select the tables you want to import
Schema: SCOTT
ACCOUNT
BONUS
DEPT
EMP
RECEIPT
SALGRADE
Add Close

FIGURE 9-4. *Table-selection dialog*

Sample Java Code Invoking the Consolidator API

The following sample code assumes that you have set up tables named a and b as well as a view named v_ab under a schema named test. You can use the mSQL utility to define the user, tables, and view, and you may want to insert a few rows of data to validate your test.

```
Owner/Schema: test
Table a
Column Name
C1 (PK)
C2
Table b
Column Name
C1
C4 (PK)
C5
View Definition:
CREATE VIEW v_ab AS
SELECT a.C1 as a_C1, C2, C4, C5
FROM a, b
WHERE a.C1 = b.C1
```

Once you have set up the sample database objects, you'll need to compile the Java program RepliView.java and produce a file named RepliView.class. When you invoke RepliView, you will need to pass two command-line arguments—the user name of the repository owner (usually mobileadmin, by default), and the repository user's password (probably mobileadmin) or whatever password you specified during installation. From a command window, enter the following:

```
RepliView mobileadmin mobileadmin
```

NOTE
You must have a Java 1.3 or greater Java runtime environment installed.

Besides the RepliView class, you will need the following code to:

1. Connect to the Mobile Server Repository.
2. Create a publication and publication items for tables a and b and the view v_ab.
3. Provide a "hint" for the primary key to the parent base table.
4. Create a mobile user named Bob.

5. Subscribe user Bob to the publication.
6. Instantiate the subscription.

NOTE
*You can use special text in a SQL statement to pass instructions, or hints, to the Oracle Lite database optimizer. The optimizer uses hints for choosing an execution plan. Hints are discussed in the Oracle9*i *Lite SQL Reference (Oracle Part No A95915-01).*

```
import java.sql.SQLException;
import java.sql.*;
import oracle.lite.sync.Consolidator;
import oracle.mobile.admin.ResourceManager;
public class RepliView
{
    static String SCHEMA;
    static String PASSWORD;
  public static void main(String argv[]) throws Throwable
  {
// Create multi table views replication support
    if(argv.length < 2)
    {
        System.out.println("Syntax: java RepliView <Schema>
            <Password>");
        return;
    }
    SCHEMA = argv[0];
    PASSWORD = argv[1];
// Connect to the Mobile Server Repository
    ResourceManager.openConnection(SCHEMA, PASSWORD);
    System.out.println("Crating Replication Environment for
       Multi Table Views ");
   try {
// Create Publication
   Consolidator.CreatePublication("T_KERNELL",
      Consolidator.OKPI_CREATOR_ID, "ViewDB.%s", null);
// Creates publication item for base table a
   Consolidator.CreatePublicationItem("pi_a", "test", "a",
      "F", "select * from a", null, null);
// Creates publication item for base table b
   Consolidator.CreatePublicationItem("pi_b", "test", "b",
      "F", "select * from b", null, null);
// Hints base table to use for updates
```

```
   Consolidator.ParentHint("test", "v_ab", "test", "a");
// Create publication item for view "v_ab"
   Consolidator.CreatePublicationItem("pi_v_ab", "test",
      "v_ab", "F", "select * from v_ab", null, null);
// Hints primary key for parent base table
   Consolidator.PrimaryKeyHint("v_ab", "a_C1", "test", "a",
      "C1");
// Hints primary key to join back to parent table from the logs.
// You only need to hint primary keys for non-parent base tables,
// when the primary key column is in the column list of the select
   statement.
   Consolidator.PrimaryKeyHint("v_ab", "C4", "test", "b", "C4");
// Need to add the publication item for the view to be replicated to
   the client.
// The other publication items (pi_a, pi_b) should not be added to
   the publication.
   Consolidator.AddPublicationItem("T_KERNELL", "pi_v_ab", null,
       null, "S", null, null);
// Create mobile user
   oracle.mobile.admin.ResourceManager.createUser("BOB","bob","BOB",
      "C");
// Create subscription for user BOB to Publication
   Consolidator.CreateSubscription("T_KERNELL", "BOB");
// Instantiate mobile user
   Consolidator.InstantiateSubscription("T_KERNELL", "BOB");
   } catch (Throwable e) {
   System.out.println("Multi table views replication
      supported generated.");
   System.out.println("Message : "+e.getMessage());
   e.printStackTrace();
   }
   ResourceManager.commitTransaction();
   ResourceManager.closeConnection();
   }
}
```

Distributed Design Considerations

The distributed environment in which offline applications exist differs quite a bit from the classic client/server model, where users are always connected by wired or wireless LANs and a single copy of the database is shared. The client/server environment also enforces a central set of business rules for the database or application, which allows developers to focus only on the user interface.

The computing demands of mobile users have led developers to focus on design considerations that must take into account the needs of disconnected users such as:

- The need for users to carry their data with them on portable handheld devices
- The need to access and exchange topical data with a central database that is often remote to mobile users
- The need to connect, using limited bandwidth networks, to the central database at irregular intervals (daily, weekly or monthly)
- The need for small-footprint infrastructures and applications that make small demands on devices with limited resources, such as telephone handsets, PDAs, and other embedded devices
- The need for applications and infrastructure software to be reliable, requiring minimal systems administration from nontechnical users

When mobile applications make a copy of data from a central database server, they become distributed systems. As such, any changes to the master site must be propagated to mobile users eventually. If the client users make changes to their copy of the database, the master site needs to reflect those changes. This exchange of data necessitates extensive checking to ensure data integrity.

When developers design distributed mobile applications, they need to understand the relationship of the data and the user. Fundamentally, three data models are available to mobile application designers:

- **Push (Data Dissemination)** Involves the dissemination of data from the Oracle back-end server to the mobile clients. An example would be price tables, product information, or customer profiles that are pushed from the server to the clients. This data may be partitioned by row or column. Usually the information is not updated on the client and there is no need for bidirectional synchronization. All updates to tables occur on the server.
- **Pull (Data Capture)** Mobile applications that are used for data capture utilize the pull technique to insert observations from the client devices to the back-end database server. This technique is used in field service applications, where field workers gather information from inspections. The completion of form-type data is inserted into the local client data store and

then pulled back to the server. In this situation, all updates to a table are carried out at the client, and typically the client data is partitioned such that each client updates its own subset of the master table.

- **Hybrid Applications** As you would guess, this model involves bidirectional synchronization of data between tables on the client and the server. This is the most complex form of synchronization. Conflicts occur when the same row is updated at two locations and can be handled by any of the standard methods of conflict detection. For more specialized cases, however, custom routines can be implemented. It is recommended that attempts be made to partition data such that each client updates its own subset of the master table.

As a developer, you should consider the following factors that influence application design:

- **Pay careful attention to the amount of data that is synchronized between clients and the server.** The synchronization payload is necessarily limited by the amount of available bandwidth. If a field worker is expecting to receive a large payload, such as a full table refresh of a catalog or price list, bandwidth latency will be a determining factor of the ultimate success of the synchronization and response time. Schema design should minimize payloads by exploiting partitioning and data subsetting.
- **Make every attempt to minimize and simplify conflict resolution.** Complex conflict detection and resolution will complicate business logic and can result in inconsistent results and poor performance. Keep conflict-resolution logic to a minimum.
- **Manage mobile applications at a minimal cost.** You need to offer centralized web-based interfaces that enable the simplified central management of users, applications, devices, and data. These management services must also easily monitor the application's synchronization load, troubleshoot any problems, and allow for simple deployment of new applications or data.
- **Application design tuning should occur before you begin the implementation of your application.** Before beginning your design, make sure you understand each of the Oracle Lite features and consider which ones best suit your requirements.

- **Work with your Oracle DBA to understand existing schema and how the Oracle master site can be tuned to accommodate your application.** Examine existing tables to see if it will be necessary to create snapshots for views or tables that do not have primary keys. Determine how tables can be partitioned to minimize replication payloads.
- **Consider the information need in relation to time.** Ask yourself these questions: Do users need immediate access to central server data? How quickly does data collected in the field need to be shared with central server?

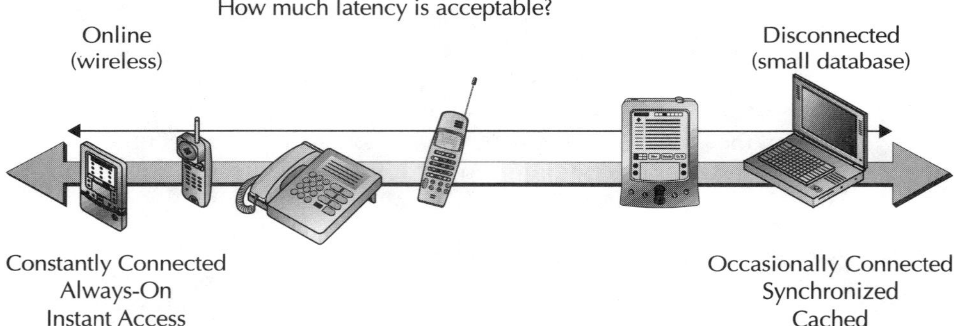

Branch Office

One of the big advantages Oracle Lite offers users is that it doesn't require local database administration. This is especially important for single users, but Branch Office extends this ease of administration to multiple users at a remote location. The Branch Office model extends access to a Branch Office database supporting up to 16 concurrent networked users (see the illustration on the next page). This is an excellent solution for distributed sites that have no technical resources, such as DBAs and system administrators, to maintain a more complicated environment.

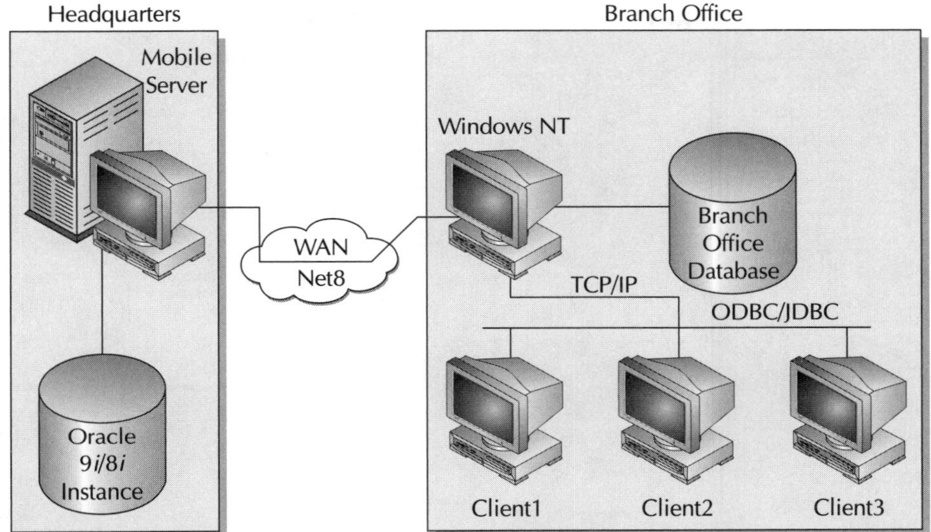

The Branch Office database synchronizes all data input by the clients with the back-end Oracle database at a company's headquarters.

The Branch Office clients connect to the Branch Office database using either ODBC or JDBC connections. The clients access and update the Branch Office database, which contains a subset of the corporate database located at company headquarters.

Each Branch Office database supports up to 16 concurrent networked users (the Branch Office *clients*), simultaneously. As shown in Figure 9-5, these clients do not require a connection to company headquarters, allowing them to work independently of the corporate database. Branch Office also supports up to 16 concurrent local ODBC/ JDBC connections to the Branch Office database. These local connections can be used for applications that perform background tasks such as reporting, making mass changes or updates, and bulk data loading. Multiple applications can run on each client.

Branch Office is administered remotely using a web-based interface known as Branch Office Control Center. Branch Office administrators use the Branch Office Control Center to monitor and configure Branch Office database services and users. Branch Office Control Center greatly simplifies administration, thus reducing costs by eliminating the need for a system administrator at each branch office.

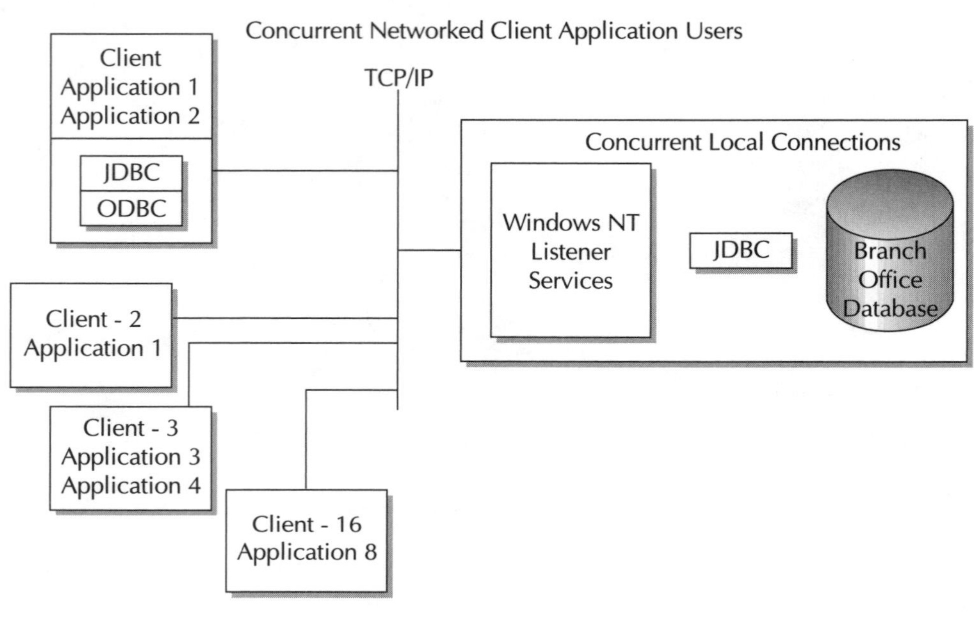

FIGURE 9-5. *Local clients accessing the Branch Office database*

Setting Up Branch Office

This section assumes you have already correctly installed an instance of Mobile Server and it is running correctly. This is a prerequisite for the installation of Branch Office. What follows is an overview of the steps that a Branch Office administrator would follow to install the Branch Office software at a remote location:

1. The Mobile Server administrator at company headquarters must create a Branch Office administrator account for each branch office and add these accounts to the Branch Administrators group. This administration task can be accomplished using the Mobile Server Control Center application by invoking the web-based interface found at http://*your_server_name*. At the prompt for authentication, log in as user "administrator" with the password "admin" as shown in the illustration.

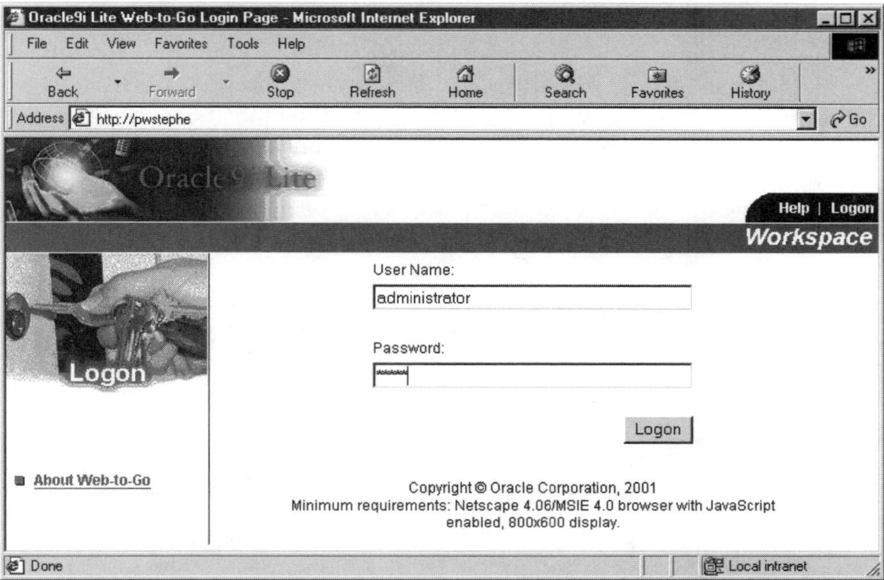

2. After the administrator logs in, he will launch the application called Control Center as shown in the illustration.

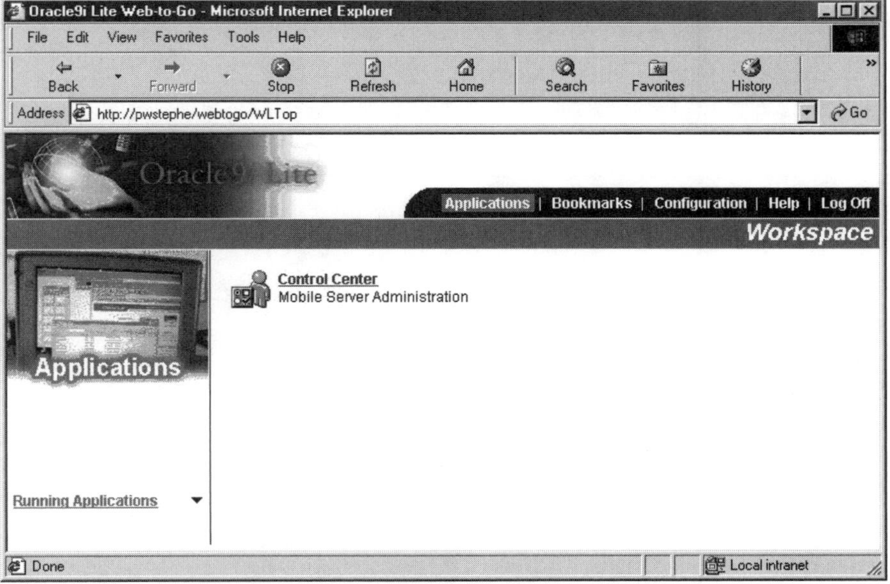

3. The administrator will select the Users tab on the left side of the workspace. Select Create User, to be presented with the dialog shown in the following illustration. The administrator will be required to supply the arbitrary full name as well as user name and password for the Branch Office Administrator. Administrators are required to set the system privilege for administrators by selecting Admin from the pull-down menu. Once all the options are completed, click Save, and a dialog will appear, indicating the success of the save operation.

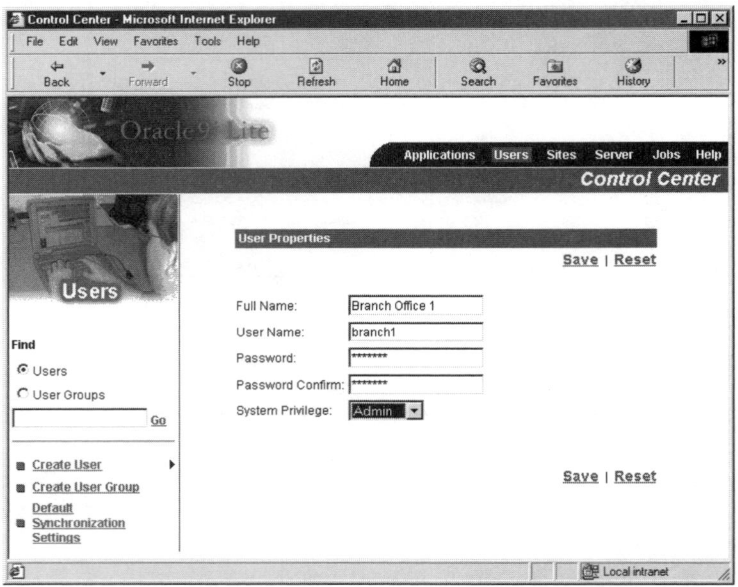

4. Once you have created a Branch Office administrator user, you must make this user part of the group of users called Branch Administrators. You must select Find User Groups by checking the User Groups option and clicking Go. You will see a list of users groups, as shown here.

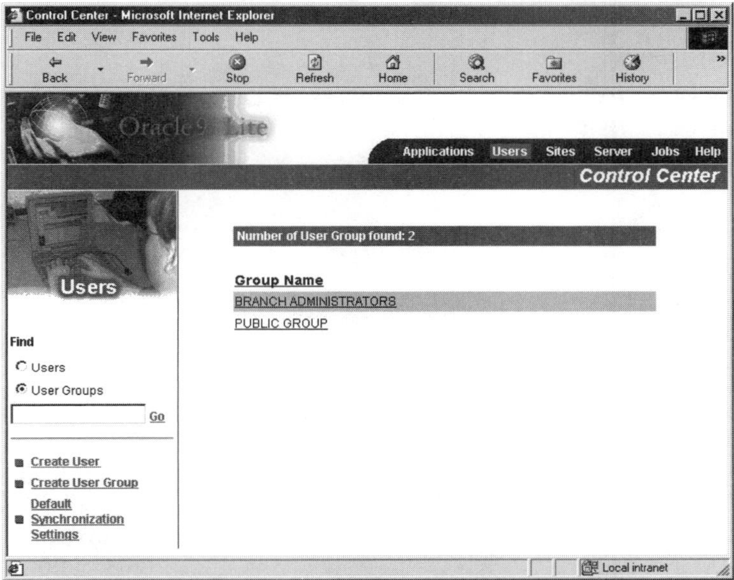

5. When you select the Branch Administrators group, you will enter the User Group Properties workspace. There, you will see all the users associated with the group and users who may be added to the group. Select the user Branch1 previously defined in the User workspace to add this new user to the group of users as shown in the following illustration. Once you have selected the Branch1 user, click Save. You will be notified that this user has been added to the user group.

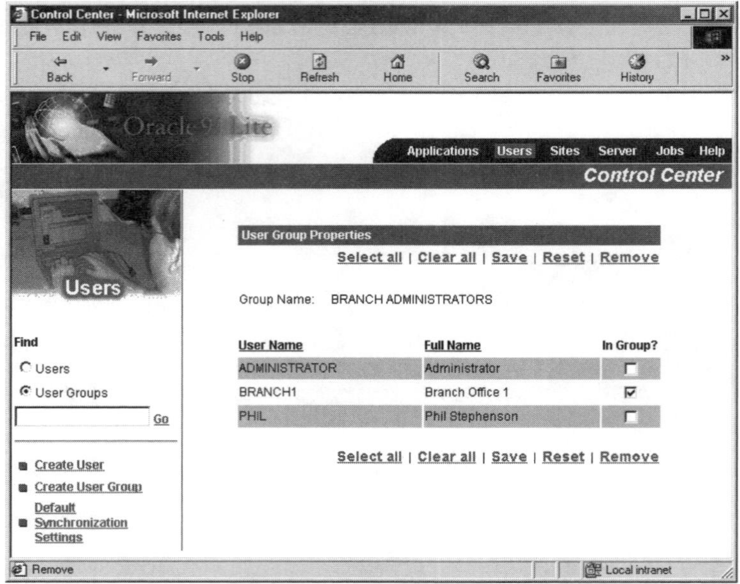

6. Next, you can download the Branch Office program from the Mobile Server. This is easily accomplished by pointing a browser at the Mobile Server using the URL http://your_mobile_server/ setup, as shown in the following illustration. Simply select the Branch Office option, and a Windows dialog will ask whether to open the setup.exe file from its current location or save the file to disk. Reply Save to Disk and specify a subdirectory, such as d:\temp. The Mobile Server will download setup.exe with all the files needed to build the Branch Office client.

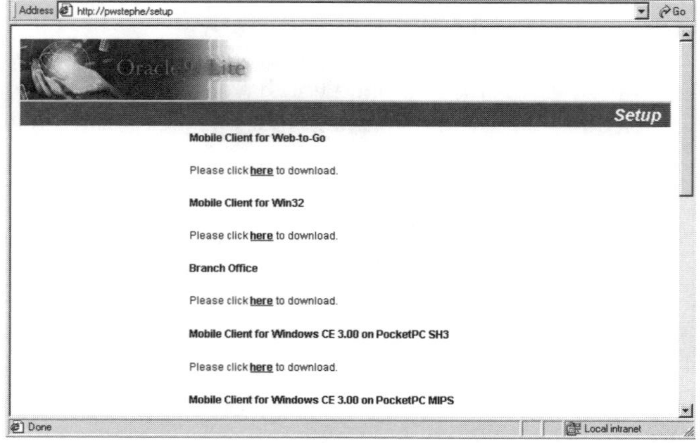

7. When setup.exe has been successfully downloaded, the Branch Office administrator will run that executable by double clicking *setup.exe*. It will install the Branch Office software on the Branch Office server. The administrator will be prompted for a directory name in which to install the software, or use the default directory as shown here.

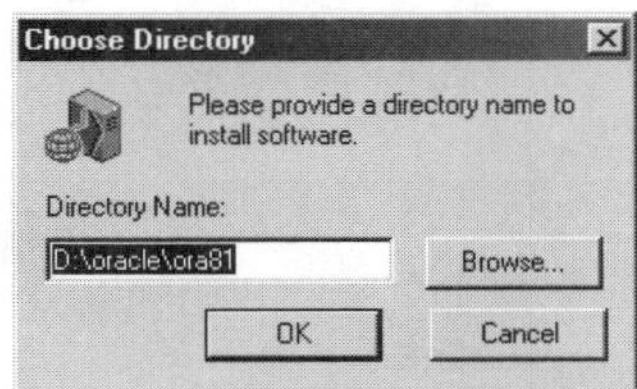

8. If another service is running on your target machine and it is using port 80, setup will prompt for a different port number as shown here.

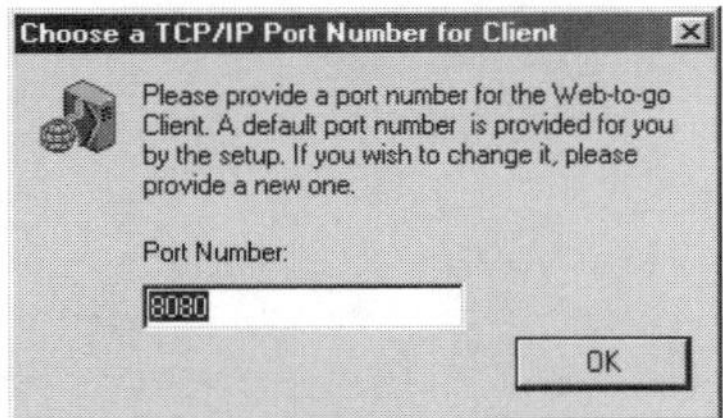

Observe that the setup program is creating directories, copying Web-to-Go client files (files named Web-to-Go are downloaded even though you are not installing the product Web-to-Go), initializing the environment, and installing the Miniserver NT service as shown in the following image. When the setup program is complete, it will launch the Miniserver, and your browser will be directed to a URL in the form of http://*your_server_name*:*your_port*.

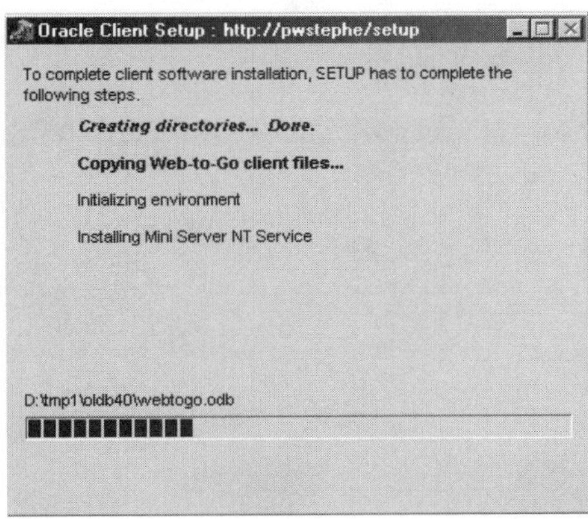

You now have the Branch Office software installed on the Branch Office client. As part of the installation, an NT service was created for the Branch Office web server. This server will be running, and you can test your Branch Office installation by invoking your local web server from the URL http://*your_local_host_name*.

When presented with the login panel as shown in the following illustration, the administrator defined on the Mobile Server can initiate a login using the user ID branch1 and the password branch1. This will give the administrator access to the Branch Office server.

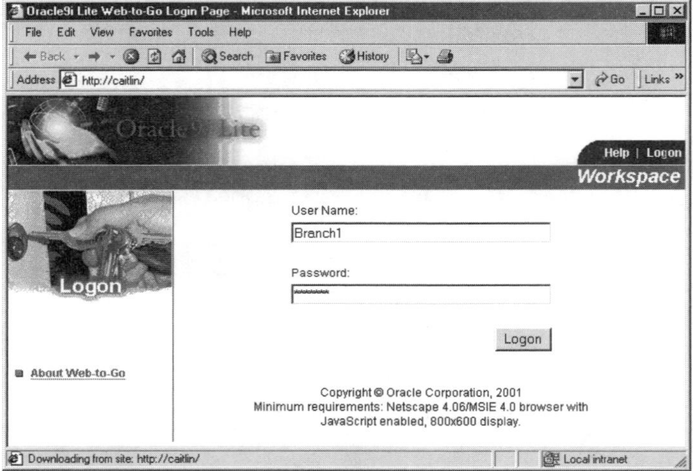

The first time the adminstrator logs in after the installation of the Branch Office software, he will receive positive confirmation that the installation of the Branch Office software was successful as shown here.

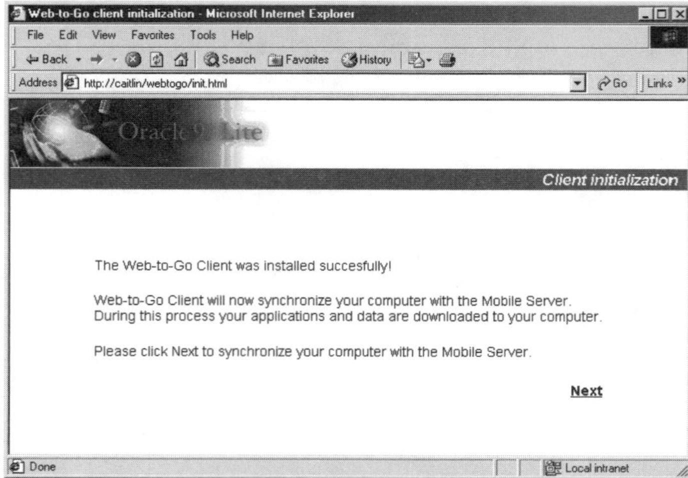

At this stage, the Web-to-Go Client will synchronize Branch Office with the Mobile Server that downloads client applications and data to the Branch Office server as shown here.

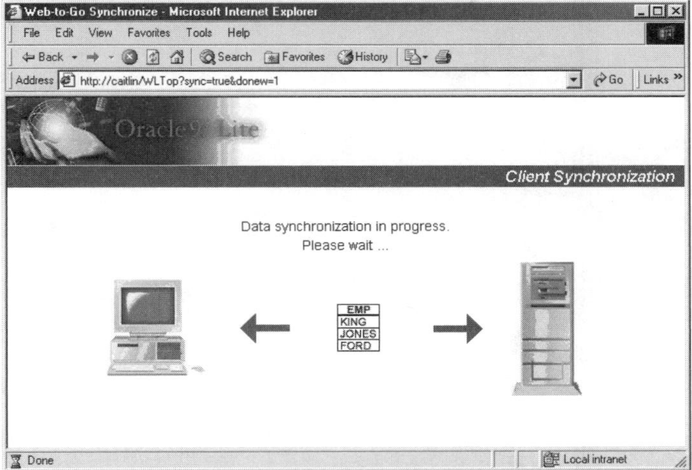

It may take a little while when applications and data are downloaded for the first time, but soon you will receive notification that this process has completed as shown here.

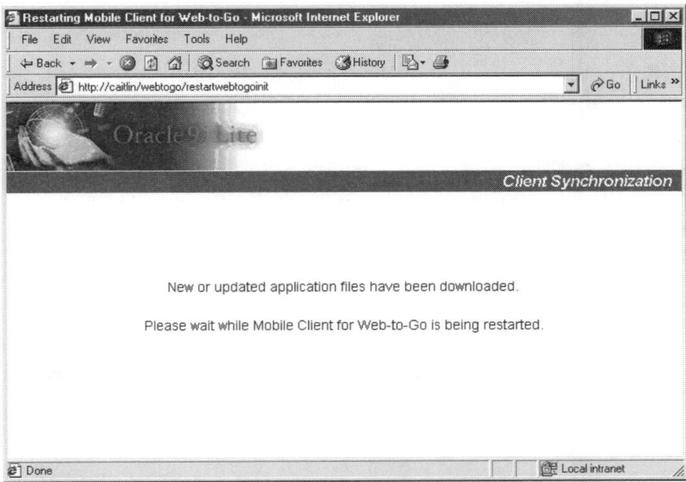

The Branch Office server will restart itself, and you will be prompted to log in using the Branch Office administrator user ID and password. When Branch Office is installed, the Branch Office Web Server service starts automatically at port 100, enabling Branch Office to allow client connections from the local area network.

Once you are again logged in as the Branch Office administrator, you will be able to launch the application Branch Office Control Center. The Branch Office Control Center allows you to manage applications and users of Branch Office and provides much of the same functionality of the Mobile Server Control Center, as shown here.

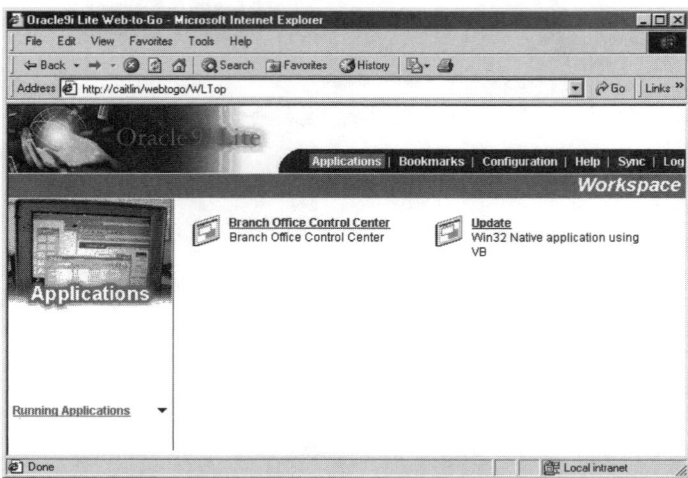

Installing the Branch Office Client Applications

With the applications and data residing on the Branch Office Server, end users in this branch may now install the appropriate client applications on their machines. Branch Office Client machines are those hosting the individual Branch Office Client applications, such as a cash register, an inventory application, or a warehouse-management application.

The Branch Office Client machines must be connected to the Branch Office database machine. To begin installation, the end user first points the Branch Office Client machine's browser to the Branch Office machine using the following URL:

```
http://<branch_office_machine>/public/download
```

This URL displays a list of all available applications that the end user can download.

Connecting Clients to the Branch Office Database Machine

The client applications connect with the Branch Office database machine over the branch office's LAN using TCP/IP. The client driver olcl2040.dll facilitates communication by connecting with the Branch Office Listener Service olsv2040.exe on the Branch Office database machine. The Listener Service establishes a separate connection thread, for every client connection, with the Branch Office database, branch.odb.

The Listener Service on the Branch Office database machine must be started before network connections can be established for concurrent Branch Office user client connections.

ODBC Connection

To make a client connection to a Branch Office database, you must first set up an ODBC data source name (DSN) using the ODBC Administrator. To connect an ODBC client application to a Branch Office database, an application must create a connection to the database. Here's an example:

```
"UID=SYSTEM;PWD=MANAGER;DSN=POLITECL;DATABASE=BRANCH"
```

Be sure to specify the keyword parameters and their formats are as follows:

- **UID** A valid database user
- **PWD** A valid password to the database
- **DSN** A data source name set up using ODBC Administrator
- **DATABASE** The name of the local Branch Office database residing in the OLDB40 folder in the *Oracle_Home* directory

Summary

This chapter reviewed how to build a Windows CE mobile application with Oracle9*i* Lite. We paid particular attention to performance tuning and scalability because they affect how well synchronization and replication of data take place with hundreds of concurrent mobile users. In order for you to gain a better understanding of these areas, we reviewed the synchronization and replication software architecture and discussed various means for optimizing performance.

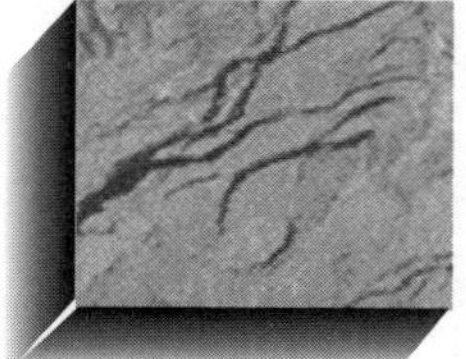

CHAPTER 10

Location-Based Services

Location-based services (LBS) comprise a basic tenet of delivering a sensible and compelling mobile user experience. Successful mobile applications are about delivering the right information and services, at the right time, at the right place. In this chapter, we review the LBS capabilities of Oracle9*i*AS Wireless by highlighting its core features as well as provide examples of how to leverage several important LBS modules. Specifically, we cover the following topics:

- Need for Location-Based Services
- Features of Oracle9*i*AS Wireless LBS
- System Architecture
- Oracle9*i*AS Wireless LBS Modules
- Module Configuration
- Sample Application

The Need for Location-Based Services

Through the combination of Internet communications with spatial technologies, location-based services are emerging from applications built with proprietary technologies in select vertical markets to packaged, scalable wireless Internet solutions that are applicable in many horizontal markets. And user groups are expanding rapidly to the mass market. You can discern location information services in every facet of your life, ranging from "Where is my overnight package?" to "How can my company optimize field services with mobile resources and assets?"

Location information is more than just real-time delivery of maps. Besides maps, which leverage visualization capability, other technologies include geocoding, spatial analysis, routing, directory, and geodemographics. Using these technologies, you can build dynamic applications and deliver a strategic differentiation to your wireless content and services.

For wireless carriers and their subscribers, wireless devices can continually transmit the location of the device, enabling location verification, store or friend finder, mapping, and related information services. On the enterprise side, delivering real-time, location-enhanced information can help automate and optimize the decision-making process for employees, partners, and suppliers. Through wireless field service solutions, for example, LBS can enable field staff to access the latest location information about company assets and customers, to capture and record this data in real time, and make just-in-time and location decisions in the field to improve performance and service delivery. We will discuss further the use of mobile technologies for real world applications in Chapter 16. For now, let's take a look at what Oracle offers in LBS capabilities.

Oracle9*i*AS Wireless LBS Features

Oracle9*i*AS Wireless helps you provide just-in-time, actionable LBS to users. The key is to create a positive experience for users and provide a means to integrate customer and corporate information necessary for e-business.

For starters, Oracle offers built-in capabilities, such as the Location Picker, to enhance user experience and service levels of any mobile applications built on top of it. That means carriers and developers alike can provision, manage, and integrate all their location services and information (such as customer location, coverage areas, and usage requirements) using standard relational database tables (Oracle8*i*/9*i* database).

For application developers, the same capability lends itself to integrating location with personalization and business processes. Wireless CRM and ERP applications are good examples, where you must have highly secure and scalable location services that can be easily incorporated into your applications.

Oracle9*i*AS Wireless enables rapid development of powerful and compelling services by providing prebuilt interfaces to LBS applications such as geocoding, mapping, and routing. You can pass data and content between these third-party applications and Oracle9*i*AS Wireless with only a few lines of Java or XML code. As a result, you can save a lot of time and effort by not having to build custom interfaces to each LBS vendor on your own. Commonly used examples include the Driving Directions and Mapping modules that ship with Oracle9*i*AS Wireless.

In addition, Oracle9*i*AS Wireless enables content syndication from online service providers via well-defined Java APIs. These, too, are now available in the form of modules, thus alleviating the need to write Java code. By combining LBS with SMS/Push technology, you can push syndicated and personalized information to wireless users (for example, local weather, news, traffic, and opt-in advertising) through the use of simple module calls. We will review how to use one of the location-based content services, Business Directory, later in this chapter.

Besides making LBS easier to build and deploy, Oracle offers a key differentiator in how these interfaces are tightly integrated with Oracle8*i*/9*i* and Oracle Spatial database (more on this later). Regardless of whether wireless carriers or business enterprises provision these services, they all share the need to provide highly capable, reliable location services to thousands and, sometimes, millions of users. Your applications must be able to handle these transactions and deliver services with no degradation in quality.

System Architecture

The LBS system architecture contains several pieces, including Oracle9*i*AS Wireless, Oracle8*i*/Oracle9*i*, Oracle Spatial, LBS providers (applications), and third-party online services and applications, as shown in Figure 10-1. The great thing about

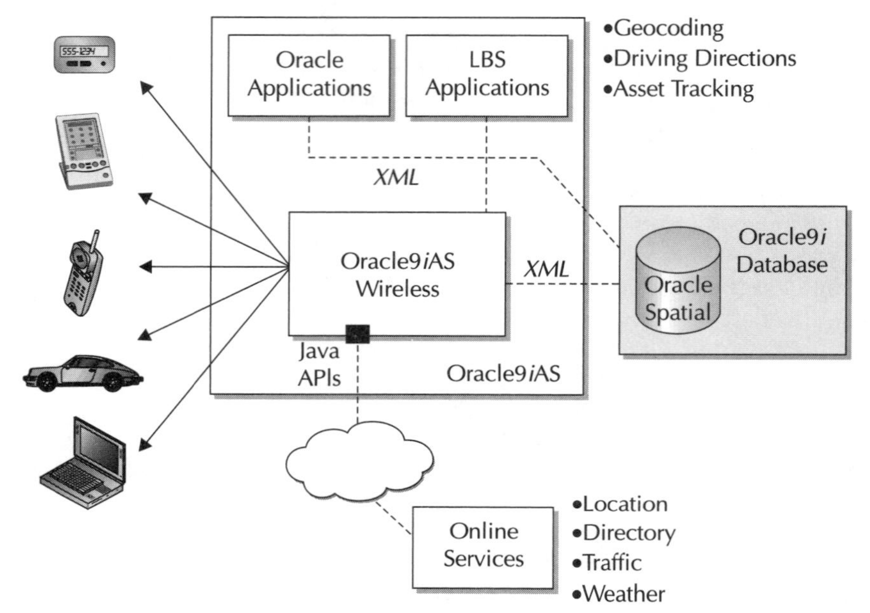

FIGURE 10-1. *Location-based services system architecture*

Oracle9*i*AS Wireless is its separation of application logic from location service access by always calling Java or PL/SQL APIs.

For example, an application developer can easily build a service to answer the questions: What is the physical location of a distress call, for emergency response purposes? Where were our service vehicles when they experienced delays in excess of 15 minutes? Features and performance requirements can be easily implemented and deployed with the Oracle9*i*AS Wireless framework. Let's look at these components:

- **Oracle9*i*AS Wireless** The key to LBS for Oracle9*i*AS Wireless is a set of APIs to ingest external location services—whether they're online services or LBS applications. The Java API enables application developers to conveniently access external service providers, and Oracle has made these LBS applications easy to use in the form of modules. Developers can quickly integrate location services with a wireless portal's front or back office applications.
- **Oracle9*i* Database** Oracle9*i* database and its unique spatial data server are proven technologies that can bring the scalability, security, integrity,

and recoverability required for mission-critical and highly scalable solutions. You can embed a geocoding server into the Java Virtual Machine (JVM) of Oracle9*i*, otherwise known as *Oracle9*i *Enterprise Java Engine* (EJE). According to Oracle, you can also embed a map-rendering and street-routing server into Oracle9*i* EJE, and utilizing Oracle9*i* Cache you can push out the compressed raster or live vector-rendering operations to wireless devices. The write capabilities to Oracle9*i* allow the user to create, move, and delete map objects.

- **Oracle Spatial** Oracle Spatial, now part of Oracle9*i*, allows you to store your own geographic or location objects in your own RDBMS and quickly serve them up in the form of maps to wireless devices. For mission-critical spatial data, Oracle Spatial provides spatial object type storage, SQL query, and fast spatial indexing. Also, it extends Oracle8*i*/9*i* to manage location data directly through a wide selection of spatial operators—all within an object-relational DBMS. New and upcoming features include version management, geoimage management, R-tree indexing, geocoding, linear referencing, and projection and coordinate system support.
- **LBS Applications** Third-party applications are offered by partner vendors that may provide Spatial Server access to spatial data stored in server-side databases. Mapping, for example, can be deployed as a servlet to take advantage of threading, fault tolerance, and load balancing in J2EE, while delegating service requests for driving directions or maps to the LBS applications. This Java component can run inside the same address space as the application server, thus eliminating context switching overhead and reducing network traffic. You can boost performance of your LBS application by tightly integrating it with Oracle8*i*/Oracle9*i*, including projection and coordination transformation, as well as via implementation of Oracle 8.1.7 Thick and Thick Bequeath JDBC drivers.
- **Third-Party Online Services and Applications** Syndication of online content and information services can be readily deployed through Java APIs that are built in for Oracle9*i*AS Wireless. As an application developer, you can write applications to invoke an online service the same way you would to implement LBS applications deployed within your firewall.

Oracle9*i*AS Wireless LBS Modules

Now we'll go into detail on four modules Oracle has created for you: Location Picker, Driving Directions, Business Directory, and Maps. Using these modules, you can build very compelling applications—whether they're location sensitive or location aware applications.

Location Picker

The Location Picker module enables users to pick and manage their frequently accessed locations. Using this module, a user can specify a location that can be used by another module, such as the Driving Directions module. This location can be the user's default location, the current location (if mobile positioning is enabled), a location mark selected by the user, a recent location used by the user, or a new location to be entered by the user.

Other location modules use the Location Picker to acquire location (or locations) from the user if the user does not have a "preferred" location or if the user specifically wants to change the location used for those modules. When used directly by the user, Location Picker provides management of the user's location marks and allows the user to set their "preferred" location, which is either the user's current location (when mobile positioning is available and on) or the user's default location marks.

You link to the Location Picker module using the following virtual URL:

```
omp://oracle/services/location/picker
```

The following table lists the input parameters that can be supplied to the Location Picker module. If none of the optional parameters are supplied, the module will ask for them once the service is invoked.

Parameter	Description	Value(s)	Notes
LOCATIONTITLE	The name of the location to be specified	Any string	Optional
LOCATIONQUALITY	The quality of the location to be specified	1 | 2 | 3 | 4 | 5 | 6 | 7 | 8 | 11	Optional
LOCATIONMASK	The mask used to specify which location fields will be available when a new location is entered	An integer derived by bitwise OR-ing together the integer values for all the location fields wanted	Optional
MOD	Used to specify a condition on the returned location	LM | unspecified	Optional

Here's an example of how location marks can be created. The preferred way is to use a web browser on a desktop PC to create them for later use on a mobile device. Here's how to use the wireless customization web tool to create a location mark:

1. Point your browser to http://oracle9iasw-server:port/customization.
2. Log in using your user name and password. Click the Location Marks tab after successful login. The LocationMark List screen appears (see Figure 10-2).
3. To create a new location mark, click the Create button. The Create LocationMark screen appears (see Figure 10-3). Fill in as much information as you possibly can so you will never have to enter the same information while on mobile devices that lack easy data-entry modality. Click the Create button after filling in all the necessary fields.
4. The newly created location mark (in this case, MyOffice SF) appears on your list now (see Figure 10-4 for how this appears on an MS PocketPC device). This location mark can now be used with the Driving Directions and Maps modules in the future. What's more, you can save new addresses as location marks from any mobile devices.

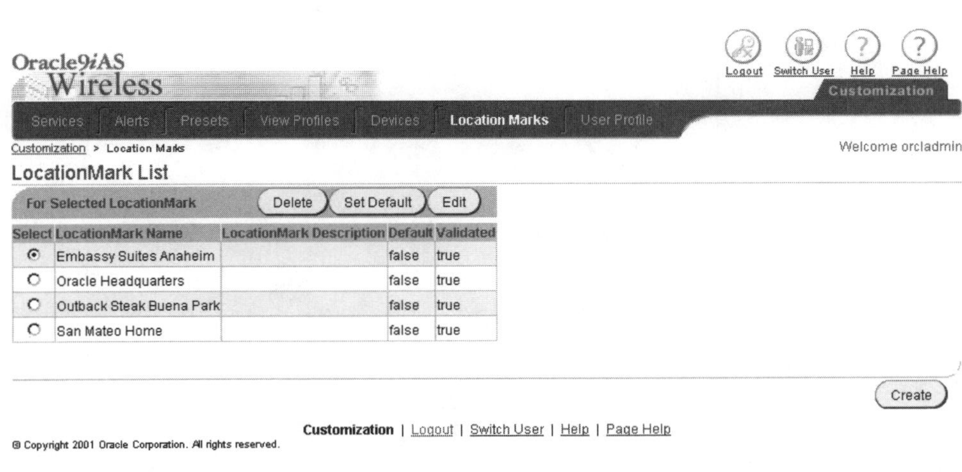

FIGURE 10-2. *LocationMark List screen*

Oracle9iAS Wireless

Logout Switch User Help Page Help

Customization

Services | Alerts | Presets | View Profiles | Devices | Location Marks | User Profile

Customization > Location Marks

Welcome orcladmin

Create LocationMark

* LocationMark Name	MyOffice SF
Description	
Label	
Company Name	MobileG Wireless
Address Line 1	2 Embarcadero Center
Address Line 2	
Address Last Line	
Block	
City	San Francisco
County	
State	CA
Postal Code	94111
Postal Code Ext	
Country	USA
Default	☐

☑ Validate this location mark

Location mark will be validated with geocoding process.

FIGURE 10-3. *Create LocationMark screen*

FIGURE 10-4. *Location marks on an MS PocketPC device*

Driving Directions

The Driving Directions module allows a mobile application to provide its users with driving directions between an originating address and a destination address. It links to the Location Picker module to enable users to select originating and destination addresses not provided by Driving Directions. The Driving Directions module also links with the Maps module for enhanced routing.

You link to the Driving Directions module using the following virtual URL:

```
omp://oracle/services/location/directions
```

The following table lists the input parameters that can be supplied to the Driving Directions module. If none of the optional parameters are supplied, the module will ask for them once the service is invoked.

Parameter	Description	Value(s)	Notes
OCOMPANYNAME	Company name of starting location	Any string	Optional
OADDRESS	Address first line of starting location	Any string	Optional
OADDRESS2	Address second line of starting location	Any string	Optional
OADDRESSLL	Address last line of starting location	Any string	Optional
OBLOCK	Block of starting location	Any string	Optional
OCITY	City of starting location	Any string	Optional
OCOUNTY	County of starting location	Any string	Optional
OSTATE	State of starting location	Any string	Optional
OZIP	Postal code of starting location	Any string	Optional
OZIPEXT	Postal code extension of starting location	Any string	Optional
OCOUNTRY	Country extension of starting location	Any string	Optional
OLAT	Latitude of starting location	Double	Optional
OLNG	Longitude of starting location	Double	Optional
ONAME	Name of starting location	Any string	Optional

Parameter	Description	Value(s)	Notes
DCOMPANYNAME	Company name of destination location	Any string	Optional
DADDRESS	Address first line of destination location	Any string	Optional
DADDRESS2	Address second line of destination location	Any string	Optional
DADDRESSLL	Address last line of destination location	Any string	Optional
DBLOCK	Block of destination location	Any string	Optional
DCITY	City of destination location	Any string	Optional
DCOUNTY	County of destination location	Any string	Optional
DSTATE	State of destination location	Any string	Optional
DZIP	Postal code of destination location	Any string	Optional
DZIPEXT	Postal code extension of destination location	Any string	Optional
DCOUNTRY	Country extension of destination location	Any string	Optional
DLAT	Latitude of destination location	Double	Optional
DLNG	Longitude of destination location	Double	Optional
DNAME	Name of destination location	Any string	Optional

Here's an example of how the Driving Directions module can be called:

1. Point your browser to http://oracle9iasw-server:port/ptg/rm and log in. Select the Location folder on your device. Pick the Driving Directions service. The starting location screen appears.
2. Select as the starting location the location mark MyOffice SF. The selection for the destination location appears (see Figure 10-5).
3. Select as the destination location the location mark Oracle Headquarters. Once the destination location is chosen, the driving directions from the starting location to the destination location appear (see Figure 10-6).
4. Two powerful features of the Driving Directions service are the Reverse Direction and Maps services. Now that you have arrived at your destination, you need directions on how to return. You can always backtrack, but there

FIGURE 10-5. *Driving directions using location marks*

are many one-way streets in metropolitan cities such as San Francisco, so this strategy does not always work! Tap the Rev button to automatically generate the reverse directions (see Figure 10-6). The other feature is the Map service. You may want a detailed map (zoom-in and zoom-out features are also available) on either your starting location or destination location. Just tap the From or To buttons, and the map is automatically generated and displayed. You can then zoom in or zoom out, as appropriate.

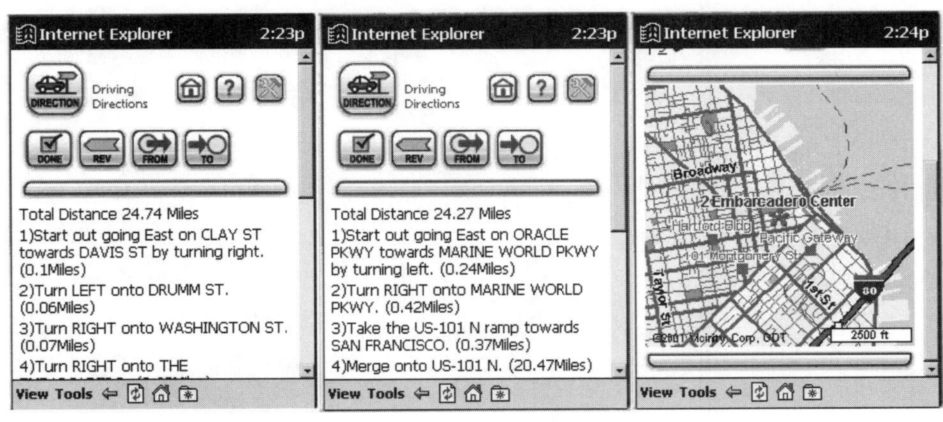

FIGURE 10-6. *Maps and reverse directions*

Business Directory

The Business Directory module provides users with a complete business directory. This module provides a Yellow Pages–type interface to look for the addresses and phone numbers of registered businesses within a given radius. It has search capabilities for business names and categories. Browsing through categories is also enabled. If no location parameters are passed to this module, the location module is invoked to obtain location data for the search.

You link to the Business Directory module using the following virtual URL:

```
omp://oracle/services/location/bizdir
```

The following table lists the input parameters that can be supplied to the Business Directory module. If none of the optional parameters are supplied, the module will ask for them once the service is invoked, or you can browse through the various categories.

Parameter	Description	Value(s)	Notes
PH	Phrase to search for	Any string	Optional
FC	Full category of the business	Any string	Optional
CN	Company name	Any string	Optional
FL	Address first line	Any string	Optional
SL	Address second line	Any string	Optional
LL	Address last line	Any string	Optional
BL	Block	Any string	Optional
CI	City	Any string	Optional
CT	County	Any string	Optional
ST	State	Any string	Optional
PC	Postal code	Any string	Optional
PCE	Postal code extension	Any string	Optional
CO	Country	Any string	Optional
LT	Latitude	Double	Optional
LN	Longitude	Double	Optional
N	Name	Any string	Optional

Here's an example of how the Business Directory module can be called:

1. Point your browser to http://oracle9iasw-server:port/ptg/rm and log in. Select the Location folder on your device. Pick the Business Directory service. The Business Directory category screen appears (see Figure 10-7).
2. Select the Automotive category. The Business Directory subcategory screen appears.
3. Select the Gas Stations subcategory. You will be taken to the Location Picker screen, where you can either choose one of your location marks (predefined or most recently used) or enter a new location (by tapping the New button). Choose the Oracle Headquarters location mark. If a business is found, it will appear on the screen. If not, you will get a message indicating no matches (see Figure 10-8).
4. You can also use the search box to look for a business by name or category.

Maps

The Maps module provides broad and detailed maps for a given location as well as supports map tiling and image map transformation for different devices. This module integrates with the Driving Directions module.

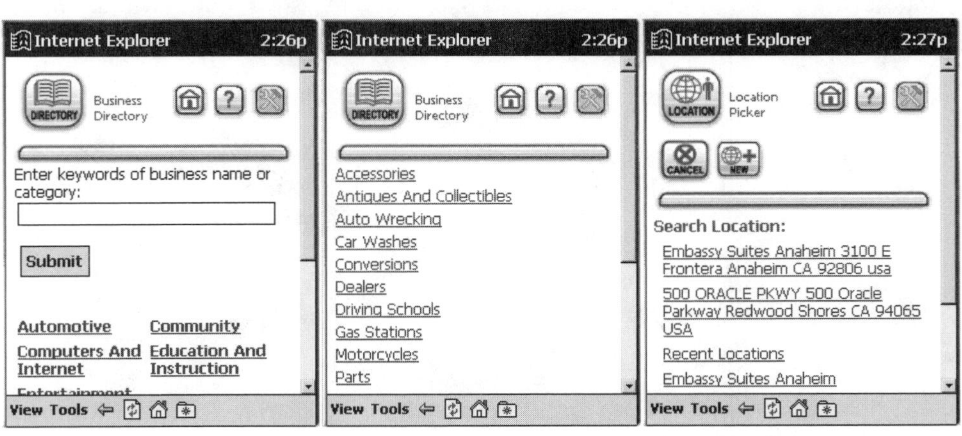

FIGURE 10-7. *Business Directory category browsing*

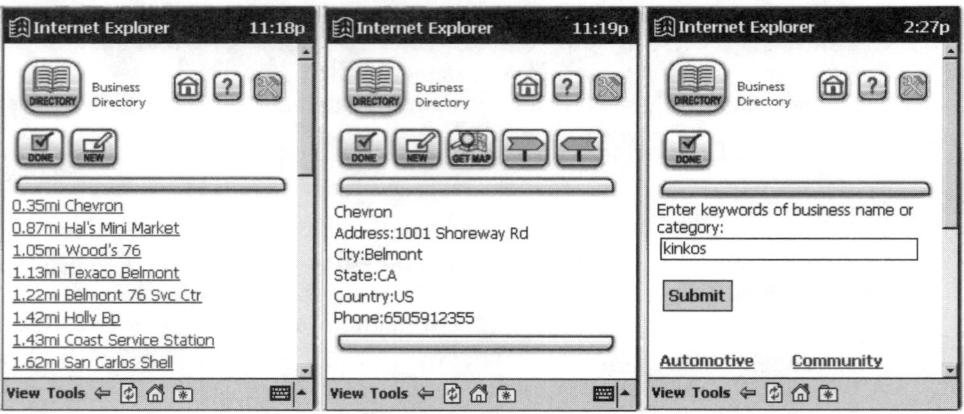

FIGURE 10-8. *Business information*

You link to the Maps module using the following virtual URL:

```
omp://oracle/services/location/maps
```

The following table lists the input parameters that can be supplied to the Maps module. If none of the optional parameters are supplied, the module will ask for them once the service is invoked.

Parameter	Description	Value(s)	Notes
CN	Company name	Any string	Optional
FL	Address first line	Any string	Optional
SL	Address second line	Any string	Optional
LL	Address last line	Any string	Optional
BL	Block	Any string	Optional
CI	City	Any string	Optional
CT	County	Any string	Optional
ST	State	Any string	Optional
PC	Postal code	Any string	Optional

Parameter	Description	Value(s)	Notes
PCE	Postal code extension	Any string	Optional
CO	Country	Any string	Optional
LT	Latitude	Double	Optional
LN	Longitude	Double	Optional
N	Name	Any string	Optional
LMN	Location mark name	Any string	Optional
STATUS	Status of the module call	ok I cancelled	Optional

Here's an example of how the Maps module can be called:

1. Point your browser to http://oracle9iasw-server:port/ptg/rm and log in. Select the Location folder on your device. Pick the Map service. The Location Picker is called and a list of location marks is presented (see Figure 10-9).
2. Tap Embassy Suites Anaheim or any of the location marks. The map is served to mobile device. You can tap the zoom-in and zoom-out icons to get more or fewer details. Tap the zoom-in icon a couple of times to get full details.
3. If you want to generate a map for a new location, tap the New button and enter the full address. The map will be generated and displayed on your mobile device, if found.

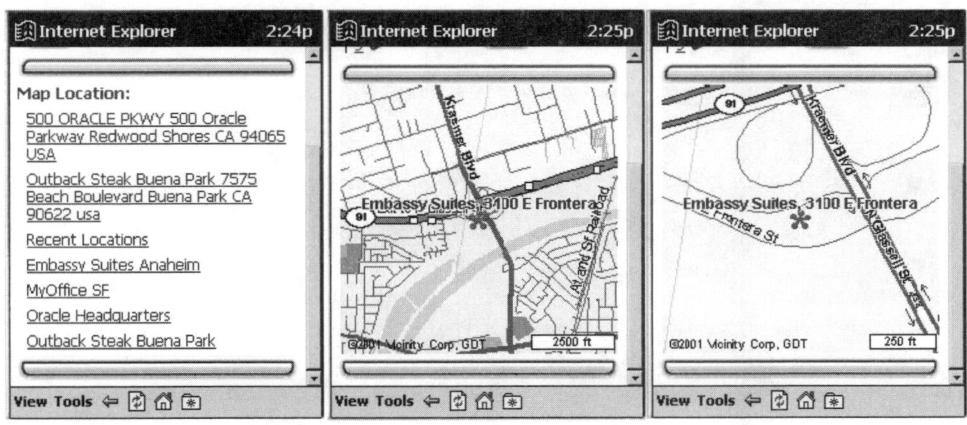

FIGURE 10-9. *Maps module usage*

Module Configuration

It is noteworthy that the LBS modules shipped in Oracle9*i*AS Wireless Release 2 run "out of the box" without additional configuration. We will show you how to get to these configuration pages using the web-based wireless tools. However, the tasks of creating and integrating custom LBS modules are beyond the scope of this book.

The core computation for location services is generally performed at an external provider web server. The external provider might be accessed over the Internet or via other means of communication, or the provider might be local. The Oracle9*i*AS Wireless Location Application Components API performs the communication and adaptation of results in a unified framework so that users are generally not aware of which provider is supplying a particular service.

To access and see what service providers are included on the available modules, and to learn more about the logic behind their usage, follow these steps:

1. Point your browser to http://oracle9iasw-server:port/webtool/login.uix and log in. Click the Site tab from the System Manager web tool. Under the Administration section, click the Location Services hyperlink. You are now presented with the Basic Configuration screen (see Figure 10-10).

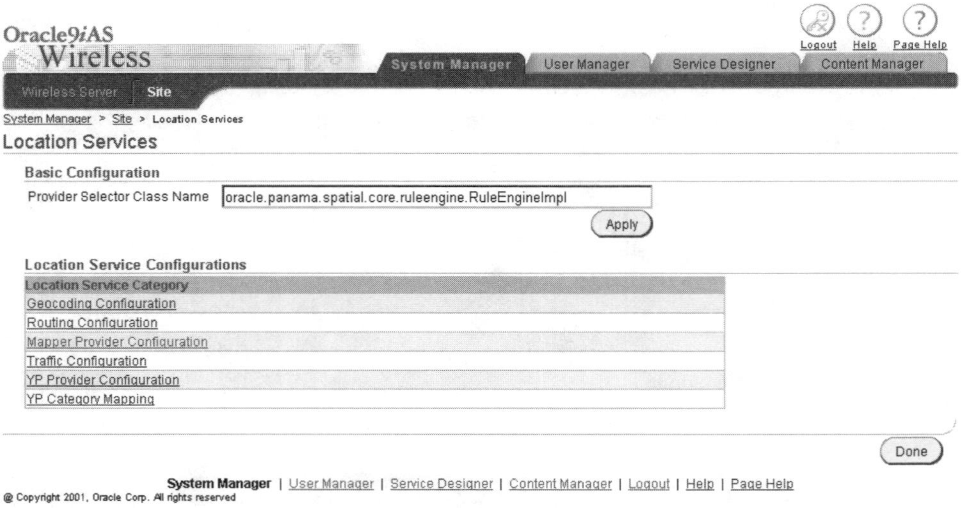

FIGURE 10-10. *LBS Basic Configuration screen*

2. Clicking any of the hyperlinks will take you into the Provider Configuration screen. For example, with the Maps module, the service providers listed include Vicinity, MapQuest, and Webraska (see Figure 10-11). Having multiple providers increases the reliability of the service.

3. You can add or delete service providers from here.

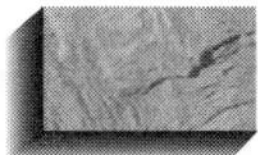

NOTE
The service providers are listed in their preferential order. The default implementation is to try each service provider until one succeeds.

Sample Application

We will now go into a simple but very practical location-based service example. We will design a store locator for Steakhouse Restaurant in California, USA. Here are some of the features of this service:

- Find a local restaurant and get its operating hours
- Get driving directions to and from the selected restaurant
- Get a map of the restaurant area

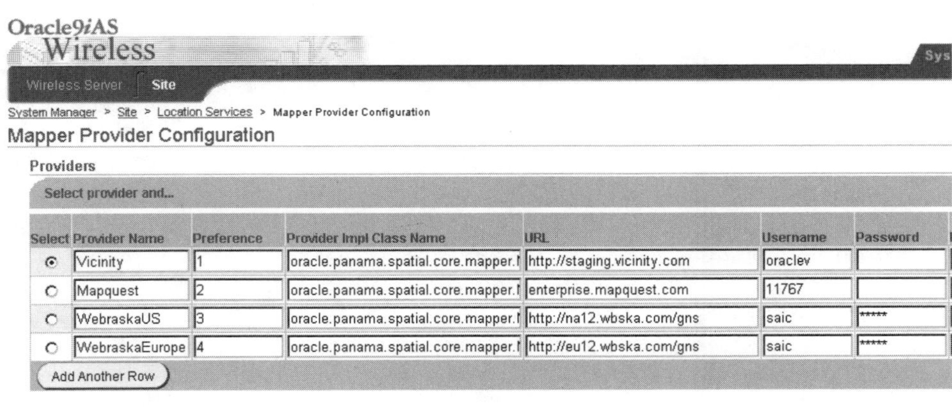

FIGURE 10-11. *Maps service providers*

To create and run this sample application, create two JSP files—*storeloc.jsp* and *info.jsp*—and place them in the following directory (see Chapter 4 for full details):

```
$ORACLE9iASW_INSTALL\wireless\j2ee\applications\examples\examples-web\book
```

Here's the code listing for storeloc.jsp:

```
<%@ page contentType="text/xml; charset=UTF-8" session="false"
language="java" import="java.util.*, java.text.*, java.net.*, java.sql.*"
%>
<%!
public String getQueryString( String queryString )
{
if ( queryString == null )
   return "";
return queryString;
}
%>
<%
String URL_startIndex = request.getParameter("startIndex");
if (URL_startIndex == null) {
   URL_startIndex = "1";
}
int i_StartIndex = Integer.parseInt(URL_startIndex);
int i_NextIndex = i_StartIndex + 9;
Class.forName("sun.jdbc.odbc.JdbcOdbcDriver");
String url_outback = "jdbc:odbc:storelocator";
String query_outback = "SELECT City+', '+State AS Label,ID
   FROM outback ORDER BY City";
Connection  conn_outback = DriverManager.getConnection(url_outback, "", "");
Statement stmt_outback = conn_outback.createStatement
   (ResultSet.TYPE_SCROLL_SENSITIVE, ResultSet.CONCUR_READ_ONLY);
ResultSet rset_outback = stmt_outback.executeQuery (query_outback);
%>
<SimpleResult>
   <SimpleContainer>
   <SimpleImage src="http://dellcomputer:9000/examples/book/outback"
   addImageExtension="yes" available="gif jpg png wbmp"
   alt="steakhouse"></SimpleImage>
   <SimpleBreak></SimpleBreak>
   <SimpleMenu>
      <SimpleTitle color="#ff0000" size="2" font="verdana">
      Select a Restaurant:
      </SimpleTitle>
<%
int accKeyIndex = 1;
int _outback_ColIndex = i_StartIndex;
rset_outback.last();
int _outback_numRows = rset_outback.getRow();
int i_NumRecs = _outback_numRows;
rset_outback.absolute(i_StartIndex);
```

```
for (int i = i_StartIndex; i <= i_StartIndex + 8; ++i)
{
   int CurrRow = rset_outback.getRow();
   try
   {
   rset_outback.getString(1);
   rset_outback.beforeFirst();
   rset_outback.absolute(CurrRow);
   }
   catch ( Exception eee )
   {
   break;
   }
%>
      <SimpleMenuItem target="info.jsp?id=
      <%=URLEncoder.encode(getQueryString(
      rset_outback.getString("ID")))%>"
      wrapmode="nowrap" accesskey="<%=accKeyIndex%>">
      <%=getQueryString( rset_outback.getString("Label") )%>
      </SimpleMenuItem>
<%
accKeyIndex = accKeyIndex + 1;
_outback_ColIndex = _outback_ColIndex + 1;
if (_outback_ColIndex > 1) {
   _outback_ColIndex = 1;
%>
<%
}
rset_outback.next();
}
%>
   </SimpleMenu>
<%
int i_PrevIndex = i_StartIndex - 9;
if (i_PrevIndex > 0) {
%>
   <SimpleHref target="storeloc.jsp?startIndex=<%=i_PrevIndex%>"
      src="http://dellcomputer:9000/examples/book/prev"
      addImageExtension="yes" available="gif jpg"
      label="Prev"></SimpleHref>
<%
}
%>
<%
if (i_NextIndex < i_NumRecs) {
%>
   <SimpleHref target="storeloc.jsp?startIndex=<%=i_NextIndex%>"
      src="http://dellcomputer:9000/examples/book/next"
      addImageExtension="yes" available="gif jpg"
      label="Next"></SimpleHref>
<%
```

```
}
%>
<%
rset_outback.close();
stmt_outback.close();
conn_outback.close();
%>
   </SimpleContainer>
</SimpleResult>
```

Here's the code listing for info.jsp:

```
<%@ page contentType="text/xml; charset=UTF-8" session="false"
language="java" import="java.util.*, java.text.*, java.net.*, java.sql.*"
%>
<%!
public String getQueryString( String queryString )
{
if ( queryString == null )
   return "";
return queryString;
}
%>
<%
String URL_ID = request.getParameter("id");
if (URL_ID == null) {
   URL_ID = "1";
}
int i_ID = Integer.parseInt(URL_ID);
Class.forName("sun.jdbc.odbc.JdbcOdbcDriver");
String url_outback = "jdbc:odbc:storelocator";
String query_outback = "SELECT * FROM outback WHERE ID = " + i_ID + "";
Connection  conn_outback = DriverManager.getConnection(url_outback, "", "");
Statement stmt_outback = conn_outback.createStatement
   (ResultSet.TYPE_SCROLL_SENSITIVE, ResultSet.CONCUR_READ_ONLY);
ResultSet rset_outback = stmt_outback.executeQuery (query_outback);
%>
<SimpleResult>
   <SimpleContainer>
   <SimpleImage src="http://dellcomputer:9000/examples/book/outback"
      addImageExtension="yes" available="gif jpg png wbmp"
      alt="steakhouse"></SimpleImage>
   <SimpleBreak></SimpleBreak>
   <SimpleText>
      <SimpleTitle color="#ff0000" size="2" font="verdana">
      Restaurant Info:</SimpleTitle>
<%
rset_outback.first();
%>
      <SimpleTextItem><%=getQueryString(
```

```
        rset_outback.getString("Address"))%>
        </SimpleTextItem>
        <SimpleTextItem><%=getQueryString(rset_outback.getString("City"))%>,
        <%=getQueryString(rset_outback.getString("State"))%>
        <%=getQueryString(rset_outback.getString("Zip"))%>
        </SimpleTextItem>
        <SimpleTextItem><%=getQueryString(
        rset_outback.getString("Phone"))%></SimpleTextItem>
        <SimpleTextItem><%=getQueryString(
        rset_outback.getString("HoursofOperation"))%>
        </SimpleTextItem>
    </SimpleText>
<%
rset_outback.first();
%>
    <SimpleHref target="omp://oracle/services/location/maps?FL=
        <%=URLEncoder.encode(getQueryString(
        rset_outback.getString("Address")))%>&amp;CI=
        <%=URLEncoder.encode(getQueryString(
        rset_outback.getString("City")))%>&amp;ST=
        <%=getQueryString( rset_outback.getString("State"))%>&amp;PC=
        <%=getQueryString( rset_outback.getString("Zip"))%>"
        src="http://dellcomputer:9000/ptg/images/location/maps/maps_small"
        addImageExtension="yes" available="gif wbmp" label="Map">Map
    </SimpleHref>
<%
rset_outback.first();
%>
    <SimpleHref target="omp://oracle/services/location/directions?DADDRESS=
    <%=URLEncoder.encode(getQueryString(rset_outback.getString("Address")))
    %>
    &amp;DCITY=
    <%=URLEncoder.encode(getQueryString(rset_outback.getString("City")))%>
    &amp;DSTATE=
    <%=getQueryString(rset_outback.getString("State"))%>&amp;DZIP=<
    %=getQueryString(rset_outback.getString("Zip"))%>"
    src="http://localhost:9000/ptg/images/location/router/direction_small"
    addImageExtension="yes" available="gif wbmp"
    label="Directions">Directions
    </SimpleHref>
    <SimpleBreak></SimpleBreak>
    <SimpleImage src="http://dellcomputer:9000/examples/book/charge_cards"
        addImageExtension="yes" available="gif jpg" alt="visa mc amex">
    </SimpleImage>
<%
rset_outback.close();
stmt_outback.close();
conn_outback.close();
%>
    </SimpleContainer>
</SimpleResult>
```

In Chapter 4, we use an Oracle database as the dynamic content feeder to the mobile application. In this example, we use an ODBC database. As you can see in the preceding code listings, it is rather straightforward to access the database using the Sun ODBC-JDBC bridge driver. We will illustrate this service using our sample user, testuser, and the MS PocketPC browser. Refer to Chapter 4 for complete details on creating this master service via the HTTP Adapter and Service Designer. Be sure to use the same user and user group settings and to publish the service to the same test group.

Here are a few items of interest:

- The URL parameter StartIndex is used to determine the starting index for our database query (storeloc.jsp). We chose to display only nine items at a time because that matches the numeric key shortcuts on cellular phones. Presentation style will be covered in Chapter 14.
- The Sun ODBC-JDBC bridge driver (sun.jdbc.odbc.JdbcOdbcDriver) is used to access the ODBC database for the store locations.
- The source URLs for images have to be absolute URLs instead of relative URLs. Oracle may change this to handle relative URLs in the future.
- We have to reset the query result set pointer (rset_outback.first) because we are re-reading the same field (column) from the result set (row) many times in our code in order to prefill all the input parameters to the Driving Directions and Maps modules (info.jsp).

Once the store locator service is created and published for the testuser account, we can check out our newly created service. Here are the steps to follow:

1. Point your browser to http://oracle9iasw-server:port/ptg/rm and log in as testuser. Select the TestService folder on your device. Pick the StoreLocatorService link (see Figure 10-12). The store locator application (storeloc.jsp) is invoked.
2. Tap the Next button. The next nine locations are shown. Select the Dublin, CA location. The store locator application (info.jsp) is again invoked. Information about that particular restaurant is shown, including address, operating hours, credit cards accepted, phone number, driving directions, and maps (see Figure 10-13). Note that we linked to the Driving Directions and Maps modules provided by Oracle9*i*AS Wireless Release 2. Tap the Map icon or link as well as the Directions icon or link and see how easily and seamlessly these location modules are tightly integrated into our store locator service (see Figure 10-14).

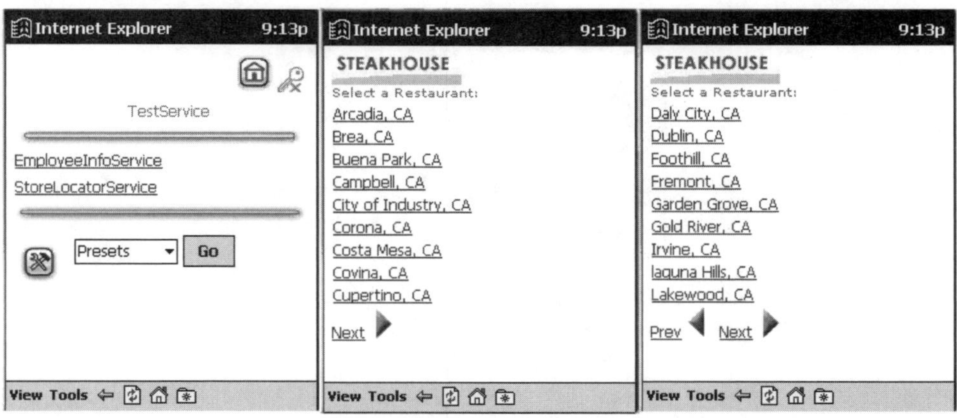

FIGURE 10-12. *Store locator service selections*

Note that the store locator service passes the destination location to the Driving Directions module so that the user only has to pick the starting location, thereby saving the user from having to enter any of that information. The same is done for the link to the Maps module.

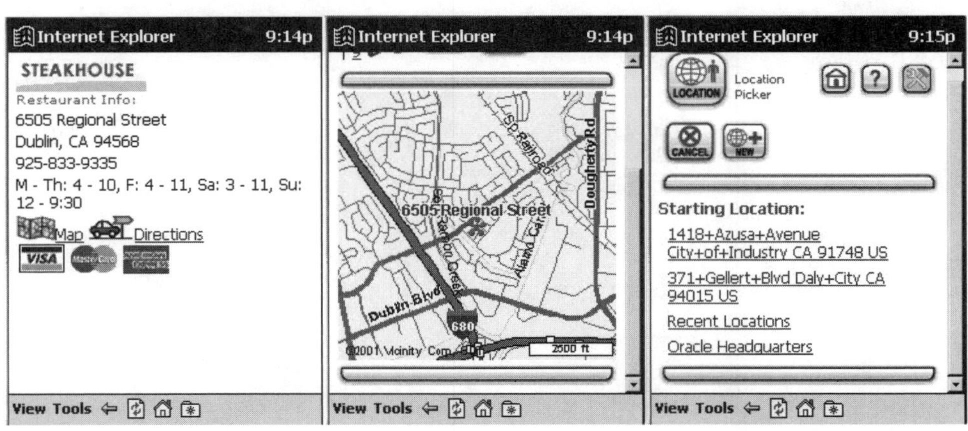

FIGURE 10-13. *Store locator service map and directions*

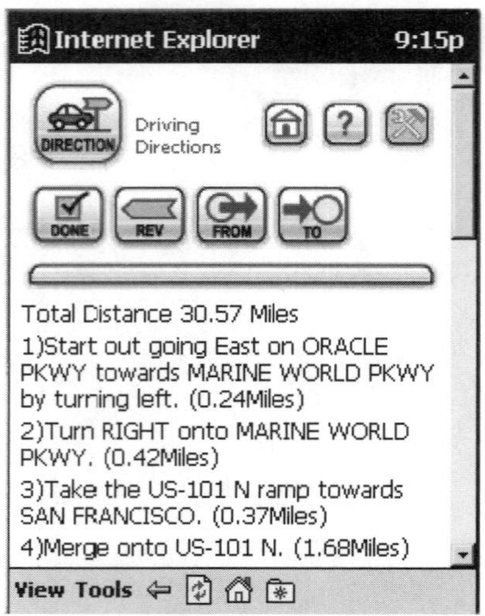

FIGURE 10-14. *Complete driving directions to restaurant*

Summary

With this chapter, you gained insights into how location-based services can be built into your applications easily and how various components fit together among Oracle9*i*AS Wireless, Oracle8*i*/9*i* database, Oracle Spatial, third-party online services, and LBS applications. By now you are well equipped to add location-based features to your mobile applications.

CHAPTER 11

Mobile PIM and E-Mail

-mail is one of the most frequently requested wireless applications. In recent years, enterprises have relied on e-mail as one of their primary channels of business correspondence. Personal information management (PIM), on the other hand, has become popular because enterprises and workgroups have found it useful to manage and coordinate their time and schedules. Together, e-mail and PIM are proven to increase productivity. Indeed, mobile workers and executives are increasingly looking for information delivered to them anytime, anywhere, thus gaining independence of physical location. In this chapter, we introduce the Mobile Personal Information Management (PIM) and Mobile E-Mail Service of Oracle9*i*AS that's shipped with Oracle9*i*AS Wireless Release 2. Specifically, we discuss the following topics:

- Extending the Office to Mobile
- Features and Architecture
- Mobile E-mail
- Mobile Directory and Address Book
- Calendar
- Instant Messaging
- Short Messaging
- Document Management
- Fax
- Tasks

Extending the Office to Mobile

Significant demand exists for business people to access services that are traditionally provided by physical office infrastructures. The idea behind the mobile office is to extend the reach of the office infrastructure to virtually any location covered by a wireless network. Although E-Mailis not specific to any business process, mobile e-mail, calendaring, and scheduling can enhance collaboration and improve communications beyond the confines of the traditional office. A case in point? Mobile e-mail is typically one of the first mobile projects an enterprise implements. Let's look at the features and architecture of the PIM and E-Mail services within Oracle9*i*AS Wireless.

Features and Architecture

The Oracle9*i*AS Wireless Personal Information Management (PIM) and E-Mail Service enables integration of corporate e-mail, directory, address book, calendaring, and instant-messaging applications with mobile enterprise portals. Each of these applications is built as a module that can be called either directly by mobile users from their devices or by other applications. These mobile PIM and e-mail applications are fully integrated within one another, enabling a user to access such features as an address book or a directory when composing e-mail messages. You can leverage PIM service modules in your own or third-party applications. For example, you can add communication features to your wireless services, retrieve corporate directory information, or add and manage appointments for users, such as travel or dining reservations.

The PIM service modules are based on standard protocols, allowing for a simple integration into existing environments. The Mobile E-Mail client gives access, from any mobile devices, to any IMAP4 or POP3 server, including Microsoft Exchange and Lotus Domino. The Mobile Directory client connects to any LDAP directory server. The Mobile Calendar client integrates natively with MS Exchange and Lotus Servers, and through published interfaces, these PIM modules can be customized to support any calendar server.

The PIM solution has a universal user interface (UI) used across all backends. The idea is to have PIM business objects between the UI and the backend implementation so that the same UI can be used for different backends. What's more, the same UI can be reused for any new backends that may hit the market.

Features

An out-of-the-box J2EE application, Oracle9*i*AS Wireless PIM and E-Mail Service supports popular PIM and e-mail protocols. Let's look at the features and components:

- **Configuration** The starting day of the week and the display of week numbers can be configured through user preferences.
- **Localization** Localized interfaces can be branded for individual users. You can format the localization of text strings, dates, and times (in the calendar) in a locale-sensitive manner.
- **Document Management** By integrating PIM and E-Mail with Oracle iFS, you can enhance file attachments to e-mail. Likewise, using RightFax, an Oracle partner utility, you can enable document printing by fax.
- **Branding** You can extend and maintain customer's brands on mobile devices. Brand names can be specified for page and menu titles throughout the application. Because PDAs have fewer screen constraints when compared to those of most phones, you can present customer logos in the application.

Architecture

Devices from phones to PDAs and laptops have generally built-in support for access to e-mail accounts using standard Internet e-mail protocols such as POP3 or IMAP4. Oracle does it a bit differently, however, as you'll see in this section.

Although the Oracle Mobile PIM and E-Mail Service works with basic LAN or workgroup topology, it sports an open XML API to support tight integration with popular systems. Essentially, it emulates the backend server environment of Microsoft Exchange Server or Lotus Domino Server, while supporting the front end of these PIM and e-mail systems. Seamless integration with wireless enterprise portals and accessibility to file systems such as Oracle iFS allow developers to merge applications with these modules and provide true anytime, anywhere access.

Access to other people's calendars requires online linkage to a shared calendar system. Besides the ability to retrieve directory and appointment information, users can also access corporate e-mail systems such as Microsoft Exchange directly or, in other cases, through synchronization with a PC.

Other integration points include LDAP (the default server port number is 389). Users can send e-mail messages directly to others if the e-mail addresses of the target recipients are displayed from LDAP.

Mobile E-Mail

The Mobile E-Mail module enables users to access their e-mail messages from any mobile device. Mobile E-Mail integrates with any POP3 or IMAP4 server, including Microsoft Exchange and Lotus Domino Servers. You link to the e-mail service using the virtual URL `omp://oracle/services/pim/mail`, and its three parameters, action, mailto and attach, are listed in Table 11-1.

For example, you can send an e-mail message using the following code:

```
<SimpleMenuItem target="omp://oracle/services/pim/mail?
   action=messageto&amp;mailto=bookauthors@oraclepress.com">
   Send E-mail to Authors
</SimpleMenuItem>
```

NOTE

The target attribute of <SimpleMenuItem>, <SimpleAction>, <SimpleHref>, and <SimpleForm> is used for linking to a mobile module and is mandatory. The value of the target attribute starts with omp:// for accessing modules.

Mobile module services operate in a friendly manner. If they are called without any of the optional parameters, they will ask you to input them. If they

Parameter	Description	Value(s)	Notes
action	The action the e-mail module should perform.	messageto | messagecc | sendasattachment	Required
mailto	The e-mail address to which the message is sent.	Any string	Optional
attach	The fully qualified path of the local file that is sent as an attachment to the e-mail.	Any string	Optional

TABLE 11-1. *Mobile E-Mail Input Parameters*

are called with the appropriate parameters, they will use them without further questions. So if you do not know what the optional input parameters are, you can just make a call from your application to the virtual URL of that module, and the module handles the rest from then on—very user friendly.

Configuring the E-Mail Service

Before you can use the mobile e-mail service, you must first configure it. You can configure the mobile e-mail service using the *Service Designer* and drill down through the appropriate folders to find that particular service. Once the mobile e-mail service is found, click the *Input Parameters* link on the left side of the *Edit Master Service* configuration screen. The Input Parameters screen appears. Most of the fields are self-explanatory. Refer to the Oracle documentation for the complete field listings, which are too detailed to be covered here.

Once the service is configured, you are ready to use it. Using the example in the previous section, let's see what happens next when we invoke the Mobile E-Mail service on a mobile device.

Mobile E-Mail Example

Using the e-mail example from the previous section, we'll simply create a service using the HTTP Adapter and the Service Designer. Let's see what it looks like when viewed from the MS PocketPC browser. In Figure 11-1 and Figure 11-2, you can see that the Compose screen is presented because we are composing a new e-mail message. Our code only provides an action parameter, but you can choose to include an attachment, if desired.

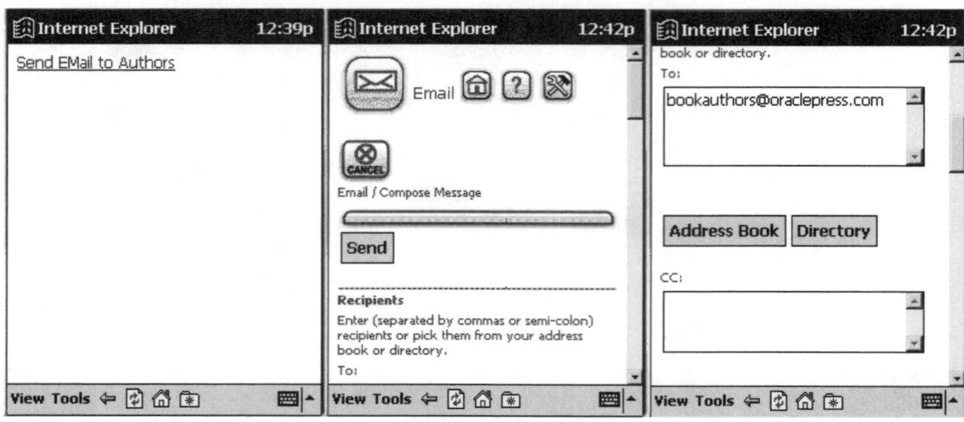

FIGURE 11-1. *Mobile E-Mail using MS PocketPC browser, Part 1*

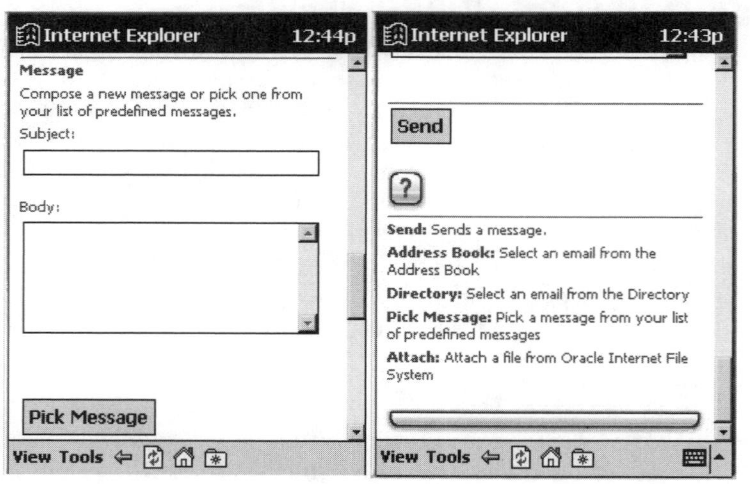

FIGURE 11-2. *Mobile E-Mail using MS PocketPC browser, Part 2*

To complete the task, enter the rest of the information via the mobile device and click the Send button to send the e-mail. Here are a few items worth noting:

- You can use the linked address book to get an e-mail address instead of having to key in the e-mail address. Just select the e-mail address from the address book after you find the desired entry. More details in the "Mobile Address Book" section of this chapter.
- You can also use the linked directory to search for a person by name to get additional information, such as an e-mail address, instead of having to key it in manually. Again, just select the e-mail address from the directory after you find the desired entry. More details in the "Mobile Directory" section of this chapter.
- You can also use the Pick Message option to select a previously used or predefined messages that you created earlier using other, more favorable input means. Once you select the message, it will automatically be pasted into the body message box of your Compose screen. This feature is especially useful for mobile phone uses when keyboards are not available.

Obviously, all the other features of a typical e-mail service are included, such as your inbox and folders. We will now show you more Mobile E-Mail module features by accessing the popular Yahoo! mailbox using the POP3 and SMTP interface. We will access a fictional e-mail account on Yahoo! Mail called np@yahoo.com. Here, we configure the E-Mail module to point to POP3 and SMTP servers at yahoo.com. As a result, your mobile UI will share the same universal interface among the mailboxes you access, including Yahoo! Mail and your corporate e-mail. Our service is configured using the following input parameters in the Content Manager:

ORACLE_SERVICES_PIM_MAIL_SERVER_NAME	pop.mail.yahoo.com
ORACLE_SERVICES_PIM_MAIL_SMTP_SERVER_NAME	smtp.mail.yahoo.com

As shown in Figure 11-3, you have the standard organization (inbox and folders) to navigate in. Actions on messages include Read, Compose, Reply, Delete, and Forward (see Figure 11-4).

One unique feature of Mobile E-Mail is the integration of fax. You can see the Fax icon in the bottom-right corner of an e-mail message screen. By clicking the Fax icon, your e-mail message is automatically converted and faxed to your desired destination (for example, to the front desk of the hotel you're staying in or to the nearest Kinko's fax center).

Oracle9*i*AS Wireless supports multiple locales and multiencoding. Most of this is done automatically for the user. You can get a taste of that by simply setting the

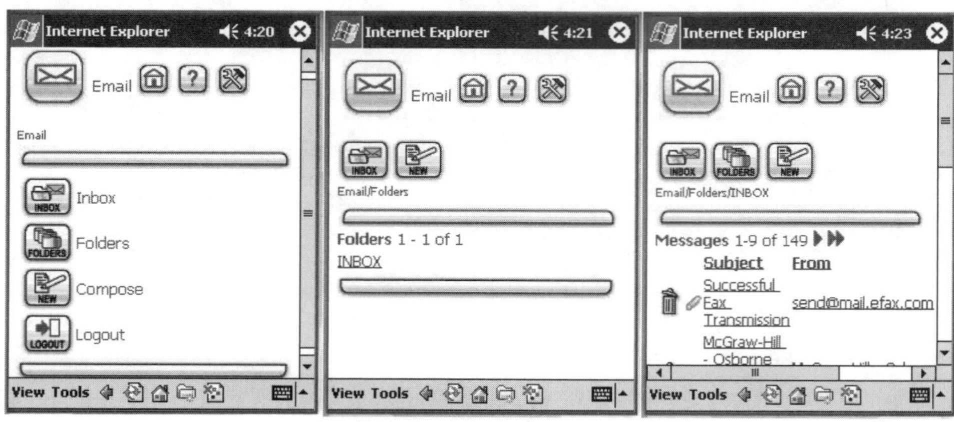

FIGURE 11-3. *Yahoo! e-mail from a mobile device*

Language pull-down option in the User Profile of the Customization web tool. E-mail via Oracle9*i*AS Wireless can now be viewed using two popular languages: Chinese (see Figure 11-5) and Japanese.

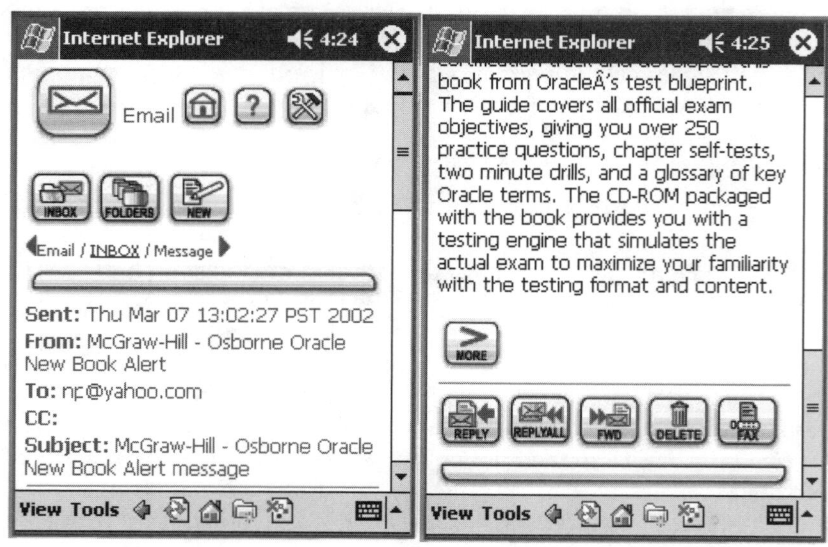

FIGURE 11-4. *Yahoo! e-mail composition screen*

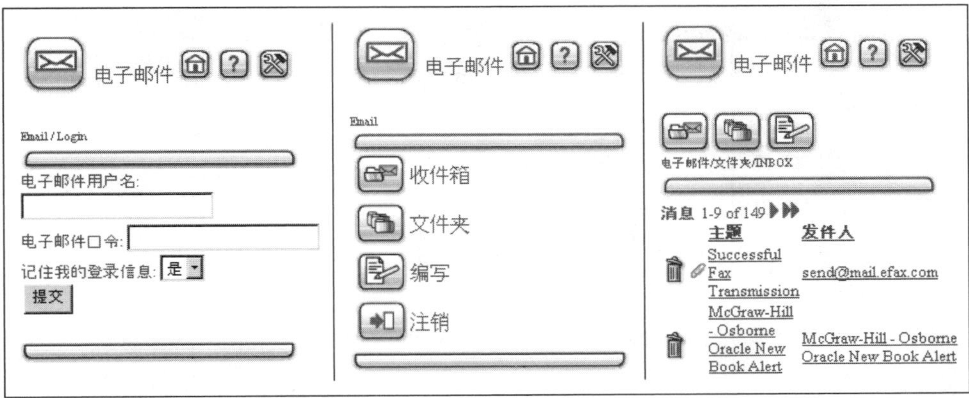

FIGURE 11-5. *Chinese Mobile E-Mail user interface*

Mobile Directory

The Mobile Directory module enables users to access LDAP directory servers from any device. The Directory module is integrated with the Mobile E-Mail module, enabling users to browse their corporate directory and then send an e-mail to a particular contact, or to compose a recipient list from the directory. You link to the Directory service using the virtual URL `omp://oracle/services/pim/directory`.

No input parameters are required. Notice that your administrator should have configured the service using the Service Designer and pointed it to a private or public LDAP server.

Using the Directory service, the lookup is done via Search by Name. Once matching entries are found, you can click the First Name or Last Name field to get record details displayed. You can also click the E-Mailfield to send an e-mail; you will be taken to the familiar Mobile E-Mail module (see Figure 11-6).

Mobile Address Book

The Mobile Address Book enables users to manage their own address books and contacts as well as enables call functions from wireless phones. The Mobile Address Book integrates with the Mobile E-Mail module to allow users to compose a message's recipient list from their address book. You can link to the Address Book service via the virtual URL `omp://oracle/services/pim/addressbook` and the parameters listed in Table 11-2.

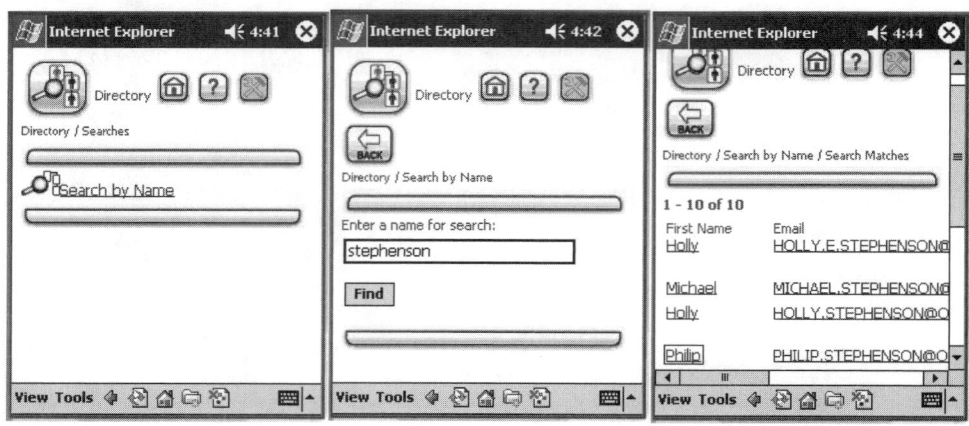

FIGURE 11-6. *Directory*

Using the Address Book service, the lookup is done with a string search. Once matching entries are found, you can click on the Name field to get record details displayed (see Figure 11-7). You can also click the E-Mailfield to send an e-mail—and be taken to the Mobile E-Mail module. If you select the Phone Number field, you will be taken to the linked SMS module to send a voice message (alternatively, you can send an SMS, e-mail, or fax instead of a voice message). Once you find a contact, you can also edit the contact information or delete a contact.

Parameter	Description	Value(s)	Notes
screen	Displays the list of contacts or adds the contact information supplied	0 | 51	Optional
srchstr	The string to search for	Any string	Optional

TABLE 11-2. *Mobile Address Book Input Parameters*

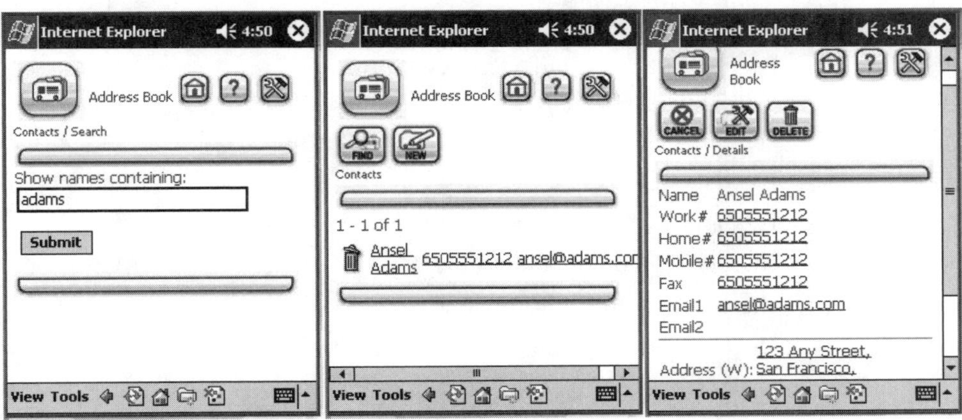

FIGURE 11-7. *Address Book*

Calendar

The Calendar module enables users to manage their schedules and tasks via mobile access to popular calendar servers, such as Microsoft Exchange and Lotus Domino. You link to the Calendar service using the virtual URL `omp://oracle/services/pim/calendar` and the parameters listed in Table 11-3.

You're probably familiar with the Calendar module, shown in Figure 11-8, because it is not significantly different from those featured on PDAs such as MS PocketPC 2002 OS. You have the Weekly view in addition to the Daily view. You can add, modify, and delete appointments as well as sequentially navigate through each appointment in your calendar.

Instant Messaging

The Instant Messaging module provides presence management, enabling users to exchange instant messages from mobile devices. It is also fully integrated with the Jabber Instant Messaging server as well as the MSN and Yahoo! networks. You link to the Instant Messaging service using the virtual URL `omp://oracle/services/pim/instantmessaging` and the IMMessage parameter, as detailed here:

Parameter	Description	Value(s)	Notes
IMMessage	The text of the message	Any string	Optional

Parameter	Description	Value(s)	Notes
ID	The input ID required to retrieve appointment details	Any string	Mandatory
title	The title of the appointment	Any string	Mandatory
date	The date of the appointment	Any string	Mandatory
time	The time of the appointment	Any string	Mandatory
duration	The duration of the appointment	Any string	Mandatory
notes	The notes for the appointment	Any string	Optional
type	The type of the appointment	appointment | anniversary | all day event | meeting | reminder	Mandatory
location	The location of the appointment	Any string	Mandatory
remind	The time interval before the event reminder occurs	Any string	Mandatory
sharing	The flag that enables or disables sharing of the appointment	true | false	Mandatory

TABLE 11-3. *Calendar Input Parameters*

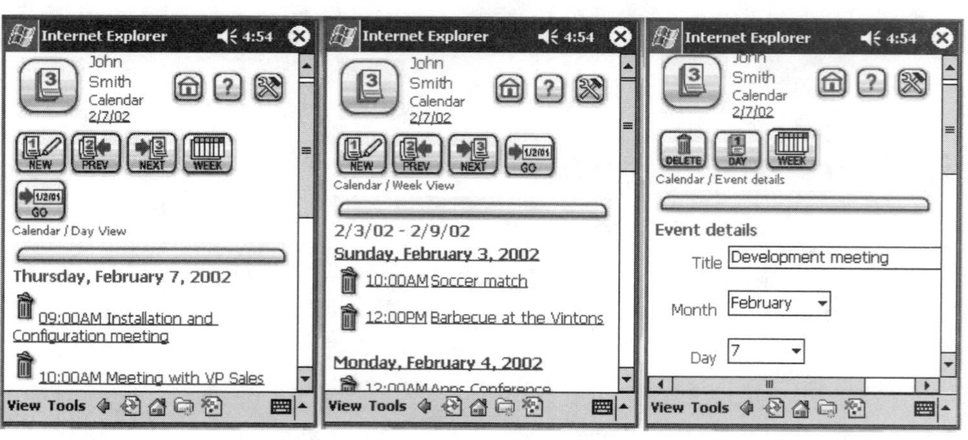

FIGURE 11-8. *Calendar*

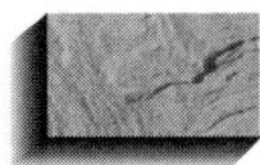

NOTE
Jabber is an open, XML-based protocol for instant messaging and presence. Jabber-based software is deployed on thousands of servers across the Internet and is used by over a million people worldwide. The protocol itself is managed by the Jabber Software Foundation.

You don't have to install your own Jabber server in order to use this module. Point your browser to the URL `http://www.jabberview.com` to see a list of all the public Jabber servers. Select one of the servers and see what services (Yahoo, MSN, ICQ, AIM, and so on) it supports and use that information (JID and JUD) to configure your Instant Messaging module using the Content Manager (see Figure 11-9).

We'll now run through an example of using the Instant Messaging module, in which we'll add our friend Nick to our Alumni Group. Nick has an IM account on Yahoo! (np@yahoo.com), but we only need to select the Yahoo radio button, enter **np**, and click Add (see Figure 11-10). The user entered will be validated and a status message will be sent immediately.

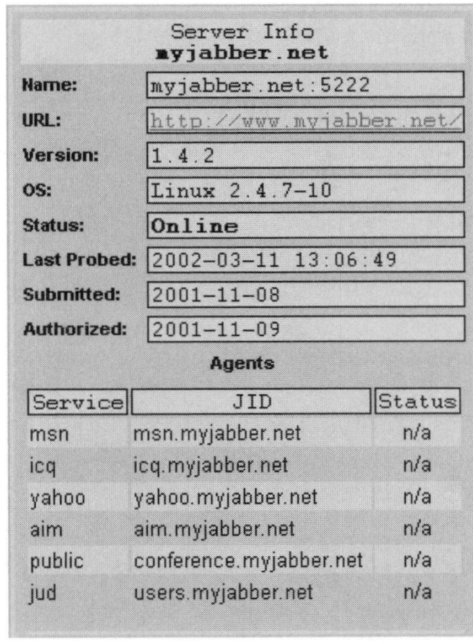

FIGURE 11-9. *Public jabber server service agents*

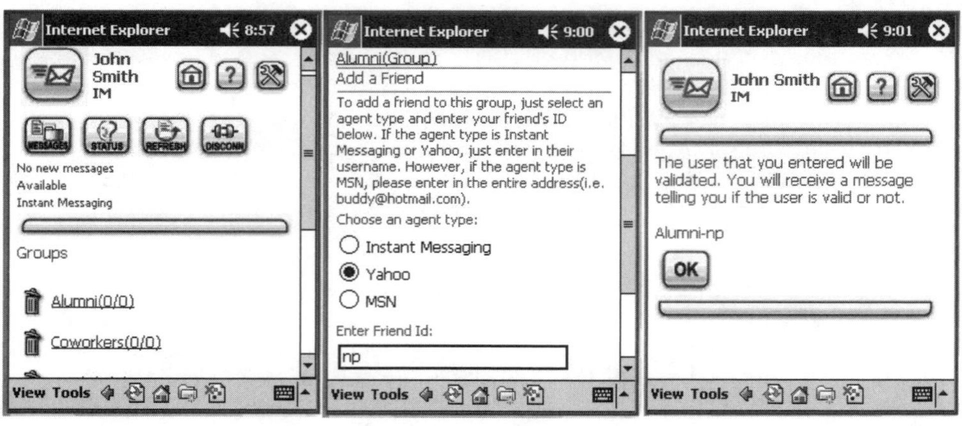

FIGURE 11-10. *Adding a friend from Yahoo! IM*

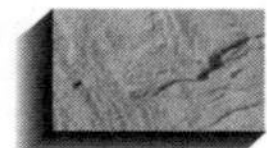

NOTE
*If the agent type is MSN, be sure to enter the entire address. For example, enter **myfriend@hotmail.com** instead of **myfriend**.*

Once the newly added account is validated, it will show up on your screen under the Online or Offline Friends lists (see Figure 11-11). Click np@yahoo.com to send an instant message to Nick.

In the main IM menu (envelope icon), you will now see that we have a new message from one of our friends (english@omdemo1), asking to join him for lunch (see Figure 11-12). We simply click that message in the menu, enter our reply, and finish by clicking Send.

This scenario illustrates how easy it is for a mobile user to participate in instant messaging with a variety of users on other proprietary IM systems, which is now made possible by the open Jabber protocol and simplified for developers by Oracle9*i*AS Wireless, all done via the web with no proprietary client installations required!

Short Messaging

The Short Messaging module enables users to send messages through such media as voice, e-mail, fax, and SMS messaging. To send a short message, a user sends the service four parameters: the type of message to be sent (e-mail, SMS, voice, or fax),

FIGURE 11-11. *Instant message to new friend*

the destination address of the message, the subject text, and the body text of the message (see Figure 11-13).

The subject and body text are translated into the medium appropriate to the message type and then sent to the destination. You link to the Short Messaging service using the virtual URL `omp://oracle/services/pim/shortmessaging` and the parameters listed in Table 11-4.

FIGURE 11-12. *Instant messaging between Oracle9iAS Wireless and Yahoo! IM*

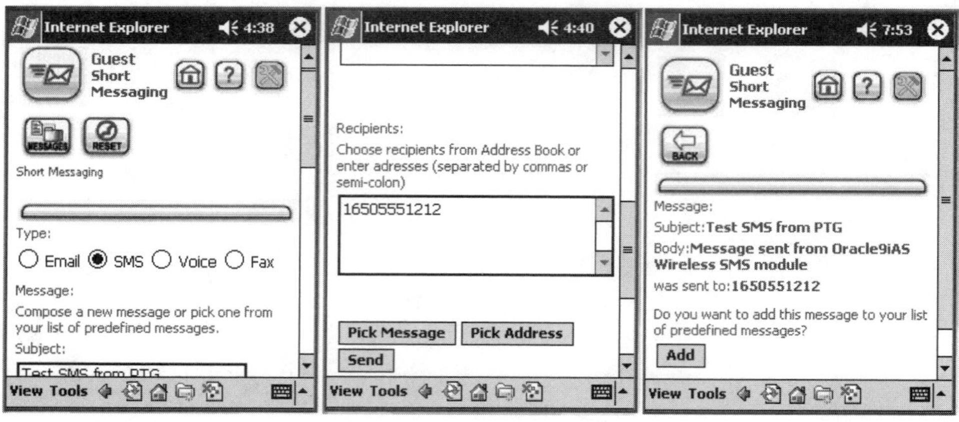

FIGURE 11-13. *SMS via an MS PocketPC mobile device*

NOTE
After sending a message, you can optionally add that message to your list of predefined messages!

Parameter	Description	Value(s)	Notes
type	The type of medium through which the message is sent	e-mail | sms | voice | fax	Optional
destinationAddress	The address to which the message is sent	Any string	Optional
subjectText	The subject of the message to be sent	Any string	Optional
bodyText	The body text of the message to be sent	Any string	Optional
sendMessage	Specifies whether the service should send the message or not (explicitly)	yes | no	Optional

TABLE 11-4. *SMS Input Parameters*

An SMS message instantaneously shows up on your mobile phone, most likely with the sender's area code. Only one-way SMS is supported in Release 2 because the reply number is invalid—it does not use the sender SMS number from the User Profile. In future releases of Oracle9*i*AS Wireless, you will be able to specify a return SMS number when you send it or at least use the one from your User Profile.

Document Management iFS

The Oracle Internet File System (iFS) module enables users to upload files to or download files from an Oracle iFS server. The iFS module is integrated with other modules, such as the E-Mail and Fax modules. You link to the Document Management service using the virtual URL `omp://oracle/services/pim/ifs` and the parameters listed in Table 11-5.

This is a convenient way to select documents for use with the other modules. What's more, it can be from any Oracle iFS server you have access to—both locally and remotely.

Fax

The Fax module enables users to send a fax, check the status of a fax, and forward or delete a fax from any wireless device. By combining E-Mail or iFS services, the Fax module also supports faxing documents through mobile devices. You link to the Fax service using the virtual URL `omp://oracle/services/pim/fax` and the FAXTODO parameter, detailed here:

Parameter	Description	Value(s)	Notes
FAXTODO	The type of action to be performed	NEWFAX | STATUS | DELETE | FWD	Mandatory

Parameter	Description	Value(s)	Notes
IFSAction	The type of action to be performed	upload | download	Mandatory
LOCALPATH	The absolute local path of the file to be uploaded to the iFS server	Any string	Mandatory
OBJNAME	Enables file renaming	Any string	Optional

TABLE 11-5. *Document Management Input Parameters*

You will need to install the RightFax server on the machine that Oracle9*i*AS Wireless is running on because the wireless web server uses the RightFax Java API for connecting to a RightFax server.

Composing a fax to send is similar to sending a standard e-mail message. Instead of an e-mail address, the telephone number of the fax machine or service is used instead. You can alternatively pick a recipient from the Address Book or pick a message from your list of predefined messages (see Figure 11-14). Once you click the Send button, your fax will be converted to the right format for sending automatically and inserted into the scheduler for faxing. Once it is completed, the status of your fax becomes OK (see Figure 11-15). Other status conditions include Fax Number Busy, Sending, and so on, as typically found in a fax machine.

NOTE
The fax cover page is configured according to your RightFax server installation and is independent of Oracle9iAS Wireless. See your RightFax Administrator's Guide for detailed instructions.

Tasks

The Tasks module enables users and applications to schedule and manage tasks. This module integrates with Lotus and Exchange Servers. You link to the Tasks service using the virtual URL `omp://oracle/services/pim/tasks` and the parameters listed in Table 11-6.

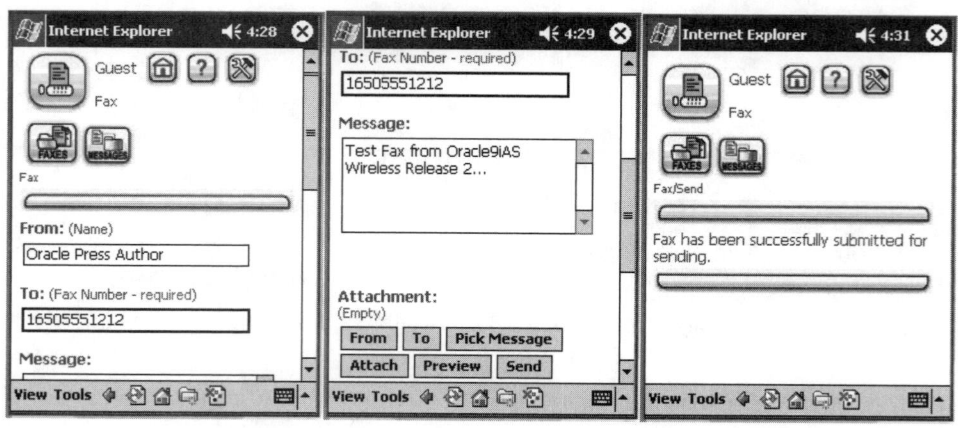

FIGURE 11-14. *Composing a fax*

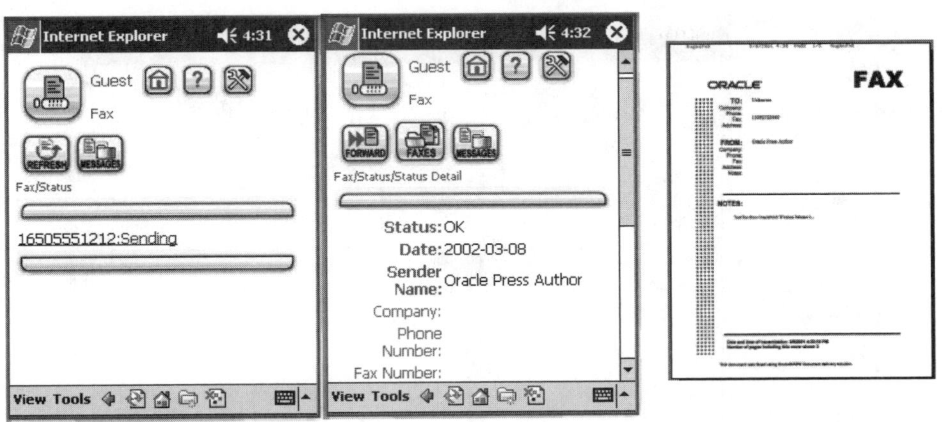

FIGURE 11-15. *Sending and receiving a fax*

Tasks should be familiar to most MS Outlook and Lotus Domino users. In the Oracle9*i*AS Wireless version, you are presented with a menu in which you can add, delete, or edit tasks (see Figure 11-16).

Parameter	Description	Value(s)	Notes
title	The title of the task	Any string	Mandatory
startdate	The start date of the task	Any string	Mandatory
duedate	The due date of the task	Any string	Mandatory
priority	The duration of the task	low I medium I high I none	Mandatory
notes	The notes for the task	Any string	Optional
category	The type of the task	holiday I vacation I projects I clients I phone calls I travel	Mandatory
sharing	The flag that enables or disables sharing of the tasks	true I false	Mandatory

TABLE 11-6. *Tasks Input Parameters*

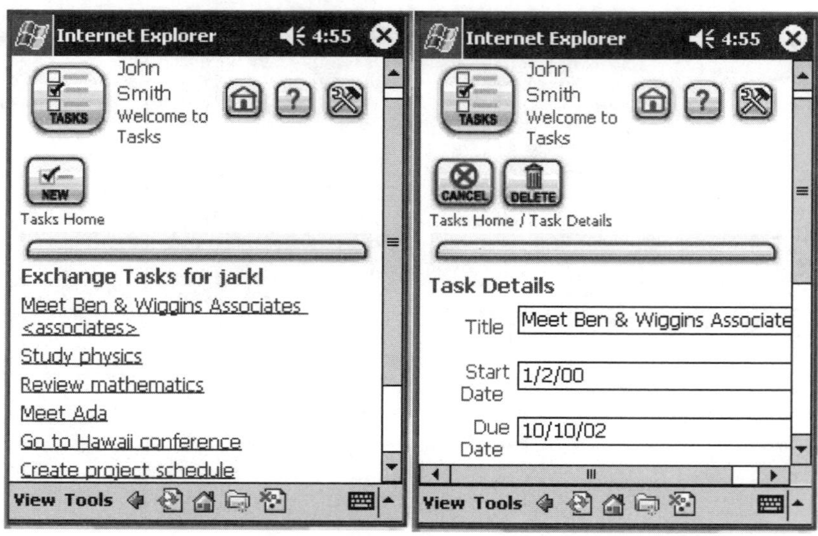

FIGURE 11-16. *Tasks*

Summary

The Mobile PIM and E-Mail Service of Oracle9*i*AS Wireless enables you to easily create multichannel communication services as well as wireless and voice-enabled e-mail, calendar, corporate directory, and other office functions—all with your mobile devices. The iFS and Fax modules are particularly useful for road warriors and other mobile workers who need access to vital and timely information and services on the go. With a universal user interface, these modules provide a consistent user experience with different backends, such as Lotus Domino, MS Exchange, Yahoo! E-Mail, and so on. You can extend these modules to easily handle new backends that may hit the market in the future. You can configure and enable users to send short messages in voice and SMs, and exchange instant messages via mobile devices.

CHAPTER 12

Mobile Commerce

he Oracle9*i*AS Wireless Mobile Commerce (m-Commerce) Service comprises several key modules to facilitate the secure storage of user profiles, authorization of sharing transactional information with merchants, and enabling of online payments. Oracle9*i*AS Wireless offers a preinstalled Mobile Wallet server that can integrate mobile commerce services with third-party applications. It also includes a Form Filler module to easily fill out forms for shopping carts and provides a Translator module to transcode existing WML commerce applications into XML. This allows *legacy* WML applications to participate in commerce transactions with the ease of the one-click or one-tap shopping experience offered by the Form Filler service. Specifically, the following topics are discussed in this chapter:

- Features and Functionality
- Architecture and Security
- Mobile Commerce Modules
- Example: Single-Tap Checkout

Features and Functionality

To make it easy to buy goods and services with mobile devices, Oracle9*i*AS Wireless offers out-of-the-box functionality to both carriers and enterprises to extend m-commerce capabilities to their subscribers and users. Today, it's still quite difficult to buy even the simplest consumer item with mobile devices due to their small form factor and limited input capabilities. Besides the navigational challenge to reach the m-commerce site and select the items, you have tap in your payment information, along with the billing and shipping instructions.

The Oracle9*i*AS Wireless m-Commerce Service simplifies all that and enables easy input and secure storage of user information while allowing authorized applications to receive this information at any time from any device. The key features of this service include the following:

- **Secure Online Transactions** Enable the mobile phones or PDAs to become "trusted devices" for mobile users, within an environment where secure transactions take place and online payments can be made through Public Key Infrastructure (PKI) and other measures.
- **Automatic Form-Filling** Buying through a mobile device is inherently difficult. You have to tap in your credit or debit card information, along with billing and shipping address information. The user experience is so challenging that most of us would simply call an operator to place the

order instead. Oracle provides the Form Filler module to solve this problem. By simply mapping and filling out forms automatically, you can build applications that spare users from entering information from a mobile device. Stored information could include credit, debit, and loyalty program card details as well as shipping and billing information.

- **Secure Storing of Payment Instruments in Wallet** Mobile Wallet (m-Wallet) enables users to manage their profile from mobile devices and participate in m-commerce transactions and track their activities. The m-Wallet module securely stores a user's payment instrument information, such as credit cards, bank accounts, and shipping address. Upon user approval, other m-commerce applications can retrieve this information to process payments. In some ways, a mobile wallet is like a real wallet, because it's the place where you store information about your credit cards and your address. These m-wallets basically make consumer payment information available to merchants without requiring the user to enter this information manually. With built-in Mobile Wallet inside Oracle9*i*AS Wireless, you can create a wallet out of the box, leveraging Oracle's infrastructure and partnerships.
- **Access to Transactions History** The built-in repository capability of the m-Commerce Service facilitates access to any transaction history. Potentially, you can use it to support all forms of m-commerce, including micropayments, online purchases, advertising, coupon-serving, alerts, and messaging.
- **Online Support for Payment Systems** Integrating payment processing with Oracle9*i*AS Wireless lets mobile users pay for goods and services using a number of options. For example, with built-in linkages to financial institutions on Oracle9*i*AS Wireless, mobile users can charge their purchases to a bank account or simply add the amount to their wireless phone bills. That way, users can have the amount deducted from their bank accounts or have it billed to their prepaid phones through the mobile commerce infrastructure and applications; for instance, through their SIM cards.

Architecture and Security

The Oracle9*i*AS Wireless m-Commerce Service is a carrier-grade mobile solution featuring scalable, robust architecture and strong security infrastructure. Here, Oracle provides a framework that separates application program interfaces (APIs) from payment management and specific transaction processing so that each of the components can evolve independently (see the following illustration). Besides offering Java and HTTP APIs, the m-Commerce Service provides easy-to-deploy wallet management and seamless integration with leading electronic payment systems for secure mobile transactions from any mobile device, using any means of payment, including credit cards, micropayments, existing online merchant accounts, and monthly wireless bills.

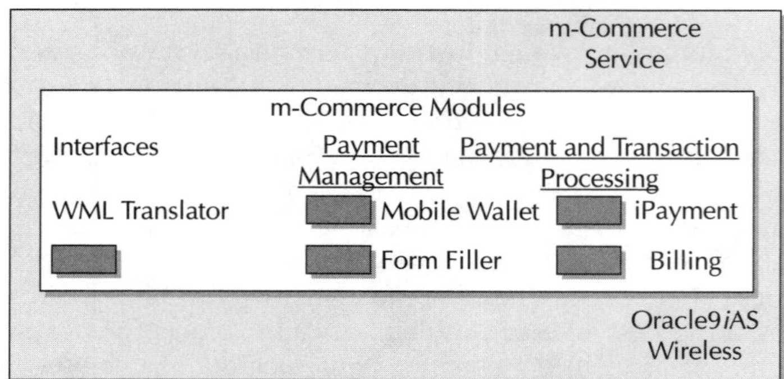

Mobile Commerce Architecture

Let's review the application program interfaces (APIs), payment management, and transactional processing in Oracle9*i*AS Wireless.

Application Program Interfaces

You can build your m-commerce application by calling the m-Commerce Service. Simply add the URL links to the modules that comply with their APIs. If you have existing m-commerce websites developed in WML, you can take advantage of the WML Translator module to translate (or transcode) the transactional links, as shown in Figure 12-1.

Payment Management

There are two ways to enable mobile wallets. One way is to incorporate a wallet application feature that facilitates online payments inside the mobile device (or desktop terminal) using a smart card (or SIM card). The data inside the device is secured with a special code to authenticate the user to the application. The wallet application makes use of the virtual card and simplifies the storage and retrieval of personal information in mobile transactions. By enabling Internet-type payments using the Electronic Commerce Modeling Language (ECML) standard, the wallet offers service providers easy adaptation of their current e-business to the mobile world. Other examples include Nokia 6310–6340 phones, which come with a built-in wallet for fast and secure wireless transactions.

Rather than having the information held directly inside the device, another approach is to host this information on a secure server somewhere. This is often

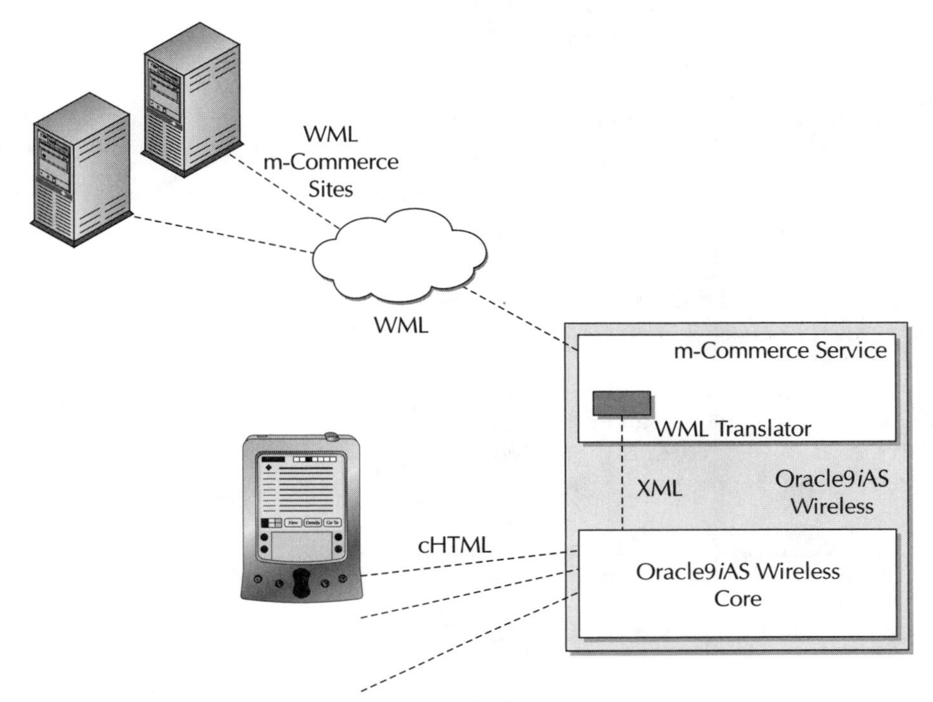

FIGURE 12-1. *WML Translator module for WML sites*

referred to as *having a wallet on a remote server,* and it's common practice in many of the original Internet payment solutions. Oracle has done this one better by incorporating a mobile wallet module (m-Wallet) inside Oracle9*i*AS Wireless.

Mobile commerce transaction and credential presentation in the mobile wallet can be summarized in the following steps (see Figure 12-2):

1. If a user wants to purchase a product (for example, some cinema tickets), he or she goes to the merchant's store and submits an order.
2. In response, the merchant's server sends back a request for payment information.
3. The phone, upon receiving this request, initiates a dialog with the user's mobile wallet server.

4. The user is prompted to enter his or her password, after which the user can then specify the payment method and the address to which the goods are to be delivered.
5. Once the user has completed filling in this information, the wallet server separately contacts the merchant server and sends it all the payment details.
6. The merchant server then finally returns a notification to the user's mobile device to acknowledge the purchase.

Payment and Transaction Processing

By bridging the security issues and enabling robust payment processing to mobile Internet merchants, Oracle9*i*AS Wireless works with financial institutions to support multiple payment protocols that are built on open, standards-based technology. Simply put, the iPayment and Billing modules within Oracle9*i*AS Wireless work with merchant software systems and provide cash register-like functionality to manage payment processing. This payment and billing framework represents a

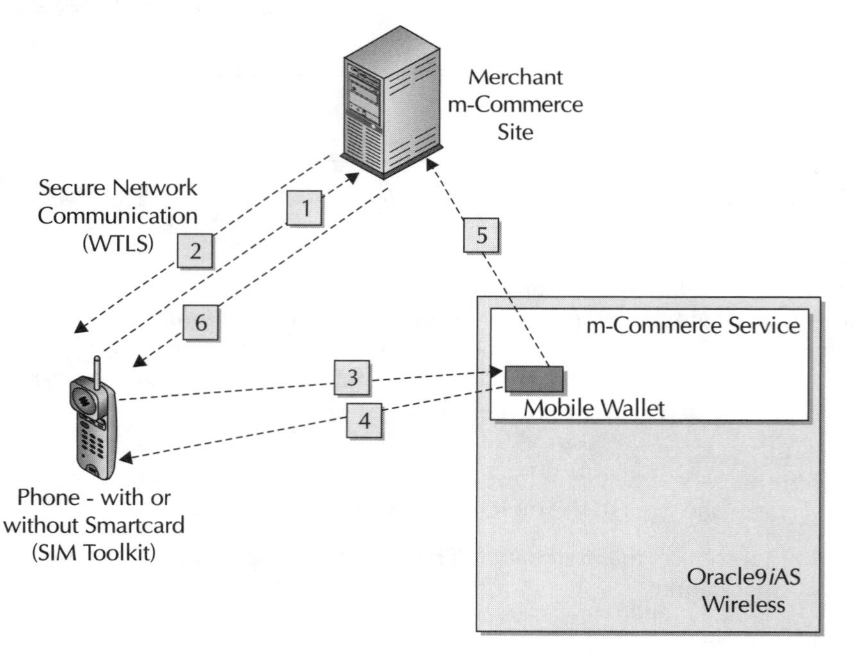

FIGURE 12-2. *Mobile wallet execution flow*

flexible, yet extensible way to accommodate payment requirements on the Internet (and the Wireless Web) for merchants who need to accept multiple payment methods.

Security

The ability to complete a transaction anytime, anywhere places a great demand on security to protect the transaction's integrity and confidentiality. It is also necessary to authenticate the user in a way that protects the legality of the transaction and ensures its nonrepudiation.

Wireless Transport Layer Security (WTLS) is the most common way of encrypting a mobile transaction. Encryption is applied to the connection between the gateway and the devices, while Secure Socket Layer (SSL) encrypts the connection from the server to the gateway. Oracle9*i*AS Wireless fully supports the WTLS and SSL 3.0 standards, ensuring secure end-to-end communications between the device and the mobile commerce site. Previously, there was a security gap in which the gateway had to manage the conversion between WTLS and SSL, thus exposing the data in an unencrypted fashion. This "data in the clear" problem has been addressed in WAP 2.0. As a result, wireless carriers and wireless application service providers now have an opportunity to establish the mobile phone or wireless PDA as a "trusted device" to encourage secured transactions and payment making.

On the payment side, the mobile payment solutions are based on Wireless Public Key Infrastructure (WPKI) and implemented with or without digital certificates. The private key, which enables digital signatures, can be stored on the mobile device's SIM card when the financial functions are initiated. With Public Key Infrastructure (PKI), transactions can be secured using the same security scheme, regardless of the device used by the customer. Many unsecured devices can be used in combination with a PKI-enabled mobile device to finalize purchases and execute secure transactions. Indeed, applications using SIM cards have been created with the SIM Application Toolkit and are activated via infrared or Bluetooth. With Oracle9*i*AS Wireless, the mobile wallet is equipped to encrypt and decrypt all information stored in the repository with a three-part key made up of a system key, a user-specific key, and the user's trading password.

Mobile Commerce Modules

Oracle9*i*AS Wireless implements a number of modules that accelerate the build-out of mobile commerce service. The end user typically sees this service as a menu item on a handset or a link on a web page. End users invoke the m-Commerce Service by choosing menu items in their device interface. The service then returns the data, including text and applications.

WML Translator

The Translator module enables any site written in WML to be rendered on any device by converting its contents to Oracle9*i*AS multichannel XML. It also enhances the navigation of sites originally authored in WML by adding links to Oracle9*i*AS Wireless Core services. Currently, only WAP sites are supported. There is no output parameter; the Translator module internally consumes the translated result and status code.

You link to the WML Translator module using the virtual URL `omp://oracle/services/commerce/translator`.

Table 12-1 lists the input parameters that can be supplied to the WML Translator module.

Here's an example of how the Translator module can be called:

1. Point your mobile browser to the URL **http://oracle9iasw-server:port/ptg/rm** and log in. Select the Commerce folder on your device. Pick the Translator service. The translator URL entry screen appears (see Figure 12-3).

2. Enter the URL **http://updev.phone.com/dev/wml/devhome4.wml** and click Submit. This should point to the starting page of the Openwave Developer's Portal. The WML site is now translated to Oracle9*i*AS multichannel XML, presented to the Wireless Core and transformed to the markup language for displaying on the mobile device.

Parameter	Description	Value(s)	Notes
XLTORSITE	Source URL of the WML site whose content will be translated to 9*i*AS multichannel XML	Valid URL string	Mandatory
XLTORLANG	Source language of the WML site	WML	Optional
EXTENSIONACTION	Actions other than translating the URL	HELP | DELPRESET	Optional
PRESETLABEL	Label of preset that will be deleted (normally a site name)	Any string	Optional

TABLE 12-1. *WML Translator Input Parameters*

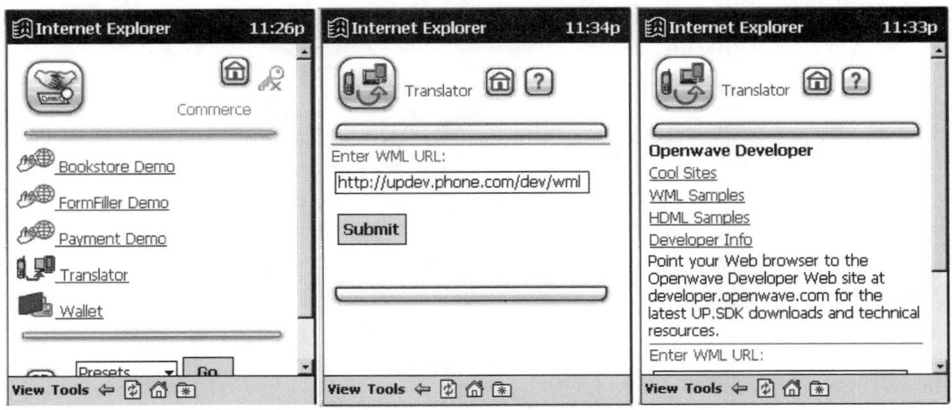

FIGURE 12-3. *Translating a WML site*

3. You can view the same URL on a WAP browser and compare the resulting display with other mobile devices.

You can see that existing WML sites can be quickly transformed into multichannel mobile sites with no extra work on the part of the developer.

Mobile Wallet

The use of m-Wallet is potentially one of the most secure methods of mobile payments, where none of the user's details are being broadcast directly across the Internet or the airwave. The implication here is, of course, that the merchant has to support the use of the Mobile Wallet server and has some sort of private line connection to it. This method is not commonly used in the PC environment because of the general lack of knowledge about payment methods other than sending credit card details over HTTPS. Such a system is ideally suited for the mobile environment, but mobile phone users are generally less computer savvy, and it will require some education in order for such technologies to become widely adopted.

The m-Wallet module securely stores a user's payment instrument information, such as credit card numbers, bank accounts, Internet accounts, personal profile, extended information, and shipping addresses (see Figure 12-4). Upon user approval, other m-commerce applications can retrieve this information to process payments or personal information form filling. The m-Wallet is divided into *compartments* that can hold one or more instruments. For example, the Credit Cards compartment holds as many different credit card numbers as the user feels the need for. It may

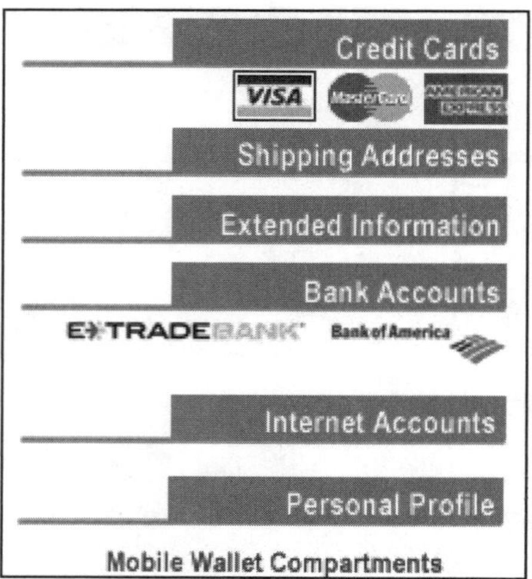

FIGURE 12-4. *m-Wallet module*

contain business or personal credit cards from Visa, MasterCard, Sears, Costco, American Express, and so on. The Personal Profile and Extended Information compartments, however, each hold only one information set.

M-Wallet provides a convenient one-click (or, more precisely, one-tap) commerce payment mechanism. It is a server-side, encrypted entity that contains payment instrument, identification, and address information for registered users. M-Wallet enables users to store all the information required to fill out commerce-related forms from any application. It processes requests for personal and payment instrument information issued through mobile forms by third parties and presents them to users, who decide what information gets sent back to the third party (merchant). The wallet stores this information securely for users, providing them an easy, secure shopping experience, and freeing them from repeatedly entering information.

Configuring the Wallet

Because the wallet is core to all commerce activity, it has to be configured before you can use the other modules, such as the Form Filler module. You must install and configure the Secure Key Server before using the wallet. Follow these steps carefully to configure the server:

1. Open a console or shell window. Locate the setup script (security.bat or security.sh) in the folder $ORACLE9iASW_INSTALL\wireless\j2ee\applications\modules\modules-web\commerce\setup\scripts.

2. Modify the script to reflect your setup using the examples within the script as a guide.

3. Check and make sure you have the necessary Java Cryptography Extension (JCE) JAR files placed in your JAVA13_HOME/jre/lib/ext folder. These include jce1_2_1.jar, local_policy.jar, ojcae.jar, sunjce_provider.jar, and US_export_policy.jar. If you don't have these files, they can be downloaded from Sun at http://java.sun.com/products/jce/index-121.html.

4. Run the security script. This generates a secure file, called KeyMgmtProps.enc, in the current directory. It also generates, encrypts, and inserts the System Encryption Key into the database as well as prints out the directory path for the security file. This path to the file is used as a service input parameter value.

5. Log into the web-based Wireless Tool and access the Service Designer. Navigate through the folders until you get to the Commerce folder set of services. Select the Security radio button and click Edit. Click Input Parameters and modify the default value of the input parameter ORACLE_SERVICES_COMMERCE_SECURITY_PROPS_PATH for the security server. Use the value from the previous step (without the filename). Click Apply.

NOTE
For testing out your mobile application with the wallet, you don't need to configure HTTPS on your web server. Make sure you edit the appropriate entry in the module.properties file to reflect that.

6. The module.properties file needs to be configured with the correct paths for both the HTTP and HTTPS listeners. This file is located in the folder at ORACLE9iASW_INSTALL\wireless\server\classes\messages\oracle\panama\module\common.

7. If you are not using HTTPS, there is one more step you have to manually edit to complete the configuration. This step seems to be undocumented in any of the Oracle documents. Edit the file WalletHelper.jsp, located at $ORACLE9iASW_INSTALL\wireless\j2ee\applications\modules\modules-web\commerce\wallet\jsp,and set the WALLET_PROTOCOL value to *false* (indicating nonsecure).

8. Restart the Wireless Web server. Your m-Wallet is at your service for initialization and usage.

To mimic the actual production environment, you can use a test certificate for HTTPS. Refer to your web server documentation for setting up Secured Sockets Layer (SSL). Setting up a production machine requires an actual certificate for HTTPS.

Using the Wallet

You link to the m-Wallet module using the virtual URL `omp://oracle/services/commerce/wallet`.

Table 12-2 lists the input parameters that can be supplied to the m-Wallet module. If none of the optional parameters are supplied, the module will ask for them once the service is invoked.

The m-Wallet data structure is defined in the wallet.properties file. This m-Wallet structure definition file is located in the directory $ORACLE9iASW_INSTALL\wireless\server\classes\messages\oracle\panama\module\commerce\wallet.

This file contains the definitions for credit cards, bank accounts, and extended information, plus the definition of the formats to be used for each field. You can

Parameter	Description	Value(s)	Notes
WALLET_ACTION	The action to perform	GETSTRUCTURE | GET_FORM_DATA | GET_INET_ACCT | GEN_USER_PASS	Mandatory
FORM_TITLE	The title to be displayed during the duration of the call	Any string	Mandatory
GET_DATA	A comma-separated list of tokens of values to retrieve	CC | BA | FN | LN | EMAIL | PHONE | INT_ACCT | SHIP	Mandatory
APPLICATION	The application name	Any string	Optional
ISEXCLUSIVE	The credit card or bank account used by the Payment module	true | false	Optional
DOMAIN	The domain name	Any string	Mandatory
ACCOUNT_ID	The account	Any string	Mandatory
PASSWORD	The password	Any string	Mandatory

TABLE 12-2. *Mobile Wallet Input Parameters*

configure the structure of the m-Wallet so that its contents can be extended and personalized according to usage. You simply edit the definition file and add compartments and fields as needed.

NOTE
Because the m-Wallet is extensible and can be personalized, the attributes of the input parameters as well as the output parameters that can be requested by services from the m-Wallet (for example, the GET_DATA parameter) could change accordingly.

Before the wallet can be used, it must be initialized with data. This is usually done on a desktop PC where data entry is done at your convenience and with a keyboard. When the wallet is invoked the first time, you will be asked to create a new password. This password will need to be entered every time you try to access your wallet (see Figure 12-5).

You will also be asked to create new accounts or new information for each of the compartments in the wallet. For example, you might be entering all the relevant Visa and MasterCard information in your Credit Card compartment. Once all the desired information has been entered and saved in the wallet, you are ready to use this wallet (see Figure 12-6).

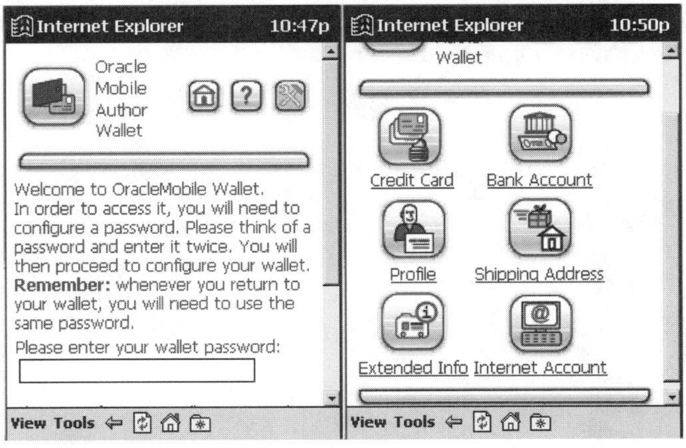

FIGURE 12-5. *Initializing the wallet*

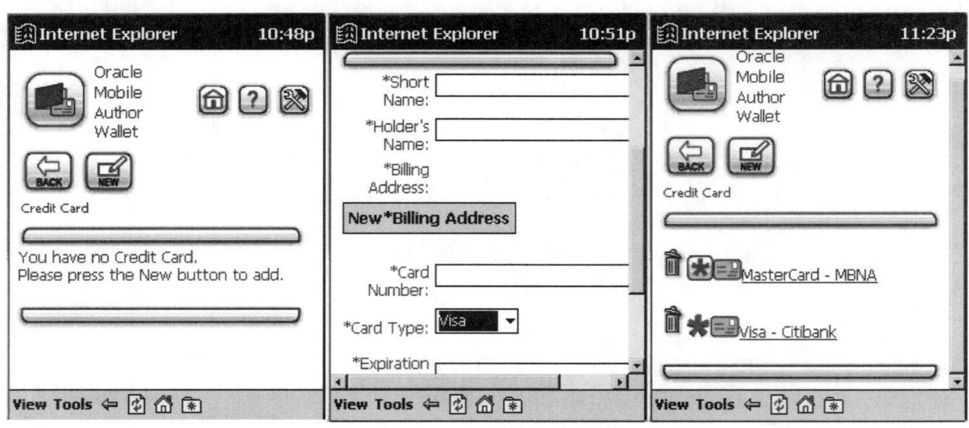

FIGURE 12-6. *Wallet ready for use*

As mentioned before, every time you use the wallet, you will be asked for the wallet password on a unique session basis. Additionally, you will also be asked for the password again every time you access a new compartment to pass the secure information to a third party.

NOTE
The wallet cannot be accessed by guest users. You will need to be a registered user to access this service.

To illustrate how simple it is to use the m-Wallet module to capture secured information, let's build a simple example:

```
<SimpleResult>
   <SimpleContainer>
   <SimpleMenu>
   <SimpleTitle wrapmode="nowrap" size="3">
      <SimpleStrong>Get Wallet Info</SimpleStrong>
   </SimpleTitle>
   <SimpleMenuItem
      target="omp://oracle/services/commerce/wallet?
      WALLETACTION=GET_FORM_DATA&amp;
      FORM_TITLE=getSecuredInfo&amp;
```

```
        APPLICATION= Oracle+Press&amp;
        GET_DATA=FN,LN,CC"
        callbackurl="https://localhost:9000/book/wallet_resp.jsp" >
        Credit Card, First Name, Last Name
    </SimpleMenuItem>
    </SimpleMenu>
    </SimpleContainer>
</SimpleResult>
```

This XML example calls the m-Wallet module and requests first name and last name information from the Profile compartment and also the credit card number and expiration date from the Credit Card compartment (see Figure 12-7).

NOTE
The default payment instrument is always presented to the user. You can always choose another payment instrument by selecting the instrument in question and making your selection changes before submitting the information using the Done key.

The user will be asked to enter the password to the wallet, and the information from the secured m-Wallet is displayed to the user for verification before submission

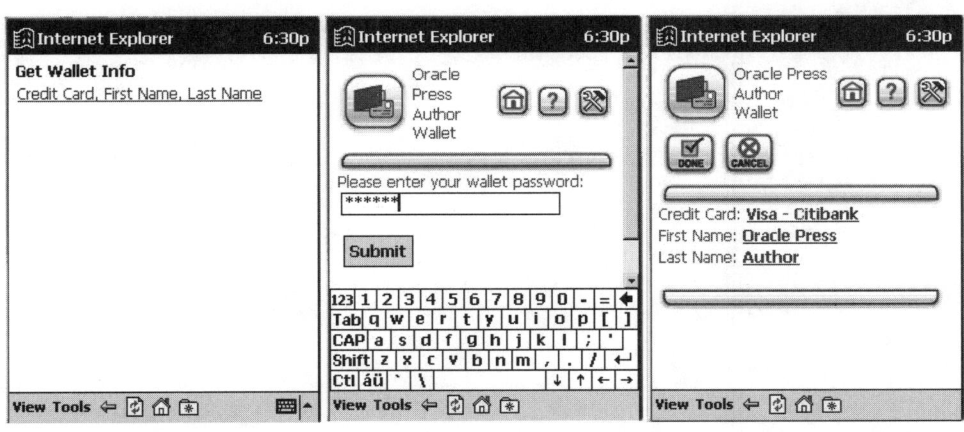

FIGURE 12-7. *m-Wallet module captures secure information*

to the third party. The final verification step may be skipped if the user configures it as such (see Figure 12-8).

The following code snippet will display the output parameters passed back from the m-Wallet module:

```
<%
String URL_WALLET_SELECT = request.getParameter("WALLET_SELECT");
   if (URL_WALLET_SELECT == null) {
      URL_WALLET_SELECT = "N/A";
}
String URL_CC_NUMBER = request.getParameter("CC_NUMBER");
   if (URL_CC_NUMBER == null) {
      URL_CC_NUMBER = "N/A";
}
String URL_CC_EXPIRATION_DATE = request.getParameter("CC_EXPIRATION_DATE");
   if (URL_CC_EXPIRATION_DATE == null) {
      URL_CC_EXPIRATION_DATE = "N/A";
}
String URL_FIRSTNAME = request.getParameter("FIRSTNAME");
   if (URL_FIRSTNAME == null) {
      URL_FIRSTNAME = "N/A";
}
String URL_LASTNAME = request.getParameter("LASTNAME");
   if (URL_LASTNAME == null) {
      URL_LASTNAME = "N/A";
}
%>
<SimpleResult>
   <SimpleContainer>
   <SimpleTitle wrapmode="nowrap" size="3">
      <SimpleStrong>Wallet Info Captured</SimpleStrong>
   </SimpleTitle>
   <SimpleBreak rule="true" />
   <SimpleText>
   <SimpleTextItem>WALLET_SELECT: <%=URL_WALLET_SELECT%></SimpleTextItem>
   <SimpleTextItem>CC_NUMBER: <%=URL_CC_NUMBER%></SimpleTextItem>
   <SimpleTextItem>
      EXPIRATION_DATE: <%=URL_CC_EXPIRATION_DATE%>
   </SimpleTextItem>
   <SimpleTextItem>FIRSTNAME: <%=URL_FIRSTNAME%></SimpleTextItem>
   <SimpleTextItem>LASTNAME: <%=URL_LASTNAME%></SimpleTextItem>
   </SimpleText>
   </SimpleContainer>
</SimpleResult>
```

A special module utilizing the m-Wallet module is the Form Filler module. The Form Filler module puts an intelligent wrapper around the m-Wallet module and takes a guess at getting the correct instruments to match the form input variables. Full details can be found in the next section, *Form Filler.*

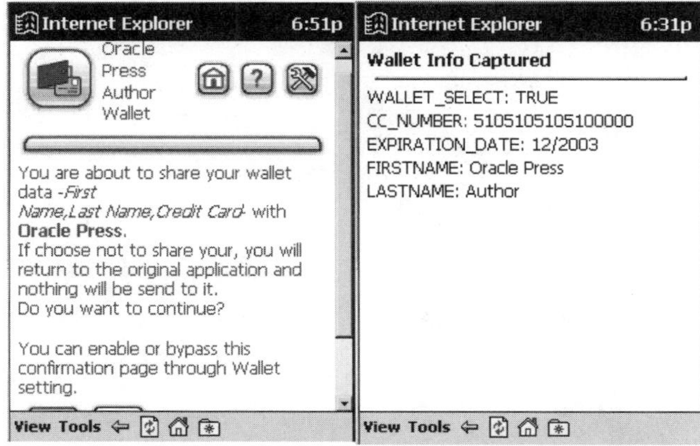

FIGURE 12-8. *Sharing data*

Accessing Wallet Output Parameters

Once the m-Wallet module returns to your "callbackurl" page, it passes the output URL parameters—credit card numbers, first name, last name, and so on—to your application. These predefined variable names are shown in Table 12-3.

Because the m-Wallet is extensible, your personalized or extended output parameters may be different from the defaults listed here.

Parameter Name	Description
	Core and Shipping Address
FIRSTNAME	User's first name
LASTNAME	User's last name
EMAIL	User's e-mail address
WALLET_SELECT	Status of operation (true or false)
ADDRESS_LINE1	User's address line 1
ADDRESS_LINE2	User's address line 2
CITY	User's city

TABLE 12-3. *Mobile Wallet Output Parameters*

Parameter Name	Description
STATE	User's state
ZIPCODE	User's ZIP code
COUNTRY	User's country
Credit Card	
CC_HOLDER_NAME	Name of credit card holder
CC_HOLDER_ADDRESS_LANDMARK	Billing address of credit card holder
CC_NUMBER	Credit card number
CC_EXPIRATION_DATE	Expiration date of credit card
CC_LANDMARK_NAME	The location mark of credit card
CC_ADDRESS_LINE1	Billing address line 1 of credit card holder
CC_ADDRESS_LINE2	Billing address line 2 of credit card holder
CC_CITY	Billing city of credit card holder
CC_STATE	Billing state of credit card holder
CC_ZIPCODE	Billing ZIP code of credit card holder
CC_COUNTRY	Billing country of credit card holder
Bank Account	
BA_HOLDER_NAME	Name of bank account holder
BA_HOLDER_ADDRESS_LANDMARK	Statement address of bank account holder
BA_ACCT_NUMBER	Bank account number
BA_ACCT_TYPE	Bank account type
BA_FI_ROUTING_NUMBER	Bank routing number
BA_FI_NAME	Name of bank
BA_LANDMARK_NAME	The location mark of bank address
BA_ADDRESS_LINE1	Statement address line 1 of bank account holder

TABLE 12-3. *Mobile Wallet Output Parameters* (continued)

Parameter Name	Description
BA_ADDRESS_LINE2	Statement address line 2 of bank account holder
BA_CITY	Statement city of bank account holder
BA_STATE	Statement state of bank account holder
BA_ZIPCODE	Statement ZIP code of bank account holder
BA_COUNTRY	Statement country of bank account holder
Extended Information	
ID_SSN	Social security number
ID_DL	Driver's license number
ID_DL_STATE	Driver's license state
ID_DL_EXP_DATE	Driver's license expiration date
ID_PASSPORT	Passport number
ID_PASSPORT_EXP_DATE	Passport expiration date

TABLE 12-3. *Mobile Wallet Output Parameters* (continued)

Form Filler

The Form Filler module maintains mappings between application form fields and wallet elements. The Form Filler accepts a URL and a list of label and variable names as input parameters, and it checks whether there is a stored mapping from the given labels and variables to wallet fields. If there is no such mapping, it enables you to create a new mapping into wallet fields. Once a mapping is retrieved or created, the Form Filler automatically calls the wallet asking it for the given mapped information. You may be asked to provide a password based on your wallet configuration. Upon successful completion, the module will return the wallet values corresponding to the label/variable name list. Otherwise, a status code of FAILURE will be returned.

If a mapping is not available, authorized users are allowed to select fields from their m-Wallets to fill in values for the input fields in the mobile application. By default, the Form Filler module uses a name-guessing heuristic to automatically suggest default values to the user. As a result, the manual user mapping process is minimized. The guessing heuristic uses keys that are defined in the service parameters for the Form Filler Master Service. You can implement your own guessing heuristics by creating a Java class and overriding the default by adding a new input parameter named ORACLE_SERVICES_COMMERCE_FORMFILLER_HEURISTIC to the service and assigning a fully qualified class name.

You link to the Form Filler module using the virtual URL `omp://oracle/services/commerce/formfiller`.

Table 12-4 lists the input parameters that can be supplied to the Form Filler module. If none of the optional parameters are supplied, the module will ask for them once the service is invoked.

An example of a call to the Form Filler module for a typical registration form might look like this:

```
<SimpleResult>
   <SimpleContainer>
   <SimpleForm target="https://localhost:9000/book/register.jsp"
      layout="tabular">
   <SimpleTitle size="3">
      <SimpleStrong>User Registration</SimpleStrong>
   </SimpleTitle>
   <SimpleFormItem name="FNAME" value="">
      <SimpleTitle>First Name:</SimpleTitle>
   </SimpleFormItem>
   <SimpleFormItem name="LNAME" value="">
      <SimpleTitle>Last Name:</SimpleTitle>
   </SimpleFormItem>
   <SimpleFormItem name="EMAIL" value="">
      <SimpleTitle>Email:</SimpleTitle>
   </SimpleFormItem>
   <SimpleFormItem name="ADDRESS" value="">
      <SimpleTitle>Address:</SimpleTitle>
   </SimpleFormItem>
   <SimpleHref
      target="omp://oracle/services/commerce/formfiller?
      FORMFILLURL=http://www.userreg.com&amp;
      APPLICATION=UserReg&amp;
      FORMFILLPARAMS=First+Name:FNAME,Last+Name:LNAME,
      Email:EMAIL,Address:Address"
      callbackurl="https://localhost:9000/book/register.jsp"
      label="Use FormFiller" />
   </SimpleForm>
   </SimpleContainer>
</SimpleResult>
```

For each call, the module returns the label (FORMFILLURL parameter), a return code (SUCCESSCODE) of True or False, and the filled-in parameter list

Parameter	Description	Value(s)	Notes
FORMFILLURL	The URL of the form to be filled	Any valid URL string	Mandatory
FORMFILLPARAMS	A comma-separated, ordered list of parameters inside the form	Any string	Mandatory
APPLICATION	The application name	Any string	Optional

TABLE 12-4. *Form Filler Input Parameters*

(FORMFILLPARAMS). In the preceding example, a successful call will return the following FORMFILLPARAMS parameter:

```
FORMFILLPARAMS: First Name:FNAME:Oracle Press,
Last Name:LNAME:Author,Email:EMAIL:om@oraclepress.com,
Address:ADDRESS:2 Embarcadero Center
```

Your program will just have to parse the FORMFILLPARAMS variable string value to extract the individual components or instruments (see Figure 12-9).

So, what is the difference between using the m-Wallet versus the Form Filler? The Form Filler removes a lot of the guesswork for the user and leverages heuristics

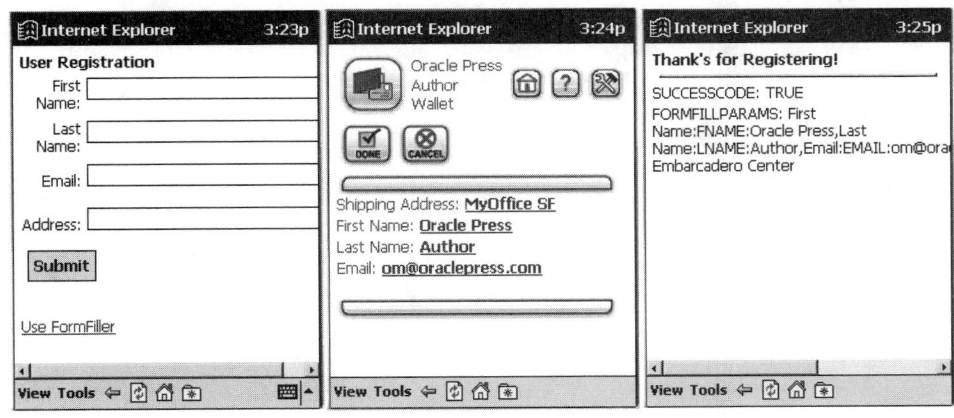

FIGURE 12-9. *The Form Filler*

and the m-Wallet to simplify the task. Unlike with the m-Wallet, the form variable names do not have to be exact matches. For example, we used FNAME for the First Name form field. This got matched to FIRSTNAME from the m-Wallet Profile compartment without the user having to perform the lookup. For forms that are generated dynamically from database queries or driven by XML files, this module is extremely useful.

iPayment

Providing mobile users a choice of payment options is the philosophy behind Oracle's iPayment module. Although credit cards will probably remain the most common way to pay for such goods in the United States, prepaid plans have found great success in Europe as a viable way to sell time for use with mobile phones. That model has been extended to other goods users can buy on their phones. By making a payment up front, your account is debited as you purchase goods, services, or information on your mobile device.

The iPayment module, which integrates with the Oracle CRM iPayment module, processes credit card and bank account transactions, thus allowing transactions to be processed directly through the platform rather than through a processing infrastructure deployed by merchants. Oracle iPayment, which is part of Oracle 11*i* E-Business Suite, is beyond the scope of this book. Therefore, refer to http://www.oracle.com/applications for details.

Billing Mechanism

Whenever any of the mobile services are invoked by an end user—be it a guest or a registered user—an entry is logged into the Oracle database table PTG_SERVICE_LOG. The log table contains a record with information of the service ID, service name, user ID, time stamp, and many related values (see the illustration). A billing mechanism can easily be implemented using these records. For example, a query can be made to report all usages of the Map Generation module by user orcladmin.

SERVICE_NAME	INVOCATION_TIME	RESPONSE_TIME	USER_NAME	REMOTE_ADDRESS	LOGICAL_DEVICE	ADAPTOR_TIME	TRANSFORMATION
/Location/Maps	11-Feb-2002 08:22:59 AM	1903	orcladmin	192.168.0.7	TINY_HTML	1583	310
/Location/Maps	11-Feb-2002 08:23:03 AM	7451	orcladmin	192.168.0.7	TINY_HTML	6710	721
/Location/Maps	11-Feb-2002 08:55:04 AM	70	orcladmin	192.168.0.7	WML11_OPENWAVE	40	20
/Location/Maps	11-Feb-2002 08:55:27 AM	911	orcladmin	192.168.0.7	MS_POCKET_PC	811	90

Based on the result set, charges can be made according to your own customized billing system—be it a per-usage charge method or an adapter/transformation time method, or a time-of-day use or any other combination of usage variables. Table 12-5 provides brief descriptions of some of the fields/columns from the PTG_SERVICE_LOG table that can be used to develop your billing mechanism.

NOTE
The Performance Monitor must be enabled and started for logging to occur. Because these tables grow over time, periodic purging or archiving of these tables is required.

Column Name	Description
SERVICE_ID	The object identifier of the invoked service
SERVICE_NAME	The name of the invoked service
INVOCATION_HOUR	The hour when the service was invoked
INVOCATION_TIME	The date when the service was invoked
RESPONSE_TIME	The response time for the service
USER_ID	The object identifier of the user
USER_NAME	The name of the user
LOGICAL_DEVICE	The logical device from where the service was invoked
ADAPTOR_TIME	The time taken by the adapter to service this request
TRANSFORMATION_TIME	The time taken by the transformer to service this request
TIMESTAMP	The logged event timestamp generated by the trigger

TABLE 12-5. *PTG_SERVICE_LOG Field Names*

Example: Single-Tap Checkout

We will now go through an example of using the m-Wallet to facilitate a "single-tap" checkout process from a shopping cart. Before we begin, it is assumed that the user has already configured his or her m-Wallet and has entered all the relevant data via a desktop PC or equivalent device. We will start from the shopping cart at the m-commerce site (RingTones Central), where a few ring tones are in the cart. The goal is to pay for these ring tones with a single tap, without the user having to enter any credit card or personal information. All the required information is retrieved from the m-Wallet with a final verification by the user before submitting to the third party (RingTones Central, in this example). The code to display the shopping cart and set up for single-tap checkout, leveraging Oracle9*i*AS Wireless m-Wallet, follows:

```
<SimpleResult>
   <SimpleContainer>
   <SimpleImage src="http://localhost:9000/book/rt"
      addImageExtension="true" available="gif jpg" />
   <SimpleImage src="http://localhost:9000/book/cart"
      addImageExtension="true" available="gif jpg" />
   <SimpleTable>
   <SimpleRow>
      <SimpleCol></SimpleCol>
      <SimpleCol><SimpleStrong>Name</SimpleStrong></SimpleCol>
      <SimpleCol><SimpleStrong>Artist</SimpleStrong></SimpleCol>
      <SimpleCol><SimpleStrong>SKU</SimpleStrong></SimpleCol>
   </SimpleRow>
   <SimpleRow>
      <SimpleCol><SimpleImage src="http://localhost:9000/book/music"
      addImageExtension="true" available="gif" /></SimpleCol>
      <SimpleCol>Stan</SimpleCol>
      <SimpleCol>Eminem</SimpleCol>
      <SimpleCol>105859</SimpleCol>
   </SimpleRow>
   <SimpleRow>
      <SimpleCol><SimpleImage src="http://localhost:9000/book/music"
      addImageExtension="true" available="gif" /></SimpleCol>
      <SimpleCol>Mission Impossible</SimpleCol>
      <SimpleCol>Movie Theme</SimpleCol>
      <SimpleCol>101779</SimpleCol>
   </SimpleRow>
   <SimpleRow>
      <SimpleCol><SimpleImage src="http://localhost:9000/book/music"
      addImageExtension="true" available="gif" /></SimpleCol>
      <SimpleCol>Take On Me</SimpleCol>
      <SimpleCol>AHA</SimpleCol>
      <SimpleCol>101830</SimpleCol>
```

```
  </SimpleRow>
  <SimpleBreak rule="true" />
  </SimpleTable>
  <SimpleTable>
  <SimpleRow>
     <SimpleCol><SimpleStrong>Total:</SimpleStrong></SimpleCol>
     <SimpleCol>$3.00</SimpleCol>
     <SimpleCol>
     <SimpleHref target="omp://oracle/services/commerce/wallet?
     WALLETACTION=GET_FORM_DATA&amp;FORM_TITLE=getSecuredInfo&amp;
     APPLICATION=Ringtone+Central&amp;GET_DATA=FN,LN,CC,EMAIL,SHIP"
     callbackurl="https://localhost:9000/book/responseWallet.jsp" >
     <SimpleImage src="http://localhost:9000/book/co"
     addImageExtension="true" available="gif jpg" border="0" />
     </SimpleHref>
     </SimpleCol>
  </SimpleRow>
  <SimpleBreak rule="true" />
  </SimpleTable>
  </SimpleContainer>
</SimpleResult>
```

The user has three items in the cart (see Figure 12-10). Tapping the CheckOut button will activate m-Wallet. The next few screens are part of m-Wallet. At this point, the walletCart.jsp page on RingTones Central calls the user's m-Wallet

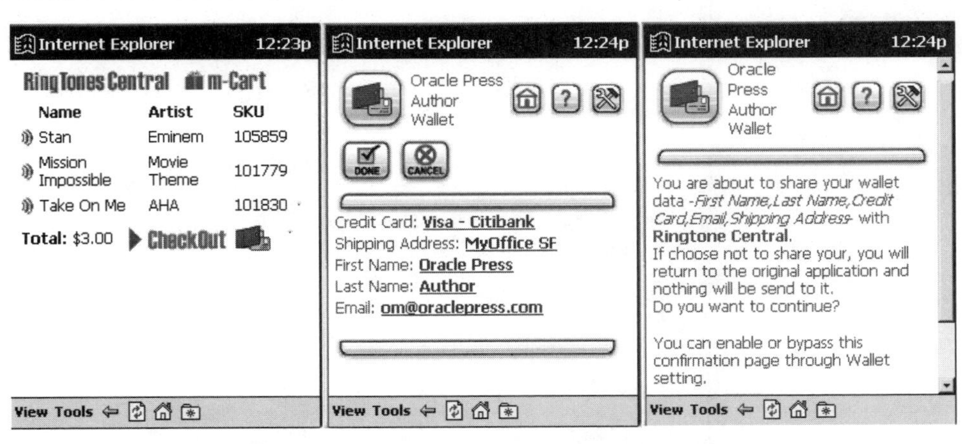

FIGURE 12-10. *Single-tap checkout*

on Oracle9*i*AS Wireless. A dialog between the mobile device and Oracle9*i*AS Wireless ensues.

Once the user has confirmed and approved the transmission of his or her information to RingTones Central, the parameters are passed to the callback URL, responseWallet.jsp, where the data is captured from the HTTPS URL.

The code snippet for extracting the URL parameters and displaying them is shown next. Any real-world code you might write would actually write these parameters into a database and dynamically generate a transaction number, send an e-mail receipt, and build the real download links for the ring tones.

```
<SimpleResult>
   <SimpleContainer>
   <SimpleTitle wrapmode="wrap" size="3">
      <SimpleStrong>Successful Transaction:
RTDL-00015389</SimpleStrong>
   </SimpleTitle>
   <SimpleBreak rule="true" />
   <SimpleText>
      <SimpleTextItem>FIRSTNAME: <%=URL_FIRSTNAME%></SimpleTextItem>
      <SimpleTextItem>LASTNAME: <%=URL_LASTNAME%></SimpleTextItem>
      <SimpleTextItem>ADDRESS: <%=URL_ADDR1%>,
      <%=URL_CITY%>, <%=URL_STATE%> <%=URL_ZIPCODE%></SimpleTextItem>
      <SimpleTextItem>EMAIL: <%=URL_EMAIL%></SimpleTextItem>
      <SimpleTextItem>CC_NUMBER: <%=URL_CC_NUMBER%></SimpleTextItem>
      <SimpleTextItem>EXPIRATION_DATE: <%=URL_CC_EXPIRATION_DATE%>
      </SimpleTextItem>
   </SimpleText>
   <SimpleBreak rule="true" />
   <SimpleHref target="">
      <SimpleImage src="http://localhost:9000/book/dl"
       addImageExtension="true" available="gif jpg"
       border="0" />Download Tones
   </SimpleHref>
   <SimpleBreak />
   <SimpleHref target="omp://oracle/services/pim/mail">
      <SimpleImage src="http://localhost:9000/book/mail_small"
      addImageExtension="true" available="gif jpg" border="0" />
      m-Receipt Mail
   </SimpleHref>
   </SimpleContainer>
</SimpleResult>
```

As shown in Figure 12-11, the crucial information for completing this transaction is passed from the m-Wallet to the third-party server. This server then grants download privileges to the paid user. You can also link to the Mobile E-mail module to read the m-Receipt.

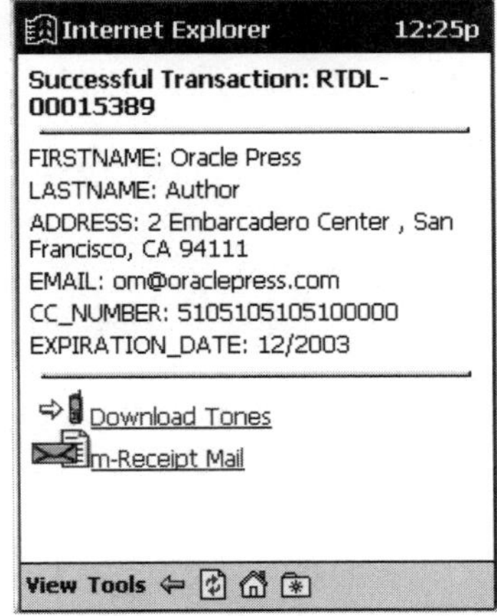

FIGURE 12-11. *m-Receipt*

Summary

From the core commerce modules supplied by Oracle9*i*AS Wireless, you have seen the simplicity with which mobile commerce can be accomplished—maybe even easier than can be done with e-commerce! You can focus only on your business logic and content and utilize the commerce modules to handle the form filling and payment with ease. Your end users will only have to configure their mobile wallets once. They may never have to enter any personal information, such as credit card numbers, billing and shipping addresses, e-mail address, with the unfriendly keypads on their mobile devices again. What's more, they can avoid making any tapping mistakes in entering long sequences of alphanumeric data!

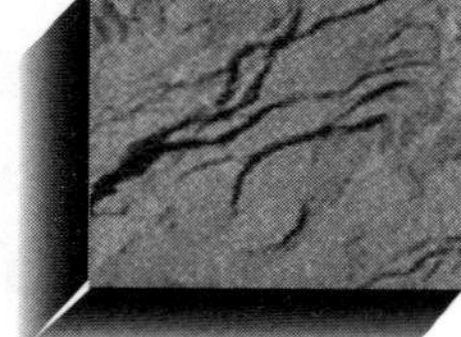

CHAPTER 13

Mobile Studio

he Oracle9*i*AS Wireless Studio, or *Mobile Studio,* is an environment for building, testing, and deploying wireless applications quickly. It lets any developer, systems integrator, or independent software vendor build mobile applications that are immediately accessible from all devices. By offering web-based access to the latest mobile services and tools, Mobile Studio is a unique development environment that can help you shorten time to market, increase productivity, and dramatically simplify your testing cycle. Whereas Oracle9*i*AS Wireless enables you to focus on your business logic by hiding the device and network complexity, Mobile Studio allows you to extend this simplicity to your customers—whether they are in-house or external developers—without them having to deploy their own wireless servers. To facilitate your development effort, we'll look at the steps you need to take to become productive with the Oracle9*i*AS Wireless Studio. In this chapter, we go into the following topics:

- Customizing the Studio Design Environment
- Building Mobile Applications
- Testing Mobile Applications
- Deploying Mobile Applications
- Oracle Mobile Modules (Wireless Services)

Customizing the Studio Design Environment

New to Release 2, Mobile Studio is shipped with Oracle9*i*AS Wireless. This bundled version allows application developers to reap the benefits of Mobile Studio in an internal corporate setting or an extranet setting. For example, you can run Mobile Studio within your firewall in a corporate intranet environment to allow collaboration without exposing your application to the external world. In an extranet setting, on the other hand, Mobile Studio is accessible by any developer from the public Internet.

Mobile Studio's web administration tool allows an enterprise or a wireless carrier to rapidly create a compelling developer portal that can serve both as an interactive development tool and as a one-stop source for up-to-date information and collateral on the wireless server platform. This makes it easy for service providers to support their developer communities and attract new developers. For example, a fictitious carrier, MobileG Wireless, can configure Mobile Studio at http://studio.mobilegwireless.com and make this available to their own developer community, coupled with their own sample applications and a select set of mobile modules (Wireless Services).

Oracle has launched an instance of Mobile Studio that is available to all developers. This Oracle-hosted environment, named *Oracle Mobile Online Studio,* is essentially a free, online resource with a basic set of mobile modules available as building blocks for application development. The types of mobile modules and their usage are described in the Oracle Mobile Modules section. Developers can quickly prototype mobile applications and test them in a live environment through the http://otn.oracle.com website.

There is a growing demand for speech and short message capabilities to make up for the limited input capabilities (such as small keypads) and lack of text display area on handheld devices. A unique feature of Oracle Mobile Online Studio is its integration with carrier-grade voice portals and gateways, including automatic voice recognition (AVR), text-to-speech (TTS) and Short Message Service (SMS) capabilities. This makes the Oracle Mobile Online Studio very compelling for developing, testing, and deploying voice and SMS applications.

The Mobile Studio Model

Mobile Studio's build/test/deploy model, shown in the illustration, is new and unique to software development. It presents a hosted approach to developing dynamic content. You do not need to download any software or tools to start using the Studio. All you need is to access the Studio website, register, and log in. Once authenticated, you have access to reusable modules, sample code, documentation, runtime information, and other useful resources.

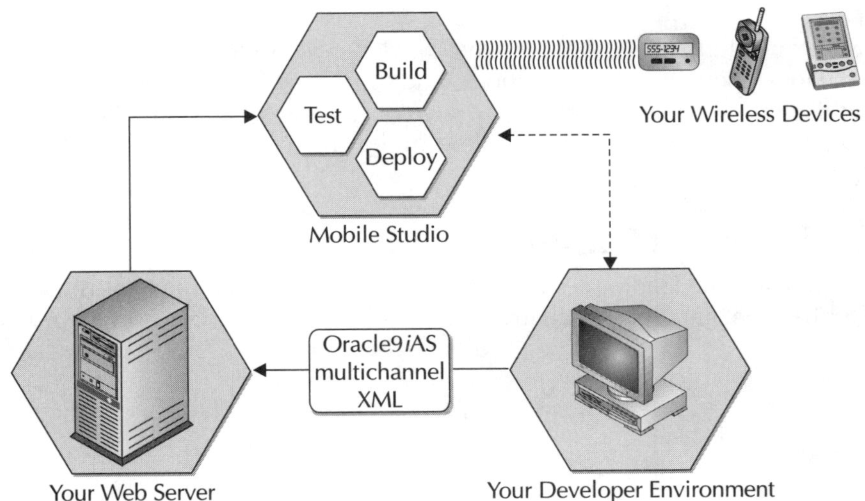

Key features for developers include the following:

- A 100-percent online, hosted environment with nothing to download or maintain
- A simple, web-based user interface targeting mobile application developers
- Instant access to developed applications from any device or simulator, including voice
- Instant debug log access for interactive testing
- One-click deployment to production

Key features for service providers include these:

- Serves as a developer portal, attracting new developers while supporting existing ones
- Easy to brand and customize using web-based administrative tools
- Supports multiple look-and-feel settings in various languages and character sets out of the box
- Targeted to web developers of their own platforms with simple customization pages

Minor differences exist between the Oracle-hosted Oracle Mobile Online Studio and the local, corporate-hosted Mobile Studio. These differences will be pointed out in due course. In this chapter, any references to "Studio" are applicable to both the Oracle-hosted Oracle Mobile Online Studio and the local, corporate-hosted Mobile Studio.

Configuring Mobile Studio

The default Mobile Studio site shipped with Release 2 can be used "as is," without any further configuration. To change the default configuration, however, you need to log into the Mobile Studio administrative web tool at http://oracle9iasw-host:port/studio/admin/login.jsp. Here are the steps you'll follow:

1. Enter an administrator user name (for example, **orcladmin**).
2. Enter the password (for example, **manager**).

Once logged in, you will see a screen like the one shown here.

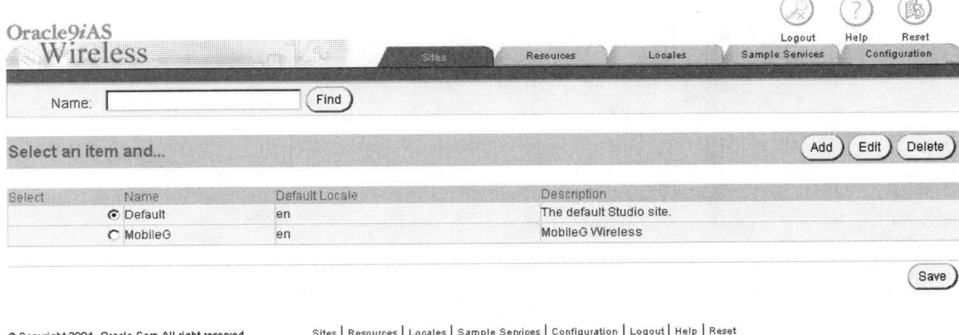

To begin creating a new look and feel, you need to follow these steps:

1. Click the Sites tab to create a new site.
2. Click the Resources tab to customize the resources for your site.
3. Click the Configuration tab to set the parameter oracle.panama.studio.resource.defaultSite to the name of the your site.
4. Click the Reset button to make your changes viewable to end users.

Defining a New Mobile Studio Site

The first step in creating a new Mobile Studio site is to click the Add button on the Sites tab. You will be taken to another web page (see illustration), where you can enter a name and description for your new site.

Oracle9*i*AS Wireless

Logout Help Reset

Sites | Resources | Locales | Sample Services | Configuration

Add/Edit Site:

Name: MobileG

Description: MobileG Wireless

Default Locale: English [en]

Save | Cancel

© Copyright 2001, Oracle Corp.All right reserved

Sites | Resources | Locales | Sample Services | Configuration | Logout | Help | Reset

Click the Save button to save your changes. From here on, the new site label is available in the pull-down menus of the other configuration web pages.

A common practice for developers and administrators alike is to make modifications to the default site. Unfortunately, the default site cannot be modified—the only item that can be modified for the default site is its description. This is obviously set up so that you can always have a working default configuration to revert back to at any time.

NOTE

You can create multiple sites, but only one can be activated with the instance of Mobile Studio running on your Oracle9iAS Wireless server.

Configuring the New Mobile Studio Site

You configure the bulk of your new site in two places: the Resources tab and the Sample Services tab. From the Resources tab, you configure the text and images. The resources are displayed in a fashion similar to a file directory structure. To drill down to a folder, click the name of the folder. For example, to change the page title of the main login page, you drill down through the login folder, to the login.text folder, and finally select the login.text.title literal. Click the Add button to add new text (for example, "Welcome To MobileG Developer Mobile Studio!" for the fictitious MobileG site label, as shown in the illustration).

Oracle9iAS Wireless

Logout Help Reset

Sites | Resources | Locales | Sample Services | Configuration

Resource

Name login.text. title

Description

Type FILE HTTP LITERAL

Default Locale English [en]

Values

Select	Site	Locale	Value
◉	MobileG	English[en]	Developer Mobile Studio!
○	Default	en	Welcome To The Oracle 9iAS Wireless Mobile Studio

Add Delete Undelete

Save

© Copyright 2001, Oracle Corp.All right reserved

Sites | Resources | Locales | Sample Services | Configuration | Logout | Help | Reset

Repeat this for any other parameters you want to replace with customized text or images.

From the Sample Services tab, you can add or remove sample services for your developers to start experimenting with (see the illustration). You just need to specify the name, description, and URL of the service. Each service can be taken offline for debugging but left there for activation later simply by clicking the appropriate Visible radio button.

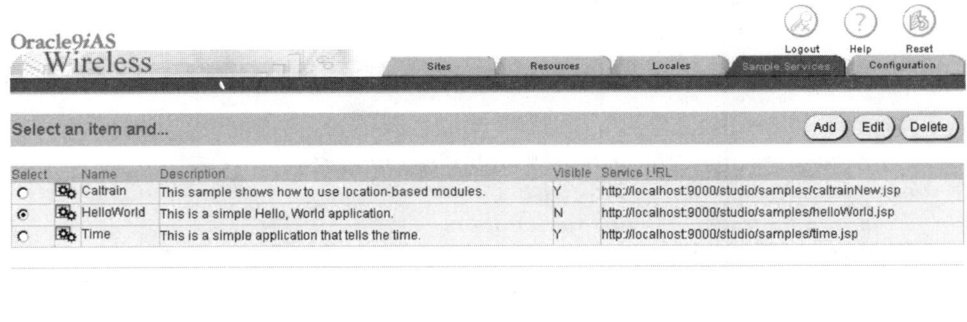

Publishing the New Mobile Studio Site

To publish the newly created site, you click the Configuration tab. The key to publishing a new site is to define the parameter oracle.panama.studio.resource.defaultSite and assign it the value of the site label. For example, by assigning it to our fictitious MobileG site label, we can publish that specific configuration of Mobile Studio, as shown here.

Oracle9*i*AS Wireless

Logout Help Reset

Sites | Resources | Locales | Sample Services | Configuration

Add/Edit Configuration Parameters:

Parameter

Name: oracle.panama.studio.resource.defaultSite

Description: MobileG

Values

Select | Value

MobileG

Add | Delete | Move Up | Move Down

Save | Cancel

© Copyright 2001, Oracle Corp.All right reserved

Sites | Resources | Locales | Sample Services | Configuration | Logout | Help | Reset

After clicking the Save button, you need to click the Reset button to make the site available to the end users. Figure 13-1 shows a newly customized version of our fictitious MobileG Mobile Studio running.

NOTE

If any changes made through the administration web pages are to be visible to end users, the administrator must click the Reset button located on the top-right side of the pages.

User Setup

To access Mobile Studio on your Oracle9*i*AS Wireless instance, point your web browser to http://<oracle9iasw-host:port>/studio. For example, http://compaq9iasw:9000/studio would be a typical URL for your corporate instance

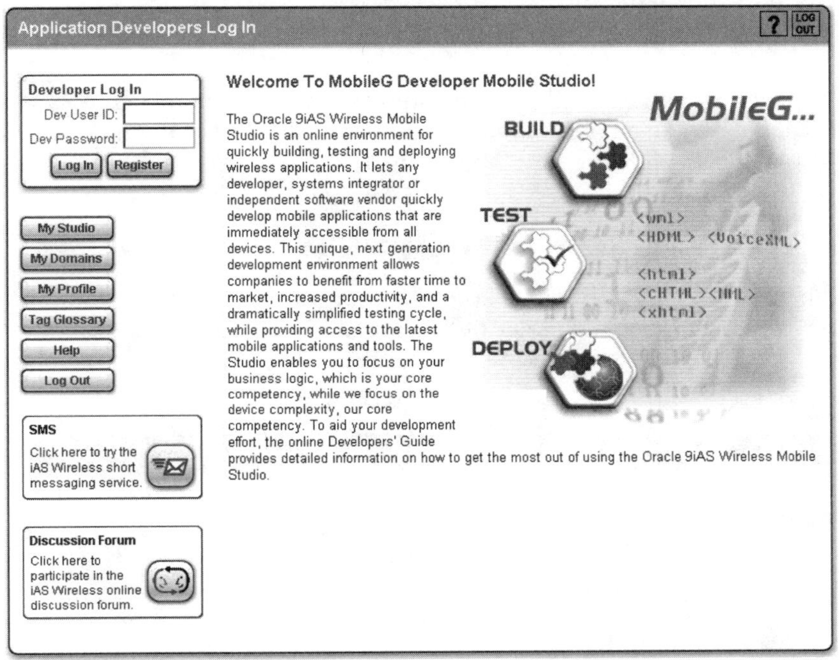

FIGURE 13-1. *Mobile Studio MobileG site*

of Mobile Studio. The Oracle-hosted Mobile Studio is at http://otn.oracle.com. A developer must register with the instance of Studio to access the Studio website. You can register and create a user account by following these steps:

1. Point your browser to your instance of Studio.
2. Click the Register button on the home page and provide the required details to register.
3. In creating this account, you want to enter as much information as possible so when you access Studio from mobile devices, you don't have to enter the same information all over for each device. Your personalized information, such as landmarks (for example, your home and office addresses) and communications channels (for example, your e-mail address and mobile phone number), is what makes or breaks the adaptation of certain mobile devices.

4. Once your account is created, you will automatically be logged in and taken into the Studio development environment, called *My Studio* (see Figure 13-2).

5. You now have an account on Studio. All the tools for developing, testing, and deploying mobile applications are now available at your fingertips. We will explore some of them in the next few sections of this chapter.

Building Your Mobile Application

You can build your mobile application with your own tools and platform because your development infrastructure is transparent to Studio. This allows you to leverage

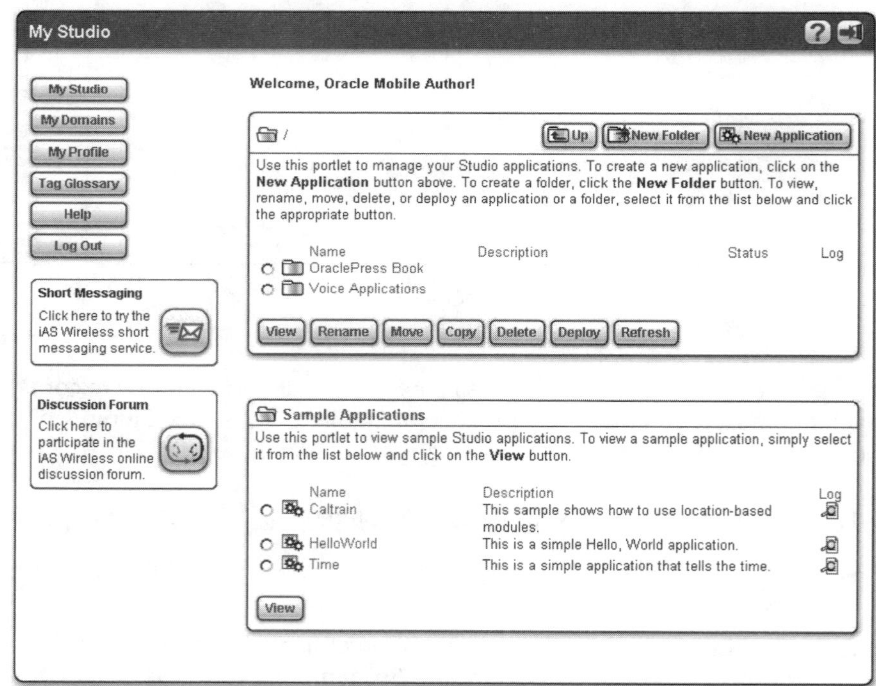

FIGURE 13-2. *The My Studio user interface*

your existing infrastructure investment. Studio is also transparent to the mechanism used to generate the presentation logic of your mobile application. This allows you to leverage your existing skill sets. Examples of these mechanisms are CGI, JavaServer Pages, and Active Server Pages. For Studio to work, the presentation logic of your application must return content that is compliant with the DTD for Oracle9*i*AS multichannel XML. As described in Chapter 3 Oracle9*i*AS multichannel XML consists of a set of device-neutral XML tags specifically designed for small-screen devices and voice.

You can develop dynamic content on your own web server and provide the Studio with a link to that content through your web server (see the illustration). You simply need to set up an HTTP URL to link to your application's entry point, which contains code that generates Oracle9*i*AS multichannel XML. This XML will be transformed by Studio to the individual device content formats understood by each unique device (for example, WML for WAP-compliant devices).

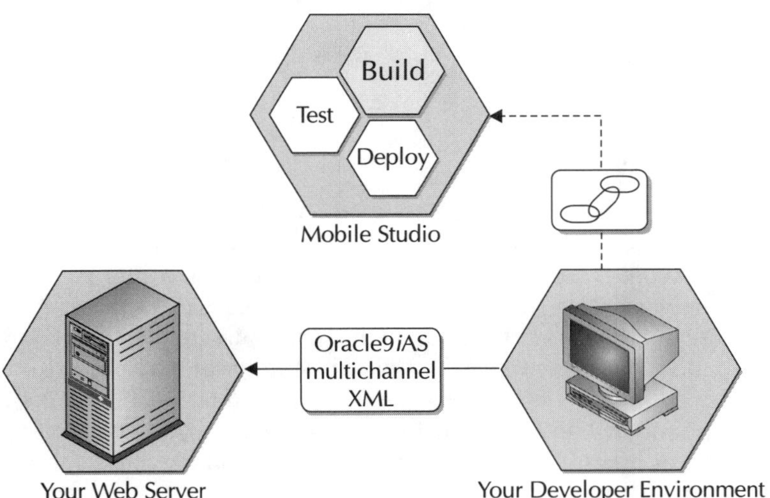

Once you have written application code to generate Oracle9*i*ASW multichannel XML and have defined an HTTP URL to your web server, you can add an application in Studio to link to that XML content. Follow these instructions:

1. Click My Studio on the navigation bar. Log in if you haven't already.

2. Click either the New Application or New Folder button, depending on how you want to organize your applications (see the illustration).

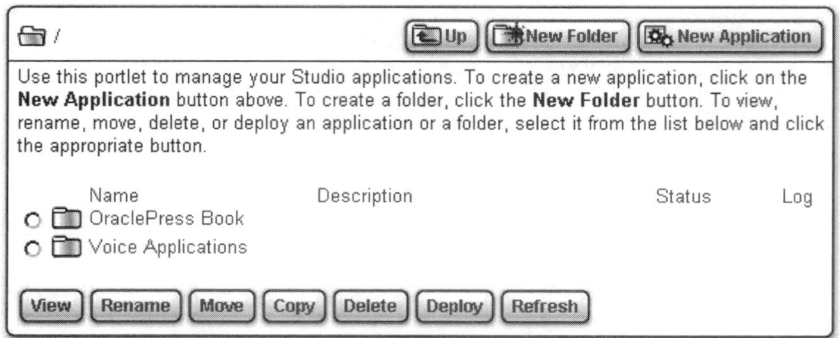

3. When the new application web page is displayed, edit the application details as follows:

   - **Name** The name of your new application (for example, Mobile Contexts).
   - **Remote URL** The HTTP URL to your content. If you're hosted on Oracle Mobile Online Studio, your content must be accessible on the Internet. Your web server must be outside any corporate or personal firewall. The Online Studio needs to make HTTP requests to your web server. Because of firewall architectures, the requests can only be made to web servers visible to the public Internet because firewalls block web servers within them from the public Internet. If your content is on an intranet and you're using Mobile Studio, your web server just has to be accessible on the local network (for example, http://mobileappsvr: studio/mobile_contexts.jsp).
   - **Description** A description of your new application. This will appear in the modules list as the description of your application if you decide to make it a module.
   - **Keywords** Searchable keywords used by the search feature to find your application.
   - **Comments** Private comments.

4. Click the Create button. Your application is now registered in Studio (see the illustration).

Here's a sample application we'll be testing with (using the cut-and-paste method) named "Mobile Contexts":

```
<SimpleResult>
   <SimpleContainer>
      <SimpleText>
         <SimpleTextItem>
            <SimpleStrong>Mobile Contexts</SimpleStrong>
         </SimpleTextItem>
         <SimpleTextItem>
            %value user.id% (user.id)
         </SimpleTextItem>
         <SimpleTextItem>
            %value user.name% (user.name)
         </SimpleTextItem>
      </SimpleText>
   </SimpleContainer>
</SimpleResult>
```

You're now ready to test your newly created application in Studio from a mobile device.

Testing Your Mobile Application

Once you have specified the URL to your application in Studio, you can start running and testing it with actual mobile devices or simulators (see the illustration).

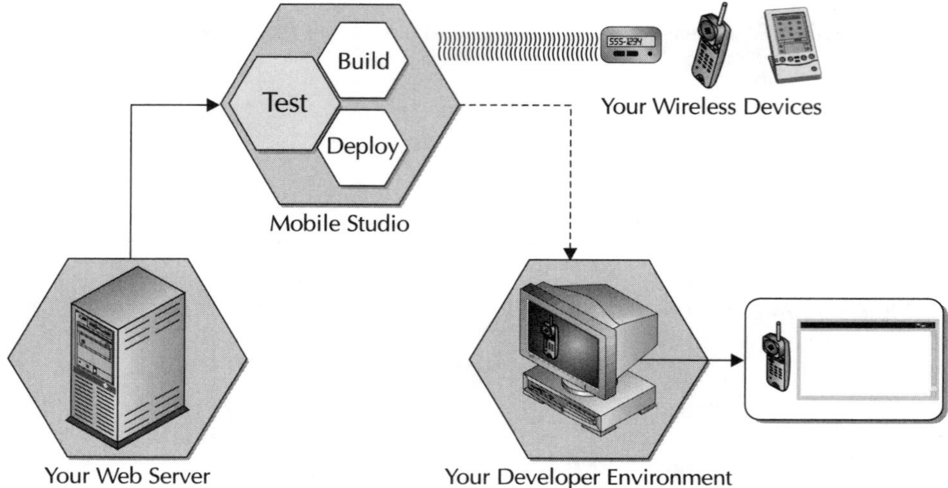

Invoke your application from a mobile device or simulator as follows:

1. Using a small-screen mobile device or simulator, point your device browser to http://studio.oraclemobile.com or http://compaq9iasw:9000/ptg/rm.
2. Log in with the same user name/password as you did for the Studio web site.
3. Navigate and select your new application from the list.

Using the Mobile Contexts sample application, we can view the results using the Openwave 5 WML/XHTML simulator, as shown in Figures 13-3 and 13-4.

As you interact with your mobile application, you can view runtime messages in the debug log file. To view the log file for your new application, navigate through your folders to find your newly created application. Select the log icon button and click it. A pop-up window will appear (see Figure 13-5). From here, you can show many time-stamped versions of the log entries for extensive debugging.

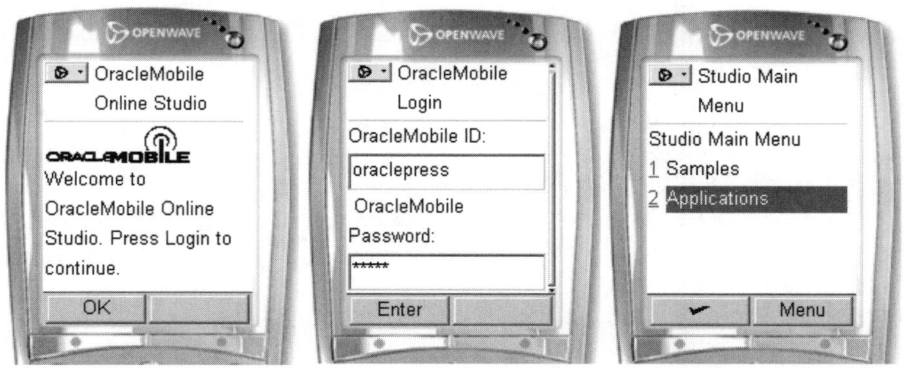

FIGURE 13-3. *Logging into the Openwave 5 simulator sample application*

If an error occurs, you can use the messages in this window for debugging. This window also shows the XML code generated by your application so you can see whether there are any errors.

Notice that we're using the Openwave simulator for debugging the sample application. You can obtain the latest Openwave WML/XHTML simulator from http://developer.openwave.com. Once your mobile application is working as planned, you can deploy it.

FIGURE 13-4. *Accessing the Openwave 5 simulator sample application*

FIGURE 13-5. *View Log Message window*

Deploying Your Mobile Application

Once you have finished testing your application, you may choose to deploy it on a production instance of Oracle9*i*AS Wireless (see the illustration). However, before you can do so, you must set up a deployment domain first.

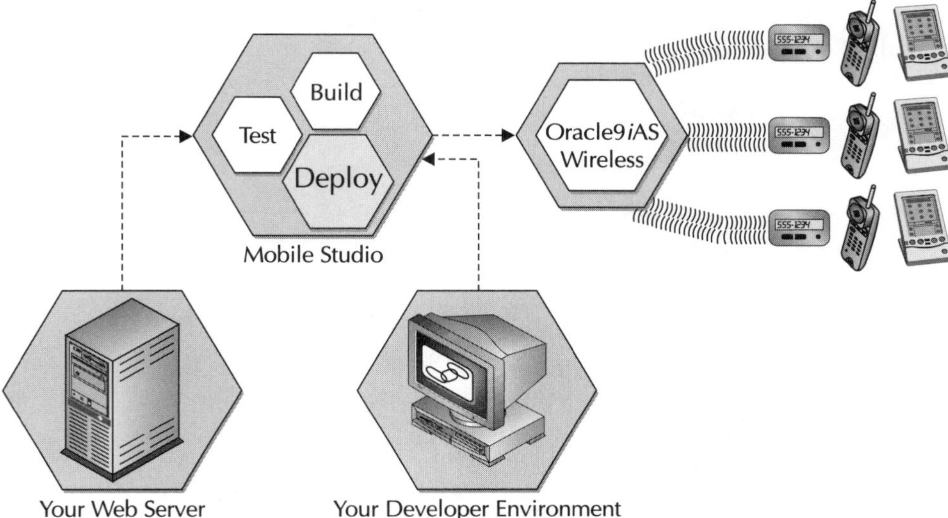

Oracle9*i*AS Wireless domains (no relation to Internet domains, such as mobilegwireless.com) are namespaces used to group related applications deployed from the Mobile Studio to a production instance.

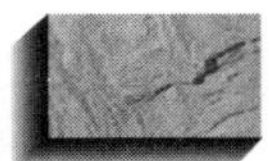

NOTE
Domain names must be unique within an Oracle9iAS Wireless instance, and application names must be unique within a domain.

Any developer can use the Mobile Studio to create as many domains as needed. Each domain has a domain password set by the original creator, which is used to prevent unauthorized deployment of applications to that domain. You can invite others to deploy applications to your domain by sharing the domain password with them.

In order to deploy an application to a production server, you must first *join* a domain. You can join a domain either by creating a new domain for yourself or by joining someone else's domain by acquiring the domain password from its owner. To create or join a domain, click on the My Domains menu button from the My Studio page to go to the domain-management page shown in Figure 13-6.

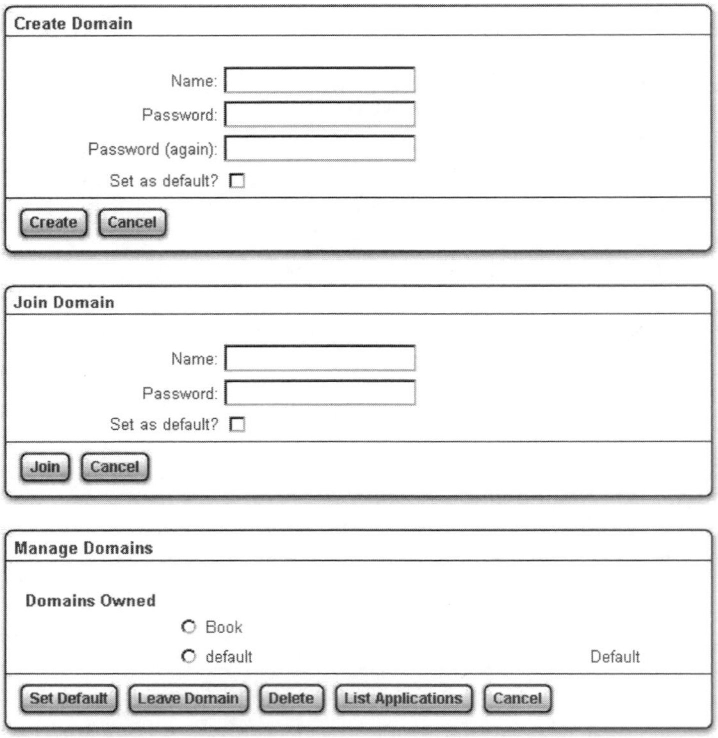

Create Domain

Name:
Password:
Password (again):
Set as default?

Create | Cancel

Join Domain

Name:
Password:
Set as default?

Join | Cancel

Manage Domains

Domains Owned

- Book
- default — Default

Set Default | Leave Domain | Delete | List Applications | Cancel

FIGURE 13-6. *Domain-management page*

Once you have successfully joined a domain, you can go back to the My Studio page, select the application you want to deploy, and click the Deploy button. Verify the information shown on the deployment page and then click the Deploy button to deploy your application to the server indicated. In Mobile Studio, the status of your application is changed from Development to Deployed (see the illustration).

Once an application has been deployed to the production server, end users on the production server will be able to link it to their home pages. In order to make it easier for your end users to link to your application, the Mobile Studio generates a snippet of HTML code you can include on your website. End users who visit your web site will be able to use this QuickLink Wizard to link to your application.

You're now done with your mobile application! In the next section, we will discuss some of the out-of-the-box modules provided by Oracle9*i*AS Wireless Release 2 as well as the Oracle-hosted Oracle Mobile Online Studio. They're designed for ease of use and integration with your custom mobile applications.

Oracle Mobile Modules (Wireless Services)

Seventeen mobile modules (or Wireless Services) are shipped with Oracle9*i*AS Wireless Release 2. These are available to any customer of the wireless server.

However, the Oracle-hosted Oracle Mobile Online Studio offers only a subset of these to its developers. These modules are reusable application components that allow you to link pre-built applications to your own, thus adding functionality beyond the scope of your applications. Table 13-1 lists the mobile modules that are available on Oracle Mobile Online Studio, as of this writing.

Modules are constantly being added to or deleted from Oracle Mobile Online Studio based on suitability and agreements between Oracle and its partners. Check with Oracle Mobile Online Studio at http://otn.oracle.com for the latest modules available and full descriptions.

Here's a sample usage: If you are developing a Movie Finder application, you can link the address of a movie theater showing a specific movie to the Driving Directions module. A user of your service can select a movie theater and obtain driving directions to it from an originating address. Before driving there, the user may want to find an ATM machine around the Oracle campus to withdraw some cash for purchasing movie tickets and refreshments. This can be done without you having to write another application to generate driving directions. You only need to specify the module's namespace reference in the "target" attribute of your service's XML tags and provide callback information to the module in the form of attributes.

Module	Function	Virtual URL
Driving Directions	Provides detailed driving directions between two locations (U.S. addresses only)	omp://oracle/services/location/directions
Location	Provides landmarks or previously used addresses automatically to the user	omp://oracle/services/location/picker

TABLE 13-1. *Mobile Modules Available on the Online Studio*

An example of how to use one of these modules on Oracle Mobile Online Studio follows:

```
<SimpleResult>
   <SimpleContainer>
      <SimpleMenu title="Select a task:">
      <SimpleMenuItem
      target="omp://oraclemobile/atmlocator?ADDRESS=500+Oracle+Parkway
      &amp;CITY=Redwood+City&amp;STATE=CA&amp;SORTBY=distance
      &amp;RADIUS=5">
      Find an ATM
      </SimpleMenuItem>
      </SimpleMenu>
   </SimpleContainer>
</SimpleResult>
```

This sample application uses the ATM Finder mobile module to look for an ATM within a five-mile radius from Oracle World Headquarters in Redwood City, California.

Figures 13-7 and 13-8 show how this looks when viewed with the Openwave 5 WML/XHTML browser.

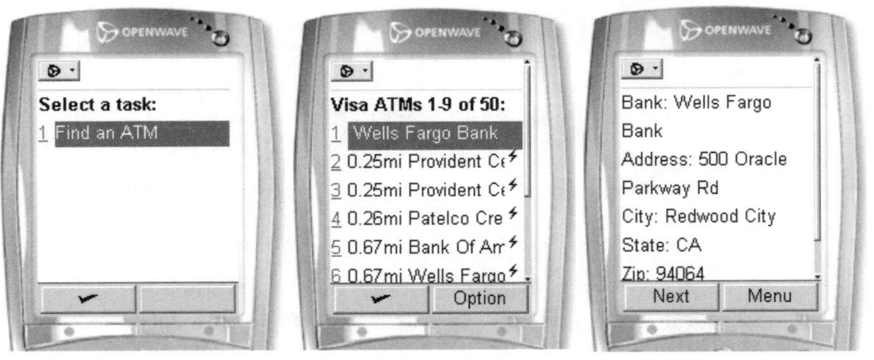

FIGURE 13-7. *ATM Finder results*

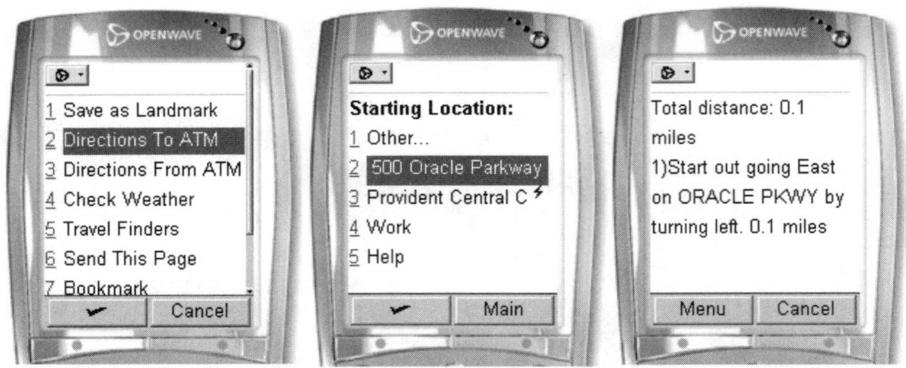

FIGURE 13-8. *Directions to the ATM*

When ATMs are located, the ATM names and distances from a specific location are shown. The user then has the options of getting driving directions or saving any of these ATM addresses as a landmark, once a specific ATM is chosen. You can build user-friendly applications by simply calling these location-based services modules in your code.

If you are building applications with the Mobile Studio hosted within your own firewall, you can use the 17 mobile modules shipped with Oracle9*i*AS Wireless Release 2 and link them the same way as earlier, using slightly different URLs. Table 13-2 lists the shipped modules and their virtual URLs.

Module	Function	Virtual URL
Mobile E-Mail	Allows users to access e-mail messages from any mobile device (IMAP4 or POP3 servers).	omp://oracle/services/pim/mail
Mobile Directory	Allows users to access LDAP directory servers from any mobile device.	omp://oracle/services/pim/directory
Mobile Address Book	Allows users to manage address books and contacts from any mobile device.	omp://oracle/services/pim/addressbook

TABLE 13-2. *Shipped Modules and Their URLs*

Module	Function	Virtual URL
Calendar	Allows users to manage schedules from any mobile device.	omp://oracle/services/pim/calendar
Instant Messaging	Allows users to exchange instant messages from any mobile device.	omp://oracle/services/pim/instantmessaging
Short Messaging	Allows users to send voice, e-mail, fax, or SMS messaging from any mobile device.	omp://oracle/services/pim/shortmessaging
Document Management	Allows users to upload or download to/from the Oracle Internet File System from any mobile device.	omp://oracle/services/pim/ifs
Fax	Allows users to send a fax, check status, forward, or delete a fax from any mobile device.	omp://oracle/services/pim/fax
Tasks	Allows users to schedule and manage tasks from any mobile device.	omp://oracle/services/pim/tasks
Mobile Wallet	Stores and retrieves user payment instrument information, such as credit cards, bank accounts, and shipping addresses, to process payments.	omp://oracle/services/commerce/wallet
Translator	Allows users to translate any site written in WML to be rendered on any mobile device by converting its contents to XML.	omp://oracle/services/commerce/translator
iPayment	Processes credit card and bank account transactions; integrated with Oracle CRM iPayment module.	omp://oracle/services/commerce/payment

TABLE 13-2. *Shipped Modules and Their URLs* (continued)

Module	Function	Virtual URL
Form Filler	Self-teaching form filler that maintains mappings between application form fields and wallet elements.	omp://oracle/services/commerce/formfiller
Business Directory	Provides users with a Yellow Pages–type interface to look for the addresses and phone numbers of registered businesses in a given radius.	omp://oracle/services/location/bizdir
Directions	Provides users with driving directions between an originating address and a destination address.	omp://oracle/services/location/directions
Location	Allows users to pick and manage their frequently accessed locations.	omp://oracle/services/location/picker
Maps	Provides users with broad and detailed maps for a given location.	omp://oracle/services/location/maps

TABLE 13-2. *Shipped Modules and Their URLs* (continued)

For a more complete reference of the modules, OMP URLs, and inputs, along with their output values, refer to the respective chapters on these "Wireless Services" in this book.

Application developers may reuse these Wireless Services or modules to jumpstart their wireless development work, or they can develop their own modules. Mobile modules can be called from any application or module and may be instructed to return control to another application or module. A module receives information about the service it needs to return to after it is done. For example, to use Mobile E-mail, you make a call to the module and pass the *action, mailto,* and *callbackurl* attributes to the module:

```
<SimpleMenuItem
   target="omp://oracle/services/pim/mail?action=messageto
```

```
   &mailto=phil@mobilegwireless.com
   "callbackurl="%value service.home.url%">
   Send eMail
</SimpleMenuItem>
```

You've just seen how easy it is to integrate any of the Oracle mobile modules into your application and get your application up and running in minimal time.

Short Messaging Service (SMS)

A unique feature within Studio is that a user can send a short text or voice message to any phone number in the United States or to any European mobile phone (see Figure 13-9). It's as simple as entering the phone number and message into a form on a web page and submitting it to the server. You don't need to know what

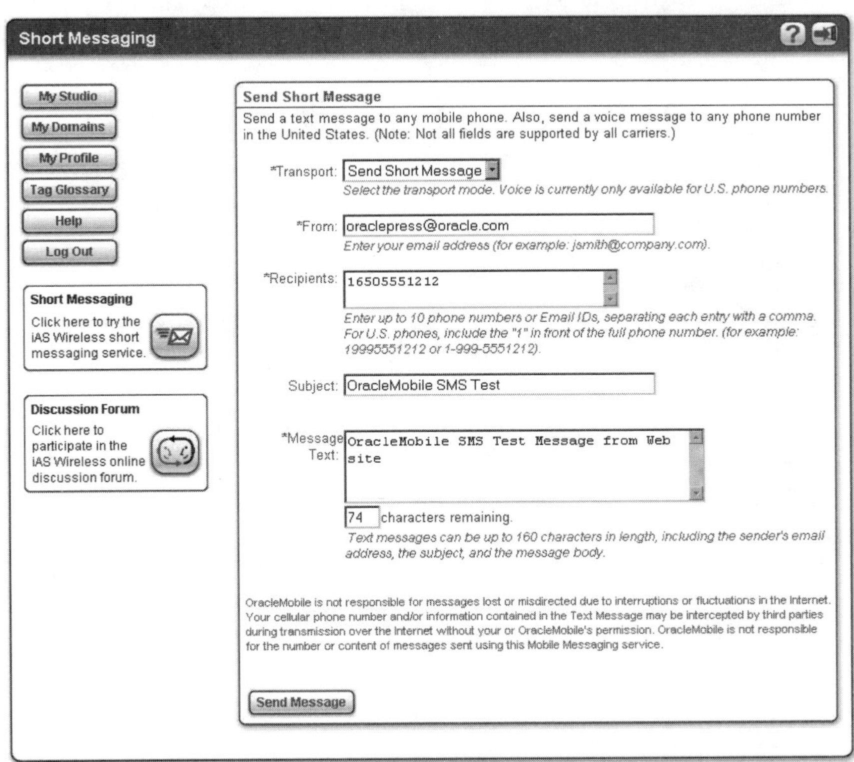

FIGURE 13-9. *Short message system*

wireless carrier the recipient subscribes to or whether the SMS services are interoperable between service providers. Through SMS brokers and other arrangements, Oracle has again shielded the complexity from you and your development work.

Two major features of Oracle9*i*AS Wireless Release 2 are push and SMS. These were covered extensively in Chapter 6. What's highlighted here is simply the convenience offered in Studio—undoubtedly a core feature in the Oracle9*i*AS Wireless platform you'll want to take advantage of.

Summary

You have just learned how to configure and use the Oracle9*i*AS Wireless Studio environment for building, testing, and deploying mobile applications. It lets you quickly develop mobile applications that are immediately accessible from all devices. This chapter has provided you with details on how to enable rapid development and deployment of mobile applications with both Oracle-hosted Oracle Mobile Online Studio and your corporate-hosted Mobile Studio.

PART III

Developing and Deploying Dynamic Applications

CHAPTER 14

Application Design and Development

In Part I, we talked about the mobile economy and Oracle's strategy and architecture. In Part II, we discussed Oracle9*i*AS Wireless core technologies and services. Now, in Part III, we'll look at real-life methodology and framework for designing and developing applications, as well as emerging platforms, devices and services. This chapter provides a simplified development methodology for project managers, service developers, architects, and content managers to review. This framework, shown in Figure 14-1, serves as a reference in our discussion on ways to build and manage mobile solutions. In Chapter 15, we will review three case studies and highlight the decision points for creating mobile services and applications. In Chapter 16, we continue to examine cases for mobile enabling enterprise information services and review successful applications such as mobile e-mail, CRM, ERP, and financial applications. In Chapter 17, we look ahead at some of the interesting developments in wireless networks, devices, protocols, technologies and services. Here, we will look at the following topics:

- Planning and Organizing for Mobile
- From Diagnostics to Defining Requirements
- Architecture Design
- Development and Coding
- Testing and Deployment

Although every organization has its own development framework, the information presented in Figure 14-1, structured with a focus on issues related to mobile computing, will highlight the points that are noteworthy for building and managing mobile solutions.

Planning and Organizing for Mobile

How are mobile projects different from any other IT endeavor? Generally, mobile assignments and their requirements do not differ significantly from any IT or e-commerce project requirements in terms of planning and organization. Mobile projects require nothing less in sound strategy development, comprehensive planning, and the fundamental process of developing the architecture. Much of the digital asset auditing, content preparation, page-level design, testing, and deployment work should be based on your existing, proven methodology.

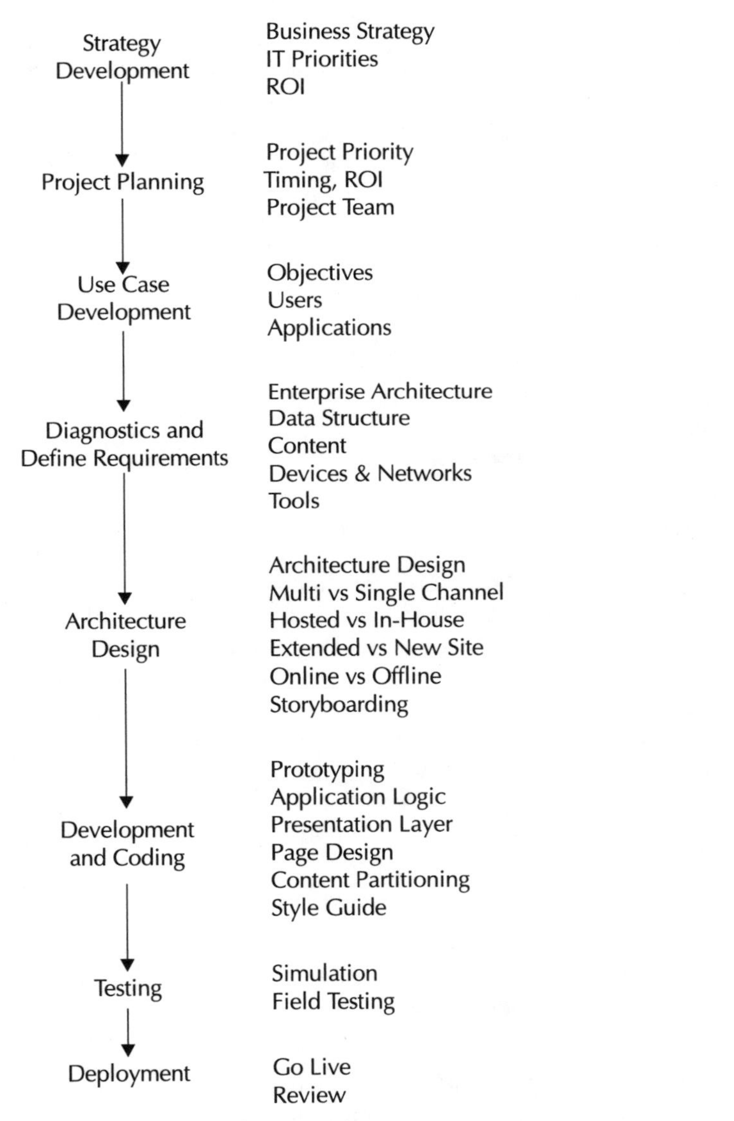

FIGURE 14-1. *Simplified mobile development lifecycle*

The key differences, though, are the considerations and driving forces for going mobile! Are you building wireless applications as a business advantage? Are you driving a new way of conducting business as the market leader in your industry? Perhaps you are responding to a competitive threat because your competitors are offering wireless portals for customers, partners, and employees to access key information. Aside from external factors, you should review your organization's internal needs. Do you know who your users are? Is a fair amount of your organization mobile? Have your competitors adopted and become successful with mobile services? Can your customers, suppliers, and partners benefit? What will they want first?

Strategy Development

Mobile has the potential to be a disruptive technology that can cause fundamental changes in an organization and bring competitive advantage to your industry. You may have to rethink the principles that drive business processes and decisions. As a result, you need to start by defining a wireless enterprise strategy and decide how that will link to your IT strategy and overall business strategy. This can help you prioritize and lead to critical reviews of key components of your mobile endeavor and the successful factors in achieving your goals.

More common objectives include making your employees and business more productive and achieving cost savings in business operations. Mobile projects could bring more timely information and real-time decision-making capabilities to those who need them. It may directly or indirectly lead to new revenues or customers.

Initially, you may not have concrete ideas about what mobile can do, let alone formulate a wireless strategy. In many cases, though, you know that mobile enabling certain business operations can bring benefits and value to your organization, just like how the Internet changed the way enterprises are now managing their businesses. You know you should do something, but you are unsure about what. Usually, these are good guidelines to follow:

- Do your business processes require time-sensitive information?
- Can you increase productivity or create value by offering your target audience real-time information and the power to act on it?
- Is your target audience mobile and do they spend a fair amount of time away from the desktop? Are they in areas so remote that always-on wireless service is unavailable, thus necessitating persistent storage?
- Can the automated interactions and/or transactions be done in a short amount of time, with few inputs or keystrokes?
- Can you succinctly identify business impacts such as reduction of operational costs or enhanced revenues and return on investment (ROI)?

Some applications can expand the scope of a business. However, you will find out only if you build a project and try it out. Invariably, even a prototype project, and the experience that comes with it, will show you the way.

Project Planning

Just like with any IT or web project, you must understand the business and IT strategy. Thereafter, you need to formulate the project plan, define functional requirements, and allocate resources.

When you're developing mobile applications, one of the first tasks is to gather functional requirements. Like other IT projects, you must decide what is needed, but you must have a clear understanding of the mobile environment, including device and wireless service constraints. Because you are adding new IT services to your organization, this may require changes to technology, business processes, people, job functions, and even the organizational structure.

Starting at the enterprise level, you are committing the organization to actively pursue wireless functionality. Through project planning, you can drill down to the system and project architectures and specify the logical and functional definition of services.

One of the biggest challenges in mobile service development is that many wireless and mobile technologies are new. Invariably, some of these capabilities and platforms have not been proven under production environments and live stresses.

Besides the architectural side, assembling a balanced, capable development team is a must. If you have developers well versed in Java and C++, these resources can be deployed to build native or offline applications. Many times these resources can help you build the application logic and expedite the efforts on synchronization or data replication. Experienced web programmers and user interface designers are required to create intuitive applications. This will ultimately affect the success or failure of your project. Remember, users won't spend time to learn to use new devices, and they are loathe to learn new applications if the applications require too much training.

Finally, user acceptance and adoption are key. Recruiting a world-class development team is only half the game. To succeed, involving end users early can help minimize risks related to project definitions and avoidance of feature creep later on in the project.

A final word on planning: Build some slack in your timetable for testing. Also, if you are experienced with enterprise IT projects, you'll probably appreciate the value of storyboarding and creating a use-case definition. We'll look at these topics next.

Use-Case Development

A good way to formalize a process is by modeling it through techniques such as using the Unified Modeling Language (UML) or by writing a use case that delineates how the process works and how the business objectives are achieved. Consider the features that will make your application compelling, user friendly, and adaptive.

A use case provides a concrete depiction of how all the actors in the system interact and achieve their goals. This step-by-step outline gives you the process flow and identifies scenarios for various success and failure steps. The use case helps you identify all the components of the system. By providing step-by-step definitions on the system, including actors such as servers, devices, networks, users, administrators, and organizations, you can gather and validate specification requirements. It helps you crystallize your designs and your implementation plan. On the other hand, it will help you avoid the pitfall of "requirement gold-plating" (that is, providing more requirements than your users want).

For example, a use case helps you decide what your application will do if wireless connection is lost, or what will happen if your service session is terminated while you are uploading data into the database server. Will you be able to recover? Will the data be backed up? Will you even know?

From Diagnostics to Defining Requirements

One important point to make is how wireless technologies may affect your existing IT investment and the architecture thinking behind them. For example, network infrastructure, related to WAP and SMS, may be sufficiently complex for you to consider outsourcing and application hosting. If you imagine your organization will never use application service providers (ASPs), wireless projects may change your mind.

Also, like creating an e-commerce site, you will need digital assets. Like e-commerce, you will need graphics in thumbnails as well as regular and expanded scales. Wireless applications may require you to provide WBMP, GIF, PNG, and other formats. Your content, in HTML, may need to be transcoded in real time or translated once and for all into XML. Team collaboration takes on new meaning when you have to worry about wireless infrastructure, handheld device usability, and integration with other enterprise systems. With all these requirements, what tools do you select? Do you even know what is available, given that tools and platforms continue to evolve? Should you use UML? Although you know who your current users are, have you considered future users and who they will be? Will your system architecture, programming model, and design become obsolete in a year? Let's look at these issues.

Enterprise Architecture

Before you start to create mobile solutions, it is important to understand the systems architecture, programming model, and management support.

If your organization has chosen Java as the platform, then obviously you are already migrating to J2EE. However, legacy or other departmental assets may still be in HTML, Active Server Pages, Perl, or PHP. For instance, if your current servers are Windows NT based using Active Server Pages, you may want to adopt the XML framework. You can go live rapidly by pointing the URL to Oracle9*i*AS Wireless for mobile provisioning. Besides middleware support, other criteria, such as processing power, expandability, battery life, memory, connectivity options, and user interface, are important under certain conditions or vertical applications.

Content and Data Structure

In a clean implementation, your data layer should house the entire back-end information specific to your applications. It should have no dependencies and knowledge of your business logic or the device your users are using to access the service.

Because many applications depend on data from multiple sources, you should not underestimate the time and effort required to extract or abstract content from the back end. This is especially true for enterprise wireless portals, where the system must fetch content locally and remotely and then integrate it into a single portal HTML page or into a multitude of mobile portal pages. Likewise, legacy applications present unique challenges—but you can web-enable them, perhaps through XML. This XML representation is made possible through an enterprise application integration (EAI) construct, and the result is delivered subsequently to the mobile devices.

Devices and Networks

For most wireless and mobile applications, your users may interact with your systems through many heterogeneous wireless networks and protocols. You must control the content presentation and format the results to be tailored for these devices—both for today and for tomorrow.

For example, if your wireless enterprise applications entail mostly text-based content and short transactions, a speed of 9.6 kbps is sufficient. You must, nonetheless, verify the latency and coverage of your network. If your coverage is spotty and you need always-on capabilities, you probably need to consider an offline or a hybrid solution that works in and out of wireless coverage.

Tools Selection

Selecting tools can be a difficult task. No hard, set rules apply here, except to go with your team's capabilities and the project on hand. For example, if you are building offline or native applications, tools from Code Warrior and AppForge may be useful. If you are building online wireless applications, Where2Net daVinci Studio could prove useful for designers, line-of-business professionals, as well as experienced JSP and Java coders. If you are building both offline and online wireless applications, you definitely want to check out Oracle9*i* JDeveloper, which is a J2EE integrated development environment (IDE) that provides end-to-end support for developing, debugging, and deploying Internet applications and Web services.

Memory Requirements

Designing applications for handheld devices requires careful consideration of memory usage. Some applications require runtime modules and may perform many functions, including translation of the application into something the operating system can handle. This can eat up anywhere between 50kB to 1MB of space on the device. For devices that have limited memory capabilities, you will need to validate their impact and ensure compatibility.

Architecture Design

A key architecture design is to determine whether you will build a single-channel or multichannel infrastructure. Let's examine the pros and cons in more details.

Multichannel vs. Single Channel

In creating a mobile application, the simplest way is to build a specific channel that supports a single markup language or device. The common one has been WML. This implementation approach is for the mobile devices to directly connect to the web server that will serve up WML pages. WAP phones accessing a mobile commerce site, via a unique URL, will be served content in WML markup.

Another approach, advocated by leading mobile platform providers, including Oracle, is to support mobile devices by using XML as the middle tier. The XML document generated from the content JSP, ASP, PHP, and Perl, and so on, will be transformed into the markup language supported by the detected mobile device browser. For example, a mobile commerce application containing JSP pages will generate Oracle9*i*AS multichannel XML, which in turn will be transformed into WML for WAP phones and into cHTML for PocketPCs, and so on.

If you plan on not supporting other channels or if your code can be easily adapted or expanded to generate XML, the single channel may provide an easy way to accomplish your goal. Otherwise, you will be better served to utilize the multichannel approach and future-proof your application code.

Another point worth considering is whether the website or application is a public one. You must decide whether there will be separate entry points for different devices/markups and web browsers (HTML) as well as whether all will use the same URL. There are some reasons related to firewalls that make using the same URL not feasible. For public mobile websites, it is simpler to offer your users the same URL for PC browsers and other mobile devices with micro-browsers. Your listener will convey the request and, based on headers, the execution flow of JSP pages will be different depending on the devices—HTML pages for PCs, and specific markup pages for other devices.

ASP vs. In-house Hosting

The decision to host wireless applications within the firewall of your enterprise may require significant upfront investments in time and effort. The cost considerations in setting up, implementing, and maintaining network infrastructure, servers, hardware, load-balancing, security, and failover measures all add to the cost. It is less expensive to utilize a wireless ASP, because the pay-per-use approach typically requires a setup fee and a monthly per-user fee. One key criterion will be how you handle security as the data goes through a third party's network. It can become more expensive in the longer term unless ongoing support and upgrades with the latest technologies help justify the perpetual fee as well. The advantages of sharing infrastructure bandwidth and costs may help justify the use of wireless ASPs.

Time to market quite often is a consideration and if there's good economic justification, one strategy is to quickly host applications on an ASP while building your own infrastructure for hosting. Once your infrastructure is complete, the hosted applications can be hosted in your infrastructure.

Extended vs. New Site

Another key question is whether to extend an existing site, perhaps through transcoding, or to create a completely "multichannel" site.

By bringing an existing website or application to mobile devices, it is important to understand whether you need to extend any existing PC browser-accessible content and application logic to small form factors and limited bandwidth. The presentation and business logic, written specifically for HTML browsers, may not be applicable for micro-browsers used in handheld devices. Hence, the transcoding approach is not usually recommended, unless the scope is very limited or the purpose is for proof of concept.

On the other hand, the decision to abandon an existing, proven and working e-commerce site to opt for a truly multichannel site is not only hard to justify in terms of cost, but pragmatically, it is hard to pull off and transition well. An approach that uses existing HTML content protects current investments and is a fast way to get up and running, but in the long run a transcoding approach will have formidable limitations.

When you're designing a mobile site from scratch, many design issues could impact how the application functions seamlessly in different channels, such as web, WAP, voice, and push. Also, this approach can have implications during runtime. This is because XML applications may prove to be too slow for a heavy-traffic enterprise (or e-commerce) website or application unless caching and other measures are implemented. Ultimately, your decision will hinge on what types of sites and applications your users want and how you implement them.

Online vs. Offline

Another key question is whether to build a wireless application or an offline application. This is not just another modality or channel! Building offline or native applications involves client-side application logic, synchronization/replication, and (potentially) version control of your application. What's more, it may involve a local, lightweight version of a relational database, persistent store, or other client software in the device. Therefore, you will have to deal with configuration and provisioning issues. When do you want offline or disconnected applications? Are they always available, or do you need a local data store? Is it because you don't have coverage? Is it just to save connection airtime? Here are the criteria generally used to decide:

- Do you need a persistent data store on the device?
- Will there be heavy-duty data access and capture?
- Is wireless coverage spotty?
- Is bandwidth inadequate or expensive?
- Will the devices used be mostly PDAs, not WAP phones or SMS phones?
- And ultimately, what is the time value of information for your target audience?

Offline applications can handle data transfers where the user is not connected to the server or a central database on a real-time basis. Instead of instant data transfer, the user occasionally synchronizes the data in their mobile device with either a PC or a server through a wireless, WLAN, or cradle connection. Synchronization applications must work with a thick client that contains most or all of the data.

Another category worth mentioning is the so-called "intermittently connected" or hybrid applications. The term "intermittent" is being used to distinguish these applications from the ones that require no persistent storage because they have constant access to wireless network resources. These hybrid applications typically have a thick client—one that will process interactions in real time, if the real-time connection can be established, but can cache or queue the transaction when the connection is not available. When the connection becomes available again, the queued interactions are processed at that time.

Many hybrid applications can detect the connection and then choose whichever means of connectivity is most applicable. Most often, the users do not need to even know whether the connection is on. The applications will handle the connectivity monitoring and render it mostly transparent to the users. If you need real-time access for a database query, for example, and you're not connected, you will receive an error message. However, with caching, these applications can prefetch and make the information available with some degree of currency, even if the wireless connection is not available at the exact time of processing. It is important to consider the time value of the information for applications. The time value of information helps determine if we should use a model for an application that is constantly connected to the network or a model for application that is only occasionally connected to a network.

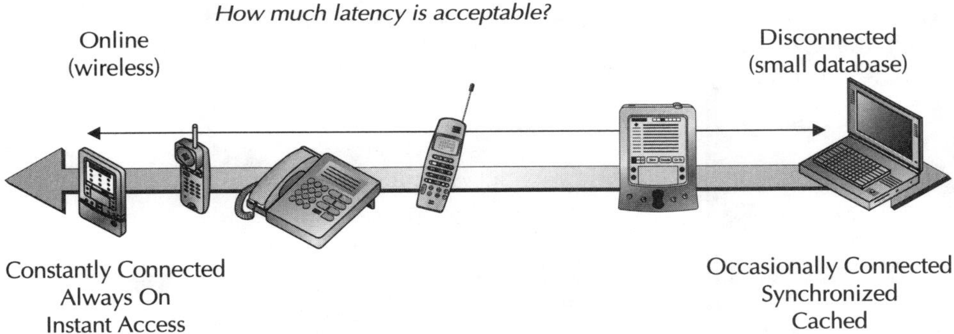
Time Value of Information
Do users need immediate information from a central server; does the data collected in the field need to be shared with the central server immediately?
How much latency is acceptable?
Online
(wireless)
Disconnected
(small database)
Constantly Connected
Always On
Instant Access
Occasionally Connected
Synchronized
Cached

If our data or applications information loses its value quickly over time we must remain connected with always-on services. But, if our information doesn't lose its significance for days, weeks, or months, then we require persistence for data but not continuous connectivity. More will be covered later on in this chapter.

Storyboarding

Creating a storyboard is particularly useful for building multichannel applications, because multichannel applications may involve a variety of users and use cases. For example, a user may access the application via a desktop PC for full-fledged functionality, and the same user may access the same application from a WAP browser later on. The HTML pages served will have multimedia and rich content, whereas the mobile pages (perhaps in WML or cHTML) will be limited to display in a small form factor device. The mobile access may be restricted to certain content or functionality. Also, mobile users may be amenable to SMS alerts or voice alerts.

In most cases, you should use separate storyboards for the HTML and mobile channels because of the distinctly different user experience. Also, separate storyboards may be made for different roles and even different modalities. For example, a voice channel will entail different interactions than a WAP channel.

You will see more of these differences in content, execution flow, and modalities in later sections of this chapter. In any case, once validated, your storyboards could become the sitemaps of these channels.

Development and Coding

Let's take a closer look at native application or wireless service development, especially on page design and coding.

Prototyping

Needless to say, many of you appreciate the value in prototyping, or building a proof of concept service. This is a legitimate way to start making some progress immediately with your project while you are still developing your functional requirements or refining your wireless strategy. By creating and delivering a small, limited-functionality service to a subset of users, you can achieve several goals:

- Provide meaningful services without significant upfront investments
- Gain experience quickly with actual implementation
- Obtain inputs on how your services will play out in the real world
- Build support and interest for wireless services in your organization

Business Logic

Web and mobile channels have fundamentally different use cases and form factors. For example, you can easily fill in a form using a keyboard while typing away in the office. But you expect a short one-way or two-way message if you sign onto SMS alert services. Therefore, your application layer, which houses all the business logic and system application components, should be carefully examined to determine which user roles and devices will be allowed to access certain functions of your applications. Only after that should you decide what the presentation format will look like.

For designing the business logic, and by the same token, the presentation style, there are generally two approaches:

- Design for the *lowest common denominator* user role and device. You look for and fulfill the minimal requirements in screen size, screen resolution, memory size, color capability, and browser support.
- Design for one or several target user roles and devices that represent the largest (or most important) fractions and create a lowest-common-denominator profile for the rest. This approach is preferred because user experience is so important.

The first approach is the easiest because you can create one group and be done with the effort. However, that belies the criticality of offering seamless and intuitive services to mobile users with handheld devices. Therefore, you might want to start with the first approach to create a lowest-common-denominator role and then build on top of the lowest denominator to optimize for one or more user roles. This way, you can gradually optimize services and have migration paths for practically all users. If you built your applications using the single-channel approach, you will have to modify the code based on device constraints, use case (execution flow), and input capabilities. Your workload will increase if you have to build code for each of the channels based on user roles and devices.

Inherently, this is not scalable. On the other hand, if you opt for the XML multichannel approach, you can easily add support by adding style sheets for each user role or mobile device. This lessens your development cycle time, especially if you can leverage framework like Oracle9*i*AS Wireless. When new user roles and devices come along, you can add support handily. This method is actually made easy with built-in capabilities and style sheets provided in Oracle9*i*AS Wireless, and you can support literally tens of devices and browsers.

Presentation Layer

The presentation layer is tasked with provisioning users with data and content in the correct format for specific devices. Unlike the application layer, the presentation layer has specific knowledge of the environment (including devices and the network) from where the user makes the request.

The J2EE application server platform provides a clean separation of the application code and presentation style and allows developers and service designers to focus on their specific tasks. Naturally, you are encouraged to keep the presentation layer code as separate as possible from business logic to minimize the maintenance cost.

Personalization and Integration

The personalization or customization layer is responsible for housing all business logic to apply personalization parameters, such as preferred language, home location, address, and preferred screen layout.

This layer is also responsible for integrating external parties into the system. For instance, if an ERP system has been integrated into your system, this layer will need to work with your back-end to replicate data. Alternately, this layer may have the transaction logic to allow the system to form synchronous requests to the ERP system.

Page Design and User Interface

When you're designing for small form-factor devices, interface design and creative methods for streamlining and simplifying inputs are critical. Providing users with visual feedback on their inputs as well as successful uploads (to the server) will go a long way toward improving the user experience.

If the design emphasis is on expediency rather than quality, you tend to need several, ultimately time-consuming design cycles before you can finally complete the system.

A user (presumably a worker who has performed his job via a paper process) will not adopt a mobile device quickly if he doesn't feel it is easy to use. The new user will not embrace the mobile process if he now has to do more just to adjust to the wireless system. To avoid this pitfall, you should simplify the design from the full-fledged desktop application and only provide the features that are relevant for mobile and timely usage.

Content Partitioning and Grouping

As a rule of thumb, you should put the most pertinent items at the top of each page and allow the users to drill down to more details through successive hyperlinks. Content partitioning makes information more accessible to mobile users who are in a hurry and are using handheld devices with limited screen and input capabilities. Hence, as a developer, you must make a tradeoff between how much information (for example, the number of hyperlinks) to display on a page, versus how many pages to accomplish a task. Because your application should be direct and get the users to the right information or interaction point, you should not take up too much of their time. Also, they shouldn't need to tap too many keys and go through too many pages to get there. Scrolling may be awkward, and text entry or input other than selecting is difficult.

Because you may have to partition content, you then are also left with a decision on how to group content for different devices and protocols. Usually, different channels will have the code developed and stored in different folders. Through device detection and user agents, the web server will direct the execution flow to the right folders, and the correct server pages (JSP, HTML, ASP, PHP, Perl, and so on) will be loaded and executed for the specific device.

Style Guide

A style guide for small form-factor or mobile devices could easily fill up an entire book. This section provides some basic guidelines and several examples. Many device manufacturers and carriers provide style guides for their devices and simulators that serve as a good reference. In general, when designing for mobile, you should do the following:

- Minimize text and the length of text; use abbreviations where possible.
- Avoid free-form text inputs. Try to provide check boxes or list items. Entering data on handheld devices is very daunting.

- Use graphics judiciously due to bandwidth overhead and because graphics may display differently even among the same WAP browsers within different brands of devices.
- Reduce the content served to minimize scrolling—vertical or horizontal.
- Design for minimal latency and memory size.
- Leverage the built-in elements such as icons and images.

Style for Multichannel

With Oracle9*i*AS Wireless, the approach taken is a multichannel write-once run-everywhere solution that has the following components:

- An XML DTD that defines a multichannel language, such as Oracle9*i*AS multichannel XML or a class library for J2EE
- A runtime engine that detects device type and characteristics (logical and physical)
- A runtime engine that converts documents written in the multichannel language to a device-specific markup language
- Out-of-the-box services that can provide data access to content and business logic

With this kind of approach, you, as a developer, can just focus on the business logic and generate Oracle9*i*AS multichannel XML. You learn only one language and don't have to worry about the new tags from WML1.3, XHTML, i-mode, VoiceXML, and so on. The Oracle core will handle all the different devices such that the correct markup language and physical device characteristics are taken into account and maintained by Oracle—you never have to keep up with what's coming to the market! See Appendix B for the complete set of available Oracle9*i*AS multichannel XML tags in Release 2.

There are times when your application needs specific tweaking for certain physical models of WAP phones. Or you might want to add a new phone or user agent that Oracle does not support yet. As a developer, you have access to all the style sheets used by Oracle9*i*AS Wireless for transforming the multichannel XML to the target device markup language (logical device), coupled with the specific device characteristics. Let's look at both of these in detail.

User Agents A logical device in Oracle9*i*AS Wireless represents either a physical device, such as a Nokia 9210 mobile phone, or an abstract device, such as e-mail. The logical device also stores the attributes of the physical device/browser and device transformers. The Oracle9*i*AS Wireless server uses the device transformer of the logical device associated with the request to transform the XML service results to the associated device markup language. Oracle9*i*AS Wireless server ships with a set of prebuilt logical devices, but you can add additional logical devices or modify existing logical devices if any of your physical devices cannot be mapped.

A user agent is used by the device implementation to find a logical device corresponding to an Oracle9*i*AS Wireless request. In previous releases of Oracle9*i*AS Wireless, this "user agent string to logical device" mapping was specified in the *UserAgents.properties* file. A logical device is now an object in the Wireless repository. You can modify or add new logical devices via the System Designer from the wireless web tool. Click the Logical Devices tab to see the list of available devices and make any modifications, as shown here:

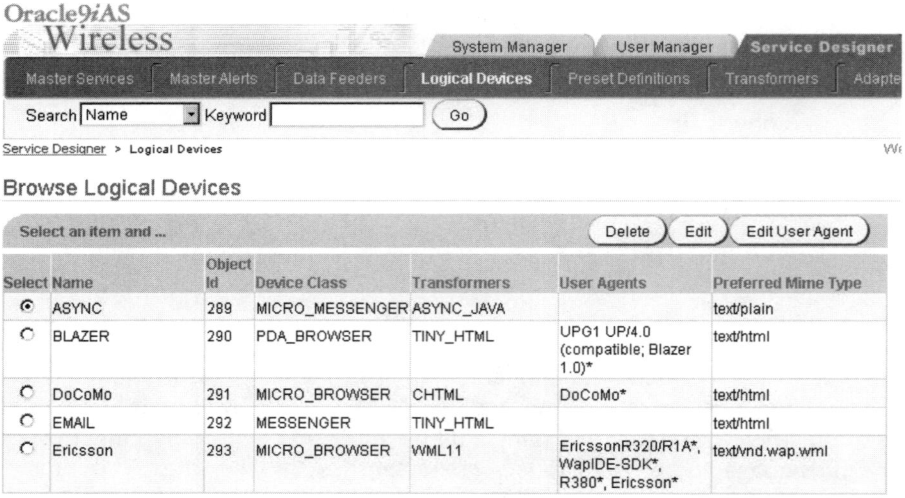

Oracle9*i*AS Wireless

System Manager | User Manager | Service Designer

Master Services | Master Alerts | Data Feeders | Logical Devices | Preset Definitions | Transformers | Adapte

Search Name Keyword Go

Service Designer > Logical Devices

Browse Logical Devices

Select an item and ... Delete Edit Edit User Agent

Select	Name	Object Id	Device Class	Transformers	User Agents	Preferred Mime Type
◉	ASYNC	289	MICRO_MESSENGER	ASYNC_JAVA		text/plain
○	BLAZER	290	PDA_BROWSER	TINY_HTML	UPG1 UP/4.0 (compatible; Blazer 1.0)*	text/html
○	DoCoMo	291	MICRO_BROWSER	CHTML	DoCoMo*	text/html
○	EMAIL	292	MESSENGER	TINY_HTML		text/html
○	Ericsson	293	MICRO_BROWSER	WML11	EricssonR320/R1A*, WapIDE-SDK*, R380*, Ericsson*	text/vnd.wap.wml

For example, you might want to add support for the new Openwave 5.1 Universal browser, which supports both WML 1.3 and XHTML Mobile Profile (XHTML-MP). Here are the user agent strings for these two:

WML	OPWV-GEN-02/UNI10 UP/5.0.2.375 (GUI) UP.Browser/5.0.2.375 (GUI)-XXXX UP.Link/5.0.HTTP-DIRECT
XHTML	OPWV-GEN-99/UNI10 UP.Browser/6.0.2.221 (GUI) HTTP-DIRECT/5.1

You could create a new logical device for WML13 or add another user agent string row to the existing WML11_OPENWAVE entry. Use something such as "UP.Browser/5*" or "OPWV-GEN-02*" for the user agent name string row to be added. Similarly for XHTML, you can use something such as "UP.Browser/6*" or "OPWV-GEN-99*" for the user agent name string row to be added.

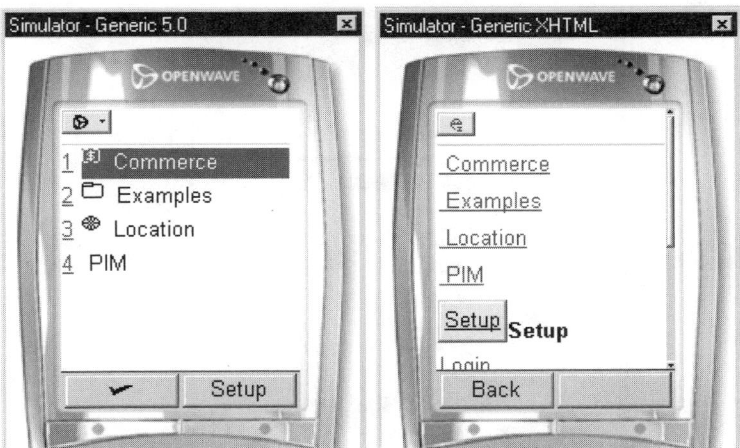

You might need to *restart* the wireless web server for this to take effect. Without any of the user agent strings, pointing the Openwave 5.1 browser to the wireless web server (for example, http://localhost:9000/ptg/rm) will result in a server error (HTTP 500).

Device Transformation Similarly, if a shipped device transformer is not sufficient for a logical device, you can modify or add new device transformers via the System Designer from the wireless web tool, as shown here:

Oracle9iAS Wireless

System Manager | User Manager | Service Designer

Master Services | Master Alerts | Data Feeders | Logical Devices | Preset Definitions | Transformers | Adapte

Service Designer > Transformers

Browse Transformers

Select an item and ... Delete Edit

Select	Name	Object Id	MIME Type	Simple Result DTD Version
◉	ASYNC_JAVA	288	text/plain	1.1.0
○	CHTML	284	text/html	1.1.0
○	HDML	277	text/x-hdml	1.1.0
○	MML	285	text/html	1.1.0
○	PLAIN_TEXT	278	text/plain	1.1.0
○	PLAIN_TEXT_JAVA	287	text/plain	1.1.0
○	PTG	279	text/vnd.oracle.mobilexml	1.1.0
○	TINY_HTML	280	text/html	1.1.0

For example, you might want to modify the TINY_HTML XSL to draw your corporate color horizontal rule for the <SimpleBreak rule="true"> tag instead of the default black line.

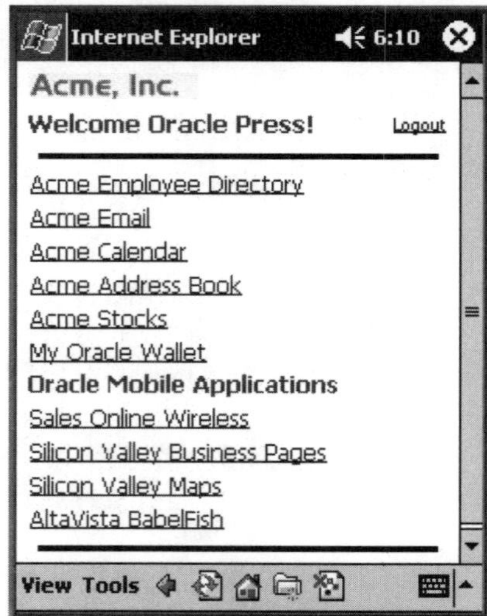

To do this, you simply select the TINY_HTML transform, click Edit, and the Edit Transformer screen shows up. You can edit the text within the text area of the input form or you can import from a file. The existing XSL is shown here:

```
<xsl:template match="SimpleBreak">
   <xsl:text disable-output-escaping="yes">__LT__br /></xsl:text>
</xsl:template>
<xsl:template match="SimpleBreak[@rule='true']">
   <xsl:text disable-output-escaping="yes">__LT__hr /></xsl:text>
</xsl:template>
```

Change the second template to something like this:

```
<xsl:template match="SimpleBreak">
   <xsl:text disable-output-escaping="yes">__LT__br /></xsl:text>
</xsl:template>
<xsl:template match="SimpleBreak[@rule='true']">
   <xsl:text disable-output-escaping="yes">
      __LT__hr color="#66633" />
   </xsl:text>
</xsl:template>
```

You could be more sophisticated and add a color attribute to the <SimpleBreak> tag or invent a new tag instead, such as <SimpleRule>. There's no limit!

NOTE
Edit TINY_HTML with care. This transformer is used for the browser version of the wireless portal (http://localhost:9000/ptg/rm). If the XSL is invalid, you will not be able to access the wireless portal! Be sure to make a copy before editing.

Style for WAP

If you are designing your mobile applications for a single channel only (WAP, in this case), you could still use Oracle9*i*AS multichannel XML. Besides not having to learn WML, there are a lot of other benefits, such as leveraging the various mobile modules or services shipped with Oracle9*i*AS Wireless. However, if you still choose to design in WML only, this section provides you with some tips.

The user's experience with an application may determine whether or how often the user will revisit the application—the first impression is everything when a mobile user is pressed for time, connectivity, and accessibility. The following design guidelines should be kept in mind when building an application for a WAP browser phone:

- **Usability is critical.** Mobile phones are optimized for voice communications, not data services. Don't make it harder to use your mobile applications or web sites. Otherwise, the users will just call the operator instead!
- **Entering text is difficult.** Triple-tap is still challenging to most users. Too much data entry will not earn repeat users. Give users an alternative to text entry, such as selection lists, if possible. This also reduces user-entry errors.
- **Choose content carefully.** Customize content specifically for the targeted user and target only information that is essential.
- **Airtime has a cost.** A number of systems are still circuit switched, which means you get billed on a per-minute basis. With packet technology, users are charged on a flat-fee basis or by the packet. Don't waste your users' time because they are paying for it.
- **It's a phone first until smart phones are mainstream.** Users buy phones for voice quality and size. The browser comes second. If your application doesn't run well on a phone, users won't use it.
- **A phone browser is for information retrieval, not browsing.** Mobile users access their phone browsers for quick access to timely content. Browsing is usually done on a PC.

- **Wireless data is not fast yet.** Every byte counts because the users pay for them. Don't send unnecessary content. Even with 3G networks, phones will still utilize less-expensive, low-bandwidth solutions.
- **Every keystroke costs usability.** Users will get lost or frustrated in applications requiring a lot of keystrokes to navigate to get to what they want. High-value areas should be exposed immediately or with very few keystrokes.
- **Brevity usually outweighs breadth of content.** Display only the relevant content in a summarized format. Users can always request more details, if desired.
- **Displays are small.** The masses have micro-browsers within small phones. Don't develop for specialty phones. Keep in mind the display constraints.
- **Keep soft key labels to five characters or less.** Most devices cannot display more than four or five letters and will truncate your labels if they have more letters than allowed.
- **Assign most common actions or tasks to soft keys.** You can make it easier for the users by them just having to press a single key, such as the accept (OK) key.
- **Allow users to dial using a single key.** Use the Wireless Telephony Application Interface (WTAI) to allow a phone call to be made from an application via a soft key (for example, <go href="wtai://wp/mc;6505551212"/>) .
- **Ensure decks are smaller than 500 bytes.** Download latency can be large, and users' perception of a download can be longer than it really is—if all they are allowed to do is wait for the response.
- **Use built-in local icons.** You can reduce transmitting icons over the air by referring to them in your pages. For example, instead of creating an e-mail icon, use the following code:

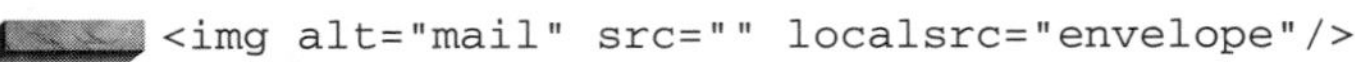

```
<img alt="mail" src="" localsrc="envelope"/>
```

An example of an application following some of these guidelines can be seen in Figure 14-2. This example uses a maximum of three levels of navigation, simple menu names with associated shortcut accelerator keys or access keys (numbers 1 through 9), and soft keys (left or right) for sending e-mail to an employee or dialing the mobile phone number of an employee—all without much key entry other than navigation via the OK (accept) soft key or the accelerator keys. The searched-for employee contact information is shown in Figure 14-3.

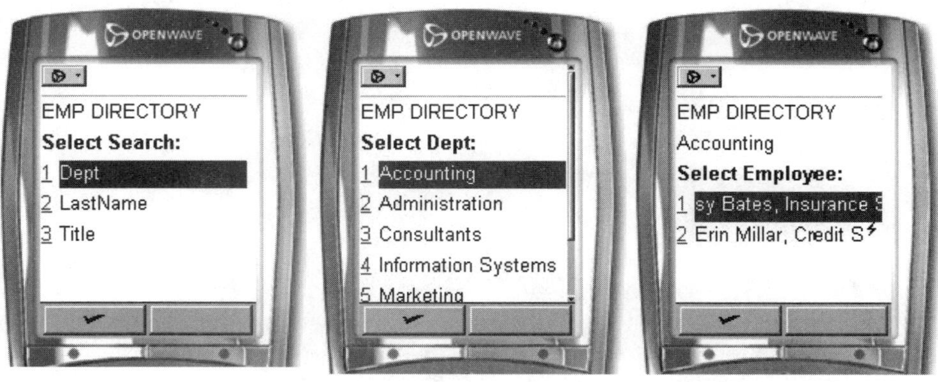

FIGURE 14-2. *Employee lookup in WAP*

Major WAP browser manufacturers, such as Nokia, Ericsson, and Openwave, have implemented different presentation layers and functionality in their products. That means the same site, delivered in WML, may look and behave very differently when accessed by different WAP browsers. Presentation and functional differences can cause major usability issues and therefore warrant extensive testing with different WAP browsers.

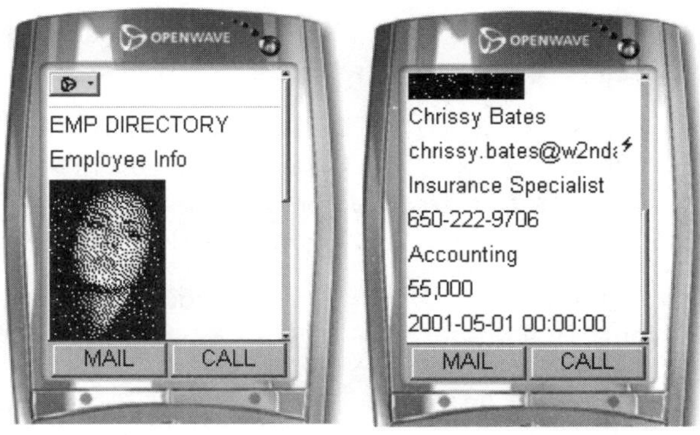

FIGURE 14-3. *Employee contact information*

We have just touched on some of the main points of design style for WAP devices. Complete details and examples can be found in the following references:

- *Openwave WML Application Style Guide.* Designing and developing WML applications (http://developer.openwave.com).
- *Openwave Developing User-Friendly Applications* (http://developer.openwave.com).
- *Sprint WML Style Guide* (http://developer.sprintpcs.com).

Style for Palm, PocketPC, and i-mode

As mentioned in the previous section, if you are designing your mobile applications for a single channel only, compact HTML, tiny-HTML, or i-mode cHTML, you can still use Oracle9*i*AS multichannel XML. Besides not having to learn the variants of compact HTML, you gain a lot more benefits, as stated before. However, if you choose to design in compact HTML only, here are some tips.

- **Choose content carefully.** Customize content specifically for the targeted user and target only information that is essential.
- **Organize information effectively.** Split long documents into pieces (content partitioning) and create indexes whenever possible.
- **Pay attention to graphics.** Master design small bitmapped graphics to make an outstanding page.
- **Focus on content, not display.** Keep it simple and elegant. Use only supported HTML tags and avoid tables, especially embedded tables, if practical to preserve screen space.
- **Keep the user interface simple.** Don't make the interface keyboard intensive, because this can lead to errors or inaccuracies.
- **Allow customization or personalization.** The user should decide on content, selections, or preferences, and the system should not have to explicitly ask the user for types of content to display, color and font preferences, etc. every time when serving up content.
- **Page organization.** A balance has to be made between page hierarchy depth and the length of individual pages, because it is difficult to find one's place in a lengthy section using a scroll bar.

- **Use local images or built-in icons.** Reduce transmitting images or icons over the air by building them into your applications and referring to them in your pages.
- **Don't cover input fields with pop-up keyboards.** When a pop-up keyboard is used for data entry, make sure it does not cover the input fields such that the user has to scroll to enter the information.

An example of an application following some of these guidelines can be seen in Figure 14-4.

As stated earlier, one often-overlooked guideline involves the pop-up keyboard. When a page is designed with a form that the user has to fill in, the keyboard may automatically launch. This could cover the form and may require the user to scroll up or down to fill in any of the fields. As a good practice, avoid having your form in the area that will be covered by the pop-up keypad (see Figure 14-5).

The two most popular PDAs—Palm and PocketPC—both have smaller usable screen sizes for content than you might think. Although several Palm licensees (e.g., Sony Clié) offer larger screens, typical Palm PDAs have a display resolution

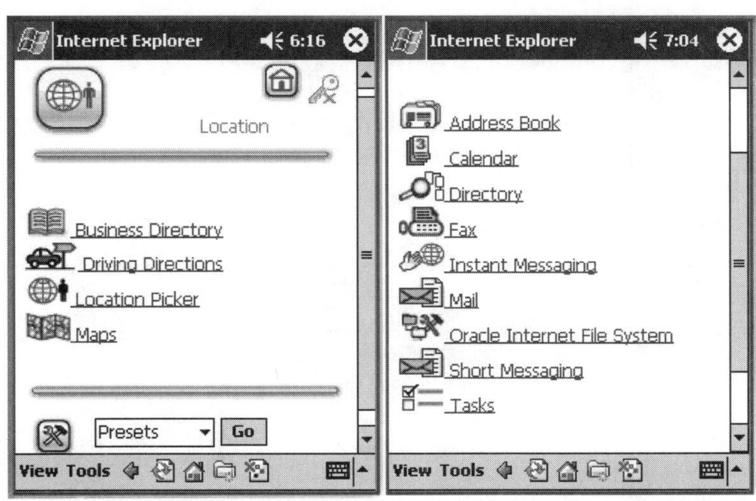

FIGURE 14-4. *Sample PocketPC application*

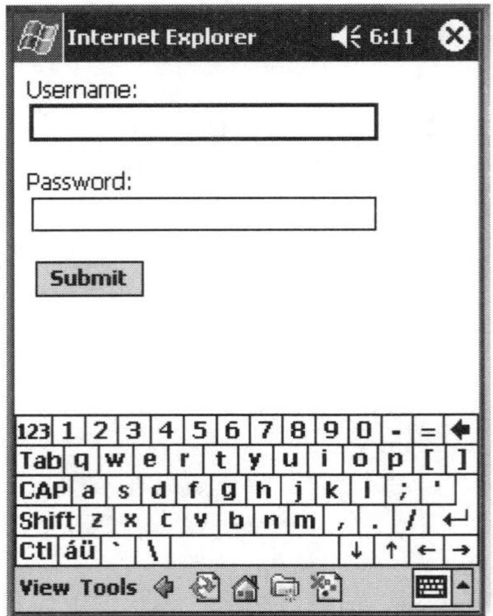

FIGURE 14-5. *A pop-up keyboard for the PocketPC*

of 160 pixels by 160 pixels (color or monochrome) but only 150 pixels by 150 pixels are usable for content due to the title display and scroll bars (see Figure 14-6).

On the PocketPC, the screen size has been referred to as having a display resolution of 240 pixels by 320 pixels. However, only 230 pixels by 255 pixels are usable for content due to the address bar, scroll bars (vertical and horizontal), and the menu bar (see Figure 14-7).

FIGURE 14-6. *The Palm application area*

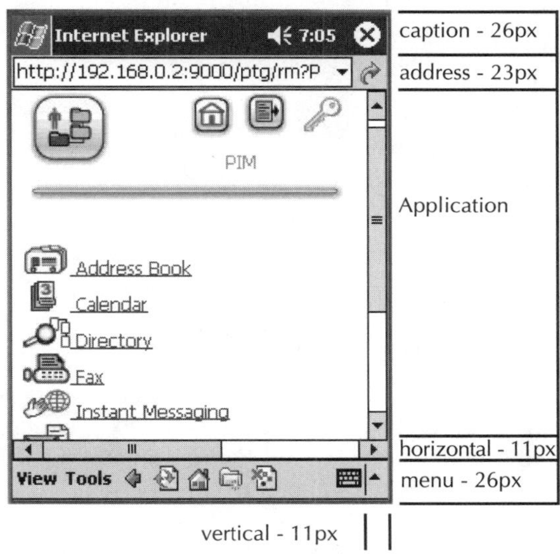

FIGURE 14-7. *The PocketPC application area*

For the i-mode phone, only 250 characters are displayed—anything over this limit will be truncated (see Figure 14-8).

FIGURE 14-8. *The i-mode application area*

Again, we have just touched on some of the main points of design style for PocketPC or PDA devices that support compact HTML. Complete details and examples can be found in these great references:

- *Palm Web Clipping Developer's Guide* (http://www.palmos.com/dev)
- *Microsoft Pocket PC Developer* (http://www.microsoft.com/mobile/developer/)
- *i-mode Service Guidelines* (http://www.nttdocomo.com)

Style Guide: Voice

We have discussed multichannel design previously, but we did not touch on one of the emerging channels yet—voice. A majority of the population has a landline or mobile phone primarily for voice communications. Using automatic speech recognition to navigate the Wireless Web for mobile services creates an interesting design problem for the developer. Fortunately, if you are designing using Oracle9*i*AS multichannel XML, you don't have to learn VoiceXML or VoXML. If you are just using voice for your navigation UI, then you probably don't need to develop custom grammar or vocabulary libraries using tools from TellMe, BeVocal, VoiceGenie, Motorola, SpeechWorks, Nuance, and so on.

The following methodology is recommended by Oracle for voice application development using Oracle9*i*AS multichannel XML:

1. Write a basic version of the service using exactly the same flow and markup for small-screen devices and audio interfaces.
2. Test on small-screen devices and voice telephones. If the result is acceptable, you are done.

   This methodology has worked well for a large class of services. Nonetheless, there are a few things you can do to improve it, as discussed in the remaining steps.
3. Adjust certain Oracle9*i*AS multichannel XML tag attribute values to enhance the interface for one of the device classes.
4. Selectively include or exclude certain elements from the user interface, depending on the device classes.
5. Alter the user interface flow by selectively following different paths through a service, depending on the device classes.

Generally, voice gateways provide a text-to-speech (TTS) engine that reads out text content from tags such as <SimpleStrong>, <SimpleTextItem>, and so on. For the TTS to sound intelligible, proper spacing and punctuation is required. Oracle9*i*AS multichannel XML voice tags such as <SimpleFormOption> and <SimpleMenuItem> should never have text punctuation unless the deviceclass attribute has been set to a value other than "voice". This is because the text in these tags is used to produce speech-recognition grammars, and nonalphabetic characters foil most grammars. Speech recognition works only when there is a very narrowly prescribed vocabulary to listen for. If you wish to avoid using the synthesized message, you may specify a prerecorded audio file to be played. End user experience of TTS is often considered unpleasant. Prerecorded human sounds should be used as much as possible instead of TTS.

Here are some guidelines on enhancing voice features:

- The voice experience can be enhanced with prerecorded audio using the <SimpleAudio> element. The supported format is CCITT mu-law, 8 bit, and 8 kHz WAV.
- Use confirmation by echoing the recognized utterance. Allow the user to cancel if an input has been incorrectly recognized.
- Always provide context-sensitive help. Use <SimpleCatch> as a child tag for this.
- Use the deviceclass attribute to tailor audio and text messages to voice.
- Always provide the user with the option of continuing a service by providing an appropriate command leading to the place the user wants to go to.
- Provide special event handlers for recognition failures (for example, noinput and nomatch) and Internet fetch failures where appropriate. If the user says nothing, the system will prompt the user with a system default noinput message, "Please speak up, or say Help." If the user says something and the system is unable to recognize it, the system default nomatch message, "Please say that again," is played. The <SimpleCatch> tag can be used with the count attribute to handle multiple recognition failures, thereby having the system say different messages depending on the count.
- If the type attribute is omitted in a voice tag or if the type specified is not a recognized type, the system defaults to the "digits" input type and asks the user to enter information one digit at a time. Therefore, every <SimpleFormItem> tag must have a type attribute specified.
- Within each <SimpleContainer>, if there are no form submission or action tags, the system automatically announces, "You may say Main menu or Exit," and waits for a command.
- Speech recognition is only supported for written English words or phrases in a <SimpleMenuItem> or <SimpleFormItem> tag or in inputs of the following types: number, digits, date, time, and currency. There should not be any nonalphabetic characters or punctuation.

- The deviceclass attribute provides a way to switch between one format and another depending on the modality (small-screen or voice) of a device. If the modality (deviceclass) of the user agent is "voice," then the system will include all elements that have "deviceclass=voice" and all elements that do not have a deviceclass attribute or that have an empty deviceclass attribute, and it will exclude all others.
- You can suppress the automatic TTS options message and use a custom or prerecorded one by setting the autoprompt attribute to false for <SimpleFormSelect> or <SimpleMenu> tags.

The next few sections will go through an example of using Oracle Mobile (OM) Online Studio to write a single application that can be accessed via both wireless and voice interfaces, including landline telephones. Refer to Chapter 13 for details on how to create mobile applications using Mobile Studio. Follow these steps to develop and test voice services on the OM Online Studio:

1. Call (877) 672-0807 from anywhere in the U.S. or (650) 607-1039 from any place else. This number is subject to change, so check the Oracle Mobile website for the latest telephone number.
2. Enter or say your OM Online Studio account number. This is not the same as your Studio ID. If you don't remember or don't know your account number, you can find it under My Preferences. Your account number is displayed prominently on the top of the page.
3. Enter or say your PIN.
4. Listen to the instructions. Say "help" for assistance or "main menu" if you wish to return to the main menu.

Although OM Online Studio automatically provides an audio interface for any service written to the Oracle9*i*AS multichannel XML DTD, the system is not intended to be a "speech-controlled small-screen device browser," where speech is added as an extension or afterthought. Instead, Oracle encourages developers to use OM Online Studio to create services that are designed specifically for the modalities where their respective strengths (small screen versus audio) can be used to an advantage. Therefore, wireless interfaces should have very good small-screen interfaces, and voice-based interfaces should be easy to navigate and intuitive with speech.

Basic Voice Commands The following universal commands are available to users at all times. The user can barge in (speak over the prompt) anytime except when you disallow this with the voice tags <SimpleTitle> and <SimpleTextItem> by setting the bargein attribute to false.

Main Menu	Can be uttered at any time and by default takes the user to the main Oracle9*i*AS Wireless menu.
Goodbye	Ends a session with one Oracle9*i*AS Wireless instance. Alternatively, the user may just hang up.
Exit	Same as Goodbye.
Help	Context-sensitive help.
Cancel	Aborts or restarts a dialogue when the system incorrectly recognizes a command or input.

Tip Calculator Voice Example In this section, we'll go through the voice application development process—from being small screen friendly to being voice user friendly—by applying some of the guidelines in the previous sections. The Tip Calculator service is a great example because it blends different input types (currency and digits) and has lots of potential for incorrect voice recognition and TTS. This service calculates the tip on a restaurant bill. It collects the amount on the bill, the number of people splitting the bill, and the size of the tip. It then reports the amount of the tip, the total bill including the tip, and the portion each diner would owe, assuming the bill is evenly divided.

Let's start off with a version that works great on a small-screen device such as the Openwave 5 browser or the Microsoft PocketPC browser. The Oracle9*i*AS multichannel XML code would look like the following:

```
<SimpleResult>
   <SimpleContainer>
      <SimpleForm target="tipcalc.jsp">
         <SimpleFormItem name="howmuch" type="currency">
            <SimpleTitle>How much is the bill? </SimpleTitle>
         </SimpleFormItem>
         <SimpleFormItem name="howmany" format="N*" type="number">
            <SimpleTitle>How many are in your party? </SimpleTitle>
         </SimpleFormItem>
         <SimpleFormSelect name="howbig">
            <SimpleTitle>Choose tip size: </SimpleTitle>
            <SimpleFormOption value="10">10 percent</SimpleFormOption>
            <SimpleFormOption value="15">15 percent </SimpleFormOption>
            <SimpleFormOption value="20">20 percent </SimpleFormOption>
         </SimpleFormSelect>
      </SimpleForm>
   </SimpleContainer>
</SimpleResult>
```

The Oracle9*i*AS multichannel XML would be rendered on both these browsers as shown in Figure 14-9. For other small devices, such as the Openwave 4 WML browser, it would be presented in three separate screens (see Figure 14-10).

For the voice channel, the following dialogue is presented:

System:	How much is the bill?
User:	One hundred twenty-three and forty-five.
System:	How many are in your party?
User:	Two.
System:	Choose tip size. Select one from the following options: 10 percent, 15 percent, 20 percent.
User:	15 percent.

While going through this dialogue on a voice channel, you'll notice that the system encounters many potential errors, including the following:

- Incorrect bill amount due to incorrect currency input.
- Inputs are not echoed back for confirmation.
- There is no context help.
- There is no distinction between small-screen devices and voice.

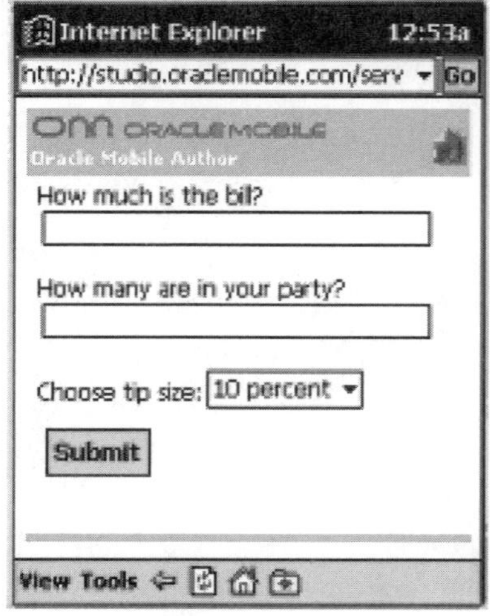

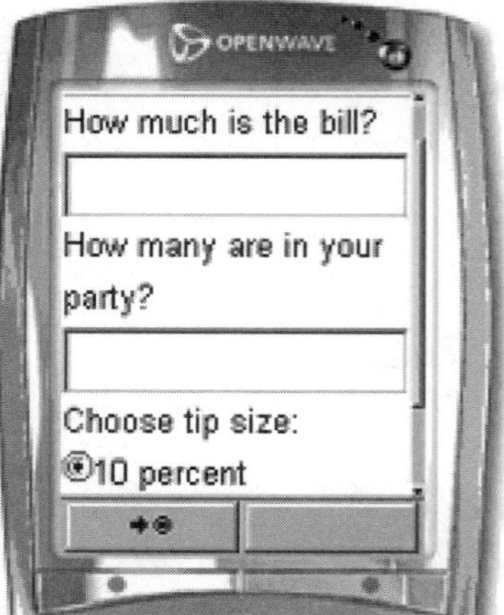

FIGURE 14-9. *The tip calculator on Openwave 5 and PocketPC browsers*

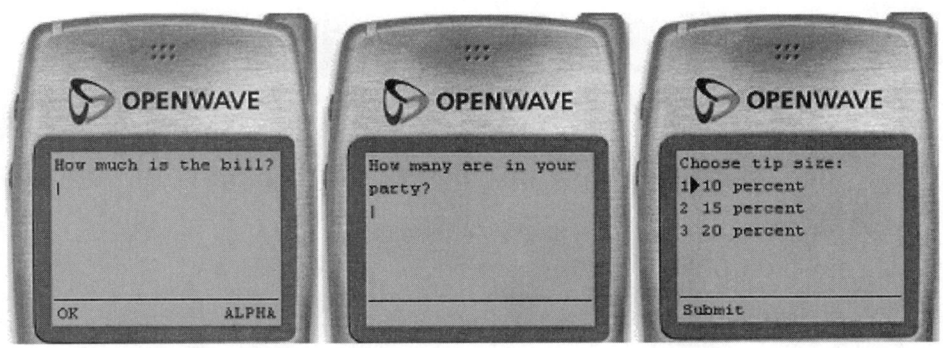

FIGURE 14-10. *The tip calculator on the Openwave 4 WML browser*

Let's enhance the basic tip calculator application with some of the basic voice user interface guidelines, thus making it more voice friendly. Our code now looks like this:

```
<SimpleResult>
   <SimpleContainer>
      <SimpleForm target="tipcalc.jsp">
         <SimpleFormItem name="howmuch" type="currency">
            <SimpleTitle>How much is the bill? </SimpleTitle>
            <SimpleCatch type="help">
            Help. Say the amount of the bill in dollars and cents.
            For example, twenty-five dollars and ten cents
            </SimpleCatch>
            <SimpleCatch type="cancel">Canceling.
            <SimpleClear name="howmuch"/>
            </SimpleCatch>
         </SimpleFormItem>
         <SimpleFormItem name="howmany" format="N*" type="number">
            <SimpleTitle>How many are in your party? </SimpleTitle>
            <SimpleCatch type="help">
            Help. Say the number of people to split the bill.
            </SimpleCatch>
            <SimpleCatch type="cancel">Canceling.
            <SimpleClear name="howmuch"/>
            <SimpleClear name="howmany"/>
            </SimpleCatch>
         </SimpleFormItem>
         <SimpleFormSelect name="howbig" deviceclass="microbrowser
```

```
             pdabrowser pcbrowser micromessenger messenger">
            <SimpleTitle>Choose tip size: </SimpleTitle>
            <SimpleFormOption value="10">10 pct</SimpleFormOption>
            <SimpleFormOption value="15">15 pct</SimpleFormOption>
            <SimpleFormOption value="20">20 pct</SimpleFormOption>
         </SimpleFormSelect>
         <SimpleFormSelect name="howbig" deviceclass="voice"
            autoprompt="false">
            <SimpleTitle>
            How big do you want your tip to be?
            For 'ten percent' say 'small',
            for 'fifteen percent' say 'medium',
            for 'twenty percent' say 'large'.
            </SimpleTitle>
            <SimpleFormOption value="10">small</SimpleFormOption>
            <SimpleFormOption value="15">medium</SimpleFormOption>
            <SimpleFormOption value="20">large</SimpleFormOption>
            <SimpleCatch type="nomatch">
            Sorry I didn't get that. Please say that again.
            </SimpleCatch>
            <SimpleCatch type="cancel">Canceling.
            <SimpleClear name="howmuch"/>
            <SimpleClear name="howmany"/>
            <SimpleClear name="howbig"/>
            </SimpleCatch>
         </SimpleFormSelect>
      </SimpleForm>
   </SimpleContainer>
</SimpleResult>
```

We've added the following enhancements for both small-screen devices and voice channel:

- By using the deviceclass attribute, we have created an alternative format for small-screen browsers and one for voice only. The small screen format also uses "pct" for percent to save size. The voice format has added instructions and better TTS options.
- Context help is now available for each of the inputs being requested, and the instructions are more voice-user friendly.
- Cancellations are handled more gracefully.
- Error messages are now more voice friendly.

The voice channel dialogue now sounds like this:

System:	How much is the bill?
User:	One hundred twenty-three dollars and forty-five cents.
System:	How many are in your party?
User:	Help.
System:	Help. Say the number of people to split the bill.
User:	Two.
System:	How big do you want your tip to be? For ten percent say "small," for fifteen percent say "medium," for twenty percent say "large."
User:	Huh?
System:	Sorry I didn't get that. Please say that again.
User:	Medium.

You can still improve this application further by echoing all input values back to the user so that they have a chance to verify each one by saying "yes" or "no" and repeating the input values that are incorrectly recognized by the system.

The TTS within the current Oracle Mobile Voice System is very good. However, if you are not satisfied with the TTS prompts, you can always record your own audio WAV files. For example, if you want to make "How much is the bill?" better or use a touch of a local accent, you can try the following code snippet:

```
<SimpleTitle deviceclass="microbrowser pdabrowser pcbrowser
   micromessenger messenger">How much is the bill? </SimpleTitle>
   <SimpleTitle deviceclass ="voice">
   <SimpleAudio
   src="http://studio.oramobile.com/omp/voice/audio/tc/tc_howmuch.wav">
   </SimpleAudio >
</SimpleTitle>
```

Refer to Appendix B for complete details on the voice tags used in these examples.

Style Guide: Disconnected or Offline

As discussed in Chapter 8, Oracle9*i*AS Wireless/Offline Management (Oracle9*i* Lite 5.0) can simplify the task of developing and deploying offline mobile applications.

Here's a list of the top issues and guidelines that any offline mobile application developer has to examine before selecting a solution:

- **Careful consideration should be given to the distributed database design.** There are typically three generic application models, including pushing data, pulling data, and pushing/pulling data to and from the back-end server. Here are some specifics:
    - **Push** Involves the dissemination of data from the Oracle back-end server to the mobile clients. An example would be price tables, product information, or customer profiles being pushed from the server to the clients. This data may be partitioned by row or column. Usually the information is not updated on the client, there is no need for bidirectional synchronization, and all updates to tables occur on the server.
    - **Pull** Mobile applications that are used for data capture utilize the pull technique to insert observations from the client devices to the back-end database server. You see this technique used in field service applications, where field workers gather information from inspections, and the completion of form-type data is inserted into the local client datastore and then pulled back to the server. In this situation, all updates to a table are carried out at the client, and typically the client data is partitioned such that each client updates its own subset of the master table.
    - **Hybrid applications** As you would guess, this model involves bidirectional synchronization of data between tables on the client and the server. This is the most complex form of synchronization. Conflicts occur when the same row is updated at two locations. This can be handled by any of the standard methods of conflict detection or, for more specialized cases, custom routines can be implemented. It is recommended that attempts be made to partition data such that each client updates its own subset of the master table (see Chapters 8 and 9 for a more complete discussion of synchronization and conflict detection and resolution).
- **Careful attention should be paid to the amount of data that is synchronized between clients and the server.** The synchronization payload is necessarily limited by the amount of available bandwidth. If a field worker is expecting to receive a large payload, such as a full table refresh of a catalog or price list, bandwidth latency will be a determining factor of the ultimate success of the synchronization and response time.

- **Every attempt should be made to minimize and simplify conflict resolution.** Complex conflict detection and resolution will complicate business logic and can result in inconsistent results and poor performance.
- **Ensure that the application is portable across today's and tomorrow's devices.** New devices will come out with different operating systems, thus depreciating your mobile investment. Your mobile application should be developed using a lightweight relational database that supports all of today's devices with open APIs.
- **Support mobile users as well as online users.** You need a mobile platform that offers support for online web-based access and offline access without the need to develop two separate applications, which increases cost and complexity. Until this platform is generally available, developers must understand and make distinctions between development for browser-based applications and native client applications.
- **Provide the ability to provision mobile applications to thousands of devices.** Enterprises with tens of thousands of mobile devices deployed globally cannot afford to install the mobile application one device at a time. You will need to develop a centralized provisioning infrastructure.
- **Synchronize data in thousands of devices with a central information system.** You will need infrastructure to synchronize between each mobile device and central servers. Synchronization must be bidirectional to ensure data integrity and should be able to handle thousands of simultaneous requests during peak hours. Synchronization must implement fast-refresh (synchronizing only the delta differences), compression, and asynchronous building of payloads on the server so that limited bandwidth can be more fully exploited and support of large numbers of concurrent users is possible.
- **Ensure security throughout the application.** Because devices will be lost, synchronized data must be encrypted and employee access to enterprise systems must be enforceable.
- **Manage mobile applications at a minimal cost.** You need to offer centralized web-based interfaces that enable the simplified central management of users, applications, devices, and data. These management services must also easily monitor the application's synchronization load, troubleshoot any problems, and allow for simple deployment of new applications or data.

Oracle9*i* Lite 5.0 addresses and provides solutions to all these design issues. Let's see how developers and IT departments can dramatically simplify the amount of integration work required in their mobile application development and support. Here are some key points:

- The Oracle9*i* Lite database, a lightweight fully relational database, supports the Palm computing platform, Microsoft PocketPC, Symbian EPOC, Linux, and Windows 95/98/NT/2000. With broad visual tool support, you can rapidly build offline mobile applications for different devices. Also, because Oracle9*i* Lite exposes open APIs such as ODBC and JDBC to the mobile application developer, mobile applications may be rapidly ported to new platforms as the business need arises.
- Oracle9*i* Lite's Web-to-Go feature enables browser-based web applications to be developed and deployed once and then be immediately accessible by both online users connected to the enterprise's network and offline mobile users.
- You can centrally provision and deploy all offline applications from a central web-based management console.
- You can enable the simple synchronization of data between thousands of mobile devices and central servers. Oracle9*i* Lite's enhanced asynchronous synchronization scales to support thousands of simultaneous sessions to address the needs of the largest enterprises.
- Because data may be encrypted on the device and during synchronization exchanges, you can ensure end-to-end security of your offline applications. You can conveniently manage them from the web-based management console as you provisioned them.
- You can easily manage users, roles, devices, data, and applications using centralized web-based administration interfaces.

In terms of development tools and the selection of development environments, you might consider these rule-of-thumb guidelines (mentioned previously in Chapter 8):

- **Developing Win32, CE, or PPC applications** Are you tackling any of the following design requirements?
  - You are writing a prototype or quick demo that uses few forms.
  - You want to build an application in the quickest timeframe.
  - Your application does not involve complex database operations.

If so, use the following:

- EVT Visual Basic
- Oracle Lite (ADOCE, if CE)
- mSync for COM, AppForge for CE

- **Developing Win32 or CE 3.0 native applications** Are you tackling any of these design requirements?
  - Your application needs to be professional looking.
  - Your application needs a very good user interface and is relatively large.
  - Your development staff has lots of good MFC programmers available.

  If so, use the following:

  - EVT MFC
  - Oracle Lite ODBC
  - mSync API
- **Developing Win32 native applications** Are you tackling any of these design requirements?
  - The application is very UI and CPU intensive and requires optimal response time.
  - You have lots of excellent engineering resources to spend.

  If so, use the following:

  - EVT MFC or Win32API
  - Oracle Lite OKAPI
  - mSync COM
- **Developing Java native applications for Win32, CE 3.0, or Palm OS** Are you tackling any of these design requirements?
  - Your application is for production and does not need a lot of fancy user interfaces, and you want to write it once and run it on all CE devices and possibly Palm OS (if you do the layout properly with AWT and SWING).
  - You don't mind performance that is less than applications developed with MFC.

If so, use the following:

- Java with Oracle Lite JDBC
- mSync for Java

Style Guide: 3G and Smart Phones

We cannot leave the style guide section without having touched on the latest smart phones that will hit the market in late 2002. Undoubtedly some of you will be developing for these state-of-the-art mobile phones in your job in addition to using some of the latest user interface technologies, such as Macromedia Flash MX for mobile UI application design. Most of these phones will have a Flash MX player—either standalone or as a mobile browser plug-in—and they all will have one or more micro-browsers (WAP or XHTML). Additionally, they will sport a built-in digital camera or an MP3 player and play Real or Windows media. All will be able to download ringtones and wallpaper graphics as well as have enhanced messaging capabilities.

Some of the 3G concept phones from Nokia can be seen in Figure 14-11. The latest smart phones from Nokia and Sony Ericsson can be seen in Figure 14-12.

We will touch on just the content presentation for the Nokia 9200 series Communicator as well as using Flash MX as the alternative multichannel format for smart phones in the following subsections. Other smart phones will share the same approach and guidelines.

Nokia 9200 Series Communicator The Nokia Communicator comes with two micro-browsers—WAP and WWW HTML. For normal web browsing, you can use

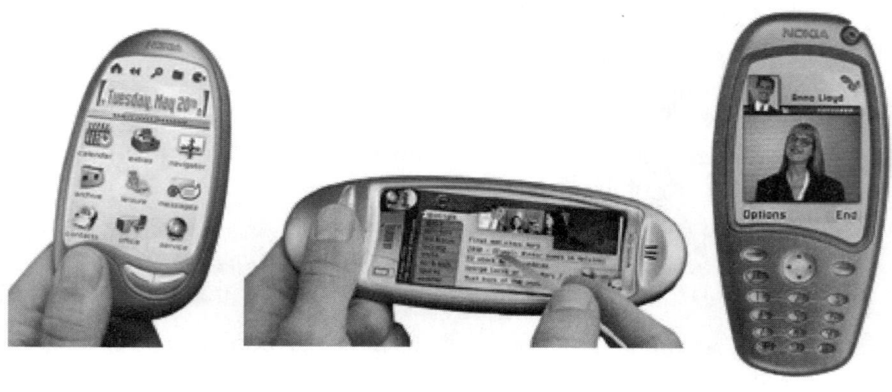

FIGURE 14-11. *Nokia 3G concept phones*

FIGURE 14-12. *Latest smart phones from Nokia and Sony-Ericsson*

the WWW browser. For mobile services, use the WAP browser. This mobile device has a display resolution of 640 pixels by 200 pixels. However, only 490 pixels by 165 pixels are usable for the application content due to the command buttons and indicator areas (see Figure 14-13).

One cool feature is that the Nokia Communicator does allow full screen mode—the button and indicator areas are no longer displayed and must be accessed via the keyboard. This may be perfect for viewing video or images! When the keyboard is used, the button and indicator areas will reappear and overlap whatever is displayed full screen. Other features include frames, cookies, and SSL support.

Navigation is done using the pointer or keypad. The functionality of the pointer is similar to a mouse, but you control it using the arrow and Enter keys. Also, you can change the size of a selected frame so that you can better view its content.

Which browser (WWW or WAP) should you design for? With a WAP browser, you will have to deal with two additional items:

- To access WAP services, you need to define WAP access points from your WAP service providers and configure Communicator. Your WAP service provider can send a WAP access point via a short message!
- Certain bookmarks can be accessed through specific WAP access points only.

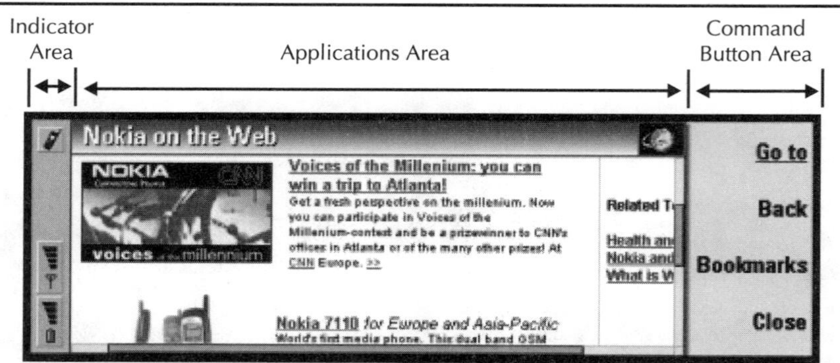

FIGURE 14-13. *Nokia 9210 displayable area*

Therefore, if you are not planning on providing specific WAP services, you can publish for the Nokia Communicator via a regular website in HTML. Keep the HTML simple, consistent, and clear.

In a nutshell, there is nothing magical about smart phones—they all have micro-browsers. This is almost identical to the PDA (Palm, PocketPC, and i-mode) style guide discussed earlier. The only difference is the displayable content area and screen orientation (more landscape versus portrait in most smart phones). As a developer, you should leverage these features whenever possible to maximize the available screen size, albeit small.

Flash MX Multichannel Approach A newcomer in the client-side technology platform is Macromedia Flash MX. Macromedia Flash MX provides a rich client environment for mobile content and applications, and it provides a model for using remote services provided by back-end components hosted in an application server or accessed as XML web services.

We'll briefly review Macromedia Flash MX and its multichannel approach here. Macromedia Flash MX provides a runtime for code, content, and communications. Flash runtime executable (SWF files) combines code, media, and data into a compact, compiled file format that can be easily delivered. Using a high-performance compression/decompression model and its core graphics-rendering engine, you can deliver full images, animations, or simple user interface controls to your mobile devices. Unlike bitmapped interfaces that must send data for each pixel in a screen, vector-based interfaces need only send the mathematical description of the interface, thus resulting in much smaller files and faster transmission. What's more, vector graphics scale much more easily to a variety of different form factors—whether you're dealing with smaller monitors with constrained screen space on a desktop or new device formats that we have yet to consider, such as tablet PCs and PDAs.

Macromedia Flash MX includes an ECMAScript-compliant programming language called ActionScript. ActionScript provides an object-oriented scripting model for controlling and extending Macromedia Flash applications. There is also built-in support for integrating data via HTTP, sockets and XML. Flash MX can therefore work with data generated from almost any server-side application environment.

Here's an approach that can be taken with Flash MX:

- On the server side, use the Oracle9*i*AS Wireless infrastructure of logical devices and device transformers for maintaining the different flavors of Flash files that will be served to the client based on the device form factor.
- Also on the server side, store the various Flash files that will be served to the devices in the Oracle 8*i*/9*i* database or the Oracle Internet File System. You may have slightly different form factor versions (square, landscape, portrait, and so on) of these files.
- The ActionScript in all these files should be identical because only the presentation differs due to vector scaling. The server-side interaction is transparent to the end user.
- Test the application Flash file against all targeted mobile devices. Maybe one file is all you need. Utilize the Flash parameters as much as possible before creating specific files if the original Flash file does not render nicely on these mobile devices. For example, the Flash parameter Scale (HTML <embed> or <object> tag) can be set to ExactFit or NoBorder instead of the default ShowAll. ExactFit makes the entire movie visible in the specified area without trying to preserve the original aspect ratio. Therefore, distortion may occur. NoBorder scales the movie to fill the specified area, without distortion but possibly with some cropping, while maintaining the original aspect ratio of the movie. ShowAll, the default, makes the entire movie visible in the specified area without distortion, while maintaining the original aspect ratio of the movie. Borders may appear on two sides of the movie.

Figure 14-14 shows a sample Flash MX file from the Flash Lessons directory that is being sent to the various mobile devices based on user agent detection by Oracle9*i*AS Wireless.

FIGURE 14-14. *Flash MX for Nokia 9110i Communicator*

Here are a few noteworthy items:

- The original file fits nicely on a Nokia 9110i Communicator device without any extra work (see Figure 14-14).
- The same file, when served to a Nokia 9210 Communicator device, works but it has the annoying borders. However, setting the Scale parameter to ExactFit makes a big difference.

- The same file on a PocketPC wastes a lot of screen space. Changing the Scale parameter to ExactFit makes it worse, with big distortions. In this situation, another Flash file will have to be created slightly differently for the user interface so that it renders nicely for the PocketPC or Palm platform.

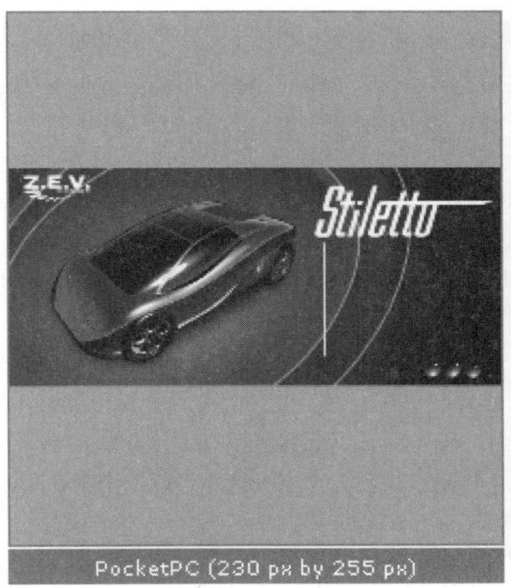

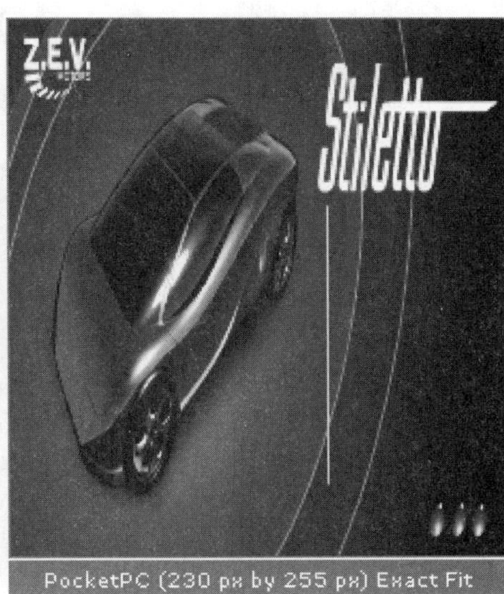

Once the presentation issues are resolved, the back-end server support is where all the application development is focused. A basic Flash file is used in this example for illustrating the UI elements only. The UI could be a full-blown mortgage calculator or contain complex forms, spreadsheets, and so on. You are only limited by your creativity. The back-end is driven by Oracle or SQL databases and server languages such as JSP, ASP, Perl, PHP, ColdFusion, and so on. Flash MX has opened up many possibilities for mobile application development. With a rich client that is small and fast and resides on the mobile device in Flash MX, you can use Oracle9*i*AS Wireless as your mobile back-end, and leverage Flash MX, either as a browser plug-in or as a standalone application!

Localization and Globalization

As a last point, you should keep in mind that mobile users tend to cross borders when traveling. For example, a Belgian mobile user may travel to Germany or France. A user accustomed to complex Chinese characters may travel to China where simplified Chinese characters are widely used. Therefore, your application should have built-in natural language and character-encoding translation capabilities. Besides encoding, subtle differences such as numerical, monetary, and date and time formats exist. Even sorting algorithms and text display directions can be different.

One way to cope with this is to use a localized user agent, which allows you to display local natural languages and can understand limited numbers of encoding.

Testing and Deployment

Simulators are just simulators. They don't always model the network issues associated with real-world uses. Therefore, field testing is crucial. We'll now look at some of the issues involved in the testing and deployment of your mobile applications.

Simulators and Simulation

In mobile service development, it is highly desirable and cost effective to use device simulators for application testing. Phone or device manufacturers may provide the simulators, and they may include software development kits with documentation and sample code.

The simulators are best for testing out your use cases, storyboards, and especially execution flow, including links. However, you cannot rely on simulators to test out final designs and user interfaces. Often, simulators do not produce the same results as actual devices through live network environments. Most of the time, simulators can mimic the functionality of real devices, but they are not perfect. These simulators may fail to keep pace with the new models and new features manufacturers create. Also, simulators can't download plug-ins. What's more, they are known to have bugs that could hinder the proper functioning or display of pages. To minimize any surprises and avoid a false sense of usability, there is no substitution for live testing with as many mobile hardware devices as possible.

Field Testing

As with any new IT project, you will have created a test plan. After testing with simulators, you can include select devices that represent your use cases and access environment. You will be well advised to build an environment that supports real network and hardware devices. Many variations can be implemented. An intranet testing environment, especially a WLAN, may allow you to run tests without having to expose your application code outside your company's firewall.

For enterprise applications where users and devices are well understood and sometimes provisioned by the administrators, your job is easier. You can simply test them out. For public applications like m-commerce sites, field testing against possible devices, users, and network connectivity is very important. Browsers can load pages very differently with different devices, even if they are similar models made by same manufacturer.

Of course, other key requirements, such as load balancing, caching, and failover, will be addressed in the final preparation for production.

Security

Because your applications may provision a number of devices—some support cookies, some support cookies through a WAP gateway, and some don't—it may be better to opt for session management and control on the server side via URL rewriting. Be sure to validate the length and the need for a URL buffer.

Mobile devices can be easily lost or stolen. If one of your users loses a mobile phone while logged in, this poses a security threat that's much greater than it would have been at the desktop inside your firewall. You are potentially exposed to all threats and security breaches. For this reason, a login timeout must be implemented to heighten security for mobile users. You can utilize the administrative function of your wireless server platform to set the session timeout value for various instances and configurations.

Deployment of offline applications is completely different from online mobile applications. The offline application is first packaged, published into the wireless repository, and then provisioned. Next, the mobile clients are installed on the mobile devices and synchronized with centralized servers to get the application and data. For more on offline security, refer to Chapters 8 and 9.

Summary

In a nutshell, mobile development is exciting (for the developers) and can be very rewarding for the enterprise and its users. The key is to start simple and build your expertise, knowledge base, and confidence. Roll out prototypes with target user groups first, and leverage this time by exploiting applicable elements of business processes that lend themselves to the mobile venue. Remember, a simple service is not only easier to build, but easier to learn and use, thus bringing benefits faster to your users.

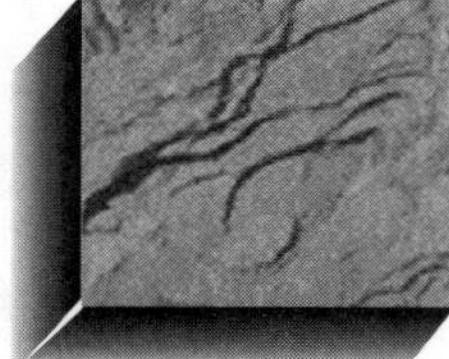

CHAPTER 15

Case Studies

In this chapter we review three case studies in which Oracle9*i*AS Wireless is implemented. The goal is to provide you with insights into the business and architecture decisions—in other words, the *what* and *why* aspects of the application design. We'll walk through the complete lifecycle of building, deploying, and enhancing mobile applications with Oracle9*i*AS Wireless, with an emphasis on the choices you would make in service and application development. We will discuss the rationale behind the decisions made in each case—and its implications and benefits. Specifically, we review these three cases:

- Case 1: Field Data Acquisition
- Case 2: Mobile Enabling Dynamic Content
- Case 3: Sales Force Automation—Forecasting

Let's look at the details—the backgrounds, application needs, use cases, strategies, and solutions—behind these cases.

Case 1: Field Data Acquisition

This case illustrates how a single-channel mobile application is designed and developed using WAP. Additionally, you'll see how to migrate the WAP application to an Oracle9*i*AS multichannel mobile application that is easy to use, build, and manage, yet is extensible and scalable.

Customer and Needs

Acme Distributors (ACME) is in the business of marketing and distributing consumer packaged goods, including snacks, over-the-counter drugs, candies, and so on. ACME is a regional player, covering several metropolitan areas, and is interested in capturing real-time or near real-time data on shelf space, in-store placement and display, promotion results, and the inventory level of the products it markets and promotes in grocery and convenience stores within its territories.

The need to capture this data has arisen because ACME frequently runs promotions on many products it distributes, and it wants to obtain immediate feedback on these campaigns. It also wants to improve its ability to monitor shelf space, product placement and inventory, as well as to track competition on a store level. Because of the changing campaigns and product mix, ACME desires near real-time data, and its field surveys, usually qualitative in nature, can change from one product to another. Also, the data collection focus for different products could change from shelf placement to inventory levels at times. This dynamic nature makes the use of a marketing firm less ideal. Instead, ACME has opted to employ its own contract workers to acquire field data and track campaign results.

Situation and Use Case

To gather data, ACME has implemented a pilot project and created a wireless application. It wanted to deploy an application that could provide real results, but would not require significant commitments in initial costs and resources. Although ACME has considered building a Palm OS native application using a barcode scanner, it rejected the idea at this stage due to the high hardware cost for the barcode scanners and development of a C++ Palm application. ACME has decided to go with a wireless browser-based application first and will add the offline applications later.

Besides the obvious expenses in creating a complex "offline" application, ACME wants to test out the human side of data collection and determine how effective it is to use independent contractors as data trackers to collect in-store data. ACME wants to avoid adding new, complex processes that require expensive software and distribution of hardware to data trackers. Also, the individual surveys for different goods change frequently and are evolving. Hence, it is difficult to define the question set and load to the PDAs in a timely fashion.

As a result, ACME chose to adopt a Wireless Markup Language (WML) programming model and has created a WAP application. This application is single channel in nature. That means this application is mobile only, with no corresponding HTML website!

Currently, ACME employs 50–100 freelance contractors to visit their assigned stores on specific days within a time window, typically 12–24 hours. This staff, many of them students, is scattered throughout the territories and has little technology background. They are low-tech workers or high-school students. Initially, ACME tested out the data forms using paper and benchmarked the latency and accuracy issues. Following that, ACME provided its data trackers with wireless WAP (Motorola) phones using Nextel iDEN network (see Figure 15-1). Because the costs of device and airtime are much less than PDAs, ACME rolled out the prototype project in several areas. Because all test sites are within different metropolitan areas, ACME found the wireless coverage to be acceptable—typically 95 percent or better. Because these sites are generally grocery and convenience stores, and not warehouses in outer regions, wireless transmission signals are decent.

Although the mobile application is rudimentary, the working site is written in a server scripting language and WML device markup language. Currently, the base applications of ACME include a mix of Active Server Pages (ASP), ColdFusion Markup Language (CFML), WML—all implemented over Internet Information Server (IIS) and Windows NT. Having chosen Java/J2EE as its future platform, ACME is migrating to JavaServer Pages/Java, XML, Apache, and Solaris.

FIGURE 15-1. *Motorola* i1000plus *phone*

Strategy

For tracking data, ACME's strategy is to eventually leverage its delivery staff to collect data, in addition to relying on dedicated, independent workers. This approach has the potential of further increasing the productivity of its mobile workforce. Because its delivery staff is more knowledgeable about ACME products, these in-house data trackers can help ACME expand the scope of its data-collection efforts.

On the device front, ACME expects to equip its mobile personnel with WAP-enabled phones. Nevertheless, ACME envisions that it may not have to provide WAP phones to all data trackers in the long run. As wireless phones become more popular, its contract workers may have their own phones instead. Hence, the mobile application should be able to handle different WML browsers and handsets. As a backup, ACME does not want to lock its application into WML only. It wants to future-proof the application from WAP phones to PDAs such as PocketPCs as well.

Although ACME uses the iDEN network and Motorola phones with push message capabilities, this application should be able to run on any network and support future devices. For now, ACME lays out the following goals and design requirements:

- Shorten time to database update
- Emphasize ease of use so that minimal training is required

- Go from just WAP to WAP and SMS/Push
- Consider going to PocketPC or Palm for larger screen size
- Reduce result latency and improve data accuracy

Solution

ACME chose a two-phase approach. Phase One involves building the WML application; Phase Two requires migrating to an XML framework, leveraging Oracle9*i*AS Wireless. ACME doesn't want to expend efforts on transcoding. It will preserve its WML application logic but create this logic in XML instead. We will go through both phases in the next few sections.

In Phase One, an end user (a data tracker) can simply type in and bookmark the site WAP URL to set up the WAP phones. The assigned data tracker would log in and get the names and locations of stores. Sometimes, the data tracker might not have assignments. Sometimes the data tracker might not log in and therefore miss the assignment. In Phase Two, we will review these shortcomings in Phase One and discuss how we can use Oracle9*i*AS Wireless to address them.

End-User Usage Scenarios

The end users for the mobile application are independent data trackers and ACME campaign managers. The data trackers are the primary users of this mobile application. The ACME campaign managers schedule and create the campaigns in addition to analyzing the collected data.

Here are two scenarios a data tracker goes through in Phase One. The differences for Phase Two will be pointed out in the relevant sections later on. In the first scenario, a data tracker logs in and checks for assignments. Naturally, data trackers can accept or reject assignment(s) and perform other tasks. In the second scenario, the data tracker would embark on an assignment, and logs in to use the ACME Data Acquisition Wizard.

The following are the steps for Scenario One:

1. A data tracker accesses the ACME system using a Nextel phone. Because the iDEN Internet access is always on, the data tracker just has to access the mobile Internet by choosing that bookmark. Alternatively, if the WAP phone is not configured previously, the data tracker will have to enter the URL manually. After successfully accessing the site, the data tracker logs in using their user ID and password.
2. The data tracker will be greeted with a menu that includes a list of assignments to accept (if any), a list of assignments to start now (if any), and the options to reject a previously accepted assignment, to make modifications to a personal profile, to check the history of all completed assignments, and to log off.

3. The data tracker chooses to see what kinds of assignments are available and whether to accept or reject them. There will be basic information describing each assignment, including the estimated length of time it takes, which stores are involved, and what products they are gathering data on. The data tracker would either reject or accept the assignment. If the assignment is accepted, it will be taken off the accept queue and inserted into the active queue. If the assignment is rejected, it will be reassigned to somebody else.
4. The data tracker either logs off or starts a new assignment (see Scenario Two).

The following are the steps for Scenario Two:

1. A data tracker logs into the ACME system using a Nextel phone and the familiar bookmark or URL.
2. As before, the data tracker is greeted with the menu from Scenario One.
3. The data tracker chooses an assignment to start now. The assignment may start before the data tracker gets to each store or when he or she arrives. When the data tracker is at the retail establishment, data tracking begins. Each posted result to the remote server is time-stamped and logged.
4. The ACME Data Acquisition Wizard will go through all the forms for data gathering that need to be performed in a sequential order. The data is posted to the server live, and once all the data is gathered, the data tracker can either log off or start another assignment.

The ACME campaign manager goes through a slightly different scenario, which is dubbed Scenario Three for the entire project implementation. A typical usage flow is as follows:

1. The campaign manager logs into the ACME system using a Nextel phone and the familiar URL or bookmark.
2. The campaign manager is greeted with a menu that includes a list of campaigns that are active, a list of completed campaigns, and the option to log off.
3. By choosing an active or completed campaign from a drill-down list, the campaign manager can view the results in real time (for active campaigns) as they get posted by data trackers in the field, or they can view previously completed campaigns.

We now move on to the final design detail of the pilot project: the database needed to support it.

Database Setup

We will now touch on the tables that are stored in relational databases that will be queried based on the data tracker ID number and campaign type. Each campaign will contain a number of assignments. Each assignment is given to one data tracker and one or more retail establishment. For example, the *Potato Chips Monthly* campaign will contain five assignments given to five data trackers who will canvas Safeway, Cala Foods, Albertson's, Mollie Stone's, and Bell Market. The five data trackers will post their results, and reports will be generated based on their findings on an aggregate basis or individual basis. The database tables are briefly described next. You can skip this information if you are not interested in the details of the implementation.

Each data tracker is profiled in the tblTrackers table. This table contains the following items:

- **ID** Unique identifier for each data tracker or employee (for example, HMS007)
- **Name** Name of tracker (for example, James Bond)
- **Address** Complete address of each tracker (for example, 600 Pennsylvania Avenue, San Mateo, CA 94403)
- **HomePhone** Complete home phone number of each tracker (for example, 1-650-555-1212)
- **MobilePhone** Complete mobile phone number for SMS notifications and direct access (for example, 1-650-222-1234)
- **History** Full history of each completed task or assignment (for example, SM0009 or SM0012)
- **Preferred** Retail establishment preferred by tracker (for example, Safeway)
- **Password** Used for access to assignments (for example, shaken)

Each campaign will contain the list of assignments and is stored in the tblCampaign table. The tblCampaign table consists of the following items:

- **ID** Unique identifier for each campaign (for example, CAMP6745)
- **Desc** Description of campaign (for example, Snacks Monthly)
- **Assignments** List of assignments related to this campaign (for example, SM0088, SM0034, and SM0102)
- **Status** Either the campaign is active or inactive (for example, 0/1 boolean)

Assignments are contained in the tblAssignments table. This table contains the following items:

- **ID** Unique identifier for each assignment (for example, SM0088)
- **Name** Name of assignment (for example, Potato Chips)
- **AssignedTo** Data tracker the assignment is given to (for example, HMS007)
- **Retailers** List of retail establishments this assignment applies to (for example, GRCY001, GRCY002, GRCY004, and GRCY005)
- **AssignmentTypes** List of assignment types in this assignment (for example, 1, 2, 3, 4, and 5)
- **Categories** List of categories this assignment applies to (for example, 1)
- **StartDate** Date the assignment is active (for example, 3/20/2002)
- **EndDate** Date the assignment is done (for example, 3/22/2002)
- **EstTime** Estimated times, in minutes, this task will take (for example, 20)

Assignment types and the related product categories are stored in the tblAssignType and tblProducts tables, respectively. The tblAssignType table contains the following items:

- **Type** Unique number identifier of assignment type (for example, 1)
- **Name** Name of the assignment type (for example, Placement, Stock, or Competition)
- **Desc** Description of the assignment type (for example, Checking for Placement of Products on Shelf)
- **Choices** List of possible choices or selections for this assignment type (for example, Top, Middle, and Bottom)

The tblProducts table contains the following items:

- **CategoryID** Unique number identifier of the category (for example, 1)
- **Desc** Description of this category (for example, snacks–potato chips)

There is also a database of relevant information (tblRetailers table) for each retail establishment for the convenience of the data trackers. It contains the following items:

- **ID** Unique identifier for each retailer (for example, GRCY001)
- **Name** Name of the retail establishment (for example, Safeway)

- **Address** Complete address of the retail establishment (for example, 1100 El Camino Real, Belmont, CA 94002)
- **Phone** Complete phone number of the retail establishment (for example, 1-650-596-1730)
- **Hours** Operating hours of the retail establishment (for example, 7:00am–11:00pm)

Finally, the last database is where all the campaign results are posted to and where reports can be developed to tally the results. The tblResults table contains the following items:

- **Campaign** Campaign number (for example, CAMP6745)
- **Assignment** Assignment number (for example, SM0088)
- **Logged** Date and time the data is captured (for example, 1/23/2002 1:05pm)
- **AssignedTo** Data tracker assigned to (for example, hms007)
- **Retailer** Retail establishment (for example, GRCY001)
- **AssignmentType** Type of assignment (numeric mapping) in this campaign (for example, 1)
- **Captured** Results (numeric mapping list) captured (for example, 1)

With all these tables populated in the database, we're all set to begin a campaign. We went into some of the details here so that you can actually replicate this mobile application and see it work, as described in this book.

Phase One

This is the initial phase with just WAP access through a Motorola *i*1000*plus* phone on the Nextel iDEN network. The Nextel phone has always-on Internet access and can send or receive SMS messages as well. We will now run through the two scenarios described earlier for a campaign with a data tracker. The ACME mobile campaign example is as follows:

- Gather data on a specific brand of consumer product (yogurt, in this example) that ACME is distributing to local grocery stores.
- Send data trackers out to a number of grocery chains, such as Safeway and Albertson's.
- Data-mine and summarize the results for this campaign.

Scenario One: Accepting an Assignment The first scenario is when a data tracker logs on to accept or reject an assignment for a campaign. Figures 15-2 through 15-7 show the user interface and the steps that the data tracker goes through for this task. The data tracker logs in by providing his user ID and password (see Figure 15-2). On a successful login, the data tracker is greeted by the system (see Figure 15-3).

The data tracker is presented with a menu of choices, including updating personal information such as his address and phone number—crucial pieces of information for the campaign manager to use for scheduling and allocating assignments to data trackers (see Figure 15-4).

Next, the data tracker checks what pending assignments he has been allocated and decides whether to accept or reject them. Information available to the data tracker includes what consumer product to track, which retail establishments are involved, and an estimate of the time it takes to complete the assignment (see Figure 15-5). The data tracker can then accept or reject the assignment (see Figure 15-6).

Should the data tracker change his mind after accepting an assignment, given that the cancellation window is there, he can reject a previously accepted assignment (see Figure 15-7).

Scenario Two: Collecting Data in an Assignment The second scenario is when a data tracker logs on to start an assignment for a campaign. Figures 15-8 through 15-12 show the user interface and the steps that the data tracker goes through for this task. Before going to any of the retail establishments, the data tracker can check out their addresses and operating hours (see Figures 15-8 and 15-9).

Note that the application is designed such that the data tracker can just press the softkey to make the phone call without having to key in each number if he needs to call the retail establishment for additional information.

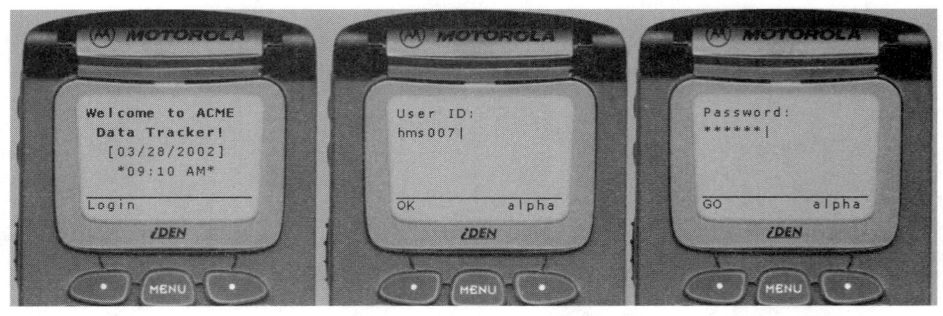

FIGURE 15-2. *Data Tracker logs into system*

FIGURE 15-3. *System greets tracker and presents menu*

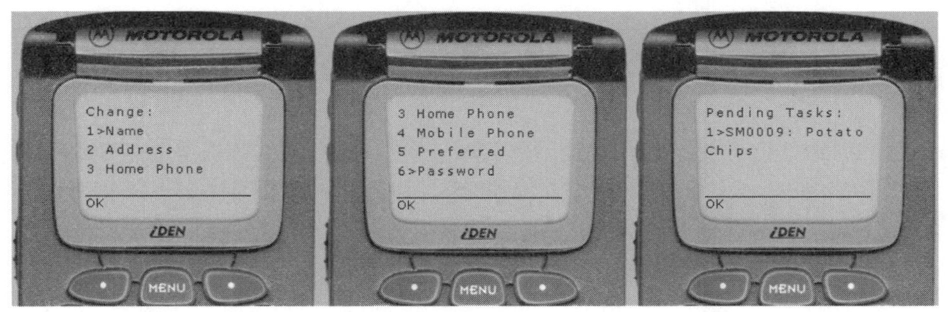

FIGURE 15-4. *Tracker can update profile and check out pending assignments*

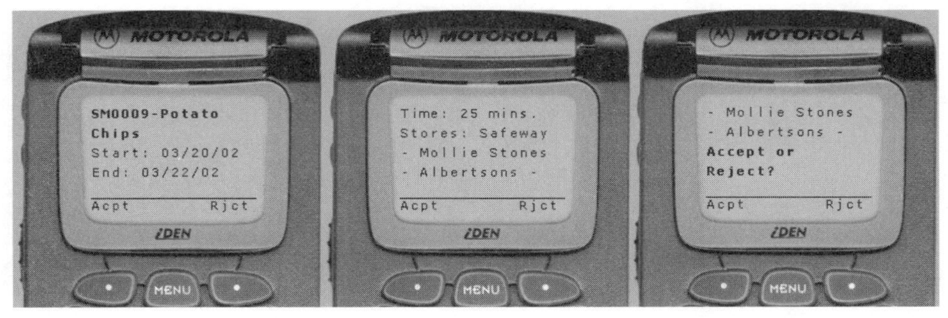

FIGURE 15-5. *Tracker can preview and accept or reject pending assignments*

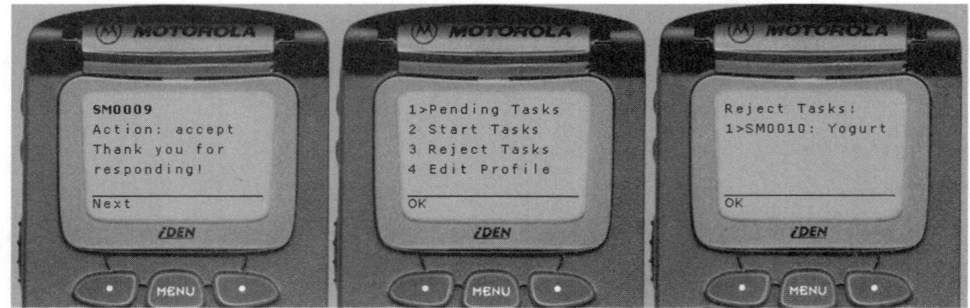

FIGURE 15-6. *Tracker accepts pending assignments*

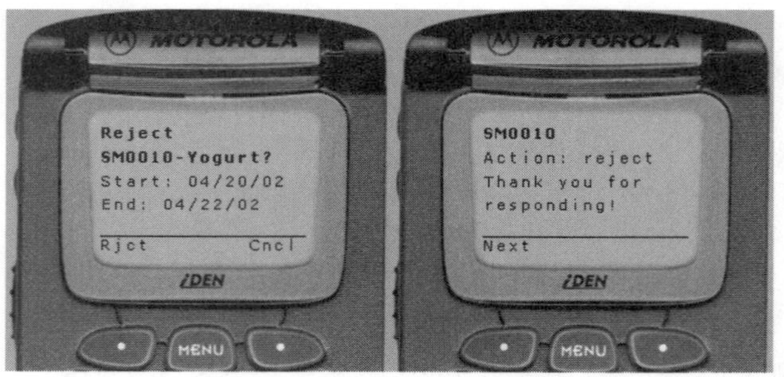

FIGURE 15-7. *Tracker rejects previously accepted assignments*

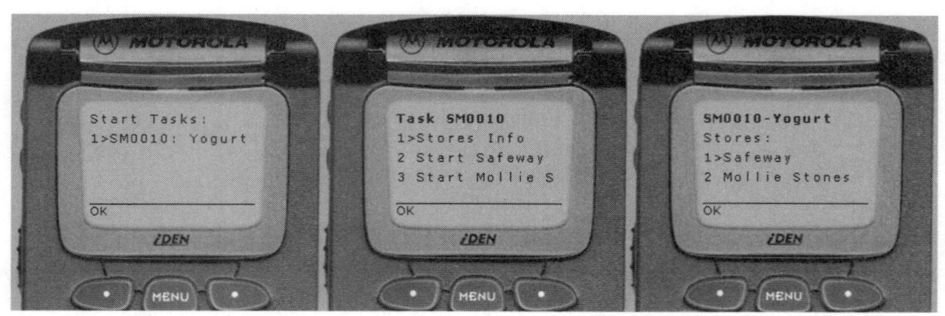

FIGURE 15-8. *Information on stores that the tracker has assignments at*

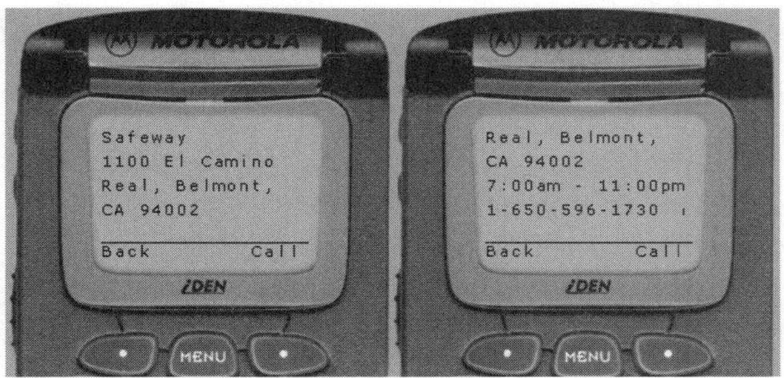

FIGURE 15-9. *Tracker can easily call a store to confirm operating hours*

The data tracker is now ready to start his assignment. The start time is logged. The first task is to check the placement of Mountain High Yogurt in the local Safeway store (see Figure 15-10). The menu-based form makes it easy for the data tracker to enter the information and submit it back to the remote server with minimal data entry, thereby reducing input errors (see Figure 15-11). He just enters it, using any of the accelerator keys and data is posted back to the central database instantly.

The data tracker continues with the remaining tasks from that store using the same simple UI to complete the tasks (see Figure 15-12). After completing all the tasks for Safeway, they move on to the next local store, Mollie Stone's. This process is repeated until all the retail establishments have been visited and data captured. Each data capture is time-stamped and can be data-mined for efficiency.

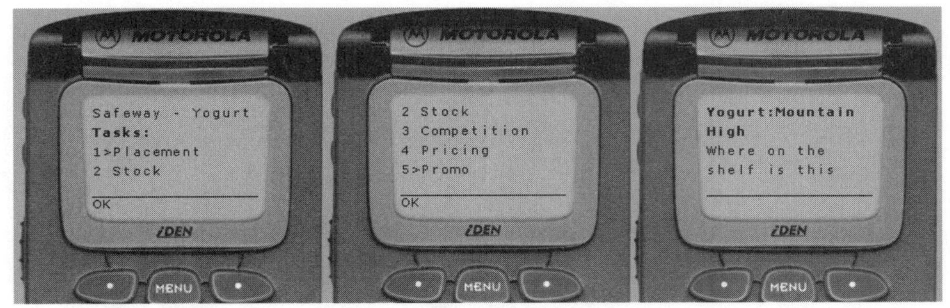

FIGURE 15-10. *Performing the assignment starting with the first data capture*

FIGURE 15-11. *Simple data captures using accelerator keys*

Some of the tasks in an assignment include the following for each consumer product:

- Whether the item is in stock or out of stock
- Whether the product is located on the top shelf, middle (eye-level) shelf, or the lower shelf
- Which brands are the competition on the shelf
- What brands are on the store's weekly specials

Scenario Three: Campaign Manager The campaign managers can see the results and can log on using their privileged accounts. Figures 15-13 and 15-14

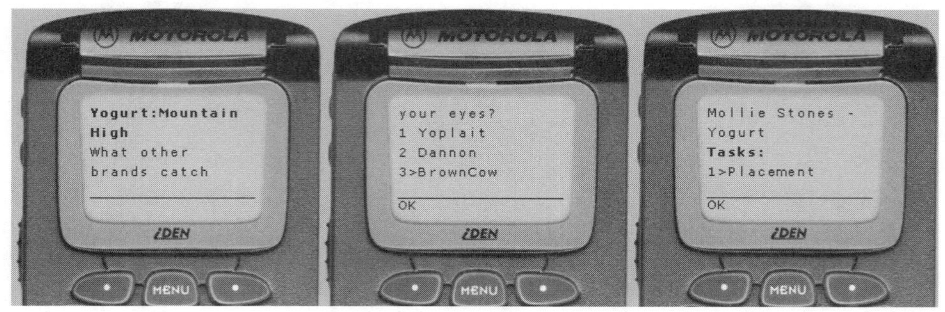

FIGURE 15-12. *More assignments*

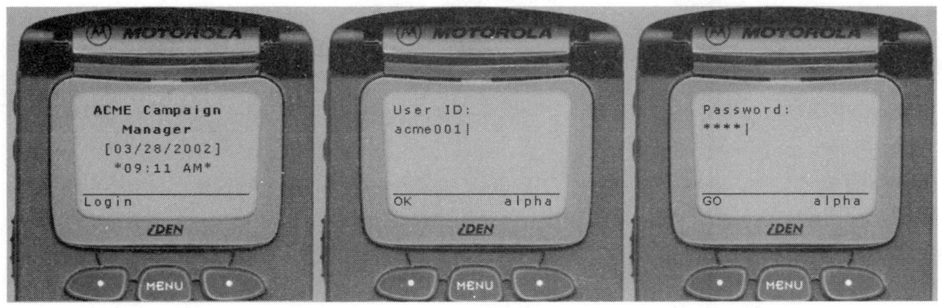

FIGURE 15-13. *Campaign manager*

show the results and the data that can be mined for this campaign. The campaign managers can also reassign any rejected tasks during the campaign cycle. A campaign manager logs in (see Figure 15-13) and is presented with a menu if successful (see Figure 15-14).

For the Yogurt Weekly campaign, the results from active campaign CAMP0714 are selected (see Figure 15-14). This campaign involves three grocery stores (Safeway, Mollie Stone's, and Albertson's) and one data tracker (hms007, James Bond). The consumer yogurt brand that ACME is distributing to these Bay Area grocery stores is Mountain High. The first report shows the placement for each grocery store and the average overall (see Figure 15-15). The times it took the data tracker to collect all the results in each grocery store and a cumulative for the whole assignment are also shown (see Figure 15-16 and Figure 15-17).

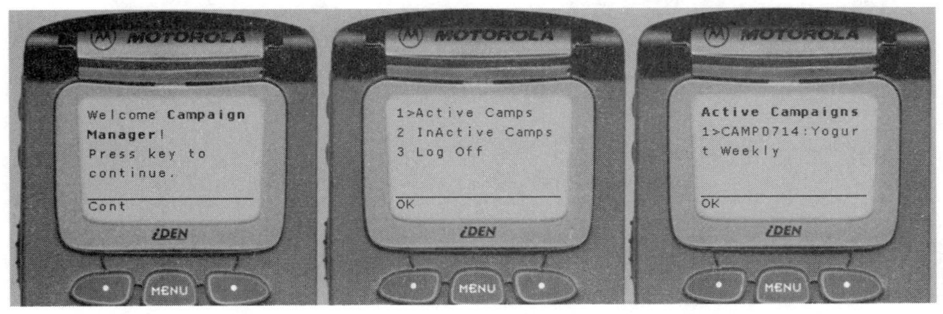

FIGURE 15-14. *Active campaigns*

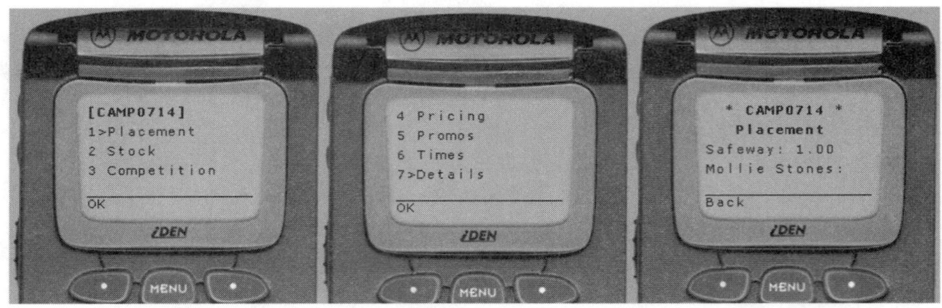

FIGURE 15-15. *Placement results*

You can see that the application is very simple and allows for remote data collection, updates to databases, and real-time viewing of results by a campaign manager. As mentioned earlier, there are still open issues with this mobile application—no automatic reminders with SMS messages so data trackers are reminded to check for assignments or start an accepted assignment, and so on. Campaign managers may want to view the results through web browsers on PCs, in addition to using their WAP phones. They may want to manually send SMS messages or simply call the data tracker using a voice phone. All require a lot of tracking on the part of the campaign manager and ACME hopes to automate this in the future.

FIGURE 15-16. *Efficiency of data tracker*

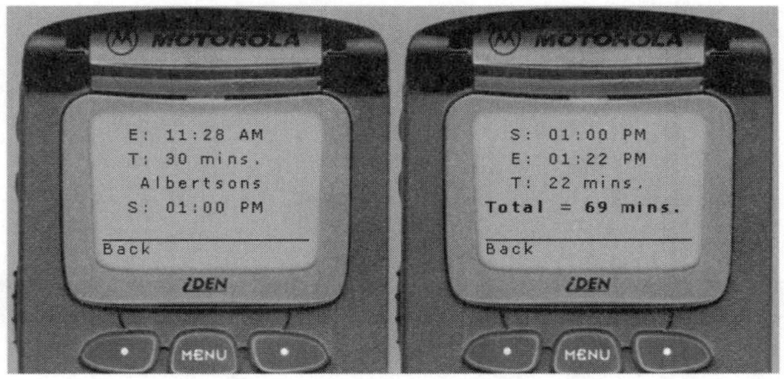

FIGURE 15-17. *Cumulative data collection times*

Phase Two

In Phase Two, ACME chose to adopt the Oracle9*i*AS Wireless platform. Here are some of the key features ACME considered for this project:

- **WML Translator** Used to leverage and get a jumpstart on converting the existing WAP application to multichannel mobile while developing a native Oracle9*i*AS multichannel XML version. This will let ACME developers get a taste of the other devices, such as the PocketPC, and even HTML!
- **SMS** Using SMS for reminders, ACME wants data trackers to confirm engagements to eliminate no-shows. This way, if a tracker doesn't respond, the assignment is given to another data tracker.
- **Location-Based Services (LBS)** Used to provide maps and direction information to data trackers so they can complete their assignments efficiently.
- **Location Stamp** In a future phase, ACME wants to register the location at which the data is submitted from the mobile device to the database (that is, "location-stamping" the data). This will guarantee that the data is collected not only at the specified time slot but is actually taken at the designated retail establishment. This location stamp will help ensure a visit is made to the retail store and true data is collected for each assignment.

Jumpstart Using Oracle9*i*AS Wireless To kick off, ACME wants to get its developers to start playing with the PocketPC devices and new WAP phones (using simulators) that may be hitting the market in the near future. One way to do this is to use the WML Translator that is part of the mCommerce Service in Oracle9*i*AS

Wireless Release 2 (see Chapter 11). To do this, an end user does not even have to log into the wireless web server. Follow these steps to run the WML Translator service:

1. Point your PocketPC or other mobile device to the wireless web server. The typical URL is http://localhost:9000/ptg/rm.
2. Select the Commerce folder and then the Translator service (see the illustration).

3. Type in the URL of the ACME application (for example, http://localhost/acme/index.jsp).
4. Tap the Submit button. You will see the welcome screen from the ACME data tracker program (see the illustration). Tap the Login button, and you can log in to just the original WML application, except that you are now using it on a PocketPC.

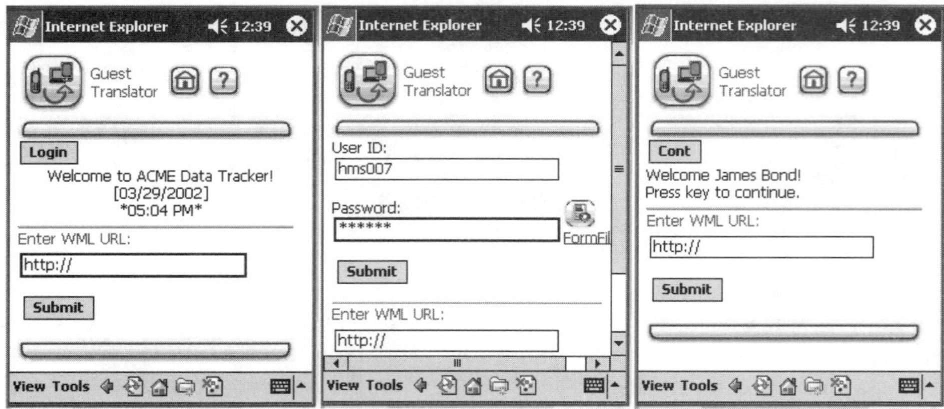

5. Notice that this is fine for testing out applications, but it's hardly usable for real-world data tracking because you lose half the screen (the WML Translator service provides an entry dialog for the user to type in a new URL to translate). It is a feature provided by Oracle for porting legacy WML pages, but not an entire mobile application. It's solely for the use of developers. To really leverage the power of Oracle9*i*AS Wireless, ACME needs to develop using the multichannel XML format—and that is what's shown in the next section.

Some of the magic can be seen in the following code listings. For example, in the Login page, the WML code is as follows:

```
<wml>
  <head>
   <meta http-equiv="Cache-Control" content="no-cache" forua="true"/>
  </head>
  <card>
  <do type="accept" label="GO">
   <go method="post" href="validate.cfm">
     <postfield name="passwd" value="$passwd"/>
     <postfield name="userid" value="$userid"/>
   </go>
  </do>
  <p>
  User ID:
  <input title="User ID" name="userid" type="text"/>
  Password:
  <input title="Password" name="passwd" type="password"/>
  </p>
  </card>
</wml>
```

The equivalent Oracle9*i*AS multichannel XML generated internally is shown here (see the sys_panama.log file):

```
<!--
  ==============================================================
            WML to MobileXML
  This file was generated automatically. Please do not edit it!
     @ Copyright 2001, Oracle Corp. All rights reserved.
  ==============================================================
-->
<SimpleContainer>
  <SimpleMenu title="You are going to fill a form with parameters &quot;
  User ID&quot;, &quot;Password&quot;. You have two choices."
  deviceclass="microbrowser" device.class="ss">
   <SimpleMenuItem target="#null"
```

```
    callbackpath="%value service.home.url%"
    callbackparam="XLTORSITE=http%3A%2F%2Flocalhost%2Facme%2Flogin.jsp"
    title="Go" label="Go">
    Go to Original Form
    </SimpleMenuItem>
    <SimpleMenuItem target="omp://oracle/services/commerce/formfiller?
    FORMFILLURL=http%3A%2F%2Flocalhost&amp;FORMFILLPARAMS=User+ID%3A
    userid%2CPassword%3Apasswd" callbackpath="%value service.home.url%"
    callbackparam="XLTORSITE=http%3A%2F%2Flocalhost%2Facme%2Flogin.jsp"
    title="Go" label="Go">
    Use FormFiller
    </SimpleMenuItem>
   </SimpleMenu>
   <SimpleForm method="post" target="translator.jsp&amp;
   XLTORSITE=http%3A%2F%2Flocalhost%2Facme%2Fvalidate.jsp%3F
   passwd%3D%24passwd%26userid%3D%24userid%26XLTOR_REQUESTMETHOD%3Dpost">
    <SimpleFormItem name="userid" type="text" default="">
    User ID:
    </SimpleFormItem>
    <SimpleFormItem name="passwd" type="password" default="">
    Password:
    </SimpleFormItem>
    <SimpleImage target="omp://oracle/services/commerce/formfiller?
    FORMFILLURL=http%3A%2F%2Flocalhost&amp;FORMFILLPARAMS=User+ID%3A
    userid%2CPassword%3Apasswd" callbackpath="%value service.home.url%"
    callbackparam="XLTORSITE=http%3A%2F%2Flocalhost%2Facme%2Flogin.jsp"
    src="/modules/images/commerce/translator/formfiller_small"
    available="gif g2.gif" width="26" height="24" device.class="ms"
    deviceclass="pdabrowser pcbrowser" border="0">
    FormFiller
    </SimpleImage>
   </SimpleForm>
</SimpleContainer>
```

Note that the wireless web server inserted the Form Filler service link to make things easier for the end user. Of course, you have all these modules at your command when you develop mobile applications using Oracle9*i*AS Wireless. Now that you have a taste of the Oracle9*i*AS multichannel XML, let's start migrating the ACME WAP application.

Full Migration Using Oracle9*i*AS Multichannel XML Migrating from WML to Oracle9*i*AS multichannel XML is pretty straightforward, because ACME only used WML for presentation or rendering of content. The business logic stays the same—only the device markup pages need to be migrated. Additionally, ACME now has the luxury of displaying images for logos, buttons, and so on, in addition to font styles, font colors, and font sizes. But care must be used, because the bandwidth for wireless is still low. Finally, ACME also has the out-of-the-box services, such as mCommerce, Location-Based Services, and PIM/E-Mail, available for integration into its mobile applications.

Let's take a look at what some of the ACME pages look like in Oracle9*i*AS multichannel XML format. The original WML for the Welcome page (index.wml) and data tracker Menu page (menu.wml) is shown here:

```
<!-- index.wml listing -->
<wml>
<head>
  <meta http-equiv="Cache-Control" content="no-cache" forua="true" />
</head>
<card>
  <do type="accept" label="Login">
   <go method="post" href="login.jsp">
   </go>
  </do>
  <p align="center" mode="wrap">
  <em>Welcome to ACME Data Tracker!</em>
  <br />
  [03/29/2002]
  <br />
  *05:04 PM*
  </p>
</card>
</wml>

<!-- menu.wml listing -->
<wml>
<head>
  <meta http-equiv="Cache-Control" content="no-cache" forua="true" />
</head>
<card>
  <p>
  <select>
   <option><onevent type="onpick">
   <go href="assignments.jsp?action=tasks_pending"/></onevent>
   Pending Tasks</option>
   <option><onevent type="onpick">
   <go href="assignments.jsp?action=tasks_starting"/></onevent>
   Start Tasks</option>
   <option><onevent type="onpick">
   <go href="assignments.jsp?action=tasks_rejecting"/></onevent>
   Reject Tasks</option>
   <option><onevent type="onpick">
   <go href="profile.jsp "/></onevent>
   Edit Profile</option>
   <option><onevent type="onpick">
   <go href="history.jsp "/></onevent>
```

```
    History</option>
    <option><onevent type="onpick">
    <go href="logoff.jsp"/></onevent>
    Log Off</option>
  </select>
  </p>
  </card>
</wml>
```

ACME has converted its server scripts from generating the WML wireless markup language to the Oracle9*i*AS multichannel XML format. The equivalent of the preceding listing follows:

```
<!-- index.xml listing -->
<SimpleResult>
  <SimpleCache ttl="0"/>
  <SimpleContainer>
  <SimpleText>
   <SimpleTextItem halign="center">
   <SimpleStrong>Welcome to ACME Data Tracker!</SimpleStrong>
   <SimpleBreak />
   [03/29/2002]
   <SimpleBreak />
   *05:04 PM*
   </SimpleTextItem>
  </SimpleText>
  <SimpleAction label="LOGIN" type="primary" target="login.jsp"/>
  </SimpleContainer>
</SimpleResult>

<!-- menu.xml listing -->
<SimpleResult>
  <SimpleCache ttl="0"/>
  <SimpleContainer>
  <SimpleMenu title="Selection Menu:" mode="nowrap">
   <SimpleMenuItem target="assignments.jsp?action=tasks_pending">
   Pending Tasks</SimpleMenuItem>
   <SimpleMenuItem target="assignments.jsp?action=tasks_starting">
   Start Tasks</SimpleMenuItem>
   <SimpleMenuItem target="assignments.jsp?action=tasks_rejecting">
   Reject Tasks</SimpleMenuItem>
   <SimpleMenuItem target="profile.jsp ">Edit Profile</SimpleMenuItem>
   <SimpleMenuItem target="history.jsp ">History</SimpleMenuItem>
   <SimpleMenuItem target="logoff.jsp ">Log Off</SimpleMenuItem>
  </SimpleMenu>
  </SimpleContainer>
</SimpleResult>
```

ACME now has a multichannel mobile application based on Oracle9*i*AS Wireless. The ACME application is now accessible by PocketPCs, WAP phones, HTML browsers, Palms or HandSprings, and many other devices supported by the Oracle9*i*AS Wireless platform.

NOTE
Server-side session variables have to be handled by the database. For example, ASP and ColdFusion server session variables will not work. They have to be redesigned for the database to be used for storing them.

ACME has added some images and text formatting in this phase (see the following illustrations).

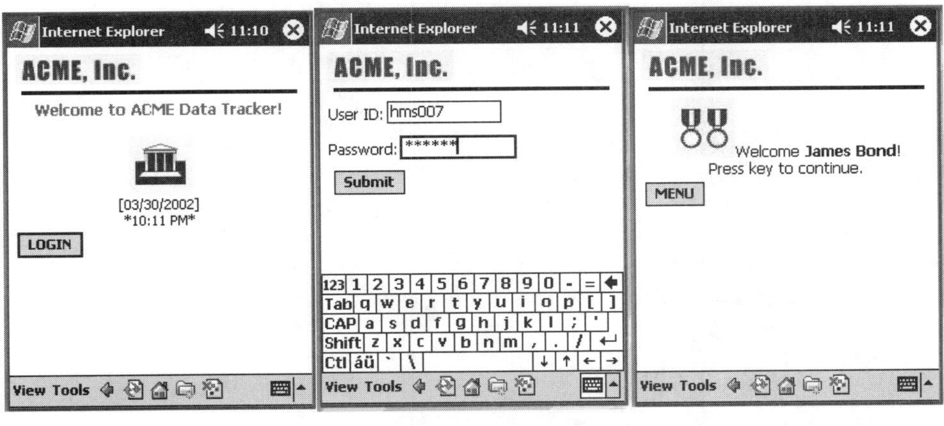

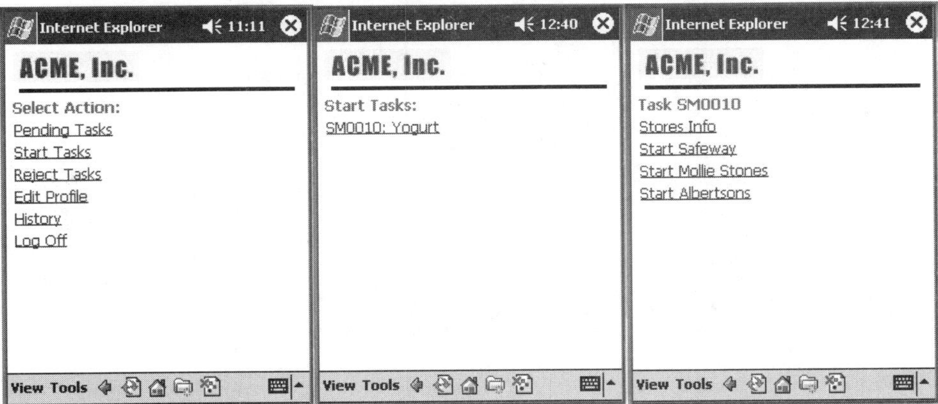

One of the interesting features, now that ACME has mobile devices that can display images, is that the campaign managers can view the results better. For example, the averages can be displayed graphically on mobile devices that support images and plain text on the others (see the illustration).

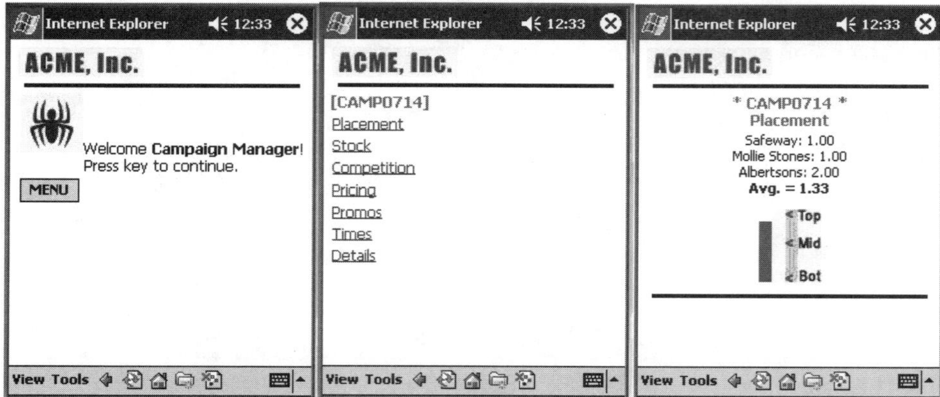

Adding LBS Feature To complete Phase Two, ACME has added maps and directions using LBS. From the Task screen (refer to the next to last illustration) for the data tracker, select the Store Info link. Based on the targeted retail establishment and the residence of the data tracker, directions to and from these two locations can be displayed in addition to a map of the retail establishment (see the illustration). Additionally, the data tracker can find directions between retail establishments for the same assignment.

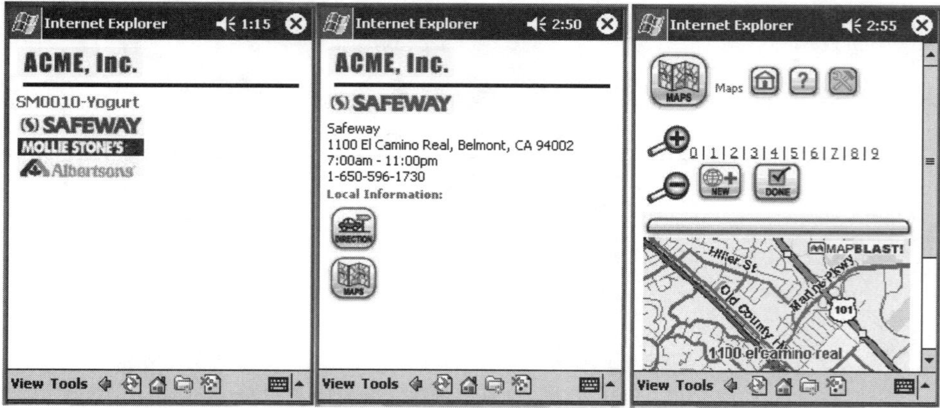

The code snippet of the store detail follows:

```
<SimpleResult>
  <SimpleCache ttl="0"/>
  <SimpleContainer>
  <SimpleImage src="http://localhost/acme/images/logo"
   addImageExtension="yes" available="jpg gif png bmp"
   alt="[ACME Logo]" />
  <SimpleBreak rule="true"/>
  <SimpleImage src="http://localhost/acme/images/safeway"
   addImageExtension="yes" available="jpg gif png bmp"
   alt="[safeway]" />
  <SimpleText>
   <SimpleTextItem halign="left" size="2" font="verdana,arial">
   Safeway
   <SimpleBreak />
   1100 El Camino Real, Belmont, CA 94002
   <SimpleBreak />
   7:00am - 11:00pm
   <SimpleBreak />
    1-650-596-1730
   </SimpleTextItem>
  </SimpleText>
  <SimpleAction label="CALL" type="primary"
   static_target="callto:1-650-596-1730"/>
  <SimpleMenu mode="nowrap">
  <SimpleTitle font="arial,verdana" size="1" color="#ff0000">
   Local Information:
  </SimpleTitle>
    <SimpleMenuItem target="omp://oracle/services/location/directions?
     OADDRESS=600+Pennsylvania+Avenue&amp;OCITY=San+Mateo&amp;
     OSTATE=CA&amp;OZIP=94403&amp;DADDRESS=1100+El+Camino+Real&amp;
     DCITY=Belmont&amp;DSTATE=CA&amp;DZIP=94002">
    <SimpleImage src="http://localhost/acme/images/directions"
     addImageExtension="yes" available="jpg gif png bmp"
     alt="directions?" />
   </SimpleMenuItem>
   <SimpleMenuItem target="omp://oracle/services/location/maps?
     FL=1100+El+Camino+Real&amp;CI=Belmont&amp;ST=CA&amp;PC=94002">
   <SimpleImage src="http://localhost/acme/images/maps"
     addImageExtension="yes" available="jpg gif png bmp"
     alt="maps?" />
   </SimpleMenuItem>
  </SimpleMenu>
  </SimpleContainer>
</SimpleResult>
```

Without any input entry from the data tracker, maps and directions are now available with the ease of a single tap or press!

Results

The bottom line is an improved ability for ACME to formulate and monitor its marketing campaigns with current information on how its products are sold. There is no paper-based process; the data is accurate and near real time, without extra steps for processing. Data trackers have seen their productivity increase with the improved user interfaces and features from Oracle9*i*AS Wireless. Because it is easier to use, it is gaining rapid acceptance by other field personnel of ACME.

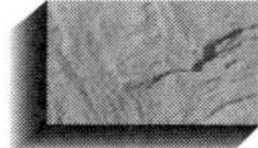

NOTE
The system has to be easy to use for the front-line worker. Many of the people using this technology are not comfortable with computers, and so the mobile computing solution really has to help them do their job better. Otherwise, it will not be adopted.

Migration took days instead of weeks, mainly because ACME started from a WAP application instead of a web-based HTML application. Decision on content is easily made because ACME chose to add instead of remove content (as in HTML applications). Additionally, ACME developers now only maintain one version of the application for all mobile devices—their original WAP application is retired after running it in parallel as a backup for about two months while they field-tested the migrated application running on the Oracle9*i*AS Wireless platform.

As ACME scales to more users, changes store assignments, and diversifies into other products, it will start to leverage the Advanced Customization and PIM features of Oracle9*i*AS Wireless to manage scheduling, provisioning, and even time tracking. ACME will also allow its developers to start using Mobile Studio to make it even easier to develop new and innovative mobile campaigns!

Case 2: Mobile Enabling Dynamic Content

This case study illustrates how to mobile enable dynamic content from a database. The content may be an XML content feed that is post-processed and stored in a database for publishing or any content that is sitting in a database independent of how it is populated. For example, it could be aggregating content using a Web service via Simple Object Access Protocol (SOAP) calls to a remote web server.

We will not go into the specifics of XML/XSLT using various parsers or discuss how Web services are implemented—the entire back-end loading of content into the database is beyond the scope of this book. We will, however, discuss how one small company mobile enables the XML data stored in a database. You'll see the XML formats and how simple it is to mobile enable the content using an XSLT stylesheet. The XSLT stylesheet will transform the XML data into the Oracle9*i*AS multichannel XML format.

Customer and Needs

MobileG Software, Inc. (MobileG) is a consulting firm specializing in mobile application development. It has expertise in WML, XML, and Oracle9*i*AS Wireless, among other platforms and wireless technologies. MobileG has implemented a number of projects extending enterprise applications to mobile devices. MobileG is interested in building up a new capability of integrating content using publicly and privately available Web services. MobileG believes there will be significant demands for mobile assignments to adapt content from both internal data stores (within the firewall) and external sources as well as to subsequently deliver the content to various mobile devices. It wants to leverage Oracle9*i*AS Wireless as part of the core platform. Additionally, it wants to use this implementation to deepen the expertise of its technical consultants and developers in mobile development, SOAP, and XML/XSLT.

All the MobileG consultants have PocketPCs or WAP phones and have access to their local LAN or wireless LAN. Although many MobileG consultants are Java developers, a great deal of MobileG's customers use Active Server Pages (ASP) and ColdFusion Markup (CFM) server scripts for their web applications. Hence, MobileG wants to implement a solution that is applicable to JSP, ASP, or CFM scripts, with minor modifications, if at all. As long as these customers can publish in Oracle9*i*AS multichannel XML, it does not matter what server languages they use!

Situation and Use Case

Keeping up with the latest developments in mobile and wireless arenas has been a challenging task for anyone involved in the high-technology workforce. You are always learning new technologies and languages—within six months, the cycle repeats. MobileG's clients expect the firm to be up to date with whatever technology is available worldwide. Customers are interested in technologies such as i-mode, 3G, GSM, and GPRS, which are not abundantly available in the United States. For technologies that are already available in the U.S. (WAP-enabled phones and PocketPC devices with wireless access), their customers expect them to be experts.

Using WAP-enabled phones and PocketPC devices to access mobile applications or Internet content requires a great UI model, as already discussed in Chapter 14. What a developer considers a good UI may be totally off base for an end user. If a developer uses whatever they have created (have your cake and eat it too) on a daily basis, they will learn real quickly when things break. Apply that to all the consultants, and you have great data points!

These mobile applications are meant to display relevant news abstracts. The details or full articles should be accessible from a desktop PC or sent by e-mail to the end user for later reading on their desktop PCs. Also, the full article can be made available for those who really want it. Additionally, these news sources can come from many different web servers in many different XML formats, including raw SOAP responses. MobileG's main goal is to make its employees aware of these technologies so they can pursue the details at their own pace.

Strategy

As MobileG's employees get used to using mobile devices as part of their daily routine, MobileG's expertise also grows. MobileG is its own sandbox for testing new mobile applications and new mobile devices. Its best customers are its employees!

Content aggregation is only part of MobileG's strategy. Creating news portals using diverse technologies is a requirement for MobileG's business. Being able to aggregate and manipulate XML content feed is mandatory. MobileG is also looking at hosting the news portal for its customers. Coupled with Oracle9*i*AS Portal and Advanced Personalization in the future, this can be done easily.

Another technology of interest to MobileG is Web services. Again, being able to interact and manipulate SOAP XML messages is required knowledge for MobileG's consultants. Being able to consume a Web service is a start. Being able to publish a web service would be the next phase.

Solution

MobileG has chosen to partition the work for implementing this system. The Feeds group does all the back-end server-side population of the databases. This group handles all the code necessary for accessing the XML content feeds using HTTP or XML Remote Procedure Calls (RPC) protocols. This group is also responsible for populating the databases with SOAP responses from select Web services using XML RPC or similar technologies. From the databases onward, the Content group will handle all the processing and publish the content in Oracle9*i*AS multichannel XML format. This is where they will create services using the HTTP Adapter from the Oracle9*i*AS Wireless platform.

Two basic scenarios are described here. The first one is using XSLT to transform one of the XML content feeds into the Oracle9*i*AS multichannel XML format. The second scenario is also using XSLT but transforming a SOAP response to the Oracle9*i*AS multichannel XML format. We will not go into the performance issues of full-scale content aggregation, because MobileG is not at that stage yet. Note that the Oracle9*i*AS Portal product can be used for such an enterprise portal solution.

Oracle is making it easier to mobile enable portals and will release a much better integrated product (Portal and Wireless platform) in the near future.

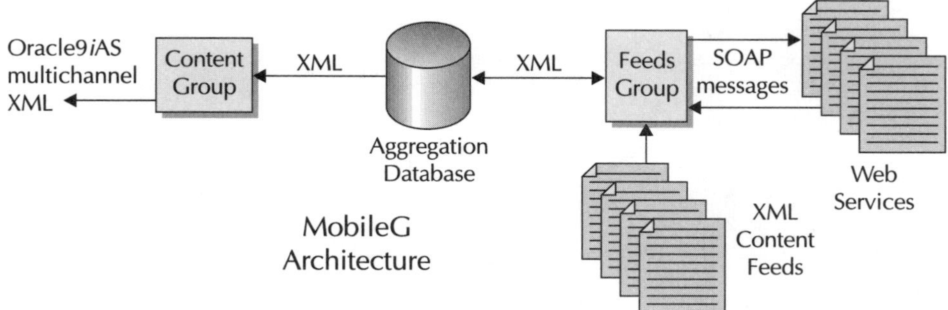

Additionally, we will apply some of the design guidelines from Chapter 14 when presenting these content pages on mobile devices. We will now go into these two scenarios and look at the code MobileG used to create the content-aggregation service.

XML Content Feed

A very interesting XML content feed from Norway that is available for free and contains compelling content on the mobile handheld platform is a website called InfoSync (http://www.infosync.no). Its XML content feed (headlines and abstracts) URL is http://www.infosync.no/feed/infosync.php.

This is a free service, but a premium service is also available, where you get the full text for a fixed monthly charge. The DTD can be found at http://www.infosync.no/feed/dtd/infosync.dtd.

A snapshot of the XML content feed is shown here:

```
<?xml version="1.0" encoding="windows-1252" ?>
<infosync xmlns:infosync="http://www.infosync.no/feed/dtd/infosync.dtd">
  <story>
   <title>Teaching Flash for mobile devices</title>
   <url>http://www.infosync.no/show.php?id=1628</url>
   <abstract>Albeit a relatively new possibility, that hasn"t stopped
    11 authors from teaming up to create the very first book on
    designing Flash for mobile devices such as Pocket PCs.
   </abstract>
   <timestamp>20020328124821</timestamp>
  </story>
  <story>
   <title>Sun continues to push mobile Java</title>
```

```
    <url>http://www.infosync.no/show.php?id=1627</url>
    <abstract>Sun has introduced new virtual machines that the company
    expects to improve performance of Java technology-based devices up
    to 10 times higher than existing virtual machines.
    </abstract>
    <timestamp>20020328124754</timestamp>
   </story>
   <story>
    <title>English swivel CLIEs coming up</title>
    <url>http://www.infosync.no/show.php?id=1626</url>
    <abstract>When news first broke about the new super-swivel-CLIE
    NR70 series from Sony, speculations ran high on how soon English
    versions would be announced. Now, the cat"s out of the bag.
    </abstract>
    <timestamp>20020327145543</timestamp>
   </story>
   <story>
    <title>HSCSD by the millions</title>
    <url>http://www.infosync.no/show.php?id=1625</url>
    <abstract>While the GSM standard in its most basic form is
    incredibly popular, its HSCSD high-speed add-on isn"t lost
    either; it"s now available to over 100 million users in 27
    countries.
    </abstract>
    <timestamp>20020327145457</timestamp>
   </story>
</infosync>
```

MobileG's Feeds group created an XSLT stylesheet that will process this XML content and populate the database. The XML data is stored in two different ways: the complete XML feed and XML fragments for each news story. Here's what one of these XML fragments would look like:

```
<story>
 <title>Teaching Flash for mobile devices</title>
 <url>http://www.infosync.no/show.php?id=1628</url>
 <abstract>Albeit a relatively new possibility, that hasn"t stopped
  11 authors from teaming up to create the very first book on
  designing Flash for mobile devices such as Pocket PCs.
 </abstract>
 <timestamp>20020328124821</timestamp>
 <next>20020328124754</next>
 <previous>20020327145457</previous>
</story>
```

This is indexed by a time-stamp, which is unique for each story. The extra XML tag extended by the Feeds group is for going to the next and previous abstracts.

The job of the Content group is to retrieve this data from the database, apply the XSLT stylesheet, and generate Oracle9*i*AS multichannel XML from it. We have already discussed how to create a mobile service, so we won't cover how MobileG does that.

The XSLT stylesheet that can be used to process this XML content is shown next (one for the headlines/menu, and one for the abstracts):

```
<!--infosync_menu.xsl listing -->
<?xml version="1.0" ?>
  <xsl:stylesheet xmlns:xsl="http://www.w3.org/1999/XSL/Transform"
version="1.0">
  <xsl:output method="xml" omit-xml-declaration="yes"/>
  <xsl:template match="/">
   <SimpleResult>
     <SimpleContainer>
     <SimpleImage halign="center" src="http://localhost/book/MobileG"
      addImageExtension="yes" available="jpg gif png bmp"
      alt="[MobileG]" />
     <SimpleBreak />
      <xsl:apply-templates select="//infosync" />
   </SimpleContainer>
  </SimpleResult>
</xsl:template>
<xsl:template match="infosync">
  <SimpleMenu>
   <SimpleTitle color="#ff0000" font="verdana,arial" size="3">
      Select an Article:
   </SimpleTitle>
   <xsl:for-each select="//story">
     <SimpleMenuItem>
      <xsl:attribute name="target">infosync_abstract.cfm?timestamp=
      <xsl:value-of select="./timestamp" /></xsl:attribute>
      <xsl:attribute name="wrapmode">nowrap</xsl:attribute>
      <xsl:value-of select="./title" />
     </SimpleMenuItem>
   </xsl:for-each>
  </SimpleMenu>
  <SimpleAction label="INFO" type="secondary" target="info.cfm"/>
</xsl:template>
</xsl:stylesheet>

<!--infosync_abstract.xsl listing -->
<?xml version="1.0" ?>
  <xsl:stylesheet
      xmlns:xsl="http://www.w3.org/1999/XSL/Transform"
      version="1.0">
  <xsl:output method="xml" omit-xml-declaration="yes"/>
```

```
  <xsl:template match="/">
  <SimpleResult>
   <SimpleContainer>
   <SimpleImage halign="center" src="http://localhost/book/MobileG"
     addImageExtension="yes" available="jpg gif png bmp"
     alt="[MobileG]" />
   <SimpleBreak />
   <xsl:apply-templates select="//infosync" />
   </SimpleContainer>
  </SimpleResult>
</xsl:template>
<xsl:template match="infosync">
  <SimpleText>
  <SimpleTitle color="#ff0000" font="verdana,arial" size="3">
      Article Abstract
  </SimpleTitle>
  <SimpleBreak />
   <SimpleTextItem>
     <xsl:value-of select="./story/abstract" />
   </SimpleTextItem>
  </SimpleText>
  <SimpleAction>
   <xsl:attribute name="label">NEXT</xsl:attribute>
   <xsl:attribute name="type">secondary</xsl:attribute>
   <xsl:attribute name="target">infosync_abstract.cfm?timestamp=
   <xsl:value-of select="./story/next" /></xsl:attribute>
  </SimpleAction>
  <SimpleBreak />
  <SimpleAction>
   <xsl:attribute name="label">PREV</xsl:attribute>
   <xsl:attribute name="type">primary</xsl:attribute>
   <xsl:attribute name="target">infosync_abstract.cfm?timestamp=
   <xsl:value-of select="./story/previous" /></xsl:attribute>
  </SimpleAction>
</xsl:template>
</xsl:stylesheet>
```

A quick explanation of the preceding XSLT code is necessary. In the first stylesheet (infosync_menu.xsl), the first template (<xsl:template match="/">) is simply the Oracle9*i*AS multichannel XML wrapper for the content. The work is done by the second template (<xsl:template match="infosync">). The XSL statement <xsl:for-each select="//story"> looks for all occurrences of the tag element *story* at all levels from the root tag in this template (<infosync>). For every match, a <SimpleMenuItem> tag is created with the appropriate tag attributes based on the value of the <title> and <timestamp> XML tags. For the second stylesheet (infosync_abstract.xsl), the first template is again the Oracle9*i*AS multichannel

XML wrapper for the content, as in the first stylesheet. Again, the second template (<xsl:template match="infosync">) does all the work. The abstract content is extracted from the <xsl:value-of select="./story/abstract" /> XSLT statement. The rest of the XSLT statements set up the navigation (Next and Previous) for the article itself, so the user can easily go back to the previous article or to the next article without having to always start from the menu-selection screen.

From the two stylesheets, MobileG generated two mobile pages—one for the menu/headlines, and one for the abstract chosen from the menu. MobileG uses ASP and CFM for some of its clients, but it also uses JSP internally, so MobileG has a pretty diverse bunch of programmers. The resulting Oracle9*i*AS multichannel XML looks like this:

```
<!--infosync_menu Oracle9iAS XML listing -->
<SimpleResult>
  <SimpleContainer>
  <SimpleImage halign="center" src="http://localhost/book/MobileG"
   addImageExtension="yes" available="jpg gif png bmp"
   alt="[MobileG]" />
  <SimpleBreak />
  <SimpleMenu>
  <SimpleTitle color="#ff0000" font="verdana,arial" size="3">
   Select an Article:
  </SimpleTitle>
   <SimpleMenuItem
     target="infosync_abstract.cfm?timestamp=20020402073914"
     wrapmode="nowrap">NTT DoCoMo piloting 4G
   </SimpleMenuItem>
   <SimpleMenuItem
     target="infosync_abstract.cfm?timestamp=20020402061606"
     wrapmode="nowrap">Quickoffice improved
   </SimpleMenuItem>
   <SimpleMenuItem
     target="infosync_abstract.cfm?timestamp=20020402052236"
     wrapmode="nowrap">Phones as wallets gets strong support
   </SimpleMenuItem>
   <SimpleMenuItem
     target="infosync_abstract.cfm?timestamp=20020328124821"
     wrapmode="nowrap">Teaching Flash for mobile devices
   </SimpleMenuItem>
   <SimpleMenuItem
     target="infosync_abstract.cfm?timestamp=20020328124754"
     wrapmode="nowrap">Sun continues to push mobile Java
   </SimpleMenuItem>
   <SimpleMenuItem
     target="infosync_abstract.cfm?timestamp=20020327145543"
     wrapmode="nowrap">English swivel CLIEs coming up
```

```
    </SimpleMenuItem>
    <SimpleMenuItem
      target="infosync_abstract.cfm?timestamp=20020327145457"
      wrapmode="nowrap">HSCSD by the millions
    </SimpleMenuItem>
    <SimpleMenuItem
      target="infosync_abstract.cfm?timestamp=20020326123218"
      wrapmode="nowrap">In-Stat checks out Bluetooth
    </SimpleMenuItem>
    <SimpleMenuItem
      target="infosync_abstract.cfm?timestamp=20020326115417"
      wrapmode="nowrap">Palm snuggles up to OS X
    </SimpleMenuItem>
    <SimpleMenuItem
      target="infosync_abstract.cfm?timestamp=20020326102727"
      wrapmode="nowrap">Look into the mobile phone, please
    </SimpleMenuItem>
  </SimpleMenu>
  <SimpleAction label="INFO" type="secondary" target="info.cfm" />
</SimpleContainer>
</SimpleResult>

<!--infosync_abstract Oracle9iAS XML listing -->
<SimpleResult>
  <SimpleContainer>
  <SimpleImage halign="center" src="http://localhost/book/MobileG"
     addImageExtension="yes" available="jpg gif png bmp"
     alt="[MobileG]" />
  <SimpleBreak />
  <SimpleText>
  <SimpleTitle color="#ff0000" font="verdana,arial" size="3">
  Article Abstract</SimpleTitle>
  <SimpleBreak />
   <SimpleTextItem>NTT DoCoMo is currently in the early stages of
     setting up an experimental pilot system for 4G services with data
     transfer speeds in excess of 100 Mbps downlinks and 20 Mbps
     uplinks.
   </SimpleTextItem>
  </SimpleText>
  <SimpleAction label="NEXT" type="secondary"
   target="infosync_abstract.cfm?timestamp=20020402061606" />
  <SimpleBreak />
  <SimpleAction label="PREV" type="primary"
   target="infosync_abstract.cfm?timestamp=20020326102727" />
  </SimpleContainer>
</SimpleResult>
```

MobileG has just mobile enabled its InfoSync XML content feed! This is how it looks when displayed on mobile devices (see the following illustrations).

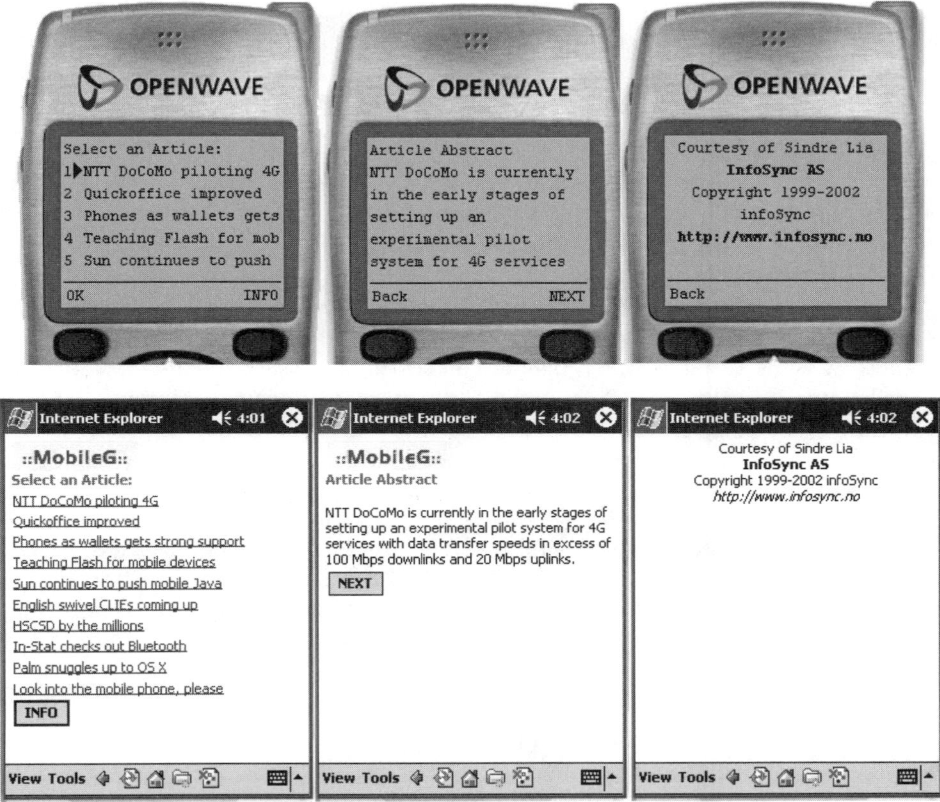

MobileG will make a few improvements that are based on the style guide for PocketPC in Chapter 14. First, it has to make sure each screen only displays nine or fewer headlines. This way, the accelerator keys on WAP phones can be used to select the headlines without the user having to scroll up and down using the keypad on the phone. Second, MobileG will publish the abstract and provide a link for the full article. Lastly, the full article will be divided into multiple parts, each with less than 200 bytes, and with Next and Previous links for easy navigation. Initial feedback showed that this is the optimal UI, and some users preferred the full article in one screen rather than over multiple screens (this can be implemented in the future through personalization so that users can customize to their hearts' content).

Numerous other XML-based content feeds are available that can be integrated into MobileG's content aggregation system, thus expanding the vast knowledge of wireless and mobile technologies to all the employees. One other popular content provider is MoreOver Technologies, Inc., located at http://www.moreover.com. MoreOver carries a lot of relevant mobile technology news, including daily news articles on handhelds and 3G technologies.

SOAP Response XML

MobileG wants to explore and deploy Web services within its intranets and at the same time have its employees exposed to Web services so that feedback and improvements can be made in-house. MobileG's customers will again indirectly gain such knowledge from this exercise.

A 30-second primer on SOAP is next. SOAP, or *Simple Object Access Protocol*, is an XML-based protocol for exchanging information in a distributed environment. Because SOAP is XML-based, it is platform and operating system independent, making it easily implementable for all of MobileG's customers. Because of the openness and extensibility, SOAP is emerging as the de facto standard for delivering content over the web.

Each SOAP message consists of a SOAP header/envelope and a SOAP body. Requests are made to invoke a method as a service (which includes input parameters). For each SOAP request, you will get a SOAP response (which includes a return value, output parameters, and error parameters). Let's look at an example. A SOAP request, FindMP3, is sent to the XMLRAD MP3 directory Web service. This request takes two string parameters, SearchString and MaxReturn, and returns a list of MP3 songs with the name, URL, and size in the SOAP response. The XML document represents the SOAP message. The SOAP envelope is the top element of the XML document. The following example uses the HTTP transport protocol and is similar to what one of MobileG's client wants to implement—an MP3 music download service. The SOAP request message embedded in the HTTP request looks like this:

```
POST /FindMP3 HTTP/1.1
Content-Type: text/xml
SOAPAction: FindMP3
<SOAP-ENV:Envelope
  xmlns:SOAP-ENV="http://schemas.xmlsoap.org/soap/envelope/"
  SOAP-ENV:encodingStyle="http://schemas.xmlsoap.org/soap/encoding/">
  <SOAP-ENV:Body>
   <FindMP3>
     <SearchString>Cartoon</SearchString>
     <MaxReturn>10</MaxReturn>
   </FindMP3>
  </SOAP-ENV:Body>
</SOAP-ENV:Envelope>
```

The SOAP response HTTP message containing the XML message with SOAP as the payload looks like this:

```
<SOAP-ENV:Envelope
   xmlns:SOAP-ENV="http://schemas.xmlsoap.org/soap/envelope/"
   SOAP-ENV:encodingStyle="http://schemas.xmlsoap.org/soap/encoding/">
  <SOAP-ENV:Body>
   <FindMP3Response>
   <MP3Results>
     <MP3>
      <FileName>Cartoon Theme - Simpsons.mp3</FileName>
      <URL>http://xmlrad.com/MP3/Cartoon Theme - Simpsons.mp3</URL>
      <FileSize>721682</FileSize>
     </MP3>
     <MP3>
      <FileName>Cartoon Theme - Super Chicken.mp3</FileName>
      <URL>http://xmlrad.com/MP3/Cartoon Theme - Super Chicken.mp3</URL>
      <FileSize>528759</FileSize>
     </MP3>
     <MP3>
      <FileName>Cartoon Theme - X-Men.mp3</FileName>
      <URL>http://xmlrad.com/MP3/Cartoon Theme - X-Men.mp3</URL>
      <FileSize>943461</FileSize>
     </MP3>
   </MP3Results>
   </FindMP3Response>
  </SOAP-ENV:Body>
</SOAP-ENV:Envelope>
```

You can see that the SOAP message is just a simple XML fragment and can easily be transformed by an XSLT stylesheet for publishing into the Oracle9*i*AS multichannel XML format. The following XSLT stylesheet can be used to transform the SOAP message:

```
<?xml version="1.0" ?>
  <xsl:stylesheet
   xmlns:xsl="http://www.w3.org/1999/XSL/Transform"
   version="1.0">
  <xsl:output method="xml" omit-xml-declaration="yes"/>
  <xsl:template match="/">
   <SimpleResult>
     <SimpleContainer>
     <SimpleImage halign="center" src="http://localhost/book/MobileG"
      addImageExtension="yes" available="jpg gif png bmp"
      alt="[MobileG]" />
     <SimpleBreak />
     <xsl:apply-templates select="//FindMP3Response" />
```

```
      </SimpleContainer>
    </SimpleResult>
  </xsl:template>
  <xsl:template match="FindMP3Response">
  <SimpleMenu>
  <SimpleTitle color="#ff0000" font="verdana,arial" size="3">
    Select a Song:</SimpleTitle>
   <xsl:for-each select="//MP3">
   <SimpleMenuItem>
     <xsl:attribute name="static_target">
      <xsl:value-of select="./URL" />
     </xsl:attribute>
     <xsl:attribute name="wrapmode">nowrap</xsl:attribute>
    <SimpleImage halign="left" src="http://localhost/book/rt_item"
     addImageExtension="yes" available="jpg gif png bmp" alt="" />
     <xsl:value-of select="./FileName" />
     (<xsl:value-of select="./FileSize" /> bytes)
   </SimpleMenuItem>
   </xsl:for-each>
  </SimpleMenu>
  </xsl:template>
</xsl:stylesheet>
```

Here's the resulting Oracle9*i*AS multichannel XML:

```
<SimpleResult>
  <SimpleContainer>
  <SimpleImage halign="center" src="http://localhost/book/MobileG"
   addImageExtension="yes" available="jpg gif png bmp"
   alt="[MobileG]" />
  <SimpleBreak />
  <SimpleMenu>
  <SimpleTitle color="#ff0000" font="verdana,arial" size="3">
  Select a Song:</SimpleTitle>
   <SimpleMenuItem
   static_target="http://xmlrad.com/MP3/Cartoon Theme - Simpsons.mp3"
   wrapmode="nowrap">
   <SimpleImage halign="left" src="http://localhost/book/rt_item"
     addImageExtension="yes" available="jpg gif png bmp" alt="" />
     Cartoon Theme - Simpsons.mp3 (721682 bytes)
   </SimpleMenuItem>
   <SimpleMenuItem
   static_target="http://xmlrad.com/MP3/Cartoon Theme - Super Chicken.mp3"
   wrapmode="nowrap">
   <SimpleImage halign="left" src="http://localhost/book/rt_item"
     addImageExtension="yes" available="jpg gif png bmp" alt="" />
```

```
      Cartoon Theme - Super Chicken.mp3 (528759 bytes)
    </SimpleMenuItem>
    <SimpleMenuItem
    static_target="http://xmlrad.com/MP3/Cartoon Theme - X-Men.mp3"
    wrapmode="nowrap">
    <SimpleImage halign="left" src="http://localhost/book/rt_item"
      addImageExtension="yes" available="jpg gif png bmp" alt="" />
      Cartoon Theme - X-Men.mp3 (943461 bytes)
    </SimpleMenuItem>
   </SimpleMenu>
   </SimpleContainer>
</SimpleResult>
```

The following illustration shows how the page is displayed on a WAP phone and a PocketPC. For those devices that have built-in MP3 players, you can simply tap or select the link and the music will start to play.

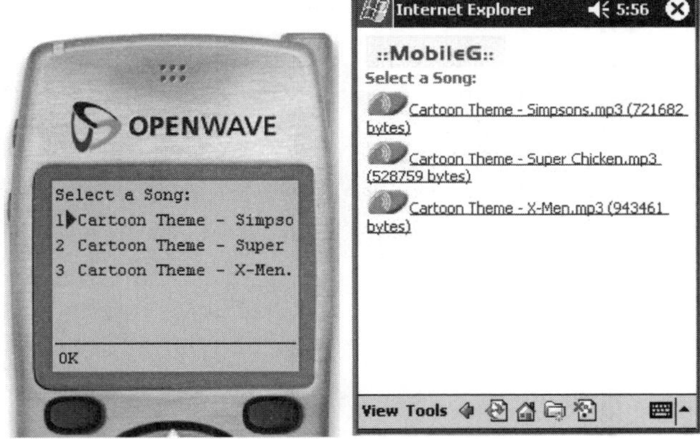

MobileG is also working on making the Web service "real time" by incorporating some of the code developed by the Feeds group to make the SOAP request and by accepting a dynamic search string.

One missing item that we did not touch on in the preceding example is the Web Services Description Language (WSDL). The WSDL is an XML format for describing the network services offered by the server. You use the WSDL to create a file that identifies the services provided by the server and the set of operations within each service that the server supports. For each of the operations, the WSDL file also describes the format that the client must follow in requesting an operation. Because the WSDL file sets up requirements for both the server and the client, this file is like a contract between the two. The server agrees to provide certain services only if the client sends a properly formatted SOAP request. The WSDL for the FindMP3 service is shown here:

```
<definitions name="WSFindMP3"
  targetNamespace="http://xmlrad.com/WSFindMP3Bin/WSFindMP3.dll/wsdl"
  xmlns:tns="http://xmlrad.com/WSFindMP3Bin/WSFindMP3.dll/wsdl"
  xmlns:soap="http://schemas.xmlsoap.org/wsdl/soap/"
  xmlns:xsd="http://www.w3.org/2000/10/XMLSchema"
  xmlns="http://schemas.xmlsoap.org/wsdl/">
<message name="FindMP3">
  <part name="SearchString" type="xsd:string"/>
  <part name="MaxReturn" type="xsd:string"/>
</message>
<message name="FindMP3Response"/>
<portType name="WSFindMP3PortType">
  <operation name="FindMP3">
   <input message="tns:FindMP3" name="FindMP3"/>
   <output message="tns:FindMP3Response" name="FindMP3Response"/>
  </operation>
</portType>
<binding name="WSFindMP3Binding" type="tns:WSFindMP3PortType">
  <soap:binding style="rpc"
    transport="http://schemas.xmlsoap.org/soap/http"/>
  <operation name="FindMP3"><soap:operation soapAction="FindMP3"/>
   <input>
     <soap:body use="encoded"
     namespace="http://xmlrad.com/WSFindMP3Bin/WSFindMP3.dll/wsdl"
     encodingStyle="http://schemas.xmlsoap.org/soap/encoding/"/>
   </input>
   <output>
     <soap:body use="encoded"
      namespace="http://xmlrad.com/WSFindMP3Bin/WSFindMP3.dll/wsdl"
      encodingStyle="http://schemas.xmlsoap.org/soap/encoding/"/>
   </output>
  </operation>
</binding>
<service name="WSFindMP3Service">
  <documentation>
   Provides access to all XMLServices defined in WSFindMP3
  </documentation>
  <port name="WSFindMP3Port" binding="tns:WSFindMP3Binding">
   <soap:address
location="http://xmlrad.com/WSFindMP3Bin/WSFindMP3.dll"/>
  </port>
</service>
</definitions>
```

From the WSDL file, we can determine what input parameters are required from this service and what output parameters are returned from the Web service. A list of *methods* available for this service is also described by the WSDL file.

Again, the members of the Feeds group are the folks making the SOAP requests and populating the databases with the SOAP responses. The members of the Content group are the ones making the database queries and generating the XML for the Oracle9*i*AS Wireless platform.

Results

MobileG is killing two birds with one stone. Its employees are learning about the latest mobile and wireless technologies, in addition to Web services. Because MobileG has used this as the sandbox and has its employees performing the field testing, it has developed the technology and infrastructure for aggregating content—not just any content, but content that the employees can actually use. By republishing the content using the Oracle9*i*AS Wireless platform, MobileG employees have struck gold by not having to create focus groups outside of the company—the employees are the focus when they use mobile devices such as PocketPCs and WAP-enabled phones to view the content. Oracle9*i*AS Wireless made it easy for MobileG to publish to any mobile devices supported by the software or extended by its XML and XSLT programmers. With all these real-life experiences, MobileG is ready to take on savvy clients who need wireless or mobile solutions.

Case 3: Sales Force Automation—Forecasting

This case illustrates how a simple sales force automation (SFA) application can be designed and developed using Oracle9*i*AS Wireless–Offline Management. You'll see how to create an offline Java native application that can be extended and customized as well as migrated to other packaged solutions in the long term.

Customer and Needs

King Kong Computer Company (KKCC) is a computer hardware and software reseller. It distributes and sells mobile hardware and software products, including web servers, data servers, tools, and other software products. KKCC has approximately 1,000 sales representatives, and its territories include the entire North American and Western European markets. KKCC is currently using a simple method of capturing and forecasting sales figures—via Microsoft Excel worksheets. Typically, field sales coordinators and sales reps will work with headquarters in San Francisco to input sales forecasts and account wins into an Excel worksheet that has been expressly prepared. Marketing and product management staff at headquarters then consolidates all worksheets into a master worksheet for management review and for financial planning. This methodology has been in place for over four years.

KKCC wants to improve the accuracy, timeliness, and accountability of sales reps, while keeping the cost down. Its vice president of sales and vice president of marketing have been pushing for adopting sales force automation (SFA) software. At present, KKCC wants to implement an in-house SFA software solution, because it feels that its requirements are unique and it wants time to evaluate and make the "build vs. buy" decision. KKCC is also interested in building and leveraging mobile technologies, and an offline SFA application is among its top priority for implementation. Hence, KKCC has decided to build an in-house offline application that can be extended and customized, and, at the same time, have the flexibility and compatibility to migrate to a packaged software solution such as Oracle11*i* E-Business Suite.

Situation and Use Case

Most KKCC sales reps periodically send in an updated sales worksheet to San Francisco. Headquarters runs a macro to consolidate all the data. Most sales reps are equipped with Windows CE or PocketPC devices, and they still have access through their laptops in the office or through dial-up into the corporate intranet. The major use case for the sales reps is to input data, and for the managers it's to consolidate and review the results.

Strategy

KKCC's strategy is to build upon a scalable and extensible platform as well as provide its sales staff a migration path to a full-fledged SFA implementation, starting with a simple sales-forecasting module that is easy to learn and use. In addition, KKCC wants to leverage its recent implementation of a Java/J2EE application server and an Oracle8*i* database.

Solution

KKCC chose a Java native application approach. KKCC recognizes that Oracle9*i* Lite for CE supports application development using Java tools. KKCC's developers will be able to use the Java Database Connectivity (JDBC) programming interface of Oracle9*i* Lite, which supports API for database access from within a Java program.

End-User Usage Scenarios

The two end-user groups for the KKCC mobile application are the sales representatives and the line managers. The sales reps and sales managers with direct accounts are the primary users as data acquirers and owners of this mobile application. Line managers, including sales managers, vice presidents, and KKCC's president, will generally retrieve, review, and analyze the collected data in a complete report format. Nonetheless, both user groups will need to enter, synchronize, and replicate data to perform their respective tasks.

In the first scenario, a sales rep enters data into the Java local native application and updates sales results and data. Naturally, sales reps can create new opportunities and revise confidence levels. Sales reps who have network access will log into the corporate intranet through dial-up, LAN, or other means, uploading their new or changed data. Any data that has been altered by headquarters, such as forecasted revenues, will be synchronized and downloaded. In the second scenario, line managers can sync the data and consolidate it into a master view. This allows for the creation of reports that give managers an indicator of the overall picture of their sales organization.

Creating the Mobile Sales-Forecasting Application

KKCC is building its mobile SFA solution with an Oracle database (version 8.1.6) and Oracle9*i* Lite. It follows two major steps—setting up the database and writing the Java code for the native application. We'll now look at how KKCC built the application in more detail.

Database Setup

To create the SFA application, KKCC must create the tables for the Java code (discussed later) to issue queries with and to access the results. In this example, you will need to execute the following SQL statements packages that KKCC used, in the following order, to form mSQL: Creatab, Constraint, and Insert. These statements will define the schema for the SFA application and populate the tables with some sample data for testing. The database tables are briefly described next.

Creating Database Tables, Users, and Connections

Using the information covered in the next few sections, you can actually re-create this mobile application and see how it works. You can use the following SQL statements package, Creatab, to create the database tables:

```
rem
rem Table: employees
rem Alias: emp
rem
prompt Creating database user.…
create user &owner. identified by &owner.;
Prompt Granting privileges....
grant dba, connect, resource to &owner.;
```

```
prompt Creating table EMPLOYEES....
create table &owner..employees
( id number(28) constraint pk_emp primary key not null
, username varchar2(100) not null
, full_name   varchar2(100) not null
, job varchar2(100) not null
, manager number(28)
);

rem
rem Table: regions
rem Alias: reg
rem

prompt Creating table REGIONS....
create table &owner..regions
( id number(28) constraint pk_reg primary key not null
, emp_id number(28) not null
, name varchar2(100) not null
);

rem
rem Table: territories
rem Alias: ter
rem

prompt Creating table TERRITORIES....
create table &owner..territories
( id number(28) constraint pk_ter primary key not null
, emp_id number(28) not null
, reg_id number(28) not null
, name varchar2(100) not null
);

rem
rem Table: accounts
rem Alias: acc
rem

prompt Creating table ACCOUNTS....
create table &owner..accounts
( id number(28) constraint pk_acc primary key not null
, ter_id number(28) not null
, name varchar2(50) not null
, contact    varchar2(100) not null
, phone_number varchar2(20) not null
, abbreviation varchar2(5)
, emp_id number(28)
);
```

```
rem
rem Table: status
rem Alias: sta
rem
prompt Creating table STATUS....
create table &owner..status
( id number(28) constraint pk_sta primary key not null
, name varchar2(40) not null
);
rem
rem Table: confidence
rem Alias: con
rem

prompt Creating table CONFIDENCE....
create table &owner..confidence
( id number(28) constraint pk_con primary key not null
, value number(5,2) not null
);

rem
rem Table: contracts
rem Alias: ctr

rem
prompt Creating table CONTRACTS....
create table &owner..contracts
( id number(28) constraint pk_ctr primary key not null
, name varchar2(40) not null
);

rem
rem Table: opportunities
rem Alias: opp
rem

prompt Creating table OPPORTUNITIES....
create table &owner..opportunities
( id number(28) constraint pk_opp primary key not null
, acc_id number(28) not null
, con_id number(28) not null
, sta_id number(28) not null
, ctr_id number(28) not null
, name varchar2(100) not null
, open_date date not null
, close_date date not null
, order_number varchar2(40)
```

```
, comments varchar2(2000)
, emp_id number(28) not null
);

rem
rem Table: products
rem Alias: prd
rem

prompt Creating table PRODUCTS....
create table &owner..products
( id number(28) constraint pk_prd primary key not null
, name varchar2(100) not null
);

rem
rem Table: platforms
rem Alias: pla
rem

prompt Creating table PLATFORMS....
create table &owner..platforms
( id number(28) constraint pk_pla primary key not null
, name varchar2(100) not null
);

rem
rem Table: opportunity_details
rem Alias: opd
rem

prompt Creating table OPPORTUNITY_DETAILS....
create table &owner..opportunity_details
( id number(28) constraint pk_opd primary key not null
, opp_id number(28) not null
, prd_id number(28) not null
, pla_id number(28) not null
, forecast number(28) not null
, commit_amount number(28)
, emp_id number(28) not null
);

rem
rem The sequence
rem

prompt Creating sequence SF_SEQ....
create sequence &owner..sf_seq
start with 3001 increment by 2;
```

Adding Constraints to Build the Table Relationships

The following SQL statements package, Constraint, is used to define constraints and relationships among the database tables:

```
rem
rem Add all the foreign keys
rem
rem TABLE: employees
prompt Adding constraints to table EMPLOYEES...
alter table &owner..employees
add constraint fk1_emp_emp foreign key(manager)
   references &owner..employees(id);

rem TABLE: regions
prompt Adding constraints to table REGIONS...
alter table &owner..regions
add constraint fk1_reg_emp foreign key(emp_id)
   references &owner..employees(id);

rem TABLE: territories
prompt Adding constraints to table TERRITORIES...
alter table &owner..territories
add constraint fk1_ter_emp foreign key(emp_id)
   references &owner..employees(id);
alter table &owner..territories
add constraint fk2_ter_reg foreign key(reg_id)
   references &owner..regions(id);

rem TABLE: accounts
prompt Adding constraints to table ACCOUNTS...
alter table &owner..accounts
add constraint fk1_acc_emp foreign key(emp_id)
   references &owner..employees(id);
alter table &owner..accounts
add constraint fk2_acc_ter foreign key(ter_id)
   references &owner..territories(id);

rem TABLE: opportunities
prompt Adding constraints to table OPPORTUNITIES...
alter table &owner..opportunities
add constraint fk1_opp_emp foreign key(emp_id)
   references &owner..employees(id);
alter table &owner..opportunities
add constraint fk2_opp_acc foreign key(acc_id)
   references &owner..accounts(id) on delete cascade;
alter table &owner..opportunities
add constraint fk3_opp_con foreign key(con_id)
   references &owner..confidence(id);
```

```
alter table &owner..opportunities
add constraint fk4_opp_sta foreign key(sta_id)
   references &owner..status(id);
alter table &owner..opportunities
add constraint fk5_opp_ctr foreign key(ctr_id)
   references &owner..contracts(id);

rem TABLE: opportunity_details
prompt Adding constraints to table OPPORTUNITY_DETAILS...
alter table &owner..opportunity_details
add constraint fk1_opd_opp foreign key(opp_id)
   references &owner..opportunities(id) on delete cascade;
alter table &owner..opportunity_details
add constraint fk2_opd_prd foreign key(prd_id)
   references &owner..products(id);
alter table &owner..opportunity_details
add constraint fk4_opd_pla foreign key(pla_id)
   references &owner..platforms(id);
alter table &owner..opportunity_details
add constraint fk5_opd_emp foreign key(emp_id)
   references &owner..employees(id);
```

Populating Tables with Sample Data

Now we will populate the database tables with sample data for testing. Obviously, you can modify any aspect of the data before or after successfully testing out your application. The items of each database table are briefly described in this section.

Each employee is profiled in a table called employees. This table contains the following items:

- **id** Unique number identifier of each employee (for example, 1000 - president)
- **username** User name of each employee (for example, REP1)
- **full_name** Description of employee's full name (for example, Joe Manager)
- **job** Job title of the employee (for example, MANAGER)
- **manager** ID of the manager whom this employee reports to (for example, 1100)

The regions table consists of these items:

- **id** Unique identifier for each region (for example, 1200)
- **emp_id** Identifier of the owner of this region (for example, 1110)
- **name** Name of the region (for example, Southern California)

The territories table consists of these items:

- **id** Unique identifier for each territory (for example, 1303)
- **emp_id** Identifier of the owner of this account (for example, 1121)
- **reg_id** Identifier of the region to which this territory belongs (for example, 1200)
- **name** Name of the territory—city, state, or district (for example, Los Angeles)

Accounts are contained in the accounts table. This table contains the following items:

- **id** Unique identifier for each account (for example, 1402)
- **ter_id** Identifier of the territory to which this account belongs (for example, 1301)
- **name** Account or company name (for example, EMC)
- **abbreviation** Abbreviation of the account or company (for example, CSCO, JPM, or SUNW)
- **contact** Name of the contact person at this account (for example, Smith, Andy McDough)
- **phone_number** Phone number of the contact person at this account (for example, 555-1234)
- **emp_id** Identifier of the owner of this account (account manager) (for example, 1113)

The products table contains the following items:

- **id** Unique identifier for each product (for example, 1701)
- **name** Name or description of the product (for example, Tools)

The platforms table contains the following items:

- **id** Unique identifier for each platform (for example, 1501)
- **name** Name or description of the platform (for example, Sun Solaris)

The contracts table defines the type of contracts proposed or the type of contract entered into for a specific sales opportunity (for example, Wireless Portal). It contains the following items:

- **id** Unique identifier for each contract type (for example, 1800)
- **name** Name or description of the contract (for example, None, Standard license, Non-standard, or Shrink wrap)

The confidence table describes the probability of success of the opportunity. It contains the following items:

- **id** Unique identifier for each confidence level (for example, 1850, 1851, ...1860)
- **value** Probability of success value (for example, 0.0, 0.1, ...1.0)

The status table contains the following items:

- **id** Unique identifier for each status level (for example, 1900)
- **name** Description of the status level (for example, Prospect Identified, Presentation Done, Requirements Defined, RFP/RFI, Capabilities Demonstration, Contracts Reviewed, P.O. Received, and so on)

The profile of the opportunity and its related details are stored in the opportunities and opportunity_details tables, respectively. The opportunities table consists of the following items:

- **id** Unique identifier for each opportunity (for example, 2004)
- **acc_id** Identifier of this account (for example, 1402)
- **con_id** Identifier of the confidence level of this opportunity (for example, 1854)
- **sta_id** Identifier of the status of this account (for example, 1905)
- **ctr_id** Identifier of the contract type (for example, 1803)
- **name** Name of this opportunity (for example, Wireless Portal)
- **open_date** Date at which this opportunity was opened (for example, 09-09-2002)
- **close_date** Date at which this opportunity was closed (for example, 05-02-2003)
- **order_number** Purchase order or internal tracking number of the order (for example, 4238478)
- **comments** Remarks, notes, or comments (for example, "budget just approved by CIO")
- **emp_id** Identifier of the owner of this opportunity (for example, 1112)

The opportunity_details table contains these items:

- **id** Unique identifier for each opportunity details entry (for example, 2104)
- **opp_id** Identifier of this opportunity (for example, 2002)
- **prd_id** Identifier of the product for this opportunity (for example, 1704)
- **pla_id** Identifier of the platform to which the product belongs (for example, 1501)
- **forecast** Amount in dollars, euros, or other currency the account manager has forecasted for this opportunity (for example, 100000)
- **commit_amount** Amount in dollars, euros, or other currency the customer has committed to (for example, 65000)
- **emp_id** Identifier of the account manager or owner of this opportunity (for example, 1112)

You can use the following SQL statements package, Insert, to populate the aforementioned tables in the database:

```
delete from &owner..opportunity_details;
delete from &owner..opportunities;
delete from &owner..accounts;
delete from &owner..territories;
delete from &owner..regions;
delete from &owner..employees;
delete from &owner..platforms;
delete from &owner..products;
delete from &owner..contracts;
delete from &owner..confidence;
delete from &owner..status;
commit;

rem
rem Populate the products table
rem

insert into &owner..products(id, name)
values (1700, "DataServer");
insert into &owner..products(id, name)
values (1701, "Tools");
insert into &owner..products(id, name)
values (1702, "Web Server");
insert into &owner..products(id, name)
values (1704, "Internet Lite");
insert into &owner..products(id, name)
values (1705, "Internet Lite Developer");
commit;

rem
rem Populate the contracts table
rem
insert into &owner..contracts (id, name)
values(1800, "None");
insert into &owner..contracts (id, name)
values(1801, "Standard license");
insert into &owner..contracts (id, name)
values(1802, "Non-standard");
insert into &owner..contracts (id, name)
values(1803, "Shrink wrap");
commit;
```

```
rem
rem Populate the confidence table
rem
insert into &owner..confidence (id, value)
values (1850, "0.0");
insert into &owner..confidence (id, value)
values (1851, "0.1");
insert into &owner..confidence (id, value)
values (1852, "0.2");
insert into &owner..confidence (id, value)
values (1853, "0.3");
insert into &owner..confidence (id, value)
values (1854, "0.4");
insert into &owner..confidence (id, value)
values (1855, "0.5");
insert into &owner..confidence (id, value)
values (1856, "0.6");
insert into &owner..confidence (id, value)
values (1857, "0.7");
insert into &owner..confidence (id, value)
values (1858, "0.8");
insert into &owner..confidence (id, value)
values (1859, "0.9");
insert into &owner..confidence (id, value)
values (1860, "1.0");
commit;

rem
rem Populate the status table
rem
insert into &owner..status(id, name)
values (1900, "Prospect Identified");
insert into &owner..status(id, name)
values (1901, "Presentation Done");
insert into &owner..status(id, name)
values (1902, "Requirements Defined");
insert into &owner..status(id, name)
values (1903, "Competition Identified");
insert into &owner..status(id, name)
values (1904, "RFP/RFI");
insert into &owner..status(id, name)
values (1905, "Capabilities Demonstration");
insert into &owner..status(id, name)
values (1906, "Favorable Decision");
insert into &owner..status(id, name)
values (1907, "Negotiation");
```

```
insert into &owner..status(id, name)
values (1908, "Contracts Reviewed");
insert into &owner..status(id, name)
values (1909, "P.O.Received");
insert into &owner..status(id, name)
values (1910, "Dead Deal");
commit;

rem
rem Populate the employees table
rem

insert into &owner..employees(id, username, full_name, job, manager)
values (1000, "KING", "King Kong", "PRESIDENT", null);
insert into &owner..employees(id, username, full_name, job, manager)
values (1100, "VP1", "Mr. VP 1", "VICE PRESIDENT", 1000);
insert into &owner..employees(id, username, full_name, job, manager)
values (1200, "VP2", "Mr. VP 2", "VICE PRESIDENT", 1000);
insert into &owner..employees(id, username, full_name, job, manager)
values (1110, "MANAGER", "Bob Manager", "MANAGER", 1100);
insert into &owner..employees(id, username, full_name, job, manager)
values (1120, "MAN12", "Joe Manager", "MANAGER", 1100);
insert into &owner..employees(id, username, full_name, job, manager)
values (1210, "MAN21", "John Manager", "MANAGER", 1200);
insert into &owner..employees(id, username, full_name, job, manager)
values (1220, "MAN22", "Robert Manager", "MANAGER", 1200);
insert into &owner..employees(id, username, full_name, job, manager)
values (1111, "REP1", "Mr. Brown", "SALES REP", 1110);
insert into &owner..employees(id, username, full_name, job, manager)
values (1112, "REP2", "Mr. Pink", "SALES REP", 1110);
insert into &owner..employees(id, username, full_name, job, manager)
values (1113, "REP3", "Mr. Gray", "SALES REP", 1110);
insert into &owner..employees(id, username, full_name, job, manager)
values (1121, "REP121", "Mr. Yellow", "SALES REP", 1120);
insert into &owner..employees(id, username, full_name, job, manager)
values (1122, "REP122", "Mr. Green", "SALES REP", 1120);
insert into &owner..employees(id, username, full_name, job, manager)
values (1211, "REP211", "Mr. White", "SALES REP", 1210);
insert into &owner..employees(id, username, full_name, job, manager)
values (1212, "REP212", "Mr. Black", "SALES REP", 1210);
insert into &owner..employees(id, username, full_name, job, manager)
values (1221, "REP221", "Mr. Blue", "SALES REP", 1220);
insert into &owner..employees(id, username, full_name, job, manager)
values (1222, "REP222", "Mr. Purple", "SALES REP", 1220);
commit;
```

```
rem
rem Populate the regions table
rem

insert into &owner..regions(id, emp_id, name)
values (1200, 1110, "Northern California");
insert into &owner..regions(id, emp_id, name)
values (1201, 1120, "Southern California");

commit;
rem
rem Populate the territories table
rem

insert into &owner..territories(id, emp_id, reg_id, name)
values (1301, 1111, 1200, "San Francisco");
insert into &owner..territories(id, emp_id, reg_id, name)
values (1302, 1112, 1200, "Sacramento");
insert into &owner..territories(id, emp_id, reg_id, name)
values (1304, 1113, 1200, "San Jose");
insert into &owner..territories(id, emp_id, reg_id, name)
values (1303, 1121, 1201, "Los Angeles");
commit;

rem
rem Populate the accounts table
rem

insert into &owner..accounts(id, ter_id, name, abbreviation, contact,
  phone_number, emp_id)
values (1401, 1301, "Ascend Comm", "ASND", "Michelle", "555-1234",
1111);
insert into &owner..accounts(id, ter_id, name, abbreviation, contact,
  phone_number, emp_id)
values (1402, 1301, "Pfizer Inc", "PFE", "Robert", "555-2312", 1111);
insert into &owner..accounts(id, ter_id, name, abbreviation, contact,
  phone_number, emp_id)
values (1403, 1302, "Cisco Systems", "CSCO", "Andy", "555-1222", 1111);
insert into &owner..accounts(id, ter_id, name, abbreviation, contact,
  phone_number, emp_id)
values (1404, 1301, "JP Morgan", "JPM", "Smith", "666-2946", 1111);
insert into &owner..accounts(id, ter_id, name, abbreviation, contact,
  phone_number, emp_id)
values (1405, 1301, "Broadcom", "BRCM", "Nicholas", "666-9900", 1111);
insert into &owner..accounts(id, ter_id, name, abbreviation, contact,
  phone_number, emp_id)
```

```
values (1406, 1301, "Qualcomm", "QCOM", "Rulian", "777-3434", 1111);
insert into &owner..accounts(id, ter_id, name, abbreviation, contact,
  phone_number, emp_id)
values (1407, 1301, "EMC Corp", "EMC", "Mike", "506-3333", 1111);
commit;

rem
rem Populate the platforms table
rem

insert into &owner..platforms (id, name)
values (1500, "N/A");
insert into &owner..platforms (id, name)
values (1501, "Sun Solaris");
insert into &owner..platforms (id, name)
values (1502, "IBM");
insert into &owner..platforms (id, name)
values (1503, "HP");
insert into &owner..platforms (id, name)
values (1504, "Dec Alpha");
insert into &owner..platforms (id, name)
values (1505, "Windows NT");
insert into &owner..platforms (id, name)
values (1506, "Windows 95");

commit;

rem
rem Populate the opportunities table
rem

insert into
&owner..opportunities(id,acc_id,con_id,sta_id,ctr_id,name,open_date,
  close_date,order_number,comments,emp_id)
values(2000, 1401, 1857, 1901, 1802, "CRM", sysdate-20, sysdate+30,
  "242398", null, 1111);
insert into &owner..opportunities(id,acc_id,con_id,sta_id,ctr_id,name,
  open_date,close_date,order_number,comments,emp_id)
values(2001, 1401, 1855, 1907, 1801,
"m-Commerce",sysdate-30,sysdate+15,
  "435348", null, 1111);
insert into &owner..opportunities(id,acc_id,con_id,sta_id,ctr_id,name,
  open_date,close_date,order_number,comments,emp_id)
values(2002, 1402, 1858, 1904, 1803, "Mobile Studio", sysdate-20,
  sysdate+28, "212397", null, 1111);
insert into &owner..opportunities(id,acc_id,con_id,sta_id,ctr_id,name,
  open_date,close_date,order_number,comments,emp_id)
```

```
values(2003, 1403, 1854, 1906, 1803, "Wireless Portal", sysdate-22,
  sysdate+4, "4238478", null, 1112);
insert into &owner..opportunities(id,acc_id,con_id,sta_id,ctr_id,name,
  open_date,close_date,order_number,comments,emp_id)
values(2004, 1404, 1857, 1901, 1802, "e-Commerce", sysdate-20,
  sysdate+30, "242397", null, 1111);
insert into &owner..opportunities(id,acc_id,con_id,sta_id,ctr_id,name,
  open_date,close_date,order_number,comments,emp_id)
values(2005, 1405, 1855, 1907, 1801, "External Web Site", sysdate-30,
  sysdate+15, "435349", null, 1111);
insert into &owner..opportunities(id,acc_id,con_id,sta_id,ctr_id,name,
  open_date,close_date,order_number,comments,emp_id)
values(2006, 1406, 1858, 1904, 1803, "Euro Conversion", sysdate-20,
  sysdate+28, "222397", null, 1111);
insert into &owner..opportunities(id,acc_id,con_id,sta_id,ctr_id,name,
  open_date,close_date,order_number,comments,emp_id)
values(2007, 1407, 1854, 1906, 1803, "System Upgrade", sysdate-22,
  sysdate+4, "4238478", null, 1112);

commit;
rem
rem Populate the opportunity_details table
rem

commit;

insert into &owner..opportunity_details(id, opp_id, prd_id, pla_id,
  forecast, commit_amount, emp_id)
values(2100, 2000, 1700, 1500,80000,60000,1111);
insert into &owner..opportunity_details(id, opp_id, prd_id, pla_id,
  forecast, commit_amount, emp_id)
values(2101, 2000, 1702, 1500,30000,10000,1111);
insert into &owner..opportunity_details(id, opp_id, prd_id, pla_id,
  forecast, commit_amount, emp_id)
values(2102, 2001, 1702, 1502,100000,65000,1111);
insert into &owner..opportunity_details(id, opp_id, prd_id, pla_id,
  forecast, commit_amount, emp_id)
values(2104, 2002, 1704, 1501,35000,25000,1111);
insert into &owner..opportunity_details(id, opp_id, prd_id, pla_id,
  forecast, commit_amount, emp_id)
values(2106, 2003, 1702, 1506,170000,100000,1112);
insert into &owner..opportunity_details(id, opp_id, prd_id, pla_id,
  forecast, commit_amount, emp_id)
values(2107, 2003, 1705, 1506,49000,30000,1112);
commit;
```

Writing Java Source Code

As described in Chapter 8, KKCC took the following requisite steps in creating the source code for its native Java application, sales.java:

- Modify the CLASSPATH to include olite40.jar during Oracle Lite installation and ensure a Sun JDK is in its environment.
- Load the JDBC driver into your application. Your application must first load the Oracle9*i* Lite JDBC driver.
- Connect to the Oracle Lite database via the Native Driver Connection URL syntax.

For this offline application, KKCC used Java AWT to build the user interface. The Java code for the KKCC Sales Force Automation–Forecasting application follows:

```
import oracle.lite.msync.*;
import java.awt.*;
import java.awt.event.*;
import java.awt.image.*;
import java.sql.*;
import java.lang.Integer;
import java.util.*;
import java.awt.List;
import java.io.*;
import java.lang.String;

public class sales extends Frame implements ItemListener,
    ActionListener {
   CheckboxGroup g;
   static Checkbox account, opport;
   Button quit, options, sync;
   String[] colName;
   int colNum, i;
   List list;
   Label lbl = new Label();

   static Font fixed = new Font("Courier", 0, 10);
   int[] padLen;
   int[] padLen1;
   public sales() {
      //super("Sales Forecasting Application");
      super(title);
      mw = this;
      setFont(fixed);
      setLayout(new GridBagLayout());
      GridBagConstraints gbc = new GridBagConstraints();
```

```
gbc.gridy = 0;
gbc.weightx = 100;
g = new CheckboxGroup();
account = new Checkbox("Accounts", g, true);
opport = new Checkbox("Opportunities", g, false);
quit = new Button("Quit");
options = new Button("Options");
sync = new Button("Sync");
sync.setVisible(false);
add(account, gbc);
add(opport, gbc);
gbc.gridy++;
gbc.anchor = gbc.WEST;
add(options, gbc);
add(sync, gbc);
add(quit, gbc);
gbc.gridy++;
gbc.weightx = 1;
gbc.gridwidth = 5;
gbc.fill = gbc.HORIZONTAL;
gbc.anchor = gbc.WEST;
add(lbl, gbc);
gbc.gridy++;
gbc.weighty = 1;
gbc.fill = gbc.BOTH;

account.addItemListener(this);
opport.addItemListener(this);
options.addActionListener(this);
sync.addActionListener(this);
quit.addActionListener(this);

list = new List(4, false);
list.addItemListener(this);
add(list, gbc);

Toolkit tk = Toolkit.getDefaultToolkit();
Dimension d = tk.getScreenSize();

w = d.width;
if (w < 250) {
   setSize(new Dimension(d.width, d.height/4*3));
} else {
   setSize(new Dimension(d.width/2, d.height/4*3));
}

Sync sc = new Sync(user, passwd, url, useProxy, proxy,
      proxyPort);
sc.getInfo();
```

```
    user = sc.getUserInfo();
    passwd = sc.getPasswdInfo();
    url = sc.getUrlInfo();
    proxy = sc.getProxyInfo();
     useProxy = sc.getUseProxyInfo();
    proxyPort = sc.getProxyPortInfo();

//
 // The DriverManager is the class responsible for loading database
 // driver and creating a new database connection. Loading the driver
 // manager code so that the program can use it.
 //
    try {
       Class.forName("oracle.pol.poljdbc.POLJDBCDriver");

    } catch (Throwable t) { }
    try {
       Class.forName("oracle.lite.poljdbc.POLJDBCDriver");
    } catch (Throwable t) { }
 //
 // Create a database connection with the given database source name.
 //
    try {
       conn = DriverManager.getConnection("jdbc:polite:sales",
          "system", "holi");
       stmt = conn.createStatement();
    } catch (SQLException ex) {
       System.out.println("SQLException: " + ex);
    } catch (java.lang.Exception ex) {
       System.out.println("Exception: " + ex);
    }

    tableName = "ACCOUNTS";
    printColName();
    printRow();
 }

 public static void close() {
 //
 // Before synchronizing with the server, the program needs to commit
 // and also close the current connection.
 //
    try {
       conn.commit();
       stmt.close();
       conn.close();
    } catch (SQLException ex) {
       System.out.println("SQLException: " + ex);
    }
 }
```

```
public static void setConn() {
//
// After synchronizing with the server, in order to bring back
// the application, the program needs to reinitialize the connection.
//
   try {
      conn = DriverManager.getConnection("jdbc:polite:sales",
        "system","holi");
      stmt = conn.createStatement();
   } catch (SQLException ex) {
      System.out.println("SQLException: " + ex);
   }
}

public void setTableName(String tabName) {
   tableName = tabName;
}

String pad(String s, int len) {
   StringBuffer sb = new StringBuffer(s);
   while (sb.length() < len) {
      sb.append(" ");
   }
   return sb.toString();
}

public void printColName() {
   try {
      if (tableName.equals("ACCOUNTS")) {
         rs = stmt.executeQuery("SELECT NAME,
            CONTACT, PHONE_NUMBER FROM " + tableName);
            padLen1 = new int[] {15, 10, 10};
            padLen = new int[] {15, 10, 10};
      } else if (tableName.equals("OPPORTUNITIES")) {
         rs = stmt.executeQuery(
         "SELECT NAME, OPEN_DATE, CLOSE_DATE,
            ORDER_NUMBER FROM " + tableName);
         if (w < 250) {
            padLen1 = new int[] {5, 10, 11, 0};
            padLen = new int[] {15, 12, 12, 0};
         } else {
            padLen1 = new int[] {15, 12, 12, 0};
            padLen = new int[] {15, 12, 12, 0};
         }
      }
      rsmd = rs.getMetaData();
      colNum = rsmd.getColumnCount();
      colName = new String[colNum];
      for (i = 1; i <= colNum; i++) {
```

```
            colName[i-1] = rsmd.getColumnName(i);
         }
      } catch (SQLException ex) {
         System.out.println("SQLException: " + ex);
      } catch (Exception e1) {
         System.out.println("Exception: " + e1);
      }

      StringBuffer sb = new StringBuffer();
      for (i = 0; i < colNum; i++) {
         sb.append(pad(colName[i], padLen1[i]));
      }
      lbl.setText(sb.toString());
      validate();
   }

   public void printRow() {
      list.removeAll();
      try {
         if (tableName.equals("ACCOUNTS")) {
            while (rs.next()) {
               StringBuffer sb = new StringBuffer();
               for (i = 0; i < colNum; i++) {
                  sb.append(pad(rs.getString(i+1),
                     padLen[i]));
               }
               list.add(sb.toString());
            }
         } else if (tableName.equals("OPPORTUNITIES")) {
            while (rs.next()) {
               StringBuffer sb = new StringBuffer();
               for (i = 0; i < colNum; i++) {
                  if (i == 0 || i == 3)
                     sb.append(pad(rs.getString(i+1),
                        padLen[i]));
                  else if (i == 1 || i == 2) {
                     String s = rs.getString(i+1);
                     sb.append(pad(s.substring(0,10),
                         padLen[i]));
                  }
               }
               list.add(sb.toString());
            }
         }
         validate();
      } catch (SQLException ex) {
         System.out.println("SQLException: " + ex);
      }
   }
```

```
public void itemStateChanged(ItemEvent evt) {
   if (evt.getItem().equals("Accounts")) {
      tableName = "ACCOUNTS";
      printColName();
      printRow();
   } else if (evt.getItem().equals("Opportunities")) {
      tableName = "OPPORTUNITIES";
      printColName();
      printRow();
   } else {
      if (tableName == "ACCOUNTS") {
         int index = list.getSelectedIndex();
         ad = new accountDialog(this, index);
         ad.show();
      } else if(tableName == "OPPORTUNITIES") {
         int index = list.getSelectedIndex();
         od = new opportDialog(this, index);
         od.show();
      }

   }
}
public void actionPerformed(ActionEvent evt) {
   String arg = evt.getActionCommand();
   if (arg.equals("Options")) {
      if (opd == null) // First time
         opd = new optionsDialog(mw);
      opd.show();
   } else if (arg.equals("Sync")) {

      if ((user == null) || (passwd == null) || (url == null) ||
       (user.equals("")) || (passwd.equals("")) ||
       (url.equals(""))) {
         if (ed == null) {
            ed = new errDialog(mw);
}
      if (user == null)
         user = " ";
      if (passwd == null)
         passwd = " ";
      if (url == null)
         url = " ";
         ed.show();
         return;
      }
      if (sd == null) { // First time
         sd = new syncDialog(mw);
      } else {
         syncDialog.lb.setText("Sync......");
```

```
            }
         //
         // Close the current connection before synching with server.
         //
            Sync sc = new Sync(user, passwd, url, useProxy, proxy,
              proxyPort);
            try {
               sc.doSync();
            } catch(SyncException e){
               syncDialog.lb.setText("Error!");
            }
            syncDialog.lb.setText("Success!");
            validate();
            sd.show();
         } else if (arg.equals("Quit")) {
            System.exit(0);
         }
      }

      public static String getTitle(String f, String key, Locale lc) {
         String s = null;
         try {
            ResourceBundle rb = ResourceBundle.getBundle(f, lc);
            s = rb.getString(key);
         }
         catch (MissingResourceException e) {
            s = null;
         }
         return s;
      }
      public static void main(String args[]) {
         String fn = "Title";
         String mornkey = "sfa";
         Locale ger = Locale.GERMAN;
         Locale eng = Locale.ENGLISH;
         title = getTitle(fn, mornkey, ger);
         sales f = new sales();
         f.show();
      }

      static Connection conn;
      static Statement stmt;
      static sales mw;
      ResultSet rs;
      ResultSetMetaData rsmd ;
      private String tableName;
      private accountDialog ad;
      private opportDialog od;
```

```
    private syncDialog sd;
    private optionsDialog opd;
    private errDialog ed;
    static String user, passwd, url, proxy;
    static short useProxy, proxyPort;
    static int w;
    static String title;
}
class accountDialog extends Dialog implements ActionListener {
    TextField tf1, tf2, tf3;
    String id;
    static String accId;
    public accountDialog(Frame parent, int index) {
        super(parent, "Account", true);
        Toolkit tk = Toolkit.getDefaultToolkit();
        Dimension d = tk.getScreenSize();
        setSize(new Dimension(d.width, d.height));
        Panel p = new Panel();
        Button save = new Button("Save");
        Button cancel = new Button("Cancel");
        p.add(save);
        p.add(cancel);
        add(p, "South");
        save.addActionListener(this);
        cancel.addActionListener(this);
        printField(index);
        pack();
    }

    public accountDialog(Frame parent) {
        super(parent, "Account", true);
        Toolkit tk = Toolkit.getDefaultToolkit();
        Dimension d = tk.getScreenSize();
        setSize(new Dimension(d.width, d.height));
        Panel p = new Panel();
        Button save = new Button("Save");
        Button cancel = new Button("Cancel");
        p.add(save);
        p.add(cancel);
        add(p, "South");
        save.addActionListener(this);
        cancel.addActionListener(this);
        printAccount();
        pack();
    }
    public void printField(int index) {
        try {
            rs = sales.stmt.executeQuery(
```

```
            "SELECT ID, NAME, CONTACT, PHONE_NUMBER FROM ACCOUNTS");
            rsmd = rs.getMetaData();
            colNum = rsmd.getColumnCount();
            colName = new String[colNum];
            for (i = 1; i <= colNum; i++) {
               colName[i-1] = rsmd.getColumnName(i);
            }
            for (i = 0; i <= index; i++) {
               rs.next();
            }
            id = rs.getString(1);
            tf1 = new TextField(rs.getString(2));
            tf2 = new TextField(rs.getString(3));
            tf3 = new TextField(rs.getString(4));
         } catch (SQLException ex) {
            System.out.println("SQLException: " + ex);
         }
         Panel p = new Panel();
         p.setLayout(new GridBagLayout());
         GridBagConstraints dbc = new GridBagConstraints();
         dbc.fill = dbc.HORIZONTAL;
         dbc.gridx = dbc.RELATIVE;
         dbc.gridy = 0;
         add(p, "Center");
         p.add(new Label(colName[1]), dbc);
         dbc.weightx = 1;
         p.add(tf1, dbc);
         dbc.weightx = 0;
         dbc.gridy++;
         p.add(new Label(colName[2]), dbc);
         p.add(tf2, dbc);
         dbc.gridy++;
         p.add(new Label(colName[3]), dbc);
         p.add(tf3, dbc);
         pack();
      }
      public void printAccount() {
         try {
            String sql;
            sql = "SELECT ID, NAME, CONTACT,
              PHONE_NUMBER FROM ACCOUNTS WHERE ID = ""+accId+""";
            rs = sales.stmt.executeQuery(sql);
            rsmd = rs.getMetaData();
            colNum = rsmd.getColumnCount();
            colName = new String[colNum];
            for (i = 1; i <= colNum; i++) {
               colName[i-1] = rsmd.getColumnName(i);
            }
```

```
      if (rs.next()) {
         id = rs.getString(1);
         tf1 = new TextField(rs.getString(2));
         tf2 = new TextField(rs.getString(3));
         tf3 = new TextField(rs.getString(4));
      }
   } catch (SQLException ex) {
      System.out.println("SQLException: " + ex);
   }
   Panel p = new Panel();
   p.setLayout(new GridBagLayout());
   GridBagConstraints dbc = new GridBagConstraints();
   add(p, "Center");
   dbc.fill = dbc.HORIZONTAL;
   dbc.gridx = dbc.RELATIVE;
   dbc.gridy = 0;
   p.add(new Label(colName[1]),dbc);
   p.add(tf1,dbc);
   dbc.gridy++;
   p.add(new Label(colName[2]),dbc);
   p.add(tf2,dbc);
   dbc.gridy++;
   p.add(new Label(colName[3]),dbc);
   p.add(tf3,dbc);
   pack();
}
public void actionPerformed(ActionEvent evt) {
   String arg = evt.getActionCommand();
   if (arg.equals("Save")) {
      String sql;
      sql = "UPDATE ACCOUNTS SET "+colName[1]+"=""+tf1.getText()+
         "", ";
      sql += colName[2]+"=""+tf2.getText()+"", ";
      sql += colName[3]+"=""+tf3.getText()+"" ";
      sql += "WHERE ID = ""+id+""";
      try {
         sales.stmt.executeUpdate(sql);
         sales.conn.commit();
         sales.account.setState(true);
         sales.mw.setTableName("ACCOUNTS");
         sales.mw.printColName();
         sales.mw.printRow();
         dispose();
      } catch (SQLException ex) {
         System.out.println("SQLException: " + ex);
      }
   } else if (arg.equals("Cancel")) {
      dispose();
```

```
        }
    }
    private ResultSet rs;
    ResultSetMetaData rsmd;
    int colNum, i;
    String[] colName;
}
class opportDialog extends Dialog implements ActionListener {
    TextField tf1, tf2, tf3, tf4;
    String id;
    String accId;

    public opportDialog(Frame parent, int index) {
        super(parent, "Opportunity", true);
        Toolkit tk = Toolkit.getDefaultToolkit();
        Dimension d = tk.getScreenSize();
        setSize(new Dimension(d.width, d.height));
        Panel p = new Panel();
        Button save = new Button("Save");
        Button cancel = new Button("Cancel");
        Button account = new Button("Account");
        p.add(save);
        p.add(cancel);
        p.add(account);
        add(p, "South");
        save.addActionListener(this);
        cancel.addActionListener(this);
        account.addActionListener(this);
        printField(index);
        pack();
    }
    public void printField(int index) {
        try {
            rs = sales.stmt.executeQuery(
                "SELECT ID, ACC_ID, NAME, OPEN_DATE, CLOSE_DATE,
                    ORDER_NUMBER FROM OPPORTUNITIES");
            rsmd = rs.getMetaData();
            colNum = rsmd.getColumnCount();
            colName = new String[colNum];
            for (i = 1; i <= colNum; i++) {
                colName[i-1] = rsmd.getColumnName(i);
            }
            for (i = 0; i <= index; i++) {
                rs.next();
            }
            id = rs.getString(1);
            accId = rs.getString(2);
            tf1 = new TextField(rs.getString(3));
            tf2 = new TextField(rs.getString(4));
```

```
      tf3 = new TextField(rs.getString(5));
      tf4 = new TextField(rs.getString(6));
   } catch (SQLException ex) {
      System.out.println("SQLException: " + ex);
   }

   Panel p = new Panel();
   p.setLayout(new GridBagLayout());
   GridBagConstraints dbc = new GridBagConstraints();
   add(p, "Center");
   dbc.fill = dbc.HORIZONTAL;
   dbc.gridx = dbc.RELATIVE;
   dbc.gridy = 0;
   p.add(new Label(colName[2]),dbc);
   p.add(tf1,dbc);
   dbc.gridy++;
   p.add(new Label(colName[3]),dbc);
   p.add(tf2,dbc);
   dbc.gridy++;
   p.add(new Label(colName[4]),dbc);
   p.add(tf3,dbc);
   dbc.gridy++;
   p.add(new Label(colName[5]),dbc);
   p.add(tf4,dbc);
   pack();
}

public void actionPerformed(ActionEvent evt) {
   String arg = evt.getActionCommand();
   if (arg.equals("Save")) {
      String sql;
      sql = "UPDATE OPPORTUNITIES SET "+colName[2]+
         "=""+tf1.getText()+"", ";
      sql += colName[3]+"=""+tf2.getText()+"", ";
      sql += colName[4]+"=""+tf3.getText()+"", ";
      sql += colName[5]+"=""+tf4.getText()+"" ";
      sql += "WHERE ID = ""+id+""";
      try {
         sales.stmt.executeUpdate(sql);
         sales.conn.commit();
         sales.opport.setState(true);
         sales.mw.setTableName("OPPORTUNITIES");
         sales.mw.printColName();
         sales.mw.printRow();
         dispose();
      } catch (SQLException ex) {
         System.out.println("SQLException: " + ex);
      }
```

```
      } else if (arg.equals("Cancel")) {
         dispose();
      } else if (arg.equals("Account")) {
         accountDialog.accId = accId;
         accountDialog ad = new accountDialog(sales.mw);
         ad.show();
      }
   }
   private ResultSet rs;
   ResultSetMetaData rsmd;
   int colNum, i;
   String[] colName;

}

class syncDialog extends Dialog implements ActionListener {
   syncDialog(Frame parent) {
      super(parent, "Sync", true);
      Toolkit tk = Toolkit.getDefaultToolkit();
      Dimension d = tk.getScreenSize();
      if (sales.w < 250)
         setSize(new Dimension(d.width/2, d.height/3));
      else
         setSize(new Dimension(d.width/4, d.height/3));
      Panel p = new Panel();
      Button ok = new Button("Ok");
      lb = new Label("Sync......");
    p.add(lb);

      add(lb, "Center");
      p.add(ok);
      add(p, "South");
      ok.addActionListener(this);
   }

   public void actionPerformed(ActionEvent evt) {
      String arg = evt.getActionCommand();
      if (arg.equals("Ok")) {
      //
      // Reinitializing the connection after synchronizing
      // with server.
         reConnect();
         setVisible(false);
      }
   }

   public void reConnect() {
      sales.setConn();
   }
```

```
   TextField tf1, tf2, tf3;
   static Label lb;
   Connection conn;
   Statement stmt;
   ResultSet rs;
   sales mw;
}

class optionsDialog extends Dialog implements ActionListener,
ItemListener {
   optionsDialog(Frame parent) {
      super(parent, "Options", true);
      Toolkit tk = Toolkit.getDefaultToolkit();
      Dimension d = tk.getScreenSize();
      setSize(new Dimension(d.width, d.height));
      Panel p1 = new Panel();
      Button ok = new Button("Ok");
      Button cancel = new Button("Cancel");
      p1.add(ok);
      p1.add(cancel);
      add(p1, "South");
      ok.addActionListener(this);
      cancel.addActionListener(this);
      Panel p2 = new Panel();
      p2.setLayout(new GridBagLayout());
      GridBagConstraints dbc = new GridBagConstraints();
      dbc.fill = dbc.HORIZONTAL;
      dbc.gridx = dbc.RELATIVE;
      dbc.gridy = 0;
      add(p2, "Center");

      Label name = new Label("User Name");
      p2.add(name,dbc);
      dbc.weightx = 1;
      tf1 = new TextField(20);
      tf1.setText(sales.user);
      p2.add(tf1,dbc);
      dbc.weightx = 0;
      dbc.gridy++;
      Label passwd = new Label("Password");
      p2.add(passwd,dbc);
      tf2 = new TextField(20);
      tf2.setText(sales.passwd);
      p2.add(tf2,dbc);
      dbc.gridy++;
      Label ip = new Label("URL");
      p2.add(ip,dbc);
      tf3 = new TextField(20);
```

```
      tf3.setText(sales.url);
      p2.add(tf3,dbc);
      dbc.gridy++;
      c = new Checkbox("Use Proxy");
      c.addItemListener(this);
      dbc.gridwidth = 2;
      p2.add(c, dbc);

      if (sales.useProxy == 1)
         c.setState(true);
      else
         c.setState(false);
      dbc.gridy++;
      dbc.gridwidth = 1;
      Label proxy = new Label("Proxy");
      p2.add(proxy, dbc);
      tf4 = new TextField(20);
      tf4.setText(sales.proxy);
      p2.add(tf4, dbc);
      dbc.gridy++;
      Label port = new Label("Port");
      p2.add(port, dbc);
      tf5 = new TextField(4);
      tf5.setText(Short.toString(sales.proxyPort));
      p2.add(tf5, dbc);

      pack();

   }

   public void actionPerformed(ActionEvent evt) {
      String arg = evt.getActionCommand();
      if (arg.equals("Ok")) {
         String s1 = tf1.getText();
         String s2 = tf2.getText();
         String s3 = tf3.getText();
         short s4, s6;
         String s5;
         if (c.getState()) {
            s4 = 1;
            s5 = tf4.getText();
            s6 = Short.parseShort(tf5.getText());
         } else {
            s4 = 0;
            s5 = "\0";
            s6 = 0;
         }
```

```
            sales.user = s1;
            sales.passwd = s2;
            sales.url = s3;
            sales.useProxy = s4;
            sales.proxy = s5;
            sales.proxyPort = s6;
            sc = new Sync(s1, s2, s3, s4, s5, s6);
            try {
               sales.close();
               sc.saveInfo();
               sales.setConn();
            } catch(SyncException e){
            }
            setVisible(false);
         } else if(arg.equals("Cancel"))
            setVisible(false);
      }

      public void itemStateChanged(ItemEvent evt) {
      }

      TextField tf1, tf2, tf3, tf4, tf5;
      Checkbox c;
      Sync sc;
   }
   class errDialog extends Dialog implements ActionListener {
      errDialog(Frame parent) {
         super(parent, "Error", true);
         Toolkit tk = Toolkit.getDefaultToolkit();
         Dimension d = tk.getScreenSize();
         setSize(new Dimension(d.width/4, d.height/3));
         Panel p = new Panel();
         Button ok = new Button("Ok");
         Label lb = new Label("Please enter user info!");
         add(lb, "Center");
         p.add(ok);
         add(p, "South");
         ok.addActionListener(this);
      }

      public void actionPerformed(ActionEvent evt) {
         String arg = evt.getActionCommand();
         if (arg.equals("Ok")) {
            setVisible(false);
         }
      }
   }
```

Here are a couple of usage pointers when building and using this Java program:

- **Commit a transaction**. Use the commit method to commit a transaction:

```
conn.commit();
```

When you no longer need the database connection, the application can disconnect using the following code:

```
conn.close();
```

- **Compile and run the example**. To compile the example, type

```
javac sales.java
```

As a guide, follow the publication procedures outlined earlier in Chapters 8 and 9 to define this application to your mobile server and publish the *sales.class* file. Also, be certain that you perform the following tasks:

- Prior to publishing the application, make sure you have correctly created all the base tables and the schema on the Oracle back-end database server.
- Using the Packaging Wizard, you need to package the application (sales.class) and the related meta data into a JAR file and publish the JAR into the Mobile Server Repository.

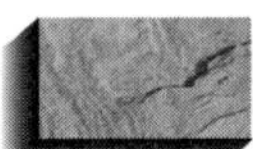

NOTE
It is very important that the client database name in the Packaging Wizard's Database panel be set to the DSN named in the getConnection() statement.

- From the client device, you must provision the Oracle Lite runtime environment by invoking the Mobile Server bootstrap for the correct version of the runtime environment for your particular CE device, as detailed in Chapters 8 and 9.
- Remember to define a user using the Mobile Server Control Center and associate the user with the sales application.
- Install the JVM on the CE device. This involves installing a third-party Java runtime environment—either Jeode from Insignia Solutions or Sun's Personal Java. The Java Virtual Machine is processor specific, so if your CE

device uses a SH3 or StrongARM processor, you must install the SH3 version of the JVM. The Java runtime environment can be installed using the Microsoft ActiveSync utility.

- After the JVM environment is installed and the setup bootstrap operation has installed the Oracle9*i* Lite client runtime environment, invoke the mSync utility to use synchronization to provision the sales application environment and client databases on the client from the client device. Launch the Mobile Sync application on the client, specifying the Mobile Server user ID you created, the password, and the URL pointer to the mobile server, and then click Sync.
- You should also include a statement to create an icon to start the program on your PocketPC device. The following statement invokes the Jeode JVM, in this case pointing to the Java archive for Oracle9*i* Lite, and invokes the Java class, *sales*:

```
\Windows\evm.exe -cp "/oracle/olitejdbc40.jar;." sales
```

Running sales.java on a PocketPC

Browse for the sales-forecasting application (named SFA) using the File Explorer on the PocketPC and invoke the application. The sales-forecasting application will launch the Java Virtual Machine and the application user interface (see the illustration).

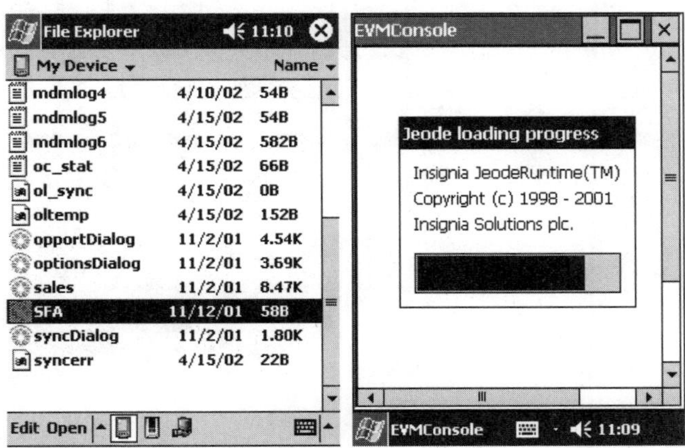

When the application is deployed from your device, you should be able to do the following:

- Browse the Accounts and Opportunities views.

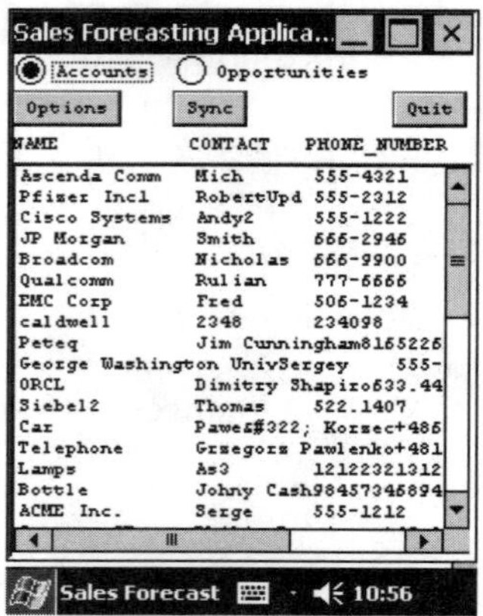

- Tap on any account to modify the name, contact, or phone number information.

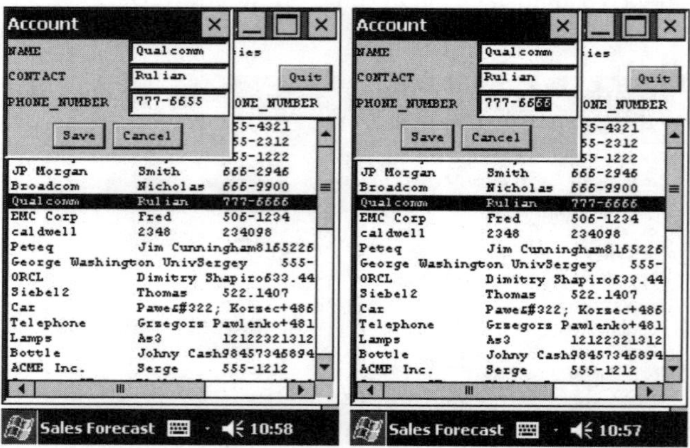

- Change to Opportunities view and then tap on any opportunity to change the name, open date, close date, order number, and other information.

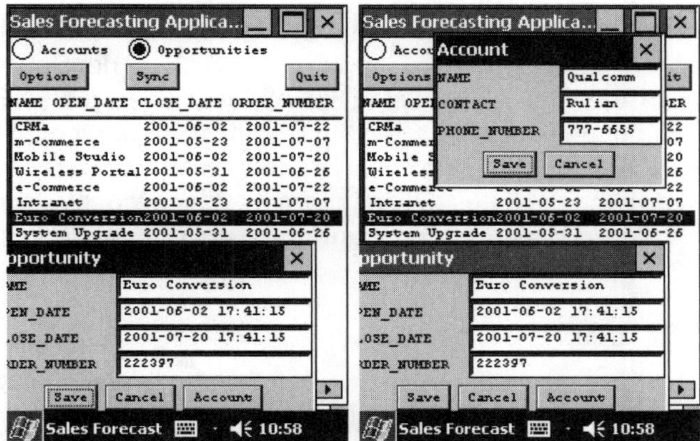

- Tap on the Account button from the Opportunities view to browse/modify the associated account information.
- Change the synchronization preferences (user name, password, server URL, proxy) by tapping the Options button from main screen.

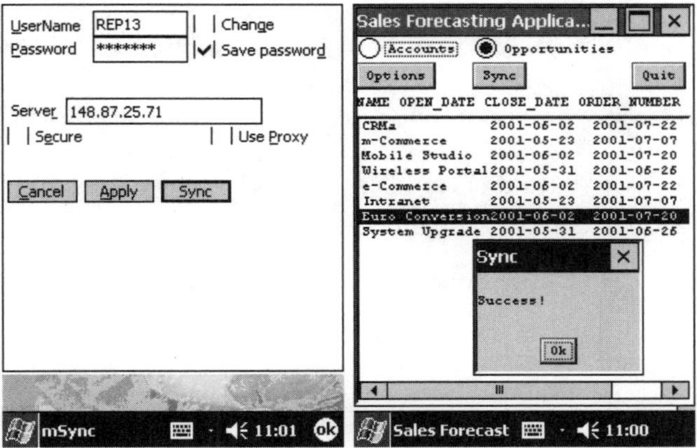

Results

Using Oracle9*i* Lite, KKCC was able to quickly and easily build the mobile SFA application to support its sales-forecasting process. It achieved several objectives:

upgrade its forecasting capability, evaluate mobile platforms and SFA options, and, of course, build skills and experience in mobile application development. Because the user interface is very intuitive and the SFA application itself takes less time to use, sales reps and line managers have embraced this SFA approach. Now, all sales reps can spend more time with customers and less time inputting data and planning. Line managers have the most up-to-date information by accounts, sales reps, and sales regions. Management can act more quickly to respond to sales wins and losses.

Summary

The applications discussed in this chapter are distinctly different. For ACME, data collection and input must be in near real time, and simplicity of use is crucial. Starting with WAP, ACME met these requirements. By migrating from a single- channel WAP to the Oracle9*i*AS Wireless platform, ACME has improved user experience and greatly increased the functionality of its application—more devices, better UI, better display of results, and Location-Based Services such as maps and directions. For MobileG, its focus has been to aggregate feeds, especially via XML, parse the data, and deliver relevant information to mobile workers. By implementing this application, MobileG brings instant benefits to its employees— enabling them to be more skilled with SOAP, XML, and mobile, while keeping up with the latest news in mobile technologies. More importantly, MobileG now has a live XML/mobile application running internally that can be extended to serve clients elsewhere. KKCC, on the other hand, was able to quickly build a mobile SFA application to support its sales-forecasting process. The SFA application is very intuitive and takes less time to use, so sales reps can spend more time with customers and less time on maintenance and data inputs.

CHAPTER 16

Mobile Applications: A Survey

e have covered a lot of grounds in providing an end-to-end view of Oracle's mobile technology. In this process, we have discussed the challenges of building mobile solutions, reviewed Oracle's offerings, and detailed how to build mobile services on the Oracle9*i*AS Wireless platform. In Chapters 14 and 15, we examine the issues related to the design and implementation of mobile solutions. We assess possible solutions, in terms of design criteria and case studies, and build pilot solutions, giving you the opportunity to test and evaluate them before you invest in an enterprise-wide deployment. Here, we review some of the popular and successful implementations of mobile applications that have been or can be built with Oracle9*i*AS Wireless. By identifying the use cases and the technology these solutions employ, we hope you can gain insight into how you can use the various features and capabilities of Oracle9*i*AS Wireless to build your own solutions.

We focus on the key characteristics of these mobile solutions and the technology and platforms on which they are deployed. We put an emphasis on defining the specific solution that is rooted in real business needs and prioritized for high-payback deployment. We will also cover the benefits they bring to the users. Specifically, we cover the following topics:

- Wireless Portals
- Mobile Office and E-Mail
- Field Force Automation
- Sales Force Automation
- Mobile Banking and Brokerage
- Warehouse and Inventory Management
- Wireless Dispatch and Package Delivery
- Other Applications

This list of applications is by no means comprehensive, and new applications are being developed and implemented everyday. These applications, however, all share several common attributes—the need for timely and accurate information, as well as the element of mobility.

Invariably, these cases may entail provisioning wireless services to phone users, or extending applications to mobile workers, as well as bringing automation to mobile devices for ERP and Supply Chain Management. They involve giving access to such enterprise applications as CRM and Financials on smart phones. These enterprise applications can bring value to your company by making your employees and partners more efficient and improving your business processes.

Wireless Portals

Portals are an important wireless solution, especially among mobile phone operators who want to offer compelling data services to their existing cellular voice customers. Wireless data services, such as SMS, help phone subscribers communicate better. This in turn can increase customer loyalty, reduce customer churn, and increase average revenue per user (ARPU) for the mobile operators. Typically, mobile operators aggregate content from multiple sources, both public and private, and tie it together in one or multiple WAP services. Through personalization capabilities and location-based services, mobile operators can give users a positive wireless Internet experience.

Carriers and service providers enhance their offerings through the creation of targeted public-facing portals with customized content based on subscribers' geography, specific user community interests, or other criteria that enhance a user's experience. This type of branded portals drives ARPU, increases m-business revenue and creates subscriber loyalty or stickiness.

Content providers, who offer weather, news, and traffic information, are increasingly offering wireless services as an adjunct to their websites, in addition to provisioning these services to mobile operators. These wireless websites can be accessed directly by wireless subscribers. Many of them also provide e-mail, SMS, and even voice alerts to their subscriber bases. Increasingly, they are building tighter relationships with their customers by instantly providing personalized information that mobile users need.

Their services can reach customers both domestically and abroad and provide access to services at any time. With business travelers carrying mobile devices on their trips, wireless applications offering travel and leisure services can be particularly useful for these road warriors, not just when they're at home, but also when they are in transit, or at their final destinations.

Another important use case of wireless portals is in the area of business intelligence, a valuable resource for employees and managers, as well as business partners such as sales reps and resellers, to tap into.

Platform and Solutions

Creating a customer-facing mobile application today is extremely complex due to the variety of protocols and standards. For a wireless portal application to be successful, all customers (users) must have access to the information. Consequently, it must be developed from a multichannel perspective, and not from the viewpoint of any single mobile device, due to the broad spectrum of protocols and devices these users may use.

Based on wireless application server platforms, including push and SMS capabilities, wireless portals are regarded as the pure play of mobile applications as they are usually built from the ground up by the mobile operators solely for their subscribers. For mobile operators, scalability must be carrier-grade in support of multiple millions of customers.

Many mobile websites and applications have evolved from HTML websites. Figure 16-1 shows the simplified evolution of wireless and mobile services, from wireline to wireless. While the change is not monolithic, mobile solutions are evolving from one-way, informational-only sites to bi-directional applications that are not only interactive but also transactional. Initially, many applications simply added a new channel, such as WAP or SMS, which usually has a simple, cleanly tailored user interface. Now many of these solutions are multichannel in nature, where you access the information and services with many devices, gateways, networks, and protocols. Taking it one step further, you can switch modes from voice to data, and back to voice, when these applications become multi-modal, all within the same user session.

As mobile development matures, most services will be integrated with other data, content, and applications, equipped with location-sensitive or -aware capability, and of course, personalized to the user and tailored to meet that user's business or communication needs.

There is tremendous interest in private portals for enterprises and their employees, customers, and trading partners. Enterprise users are able to build private role-based portals that provide individual users a unique set of content based on their roles within

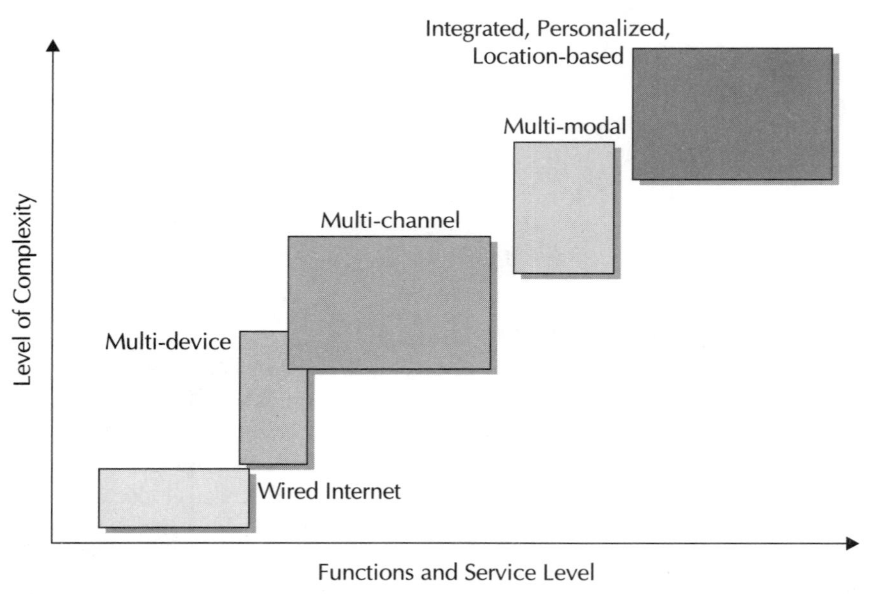

FIGURE 16-1. *Evolution and increasing complexity of mobile applications*

the enterprise. The content provided includes a base set of company information such as corporate e-mail, an employee's HR information, and corporate self-service applications.

In addition to the base corporate content, these portals contain content specific to users based on their job function that becomes available when the user authenticates. Managers receive content for managers, whereas service or field workers receive specific content and applications for their job functions, all as a result of customization and personalization. All users may be allowed access to public content such as weather, traffic, and driving directions on the same portal. The same enterprise portal might give specific customers access to value-added services and enable suppliers to authenticate to receive sets of content unique to their roles for the enterprise.

Wireless portal implementations can take on very interesting forms, especially within a vertical industry. Consider this example of a reusable resource network.

Many of the materials generated from work on construction and demolition sites can be reused or readily recycled and kept out of landfills. A commercial portal for reusable resources has been created to assist with this process. The main materials that make up the construction and demolition (C&D) waste stream include fill, concrete, bricks, asphalt, wall paneling, metal, glass, and packaging (cardboard, plastic, and wood).

At present, approximately 30 percent of demolition waste is recovered for reuse or recycling. A major component of demolition waste, concrete, and asphalt rubble, is readily reused in road construction as road base. Many internal fittings as well as roof and structural materials are also resold and reused following demolition, as this has proved more profitable than disposal to landfill for many C&D industry members.

The reusable resource portal offers an important service, enabling the Construction and Demolition sector to make connections with recyclers and other users who will collect or deliver the specific types and quantities of materials generated or needed. It includes an online trading site, where businesses and individuals can list the reusable goods and materials they no longer need, or they can place a request for those reusable items.

The reusable resource portal wirelessly enabled its online trading site using Oracle9*i*AS Wireless.

Using wireless access to the reusable portal, workers in the Construction and Demolition industry can use their Web-enabled phones directly from work sites to reuse materials and reduce landfill waste.

Customers register their profiles on the reusable resource portal, personalizing presets that indicate interest in their profile. This profile may say, "Interested in old bricks." If someone says, "I am dumping some bricks," the network matches both parties. The portal generates alerts to construction contractors via mobile phones on the availability of materials that would otherwise be dumped into landfill.

The total implementation took less than two months, and this translated to a reduction in total cycle time for the project. That in turn meant cost savings and much faster time to market; hence higher return on investment. (Refer to: http://www.arrnetwork.com.au/pls/workplace/sb_sab.main)

Benefits

Obviously, for wireless operators, a wireless portal is an essential offering of wireless data services, which augment the voice services. The direct effect is to provide additional capability. For the operators, the wireless portals are a crucial part of the data service that can help increase ARPU.

For the enterprises, wireless portals can empower their mobile workforces and enable their enterprise infrastructure to handle wireless data securely and efficiently. Role-based personalization provides specific users access to enterprise content that reflects a domain of information unique to a user's job function.

Mobile Office and E-Mail

When it comes to mobile strategy, "helping mobile workers stay connected" seems to be the most common objective in many enterprise IT plans. Businesses want to enable their employees to access information wherever they are—using the Web, wireless, push, or voice—so that they perform their duties and make decisions instantly without being tied to a desk or a desktop computer.

An enterprise may adopt mobile technologies in order to do one or more of these things (see Figure 16-2):

- **Improve Services** To support customers in a competitive marketplace with timely information and services
- **Enhance Productivity** To utilize software automation in support of a very mobile workforce
- **Generate Revenue** To gain the ability to reach and serve customers, bringing more sales and profits
- **Reduce Cost** To streamline methods and processes of conducting business, making it more cost effective to serve customers or produce goods and services

Among the first enterprise mobile applications many enterprises adopt is "mobile office and e-mail." In many ways, this choice is logical, as business communications are the most important means of extending the reach of office functionality to mobile

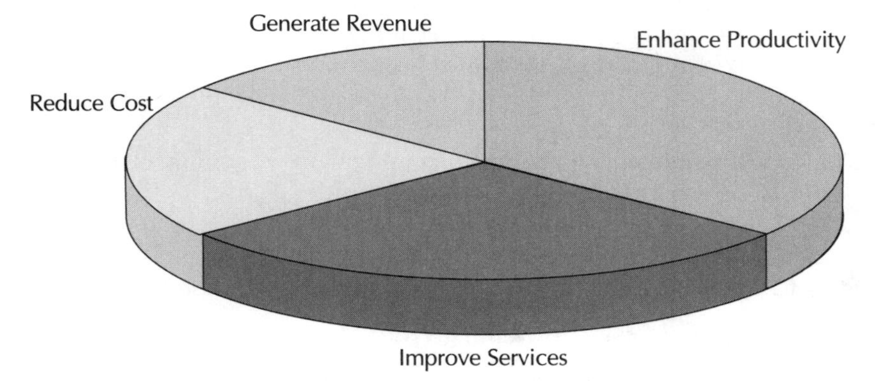

FIGURE 16-2. *Typical drivers for implementing mobile solutions*

employees. The mobile office starts with marking enterprise e-mail remotely available to the organization's employees. A corporate directory, customer information, PIM, quote approval, and documentation sharing and management are just a few examples of the business resources and processes mobile office and e-mail can engender. Inherent in these solutions are the needs to filter e-mail and make selections as to what should be displayed on the mobile devices. In addition to real-time messaging, PDA users without wireless connectivity need to have a synchronization process that periodically connects with the network to retrieve and respond to e-mail.

The questions that arise for users include "what to filter and what to block?" Or "Can the mobile office platform deliver and handle attachments? Can you view these attachments?"

Platforms and Solutions

The mobile office and e-mail are parts of a greater set of wireless services. Other services may entail push and SMS, as well as additional wireless and offline functionality. In Chapter 11, we discuss how Oracle9*i*AS Wireless supports both Microsoft Exchange and Lotus Domino for mobile office functionality, and how it includes real-time access to e-mail, calendars, contact data, and attachments, while also including the ability to securely authenticate the device and user prior to giving wireless access to an e-mail account. Nowadays, an important trend is to adopt unified messaging services, including providing voice, SMS/push, wireless, and e-mail all in "one box."

Going forward, EMS and MMS will become as much a consumer application as a corporate communication platform. Witness how e-mail is being used by your CEO, as well as your grandma, for everyday communication. Some of the common features include:

- Receiving immediate notification of e-mail messages and events that are new, critical, or preset
- Reading, responding to, forwarding, creating, and deleting e-mail messages
- Managing basic and advanced PIM functions, such as address books and tasks
- Viewing, editing and forwarding Word, PowerPoint, Excel, Acrobat, and other documents with or without attachments
- Strongly authenticating both the user and the device for secure wireless e-mail access using wireless PKI certificate technology

Of these features, handling attachments and security pose critical challenges. At present, attachments are typically stripped and presented in a format suitable for the device. A user can retrieve documents at a summary level or by section. This way, users can drill down into essential information and avoid the struggle of viewing large documents in a small screen.

In terms of security, enterprises are using strong authentication to ensure the integrity of their information and infrastructure. In addition, businesses are increasingly requiring digital certificates as an extra layer of security.

Benefits

As mentioned earlier, most enterprises start harnessing mobile technologies by deploying wireless e-mail. The reason: the return on investment (ROI) can be very fast, four to six months being typical. Without using any specialized networks, mobile office solutions can enable anyplace, anytime, anywhere access to e-mail and thereby improve corporate communications.

After mobile enabling corporate e-mail, enterprises may expand to other applications that are often proprietary or legacy in nature. Enterprises get hooked on wireless e-mail and then look beyond the mobile office and PIM for what other mobile applications can bring them benefits.

This way, they can reap the business benefits and further develop and deploy an integrated, end-to-end mobility solution in less time across the enterprise—and with less risk.

According to Cahners In-Stat Group, wireless e-mail by 2005 could lead to productivity gains of up to $12,900 per employee per year. Longueuil also claims that wireless e-mail can boost productivity up to $9,300 per employee per year. According to Research Portal, only 2.3 percent of the 43 million Americans who telecommute currently access their e-mail through a handset or wireless-enabled handheld. From *Investor's Business Daily:* "It would be a reasonable expectation, based on experience, that mobile e-mail and PIM save 5–6 hours per mobile employee per week."

Field Force Automation

Field force automation (FFA), part of CRM, is another enterprise mobile application that is used heavily within the confines of a corporation and now is being expressly designed to reach the mobile workforce.

Field force automation has been used for a number of years, built on and provisioned by specialized networks and carriers. There are many flavors of these applications, with varying functions, but the mode of interaction is via synchronization, rather than network or wireless connection. As in the case of the mobile office and e-mail, the reason for widespread acceptance of mobile field force applications is that the return on investment can be calculated and achieved easily.

Field force automation should give field service personnel application access via a simple, small device with intuitive software that is very easy to use. FFA solutions appear in specific implementations for utilities, copier, telecommunications, HVAC, and office-supply industries, among others. Field service users can get instantaneous access to the information required to successfully complete their tasks at a customer's site.

Platforms and Solutions

Usually run on offline applications, mobile FFA enables users to do the following:

- Enter real-time data, including field symptoms and parts failure data, via fill-in forms. This is subsequently entered in near real-time into corporate field service and design systems.
- Easily assess customer contact, contract, and historical information during a service call including location, billing, contact, service history, etc.
- Gain an up-to-the-minute view of service status. Wirelessly dispatch field engineers who can accept the assignment or be reassigned according to availability, location, and skill set.
- Look up spare parts availability and parts usage in real time.

- Communicate by e-mail with expert groups and the corporation as a whole.
- Access data directly from back-end information systems. Blend voice and data in the format best suited for the mobile field personnel.

Benefits

Increasing the competitiveness of the enterprise—improving services and responsiveness—is frequently cited as the driver for implementing mobile field force solutions. The ability to access critical back-end systems can raise the bar for customer support in a particular industry and take field services to the next level. These solutions enable the entire field service organization to better allocate resources, share or disseminate knowledge, and foster a better relationship with customers.

As a result, mobile FFA frequently provides an extremely quick payback period, measured by additional calls serviced per day or a decrease in time spent idle between customer visits. If the field service rep is equipped with wireless and messaging services, the enterprise can dynamically reroute a field person's schedule as emergencies arise. This tends to simplify, streamline, and eliminate routine tasks and optimize productivity.

Customers using FFA often see a 15 percent average reduction in total cost per service call, resulting in operational cost savings and increased customer satisfaction. These benefits are difficult to measure, but nonetheless, FFA contributes to reductions in costs and increases in revenues. For additional information, see *Mobile E-Business—Cut Costs and Drive New Revenue*, an Oracle White Paper, December 2001.

Sales Force Automation

Mobile enterprise solutions enable companies to differentiate the way that they serve and support their customers. *Sales force automation (SFA),* also part of CRM, is a key area where providing real-time information to large mobile workforces can directly and sometimes dramatically improve their ability to do their jobs.

Recently, SFA has emerged as a key component of an integrated corporate sales strategy. SFA software typically provides contact, opportunity, and marketing information. A structured approach to sales management can lead to increased productivity. Because the return on investment can be phenomenal, as shown in many successful implementations, adding mobile access to real-time data, including inventory levels, customer records, billing records, price levels, and other key data, can afford your company the ability to speed internal information flow and reduce cycle times.

Platforms and Solutions

The payoffs associated with an SFA system investment include the ability to impose best practices, automate segments of the sales process, assist the sales organization with pipeline management, improve sales force targeting, and improve order and billing mechanisms. Over the last few years, SFA has matured such that adoption is now accelerating worldwide. A typical SFA package may include the following types of functionality:

- Account management
- Forecasting and pipeline management
- Sales process management
- Product information, including collaterals, pricing, and competitive positioning
- Sales configuration systems to assemble and price product bundles
- Service request history

Benefits

These SFA tools have helped sales forces become more productive. Mundane tasks have been automated, while tools for more complex processes, such as bundling and pricing, have simplified the salesperson's workload. Managers can receive quote requests and proposals, and approve them in a timely manner. This results in better response and service to the customer as well as additional time for the sales force to be out selling.

Another immediate benefit is the ability for sales reps to check the pricing of products in real time, in addition to inventory levels, while on the road or face-to-face with the customer.

Mobile solutions enable the sales force to maintain closer contact with the customer and make the sales force more familiar with historical account information. As a result, sales reps become better prepared to educate customers and answer questions about the products they sell, and can respond to competitive questions more effectively. With instant access to the back-end and the ability to receive management approvals quickly, they commit to delivery and close the deal on site. In a nutshell, by creating a mobile solution, the total sales process can be improved, resulting in the following benefits:

- Higher customer loyalty
- Enhanced product knowledge
- Improved response time
- Better product delivery capability

- Reduced inventory costs
- Quicker sales cycles
- A more productive sales force

According to Oracle, mobile SFA can result in a 15-20% sales revenue uplift. (See *Mobile E-Business—Cut Costs and Drive New Revenue*, an Oracle White Paper, December 2001.)

Mobile Banking and Brokerage

Wireless technology is beginning to transform the financial sector, including the Banking and Brokerage industries. Customers, having become accustomed to the convenience of ATMs, voice-based telephony systems, and branch offices within grocery stores, are seeking Internet and mobile access to financial data anytime and anyplace.

Mobile devices represent an additional means for financial institutions to retain current customers and attract new ones. By offering compelling wireless services, banks and brokerage firms can increase their revenues and reduce costs.

Platforms and Solutions

Wireless Internet banking may be one of the latest "cool" applications of technology, but financial institutions are not launching Internet banking services just because they like wireless technology. Banks want to give their customers another choice for banking by offering wireless banking services and the choice of another channel for them to do banking business.

There are financial institutions that have offered data services to bank customers for over two years, and these services allow customers to bank not only via traditional channels, such as regular retail branches and telephone, but by using "wired" and wireless Internet devices. In mobile banking, users can typically view balances, search transaction histories, transfer funds, inquire about foreign exchange and unit trust rates, and make payments via mobile devices. You, of course, will need a secure, robust, and scalable solution to deliver these personalized financial services.

As for brokerage applications, users want to access stock prices, news, and research information. They may opt for price or market alerts through pagers, mobile phones, or PDAs. Users can place trades, get quotes, and access their account information. Specifically, these applications may enable users to

- View real-time news and alerts on watch lists
- Trade stocks and options

- Place extended-hours orders
- View charts and research
- Review open orders and trading history

Real-time quotes for equities and market indices are now readily available on most wireless devices. You can access your accounts and set up one or more e-mail addresses, SMS addresses, and phones to receive alerts messages in HTML e-mail, SMS, or voice. Upon successful placement of an order, you will receive a time-stamped notification delivered to your chosen preset channels. If you do not wish to receive confirmations via alerts, you can of course use your wireless device to check your order status.

Secure transactions and privacy are big issues. Problems related to the longer transmission delays in wireless communication must be addressed. Also, if you travel out of the wireless coverage area for an extended period, your session will expire. Of course, you will be able to begin another session and use the service again when you return to a coverage area.

Obviously, all trades placed through wireless devices must be secure. Security technologies vary by device. Security between the wireless Web phones and the carrier's WAP server can be implemented by over-the-air encryption and authentication, as is done, in the case of Palm VII, between the Palm VII devices and the Palm.Net proxy server. For mobile devices such as Windows CE or web phones running on CDPD / Mobitex, security is done through CDPD encryption, where information and account data are encrypted in digital transmission bursts (packets) securely and efficiently. Data transmission is indecipherable to anyone but the intended recipient. In addition, the CDPD network, which the Minstrel III utilizes, is secured with advanced RSA Public Key Encryption technology. Secure Socket Layer (SSL) is also used for securing the RIM devices on GoAmerica's Go.Web wireless Internet service, between the Go.Web server and the wireless applications.

Benefits

Mobile services, banks and brokerage firms believe, can reduce customer calls and visits, thereby lowering their customer service costs while improving services. Their customers welcome the new freedom to be able to view their balances and conduct transactions from virtually any wireless device and pay bills instantly. It's truly a unique way to expand and enhance customer relationships.

With mobile technology, banks and brokerage firms can offer new services that are not feasible otherwise. For example, alerts on new financial products can be delivered to the personalized devices of their customers, not just to desktop PCs.

Indeed, alerts can even take the form of third-party research reports, and customers can make a buy or sell order directly after viewing the research page. Real-time access to information, via wireless websites and alerts, can let financial institutions' customers respond faster to changes and better manage their finances. That in turn will generate trades, fees, and profits for these institutions.

Since most wireless services are offered at no additional charges, banks and brokerage firms do, however, expect a well-defined, achievable path for gaining a return on their investment, initially through cost savings from a lower demand on their phone centers, and eventually through new revenues as information on financial products and services is disseminated to those who want and need it at the right time, at the right place.

Financial institutions have managed to get wireless applications up and running in record time. In some cases, the time from project approval to pilot launch was only two months, and many banks were able to hit the market earlier than competitors. A custom wireless solution also allows users to be independent of "telcos" who tend to lock subscribers into a single or limited financial service.

Warehouse and Inventory Management

For many enterprises, especially those in the manufacturing sector, there is a strong need for wireless warehouse management systems (WMS) and inventory systems, mainly to provide data collection and inventory management capabilities on the warehouse floor. Using wireless technology, they want access into their existing local area network, obtaining links to data such as location history, asset status, and reporting.

Platforms and Solutions

A typical warehouse solution may involve a wireless local area network (WLAN) and an offline WMS application (see Figure 16-3). More often, warehouse management system and mobile supply chain applications are accessible via any devices, such as through Telnet on a wireless LAN from industrial, radio frequency devices. This solution is an asset management scenario in a typical warehouse. On the network, you can expect devices including a stationary tag reader and a barcode printer as well. You can also find wireless tags, which can be read by fixed-position readers as the inventory is moved through the warehouse floor. Equipped with mapping software, you can locate inventory within one to two meters in both indoor and outdoor environments.

Mobile devices such as laptop PCs, vehicle-mounted computers, and portable label printers can access the wireless infrastructure via a series of radio frequency (RF)–based access points or cells in a wireless LAN or 802.11b environment. The wireless segment is linked to the local area network (LAN) through a controller and a gateway. Through the firewall, the data can be transmitted remotely to other infrastructure and the wide area network (WAN) of the enterprise.

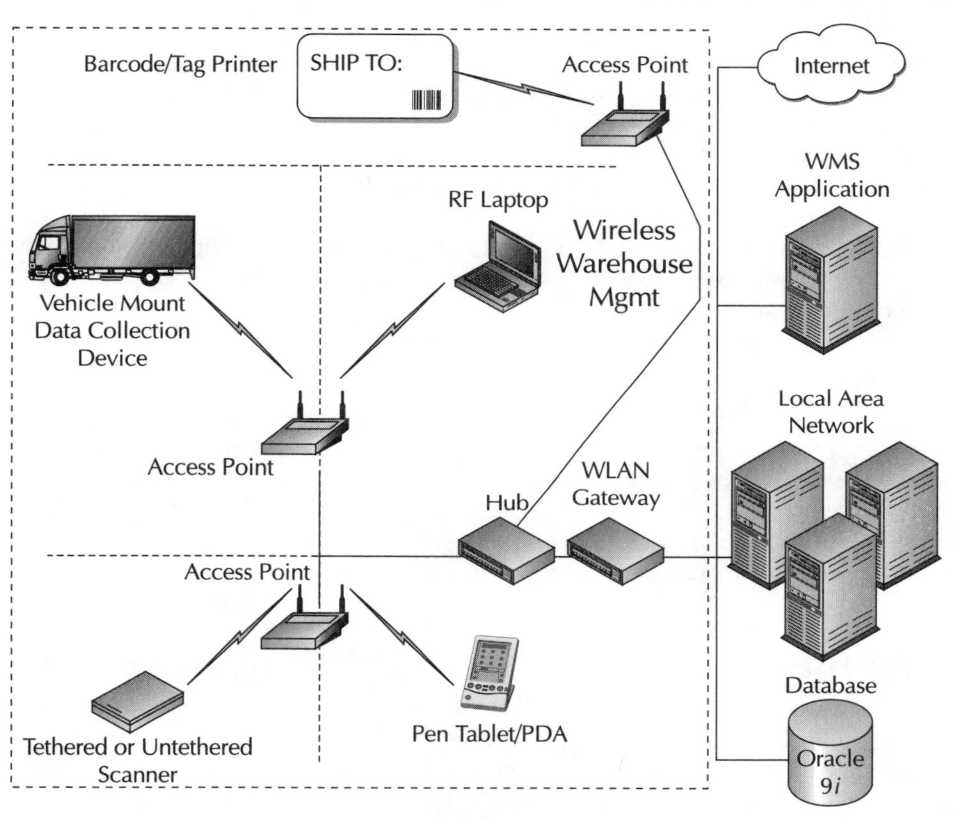

FIGURE 16-3. *Wireless warehouse management system*

The application model used by an application depends strongly on its data needs and the environment in which it operates. A common approach is to build a hybrid solution, with a rich or smart client, and leverage the strengths of offline and/or always-on applications. Because the enterprise has control over its choices of client devices and because most of the data required by the client is relatively static, an offline application is ideal for WMS solutions.

By using 802.11b networks, you can leverage existing wired networks and provide convenient access to network resources for workers carrying portable computers and handheld devices within the warehouse. WiFi or 802.11b networks can be implemented in "infrastructure" mode, where each wireless client "associates" itself with an access point via a radio link. The client device connects to the wireless LAN at 10/100 megabits per second (Mbps), via the access point provisioned by a standard Ethernet cable.

In designing an effective WMS solution, care must be given to well-planned access point placements and RF channel design. Often, a thorough site survey is conducted before access points are installed, and thorough testing of signal strength is needed after installation. This is especially true for the wireless local area networks, where environmental obstacles can impede radio frequency (RF) signal transmissions. Successful deployment of an 802.11b network also requires consideration of such factors as coverage requirements, device types and capabilities, number of users, and equipment selection.

Benefits

With wireless LAN and mobile WMS applications, you can support your warehouse floor, for instance, with a wireless pick and pack inventory management solution. This wireless WMS system can be part of a solution that provides total resource visibility to the enterprise, offering information on a real-time basis. As a result, the wireless WMS solution can be deployed to help lower operating costs; increase returns on assets; and track work orders in process, inventory, and assets.

Wireless Dispatch and Package Delivery

With a wide range of demands for mobile solutions in the transportation, automotive, and distribution marketplaces, there is an expanding suite of wireless, Internet-enabled, or offline solutions that provide enterprises with the power and flexibility to meet their mobile management needs, including pick-up and delivery automation, fleet and driver management, asset and freight tracking, and telematics solutions for the automotive and trucking industries.

There are many use cases; United Parcel Service (UPS) customers, for example, can find out the status of their packages from their office desktop PCs, without having to call a UPS call center. This is because UPS (and FedEx too) wirelessly tracks these packages, from drop-off locations to their final destinations, with barcode, scanning, and wireless/Internet communication, and the company delivers that information to its websites, now including wireless sites.

Platforms and Solutions

Wireless dispatch and package delivery services allow customers to access shipment information and support tracking and communications for delivery personnel when they are mobile. This is an area that drives competitive advantages for many package delivery firms and couriers. Features such as signature capture, routing, and package tracking are driving the use of synchronization and replication technology within the offline environment.

Many of these dispatch and tracking solutions have been custom built and proprietary. Nowadays, with platforms like Oracle9*i*AS Wireless, you can build a robust solution at a much lower cost, even combining land-based and satellite technology in the network mix. This combination of mobile messaging services with a powerful online/offline solution may also require the use of push/SMS and wireless technology.

Benefits

To sum up, the fundamental drivers of benefits are speed and quality. Like other enterprises, a courier service company such as UPS would justify its wireless projects by citing improved services, costs savings, and the potential for additional revenues. Major benefits in adopting mobile package delivery capabilities include customer acquisition, customer retention, and productivity improvements. As for transportation dispatch, drivers using the latest handheld devices can capture critical information and make it immediately available over the Internet. This can improve productivity, shorten billing cycles, eliminate Proof of Delivery write-offs, and improve customer service.

Other Applications

Besides the applications we covered earlier, wireless auction, marketing/promotion, and other vertical applications are rapidly gaining traction. Wireless devices can be used to track and respond to auctions. Marketing and promotion campaigns can be driven through SMS. And if you are involved in health care, you are probably aware that Health Insurance Portability and Accountability Act (HIPAA) regulations dictate many of the security standards that health care systems must adhere to. Mobile devices and automation software have enabled health care workers, such as physicians, to optimize billings, save costs, and most importantly, abide by the law.

Specifically, wireless applications can help health care workers deal with charge capture and reimbursement. For Medicare, Medicaid, and managed health care organizations to be reimbursed for services, health care workers need to use an alphanumeric system for translating medical diagnoses into codes that insurance companies accept. There are literally thousands of procedure codes and over 10,000 diagnostic codes. And there are rules that govern the provision of care and procedures. If these rules are not abided by, health care workers may not get reimbursed. As a result, many of the tedious and frustrating tasks are being automated and brought to the health care workers via wireless networks and devices. The benefits are measurable, and return is immediate.

E-government is another area where Internet communication is increasingly harnessed in a very public way. E-government is about using a home computer to view through real-time traffic cameras, find polling locations, or request removal of an abandoned vehicle. M-government takes that power to the streets, allowing you to use your mobile phones and other wireless or Internet-enabled devices to do all that and more. Either way, it's a mechanism to improve delivery of government services.

For the municipality of New York, those mobile government interactions can range from locating your towed vehicle to viewing a calendar of events or checking out restaurant sanitation records. Already, pilot programs are successfully underway for these wireless applications. Want to know, for example, if that corner café is as "sanitation challenged" as it looks? Spare yourself the bout of botulism with the power you've got in your palm. Use your handheld device to check out the inspection records at the NYC.gov website, which is powered by the Oracle Database and Oracle9*i*AS Wireless.

When the restaurant inspection application was first released, it received 38,000 hits per hour, and this application is just one of the many online services proving so popular with the populace. With over 80 city agencies, authorities, and other entities contributing to the site, NYC.gov offers more than 140 types of online transactions, along with more than 50,000 pages of content. Eventually, citizens will have wireless access to a whole suite of online offerings.

The city began to see the enormous potential of wireless technology after the terrorist attacks of September 11, when traffic to the city's wireless website soared to 1.67 million page views in one day—on September 14—and to 7.2 million page views the following week. In the future, city authorities hope to offer wireless access to crucial information about emergency evacuation routes and shelter locations.

Summary

We've looked at various applications that leverage different services and modes (wireless, offline, voice, and push) of communications. By going through them, you can gain insights into their use cases and application needs. You can obviously leverage Oracle9*i*AS Wireless to build and deploy many of these vertical and horizontal mobile applications.

CHAPTER 17

Looking Ahead

obile devices, applications, and technologies are at an inflection point. Progress is being made on all fronts that can positively impact other areas of advancement. In this chapter, we look ahead at some of the interesting developments in wireless networks, devices, protocols, technologies, and services. Undoubtedly, these advances will become an integral part of many mobile application development efforts.

While it is always risky to predict what Oracle may do in the future, we will indicate where Oracle has announced product releases and support. For now, we focus on the following topics:

- Developments in Wireless Networks and Devices
- Java 2, Micro Edition (J2ME)
- Extensible Hypertext Markup Language (XHTML)
- Multimedia Messaging Service (MMS)
- Voice and VoiceXML

Developments in Wireless Networks and Devices

In Chapter 1, we point out that this is an exciting time for mobile application developers as wireless networks and infrastructure are being deployed around the globe, and truly usable mobile devices are finally hitting the market. In this chapter, let's look at what has happened recently.

GPRS and 3G Networks

In the Americas, Europe, Japan, and the rest of Asia, 2.5G and 3G networks are being deployed and built on top of the success of 2G networks. Not only are extensive field trials run to ensure success, mobile operators in Norway, Hungary, Japan, the U.K., and the U.S., just to name a few countries, are set to roll out 2.5G and 3G wireless data services. In 2002, for instance, Telenor Mobil of Norway was successful in launching its Multimedia Messaging Service (MMS) within a high-speed 3G network, not too far behind the 3G rollout in Japan.

MMS enables mobile phone users to send text, graphics, photographs, audio sound, and animations from mobile phones to other mobile devices and desktop PCs. While pricing will continue to change, the economics of sending MMS messages will be quite feasible, perhaps around one U.S. dollar per message or less, if sent from a mobile phone. Receiving an MMS message will remain free, we presume. Naturally, content providers are being courted by mobile operators and market forces to build services for 2.5G and 3G.

What that means is that new 2.5G and 3G capabilities such as MMS are finally becoming reality. Following that come new protocols and technologies, such as XHTML, and new devices, including mobile phones with built-in digital cameras. We will take a look at some of these devices in the following section!

Mobile Devices and Browsers

Launched in mid-2002, the Nokia 7650 imaging "smart phone" (see the illustration on the right hand side of this page) is equipped with a color display, built-in camera, and MMS capability. While many of these phones use new mobile browsers, from Nokia or Openwave, for example, many phones from Nokia and Sony Ericsson adopt the Symbian OS, which has become a major force in shaping the future direction of operating systems in handheld devices.

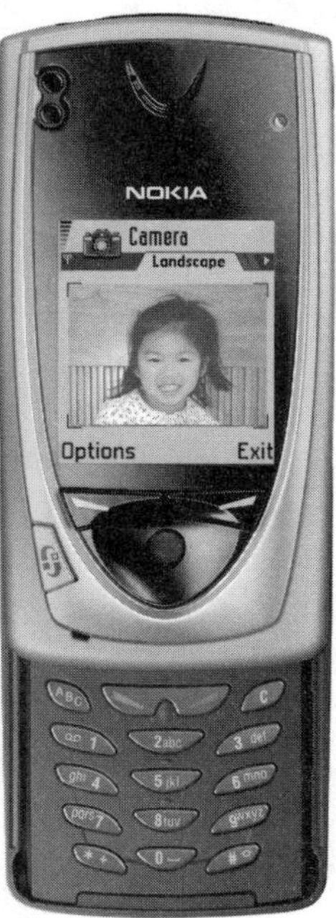

For some time, the Nokia 9210i Communicator (see the illustration below) has set the standard in terms of functionality in your pocket, having support for phone, mobile e-mail and PIM, web browsing, and word processing and spreadsheets, as well as fax. The big news has always been its bigger, full-color display and enhanced usability features.

The Nokia 9210i Communicator has bigger memory, and its browser supports JavaScript and has built-in Flash and RealOne Players. As a result, you can build rich mobile applications with your back-end server, and support it with efficient client-side technologies. Besides downloads, you can expect applications and services that come with animations, audio, and even video. Just download and play. Nokia is using the Symbian EPOC operating system in the 9210 and has partnered with Oracle to use the Oracle9*i* Lite database for native applications and persistent storage.

As for J2ME phones, the J-Phone has been quite successful in Japan, and Motorola J2ME phones have been in use with the iDEN at Nextel in the U.S. for some time. Sprint's plan has been to deploy J2ME on its PCS phones over its PCS 3G 1X network nationwide. Research-in-Motion (RIM) has come out with J2ME handheld devices, and device manufacturing heavyweights, including Nokia and Sony Ericsson, are expected to ship J2ME phones in mass quantity. For instance, both the Nokia 7210 and the Sony Ericsson Z700 (see the following illustrations) offer a color display, Bluetooth, polyphonic ringtones, dual-band GSM/GPRS, and J2ME support. NTT DoCoMo, renowned for its i-mode services, is expected to offer J2ME devices as well.

Currently, you can download and select pictures for background images, for instance, onto a Sony Ericsson T-68 phone. Motorola, Nokia, and Sony Ericsson are coming out with phones equipped with J2ME technologies, that can facilitate downloading of games and applications by any phone users. The Sony Ericsson Z700 phone is being pitched as a gaming phone and will come preloaded with games like "Men in Black" and "Charlie's Angels" when launched to the market in Q3 2002.

In terms of instant messaging, the mobile community is expecting to see services that allow mobile and desktop PC users to exchange instant messages with buddies. Openwave has been offering solutions with a uniquely friendly user interface that is conversational in nature. The "always on" experience, which does not require mobile users to log in to the wireless Web, promises to revolutionize usage in the consumer market, as well as the enterprise wireless market. As the industry device and browser vendors continue to address interoperability, starting with SMS and now instant messaging, the days grow near when SMS and instant messaging will become truly global communications platforms, like e-mail. Indeed, interoperability testing is critical as a seamless user experience, independent of the network or handset used, is a prerequisite. Mobile operators recognize that MMS services across various networks must be compatible for their customers to create a live chat with anyone, anywhere using any device.

In addition to J2ME phones, XHTML phones began shipping in quantity during 2002 and are expected to take off in 2003. Naturally, the focus is on Openwave's Mobile Browser Universal Edition (see the illustration), which provides flexible architecture to support many existing and emerging networks and technologies. Besides GPRS and 3G, Mobile Browser Universal Edition supports a range of markup languages including WML, XHTML, and cHTML.

Wireless LAN: Operator and Enterprise

To augment 2.5G and 3G, the mobile industry is witnessing heady growth in the deployment of wireless LANs (802.11b). Many believe public wireless LANs will complement 3G networks in selected dense public zones, allowing the operator to provide a completely new type of service for business users—even today.

While 802.11b is exceedingly popular, 802.11a is also coming along, but it is still priced beyond the reach of most consumers. Perhaps more interesting is the push by both enterprises and mobile operators alike to build wireless LANs for nomadic users. The operator and enterprise wireless LAN solutions can bring mobile broadband access to laptops, PDAs, and phones in such places as airports, convention centers, hotels, cafés, and other public areas.

To ensure a secure connection, most wireless LANs support the Subscriber Identity Module (SIM) services and provide user-friendly, yet secure authentication and link-up to the mobile Internet. Wireless LANs are proven technologies and can support a wide range of data services with one single SIM card through a number of access zones or points. With access speeds of up to 11 Mbps, nomadic mobile professionals armed with PDAs and laptops won't miss a beat while they are on the go.

This brings out the inevitable challenges and opportunities to link up these islands of wireless LANs and enable an always-available environment. This is an area where "smart sync" and local persistent storage may offer some advantages over the always-on environment, an area where Oracle9*i* Lite and Oracle9*i*AS Wireless may shine.

J2ME

While Java was created to allow "write once, run everywhere" regardless of devices and operating systems, Sun Microsystems soon realized that the sizable footprint of J2EE and J2SE cannot be adequately fit into small handheld devices, which are constrained in computing power, memory, and of course, battery life.

As a result, Sun has built a smaller version, called Java 2, Micro Edition (J2ME) from the ground up with its own Java Virtual Machine (JVM) and APIs. J2ME is designed as an application development platform for devices with limited memory space (such as pagers and mobile phones). Because it sits on top of the operating system, J2ME allows applications to be hardware or operating system agnostic. Thus, developers will not have to build out different applications for different handheld or limited-capability devices; manufacturers simply need to enable their operating systems to handle J2ME.

There are two common configurations for J2ME: Connected Device Configuration (CDC) for portable, full-featured Java 2 virtual machines designed for consumer electronic and embedded devices, and the Connected Limited Device Configuration (CLDC) for small, resource-constrained devices (see the illustration). Each configuration offers its own virtual machine and class libraries to support Java applications that run on devices with a 16-bit or 32-bit processor and total memories ranging from hundreds of kilobytes to 2MB. CDC runs on top of Sun's C Virtual Machine (CVM), and CLDC runs on top of its K Virtual Machine (KVM).

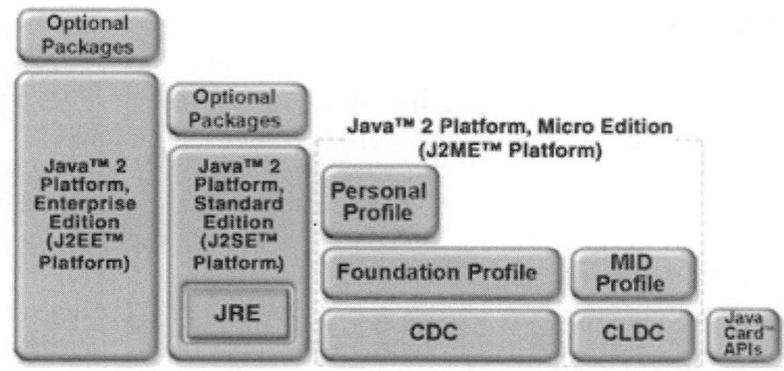

Hence, Java developers no longer have to alter their code for each client-side application for every operating system or hardware device. You can build effective user interfaces for wireless devices and take advantage of the facilities of J2ME for persistent storage and application management. The power and flexibility of J2ME can be leveraged using the APIs of the Mobile Information Device Profile (MID Profile), shown in the illustration. For more details on J2ME, visit

http://java.sun.com/j2me/

How does all this link to WAP and XHTML? From a mobile development standpoint, J2ME and WAP/XHTML come from client and server sides, respectively, and the two technologies should complement each other. Execution of local applications and availability of persistent local storage with or without network connectivity make J2ME a power platform to build upon. WAP/XHTML provides the needed browser technology and options for server-based, multimedia solutions that are vested in GPRS and 3G networks. We expect industry players, including Oracle, to provide components and services that will leverage a combination of these two technologies to work together.

Applications and Midlets

According to Sun, Java Midlets are small Java applications written in accordance with the Mobile Information Device Profile (MID Profile). Midlets, together with the CLDC, provide a complete J2ME Runtime Environment for small handheld devices such as PDAs, phones, and pagers (see the illustration). They offer the facilities to handle the user interface, messaging, sessions, security and deployment. For more information, refer to

http://java.sun.com/products/

Web Services and Oracle9*i*AS Wireless SDK

Currently, Oracle9*i*AS Wireless offers a J2ME SDK (Software Development Kit), which provides developers with the ability to extend Web Services to J2ME devices (see the illustration). The Web Services are available on the Oracle Online Mobile Studio and include the Push Service, Location Service (driving directions, yellow pages, and maps), and SQL Web Service. With Oracle9*i* Application Server acts as the back-end system for J2ME devices, these J2ME SDK applications can leverage the mobile network to invoke processing on the backend—as seamlessly as if it were done on the device.

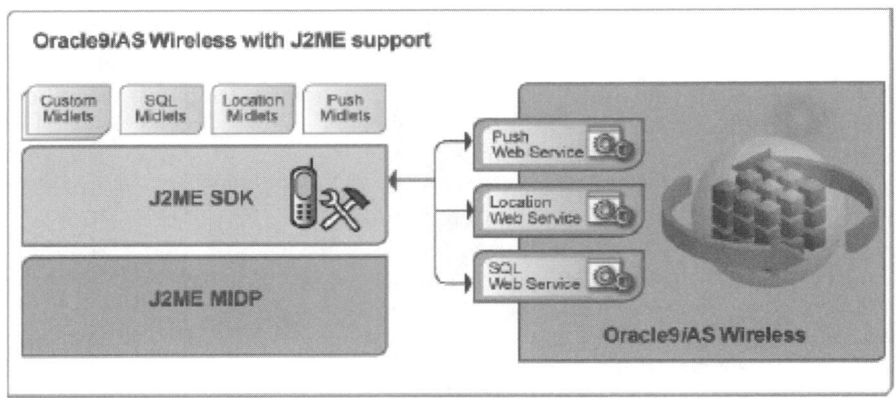

The J2ME SDK contains APIs including Push, Location, and SQL Web services; sample applications (midlets) for sending a message via e-mail, voice, fax, or SMS; Yellow Pages look-up; driving directions and maps; and location-based searching.

Like other Oracle9*i*AS Wireless components, the Push Web Service hides the complexity of sending messages to different devices on different channels. The same application can send messages through voice, e-mail, fax, or SMS. The Push Service requires only the message and the address to which the message is sent.

The SQL Web Service gives database control to J2ME developers. The SQL Web Service provides APIs to perform various DML/DDL operations, including Select, Insert, Update, Delete, and other DDL or DML operations.

XHTML

As discussed in Chapter 3, XHTML is a family of current and future document types and modules that reproduce, subset, and extend HTML 4. By defining these modules and specifying a mechanism to combine them, you can support the wide range of new devices and applications that will hit the market. XHTML Basic (W3C), XHTML Mobile (Openwave), and any XHTML flavors are supported in current or future micro-browsers. For example, Openwave's Universal Browser (version 5.1) supports both WML and XHTML.

WAP 2.0 and XHTML Basic

WAP 2.0 represents the convergence of WAP and W3C standards, bringing multiple Internet standards such as XHTML, HTTP, TCP/IP, and Transport Layer Security (TLS) together for wireless browsing and development. As you may know, WAP 1.2 derived its origin from the Handheld Device Markup Language (HDML). As new wireless devices are increasingly introduced, many of which demand heavy, complex processing capabilities, WAP continues to be upgraded. To run on faster networks with increased bandwidth and richer content, WAP 2.0 is needed.

Simply put, WAP 2.0, a welcome upgrade to WAP 1.2, is based upon the XHTML architecture using TCP and HTTP standards. For the first time, it allows the use of Cascading Style Sheets (CSS) to create applications for mobile devices as well as desktop PCs. This is a key step to address cross-platform compatibility issues, and it may help bridge the gap between wireline and wireless application development.

Various software development kits, including the Openwave SDK, provide support for content development with XHTML Mobile Profile and CSS and with legacy mobile standards (HDML, cHTML, and WML).

XHTML Modularization is a decomposition of XHTML 1.0 by referencing HTML 4 into a collection of abstract modules that provide specific types of functionality. The XHTML Basic document type includes the minimal set of modules required to be an XHTML host language document type, and in addition, it includes images, forms, basic tables, and object support. It is designed for Web clients that do not support the full set of XHTML features, for example, Web clients such as mobile phones, PDAs, pagers, and set top boxes. The document type is rich enough for content authoring. XHTML Basic is designed as a common base that may be extended. For example, an event module that is more generic than the traditional HTML 4 event system could be added or additional modules such as the Scripting Module could extend it from XHTML Modularization. The goal of XHTML Basic is to serve as a common language supported by various kinds of user agents.

XHTML Basic is a subset of WAP 2.0. With XHTML 1.0, each module specifies a set of elements and attributes associated with a certain use case. As different devices, especially hybrids, come to the marketplace, vendors can base their development on a core, like XHTML Basic, and add modules on top of that to support the capabilities of individual devices. In a way, this may become a path of convergence and agreement with Oracle9*i*AS multichannel XML as Oracle is actively promoting Oracle9*i*AS multichannel XML in relevant W3C committees. Oracle will most likely provide tools to convert Oracle9*i*AS multichannel XML to XHTML, if that is what developers want. Alternatively, it may build and include XHTML into a subset of Oracle9*i*AS multichannel XML in the near future when more modules are available that can support both voice and presentation markup in mobile devices.

As for increased functionality, developers can, for instance, create applications that include sound, images, and text. WAP 2.0 also allows for better push capabilities and provides the ability to display more advanced graphics on your device, and add audio and visual elements to messages.

XHTML Mobile Profile

A superset of XHTML Basic, XHTML Mobile Profile (MP) is the set of XHTML tags approved as the markup language for WAP 2.0. You can use CSS with your XHTML-MP applications to set their appearance; you can specify CSS style rules in external and internal style sheets for XHTML-MP elements.

Openwave has recently announced its Openwave Usability Interface (OUI), Java Edition 1.0 Beta, and XHTML Tag Library. The OUI XHTML Tag Library gives you access to OUI features through a tag interface based on XHTML-MP. OUI is a developer library for creating applications that you host on a content application server. You can use it to create WML services using a Java-based high-level interface. At runtime, this high-level library exports content optimized for browser type depending on the actual handset requesting content. Documentation on XHTML Mobile Profile is included with Openwave SDK 5.1.

What do all these mean? As HTML was officially replaced with XHTML 1.0 in 2000, there have not been (and will not be) any future upgrades or patches for HTML. The bottom line is: developers will begin to gravitate toward XHTML and, by extension, WAP 2.0 due to the closeness and linkage between XHTML and WAP 2.0. As a result, we can soon expect many HTML programmers to become well versed in WAP 2.0, one of the key mobile protocols.

Multimedia Messaging Service

Multimedia Messaging Service (MMS) promises to change the way we communicate. The good news is: It's already arrived! Let's look at some of these messaging developments and contrast them with SMS.

EMS

Enhanced Message Service, or EMS, was first submitted by Ericsson to the committees at European Telecommunications Standards Institute (ETSI) and 3G Partnership Project (3GPP). EMS is simply text messaging with images, simple animations, and short melodies on devices capable of these features. EMS allows you to send ringtones to other mobile phone users, among other things. EMS is sometimes referred to as "enhanced SMS."

Since EMS messages are sent through the same 2G networks as SMS, EMS is easy and very cost effective for mobile operators to deploy and for mobile users to use. The content-rich EMS messages are sent through the message header, and phones without EMS support will show only the unformatted text. Since EMS messages are significantly larger than a 160-character SMS text message, mobile devices with EMS (and MMS) capabilities are seeing larger memory capabilities. But possibilities that come with the memory expansion are endless. To say the least, corporate logos and navigational icons are now feasible with EMS and MMS.

Among consumers, many mobile users are using predefined images that come with their devices, and others are creating their own custom images and tunes. For enterprise solution providers, the ability to edit and create new images provides a foothold to create state-enabled messaging services, and even transactional applications on the 2G and 2.5G phones and networks.

A wide range of content, applications, and services already exist today; a list of examples and areas where messaging can be enhanced with EMS is as follows:

- **User-to-User Messaging** Messages originating from a mobile phone can include pictures, melodies, and stylized text with EMS.
- **Voice and E-Mail Notifications** Real-time notification is available for users who may have new voice or fax mail messages waiting. This includes using icons and melodies with EMS.
- **Unified Messaging** The mobile user receives a short message notifying that user of a new message in the unified messaging box. For example, an alert on "e-mail waiting" is provided in the form of a short message that details the sender of the e-mail, the subject field, and first few words of the e-mail message; in this case, stylized text is used to identify message elements.
- **Ring Signals** Ringtones can be downloaded from the Internet.
- **News** This includes general (world, sports, etc.) news and financial reports with *diagrams* and *tickers,* weather reports with *maps,* tunes from TV commercials as ringtones, etc.
- **Infotainment** This includes ringtones, e-greetings, team sports logos, horoscopes, movie previews or movie themes, TV show promotions, music artist promotions, lottery results, etc.
- **Corporate** This includes preinstalled corporate logos, company icons and ringtones, corporate e-mail notifications, call centers providing answers to questions about a product, vehicle positioning combining EMS with Global Positioning System (GPS) position information, job dispatches with customer addresses for sales calls or courier package delivery, etc.

MMS

MMS (Multimedia Messaging Service) is the new generation of messaging that allows you to send photos, audio, and even video clips in addition to text, simple melodies, and animations between phones and other terminals (see the illustration). An open standard, MMS is also approved by the 3G Partnership Project and the WAP Forum, as MMS is intended to go on the high-speed GPRS and 3G networks. As a result, major handset producers have developed handsets and network products to capitalize on its expected growth.

MMS is as easy to use as SMS and is likely to replace the SMS as the default service for messaging in future phones. In the interim, and where the device can't handle MMS, you can still get MMS messages. As in EMS, the resulting message will be an SMS which informs you of the multimedia message and provides you a link to a web site. You can click the site using your desktop PC, for instance, to view the message.

For developers, it is noteworthy that MMS messages should fit into the screen size and be compatible with the capability of the phone. This is much more complex than handling 160 characters, as in SMS. However, many of the benefits of SMS are preserved with MMS:

- MMS can be pushed to groups of recipients all at once
- Delivery is immediate and global
- Carbon copies (and blind copies) are supported
- Status and delivery reports are available

The size of an average SMS message is about 140 characters, while the average size of an MMS message will (in the early stages) be around 30,000 characters, but there is no size limit for MMS messages, unlike SMS messages being capped at 160 characters.

As a result, mobile phones and wireless PDAs can become rich multimedia, lifestyle devices overnight for consumers, and a powerful business communication device for the enterprises. At some point, this MMS platform will be seamlessly integrated with e-mail as the features and use cases coincide. It will then

- Be always available, ubiquitous
- Offer graphics, including charts, and instant video messaging for conferencing
- Be easy to use and cost effective

Rich content includes:

- **Text** As with SMS and EMS, an MMS message may consist of normal text. Besides unlimited text, the main difference is that in an MMS message, text can be accompanied not only by simple pixel images or melodies, but also by photos, graphics, audio clips, and video sequences.
- **Graphics** Graphs, tables, charts, diagrams, and layouts are just a few examples of the graphic capabilities that are feasible with MMS. Maps, drawings, sketches, and animations are likely to play a larger part in our personal lives, helping us find our way, ensure safety, express ourselves, communicate with others, and have fun.
- **Audio** MMS provides the ability to add full sound to a message. With MMS in a mobile phone, the user can also download MP3 files, and the MMS standard also supports streaming of sound as well as images.
- **Images** By using either a digital camera attached to the mobile device or a built-in digital camera, you can take snapshots and immediately send them to others. You can edit an image by adding text or voice, thus creating customized electronic postcards.
- **Video** MMS video content, once fully developed, could initially comprise something like 30-second video clips. In the future, streaming video will be possible across a full-fledged 3G network—something extremely compelling for news and entertainment services!
- **SMIL** Synchronized Multimedia Integration Language (SMIL) enables the creation and transmission of PowerPoint-style presentations on the mobile device. The idea is to allow users to customize the page timing in their PowerPoint presentations. Users can decide in what order the images and text are displayed, as well as for how long the images and text lines are to be shown.

Because MMS uses WAP as its bearer technology and is being standardized by 3GPP, it has wide industry support and offers full interoperability, which is a major benefit to service providers and end users.

Voice and VoiceXML

Voice is a natural language for a user interface. It's intuitive and requires little user training. Many industry participants expect the use of voice as an application medium to increase dramatically in the next few years as user acceptance and technologies converge.

For most mobile operators, voice is still the main revenue generator; however, the average revenue per user (ARPU) is decreasing for operators as voice communication becomes more of a commodity. In Chapter 14, we examine ways to build a voice application. With Release 2 of Oracle9*i*AS Wireless, you can already do a lot with voice. But with recent developments at Oracle, including the acquisition of a voice portal, we can expect to see more voice capabilities, such as speech recognition, Interactive Voice Response (IVR), and call control interactions, added into Oracle9*i*AS Wireless in the future. Will voice become one of the Oracle9*i*AS Wireless Services, like SMS and Push, and Offline Management? We believe so. Let's review the voice application development opportunity.

Voice Applications

Voice applications require no special client and are therefore ideal for delivering quick look-up information to a mobile user, especially in a hands-free environment.

As for consumers, voice portals take them beyond the typical IVR applications found at customer service call centers of financial institutions and credit card companies. Business users can gain access to communication and business applications behind corporate firewalls, including inventory levels, business intelligence, corporate directories, and e-mail messages.

Using natural language voice commands, a mobile user, consumer or business, can tap into any enabled applications over the phone. As long as the applications are designed for voice commands, such as using Oracle9*i*AS multichannel XML or VoiceXML, users can go through audio dialogs with recorded or synthesized speech, to accomplish their goals. Voice portals are typically applications where straightforward information, such as weather and stock quotes, can be accessed easily and quickly.

Technologies and VoiceXML

VoiceXML is the markup language for voice-based applications. Introduced by AT&T, Motorola, and others to provide a standardized, XML-based technology for the development of voice applications, VoiceXML provides the platform for applications where small amounts of information need to be accessed quickly. Support for VoiceXML and other technologies such as speech recognition and text-to-speech is critical for voice applications to be widely adopted. Recently, the Voice Browser Working Group of the World Wide Web Consortium (W3C) released the working draft and final release of the VoiceXML 2.0 specification, which includes Standardized Grammar through its support of an XML-based Speech Recognition Grammar Format, Speech Synthesis Markup Language (SSML) tags, and audio formats. The result is increased momentum and support for voice-based application development and deployment.

In terms of technology, a VoiceXML application relies on specialized voice conversion hardware and software to handle speech recognition and to interface with the actual VoiceXML processing engine. Powerful server-based speech recognition software can be evaluated from such companies as SpeechWorks and Nuance. A VoiceXML interpreter interfaces with the speech recognition software to match user requests with nodes in an XML document defined by the application developer. VoiceXML allows the developer to tie user requests to server-side scripts (such as Java servlets) or to other VoiceXML files.

Because VoiceXML applications are entirely server-based, they are excellent candidates for deployment through an application service provider (ASP) due to the cost and skills required to set up the proper mix of server hardware and software. Right now, if you want to support automatic speech recognition (ASR) and text-to-speech (TTS) features in voice, XHTML is not quite ready. While XHTML Basic has basic support for voice, it still has a way to go. Therefore, the Oracle9*i*AS multichannel XML is a good way to build voice-based services for Oracle application developers.

Summary

With high-speed networks and affordable mobile devices, rich clients and rich media are finally within reach of the mass consumer and the enterprise. These exciting developments, in wireless networks, devices, markups, and other technologies, are enabling the development and deployment of a whole new generation of mobile services, and will soon become a crucial part of your Oracle mobile development efforts. Look for some of the technologies discussed in this chapter to start showing up in future releases of Oracle9*i*AS Wireless!

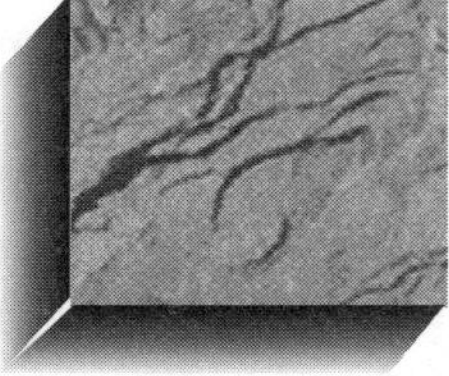

PART IV

Appendixes

APPENDIX A

Glossary

3G Third Generation. Next generation, broadband wireless, services and networks that will transform wireless communications into on-line, real-time transfer of information, regardless of time and place.

802.11b 802.11 is a family of wireless networking protocols out of the Institute of Electrical and Electronics Engineers (IEEE). The most popular of these, 802.11b, has been in commercial use since 1999. It has a maximum theoretical throughput of 11 Mbps, which is only about one-tenth the speed of common Ethernets, but much faster than broadband solutions like DSL or cable modems.

adapter A dynamically loaded Java class that acquires content from external or internal sources like websites or databases, and converts the content into Oracle9*i*AS multichannel XML. Shipped with Release 2, Oracle9*i*AS Wireless adapters include the HTTP adapter, Web Integration adapter, SQL adapter, and OC4J adapter.

AMPS Acronym for Advanced Mobile Phone Service. AMPS is used in North and South America. It is also the most common system in the Asia/Pacific region. First Generation (1G) analog service.

band In wireless communication, band refers to a frequency or contiguous range of frequencies.

Bluetooth Bluetooth is a new technology that allows devices such as mobile phones, laptops, digital cameras, personal digital assistants (PDAs), and other portable devices to communicate with each other without using cables to connect them. Bluetooth allows these devices to communicate with each other using short-range radio waves.

CDMA Acronym for Code Division Multiple Access. CDMA enables multiplexing by separating communications by code. Voice is broken into digitized bits, and groups of bits are tagged with a code. Each code is associated with a single call in the network. Groups of bits from one call are randomly transmitted along with those of other calls. Then they are reassembled in the correct order to complete the conversation.

CDPD Acronym for Cellular Digital Packet Data. It is an open wireless transmission standard allowing two-way 19.2-kbps packet data transmission over existing cellular telephone channels (AMPS with CDPD capability). In essence, CDPD technology uses idle network capacity caused by pauses in phone conversations and gaps between calls placed to transmit data.

CTIA Acronym for Cellular Telecommunications Industry Association. The membership-based CTIA is located in Washington, D.C. and represents the interests of the wireless telecommunications industry.

device transformer A transformer that converts content from Oracle9*i*AS multichannel XML format into the target device format.

DTD Acronym for Document Type Declaration. This is a file that defines the format elements for a type of XML document.

dual band A wireless phone that is capable of operating on two frequency bands such as the 900 MHz digital band and the 1800 MHz digital GSM band.

dual mode A wireless device that can operate on either an analog or digital transmission network. However, multiple digital transmission systems exist, so dual mode phone users must ensure that their dual mode phone will operate on the digital transmission system used by their selected service provider.

EMS Acronym for Enhanced Messaging Service. EMS messages contain a combination of text and simple pixel-image and/or melody. Users may download images and melodies from the Internet, or for even greater self-expression, create them on their own directly in the phone. Third Generation (3G) service.

folder Logical collection of services, which organizes and groups services based on function category, location information and user preference. Some special folders, such as User Home and Group Domain Folder, also function as ACL (Access Control List) unit enforced by the application tools. A folder can be shared by giving access permission to other groups.

GPRS Acronym for General Packet Radio Service. GPRS is a wireless data transmission service based on packet transmission. For example, if an e-mail is sent by GPRS it will be reduced into packets of information. Each individual packet travels to its destination by the quickest possible route. This means the different packets from the same mail can travel separately through different networks around the globe in order to avoid obstructions. At the pre-set destination, they are rebuilt and presented to the recipient as a whole 2.5G service.

GPS Acronym for Global Positioning System. A system using satellites, receivers and software to allow users to determine their exact geographic position.

group A logical collection of users, which supplies accessible services and alerts to its group members. On the other hand, its group members manage the contents of a group.

GSM Acronym for Global System for Mobile communications. GSM is the pan-European standard for digital cellular telephone service. It is also one of the technologies available in the Americas. GSM was designed for markets to provide the advantage of automatic, international roaming in multiple countries. GSM uses 900 MHz and 1800 MHz in Europe. In North America, GSM uses the 1900 MHz. Second Generation (2G) service.

HDML Acronym for Handheld Device Markup Language. It is a specification that allows Internet access from wireless devices such as handheld personal computers and smart phones. This language is derived from the HyperText Markup Language (HTML).

HTML Acronym for HyperText Markup Language. The document format that defines the page layout, fonts, and graphic elements, as well as the hypertext links to other documents on the Web.

IMAP Acronym for Internet Message Access Protocol. It is a method of accessing electronic mail or bulletin board messages that are kept on a mail server. The ability to access messages from more than one computer has become extremely important as reliance on electronic messaging and use of multiple computers increase. POP (Post Office Protocol) works best when one has only a single computer.

IMEI Acronym for International Mobile Equipment Identifier. It is a 15-digit number that uniquely identifies an individual wireless phone or communicator. The IMEI appears on the label located on the back of the phone. The phone automatically transmits the IMEI when the network asks for it. A network operator might request the IMEI to determine if a device is in disrepair, stolen or to gather statistics on fraud or faults.

i-mode i-mode is a highly successful 2G wireless data service offered by NTT DoCoMo. This moble platform has revolutionized the way more than 30 million people in Japan live and work. With i-mode, cellular phone users get easy access to tens of thousands of Internet sites, as well as specialized services such as e-mail, online shopping and banking, ticket reservations, and restaurant reviews.

J2EE Acronym for The Java™ 2 Platform, Enterprise Edition. J2EE defines the standard for developing multi-tier enterprise applications.

J2ME Acronym for the Java™ 2 Platform, Micro Edition. This is the edition of the Java 2 platform targeted at consumer electronics and embedded devices.

JSP Acronym for JavaServer Pages. JavaServer Pages technology separates the user interface from content generation enabling designers to change the overall page layout without altering the underlying dynamic content. JavaServer Pages programming allows web developers and designers to rapidly develop and easily maintain, information-rich, dynamic web pages that leverage existing business systems.

LDAP Acronym for Lightweight Directory Access Protocol. LDAP is a protocol for accessing online directory services. It runs directly over TCP, and can be used to access a standalone LDAP directory service or to access a directory service that is back-ended by X.500.

logical device An object that describes either a physical device, such as a cellular phone, or an application, such as e-mail. There is a default device transformer for each logical device.

master service The core implementation of a service. The master service object invokes a specific adapter, and identifies the transformer used to convert content for the target device.

MIME Acronym for Multipurpose Internet Mail Extensions. MIME is a standard for describing different types of information and extends the format of Internet mail to allow non-US-ASCII textual messages, non-textual messages, multipart message bodies, and non-US-ASCII information in message headers.

MMS Acronym for Multimedia Messaging Service. MMS messages can contain formatted text, graphics, data, animations, images, audio clips, voice transmissions and video sequences. Sending digital postcards and PowerPoint-style presentations is expected to be among the most popular user applications of MMS. Third Generation (3G) service.

module service A regular service with a virtual URL (an omp://URL) that supports callback, i.e., at the end of the service it displays a link to their caller so the user can go back to the original service.

N-AMPS Acronym for Narrowband Advanced Mobile Phone Service. Combines the AMPS transmission standard with digital signaling information to effectively triple the capacity of AMPS while adding basic messaging functionality.

Oracle9*i*AS multichannel XML format A content format that contains abstract user interface elements such as text items, menus, forms, and tables.

personalization portal A website that end users can access to select services and configure their device portal. Users can access the personalization portal from their desktop computers or mobile devices.

POP Acronym for Post Office Protocol. POP was designed to support offline mail processing—mail is delivered to a server, and a personal computer user periodically invokes a mail client program that connects to the server and downloads all of the pending mail to the user's own machine. Thereafter, all mail processing is local to the client machine.

provisioning adapter The adapter used to create, modify, and delete user objects in the Oracle9*i*AS Wireless repository.

repository An Oracle8*i*/9*i* database which stores all Oracle9*i*AS Wireless objects, such as users, groups, adapters, and services.

request A query to initiate a desired Oracle9*i*AS Wireless service. Requests are submitted on behalf of end-users to the Oracle9*i*AS Wireless server.

result transformer A transformer that converts content from Adapter Result format into Oracle9*i*AS multichannel XML format.

RMI Acronym for Remote Method Invocation. A standard for creating and calling remote objects. RMI allows Java components stored in a network to be run remotely.

service A core object used in an Oracle9*i*AS Wireless server to represent a unit of information requested by, and delivered to, an Oracle9*i*AS Wireless client. An end user typically sees a service as a menu item on a device or as a link on a Web page.

SIM Acronym for Subscriber Identity Module. SIM usually takes the form of a card commonly used in a GSM phone. The card holds a microchip that stores information and encrypts voice and data transmissions, making it close to impossible to listen in on calls. The SIM card also stores data that identifies the caller to the network service provider.

SMS Acronym for Short Messaging Service. SMS allows mobile phone users to send and receive text messages of up to 160 characters in a cost-and time-efficient manner.

SOAP Acronym for Simple Object Access Protocol. SOAP provides a simple and lightweight mechanism for exchanging structured and typed information between peers in a decentralized, distributed environment using XML.

source format The original format of content retrieved from an external data source by an Oracle9*i*AS Wireless adapter. For example, the source format of Web page content is HTML.

SQL adapter An adapter that retrieves and adapts content from any JDBC-enabled data source.

stylesheet An XSLT (eXtensible Stylesheet Language Transformation) instance that implements content presentation for XML documents. Oracle9*i*AS Wireless transformers can be either XSLT stylesheets or Java programs.

target format The format required delivering data to a specific type of client device.

TDMA Acronym for Time Division Multiple Access. TDMA utilizes GPS satellites to reference a synchronized time, and then divides the channel into time slots. As a result, channel capacity is increased because one channel has now been converted to multiple voice or data transmission vehicles. TDMA is a proven technology in cellular systems across Europe, the USA, and in Japan.

telematics A technology combining all the possibilities inherent in wireless voice and data communications with GPS location capabilities to deliver location-specific security, information, and productivity enhancing services to people on the move.

Tiny HTML A minimal version of HTML implemented by a transformer in the starter Oracle9*i*AS Wireless repository. Tiny HTML does not include support for frames, JavaScript, or other advanced features.

transformer An Oracle9*i*AS Wireless object that converts content returned by Oracle9*i*AS Wireless adapters. Result transformers convert Adapter Result documents into Oracle9*i*AS multichannel XML documents. Device transformers convert Oracle9*i*AS multichannel XML documents into the target device format.

Tri-Mode Tri-Mode phones operate on two frequency bands, such as 800MHz and 1900MHz, as well as operating in both digital and analog networks.

UML Acronym for Unified Modeling Language. It is a language for specifying, visualizing, constructing, and documenting the artifacts of software systems, as well as for business modeling and other non-software systems. The UML represents a collection of best engineering practices that have proven successful in the modeling of large and complex systems.

UMTS Acronym for Universal Mobile Telecommunications System. A 3G standard that is based on W-CDMA, UMTS will enable the wireless Information Society, delivering high-value broadband information, commerce and entertainment services to mobile users via fixed, wireless and satellite networks. UMTS will also speed convergence between telecommunications, IT, media and content industries to deliver new services and create fresh revenue-generating opportunities. Third Generation (3G) service.

unified messaging Unified messaging provides a single point of access to all message types including voice, fax, and e-mail, from virtually any communications device, telephone, personal computer or Web browser through the Internet.

user agent A special header on the HTTP request, which is used for identifying the Web client to the server. A Web server can use this header to decipher what kind of browser is making a request and then act accordingly.

VoiceXML A Web-based markup language for representing human-computer dialogs, just like HTML. VoiceXML assumes a *voice browser* with audio output (computer-synthesized and/or recorded), and audio input (voice and/or keypad tones). VoiceXML leverages the Internet for voice application development and delivery, greatly simplifying these difficult tasks and creating new opportunities.

WAP Acronym for Wireless Application Protocol. A wireless standard that aims to align industry efforts to bring advanced applications and Internet content to digital cellular phones.

WASP Acronym for Wireless Application Service Provider. It is part of a growing industry sector resulting from the convergence of two trends: wireless communications and the outsourcing of services. A WASP performs the same hosting service for wireless customers as a regular application service provider (ASP) does for wired customers: it provides Web-based access to applications and services that would otherwise have to be hosted individually by the customers themselves. The main difference with WASP is that it enables customers to access the service from a variety of wireless devices, such as a mobile smart phone or personal digital assistant (PDA).

Web Integration Adapter An adapter that retrieves and adapts Web content using WIDL files to map the source content to Oracle9*i*AS multichannel XML.

WIDL Acronym for Web Interface Definition Language. A meta-data language that defines interfaces to Web-based data and services. WIDL enables automatic and structured Web access by compatible applications.

WIDL file A file written in Web Interface Definition Language that associates input and output parameters with the source content that you want to make available in an Oracle9*i*AS Wireless service.

WML Acronym for Wireless Markup Language. A markup language optimized for the delivery of content to wireless devices.

XHTML Acronym for eXtensible HyperText Markup Language. XHTML is a family of current and future document types and modules that reproduce, subset, and extend HTML 4. XHTML family document types are XML based.

XHTML-MP Acronym for eXtensible HyperText Markup Language, Mobile Profile. XHTML-MP is a superset of XHTML Basic, which is a simpler version of XHTML. XHTML Basic is intended for smaller, non-computer devices such as mobile phones, personal digital assistants, pagers, and television-based web browsers.

XML Acronym for eXtensible Markup Language. A flexible markup language that allows tags to be defined by the content developer. Tags for virtually any data item, such as product, sales representative, or amount due, can be created and used in specific applications, allowing Web pages to function like database records.

XSLT Acronym for eXtensible Stylesheet Language Transformation. Formatting and generation of markup pages via the application of XSL (stylesheets) to XML documents. Typically involving the use of a XSLT processor.

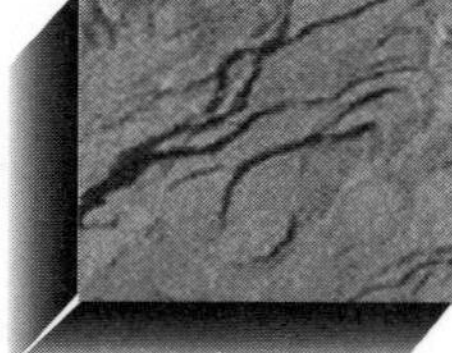

APPENDIX B

Oracle9*i*AS Multichannel XML

he Oracle9*i*AS multichannel XML tags are internal representations of the Oracle9*i*AS Wireless results returned by an adapter. If an adapter (custom) does not return a result in this format, the master service must use the result's transformer to convert the result into the Oracle9*i*AS multichannel XML format.

Oracle9*i*AS multichannel XML defines an abstract device markup language. The goal is to define one device-independent markup language that supports a variety of devices and markups. Elements in this XML represent an abstract user interface. These abstract UI elements are translated to the appropriate device-specific elements/tags. Note that the element names are case sensitive.

The list of Oracle9*i*AS multichannel XML tag elements can be found in the Document Type Definition (DTD) file SimpleResult_1_*M*_*N*.dtd (*M* and *N* are revision numbers) located locally in the $ORACLE9iASW_INSTALL_DIR/wireless/DTD folder. The latest version of the file shipped with Release 2 (as of this writing) is SimpleResult_1_1_0.dtd.

Mobile Contexts

Related to Oracle9*i*AS multichannel XML are mobile context variables. Mobile contexts are equivalent to scriptlets in JSP and scripting; they are nothing more than just context variable substitution. These variables are placeholders for the Oracle9*i*AS Wireless Core at runtime. The predefined set of variables for mobile developers to use is summarized below (they are all of the *String* data type):

Variable Name	Description
user.name	Login name of the user
user.displayname	Display name of the user
user.location.addressline1	Address line 1 of the location
user.location.addressline2	Address line 2 of the location
user.location.addresslastline	Address line 3 of the location
user.location.companyname	Company name of the address
user.location.block	Location block
user.location.city	Location city
user.location.county	Location county
user.location.state	Location state
user.location.postalcode	Location ZIP/postal code
user.location.postalcodeext	Location ZIP/postal extended code

Variable Name	Description
user.location.country	Location country
user.location.type	Profile or Auto
service.home.url	URL to home page of service
home.url	URL to Oracle9*i*AS Wireless home page
service.parent.Url	URL to folder container
module.callback.url	Callback URL for module return
module.callback.label	Display label for the module

A sample use of mobile contexts is shown here, where your application greets a user:

```
<SimpleResult>
   <SimpleContainer>
      <SimpleText>
         <SimpleTextItem>
         <SimpleStrong>Welcome %value user.displayname%</SimpleStrong>
      </SimpleTextItem>
      </SimpleText>
   </SimpleContainer>
</SimpleResult>
```

Categorized XML Tags

The Oracle9*i*AS multichannel XML tags are categorized in this section based on functionality. After finding a specific tag, you can reference it alphabetically in the "Oracle9*i*AS Multichannel XML Tag Reference" section in this appendix for a full description and its syntax.

Basic Tags

SimpleContainer SimpleMeta SimpleResult

Display and Formatting Tags

SimpleBreak	SimpleCol	SimpleEm	SimpleImage
SimpleRow	SimpleSpan	SimpleStrong	SimpleTable
SimpleTableBody	SimpleTableHeader	SimpleText	SimpleTextItem
SimpleUnderline			

Navigation Tags

SimpleAction	SimpleHref	SimpleMenu	SimpleMenuItem
SimpleTimer			

Audio and Speech Tags

SimpleAudio	SimpleCache	SimpleDTMF	SimpleGrammar
SimpleHelp	SimpleProperty	SimpleReprompt	SimpleSpeech
SimpleValue			

Forms Tags

SimpleForm	SimpleFormItem	SimpleFormOption	SimpleFormSelect
SimpleOptGroup	SimpleTextField	SimpleTitle	

Advanced User Interface Tags

SimpleBind	SimpleCase	SimpleCatch	SimpleClear
SimpleDisconnect	SimpleDisplay	SimpleEvent	SimpleExit
SimpleFinish	SimpleGo	SimpleKey	SimpleMatch
SimpleMItem	SimpleName	SimplePrev	SimpleRefresh
SimpleSubmit	SimpleSwitch	SimpleTask	

The deviceclass Attribute

The deviceclass attribute of many of the Oracle9*i*AS multichannel XML tags is a helper attribute that tells Oracle9*i*AS Wireless how to optimize the rendering of contents for specific devices. In the absence of the deviceclass attribute, the content will be rendered to both small-screen devices and voice-enabled devices.

Attribute: deviceclass	Description
voice	Indicates a voice channel for all voice devices
micromessenger	Indicates small-screen devices such as SMS, pagers, and digital cell phones (asynchronous)
messenger	Indicates medium-sized-screen devices such as e-mail clients on PDAs (asynchronous)

Attribute: deviceclass	Description
microbrowser	Indicates small-screen devices and small form factors, such as Motorola, Nokia, Ericsson, and two-way BlackBerry devices (synchronous)
pdabrowser	Indicates medium-sized-screen devices and medium form factors, such as Palm and PocketPC devices (synchronous)
pcbrowser	Indicates large-screen devices and large form factors, such as IE and Navigator running on desktop PCs (synchronous)

Oracle9*i*AS Multichannel XML Tag Reference

The Oracle9*i*AS multichannel XML tags are organized alphabetically in this section for easy reference. When the value of any attribute is referred to as **CDATA**, you can use any text string.

SimpleAction

The SimpleAction tag provides the ability to define a link or submit action. Mobile devices can associate a submit action to a number of different input methods, such as pressing an accelerator key on WAP devices or speaking a command on voice-enabled devices. Additionally, you can have SimpleTextItem as a child for rendering the tag in the voice channel.

Example

```
<SimpleResult>
   <SimpleContainer>
   <SimpleText>
      <SimpleTextItem>
         <SimpleUnderline>SimpleAction</SimpleUnderline>
      </SimpleTextItem>
   </SimpleText>
   <SimpleAction label="LEFT" type="primary" target="primary.jsp"/>
   <SimpleAction label="RGHT" type="secondary" target="secondary.jsp"/>
   </SimpleContainer>
</SimpleResult>
```

Here are a couple of items to note :

- On WAP phones, the softkeys (left and right buttons) are bound to the SimpleAction tasks. On a PocketPC, they are stacked.
- SimpleUnderline is rendered with the underline attribute in devices that support that style. In those that don't support it, the text is italicized.

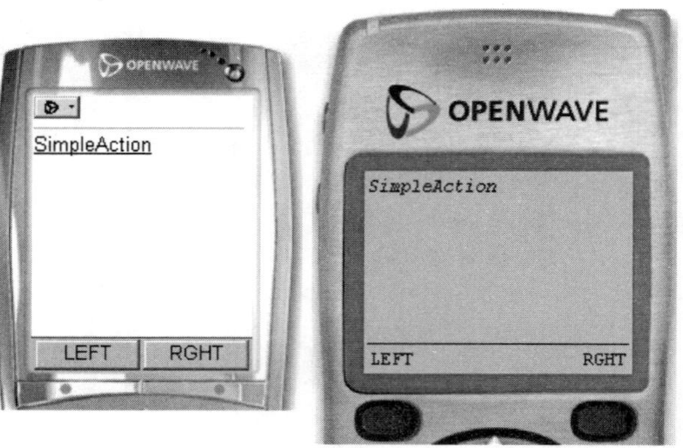

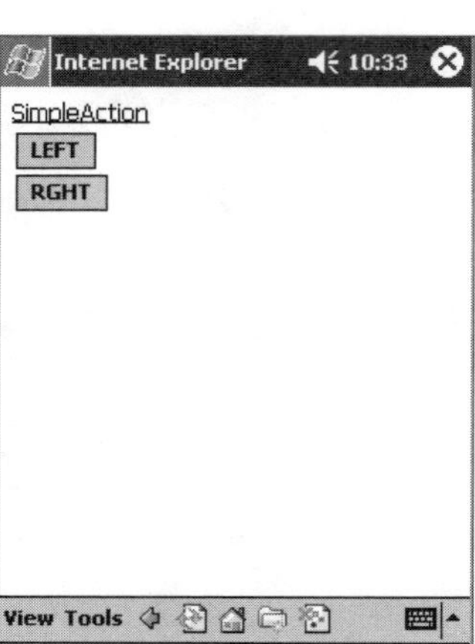

Attributes

Attribute	Description	Value(s)	Default Value
type	Defines the type of binding in the target device. Here, "primary" and "secondary" map to the primary and secondary keys, respectively, and "continue" is a special primary key that tells the voice service to continue without waiting for the user. If both continue and primary are defined, both of them will map to the primary key. The following types are also supported by the transformers for backward compatibility: accept | soft1 | option1 | option2.	continue | primary | secondary	REQUIRED

Attribute	**Description**	**Value(s)**	**Default Value**
addImageExtension	Allows the server to use the right image format from a list of available formats. The server will pick the right image to be used based on the available images (see the "available" attribute) and device browser capability.	true | false	OPTIONAL
available	The application can specify a list of available image formats in an order of preference (for example, "jpg gif g2.gif wbmp bmp"). Note that g2.gif indicates a grayscale depth 2 image for devices such as the Palm.	CDATA	OPTIONAL
callbackurl	Oracle9*i*AS Wireless module support. Indicates the URL to return back if the current action calls an Oracle9*i*AS Wireless module.	CDATA	OPTIONAL
callbackparam	Oracle9*i*AS Wireless module support. Indicates the return parameters of callbackurl. When the module returns the context back to the callee application, callbackparam is passed back for the callee to construct its application state.	CDATA	OPTIONAL
callbacksecure	Oracle9*i*AS Wireless module support. Indicates the mode of communication, when callback occurs, between the Oracle9*i*AS Wireless server and the mobile device (not the remote service).	true | false	OPTIONAL
deviceclass	This tag is interpreted only for the specified device class. The server will transform this element only for devices belonging to the specified device class. Values can be a combination of values. If not specified, the tag is interpreted for all devices.	pdabrowser | pcbrowser | voice | microbrowser | micromessenger | messenger	OPTIONAL

Attribute	Description	Value(s)	Default Value
dtmf	A digit to be pressed on a phone or DTMF tone. The dtmf attribute just takes one value (a simplified form of the voice SimpleDTMF tag). Will work on WAP devices if it's supported by the device.	CDATA	OPTIONAL
fetchaudio	Voice-only attribute. The URL of an audio clip to play while the target is being fetched.	CDATA	OPTIONAL
icon	The built-in icon name for HDML/WML. Will be used if specified.	CDATA	OPTIONAL
label	The label for an action button, displayed when an action is bound to a button on a visual device.	CDATA	OPTIONAL
mimetype	A MIME type of the target URL. If the target MIME type is not text/vnd.oracle.mobilexml, the Oracle9*i*AS Wireless server will not rewrite the URL.	CDATA	text/vnd. oracle. mobilexml OPTIONAL
name	The name identifier for the element instance.	CDATA	OPTIONAL
secure	Indicates the mode of communication, when callback occurs, between the Oracle9*i*AS Wireless server and the device (not the remote service).	true | false	OPTIONAL
src	The URL of an image to be displayed. (In SimpleAction/Href, this image needs to be used instead of the label.)	CDATA	OPTIONAL
static_target	The URL to navigate to when an action is activated. The server never rewrites this URL. If it exists, this will override the target attribute. Also supports "callto:" for phone calls and "mailto:" for e-mail support.	CDATA	OPTIONAL

Attribute	Description	Value(s)	Default Value
target	The URL to navigate to when an action is activated. This URL is rewritten by the server to point back to the Oracle9*i*AS Wireless server when the mimetype attribute is text/vnd.oracle.mobilexml. Also supports "callto:" for phone calls and "mailto:" for e-mail support.	CDATA	OPTIONAL

SimpleAudio

The SimpleAudio tag allows you to play an audio file on voice devices.

Example

```
<SimpleResult>
   <SimpleContainer>
   <SimpleText>
   <SimpleTextItem>Hello SimpleAudio</SimpleTextItem>
   </SimpleText>
   <SimpleAudio src="http://localhost/wav/hello.wav" />
   <SimpleAction label="MENU" type="secondary" target="main.jsp"/>
   </SimpleContainer>
</SimpleResult>
```

On devices that support audio, the WAV file will be played in addition to the text messages being shown.

Attributes

Attribute	Description	Value(s)	Default Value
deviceclass	This tag is applicable for voice devices only. Will not be supported on other devices, even if specified.	voice	OPTIONAL
src	The URL to an audio source file.	CDATA	OPTIONAL

SimpleBind

The SimpleBind tag is an extended action tag that can be invoked by multiple events and perform multiple tasks. An action can be triggered by events such as pressing touch-tone phone keys, speaking voice commands, and selecting a menu item. The action, in turn, may fire off a set of tasks to perform on the matching event. For example, the "submitting a form" action can happen when the user clicks the Submit button, presses a key on the device, or just says "submit" on the voice device. The SimpleBind tag defines all the events that need to match. It also defines a set of actions that are mapped to event matches (SimpleMatch). The action can include displaying an information screen informing the user of the submit action and then submitting the form (two actions for one set of events).

Example

```
<SimpleBind>
   <SimpleKey type="secondary" />
   <SimpleMatch>
   <SimpleEvent type="onpick">
   <SimpleSwitch name="cb">
      <SimpleCase value="1">
      <SimpleDisplay>
      <SimpleText>
         <SimpleTextItem>You have selected 1!</SimpleTextItem>
      </SimpleText>
      </SimpleDisplay>
      </SimpleCase>
      <SimpleCase value="2">
      <SimpleDisplay>
      <SimpleText>
         <SimpleTextItem>You have selected 2!</SimpleTextItem>
      </SimpleText>
      </SimpleDisplay>
      </SimpleCase>
   </SimpleSwitch>
   </SimpleEvent>
   </SimpleMatch>
</SimpleBind>
```

Attributes

Attribute	Description	Value(s)	Default Value
deviceclass	This tag is interpreted only for the specified device class. The server will transform this element only for devices belonging to the specified device class. Values can be a combination of values. If not specified, the tag is interpreted for all devices.	pdabrowser | pcbrowser | voice | microbrowser | micromessenger | messenger	OPTIONAL

SimpleBreak

The SimpleBreak tag creates a break or new line on text devices and causes a pause on voice devices.

Example

```
<SimpleResult>
   <SimpleContainer>
   <SimpleText>
   <SimpleTitle>Search Results</SimpleTitle>
      <SimpleTextItem>
      <SimpleEm>1 Entries Found</SimpleEm>
      <SimpleBreak msecs="500" />
      <SimpleStrong>John Smith</SimpleStrong>
      <SimpleBreak/>500 Oracle Pkwy
      <SimpleBreak/>Redwood Shores
      <SimpleBreak/>CA, 94065
      </SimpleTextItem>
   </SimpleText>
   </SimpleContainer>
</SimpleResult>
```

Here are a couple of items to note:

- On devices that support voice, a 500-millisecond (half-second) pause will occur before the text-to-speech (TTS) engine says "John Smith...."
- Devices that don't support voice will just see a break between text lines.

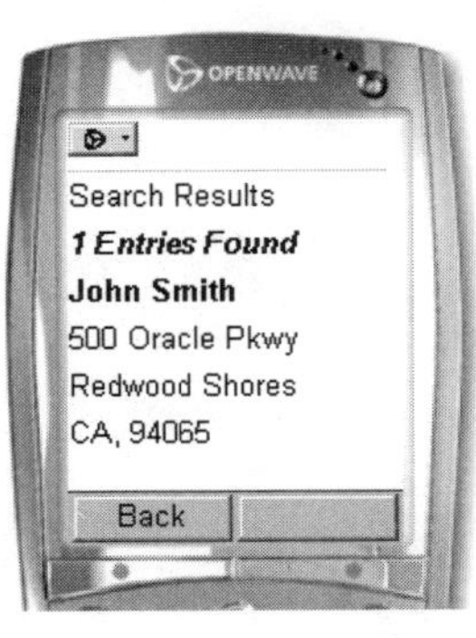

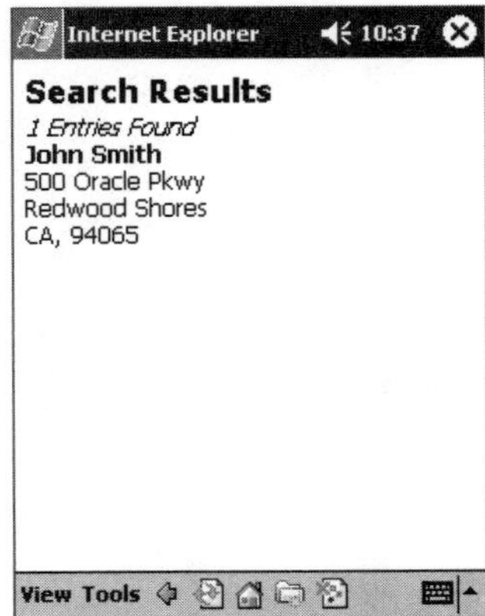

Attributes

Attribute	Description	Value(s)	Default Value
deviceclass	This tag is interpreted only for the specified device class. The server will transform this element only for devices belonging to the specified device class. Values can be a combination of values. If not specified, the tag is interpreted for all devices.	pdabrowser | pcbrowser | voice | microbrowser | micromessenger | messenger	OPTIONAL
msecs	The duration, in milliseconds, of the break for voice devices.	CDATA	OPTIONAL
rule	Generates a horizontal rule (<HR>) with this break (HTML).	true | false	false OPTIONAL
size	The size of the break (VoiceXML only).	none | small | medium | large	medium OPTIONAL

SimpleCache

The SimpleCache tag allows a URL to be cached on the gateway (such as WAP), the client, or both. It is also used when a URL needs to be prefetched while still showing the current content (only on supported devices). SimpleCache defines all these policies.

Example

```
<SimpleResult>
   <SimpleCache ttl="0"/>
   <SimpleContainer>
   <SimpleText>
      <SimpleTextItem>
      <SimpleEm>Real Time Quotes</SimpleEm>
      <SimpleBreak/>
      <SimpleStrong>ORCL</SimpleStrong>
      <SimpleBreak/>Price: 15.01
      <SimpleBreak/>
      <SimpleBreak/>Time: 12:45 PM PST
      </SimpleTextItem>
   </SimpleText>
   </SimpleContainer>
</SimpleResult>
```

Attributes

Attribute	Description	Value(s)	Default Value
deviceclass	This tag is interpreted only for the specified device class. The server will transform this element only for devices belonging to the specified device class. Values can be a combination of values. If not specified, the tag is interpreted for all devices.	pdabrowser | pcbrowser | voice | microbrowser | micromessenger | messenger	OPTIONAL
policy	Can cache on the gateway, client, both, or none. A value of public indicates to cache on the gateway (such as WAP), whereas a value of private indicates a client-only cache.	public | private | both | none	private OPTIONAL
prefetch	The prefetch policy. Certain devices can prefetch target resources, before the user requests the resources. This attribute controls the policy of such a prefetchable resource.	onload | safe | streamed	safe OPTIONAL
timeout	The time, in milliseconds, to wait while fetching a resource before failing.	Positive Int	OPTIONAL
ttl	The time-to-live value for cached data, in milliseconds.	Positive Int	OPTIONAL

SimpleCase

The SimpleCase tag provides the ability to write case statements within a SimpleSwitch tag. This allows the developer to perform client-side actions on devices. Note that support for Switch/Case is not universal and is currently supported only in WAP (HDML/WML) and voice (VoiceXML) devices.

Example

See the sample usage for the SimpleBind tag.

Attributes

Attribute	Description	Value(s)	Default Value
value	The value of the case statement (to be compared with the value of a form field, identified by the name attribute).	CDATA	REQUIRED
deviceclass	This tag is interpreted only for the specified device class. The server will transform this element only for devices belonging to the specified device class. Values can be a combination of values. If not specified, the tag is interpreted for all devices.	pdabrowser | pcbrowser | voice | microbrowser | micromessenger | messenger	OPTIONAL

SimpleCatch

The SimpleCatch tag allows for event catching and is a voice-only tag. It can be used to capture predefined voice events, such as noinput, exit, and so on, as well as to perform actions on them. For example, on a noinput event (for a form item), the user can be given some instructions and then prompted again for the input. Events also include the errors generated.

Example

See the sample usage for the SimpleMenu tag.

Attributes

Attribute	Description	Value(s)	Default Value
type	Predefined voice events. Possible values include cancel, error, exit, help, noinput, nomatch, telephone. and disconnect.	CDATA	REQUIRED
count	The occurrence of the event. The count allows you to handle different occurrences of the same event differently. The form or menu where SimpleCatch can occur maintains a counter for each event that occurs while it is being visited. These counters are reset each time the form or menu is reentered.	Positive Int	1 OPTIONAL
deviceclass	This tag is applicable for voice devices only. Will not be supported on other devices, even if specified.	voice	OPTIONAL

SimpleClear

The SimpleClear tag clears a list of client-side form fields identified by the named list (see SimpleName). Works on WML and voice devices only and is useful in voice applications where clearing a form field will allow the voice engine to prompt the user for the form field again.

Example

A code snippet from Chapter 14 follows:

```
      ...
      <SimpleForm target="tipcalc.jsp">
         <SimpleFormItem name="howmuch" type="currency">
            <SimpleTitle>How much is the bill? </SimpleTitle>
            <SimpleCatch type="help">
            Help. Say the amount of the bill in dollars and cents.
            For example, twenty-five dollars and ten cents
            </SimpleCatch>
            <SimpleCatch type="cancel">Canceling.
            <SimpleClear>
               <SimpleName name="howmuch"/>
            </SimpleClear>
         </SimpleCatch>
         </SimpleFormItem>
      ...
      </SimpleForm>
   </SimpleContainer>
</SimpleResult>
```

Attributes

Attribute	Description	Value(s)	Default Value
deviceclass	This tag is interpreted only for the specified device class. The server will transform this element only for devices belonging to the specified device class. Values can be a combination of values. If not specified, the tag is interpreted for all devices.	pdabrowser | pcbrowser | voice | microbrowser | micromessenger | messenger	OPTIONAL

SimpleCol

The SimpleCol tag defines a column in a table.

Example

```
<SimpleResult>
   <SimpleContainer>
   <SimpleTable cellpadding="2" cellspacing="2" bgcolor="#00ff00">
      <SimpleTitle>Oracle</SimpleTitle>
      <SimpleTableHeader>
         <SimpleCol colspan="3" bgcolor="#ff0000" halign="center">
         <SimpleEm>Latest Stock Price</SimpleEm>
         </SimpleCol>
      </SimpleTableHeader>
      <SimpleTableBody>
      <SimpleRow>
         <SimpleCol halign="right">Symbol</SimpleCol>
         <SimpleCol halign="right">Price</SimpleCol>
         <SimpleCol halign="right">Change</SimpleCol>
      </SimpleRow>
      <SimpleRow>
         <SimpleCol halign="right"><SimpleStrong>ORCL</SimpleStrong>
         </SimpleCol>
         <SimpleCol halign="right"><SimpleStrong>12.52</SimpleStrong>
         </SimpleCol>
         <SimpleCol halign="right"><SimpleStrong>-0.33</SimpleStrong>
         </SimpleCol>
      </SimpleRow>
      <SimpleRow>
         <SimpleCol halign="right">Date</SimpleCol>
         <SimpleCol halign="right">Volume</SimpleCol>
         <SimpleCol halign="right">Previous</SimpleCol>
      </SimpleRow>
      <SimpleRow>
         <SimpleCol halign="right">
            <SimpleStrong>3/25/2002</SimpleStrong>
         </SimpleCol>
         <SimpleCol halign="right">
            <SimpleStrong>30,843,100</SimpleStrong>
         </SimpleCol>
         <SimpleCol halign="right">
            <SimpleStrong>12.85</SimpleStrong>
         </SimpleCol>
      </SimpleRow>
      <SimpleRow>
         <SimpleCol colspan="3" halign="center">
         <SimpleImage alt="[ORCL 1-yr chart]"
          src="http://localhost/oramobile/orcl.gif"
```

```
          addImageExtension="false" />
         </SimpleCol>
      </SimpleRow>
      </SimpleTableBody>
   </SimpleTable>
   </SimpleContainer>
</SimpleResult>
```

Here are a few items to note:

- The content is displayed in a tabular format on devices that support tables.
- The SimpleEm tag is emphasized in bold text on some devices and italicized text on others.
- On devices that do not support the GIF image, the alternate (ALT) text is displayed instead. The developer can create multiple formats, such as WBMP, PNG, JPG, and so on, make them available to the server, and let it add the image extensions automatically based on what each mobile device supports.

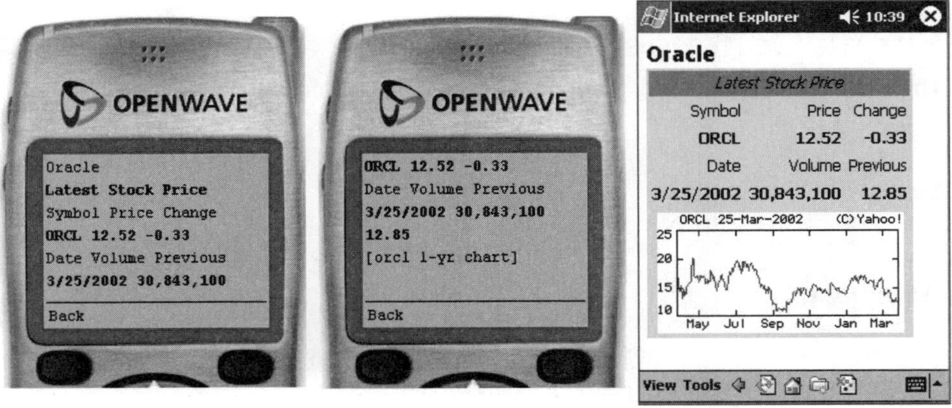

Attributes

Attribute	Description	Value(s)	Default Value
bgcolor	Background color	CDATA	OPTIONAL
bordercolor	Border color	CDATA	OPTIONAL
colspan	Column span	CDATA	OPTIONAL

Attribute	Description	Value(s)	Default Value
deviceclass	This tag is interpreted only for the specified device class. The server will transform this element only for devices belonging to the specified device class. Values can be a combination of values. If not specified, the tag is interpreted for all devices.	pdabrowser | pcbrowser | voice | microbrowser | micromessenger | messenger	OPTIONAL
halign	Horizontal alignment	left | center | right	left OPTIONAL
height	Cell height	CDATA	OPTIONAL
rowspan	Row span	CDATA	OPTIONAL
valign	Vertical alignment	top | center | bottom	top OPTIONAL
width	Cell width	CDATA	OPTIONAL
wrapmode	Text wrap mode	wrap | nowrap	wrap OPTIONAL

SimpleContainer

The SimpleContainer tag is the root element that contains all major block constructs, such as form, menu, and text.

Example

See the sample usage for the SimpleCol tag.

Attributes

Attribute	Description	Value(s)	Default Value
deviceclass	This tag is interpreted only for the specified device class. The server will transform this element only for devices belonging to the specified device class. Values can be a combination of values. If not specified, the tag is interpreted for all devices.	pdabrowser | pcbrowser | voice | microbrowser | micromessenger | messenger	OPTIONAL
id	The ID attribute of the element. Used for navigation within an XML response (target="#ID")	CDATA	OPTIONAL

SimpleDisconnect

The SimpleDisconnect tag disconnects a connection-oriented device such as a voice browser.

Example

See the sample usage for the SimpleMenu tag.

Attributes

Attribute	Description	Value(s)	Default Value
deviceclass	This tag is interpreted only for the specified device class. The server will transform this element only for devices belonging to the specified device class. Values can be a combination of values. If not specified, the tag is interpreted for all devices.	pdabrowser | pcbrowser | voice | microbrowser | micromessenger | messenger	OPTIONAL

SimpleDisplay

The SimpleDisplay tag supports all the rendering characteristics of SimpleBind (using SimpleTextItem). SimpleTextItem, a child SimpleDisplay, contains the actual rendering and display content. It is useful in two different cases: First, it provides an audible feedback (text-to-speech for the text content) for a voice device. Second, it renders the text for SimpleMenuItem when SimpleBind contains a menu (SimpleMenu tag) as a child.

Example

See the sample usage for the SimpleBind tag.

Attributes

Attribute	Description	Value(s)	Default Value
deviceclass	This tag is interpreted only for the specified device class. The server will transform this element only for devices belonging to the specified device class. Values can be a combination of values. If not specified, the tag is interpreted for all devices.	pdabrowser | pcbrowser | voice | microbrowser | micromessenger | messenger	OPTIONAL

SimpleDTMF

The SimpleDTMF tag specifies a VoiceXML DTMF grammar. DTMF grammar can be used to indicate a syntax such as the following:

```
1 {San Francisco} | 2 {Wash. DC} | 3 {New York}
```

If the syntax information is stored in a remote server, the src attribute can be used to specify the URL of the DTMF syntax file.

Example

See the sample usage for the SimpleMenu tag.

Attributes

Attribute	Description	Value(s)	Default Value
deviceclass	This tag is applicable for voice devices only. Will not be supported on other devices even if specified.	voice	OPTIONAL
scope	VoiceXML scope. The default scope of the grammar in Form/ Menu/Text/Grammar/ DTMF. If the scope is set to document, the grammar is active in the entire document.	document | dialog	OPTIONAL
src	The URL to the resource file where the DTMF and grammar is stored.	CDATA	OPTIONAL
type	The MIME type of the grammar. Represents the Grammar format and is applicable to both the remote URL Grammar file or inline Grammar text.	CDATA	OPTIONAL

SimpleEm

The SimpleEm tag displays the text or audio with emphasis. Text is usually displayed as italicized text.

Example

See the sample usage for the SimpleCol tag.

Attributes

<table>
<tr><th>Attribute</th><th>Description</th><th>Value(s)</th><th>Default Value</th></tr>
<tr><td>deviceclass</td><td>This tag is interpreted only for the specified device class. The server will transform this element only for devices belonging to the specified device class. Values can be a combination of values. If not specified, the tag is interpreted for all devices.</td><td>pdabrowser | pcbrowser | voice | microbrowser | micromessenger | messenger</td><td>OPTIONAL</td></tr>
<tr><td>level</td><td>Voice-only attribute. Indicates the level of emphasis.</td><td>strong | moderate | none | reduced</td><td>moderate</td></tr>
</table>

SimpleEvent

The SimpleEvent tag describes the possible events that would trigger a bind action. It also allows you to take advantage of device-specific event handlers and define actions that can be triggered on such events. The type attribute identifies the device-specific events. For voice applications, you can use events such as noinput, cancel, and so on. For WML, you can use events such as onenterforward, onpick, and so on.

Example

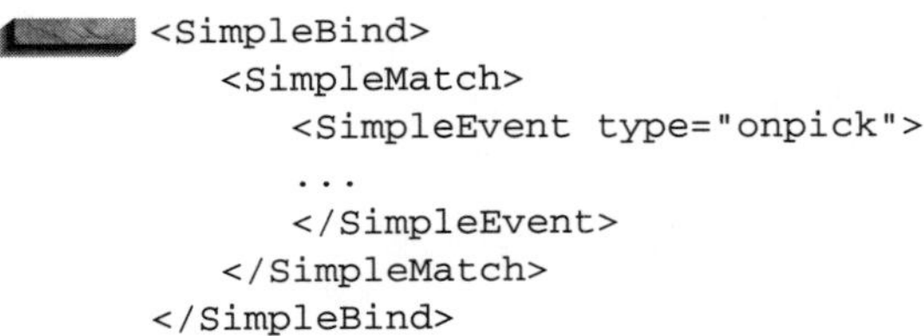

```
<SimpleBind>
   <SimpleMatch>
      <SimpleEvent type="onpick">
      ...
      </SimpleEvent>
   </SimpleMatch>
</SimpleBind>
```

Attributes

Attribute	Description	Value(s)	Default Value
type	Predefined device-level events. Possible values for voice include cancel, error, exit, help, noinput, nomatch, and telephone.disconnect. Possible values for WAP devices include onpick, onenterforward, and so on.	CDATA	REQUIRED

Attribute	Description	Value(s)	Default Value
count	Applicable to voice events only. This is the occurrence of the event (the default is 1). The count allows you to handle different occurrences of the same event differently. The form or menu, where SimpleCatch can occur, maintains a counter for each event that occurs while it is being visited. These counters are reset each time the form or menu is reentered.	Positive Int	1
deviceclass	This tag is interpreted only for the specified device class. The server will transform this element only for devices belonging to the specified device class. Values can be a combination of values. If not specified, the tag is interpreted for all devices.	pdabrowser | pcbrowser | voice | microbrowser | micromessenger | messenger	OPTIONAL

SimpleExit

The SimpleExit tag performs an application exit.

Example

```
<SimpleCatch type="exit">
   <SimpleAudio src="exit.wav">Goodbye!
   </SimpleAudio>
   <SimpleExit />
</SimpleCatch>
```

Attributes

Attribute	Description	Value(s)	Default Value
deviceclass	This tag is interpreted only for the specified device class. The server will transform this element only for devices belonging to the specified device class. Values can be a combination of values. If not specified, the tag is interpreted for all devices.	pdabrowser | pcbrowser | voice | microbrowser | micromessenger | messenger	OPTIONAL

SimpleFinish

The SimpleFinish tag indicates the finish event (voice only). This can be any event that completes a user task, such as reaching the end of the form field inputs on voice devices.

Example

```
<SimpleResult>
   <SimpleContainer>
      <SimpleForm target="tipcalc.jsp">
         <SimpleFormItem name="howmuch" type="currency">
            <SimpleTitle>How much is the bill? </SimpleTitle>
            <SimpleCatch type="help">
            Help. Say the amount of the bill in dollars and cents.
            For example, twenty-five dollars and ten cents
            </SimpleCatch>
         </SimpleFormItem>
         <SimpleFinish />
      </SimpleForm>
   </SimpleContainer>
</SimpleResult>
```

Attributes

Attribute	Description	Value(s)	Default Value
deviceclass	This tag is interpreted only for the specified device class. The server will transform this element only for devices belonging to the specified device class. Values can be a combination of values. If not specified, the tag is interpreted for all devices.	pdabrowser | pcbrowser | voice | microbrowser | micromessenger | messenger	OPTIONAL

SimpleForm

The SimpleForm tag is used for displaying one or more input fields. The fields are presented using the SimpleFormItem and SimpleFormSelect tags. If SimpleTitle is specified as a child, the title of the form will also appear.

Example

```
<SimpleResult>
   <SimpleContainer>
   <SimpleForm name="forminfo" target="process_form.jsp">
   <SimpleTitle>Form Example</SimpleTitle>
   <SimpleFormSelect name="cb" displaymode="checkbox" multiple="true">
      <SimpleTitle>Check Boxes:</SimpleTitle>
```

```
      <SimpleFormOption value="1">CB 1</SimpleFormOption>
      <SimpleFormOption value="2">CB 2</SimpleFormOption>
      <SimpleFormOption value="3">CB 3</SimpleFormOption>
   </SimpleFormSelect>
   <SimpleFormSelect name="rb" displaymode="checkbox">
      <SimpleTitle>Radio Buttons:</SimpleTitle>
      <SimpleFormOption value="1">RB 1</SimpleFormOption>
      <SimpleFormOption value="2">RB 2</SimpleFormOption>
   </SimpleFormSelect>
   <SimpleFormSelect name="select" displaymode="list">
      <SimpleTitle>Selections:</SimpleTitle>
      <SimpleFormOption value="London">London, England
      </SimpleFormOption>
      <SimpleFormOption value="Paris">Paris, France
      </SimpleFormOption>
      <SimpleFormOption value="Redwood_Shores">Redwood Shores, CA
      </SimpleFormOption>
      <SimpleFormOption value="NewYork_NY">New York, NY
      </SimpleFormOption>
   </SimpleFormSelect>
   <SimpleFormItem name="fi" default="please enter a value...">
      Form Input:
   </SimpleFormItem>
   </SimpleForm>
   </SimpleContainer>
</SimpleResult>
```

Here are a couple of items to note:

- On older WAP devices, each form input is displayed on a per-card basis. On newer WAP devices, forms are displayed in a single card.
- The rendering of check boxes and radio buttons is done nicely for PocketPC and newer WAP devices.

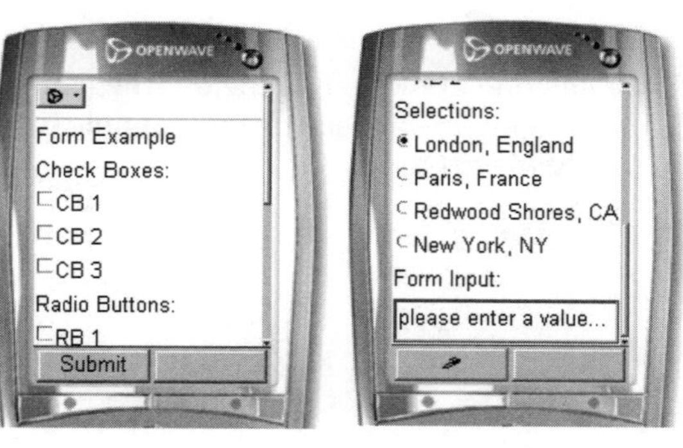

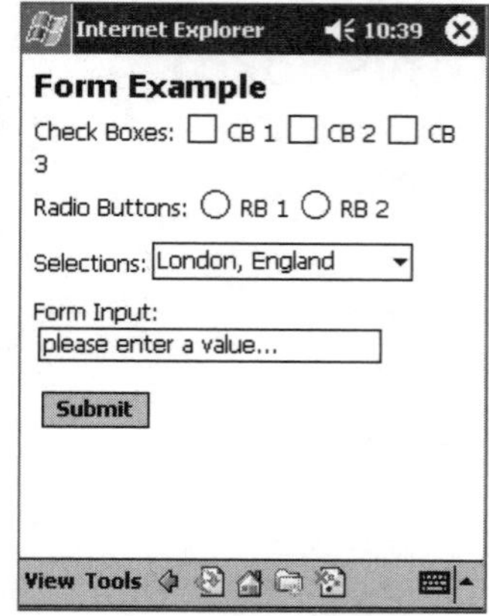

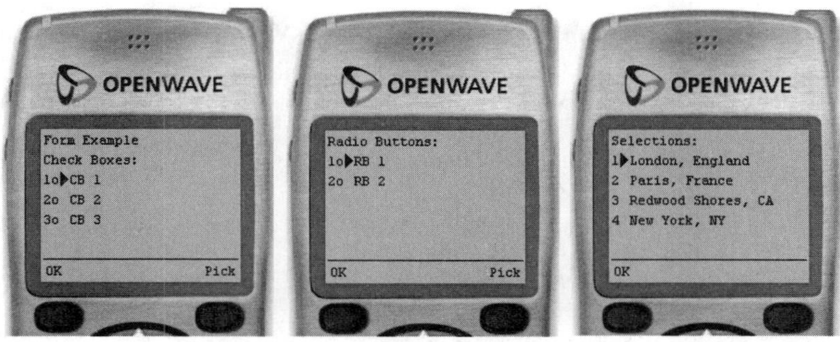

Attributes

Attribute	Description	Value(s)	Default Value
callbackurl	Oracle9*i*AS Wireless module support. Indicates the URL to return back if the current action calls an Oracle9*i*AS Wireless module.	CDATA	OPTIONAL
callbackparam	Oracle9*i*AS Wireless module support. Indicates the return parameters of callbackurl. When the module returns the context back to the callee application, callbackparam is passed back for the callee to construct its application state.	CDATA	OPTIONAL
callbacksecure	Oracle9*i*AS Wireless module support. Indicates the mode of communication, when callback occurs, between the Oracle9*i*AS Wireless server and the mobile device (not the remote service).	true | false	OPTIONAL
deviceclass	This tag is interpreted only for the specified device class. The server will transform this element only for devices belonging to the specified device class. Values can be a combination of values. If not specified, the tag is interpreted for all devices.	pdabrowser | pcbrowser | voice | microbrowser | micromessenger | messenger	OPTIONAL
fetchaudio	Voice-only attribute. This is the URL of an audio clip to play while the target is being fetched.	CDATA	OPTIONAL
id	The ID attribute of the element. Used for navigation within an XML response (target="#ID").	CDATA	OPTIONAL

Attribute	Description	Value(s)	Default Value
layout	The control layout of a form in small-screen devices. Indicates whether the form input fields should be displayed in a sequence of fields (cards) and whether there should be an enclosing page with all input field listed, thus allowing the user to select the field in an arbitrary fashion.	linear | tabular	linear OPTIONAL
method	The HTTP method get or post.	get | post	get OPTIONAL
mimetype	The MIME type of the target URL. If the target MIME type is not text/vnd.oracle.mobilexml, the Oracle9*i*AS Wireless server will not rewrite the URL.	CDATA	text/vnd.oracle.mobilexml OPTIONAL
secure	Indicates the mode of communication, when callback occurs, between the Oracle9*i*AS Wireless server and the device (not the remote service).	true | false	OPTIONAL
scope	VoiceXML scope. The default scope of the grammar in Form/Menu/Text/Grammar/DTMF. If the scope is set to document, the grammar is active in the entire document.	document | dialog	OPTIONAL
static_target	The URL to navigate to when an action is activated. The server never rewrites this URL. If it exists, this will override the target attribute. Also supports "callto:" for phone calls and "mailto:" for e-mail support.	CDATA	OPTIONAL
target	The URL to navigate to when an action is activated. This URL is rewritten by the server to point back to the Oracle9*i*AS Wireless server when the mimetype attribute is text/vnd.oracle.mobilexml. Also supports "callto:" for phone calls and "mailto:" for e-mail support.	CDATA	OPTIONAL

SimpleFormItem

The SimpleFormItem tag is used for obtaining input(s) from a user. This tag presents a prompt and waits for input from the user. The content of this tag also specifies the default values for the form item.

Example

See the sample usage for the SimpleForm tag.

Attributes

Attribute	Description	Value(s)	Default Value
name	The input field name.	CDATA	REQUIRED
type	Indicates the data types—boolean, digits, and so on. For backward compatibility, type will also accept displaymode attribute values (text | textarea | password).	none | audio | boolean | currency | date | digits | number | phone | time | transfer	REQUIRED
beep	VoiceXML beep. If this attribute is true, a tone is emitted just prior to transcription. Used when type="audio".	true | false	false OPTIONAL
bridge	VoiceXML bridge. Valid only when type="transfer". If this attribute is true, it allows the original caller to resume the current session, once the transfer/third-party call is complete.	true | false	false OPTIONAL
cols	The number of rows if displaymode is textarea.	Positive Int	OPTIONAL
connecttimeout	The VoiceXML connect timeout. Valid only when type="transfer". The time to wait while trying to connect the call before returning the noanswer condition. The default is specific to a voice gateway platform.	CDATA	OPTIONAL
dest	VoiceXML destination. Valid only when type="transfer". Specifies the phone number to transfer the call to.	CDATA	OPTIONAL

Attribute	Description	Value(s)	Default Value
deviceclass	This tag is interpreted only for the specified device class. The server will transform this element only for devices belonging to the specified device class. Values can be a combination of values. If not specified, the tag is interpreted for all devices.	pdabrowser | pcbrowser | voice | microbrowser | micromessenger | messenger	OPTIONAL
displaymode	Used to specify the display characteristics of the field, such as noecho (password), textarea, and so on.	text | textarea | noecho | hidden	text OPTIONAL
dtmfterm	VoiceXML DTMF termination. If this attribute is true, a DTMF keypress terminates the transcription.	true | false	false OPTIONAL
enctype	VoiceXML encoding type. The MIME-encoding type of the submitted document. Used when type="audio" to indicate the format of the recording requested.	CDATA	OPTIONAL
finalsilence	VoiceXML final silence. The interval of silence that indicates the end of speech	CDATA	OPTIONAL
format	A WML/HDML format attribute.	CDATA	OPTIONAL
mandatory	Specifies whether input is mandatory.	yes | no	no OPTIONAL
maxlength	The maximum length of the field.	Positive Int	OPTIONAL
maxtime	VoiceXML maximum time. Valid only when the type="transfer" and bridge="true". The time that the call is allowed to last, or 0 if it can last arbitrarily long.	CDATA	0 OPTIONAL
modal	The VoiceXML modal. If this is true, all higher-level speech and DTMF grammars are turned off while making the transcription. If this attribute is false, the grammar is scoped to the form item/select.	true | false	true OPTIONAL

Attribute	Description	Value(s)	Default Value
rows	The number of rows if displaymode is textarea.	Positive Int	OPTIONAL
size	The display size of the input field.	CDATA	OPTIONAL
slot	The VoiceXML slot. The input's grammar slot values are assigned to the corresponding field item variables. This allows the user to say one sentence and fill more than one form field.	CDATA	OPTIONAL
value	The default value (the defaultvalue attribute is also supported for backward compatibility).	CDATA	OPTIONAL

SimpleFormOption

The SimpleFormOption tag provides a predefined list of values for a form item. This tag is an item in a selectable menu. The content of this tag specifies the default values for the form item (the value attribute is required especially in voice). SimpleTextItem is used to render rich text (radio buttons and check boxes). If SimpleTextItem does not exist, the value attribute is rendered.

Example

See the sample usage for the SimpleForm tag.

Attributes

Attribute	Description	Value(s)	Default Value
value	The value of the select variable when this form item is selected.	CDATA	REQUIRED
deviceclass	This tag is interpreted only for the specified device class. The server will transform this element only for devices belonging to the specified device class. Values can be a combination of values. If not specified, the tag is interpreted for all devices.	pdabrowser | pcbrowser | voice | microbrowser | micromessenger | messenger	OPTIONAL

Attribute	Description	Value(s)	Default Value
dtmf	A digit to be pressed on a phone or DTMF tone. The dtmf attribute just takes one value (a simplified form of the voice SimpleDTMF tag). This attribute will work on WAP devices, if supported by the device.	CDATA	OPTIONAL
selected	The option selected by default (same semantics as the HTML selected tag).	true | false	false OPTIONAL

SimpleFormSelect

The SimpleFormSelect tag displays a selection using an option list, check boxes, or radio buttons.

Example

See the sample usage for the SimpleForm tag.

Attributes

Attribute	Description	Value(s)	Default Value
name	The name of the select field.	CDATA	REQUIRED
autoprompt	The VoiceXML auto prompt. Tells the voice browser not to perform an auto prompt. This is valid in menu and form Select tags. If this attribute is set to false, the voice browser will not list the items in the menu/select. This attribute is typically set to false if you need to use an audio file (listing all the menus, rather than using the TTS of the voice gateway).	true | false	true OPTIONAL
deviceclass	This tag is interpreted only for the specified device class. The server will transform this element only for devices belonging to the specified device class. Values can be a combination of values. If not specified, the tag is interpreted for all devices.	pdabrowser | pcbrowser | voice | microbrowser | micromessenger | messenger	OPTIONAL

Attribute	Description	Value(s)	Default Value
displaymode	Used to specify the display characteristics of the field, such as noecho (password), textarea, and so on.	text | textarea | noecho | hidden	text
modal	The VoiceXML modal. If this is true, all higher-level speech and DTMF grammars are turned off while making the transcription. If this attribute is false, the grammar is scoped to the form item/select.	true | false	true OPTIONAL
multiple	Used to support multiple selects.	true | false	false OPTIONAL
size	The display size of the input field.	CDATA	OPTIONAL
slot	The VoiceXML slot. The input's grammar slot values are assigned to the corresponding field item variables. This allows the user to say one sentence and fill more than one form field.	CDATA	OPTIONAL

SimpleGo

The SimpleGo tag defines the "go" task. Go is one of the many possible tasks of a bind operation (SimpleBind) and is defined as a child of SimpleTask. SimpleGo is an empty tag (no child tags).

Example

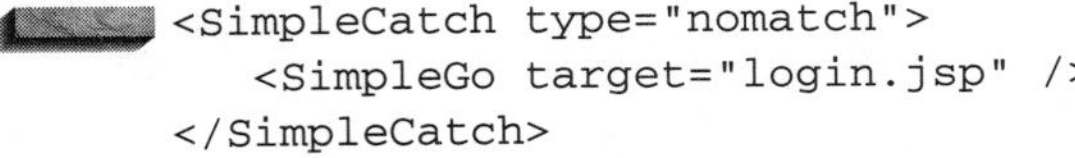

```
<SimpleCatch type="nomatch">
   <SimpleGo target="login.jsp" />
</SimpleCatch>
```

Attributes

Attribute	Description	Value(s)	Default Value
callbackurl	Oracle9*i*AS Wireless module support. Indicates the URL to return back if the current action calls an Oracle9*i*AS Wireless module.	CDATA	OPTIONAL

Attribute	Description	Value(s)	Default Value
callbackparam	Oracle9*i*AS Wireless module support. Indicates the return parameters of callbackurl. When the module returns the context back to the callee application, callbackparam is passed back for the callee to construct its application state.	CDATA	OPTIONAL
callbacksecure	Oracle9*i*AS Wireless module support. Indicates the mode of communication, when callback occurs, between the Oracle9*i*AS Wireless server and the mobile device (not the remote service).	true I false	OPTIONAL
deviceclass	This tag is interpreted only for the specified device class. The server will transform this element only for devices belonging to the specified device class. Values can be a combination of values. If not specified, the tag is interpreted for all devices.	pdabrowser I pcbrowser I voice I microbrowser I micromessenger I messenger	OPTIONAL
fetchaudio	Voice-only attribute. The URL of an audio clip to play while the target is being fetched.	CDATA	OPTIONAL
mimetype	The MIME type of the target URL. If the target MIME type is not text/vnd.oracle.mobilexml, the Oracle9*i*AS Wireless server will not rewrite the URL.	CDATA	text/vnd.oracle. mobilexml OPTIONAL
secure	Indicates the mode of communication, when callback occurs, between the Oracle9*i*AS Wireless server and the device (not the remote service).	true I false	OPTIONAL
static_target	The URL to navigate to when an action is activated. The server never rewrites this URL. If this attribute exists, it will override the target attribute. Also supports "callto:" for phone calls and "mailto:" for e-mail support.	CDATA	OPTIONAL

Attribute	Description	Value(s)	Default Value
target	The URL to navigate to when an action is activated. This URL is rewritten by the server to point back to the Oracle9*i*AS Wireless server when the mimetype attribute is text/vnd.oracle.mobilexml. Also supports "callto:" for phone calls and "mailto:" for e-mail support.	CDATA	OPTIONAL

SimpleGrammar

The SimpleGrammar tag provides the voice grammar for the enclosing item, such as *SimpleMenuItem*. For example, for a *SimpleMenuItem* tag with the enclosing text "Oracle9i AS Wireless," the voice engine would say "your options are Oracle9i AS Wireless." Use SimpleGrammar for voice if you want to invoke this menu item when the user says "'Oracle' | 'Oracle9i' | '9i' | 'Wireless.'"

Example

See the sample usage for the SimpleMenu tag.

Attributes

Attribute	Description	Value(s)	Default Value
deviceclass	This tag is applicable for voice devices only. Will not be supported on other devices even if specified.	voice	OPTIONAL
scope	The VoiceXML scope. The default scope of the grammar in Form/Menu/Text/Grammar/DTMF. If the scope is set to document, the grammar is active in the entire document.	document | dialog	OPTIONAL
src	The URL to the resource file where the DTMF and grammar is stored.	CDATA	OPTIONAL
type	The MIME type of the grammar. Represents the grammar format and is applicable to both the remote URL grammar file or inline grammar text.	CDATA	OPTIONAL

SimpleHelp

The SimpleHelp tag is used to display help information (text only) for a field. Used by PDA-style devices to display help text for the form item and Select tag. In voice, SimpleCatch with *type*="help" is used instead.

Example

See the sample usage for the SimpleTextField tag.

Attributes

Attribute	Description	Value(s)	Default Value
color	The color of the help text (HTML).	CDATA	OPTIONAL
deviceclass	This tag is interpreted only for the specified device class. The server will transform this element only for devices belonging to the specified device class. Values can be a combination of values. If not specified, the tag is interpreted for all devices.	pdabrowser | pcbrowser | voice | microbrowser | micromessenger | messenger	OPTIONAL
font	The font of the help text (HTML).	CDATA	OPTIONAL
size	The font size of the help text (HTML).	CDATA	OPTIONAL
wrapmode	The text-wrap mode.	wrap | nowrap	wrap OPTIONAL

SimpleHref

The SimpleHref tag specifies a hyperlink. It's normally used to make a phone call or send an e-mail on devices that support it.

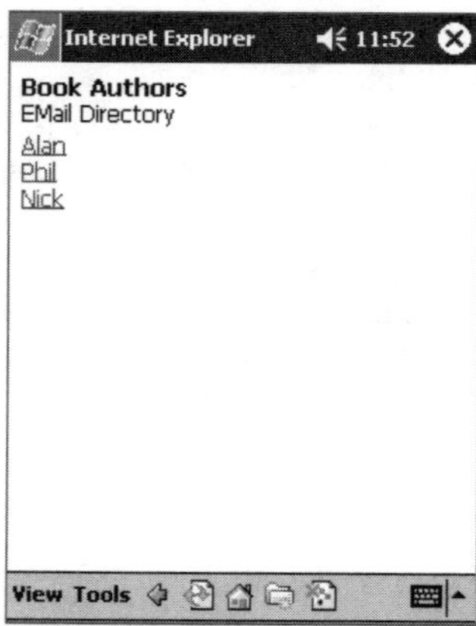

Example

```
<SimpleResult>
   <SimpleContainer>
   <SimpleText>
      <SimpleTextItem>
      <SimpleStrong>Book Authors</SimpleStrong>
      <SimpleBreak/>
      EMail Directory
      </SimpleTextItem>
      <SimpleTextItem>
      <SimpleHref static_target="mailto:oramobile@yahoo.com">Alan
      </SimpleHref>
      <SimpleBreak/>
      <SimpleHref static_target="mailto:oramobile@yahoo.com">Phil
      </SimpleHref>
      <SimpleBreak/>
      <SimpleHref static_target="mailto:oramobile@yahoo.com">Nick
      </SimpleHref>
      <SimpleBreak/>
      </SimpleTextItem>
   </SimpleText>
   </SimpleContainer>
</SimpleResult>
```

Attributes

Attribute	Description	Value(s)	Default Value
addImageExtension	Allows the server to use the right image format from a list of available formats. The server will pick the right image to be used based on the available images (see the "available" attribute) and device browser capability.	true | false	true OPTIONAL
available	The application can specify a list of available image formats in an order of preference (for example, "jpg gif g2.gif wbmp bmp"). Note that g2.gif indicates a grayscale depth 2 image, for devices such as the Palm.	CDATA	OPTIONAL

Attribute	Description	Value(s)	Default Value
callbackurl	Oracle9*i*AS Wireless module support. Indicates the URL to return back if the current action calls an Oracle9*i*AS Wireless module.	CDATA	OPTIONAL
callbackparam	Oracle9*i*AS Wireless module support. Indicates the return parameters of callbackurl. When the module returns the context back to the callee application, callbackparam is passed back for the callee to construct its application state.	CDATA	OPTIONAL
callbacksecure	Oracle9*i*AS Wireless module support. Indicates the mode of communication, when callback occurs, between the Oracle9*i*AS Wireless server and the mobile device (not the remote service).	true | false	OPTIONAL
deviceclass	This tag is interpreted only for the specified device class. The server will transform this element only for devices belonging to the specified device class. Values can be a combination of values. If not specified, the tag is interpreted for all devices.	pdabrowser | pcbrowser | voice | microbrowser | micromessenger | messenger	OPTIONAL
dtmf	A digit to be pressed on a phone or DTMF tone. The dtmf attribute just takes one value (a simplified form of the voice SimpleDTMF tag). Will work on WAP devices, if supported by the device.	CDATA	OPTIONAL
fetchaudio	Voice-only attribute. This is the URL of an audio clip to play while the target is being fetched.	CDATA	OPTIONAL

Attribute	**Description**	**Value(s)**	**Default Value**
label	The label for an action button, displayed when an action is bound to a button on a visual device.	CDATA	OPTIONAL
mimetype	The MIME type of the target URL. If the target MIME type is not text/vnd.oracle.mobilexml, the Oracle9*i*AS Wireless server will not rewrite the URL.	CDATA	text/vnd.oracle.mobilexml OPTIONAL
secure	Indicates the mode of communication, when callback occurs, between the Oracle9*i*AS Wireless server and the device (not the remote service).	true | false	OPTIONAL
src	The URL of an image to be displayed. (In SimpleAction/Href, this image needs to be used instead of the label.)	CDATA	OPTIONAL
static_target	The URL to navigate to when an action is activated. The server never rewrites this URL. If this attribute exists, it will override the target attribute. Also supports "callto:" for phone calls and "mailto:" for e-mail support.	CDATA	OPTIONAL
target	The URL to navigate to when an action is activated. This URL is rewritten by the server to point back to the Oracle9*i*AS Wireless server when the mimetype attribute is text/vnd.oracle.mobilexml. Also supports "callto:" for phone calls and "mailto:" for e-mail support.	CDATA	OPTIONAL

SimpleImage

The SimpleImage tag specifies an image. Currently, the URL to the image has to be a complete URL instead of a relative URL.

Example

See the sample usage for the SimpleCol tag.

Attributes

Attribute	Description	Value(s)	Default Value
addImageExtension	Allows the server to use the right image format from a list of available formats. The server will pick the right image to be used based on the available images (see the "available" attribute) and device browser capability.	true | false	true OPTIONAL
alt	An alternate text string to be displayed if the image is not found.	CDATA	OPTIONAL
available	The application can specify a list of available image formats in an order of preference (for example, "jpg gif g2.gif wbmp bmp"). Note that g2.gif indicates a grayscale depth 2 image, for devices such as a Palm.	CDATA	OPTIONAL
border	The width of the border around the image.	CDATA	OPTIONAL
deviceclass	This tag is interpreted only for the specified device class. The server will transform this element only for devices belonging to the specified device class. Values can be a combination of values. If not specified, the tag is interpreted for all devices.	pdabrowser | pcbrowser | voice | microbrowser | micromessenger | messenger	OPTIONAL
halign	The horizontal alignment of the image.	left | center | right	left OPTIONAL

Attribute	Description	Value(s)	Default Value
height	The height of the image.	CDATA	OPTIONAL
hspace	The horizontal spacing of the image.	CDATA	OPTIONAL
src	The URL of an image to be displayed. (In SimpleAction/ Href, this image needs to be used instead of the label.)	CDATA	OPTIONAL
valign	The vertical alignment of the image.	top | center | bottom	top OPTIONAL
vspace	The vertical spacing of the image.	CDATA	OPTIONAL
width	The width of the image.	CDATA	OPTIONAL

SimpleKey

The SimpleKey tag defines the device key for the bind operation. SimpleKey, like SimpleAction, has a type attribute that identifies the *key* on a device for the bind operation.

Example

See the sample usage for the SimpleBind tag.

Attributes

Attribute	Description	Value(s)	Default Value
type	Defines the type of binding in the target device. Here, "primary" and "secondary" map to the primary and secondary keys, respectively. The following types are also supported by the transformers for backward compatibility: accept | soft1 | option1 | option2.	primary | secondary	REQUIRED
deviceclass	This tag is interpreted only for the specified device class. The server will transform this element only for devices belonging to the specified device class. Values can be a combination of values. If not specified, the tag is interpreted for all devices.	pdabrowser | pcbrowser | voice | microbrowser | micromessenger | messenger	OPTIONAL

SimpleMatch

A bind operation (SimpleBind) can be triggered by various actions, such as pressing a key, triggering an event, or saying a key word (voice). Each of these actions are indicated by separate tags. The SimpleMatch tag is the container tag for all such possible bind invocation tags.

Example

See the sample usage for the SimpleBind tag.

Attributes

Attribute	Description	Value(s)	Default Value
deviceclass	This tag is interpreted only for the specified device class. The server will transform this element only for devices belonging to the specified device class. Values can be a combination of values. If not specified, the tag is interpreted for all devices.	pdabrowser | pcbrowser | voice | microbrowser | micromessenger | messenger	OPTIONAL

SimpleMenu

The SimpleMenu tag represents a single menu with selectable links that are defined by the children SimpleMenuItem tags.

Example

```
<SimpleResult>
   <SimpleMeta http-equiv="refresh" content="60" />
   <SimpleContainer>
      <SimpleMenu title="Mobile Tag Examples" mode="nowrap"
      deviceclass="pdabrowser pcbrowser microbrowser micromessenger
      messenger">
      <SimpleMenuItem target="simpleaction.jsp">Action
      </SimpleMenuItem>
      <SimpleMenuItem target="simpleaudio.jsp">Audio
      </SimpleMenuItem>
      <SimpleMenuItem target="simplebind.jsp">Bind
      </SimpleMenuItem>
      <SimpleMenuItem target="simplebreak.jsp">Break
      </SimpleMenuItem>
```

```
<SimpleMenuItem target="simpletable.jsp">Table
</SimpleMenuItem>
<SimpleMenuItem target="simpleform.jsp">Form
</SimpleMenuItem>
</SimpleMenu>
<SimpleMenu deviceclass="voice" autoprompt="false">
<SimpleTitle>
   <SimpleAudio src="title.wav">Mobile Tag Examples
   </SimpleAudio>
</SimpleTitle>
<SimpleMenuItem target="simpleaction.jsp">Action
<SimpleGrammar>action{} | act{} | one{}</SimpleGrammar>
<SimpleDTMF>1</SimpleDTMF>
</SimpleMenuItem>
<SimpleMenuItem target="simpleaudio.jsp">Audio
<SimpleGrammar>audio{} | sound{} | two{}</</SimpleGrammar>
<SimpleDTMF>2</SimpleDTMF>
</SimpleMenuItem>
<SimpleMenuItem target="simplebind.jsp">Bind
<SimpleGrammar>bind{} | three{}</</SimpleGrammar>
<SimpleDTMF>3</SimpleDTMF>
</SimpleMenuItem>
<SimpleMenuItem target="simplebreak.jsp">Break
<SimpleGrammar>break{} | four{}</</SimpleGrammar>
<SimpleDTMF>4</SimpleDTMF>
</SimpleMenuItem>
<SimpleMenuItem target="simpletable.jsp">Table
<SimpleGrammar>table{} | row{} | column{} | five{}</</SimpleGrammar>
<SimpleDTMF>5</SimpleDTMF>
</SimpleMenuItem>
<SimpleMenuItem target="simpleform.jsp">Form
<SimpleGrammar>form{} | six{}</</SimpleGrammar>
<SimpleDTMF>6</SimpleDTMF>
</SimpleMenuItem>
<SimpleCatch type="nospeech">
   <SimpleAudio src="nospeech.wav">
   Please speak up. You may also say help.
   </SimpleAudio>
</SimpleCatch>
<SimpleCatch type="nomatch">
   <SimpleAudio src="nomatch.wav">
   I'm sorry, I did not understand you. Please say that again
   or say help.
   </SimpleAudio>
</SimpleCatch>
<SimpleCatch type="help">
```

```
        <SimpleAudio src="help.wav">
        Help. Mobile Tags. You may say action, audio, bind, break,
        table, or form.
        </SimpleAudio>
     </SimpleCatch>
     <SimpleCatch type="telephone.disconnect">
        <SimpleDisconnect />
     </SimpleCatch>
     <SimpleCatch type="exit">
        <SimpleAudio src="exit.wav">Goodbye!
        </SimpleAudio>
        <SimpleExit />
     </SimpleCatch>
  </SimpleMenu>
  </SimpleContainer>
</SimpleResult>
```

Here are a few items to note:

- On non-voice devices (deviceclass is microbrowser, pdabrowser, and so on), the menu is displayed as text only.
- On voice devices, the menu is always prompting and waiting for the end user to speak. The speech-recognition engine is waiting to interpret and act accordingly. The grammar will guide the speech-recognition engine, and the helper code (SimpleCatch) will provide an extra convenience to the end user.
- The voice user can also press the phone numbers using touchtone (SimpleDTMF) to select from the menu.

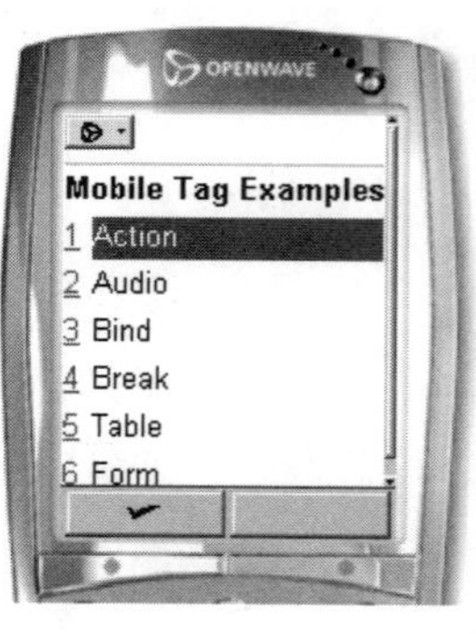

Attributes

Attribute	Description	Value(s)	Default Value
autoprompt	The VoiceXML auto prompt. Tells the voice browser not to perform an auto prompt. Valid in menu and form Select tags. If this attribute is set to false, the voice browser will not list the items in the menu/select. This is typically set to false if you need to use an audio file (listing all the menus, rather than using the TTS of the voice gateway).	true | false	true OPTIONAL
deviceclass	This tag is interpreted only for the specified device class. The server will transform this element only for devices belonging to the specified device class. Values can be a combination of values. If not specified, the tag is interpreted for all devices.	pdabrowser | pcbrowser | voice | microbrowser | micromessenger | messenger	OPTIONAL
id	The ID attribute of the element. Used for navigation within an XML response (target="#ID").	CDATA	OPTIONAL
scope	The VoiceXML scope. The default scope of the grammar in Form/ Menu/Text/Grammar/DTMF. If the scope is set to document, then the grammar is active in the entire document.	document | dialog	OPTIONAL
wrapmode	The text-wrap mode.	wrap | nowrap	wrap OPTIONAL

SimpleMenuItem

The SimpleMenuItem tag represents a single, selectable option in a menu defined by SimpleMenu.

Example

See the sample usage for the SimpleMenu tag.

Attributes

Attribute	Description	Value(s)	Default Value
callbackurl	Oracle9*i*AS Wireless module support. Indicates the URL to return back if the current action calls an Oracle9*i*AS Wireless module.	CDATA	OPTIONAL
callbackparam	Oracle9*i*AS Wireless module support. Indicates the return parameters of callbackurl. When the module returns the context back to the callee application, callbackparam is passed back for the callee to construct its application state.	CDATA	OPTIONAL
callbacksecure	Oracle9*i*AS Wireless module support. Indicates the mode of communication, when callback occurs, between the Oracle9*i*AS Wireless server and the mobile device (not the remote service).	true l false	OPTIONAL
deviceclass	This tag is interpreted only for the specified device class. The server will transform this element only for devices belonging to the specified device class. Values can be a combination of values. If not specified, the tag is interpreted for all devices.	pdabrowser l pcbrowser l voice l microbrowser l micromessenger l messenger	OPTIONAL
dtmf	A digit to be pressed on a phone or DTMF tone. The dtmf attribute just takes one value (a simplified form of the voice SimpleDTMF tag). Will work on WAP devices, if supported by the device.	CDATA	OPTIONAL
fetchaudio	Voice-only attribute. The URL of an audio clip to play while the target is being fetched.	CDATA	OPTIONAL
label	The label for an action button, displayed when an action is bound to a button on a visual device.	CDATA	OPTIONAL

Attribute	Description	Value(s)	Default Value
mimetype	The MIME type of the target URL. If the target MIME type is not text/vnd.oracle.mobilexml, the Oracle9*i*AS Wireless server will not rewrite the URL.	CDATA	text/vnd.oracle. mobilexml OPTIONAL
secure	Indicates the mode of communication, when callback occurs, between the Oracle9*i*AS Wireless server and the device (not the remote service).	true | false	OPTIONAL
separator	If defined, this attribute adds a visual separator after or before the menu item (like the "Windows" menu system).	before | after | none	none OPTIONAL
static_target	The URL to navigate to when an action is activated. The server never rewrites this URL. If this attribute exists, it will override the target attribute. Also supports "callto:" for phone calls and "mailto:" for e-mail support.	CDATA	OPTIONAL
target	The URL to navigate to when an action is activated. This URL is rewritten by the server to point back to the Oracle9*i*AS Wireless server when the mimetype attribute is text/vnd.oracle.mobilexml. Also supports "callto:" for phone calls and "mailto:" for e-mail support.	CDATA	OPTIONAL
wrapmode	The text-wrap mode.	wrap | nowrap	wrap OPTIONAL

SimpleMeta

The SimpleMeta tag defines all WML/HDML/HTML meta tags. The content is passed through to the target device.

Example

See the sample usage for the SimpleMenu tag.

Attributes

Attribute	Description	Value(s)	Default Value
content	The content of the emulated HTTP header or the associated content of the meta attribute "name".	CDATA	REQUIRED
http-equiv	The equivalent HTTP header you are emulating.	CDATA	REQUIRED
deviceclass	This tag is interpreted only for the specified device class. The server will transform this element only for devices belonging to the specified device class. Values can be a combination of values. If not specified, the tag is interpreted for all devices.	pdabrowser | pcbrowser | voice | microbrowser | micromessenger | messenger	OPTIONAL
name	A descriptive name of the meta attribute.	CDATA	OPTIONAL

SimpleMItem

SimpleMItem is an empty tag to indicate that the bind operation needs to be rendered as a menu item. This is only allowed when SimpleBind is a child of SimpleMenu.

Example

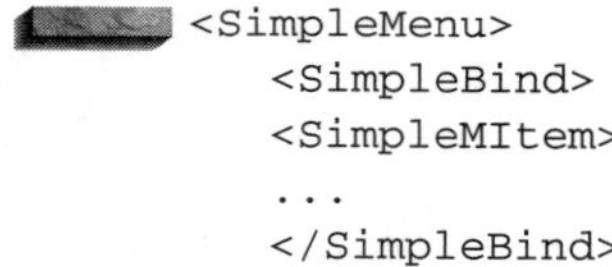

```
<SimpleMenu>
   <SimpleBind>
   <SimpleMItem>
   ...
   </SimpleBind>
</SimpleMenu>
```

Attributes

Attribute	Description	Value(s)	Default Value
deviceclass	This tag is interpreted only for the specified device class. The server will transform this element only for devices belonging to the specified device class. Values can be a combination of values. If not specified, the tag is interpreted for all devices.	pdabrowser | pcbrowser | voice | microbrowser | micromessenger | messenger	OPTIONAL

SimpleName

The SimpleName tag identifies client-side form field names. It is used to specify a list of client-side form fields that need to cleared. The SimpleName tag is useful in voice channel because the clearing of form fields leads to automatic reprompting by the voice browser.

Example

See the sample usage for the SimpleClear tag.

Attributes

Attribute	Description	Value(s)	Default Value
name	Name of Client side form field	CDATA	REQUIRED
deviceclass	This tag is interpreted only for the specified device class. The server will transform this element only for devices belonging to the specified device class. Values can be a combination of values. If not specified, the tag is interpreted for all devices.	pdabrowser | pcbrowser | voice | microbrowser | micromessenger | messenger	OPTIONAL

SimpleOptGroup

The SimpleOptGroup tag is used to group SimpleFormOption tags into a hierarchy. This provides support for small-screen devices, where a long list of options is not desirable.

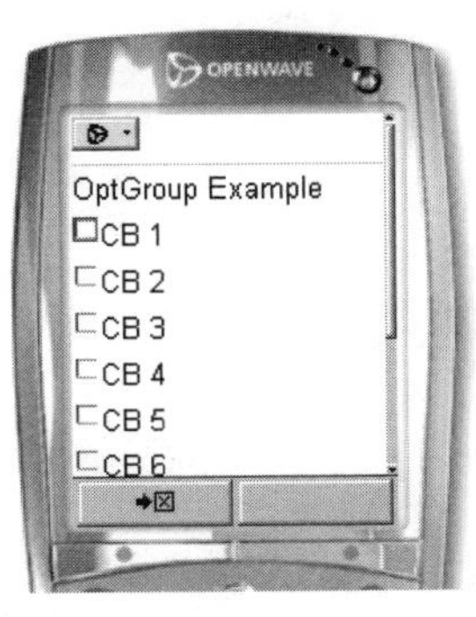

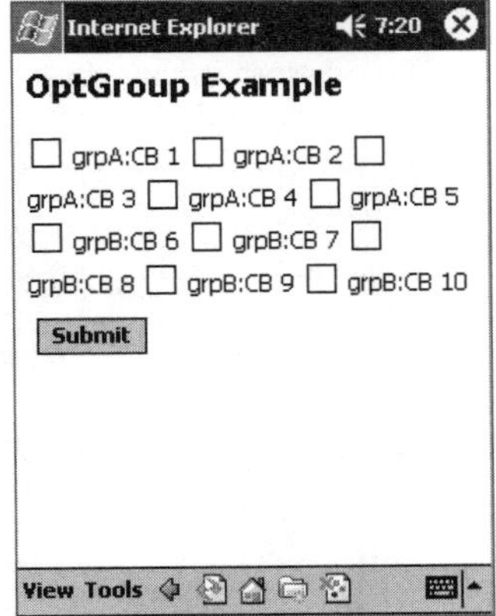

Example

```
<SimpleResult>
   <SimpleContainer>
   <SimpleForm name="forminfo" target="main.cfm">
      <SimpleTitle>OptGroup Example</SimpleTitle>
      <SimpleFormSelect name="cb" displaymode="checkbox" multiple="true">
      <SimpleBreak />
      <SimpleOptGroup label="grpA">
         <SimpleFormOption value="1">CB 1</SimpleFormOption>
         <SimpleFormOption value="2">CB 2</SimpleFormOption>
         <SimpleFormOption value="3">CB 3</SimpleFormOption>
         <SimpleFormOption value="4">CB 4</SimpleFormOption>
         <SimpleFormOption value="5">CB 5</SimpleFormOption>
      </SimpleOptGroup>
      <SimpleBreak />
         <SimpleOptGroup label="grpB">
         <SimpleFormOption value="6">CB 6</SimpleFormOption>
         <SimpleFormOption value="7">CB 7</SimpleFormOption>
         <SimpleFormOption value="8">CB 8</SimpleFormOption>
         <SimpleFormOption value="9">CB 9</SimpleFormOption>
         <SimpleFormOption value="10">CB 10</SimpleFormOption>
      </SimpleOptGroup>
      </SimpleOptGroup>
      </SimpleFormSelect>
   </SimpleForm>
   </SimpleContainer>
</SimpleResult>
```

Attributes

Attribute	Description	Value(s)	Default Value
label	For platforms that support hierarchical option lists, the label is displayed when navigating non-leaf nodes.	CDATA	REQUIRED
deviceclass	This tag is interpreted only for the specified device class. The server will transform this element only for devices belonging to the specified device class. Values can be a combination of values. If not specified, the tag is interpreted for all devices.	pdabrowser | pcbrowser | voice | microbrowser | micromessenger | messenger	OPTIONAL

SimplePrev

The SimplePrev tag is for the PREV (previous) functionality. It has SimpleGo as a child whose target attribute is the destination URL if PREV is not supported natively by the browser.

Example

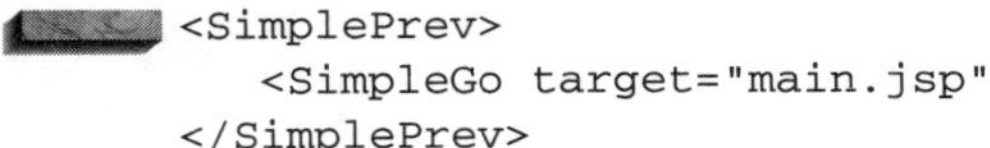

```
<SimplePrev>
   <SimpleGo target="main.jsp" />
</SimplePrev>
```

Attributes

Attribute	Description	Value(s)	Default Value
deviceclass	This tag is interpreted only for the specified device class. The server will transform this element only for devices belonging to the specified device class. Values can be a combination of values. If not specified, the tag is interpreted for all devices.	pdabrowser | pcbrowser | voice | microbrowser | micromessenger | messenger	OPTIONAL

SimpleProperty

The SimpleProperty tag allows you to set the VoiceXML engine properties.

Example

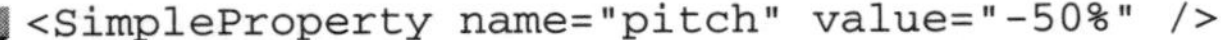

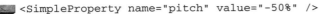

```
<SimpleProperty name="pitch" value="-50%" />
```

Attributes

Attribute	Description	Value(s)	Default Value
name	The name of the property.	CDATA	REQUIRED
value	The value of the property.	CDATA	REQUIRED
deviceclass	This tag is applicable for voice devices only. Will not be supported on other devices even if specified.	voice	OPTIONAL

SimpleRefresh

The SimpleRefresh tag performs a refresh of the device (if supported by the device).

Example

```
<SimpleResult>
   <SimpleContainer>
   <SimpleRefresh />
   <SimpleText>
      <SimpleTextItem>
      Welcome back!
      </SimpleTextItem>
   </SimpleText>
   </SimpleContainer>
</SimpleResult>
```

Attributes

Attribute	Description	Value(s)	Default Value
deviceclass	This tag is interpreted only for the specified device class. The server will transform this element only for devices belonging to the specified device class. Values can be a combination of values. If not specified, the tag is interpreted for all devices.	pdabrowser | pcbrowser | voice | microbrowser | micromessenger | messenger	OPTIONAL

SimpleReprompt

The SimpleReprompt tag explicitly reprompts the user for the field input. It's valid only in voice applications.

Example

```
<SimpleResult>
   <SimpleContainer>
      <SimpleForm target="tipcalc.jsp">
         <SimpleFormItem name="howmuch" type="currency">
            <SimpleTitle>How much is the bill? </SimpleTitle>
            <SimpleCatch type="help">
            Help. Say the amount of the bill in dollars and cents.
            For example, twenty-five dollars and ten cents
```

```
            <SimpleReprompt />
            </SimpleCatch>
         </SimpleFormItem>
      </SimpleForm>
   </SimpleContainer>
</SimpleResult>
```

Attributes

Attribute	Description	Value(s)	Default Value
deviceclass	This tag is applicable for voice devices only. Will not be supported on other devices even if specified.	voice	OPTIONAL

SimpleResult

The SimpleResult tag is the root tag of Oracle9*i*AS multichannel XML. SimpleResult encloses the complete response for a request.

Example

See the sample usage for the SimpleCol tag.

Attributes

Attribute	Description	Value(s)	Default Value
application	The VoiceXML application. This attribute is used in voice (VoiceXML) and is a URL that points to the root document for the VoiceXML generated.	CDATA	OPTIONAL
bgcolor	Sets the background color in supported mobile devices.	CDATA	OPTIONAL
lang	The language of this document. Used for voice.	CDATA	OPTIONAL

SimpleRow

The SimpleRow tag defines the row of a table.

Example

See the sample usage under the SimpleCol tag.

Attributes

Attribute	Description	Value(s)	Default Value
bgcolor	The background color.	CDATA	OPTIONAL
bordercolor	The border color.	CDATA	OPTIONAL
deviceclass	This tag is interpreted only for the specified device class. The server will transform this element only for devices belonging to the specified device class. Values can be a combination of values. If not specified, the tag is interpreted for all devices.	pdabrowser | pcbrowser | voice | microbrowser | micromessenger | messenger	OPTIONAL
halign	The horizontal alignment.	left | center | right	left OPTIONAL
valign	The vertical alignment.	top | center | bottom	top OPTIONAL
wrapmode	The text-wrap mode.	wrap | nowrap	wrap OPTIONAL

SimpleSpan

The SimpleSpan tag is used to control the style of the text display, including its font, color, and size.

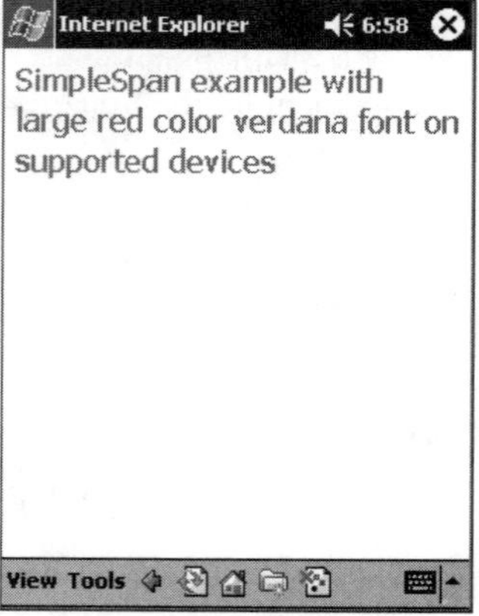

Example

```
<SimpleResult>
   <SimpleContainer>
   <SimpleText>
      <SimpleTextItem>
      <SimpleSpan color="#ff0000" font="verdana" size="15px">
      SimpleSpan example with large red color verdana font on
      supported devices.
      </SimpleSpan>
      </SimpleTextItem>
   </SimpleText>
   </SimpleContainer>
</SimpleResult>
```

Attributes

Attribute	Description	Value(s)	Default Value
color	The color of the text.	CDATA	OPTIONAL
deviceclass	This tag is interpreted only for the specified device class. The server will transform this element only for devices belonging to the specified device class. Values can be a combination of values. If not specified, the tag is interpreted for all devices.	pdabrowser | pcbrowser | voice | microbrowser | micromessenger | messenger	OPTIONAL
font	The font style of the text.	CDATA	OPTIONAL
size	The font size of the text.	CDATA	OPTIONAL

SimpleSpeech

The SimpleSpeech tag is a voice-only tag that is used to control prosody, class, and other VoiceXML text-to-speech engine parameters.

Example

```
<SimpleResult>
   <SimpleContainer>
   <SimpleText>
      <SimpleTextItem>
      You have reached
      <SimpleSpeech class="phone">
```

```
        6505551212
        </SimpleSpeech>
        </SimpleTextItem>
    </SimpleText>
    </SimpleContainer>
</SimpleResult>
```

For voice devices, the text will be rendered by the text-to-speech engine. However, the phone number needs some guidance so that it is sounded out correctly as a phone number—for example, as "six-five-zero…" instead of "six billion five hundred…."

Attributes

Attribute	Description	Value(s)	Default Value
class	The VoiceXML "sayas" class. Allows the voice browser to say something like "6505551212" as a phone number, when class="phone" (rather than saying this as a number as 6 billion ...).	phone | date | digits | literal | currency | number | time	OPTIONAL
deviceclass	This tag is applicable for voice devices only. Will not be supported on other devices even if specified.	voice	OPTIONAL
phon	The VoiceXML "sayas" phonetics. The representation of the Unicode International Phonetic Alphabet (IPA) characters that are to be spoken instead of the contained text.	CDATA	OPTIONAL
pitch	The VoiceXML prosody pitch. A numeric attribute that sets the baseline pitch in hertz. Values can be n (set volume to n) or +n or -n. They also can be +n%, -n%, or reset.	CDATA	OPTIONAL
range	The VoiceXML prosody range. A numeric attribute that sets the pitch range in hertz. Values can be n (set volume to n) or +n or -n. They also can be +n%, -n%, or reset. The pitch range represents the amount of variation in pitch above the baseline.	CDATA	OPTIONAL

Attribute	Description	Value(s)	Default Value
rate	A numeric attribute that sets the speaking rate in words per minute. The value can be an exact number such as "150" (which sets the speaking rate of 150 words per minute), or it can be +n or -n, which increases or decreases the rate by n from the current level. This can also can be +n%, -n%, or reset.	CDATA	OPTIONAL
sub	The VoiceXML "sayas" sub. Defines substitute text to be spoken instead of the contained text.	CDATA	OPTIONAL
vol	The VoiceXML prosody volume. A numeric attribute that sets the output volume on a scale of 0.0 to 1.0, where 0.0 is silence and 1.0 is maximum loudness. Values can be n (set volume to n) or +n or -n. They can also can be +n%, -n%, or reset	CDATA	OPTIONAL

SimpleStrong

The SimpleStrong tag displays the enclosed text in a stronger representation—usually bold.

Example

See the sample usage for the SimpleCol tag.

Attributes

Attribute	Description	Value(s)	Default Value
deviceclass	This tag is interpreted only for the specified device class. The server will transform this element only for devices belonging to the specified device class. Values can be a combination of values. If not specified, the tag is interpreted for all devices.	pdabrowser | pcbrowser | voice | microbrowser | micromessenger | messenger	OPTIONAL

SimpleSubmit

The SimpleSubmit tag defines the submit task of a bind operation. SimpleSubmit is child of SimpleTask. You may provide a list of form item names that has to be submitted. If a name list is provided, only those form items will be submitted. An empty SimpleSubmit tag will submit all the form items.

Example

See the sample usage for the SimpleTask tag.

Attributes

Attribute	Description	Value(s)	Default Value
name	The name of the submit button/action (like HTML). The submit name and value will be submitted back to the application as parameters.	CDATA	REQUIRED
callbackurl	Oracle9*i*AS Wireless module support. Indicates the URL to return back if the current action calls an Oracle9*i*AS Wireless module.	CDATA	OPTIONAL
callbackparam	Oracle9*i*AS Wireless module support. Indicates the return parameters of callbackurl. When the module returns the context back to the callee application, callbackparam is passed back for the callee to construct its application state.	CDATA	OPTIONAL
callbacksecure	Oracle9*i*AS Wireless module support. Indicates the mode of communication, when callback occurs, between the Oracle9*i*AS Wireless server and the mobile device (not the remote service).	true | false	OPTIONAL
deviceclass	This tag is interpreted only for the specified device class. The server will transform this element only for devices belonging to the specified device class. Values can be a combination of values. If not specified, the tag is interpreted for all devices.	pdabrowser | pcbrowser | voice | microbrowser | micromessenger | messenger	OPTIONAL

Attribute	Description	Value(s)	Default Value
fetchaudio	Voice-only attribute. The URL of an audio clip to play while the target is being fetched.	CDATA	OPTIONAL
method	The HTTP method get or post.	get | post	get OPTIONAL
mimetype	The MIME type of the target URL. If the target MIME type is not text/vnd.oracle.mobilexml, the Oracle9*i*AS Wireless server will not rewrite the URL.	CDATA	text/vnd.oracle. mobilexml OPTIONAL
secure	Indicates the mode of communication, when callback occurs, between the Oracle9*i*AS Wireless server and the device (not the remote service).	true | false	OPTIONAL
static_target	The URL to navigate to when an action is activated. The server never rewrites this URL. If this attribute exists, it will override the target attribute. Also supports "callto:" for phone calls and "mailto:" for e-mail support.	CDATA	OPTIONAL
target	The URL to navigate to when an action is activated. This URL is rewritten by the server to point back to the Oracle9*i*AS Wireless server when the mimetype attribute is text/vnd.oracle.mobilexml. Also supports "callto:" for phone calls and "mailto:" for email support.	CDATA	OPTIONAL
value	The value of the submit button/action (like HTML). The submit name and value will be submitted back to the application as parameters.	CDATA	OPTIONAL

SimpleSwitch

The SimpleSwitch tag is used to write switch statements on form field name/value pairs. It allows comparison on the value of the form field input on the client side and can branch to perform different tasks based on the result of the comparison.

Example

See the sample usage for the SimpleBind tag.

Attributes

Attribute	Description	Value(s)	Default Value
name	The name of the form field the switch is based on.	CDATA	REQUIRED
deviceclass	This tag is interpreted only for the specified device class. The server will transform this element only for devices belonging to the specified device class. Values can be a combination of values. If not specified, the tag is interpreted for all devices.	pdabrowser | pcbrowser | voice | microbrowser | micromessenger | messenger	OPTIONAL

SimpleTable

The SimpleTable tag defines a table.

Example

See the sample usage for the SimpleCol tag.

Attributes

Attribute	Description	Value(s)	Default Value
bgcolor	The background color of the table.	CDATA	OPTIONAL
border	The border width of the table.	CDATA	OPTIONAL
bordercolor	The border color of the table.	CDATA	OPTIONAL
cellpadding	The cell padding of the table.	CDATA	OPTIONAL
cellspacing	The cell spacing of the table.	CDATA	OPTIONAL
deviceclass	This tag is interpreted only for the specified device class. The server will transform this element only for devices belonging to the specified device class. Values can be a combination of values. If not specified, the tag is interpreted for all devices.	pdabrowser | pcbrowser | voice | microbrowser | micromessenger | messenger	OPTIONAL
height	The height of the table.	CDATA	OPTIONAL
id	The ID attribute of the element. Used for navigation within an XML response (target="#ID").	CDATA	OPTIONAL

Attribute	Description	Value(s)	Default Value
separator	Used when the table is not supported by the target device. If this attribute is defined, it adds a separator between column values where a table cannot be supported.		none OPTIONAL
width	The width of the table.	CDATA	OPTIONAL

SimpleTableBody

The SimpleTableBody tag defines a table body.

Example

See the sample usage for the SimpleCol tag.

Attributes

Attribute	Description	Value(s)	Default Value
deviceclass	This tag is interpreted only for the specified device class. The server will transform this element only for devices belonging to the specified device class. Values can be a combination of values. If not specified, the tag is interpreted for all devices.	pdabrowser | pcbrowser | voice | microbrowser | micromessenger | messenger	OPTIONAL

SimpleTableHeader

The SimpleTableHeader tag defines a table header.

Example

See the sample usage for the SimpleCol tag.

Attributes

Attribute	Description	Value(s)	Default Value
deviceclass	This tag is interpreted only for the specified device class. The server will transform this element only for devices belonging to the specified device class. Values can be a combination of values. If not specified, the tag is interpreted for all devices.	pdabrowser | pcbrowser | voice | microbrowser | micromessenger | messenger	OPTIONAL

SimpleTask

The SimpleTask tag is a container tag for all task items of a bind operation (SimpleBind). This tag encloses all the possible tasks, such as go, submit, exit, and so on. Tasks can also include SimpleTextItem as a child, thus allowing for the rendering of an audible feedback (text-to-speech for the text content) for a voice device or rendering the text for non-voice devices before performing an action.

Example

```
<SimpleTask>
   <SimpleSubmit target="change_PIN.jsp" name="Submit" method="post">
      <SimpleName name="currentPIN" />
      <SimpleName name="newPIN" />
   </SimpleSubmit>
</SimpleTask>
```

Attributes

Attribute	Description	Value(s)	Default Value
deviceclass	This tag is interpreted only for the specified device class. The server will transform this element only for devices belonging to the specified device class. Values can be a combination of values. If not specified, the tag is interpreted for all devices.	pdabrowser | pcbrowser | voice | microbrowser | micromessenger | messenger	OPTIONAL

SimpleText

The SimpleText tag is a container for block of texts (SimpleTextItem).

Example

See the sample usage for the SimpleAction tag.

Attributes

Attribute	Description	Value(s)	Default Value
deviceclass	This tag is interpreted only for the specified device class. The server will transform this element only for devices belonging to the specified device class. Values can be a combination of values. If not specified, the tag is interpreted for all devices.	pdabrowser | pcbrowser | voice | microbrowser | micromessenger | messenger	OPTIONAL

Attribute	Description	Value(s)	Default Value
id	The ID attribute of the element. Used for navigation within an XML response (target="#ID").	CDATA	OPTIONAL
scope	The VoiceXML scope. The default scope of the grammar in Form/Menu/Text/Grammar/DTMF. If the scope is set to document, then the grammar is active in the entire document.	document | dialog	OPTIONAL
wait	The VoiceXML wait. Tells the voice browser whether a wait has to happen before proceeding to the next construct in SimpleResult.	true | false	true OPTIONAL
wrapmode	The text-wrap mode.	wrap | nowrap	wrap OPTIONAL

SimpleTextField

The SimpleTextField tag is used to display noneditable fields inside a form—for example, changing a password where the user ID is a noneditable field.

Example

```
<SimpleResult>
  <SimpleContainer>
  <SimpleForm name="forminfo" target="change_password.jsp">
  <SimpleTitle>Make Password Changes</SimpleTitle>
    <SimpleTextField>UserID: orcladmin</SimpleTextField>
    <SimpleFormItem name="o_passwd" type="password">
```

```
        Old Password:
        <SimpleBreak />
        <SimpleHelp color="#ff0000" font="verdana" size="1">
        (help) Enter old password to validate.
        </SimpleHelp>
        </SimpleFormItem>
        <SimpleFormItem name="n_passwd" type="password">
        New Password:
        <SimpleBreak />
        <SimpleHelp color="#ff0000" font="verdana" size="1">
        (help) Enter your new password here.
        </SimpleHelp>
        </SimpleFormItem>
    </SimpleForm>
    </SimpleContainer>
</SimpleResult>
```

Attributes

Attribute	Description	Value(s)	Default Value
deviceclass	This tag is interpreted only for the specified device class. The server will transform this element only for devices belonging to the specified device class. Values can be a combination of values. If not specified, the tag is interpreted for all devices.	pdabrowser | pcbrowser | voice | microbrowser | micromessenger | messenger	OPTIONAL

SimpleTextItem

The SimpleTextItem tag contains one block of plain text, typically a single paragraph.

Example

See the sample usage for the SimpleAction tag.

Attributes

Attribute	Description	Value(s)	Default Value
bargein	VoiceXML barge in. Controls whether a user can interrupt when the text is being read by the VoiceXML browser.	true | false	true OPTIONAL

Attribute	Description	Value(s)	Default Value
color	The color of the text.	CDATA	OPTIONAL
count	The VoiceXML count. A number that allows you to activate different prompts if the user is doing something repeatedly.	CDATA	OPTIONAL
deviceclass	This tag is interpreted only for the specified device class. The server will transform this element only for devices belonging to the specified device class. Values can be a combination of values. If not specified, the tag is interpreted for all devices.	pdabrowser | pcbrowser | voice | microbrowser | micromessenger | messenger	OPTIONAL
font	The font style of the text.	CDATA	OPTIONAL
size	The font size of the text.	CDATA	OPTIONAL
timeout	The VoiceXML timeout. The interval of silence before the next construct is played.	CDATA	OPTIONAL
wrapmode	The text-wrap mode.	wrap | nowrap	wrap OPTIONAL

SimpleTimer

The SimpleTimer tag invokes a goto target task after a specified delay time.

Example

```
<SimpleResult>
   <SimpleContainer id="message">
   <SimpleTimer target="#msg1" timer="5"/>
   <SimpleText>
      <SimpleTextItem>No. 1
      </SimpleTextItem>
      <SimpleTextItem>
      <SimpleStrong>The Lord of the Rings</SimpleStrong>
      <SimpleBreak/>
      <SimpleEm>The Fellowship of the Rings</SimpleEm>
      </SimpleTextItem>
   </SimpleText>
   </SimpleContainer>
   <SimpleContainer>
   <SimpleText id="msg1">
      <SimpleTextItem>No. 2
      </SimpleTextItem>
      <SimpleTextItem>
      <SimpleStrong>Harry Potter</SimpleStrong>
      <SimpleBreak/>
      <SimpleEm>The Sorcerer's Stone</SimpleEm>
      </SimpleTextItem>
   </SimpleText>
   </SimpleContainer>
</SimpleResult>
```

Note that the timer event only works on WAP devices. It will show the cards after a brief delay, similar to a splash screen. On devices that do not have the timer capability, it just displays all the content on a single screen.

Attributes

Attribute	Description	Value(s)	Default Value
timer	Invokes a goto target task after a specified delay time. Time is in milliseconds.	Positive Int	REQUIRED
deviceclass	This tag is interpreted only for the specified device class. The server will transform this element only for devices belonging to the specified device class. Values can be a combination of values. If not specified, the tag is interpreted for all devices.	pdabrowser | pcbrowser | voice | microbrowser | micromessenger | messenger	deviceclass

Attribute	Description	Value(s)	Default Value
fetchaudio	Voice-only attribute. The URL of an audio clip to play while the target is being fetched.	CDATA	OPTIONAL
mimetype	A MIME type of the target URL. If the target MIME type is not text/vnd.oracle.mobilexml, the Oracle9*i*AS Wireless server will not rewrite the URL.	CDATA	text/vnd.oracle. mobilexml OPTIONAL
secure	Indicates the mode of communication, when callback occurs, between the Oracle9*i*AS Wireless server and the device (not the remote service).	true | false	OPTIONAL
static_target	The URL to navigate to when an action is activated. The server never rewrites this URL. If this attribute exists, it will override the target attribute. Also supports "callto:" for phone calls and "mailto:" for e-mail support.	CDATA	OPTIONAL
target	The URL to navigate to when an action is activated. This URL is rewritten by the server to point back to the Oracle9*i*AS Wireless server when the mimetype attribute is text/vnd.oracle.mobilexml. Also supports "callto:" for phone calls and "mailto:" for e-mail support.	CDATA	OPTIONAL

SimpleTitle

The SimpleTitle tag is used for the title element of form fields and the menu container (SimpleMenu).

Example

See the sample usage for the SimpleCol tag.

Attributes

Attribute	Description	Value(s)	Default Value
bargein	The VoiceXML barge in. Controls whether a user can interrupt when the text is being read by the VoiceXML browser.	true | false	true OPTIONAL
color	The color of the text.	CDATA	OPTIONAL

Attribute	Description	Value(s)	Default Value
count	The VoiceXML count. A number that allows you to activate different prompts if the user is doing something repeatedly.	CDATA	OPTIONAL
deviceclass	This tag is interpreted only for the specified device class. The server will transform this element only for devices belonging to the specified device class. Values can be a combination of values. If not specified, the tag is interpreted for all devices.	pdabrowser | pcbrowser | voice | microbrowser | micromessenger | messenger	OPTIONAL
font	The font style of the text.	CDATA	OPTIONAL
size	The font size of the text.	CDATA	OPTIONAL
timeout	The VoiceXML timeout. The interval of silence before the next construct is played.	CDATA	OPTIONAL
wrapmode	The text-wrap mode.	wrap | nowrap	wrap OPTIONAL

SimpleUnderline

The SimpleUnderline tag is used to underline text.

Example

See the sample usage for the SimpleAction tag.

Attributes

Attribute	Description	Value(s)	Default Value
deviceclass	This tag is interpreted only for the specified device class. The server will transform this element only for devices belonging to the specified device class. Values can be a combination of values. If not specified, the tag is interpreted for all devices.	pdabrowser | pcbrowser | voice | microbrowser | micromessenger | messenger	OPTIONAL

SimpleValue

The SimpleValue tag is used to substitute the value of the client-side form field variable, just like a macro. It can also be used to provide a client-side confirmation display/screen, such as "You entered 5, do you want to continue?" (where the value 5 is the value of a form item).

Example

```
<SimpleTextItem>
   You have selected to buy
   <SimpleStrong><SimpleValue name="numShares" /><SimpleStrong>
   shares. Is this correct?
</SimpleTextItem>
```

Attributes

Attribute	Description	Value(s)	Default Value
audiobase	The VoiceXML base from the value element.	CDATA	OPTIONAL
class	The VoiceXML "class" from the value element. Can take any value on the enumerated list (or can be any string).	none | audio | boolean | currency | date | digits | number | phone | time | transfer	OPTIONAL
deviceclass	This tag is interpreted only for the specified device class. The server will transform this element only for devices belonging to the specified device class. Values can be a combination of values. If not specified, the tag is interpreted for all devices.	pdabrowser | pcbrowser | voice | microbrowser | micromessenger | messenger	OPTIONAL
mode	The VoiceXML mode. This is the type of rendering. Can use the audiobase attribute to specify the base directory of the audio files.	tts | recorded	tts OPTIONAL
name	The name of the client variable to substitute.	CDATA	OPTIONAL

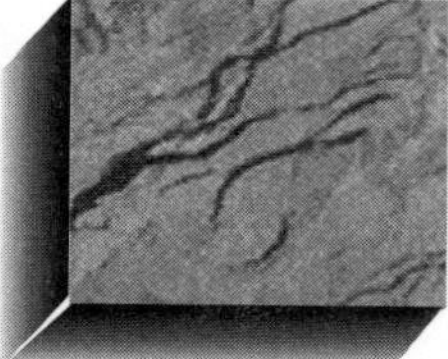

Index

Numbers

A

B

C

D

E

F

N

O

P

Q

R

S

T

U

V

W

X

Y

INTERNATIONAL CONTACT INFORMATION

AUSTRALIA
McGraw-Hill Book Company Australia Pty. Ltd.
TEL +61-2-9417-9899
FAX +61-2-9417-5687
http://www.mcgraw-hill.com.au
books-it_sydney@mcgraw-hill.com

CANADA
McGraw-Hill Ryerson Ltd.
TEL +905-430-5000
FAX +905-430-5020
http://www.mcgrawhill.ca

GREECE, MIDDLE EAST, NORTHERN AFRICA
McGraw-Hill Hellas
TEL +30-1-656-0990-3-4
FAX +30-1-654-5525

MEXICO (Also serving Latin America)
McGraw-Hill Interamericana Editores S.A. de C.V.
TEL +525-117-1583
FAX +525-117-1589
http://www.mcgraw-hill.com.mx
fernando_castellanos@mcgraw-hill.com

SINGAPORE (Serving Asia)
McGraw-Hill Book Company
TEL +65-863-1580
FAX +65-862-3354
http://www.mcgraw-hill.com.sg
mghasia@mcgraw-hill.com

SOUTH AFRICA
McGraw-Hill South Africa
TEL +27-11-622-7512
FAX +27-11-622-9045
robyn_swanepoel@mcgraw-hill.com

UNITED KINGDOM & EUROPE (Excluding Southern Europe)
McGraw-Hill Education Europe
TEL +44-1-628-502500
FAX +44-1-628-770224
http://www.mcgraw-hill.co.uk
computing_neurope@mcgraw-hill.com

ALL OTHER INQUIRIES Contact:
Osborne/McGraw-Hill
TEL +1-510-549-6600
FAX +1-510-883-7600
http://www.osborne.com
omg_international@mcgraw-hill.com

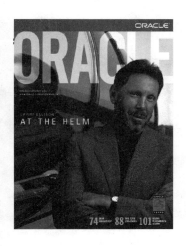

FREE SUBSCRIPTION

○ **Yes, please send me a FREE subscription to *Oracle Magazine*** ○ **NO**

To receive a free subscription to *Oracle Magazine*, you must fill out the entire card, sign it, and date it (incomplete cards cannot be processed or acknowledged). You can also fax your application to +1.847.647.9735.

Or subscribe at our Web site at www.oracle.com/oraclemagazine/

○ From time to time, Oracle Publishing allows our partners exclusive access to our e-mail addresses for special promotions and announcements. To be included in this program, please check this box.

○ Oracle Publishing allows sharing of our mailing list with selected third parties. If you prefer your mailing address not to be included in this program, please check here. If at any time you would like to be removed from this mailing list, please contact Customer Service at +1.847.647.9630 or send an e-mail to oracle@halldata.com.

signature (required) X   date

name   title

company   e-mail address

street/p.o. box

city/state/zip or postal code   telephone

country   fax

YOU MUST ANSWER ALL NINE QUESTIONS BELOW.

① WHAT IS THE PRIMARY BUSINESS ACTIVITY OF YOUR FIRM AT THIS LOCATION? (check one only)

- ☐ 01 Application Service Provider
- ☐ 02 Communications
- ☐ 03 Consulting, Training
- ☐ 04 Data Processing
- ☐ 05 Education
- ☐ 06 Engineering
- ☐ 07 Financial Services
- ☐ 08 Government (federal, local, state, other)
- ☐ 09 Government (military)
- ☐ 10 Health Care
- ☐ 11 Manufacturing (aerospace, defense)
- ☐ 12 Manufacturing (computer hardware)
- ☐ 13 Manufacturing (noncomputer)
- ☐ 14 Research & Development
- ☐ 15 Retailing, Wholesaling, Distribution
- ☐ 16 Software Development
- ☐ 17 Systems Integration, VAR, VAD, OEM
- ☐ 18 Transportation
- ☐ 19 Utilities (electric, gas, sanitation)
- ☐ 98 Other Business and Services

② WHICH OF THE FOLLOWING BEST DESCRIBES YOUR PRIMARY JOB FUNCTION? (check one only)

Corporate Management/Staff

- ☐ 01 Executive Management (President, Chair, CEO, CFO, Owner, Partner, Principal)
- ☐ 02 Finance/Administrative Management (VP/Director/ Manager/Controller, Purchasing, Administration)
- ☐ 03 Sales/Marketing Management (VP/Director/Manager)
- ☐ 04 Computer Systems/Operations Management (CIO/VP/Director/ Manager MIS, Operations)

IS/IT Staff

- ☐ 05 Systems Development/ Programming Management
- ☐ 06 Systems Development/ Programming Staff
- ☐ 07 Consulting
- ☐ 08 DBA/Systems Administrator
- ☐ 09 Education/Training
- ☐ 10 Technical Support Director/Manager
- ☐ 11 Other Technical Management/Staff
- ☐ 98 Other

③ WHAT IS YOUR CURRENT PRIMARY OPERATING PLATFORM? (select all that apply)

- ☐ 01 Digital Equipment UNIX
- ☐ 02 Digital Equipment VAX VMS
- ☐ 03 HP UNIX
- ☐ 04 IBM AIX
- ☐ 05 IBM UNIX
- ☐ 06 Java
- ☐ 07 Linux
- ☐ 08 Macintosh
- ☐ 09 MS-DOS
- ☐ 10 MVS
- ☐ 11 NetWare
- ☐ 12 Network Computing
- ☐ 13 OpenVMS
- ☐ 14 SCO UNIX
- ☐ 15 Sequent DYNIX/ptx
- ☐ 16 Sun Solaris/SunOS
- ☐ 17 SVR4
- ☐ 18 UnixWare
- ☐ 19 Windows
- ☐ 20 Windows NT
- ☐ 21 Other UNIX
- ☐ 98 Other
- 99 ☐ None of the above

④ DO YOU EVALUATE, SPECIFY, RECOMMEND, OR AUTHORIZE THE PURCHASE OF ANY OF THE FOLLOWING? (check all that apply)

- ☐ 01 Hardware
- ☐ 02 Software
- ☐ 03 Application Development Tools
- ☐ 04 Database Products
- ☐ 05 Internet or Intranet Products
- 99 ☐ None of the above

⑤ IN YOUR JOB, DO YOU USE OR PLAN TO PURCHASE ANY OF THE FOLLOWING PRODUCTS? (check all that apply)

Software

- ☐ 01 Business Graphics
- ☐ 02 CAD/CAE/CAM
- ☐ 03 CASE
- ☐ 04 Communications
- ☐ 05 Database Management
- ☐ 06 File Management
- ☐ 07 Finance
- ☐ 08 Java
- ☐ 09 Materials Resource Planning
- ☐ 10 Multimedia Authoring
- ☐ 11 Networking
- ☐ 12 Office Automation
- ☐ 13 Order Entry/Inventory Control
- ☐ 14 Programming
- ☐ 15 Project Management
- ☐ 16 Scientific and Engineering
- ☐ 17 Spreadsheets
- ☐ 18 Systems Management
- ☐ 19 Workflow

Hardware

- ☐ 20 Macintosh
- ☐ 21 Mainframe
- ☐ 22 Massively Parallel Processing
- ☐ 23 Minicomputer
- ☐ 24 PC
- ☐ 25 Network Computer
- ☐ 26 Symmetric Multiprocessing
- ☐ 27 Workstation

Peripherals

- ☐ 28 Bridges/Routers/Hubs/Gateways
- ☐ 29 CD-ROM Drives
- ☐ 30 Disk Drives/Subsystems
- ☐ 31 Modems
- ☐ 32 Tape Drives/Subsystems
- ☐ 33 Video Boards/Multimedia

Services

- ☐ 34 Application Service Provider
- ☐ 35 Consulting
- ☐ 36 Education/Training
- ☐ 37 Maintenance
- ☐ 38 Online Database Services
- ☐ 39 Support
- ☐ 40 Technology-Based Training
- ☐ 98 Other
- 99 ☐ None of the above

⑥ WHAT ORACLE PRODUCTS ARE IN USE AT YOUR SITE? (check all that apply)

Software

- ☐ 01 Oracle9i
- ☐ 02 Oracle9i Lite
- ☐ 03 Oracle8
- ☐ 04 Oracle8i
- ☐ 05 Oracle8i Lite
- ☐ 06 Oracle7
- ☐ 07 Oracle9i Application Server
- ☐ 08 Oracle9i Application Server Wireless
- ☐ 09 Oracle Data Mart Suites
- ☐ 10 Oracle Internet Commerce Server
- ☐ 11 Oracle interMedia
- ☐ 12 Oracle Lite
- ☐ 13 Oracle Payment Server
- ☐ 14 Oracle Video Server
- ☐ 15 Oracle Rdb

Tools

- ☐ 16 Oracle Darwin
- ☐ 17 Oracle Designer
- ☐ 18 Oracle Developer
- ☐ 19 Oracle Discoverer
- ☐ 20 Oracle Express
- ☐ 21 Oracle JDeveloper
- ☐ 22 Oracle Reports
- ☐ 23 Oracle Portal
- ☐ 24 Oracle Warehouse Builder
- ☐ 25 Oracle Workflow

Oracle E-Business Suite

- ☐ 26 Oracle Advanced Planning/Scheduling
- ☐ 27 Oracle Business Intelligence
- ☐ 28 Oracle E-Commerce
- ☐ 29 Oracle Exchange
- ☐ 30 Oracle Financials
- ☐ 31 Oracle Human Resources
- ☐ 32 Oracle Interaction Center
- ☐ 33 Oracle Internet Procurement
- ☐ 34 Oracle Manufacturing
- ☐ 35 Oracle Marketing
- ☐ 36 Oracle Order Management
- ☐ 37 Oracle Professional Services Automation
- ☐ 38 Oracle Projects
- ☐ 39 Oracle Sales
- ☐ 40 Oracle Service
- ☐ 41 Oracle Small Business Suite
- ☐ 42 Oracle Supply Chain Management
- ☐ 43 Oracle Travel Management
- ☐ 44 Oracle Treasury

Oracle Services

- ☐ 45 Oracle.com Online Services
- ☐ 46 Oracle Consulting
- ☐ 47 Oracle Education
- ☐ 48 Oracle Support
- ☐ 98 ther
- 99 ☐ None of the above

⑦ WHAT OTHER DATABASE PRODUCTS ARE IN USE AT YOUR SITE? (check all that apply)

- ☐ 01 Access
- ☐ 02 Baan
- ☐ 03 dbase
- ☐ 04 Gupta
- ☐ 05 BM DB2
- ☐ 06 Informix
- ☐ 07 Ingres
- ☐ 08 Microsoft Access
- ☐ 09 Microsoft SQL Server
- ☐ 10 PeopleSoft
- ☐ 11 Progress
- ☐ 12 SAP
- ☐ 13 Sybase
- ☐ 14 VSAM
- ☐ 98 Other
- 99 ☐ None of the above

⑧ DURING THE NEXT 12 MONTHS, HOW MUCH DO YOU ANTICIPATE YOUR ORGANIZATION WILL SPEND ON COMPUTER HARDWARE, SOFTWARE, PERIPHERALS, AND SERVICES FOR YOUR LOCATION? (check only one)

- ☐ 01 Less than $10,000
- ☐ 02 $10,000 to $49,999
- ☐ 03 $50,000 to $99,999
- ☐ 04 $100,000 to $499,999
- ☐ 05 $500,000 to $999,999
- ☐ 06 $1,000,000 and over

⑨ WHAT IS YOUR COMPANY'S YEARLY SALES REVENUE? (please choose one)

- ☐ 01 $500, 000, 000 and above
- ☐ 02 $100, 000, 000 to $500, 000, 000
- ☐ 03 $50, 000, 000 to $100, 000, 000
- ☐ 04 $5, 000, 000 to $50, 000, 000
- ☐ 05 $1, 000, 000 to $5, 000, 000

123101